Best Books
for Young Ad[ults]

Thir[d Edition]

Young Adult Library Services Association

Edited by Holly Koelling

Foreword by Betty Carter

AMERICAN LIBRARY ASSOCIATION
Chicago   2007

Composition by ALA Editions in Sabon and ITC Kabel typefaces using InDesign2 for a PC platform.

The paper used in this publication meets the minimum requirements of American National Standard for Information Sciences—Permanence of Paper for Printed Library Materials, ANSI Z39.48-1992. ∞

Library of Congress Cataloging-in-Publication Data

Best books for young adults / Young Adult Library Services Association.—
    3rd ed. / edited by Holly Koelling ; foreword by Betty Carter.
        p.   cm.
        Rev. ed. of: Best books for young adults / Betty Carter, with Sally Estes and Linda Waddle. 2nd ed. c2000.
        Includes bibliographical references and index.
        ISBN-13: 978-0-8389-3569-9 (alk. paper)
        ISBN-10: 0-8389-3569-9 (alk. papcr)
        1. Teenagers—Books and reading—United States—Bibliography. 2. Young adult literature—Bibliography. 3. Young adult literature—Publishing—United States. 4. Best books for young adults (1966) 5. Best books—United States.
    I. Koelling, Holly. II. Carter, Betty, 1944– Best books for young adults.
    III. Young Adult Library Services Association.
    Z1037.C34 2007
    028.1'625—dc22   2007026009

ISBN-13: 978-0-8389-3569-9
ISBN-10: 0-8389-3569-9

Printed in the United States of America

11   10   09   08   07   5   4   3   2   1

CONTENTS

PART 2 BEST BOOKS FOR YOUNG ADULTS SELECTIONS, 1966–2007

FOREWORD

When I was on the Best Books for Young Adults (BBYA) Committee in the mid-1980s, conditions were quite different from those of today. We had fewer titles published expressly for young adults, fewer advance reading copies, less access to individual books through publishers, limited capability to generate nominations electronically, and no e-mail correspondence. But there are two elements of the committee's work that have remained constant from that time through the present. The first is that a group of committed librarians is searching for those books that they believe have potential appeal and worth for young adult readers. The second is that some committee member almost always poses the question, as the pool of potential nominees begins to shrink, "This is a good book, but is it a *best* book?"

For each book selected, it's a question asked and answered both individually by each BBYA member and collectively by the group as a whole. Why this question? Because there is no set of universal criteria that constitutes a best book. Professional librarians selecting books aren't like amateur art appreciators who can say, "I don't know what's good, but I know what I like." What the librarians on these committees must do is juggle a number of philosophical balls in their heads as they try to determine what books deserve to be labeled the best. And they do.

Some librarians lean toward perceived popularity, others toward literary quality, and still others toward innovative formats, fresh content, and unique themes. What these librarians must bring to the BBYA discussion table are cogent reasons for their perceptions of "best" for each book, along with a willingness to listen to others as they plead their cases. What the collective committee must do is combine these tastes and strengths to create a list that represents the amalgamation of these points of view.

The list is never perfect, either in the present or in retrospect. As Dorothy Broderick writes, "There isn't any such animal unless you make the list just for you. Committee lists are lessons in compromise and in the art of win some, lose some graciously" (1989, 17). While individual committee members always remember at least one book they loved that didn't make the list (for me it is Clyde Edgerton's *Raney*, a book that becomes better when seen through the rose-colored lenses of my memory, but not necessarily in my estimation of literary quality, with each year that passes), and while there may be some who are "so-sorry-such-and-such-book-made-the-list," the committee as a whole understands Broderick's point about gracious compromise. What each BBYA list represents is what the majority of fifteen committee members think at a particular moment in time are the best books of any particular year. And year after year the committee produces a rock-solid list.

Sally Estes, former Books for Youth editor at *Booklist* and longtime consultant for BBYA, understood the real power of such lists when she used to say, "the reason you make a list is so others will make their own lists." The motivation that prompts Americans to cuss and discuss any list, from *People* magazine's 100 Most Beautiful People to the American Film Institute's Outstanding Films of the Twentieth Century, comes from What-Were-They-Thinking Syndrome, a condition that is alive and well in literature land. Individuals dissatisfied with some segment of any list start adding their own choices, taking away a few of the original picks, and creating in their minds a distinctive list that meets their own tastes. Far from being destructive, such second-guessing forms one of the greatest strengths of any BBYA list: it jumpstarts the conversation about young adult literature.

Such literary conversations take place when knowledgeable book people meet face to face or around symbolic water coolers on electronic discussion lists such as YALSA-BK. Adults concerned with teenagers and their reading meet head-on a variety of perspectives about literature. Here is where lovers of story narrative (*Ask Me No Questions*, by Marina Budhos; BBYA 2007) confront the beauty in related nonfiction or graphic novel formats (*The 9/11 Report*, by Sid Jacobson and Ernie Colón; BBYA 2007), while those who favor the process of historical research (*Freedom Walkers*, by Russell Freedman; BBYA 2007) can also discover the pull of historical fiction (*The Astonishing Life of Octavian Nothing*, by M. T. Anderson; BBYA 2007).

Thoughtful examination of BBYA lists allows us to move beyond our professional comfort zones. Recently a librarian told me that *Phineas Gage: A Gruesome but True Story about Brain Science*, by John Fleischman (BBYA 2003), wouldn't appeal to readers in her school. I suggested she give the book a chance, that it might appeal to children she had never seen or to those who had literary tastes different from her own. A few months later she mentioned how popular the title was on her campus and added that she had learned that perhaps she didn't know the students as well as she thought she did. Clearly, one BBYA entry had the power of challenging this librarian to think about literature in a new and productive way.

But there are also times when we talk to ourselves, when we examine various BBYA lists such as those contained in this volume, and start making our own readers' advisory lists with new books to recommend to a hard-to-please fantasy fan or a particular history buff. One book may trigger memories of forgotten titles, prompting a local list on oldies but goodies, while another title could be the impetus for an ancillary reading list for science classes. Like literary rabbits, lists spawn lists. And that's the joy and the passion this book gives to all of us.

—Betty Carter

SOURCES CONSULTED

Broderick, Dorothy M. 1989. "Good, Better, Best, or The Saga of YASD's Best Books Selection." *VOYA* 12 (April): 17.

Edgerton, Clyde. 1985. *Raney: A Novel*. Chapel Hill, NC: Algonquin.

Acknowledgments

My greatest appreciation goes to Betty Carter, a luminary in the world of teen literature, the author of the first two editions of this book, and the reason I was given the opportunity to write the third. Profound thanks to Angelina Benedetti and Pam Spencer Holley for so generously contributing time from their busy lives to write masterful annotations for many of the themed lists. You are lifesavers. A special thanks to Beth Yoke, executive director of the Young Adult Library Services Association, for her endless understanding, patience, and support. Speaking of patience, both Nichole Gilbert, YALSA's program officer, and Karyn Silverman, the 2006 BBYA chair, deserve special mention for their thoughtful and detailed responses to what may at times have seemed an endless barrage of questions. And, of course, acknowledgments would not be complete if I did not raise my glass to all the past and present chairpersons, administrative assistants, and members of the Best Books for Young Adults Committee.

PART I

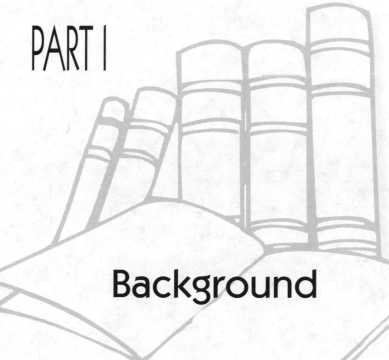

Background

Selecting the Best

A BRIEF HISTORY OF BBYA

The Best Books for Young Adults (BBYA) Committee—whose social and organizational history is explored in fascinating detail by Betty Carter in the 1994 first edition of this book—began in 1930 with three members and gradually grew to its present fifteen-member composition. The definition of young adult and both the numbers and the types of books the lists include have changed dramatically over the years. The first list was created to serve high school readers. It included thirty titles and all were adult books. Until the beginning of the 1990s, the intended audience for the lists flipped and flopped, with a tendency toward older readers and adult books. Since 1991, when YASD/YALSA officially defined young adults as between the ages of twelve and eighteen (based on the findings of a 1990 National Center for Education Statistics task force), BBYA lists have featured books for this broader age range and have been culled from a wider variety of publishing markets. New to the third edition, the 2000–2006 lists average eighty-three titles per list, making them almost three times longer than their 1930 progenitor.

Both the committee and its lists have had many names over time. In more recent history, what was known as of 1958 as the Book Selection Committee became the Committee on the Selection of Books and Other Materials in 1964 before assuming its current name, the Best Books for Young Adults Committee, in 1966. Various names for the lists have included "Books for Young People," "Adult Books for Young People," "Some of the Best Books for Young People," "Interesting Adult Books for Young People," "Significant Adult Books for Young People," and, finally, "Best Books for Young Adults."

The committee operated under a variety of divisions before the American Library Association's Young Adult Library Services Association (YALSA) was born in 1992. It began its work under the School Libraries Section in 1930, had a one-year stint in 1936 under ALA's Board on Library Service to Children and Young People, then reported to the Young People's Reading Round Table starting in 1937 before becoming part of the Division of Libraries for Children and Young People in 1945. After falling for a short spell under the Association of Young People's Librarians, the committee worked under the long-running Young Adult Services Division (YASD), formed in 1957, where it remained until 1992, when the division became known by its present name of YALSA.

The year 1966 saw the beginning of the BBYA lists as we know them today, although policies and procedures have undergone numerous changes in these forty-plus years. To respond to a changing world of library professionals, teens, and books, BBYA policies and procedures are likely to undergo many changes in the future as well.

Despite all the differences over the years, the overriding goal of this committee has not varied. The names may change, but the purpose remains the same! The fifteen-member BBYA Committee, as it is now known, is part of a much larger collective of librarians who for almost eighty years have made it their shared goal to connect teens to the best books published each year with the power to educate, entertain, and even change lives.

HOW THE BBYA COMMITTEE WORKS

In many ways, the BBYA Committee is a well-oiled machine, conceived and constructed long ago to do a heavy and ongoing job and to do it well. Since 1966, it has produced more than forty outstanding book lists for teens, parents, educators, librarians, and community caregivers. The BBYA Committee does a complex job on an aggressive time line. Its considerable power becomes more awesome with each passing year as it moves at ever increasing speeds to keep pace with the exploding market of literature aimed at or appealing to teens.

In some ways, this wonderful machine might benefit from a tune-up, or perhaps even an overhaul of sorts, to remain relevant, successfully produce its work, and meet its charge well into a rapidly changing future. Let's focus on the machine as it works now, including its formal foundation in policy and procedure, its inside workings, the book lists it produces, the characteristics of those lists, and the lists' relationships with other forms of literary distinction.

Policies and Procedures

BBYA Policies and Procedures guide and define the work of the committee and are available online (http://www.ala.org/ala/yalsa/booklistsawards/ bestbooksya/policiesprocedures.htm). YALSA also distributes a BBYA Policies and Procedures brochure at ALA's Annual Conference and Midwinter Meeting. Additional documents, including the YALSA Handbook, along with YALSA staff and elected officials, guide committee work as well. BBYA Policies and Procedures are concise, providing a basic and sometimes open-for-interpretation framework for understanding the work of the committee. They include sections defining its charge, purpose, target audience, eligibility time frame, discussion protocol, committee members, chair, voting procedures, inclusion of Printz Award titles, availability and distribution of lists, and observer comments.

CHARGE

The committee's charge bears repeating: *To select from the year's publications, significant adult and young adult books; to annotate the selected titles.* Is this an adequate charge that can be successfully met? Michael Cart—author, lecturer, consultant, and past YALSA president with a long list of leadership and committee involvements—feels that "the charge is so general that it's hard to say the committee isn't meeting it." Other past and current committee members acknowledge that the charge is not as detailed as it might be, but that this could lend it needed flexibility and become one of its primary strengths in a rapidly changing literary world. Rick Orsillo, past BBYA Committee member and teen services librarian in the King County (WA) Library System, believes that the charge is "purposefully vague in some important areas so that we can interpret the rules as the publishing industry changes. This allows the committee to reinterpret the document as teen tastes and publishing change." And Eunice Anderson, a library branch manager and past BBYA Committee member, admits that "sometimes the term 'significant' is reason for debate of some titles. However, keeping that word in focus during committee discussions makes the list good." All in all, general consensus among current and past committee members has it that, yes, the BBYA charge works well enough.

PURPOSE OF THE LISTS

The BBYA Policies and Procedures provide a handful of purpose statements that further clarify and bolster the charge, and among other details, include criteria to keep in mind when creating each year's book list.

Of particular note is the mandate to find books of "proven or potential appeal to the personal reading tastes of the young adult." Proven appeal invites the participation of teens in the BBYA Committee process, mostly at local levels but also at conferences.

The purpose statements affirm that books selected for the BBYA lists "should incorporate acceptable literary quality and effectiveness of presentation." Not unlike the charge, the purpose statements leave room for interpretation. Rick Orsillo believes that "this malleability is a double-edged sword, as we can easily interpret 'significant' [from the charge], 'acceptable literary quality,' and 'effectiveness of presentation' in so many different ways. I think that it is a balancing act among these three criteria."

BBYA books should also strive to reflect the diversity of their audience. This said, it is not a requirement that a complete BBYA list be balanced "according to subject or area of interest."

ELIGIBILITY TIME FRAME

Each year, a book is eligible to be considered for a BBYA list if it has been published in the assigned calendar year or in the last four months of the prior calendar year. For example, books being considered for nomination in 2007 must have been published between September 1, 2006, and December 31, 2007. If the book nominated is eventually selected in the final binding vote at Midwinter 2008, it will appear on the 2008 Best Books for Young Adults list.

Why sixteen months of eligibility for this selection list? Reading for the BBYA Committee is an enormous effort. It always has been a real challenge for committee members to keep up with the body of literature available for consideration. Thanks to the currently explosive teen literary market and tendencies in the adult publishing market that are producing literature of strong appeal to teens, committee members face an increasingly heavy reading load, and books published near the end of a selection year simply may get missed. By allowing a four-month eligibility crossover for each annual list, books that were not considered for nomination in the latter half of a calendar year have a chance the following year.

In contrast, the YALSA limited or single-title awards have charges that effectively narrow the literature to a more manageable volume (this statement is relative, of course!), which is one factor that allows them to keep their eligibility time frame to a single calendar year. On the other hand, Quick Picks for Reluctant Young Adult Readers, a selection list with a broader charge and greater volume of books to consider, has, at eighteen months, an even longer eligibility time frame than BBYA.

TARGET AUDIENCE

In a profession full of folks who clearly demonstrate great passion for teen literature solely on its own merits in addition to valuing its potential power for teen readers, the BBYA target audience statement is also of particular importance in keeping the committee on track: *The list is prepared for the use of young adults themselves and annotations will be written to attract the YA reader.* As mentioned above, the magnificent BBYA machine produces book lists for teens, parents, educators, librarians, and caregivers. This might appear to be in conflict with the target audience statement. It is true that the ultimate goal of the BBYA Committee is to provide a crème de la crème list of outstanding reading recommendations for teens, but it takes us all to get these lists and those books to teens! To reach teens requires the involvement and commitment of many adults, starting with the BBYA Committee.

Librarians and educators who care to promote to teens the very best books from the colossal body of literature available, selectors who buy teen materials for libraries, publishers and editors seeking feedback on their works' literary quality and appeal, and adults who simply relish reading teen literature themselves and passing the word on about their favorites—all benefit from these lists.

Nonetheless, it is important for the committee to remain focused on the primary reason for the creation of this list: making connections with teen readers.

ADDITIONAL PROCEDURES

Beyond charge, purpose and eligibility, and target audience are a variety of procedures that define and describe the makeup of the BBYA Committee, the selection of its chair, and how the committee operates. The YALSA web pages provide full details.

In brief, the committee is composed of fifteen members appointed by YALSA's vice president/president-elect on continuing, staggered rotations, one of whom is selected to chair each year. The work of the chair is guided by the BBYA Policies and Procedures, as well as by the guidelines in the YALSA Handbook. The fifteen BBYA Committee members start with a one-year term and can continue to serve for an additional two years based on participation. A committee member will only be selected to serve as chair once. An individual may serve on the BBYA Committee for more than one three-year term as long as he or she has been off the committee for a minimum of five years between terms.

The BBYA Committee is an open committee, which means its work is open for public observation and participation. Nominations may come from the field, that is, from anyone not currently serving on the BBYA Committee, as well as from committee members. If a committee member "seconds" a field nomination, it appears on the nomination list for discussion. Without a "second," such nominations are not considered. Nominations are posted regularly throughout each year on the YALSA web pages.

The committee meets twice a year, at the Annual Conference in the early summer and again at the Midwinter Meeting, usually in late January or early February. At both events, members discuss nominated books. These discussions are open to the public, and anyone who would like to speak to a nomination has an opportunity to do so. At the Midwinter Meeting, committee members vote for each year's final BBYA list and participate in the selection of the Top Ten list. Committee members may vote only on books they have read in their entirety. To make the final list a book must receive a minimum of nine "yes" votes, regardless of overall readership. That's a 60 percent majority of total possible votes. Committee members then write annotations for the final list titles, focusing on language that will attract teen readers. Discussion and voting are guided by the chair.

PRINTZ AWARD TITLES

In June 2002, the YALSA Board revised the BBYA Policies and Procedures to include a new procedure regarding Michael L. Printz Award titles. After the Printz Award and Honor books are announced at the Midwinter Meeting, the Printz titles (one award winner and up to four honor books) are added to the final BBYA list regardless of the BBYA Committee vote. The rationale for doing so is that it would appear inconsistent if the BBYA Committee did not acknowledge books selected by the Printz Award Committee for their exceptional value to young adults. A precedent exists for this in YALSA's children's services counterpart, the Association for Library Service to Children (ALSC). Four ALSC Board actions between 1976 and 2006 require that the Notable Children's Books lists include Newbery and Caldecott Medal and Honor books, the Batchelder Award books, the Sibert Medal and Honor books, the Pura Belpré Medal and Honor books, and the Theodor Seuss Geisel Medal and Honor books.

Despite the rationale and precedents, this decision remains controversial with Printz Award and BBYA Committee members alike.

An Analysis
of the Lists

In this and following sections, characteristics of the BBYA lists, as well as the BBYA Top Ten lists and BBYA unanimous votes lists, will be examined. Data for the complete lists will reflect the seven years (2000–2006) since the last edition of this book was published. As the Top Ten lists and unanimous votes lists are smaller selections of titles, a look back to 1997 provides a broader, full decade's view.

THE 2000–2006 BBYA LISTS

There are a total of 577 titles on BBYA lists between 2000 and 2006. The shortest list during these years is the one for 2003, when 71 titles "made" (were selected for) the BBYA list. The longest is 2006, with 91 titles on the list. The average BBYA list length during same span was 82 books. Looking at the past four years, during which statistics for nominations were published, there were an average of 210 nominations, from which an average of 39 percent were selected for each year's list.

> 2006: 91 titles selected from 217 official nominations (42%)
>
> 2005: 86 titles selected from 214 official nominations (40%)
>
> 2004: 84 titles selected from 207 official nominations (41%)
>
> 2003: 71 titles selected from 203 official nominations (35%)
>
> 2002: 84 titles selected
>
> 2001: 76 titles selected
>
> 2000: 85 titles selected

Characteristics of the 2000–2006 BBYA Lists

The BBYA lists are created each year by a group of librarians from around the country who specialize in teen services and who take the time to read, evaluate, discuss, and select the best books written and published for them. The BBYA lists give many of these wonderful books a longer life span than they might otherwise have had. The lists are still there even when the books have left the cultural limelight. We still have use of them, not only to make outstanding reading recommendations, but as a bellwether to track literary trends and identify patterns.

Even though the lists we are looking at here cover a fairly small range of years next to the lifespan of the BBYA Committee (in its many iterations over the years), there are trends and patterns to be detected. In this section, the focus is on statistical data of the sort that might be interesting to those in the library and information fields, in particular, data about intended market, genre and format, and comparisons with other YALSA lists and awards.

THE BBYA LISTS BY TEEN AND ADULT MARKETS

Of the 577 books selected for 2000–2006 BBYA lists, 507, or 88 percent, are teen market titles and 70, or 12 percent, are adult market titles. (Graphic novels appearing on BBYA lists that were not specifically designated for a particular audience are considered adult market titles.)

THE BBYA LISTS BY GENRE

General fiction books dominate the 2000–2006 BBYA lists. At 241 titles, they represent almost 42 percent of the books. General fiction is followed by nonfiction, fantasy and dark fantasy, and historical fiction, each coming in between about 13 and 14 percent of the total: 83, 83, and 75 titles, respectively. Biographies account for 44 books, or almost 8 percent of the total. It should be noted that biographical works and especially memoirs can be difficult to differentiate from general nonfiction, depending on a book's balance between personal information and observations about the times in which its subject lived. When in doubt, I checked a small selection of larger library systems' catalogs and went with the majority consensus on their placement. Science fiction works come in next, at 28 titles, just under 5 percent of the total. Humorous fiction and mysteries lead the rear guard, with 11 titles (1.9 percent) and 8 titles (1.4 percent), respectively, followed by poetry, with 3 titles, and horror, with 1. (See figure 1.)

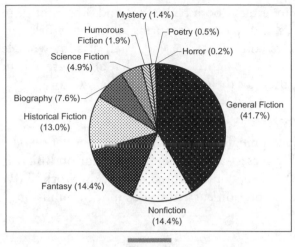

Figure 1
BBYA lists by genre, 2000–2006

THE BBYA LISTS BY FORMAT

Gone are the days when literature came in one form only, the sequential chapter narrative. Although this format is still the standard, a real artistic creativity and melding of genres is finding its way into literature for all ages, and such works are perhaps particularly intriguing to teens. As the market for these creative and genre-busting books grows and young people respond to it, more of the clearly exceptional among these works are finding their way to BBYA lists.

Fiction Formats

General fiction is a fairly amorphous category, one that includes by process of elimination just about everything fictional outside the established genres, including historical fiction, fantasy and dark fantasy, science fiction, humorous fiction, mystery, and so forth. But within this general category are stories told in increasingly creative ways and presented to readers in ways that break the boundaries of standard chapter-by-chapter narratives and traditional short story collections.

The BBYA lists of the past seven years see some unique formats creeping in. Although more than 83 percent—201 of the 241 general fiction titles— are in the traditional narrative fiction category, several other formats make a small but strong showing. Stories in verse hold their own along with traditional short story collections, each accounting for roughly 5 percent of the total. Diary and journal formats are followed by epistolary fiction

(fiction written in letters), both between 2 and 3 percent of the total. Fiction that incorporates multiple literary forms all in one work and fiction written as plays or scripts come in at the end, each at somewhat less than 1 or 2 percent of the total. (See figure 2.) And what about graphic novels? They are so noteworthy, they get their own mention below.

Nonfiction Formats

Although far less prevalent than in fiction, nonfiction works in creative formats—notably verse—are beginning to appear on BBYA lists as well. The 2000–2006 BBYA lists contain three nonfiction works in verse, which are discussed in the chapter on current trends in teen publishing.

Graphic Novels

Graphic novels are a newer yet powerful presence on BBYA lists and, as such, well worth a mention of their own. Although graphic novels are to some degree difficult to define, in essence they are stories told through or accompanied by artwork. Although BBYA lists have in the past seen books with unique artistic elements from time to time, perhaps the first true graphic novel to make a BBYA list was Katherine Arnoldi's *The Amazing True Story of a Teenage Single Mom* in 1999. Since then, graphic novels have appeared on BBYA lists in a fairly linear progression. Beginning with the 2001 BBYA list, which featured one graphic novel, the presence of this format has increased to two titles on the 2003 list, four titles on both the 2004 and 2005 lists, and five titles on the 2006 list. This is no surprise given the popularity and teen-friendliness of the format. It is also no surprise that YALSA has recently

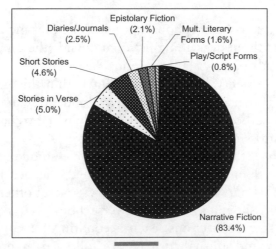

Figure 2
Fiction formats on BBYA lists, 2000–2006

responded by forming the Great Graphic Novels for Teens Committee, which selected its inaugural list at the 2007 Midwinter Meeting.

BBYA TITLES APPEARING ON OTHER YALSA AWARDS AND LISTS, 2000–2006

As all Printz Award and Honor books must appear on the BBYA lists, and as the Best of the Best lists are selected predominantly from BBYA lists, Printz titles, and Alex Award titles, the interesting statistical comparisons between the BBYA lists and these other lists will come when we look at the BBYA Top Ten lists. For now, valuable comparisons lie between BBYA lists and Quick Picks for Reluctant Young Adult Readers lists, Popular Paperbacks for Young Adults lists, and the Alex Awards.

The BBYA Lists and Quick Picks for Reluctant Young Adult Readers

A comparison between BBYA lists and Quick Picks for Reluctant Young Adult Readers lists may be of particular interest when considering that a number of books deemed meritorious by BBYA standards are also likely to have a special appeal to teens who, for whatever reason, do not like to read. BBYA and Quick Picks share seventy-seven titles over the past seven years, which means that more than one in ten BBYA books are also on Quick Picks lists. Of the seventy-seven shared titles, ten are also BBYA Top Ten titles and seventeen are also Quick Picks Top Ten titles. The two lists shared the most titles in 2000, twenty-three, a number that declines fairly significantly over the next few years until the 2004 low of six shared titles. That's roughly a 75 percent decrease. The year 2005 saw a 50 percent increase in shared titles from the 2004 low, followed by another slight rise in 2006. (See figure 3.) This may simply be a natural fluctuation and is likely dependent on the quality and content of books during any given publishing period.

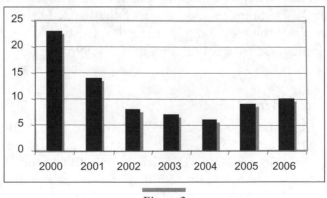

Figure 3
Titles shared between BBYA and Quick Picks,
2000–2006

The majority of the shared titles, fifty-two, are in the general fiction category, seventeen of these written in one of the creative formats. Nonfiction (including one graphic novel) and fantasy account for seven and six shared titles, respectively, followed by science fiction, with five shared titles. Mystery, historical fiction, and biography come in at three, two, and two shared titles, respectively. Again, as with the genre statistics for the BBYA lists, general fiction leads the way here, with nonfiction and fantasy in secondary placement. Science fiction rises to a more dominant position in these shared titles, with historical fiction and biography falling far behind.

The BBYA Lists and Popular Paperbacks for Young Adults

Comparisons between the BBYA and Popular Paperbacks lists may not be especially useful, as each committee serves a different purpose in the reading lives of teens. For the Popular Paperbacks Committee, popularity trumps quality, lists are produced after unique genre categories have been defined and books are found to populate them, publication year is not a consideration, and the books need to be available in a paperback format. The two lists do share one important element in common, though, that may provide an interesting connection. The BBYA Committee identifies books with "proven or potential appeal," and Popular Paperbacks focuses exclusively on this popularity aspect. Those titles that find their way to both of these lists must be especially appealing to teen readers! And, as Popular Paperback lists can consist of titles from any publication year that have, first, made it to a paperback printing and, second, are popular with teens, shared status on the two lists may serve to acknowledge and validate some of the selections made by BBYA Committees in prior years.

Between 1997 and 2006, 218 BBYA books were also identified by the Popular Paperbacks Committee as meeting the committee's purpose to find "popular or topical titles which are widely available in paperback and which represent a broad variety of accessible themes and genres." General fiction dominates, at 127 shared books, over half the total. Other fiction genres account for most of the remaining shared titles, led by historical fiction and followed by fantasy, science fiction, and mystery. Nonfiction and biography bring up the rear.

The BBYA Lists and the Alex Awards

Eight books from the 2000–2006 BBYA lists are also honored as Alex Award titles, which go to "books written for adults that have special appeal to young adults." No titles are shared between BBYA and Alex in 2001, 2003, or 2004. Two are shared in 2000, and one each in 2002 and 2005. Interestingly, the remaining half of the total are shared from the 2006 BBYA list. What might this mean? The Alex Awards, which were inaugurated in 1998, may not have a long enough track record to warrant any hard and fast conclusions, but it is possible that more adult titles with strong teen appeal are currently being published and are visible and readily available for consideration. Or perhaps more BBYA members may be focusing on adult titles for teens, actively seeking them out and bringing them to the committee's attention. Both of these factors might be at play. It may be that the existence of the Alex Awards has brought to all parties a renewed commitment to the value of adult books in the lives of teen readers. Or 2006 may have been a fluke. Only time will tell!

> Alexander, Caroline. *The* Endurance: *Shackleton's Legendary Antarctic Expedition* (2000).

> Dominick, Andie. *Needles: A Memoir of Growing Up with Diabetes* (2000).

> Vijayaraghavan, Vineeta. *Motherland* (2002).

SIX SUPERSTARS OF THE 2000–2006 BBYA LISTS AND BEYOND: BOOKS WITH EXCEPTIONAL DISTINCTION

The following six books all share recognition on BBYA, BBYA Top Ten, and BBYA unanimous votes lists, as well as receiving additional distinction elsewhere.

> Nancy Farmer's *The House of the Scorpion* also received a 2003 Printz Honor recognition, is an ALSC Notable Children's Book, and won the National Book Award in 2002.

> Angela Johnson's *The First Part Last* also appears on the 2003 Teens' Top Ten list, the 2004 Quick Picks and Quick Picks Top Ten lists, and the 2005 Best of the Best list, in addition to winning the 2004 Printz Award.

> Gordon Korman's *Son of the Mob* also appears on the 2003 Quick Picks and Quick Picks Top Ten lists, the 2005 Popular Paperbacks for Young Adults list, and the 2005 Best of the Best list.

> Kenneth Oppel's *Airborn* also appears on the 2005 Quick Picks list and the 2006 Popular Paperbacks for Young Adults list, in addition to receiving a 2005 Printz Honor recognition. It is also an ALSC Notable Children's Book.

> Gloria Whelan's *Homeless Bird* also appears on the 2002 Popular Paperbacks for Young Adults list and the 2005 Best of the Best list. It is an ALSC Notable Children's Book and won the National Book Award in 2000.

> Virginia Euwer Wolff's *True Believer* also appears on the 2005 Best of the Best list, in addition to receiving a 2002 Printz Honor recognition. It is an ALSC Notable Children's Book and won the National Book Award in 2001.

Halpin, Brendan. *Donorboy* (2005).

Buckhanon, Kalisha. *Upstate* (2006).

Gaiman, Neil. *Anansi Boys* (2006).

Galloway, Gregory. *As Simple as Snow* (2006).

Martinez, A. Lee. *Gil's All Fright Diner* (2006).

THE BBYA TOP TEN

Following the final binding vote for the full BBYA list at the Midwinter Meeting, each BBYA committee member is asked to select his or her ten favorite books from that final list. These individual top ten lists are counted and compiled into a single list, and the top ten books with the most votes are the BBYA Top Ten for that year. You might think of the BBYA Top Ten as an annual consensus snapshot of the very best of the best books for young adults. A list of ten years of BBYA Top Tens is provided in part 2.

Characteristics of the 1997–2006 BBYA Top Ten Lists

The BBYA Top Ten lists lend themselves to some of the same statistical comparisons as the complete BBYA lists, such as market and genre break-downs, and in addition offer some fascinating comparisons with other "best of the best" lists and with limited and single-title awards.

BBYA TOP TEN LISTS BY TEEN AND ADULT MARKETS

Of the one hundred books found on the past ten years of BBYA Top Ten lists, 83 percent are teen market books and 17 percent are adult market books. Compared with the complete BBYA numbers found above, the BBYA Top Ten lists demonstrate a five percentage-point higher proportion of adult titles.

Popular Authors in BBYA Top Ten Lists

There are nine authors with two or more titles in the 1997–2006 BBYA Top Ten lists. These include Laurie Halse Anderson, Susan Campbell Bartoletti, Joan Bauer, Robert Cormier, Nancy Farmer, Kimberly Willis Holt, David Levithan, Walter Dean Myers, and Adam Rapp.

Only two authors have two or more titles on both BBYA Top Ten lists and on BBYA unanimous votes lists: David Levithan and Walter Dean Myers.

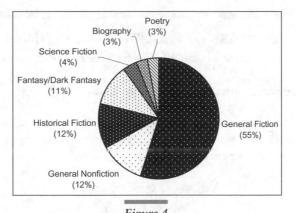

Figure 4

BBYA Top Ten lists by genre and format, 1997–2006

BBYA TOP TEN LISTS BY GENRE AND FORMAT

As with the complete BBYA lists, general fiction is the predominant genre represented on BBYA Top Ten lists, accounting for more than half the total over the past ten years. Nonfiction, historical fiction, and fantasy books nearly tie for a distant second place, with science fiction, biography, and poetry bringing up the rear. (See figure 4.)

The BBYA Top Ten lists of the past decade don't include enough titles to provide a meaningful breakdown of general fiction, but suffice it to say that creative formats (verse, diaries and letters, multiple narratives, script and play formats, graphic novels) hold their own within the total, as do humorous works. Considering all genres, the ten recent lists contain four stories in verse, two graphic novels (both fiction), and one each of script, diary, and epistolary formats.

BBYA TOP TEN TITLES APPEARING ON OTHER YALSA AWARDS AND LISTS

By virtue of their size and inclusion, there is a proportionately higher number of crossover titles between BBYA Top Ten lists and other book lists than there are between BBYA Top Ten lists and awards titles. The highest number of shared titles in the last decade is between BBYA Top Ten titles and Popular Paperbacks lists (thirty-six), followed by Quick Picks for Reluctant Readers lists (nineteen). Only four books have been on both the BBYA Top Ten list and the Quick Picks Top Ten list in the past ten years: *Among the Hidden,* by Margaret Peterson Haddix (1999 lists), *Son of the Mob,* by Gordon Korman (2003 lists), *The First Part Last,* by Angela Johnson (2004 lists), and *Twilight,* by Stephenie Meyer (2006 lists).

TEN YEARS OF PROLIFIC BBYA AUTHORS
AND THEIR BOOKS: 1997–2006

There are thirty-three authors with three books on BBYA lists between 1997 and 2006. There are eight authors with four books, eleven authors with five books, and three authors with six books. One author has more than six books on BBYA lists in the past decade: nine books by Walter Dean Myers appear on BBYA lists during that span, nearly one for each year.

Authors of Nine Selections
Walter Dean Myers

Authors of Six Selections
Paul Fleischman
Russell Freedman
Richard Peck

Authors of Five Selections

Sarah Dessen	Donna Jo Napoli	Ellen Wittlinger
Jean Ferris	Naomi Shihab Nye	Jacqueline Woodson
Margaret Peterson Haddix	Gary Paulsen	Jane Yolen
Iain Lawrence	J. K. Rowling	

Authors of Four Selections

Susan Campbell Bartoletti	Jan Greenberg and	Pete Hautman
Dennis Brindell Fradin	Sandra Jordan	Albert Marrin
Mel Glenn	Adele Griffin	Jerry Spinelli

Authors of Three Selections

Laurie Halse Anderson	E. R. Frank	Marilyn Nelson
Gary Blackwood	Neil Gaiman	Garth Nix
Tonya Bolden	Will Hobbs	Elizabeth Partridge
Martha Brooks	Kimberly Willis Holt	Philip Pullman
Dia Calhoun	Angela Johnson	S. L. Rottman
Orson Scott Card	Sherryl Jordan	Graham Salisbury
Michael Cart	Ron Koertge	Neal Shusterman
Robert Cormier	David Levithan	Sonya Sones
Charles de Lint	Chris Lynch	Vivian Vande Velde
Nancy Farmer	Carolyn Meyer	Nancy Werlin
Sharon G. Flake	Jim Murphy	Scott Westerfeld

The BBYA Top Ten Lists and the Best of the Best Lists

Perhaps of particular interest are the titles shared between BBYA Top Ten lists and the two most recent Best of the Best lists. The numbers show that although there is some consensus, the best of each annual list does not necessarily add up to the "best of the best." There is more than one kind of best! The Millennial Best of the Best list shares nine titles with the BBYA Top Ten lists of the past decade. As the Millennial list comprises titles from the inception of Best Books for Young Adults in 1966 through 1999, providing only a three-year crossover, the lower count is not surprising. The Millennial list is unique. It provides a list of books of such exceptional value that they have risen to the top of over thirty years' worth of outstanding books for young adult readers, so the nine titles that the 1997–1999 BBYA Top Ten lists share with the Millennial list are worth noting:

> Hobbs, Will. *Far North* (1997).
>
> Farmer, Nancy. *A Girl Named Disaster* (1997).
>
> Pullman, Philip. *The Golden Compass* (1997).
>
> McDonald, Joyce. *Swallowing Stones* (1998).
>
> Bloor, Edward. *Tangerine* (1998).
>
> Rowling, J. K. *Harry Potter and the Sorcerer's Stone* (1999).
>
> Sachar, Louis. *Holes* (1999).
>
> Woodson, Jacqueline. *If You Come Softly* (1999).
>
> Bauer, Joan. *Rules of the Road* (1999).

The 2005 Best of the Best list (1995–2004) provides a broader crossover (eight years) with the BBYA Top Ten lists and is perhaps a more useful comparison. At forty-four titles, the 1997–2004 BBYA Top Ten lists and the 2005 Best of the Best list share close to half their titles. Had the Best of the Best also included the past two years, that shared percentage might be even higher.

The BBYA Top Ten Lists and YALSA's Limited and Single-Title Awards

YALSA's limited or single-title awards for books (as opposed to awards for authors) are rookies compared with the veteran selection lists, so numbers are interesting but not definitive. The Alex Awards have been in existence since 1998 (officially since 2002); the Printz Award was first given in 2000. Kalisha Buckhanon's *Upstate* is the only book to appear on both a BBYA Top Ten list and an Alex Awards list. This book was honored on both in 2006. Three BBYA Top Ten books have also won the Printz Award: Walter Dean Myers's *Monster* (2000), Angela Johnson's *The First Part Last* (2004), and John Green's *Looking for Alaska* (2006). An additional six titles from BBYA Top Ten lists have received Printz Honors recognition: Laurie Halse Anderson's *Speak* (2000), Virginia Euwer Wolff's *True Believer* (2002), Nancy Farmer's *The House of the Scorpion* (2003), Jennifer Donnelly's *A Northern Light* (2004), Kenneth Oppel's *Airborn* (2005), and Markus Zusak's *I Am the Messenger* (2006).

The BBYA Top Ten Lists and the Teens' Top Ten Lists

Last but not least from YALSA is a comparison between BBYA Top Ten lists and the relatively new Teens' Top Ten lists. Beginning in 2003, the official YA Galley Group vote shared one title with the BBYA Top Ten for Angela Johnson's *The First Part Last*. The 2003 Teen Public vote shared two titles with the BBYA Top Ten: Martha Brooks's *True Confessions of a Heartless Girl* and E. R. Frank's *America*. To date, only one other title has found its way onto both the Teens' Top Ten and BBYA Top Ten lists: John Green's *Looking for Alaska*, in 2005 and 2006, respectively.

The BBYA Top Ten Lists and ALSC's Notable Children's Books

Although it takes us outside the YALSA umbrella, a comparison with ALSC's Notable Children's Books is an interesting one. The BBYA Top Ten lists share twenty-seven titles with Children's Notables across its categories for middle readers (grades 3–5, ages 8–10) and older readers (grades 6–8, ages 11–14) over the past decade. (See figure 5.)

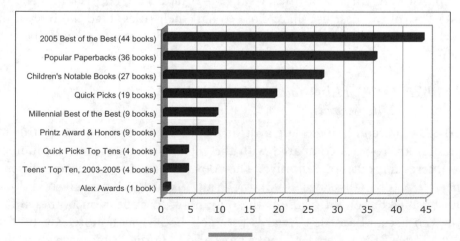

Figure 5
BBYA Top Ten books appearing on other awards and lists, 1997–2006

THE BBYA UNANIMOUS VOTES

If you frequent YALSA's Best Books for Young Adults web pages (part of Booklists and Book Awards, at http://www.ala.org/yalsa/booklists/bbya/), you may have puzzled over the differences between BBYA Top Ten lists and unanimous votes lists. Then again, you may not have paid much attention to the unanimous votes, as they appear in varying formats nestled in the introductory text, are present for some years and not others, and aren't prominently featured. Just what are the unanimous votes, how do they differ from the BBYA Top Ten, and why do they have such a spotty record?

Unanimous votes are identified after the final binding vote has been cast at the Midwinter Meeting each year. Titles that make the final BBYA list and that have full readership and unanimous yes votes from all fifteen committee members make it to the unanimous votes list. As outlined in the section on Top Ten lists, Top Ten titles are a secondary vote following the final vote for the BBYA list. They are the top ten of the compiled top tens of each of the fifteen committee members.

Top Ten titles and unanimous votes, though they share some common ground, differ in significant ways. Both lists demonstrate a strong positive reading response from committee members in general, and both contain titles that are especially notable given the body of literature read by the committee in any given year. However, without complete readership by each and every committee member, a title cannot make a unanimous votes list. And with the ever-increasing volume of literature published each year for teens or strongly appealing to teens, together with the fact that various circumstances might bring in a new committee member midway through a year, it is rare for most nominated titles to receive full readership and thus potentially earn the distinction of a unanimous vote. Were it possible for all committee members to read every nominated book every year, the unanimous votes lists would be of the utmost meaning. Given that this is not possible, the Top Ten lists provide a way for the BBYA committee to compile a short list of particularly outstanding titles from the books read by the highest number of committee members.

For the present, unanimous votes are still tallied, and if the current chair determines they have any representative value based on committee readership, the list is included in the introductory portion of each year's BBYA list. If they do not seem to be representative, they may not make an appearance. Of course, if you are surfing around in older BBYA lists and find one without a unanimous votes statement, it may simply be the case that there weren't any unanimous votes that year.

Fifty-seven titles with unanimous votes are available for the years 1999 and 2001–2005. There were three unanimous votes in 1999, five in 2001, thirteen in 2002, eleven in 2003, eleven in 2004, and fourteen in 2005.

I suggested earlier that I'd give you ten years of unanimous votes, and indeed, I tried. However, the past decade includes four years with no unanimous votes listed: 1997, 1998, 2000, and 2006. The reason why the first three of these years do not record unanimous votes is lost in the annals of YALSA history. The 2006 list was deemed nonrepresentative, and a decision was made to provide the public with a more meaningful Top Ten list only. Because the unanimous votes are spotty and may not be particularly representative, there isn't any good reason to provide any statistical breakdown here. As it hasn't been compiled anywhere, though, the full list of unanimous votes tallied in the last decade is provided for you here. Note that only two authors have more than one title in the past decade's unanimous votes lists: David Levithan and Walter Dean Myers.

A book that makes it to both the BBYA Top Ten list and a unanimous votes list is certain to be an incredible read. There are twenty-eight titles that appear on both lists between 1997 and 2006.

Titles Appearing on BBYA Top Ten (1997–2006) and on BBYA Unanimous Votes Lists (1999, 2001–2006)

Anderson, M. T. *Feed.*

Bauer, Joan. *Rules of the Road.*

Brashares, Ann. *The Sisterhood of the Traveling Pants.*

Chevalier, Tracy. *Girl with a Pearl Earring.*

Colman, Penny. *Corpses, Coffins, and Crypts: A History of Burial.*

Crutcher, Chris. *Whale Talk.*

Donnelly, Jennifer. *A Northern Light.*

Farmer, Nancy. *The House of the Scorpion.*

Flinn, Alex. *Breathing Underwater.*

Holt, Kimberly Willis. *My Louisiana Sky.*

Hoose, Phillip. *The Race to Save the Lord God Bird.*

Jenkins, A. M. *Damage.*

Johnson, Angela. *The First Part Last.*

Korman, Gordon. *Son of the Mob.*

Levithan, David. *Boy Meets Boy.*

Levithan, David. *The Realm of Possibility.*

Marchetta, Melina. *Saving Francesca.*

Maynard, Joyce. *The Usual Rules.*

Moore, Christopher. *Lamb: The Gospel according to Biff, Christ's Childhood Pal.*

Nelson, Peter. *Left for Dead: A Young Man's Search for Justice for the USS Indianapolis.*

Nye, Naomi Shihab. *19 Varieties of Gazelle: Poems of the Middle East.*

Oppel, Kenneth. *Airborn.*

Pattou, Edith. *East.*

Paulsen, Gary. *The Beet Fields: Memories of a Sixteenth Summer.*

Saenz, Benjamin Alire. *Sammy and Juliana in Hollywood.*

Taylor, Mildred D. *The Land.*

Whelan, Gloria. *Homeless Bird.*

Wolff, Virginia Euwer. *True Believer.*

Six Years of BBYA Unanimous Votes, 1999, 2001–2005

Anderson, M. T. *Feed.*

Bauer, Joan. *Rules of the Road.*

Bolden, Tonya. *Wake Up Our Souls: A Celebration of Black American Artists.*

Brashares, Ann. *The Sisterhood of the Traveling Pants.*

Chevalier, Tracy. *Girl with a Pearl Earring.*

Colman, Penny. *Corpses, Coffins, and Crypts: A History of Burial.*

Crowe, Chris. *Getting Away with Murder: The True Story of the Emmett Till Case.*

Crutcher, Chris. *Whale Talk.*

Donnelly, Jennifer. *A Northern Light.*

Fama, Elizabeth. *Overboard.*

Farmer, Nancy. *The House of the Scorpion.*

Flinn, Alex. *Breathing Underwater.*

Froese, Deborah. *Out of the Fire.*

Fusco, Kimberly Newton. *Tending to Grace.*

Greenberg, Jan, and Sandra Jordan. *Andy Warhol: Prince of Pop.*

Hearn, Lian. *Across the Nightingale Floor.*

Holt, Kimberly Willis. *My Louisiana Sky.*

Hoose, Phillip. *The Race to Save the Lord God Bird.*

Jenkins, A. M. *Damage.*

Johnson, Angela. *The First Part Last.*

Jordan, Sherryl. *The Hunting of the Last Dragon.*

Klass, David. *You Don't Know Me.*

Konigsburg, E. L. *The Outcasts of 19 Schuyler Place.*

Korman, Gordon. *Son of the Mob.*

Lawrence, Iain. *B for Buster.*

Levithan, David. *Boy Meets Boy.*

Levithan, David. *The Realm of Possibility.*

Marchetta, Melina. *Saving Francesca.*

Maynard, Joyce. *The Usual Rules.*

McCaughrean, Geraldine. *The Kite Rider.*

McCormick, Patricia. *Cut.*

Meyer, L. A. *Bloody Jack: Being an Account of the Curious Adventures of Mary "Jacky" Faber, Ship's Boy.*

Mikaelsen, Ben. *Touching Spirit Bear.*

Moore, Christopher. *Lamb: The Gospel according to Biff, Christ's Childhood Pal.*

Murphy, Jim. *An American Plague: The True and Terrifying Story of the Yellow Fever Epidemic of 1793.*

Myers, Walter Dean. *145th Street: Short Stories.*

Myers, Walter Dean. *The Greatest: Muhammad Ali.*

Nelson, Peter. *Left for Dead: A Young Man's Search for Justice for the USS Indianapolis.*

Nye, Naomi Shihab. *19 Varieties of Gazelle: Poems of the Middle East.*

Oppel, Kenneth. *Airborn.*

Pattou, Edith. *East.*

Paulsen, Gary. *The Beet Fields: Memories of a Sixteenth Summer.*

Pullman, Philip. *The Amber Spyglass.*

Rosoff, Meg. *How I Live Now.*

Saenz, Benjamin Alire. *Sammy and Juliana in Hollywood.*

Silverstein, Ken. *The Radioactive Boy Scout: The True Story of a Boy and His Backyard Nuclear Reactor.*

Smith, Sherri L. *Lucy the Giant.*

Sones, Sonya. *What My Mother Doesn't Know.*

Spinelli, Jerry. *Milkweed.*

Stratton, Allan. *Chanda's Secrets.*

Taylor, Mildred D. *The Land.*

Updale, Eleanor. *Montmorency: Thief, Liar, Gentleman?*

Vance, Susanna. *Deep.*

Whelan, Gloria. *Homeless Bird.*

Wolff, Virginia Euwer. *True Believer.*

Woodson, Jacqueline. *Miracle's Boys.*

Zusak, Markus. *Fighting Ruben Wolfe.*

BBYA AND BEST OF THE BEST LISTS

It would be remiss in a book about BBYA not to at least mention the Best of the Best lists, which are intricately linked to the work of the BBYA Committee. Conceived in the 1970s by Carol Starr and Regina Minudri of the Alameda County Library in the San Francisco Bay Area, the idea was to formalize a way for librarians to work together to find out which BBYA titles stood the test of time. Designed as a YASD preconference, the process was intended to "select good books that had remained popular with young adults" (Carter 1994, 68). Attendees of the preconference were assigned to one of three five-year periods and were asked to read and evaluate both BBYA and non-BBYA books that they believed teens were still reading and would continue to read in the future.

The first Best of the Best preconference, called "Book You," produced a list called "Still Alive in '75." There was another Best of the Best preconference in 1984, and since then there has been one about every five years, each with its own catchy nomenclature. and operating according to the same general principles up through the most recent Best of the Best list in 2005.

There have been six Best of the Best lists to date. The first list considered a fourteen-year span (1960–1974) and named seventy-one titles. The second list considered a thirteen-year span (1970–1983) and ended up with eighty-five titles. The third list considered twenty years (1966–1986) and named seventy-four titles. The fourth list considered twenty-five years (1967–1992) and was the first to mandate one hundred titles. The fifth list, developed at the "Bo Jo Jones and Beyond" preconference in 2000, considered thirty-four years of books (1966–2000) to create a list of the "100 Best Books for Young Adults." The most recent Best of the Best preconference, in 2005, looked at the previous decade (1995–2004) to produce its list of one hundred best titles. This most recent list is included in part 2.

Because of the unique character of the 2000 preconference and only six years of crossover, a comparison of the most recent two Best of the Best lists isn't particularly meaningful. Nonetheless, those books that appear on BBYA lists and on both of these Best of the Best lists have received three significant acknowledgments from three unique groups of librarians. There are twelve books found on all three, as follows:

Bloor, Edward. *Tangerine.*

Cushman, Karen. *Catherine, Called Birdy.*

Farmer, Nancy. *A Girl Named Disaster.*

Farmer, Nancy. *The Ear, the Eye, and the Arm.*

Fleischman, Paul. *Whirligig.*

Hobbs, Will. *Far North.*

Marsden, John. *Tomorrow, When the War Began.*

McDonald, Joyce. *Swallowing Stones.*

Pullman, Philip. *The Golden Compass.*

Rowling, J. K. *Harry Potter and the Sorcerer's Stone.*

Sachar, Louis. *Holes.*

Woodson, Jacqueline. *If You Come Softly.*

Although preconference guidelines encourage reading and evaluating books not found on BBYA lists during the ranges of years under consideration, and although the preconference can serve as a vehicle for acknowledging overlooked great books from the past, the majority of the books selected for the Best of the Best lists come from BBYA lists.

SOURCES CONSULTED

Anderson, Eunice. 2006. Written responses to questionnaire. January 9.

Cart, Michael. 2006. Written responses to questionnaire. February 3.

Carter, Betty. 1994. *Best Books for Young Adults: The History, the Selections, the Romance.* Chicago: American Library Association, Young Adult Library Services Association.

Orsillo, Rick. 2006. Written responses to questionnaire. February 13.

Current Trends
in Teen Publishing
and Best Books
for Young Adults

THE CURRENT TEEN BOOK WORLD

Teen literature is in a period of unprecedented growth, with teen readers clearly recognized as a potent and influential force in the American marketplace. According to Albert Greco, Fordham University marketing professor and industry analyst, teen market book sales in America have risen 23 percent between 1999 and 2005. Simultaneously, children's and adult publishing segment sales have, respectively, experienced moderate and slight declines (Beatty 2005). These strong numbers, coupled with projections for even greater future spending from the teen consumer base, have prompted a publishing response that provides teen readers with an almost dizzying selection of books in all established genres, as well as motivating publishers to proactively identify and even create new literary trends that will continue to attract teen attention.

In addition to the phenomenally popular Harry Potter books, robust adolescent demographics are in large part responsible for this increase in teen market book sales. Today's teens are right in the middle of the generation known variously as Gen Y, the Millennials, and the Echo Boomers. Their generation, which is predicted to peak well beyond the Baby Boomers' 78 million, comes armed with the greatest disposable income and marketplace influence in history. According to Don Montuori of the consumer market research company Packaged Facts, these teens "are increasingly in control of purchasing decisions, both for themselves and within families" (Packaged Facts 2002).

The more commercial teen book offerings of the past several years include both humorous and edgy chick lit series from mainstream publishers and packagers like Alloy Entertainment, as well as high-appeal series in fantasy, contemporary supernatural, and adventure/thriller genres. In addition to dedicating a regular portion of their lists to teen books, publishers have established new imprints, including Scholastic's PUSH, Simon and Schuster's Simon Pulse, and Penguin Group (USA)'s Razorbill, designed to focus on books that will connect with today's prominent and economically influential teens. These books come clad in slick, alluring packages to entice a more sophisticated audience, and entice them they do. The *Bookseller* reports that the sales threshold for high-selling teen authors has doubled in the last four to five years, rising from an average of 50,000 copies to 100,000 copies (Horn 2005).

To reach even more teens, many books are simultaneously or near-simultaneously released in audio formats, including downloadable formats. An increasing number of teen books are making it to film, with secondary market thrusts from publishers to sell more books as movie tie-ins. A few publishers are even on the vanguard of a marketing strategy to advertise new books to teens through text messages on their cell phones, in addition to maintaining an online marketing presence (Rosen 2005).

In the library world, "commercial" tends to connote "less than literary," perhaps because this has in large part proved true. Not all trends that appeal to teens or books that produce high marketplace sales are less than literary, though. Nor are all publishers motivated exclusively by commercial success. In addition to producing books that will sell, many teen book publishers look for works that resonate with them, and that they believe will resonate with teen readers now and into the future, regardless of their potential market impact. This is the case with Megan Tingley, vice president, publisher, and editor-in-chief of Little, Brown Books for Young Readers, who believes that "publishing books based on passion and vision, rather than market trends, is the best way to ensure a personal connection with readers" (Schwartz 2004). Smaller presses with smaller lines and less ability to influence the marketplace also tend to focus on originality, quality, and even debut authors. Alongside the rapidly produced commercial juggernauts is a sweeping array of lovingly crafted and caringly published books for all sorts of teens with highly diverse reading interests.

The increased activity in the teen publishing market has enhanced and expanded teen sections in bookstores and in libraries, which in turn has escalated a number of debates surrounding teen literature, almost all of which, ironically, have been generated by adults. Electronic mailing lists for teen library services and literature have become forums for debate over content in schools and communities. Since 2005 a variety of periodicals and major news services have carried reactive, biased, and factually incomplete stories on the nature of teen literature and its effect on young people. In 2006 YALSA Executive Director Beth Yoke and YALSA President Pam Spencer Holley joined forces to provide all the counterweights they could to this flak, and to educate the public on the many faces of teen literature.

Meanwhile, books for teens have been not only acknowledged but honored with increasing visibility over the past decade. In 1996, the National Book Foundation added Young People's Literature as a National Book Award category following an absence of more than twenty years for any category representing literary excellence for youth. Books receiving this honor are acknowledged for literary merit and, to date, have predominantly come from teen market titles. The year 1999 saw the inception of YALSA's Michael L. Printz Award for excellence in young adult literature, which announced its first awards in 2000 and which continues to build credibility and visibility. Particularly exciting is the new Andre Norton Award for young adult science fiction and fantasy, created in 2005 by the Science Fiction and Fantasy Writers of America.

There is no doubt it is an active and exciting, if also exasperating, time in the teen book world. Despite their detractors, and in publisher Marc Aronson's words, "motivated authors, librarians, booksellers and publishers have found ways to interject books into the slipstream of modern teenage life" (2005, 66).

TODAY'S TEENS, LITERARY TRENDS, AND THE BBYA LISTS

Currently weighing in at over 30 million strong, America's teens have been the country's most rapidly growing age group since 1990 and are projected to continue to boom in the future. They are also the most ethnically diverse population segment in the country, with one out of three teens belonging to a minority group. These teens identify with their unique ethnicities and also identify themselves as "intra-cultural," part of a larger multiethnic national and international reality, according to Mediamark Research Inc., a marketing firm that provides an annual teen profile for the Magazine Publishers of America (2004, 5). Mediamark finds that today's diverse teen population is comfortable with a fast-paced, rapidly changing, conflict-laden world with a wide range of options from which to meet interests and choose individual courses (2004, 1). These teens are smart and fairly realistic, capable of both skepticism and optimism. Well aware that they are growing up in a complex and problematic world, they are nonetheless hopeful things can come out positively in the end. They are far less individualistic (yet far more live-and-let-live) and considerably more family- and society-focused than the preceding generation, with an understanding that developing and maintaining connections is essential to achieving success in life (2004, 3).

John Bartlett published a still-well-known quotation by the influential Bostonian and Episcopal bishop Phillips Brooks in his *Familiar Quotations:* "Life comes before literature, as the material always comes before the work.

The hills are full of marble before the world blooms with statues." There is no doubt that teen life today serves as the inspiration and raw material for its literature and is reflected in it, with creative and sophisticated formatting, wide-ranging content, and areas of concentration that seem to closely mirror current knowledge about teens. Among other resources, YALSA selection lists are excellent tools for identifying some of these literary trends, both in the teen market as well as the larger literary market that publishes books with strong appeal to teens. Quick Picks for Reluctant Young Adult Readers provide a look at each year's publications with high appeal for teens who, for whatever reason, tend to shun books. The Alex Awards highlight selections from each adult publication year that show strong potential to engage the interest of teen readers. Among other trends, Popular Paperbacks for Young Adults feature a large number of books with popular and/or timely subjects that were well enough received in their first printings to merit a continued life in paperback editions.

Best Books for Young Adults showcase those books that are a combination of acceptable literary quality and proven or potential appeal to teens. And when trends are identified through BBYA lists, it can indicate that wherever they originated—author, publisher, teen demand—there is a successful connection between the interests of teens and the quality of the books meeting those interests. Trends identified in BBYA lists do not, however, mirror all publishing trends. Many prominent commercial trends in teen publishing are simply not reflected in BBYA lists, as the products of those trends do not meet the committee charge. Although they do not define themselves as marketing specifically to teens, manga publishers, for example, rely on teens and young adults to keep these Japanese serial comics among the largest and most lucrative of publishing trends in recent years. Yet no manga book to date has been recognized on a Best Books for Young Adults list.

The major trends in teen literature as seen on BBYA lists over the past seven years include more books for older teens, adult authors writing for teens, the "feminization" of teen literature, international authorship, noteworthy and innovative formats, and content trends. (Please note that a parenthetical date following a book title is the year it appeared on a BBYA list, which will not necessarily be the same as the copyright date or year of publication.)

Books for Older Teens

Gone, perhaps, are the days when authors like Ursula K. Le Guin and Robert Cormier crafted exceptional stories heedless of potential audience or any category of readership, and were somewhat befuddled to find their works labeled for a particular market in the end. There is no doubt that in the current publishing world, markets matter, and authors as well as editors and publishers are acutely aware of their works' intended audience. For precisely whom are teen market books written these days? This may seem like a foolish question, but the teen market is a moving target and the question is far less simple than it would seem. In the second edition of this book, Betty Carter noted that five editors at the 1994 YALSA Best of the Best preconference agreed that publishers saw the teen market as the younger end of adolescence, ending at fourteen years of age. By the year 2000, only a handful of years later, the teen publishing market had outgrown its previous eleven-to-fourteen age designation, and publishers were beginning to produce far more books for older teen readers (2000, 11). Since 2000, the older market has seen a continued expansion, with sophisticated, multi-plotted, ensemble-casted, experimental, and, considered by some, controversial books for older teen readers. With a more mature audience, authors are free to address complex issues in a complex fashion through older teen protagonists, to explore life's profound difficulties and questions, and to test established ideas and practices. And these authors are supported by publishers who acknowledge that there is a strong market for such books with older teen readers.

Many of these books are making appearances on BBYA lists. Laurie Halse Anderson's *Speak,* a 2000 BBYA book, explores the psychological aftermath of rape as well as the teenage and adult societies that ignore or mask such crimes. Anna Fienberg's 2001 BBYA book, *Borrowed Light,* features a teen who already plays parent to her sensitive younger brother, and who studies the cosmos and relates her life and the lives of those around her to the celestial bodies while she debates what to do about her unborn baby. K. L. Going's *Fat Kid Rules the World*, a 2004 BBYA book and 2004 Printz Honor book, takes on self-esteem, family life, suicide, drug addiction, homelessness, friendship, and music in almost equal parts through the imminently likable voice of three-hundred-pound Troy Billings. Pete Hautman's *Godless,* a 2005 Best Book and winner of the 2004 National Book Award for Young People's Literature, not only challenges the established order of family and society, it tackles belief systems in a way that allows its main protagonists to create the world anew, albeit satirically for one character and obsessively for another, demonstrating the older teenage need and inclination to see through rigid systems and hypocrisy in the quest for independence and personal meaning.

With titles for older teens come books that arguably could have been published in either the teen or the adult market. In addition to the grade school/middle school crossover book, teen literature is now seeing the older teen/adult crossover book. Although the trend is still in its relative infancy, some characteristics that often apply to this type of crossover book have been identified. According to Michael Cart:

> They're typically written by young authors, usually in their twenties; they're often first novels or novels presented in the form of the currently fashionable

collection of linked stories. Their protagonists may be teens, but just as often they are in their twenties. Coming-of-age or rite-of-passage issues drive their plots. And, perhaps most importantly, they are published as *adult* novels. (Cart 2004, 734)

A common debate among teen services librarians revolves around which books published for teens could have been published for adults and vice versa. The YALSA President's Program panel presentation at the 2006 Annual Conference in New Orleans, "How Adult Is Young Adult: The Sequel," confirmed that editors and publishers are also engaged in this debate, and common consensus has it that it is a case-by-case determination for which market any particular teen/adult crossover book will be published. In some cases, the most economical publishing process and the market most likely to turn a profit wins out (usually adult), in others, the best content-to-audience match holds sway. One thing is certain: all publishing houses are receiving an increased number of manuscripts for teen novels, and adult publishing houses are paying attention to them. Perhaps a happy result of this shared market, or books that in Michael Cart's words are "happy hybrids," will be an increased interest and engagement in the adolescent experience and an increased appreciation among adult readers for literature about adolescents.

The past several years have seen a strong increase in these older teen/adult crossover books on BBYA lists. Teen books on BBYA lists that might arguably have been published for adults include titles like Aidan Chambers's *Postcards from No Man's Land* (2003), Benjamin Alire Saenz's *Sammy and Juliana in Hollywood* (2005), Meg Rosoff's *How I Live Now* (2005), David Levithan's *Are We There Yet?* (2006), Markus Zusak's *I Am the Messenger* (2006), and John Green's *Looking for Alaska* (2006). Of note, Rosoff's book was published in Britain as a crossover title, with two publicity and sales teams, one for each market (Corbett 2005, 31). Interestingly, three of these books are Printz Award winners and another is a Printz Honor book.

As for books published for adults that could have been marketed to teens, the recent BBYA lists have seen quite a few, notably beginning in 2000 with Stephen Chbosky's *The Perks of Being a Wallflower*. Among many others are particularly notable books such as Tracy Chevalier's *Girl with a Pearl Earring* (2001), Vineeta Vijayaraghavan's *Motherland* (2002), Alice Sebold's *The Lovely Bones* (2003), Mark Haddon's *The Curious Incident of the Dog in the Night-Time* (2004), Joyce Maynard's *The Usual Rules* (2004), Brendan Halpin's *Donorboy* (2005), Kalisha Buckhanon's *Upstate* (2006), and Gregory Galloway's *As Simple as Snow* (2006). Mark Haddon's book is a particularly strong example of walking the market line. Haddon played a role in its market designation, specifically requesting it be published as an adult title to distance it from his other books for young readers. His request was granted in the United States, but his book was published concurrently in both teen and adult editions in Great Britain, each with unique, market-specific packaging (Corbett 2005, 30). Among these notable examples five are also honored as Alex Award titles, perhaps another indicator of the current blurring of teen and adult publishing markets.

Adult Authors Writing for Teens

A related trend has well-known adult market authors writing books for the teen market, which is evidenced on BBYA lists. Among the more celebrated in this trend is Carl Hiaasen, whose 2002 teen novel, *Hoot,* was recently adapted as a feature film. Hiaasen admits that the idea to write for a younger audience was not his own, but rather a request from an editor. Although he thought "it was nuts at first," the beloved author of humorous, society-mocking adult mysteries wrote a humorous, society-mocking teen novel with an ecological bent (Taylor 2005, 1). With *Hoot* and its burrowing owls very well received, including a place on the 2003 BBYA list, Hiaasen went on to write *Flush,* which made the 2006 BBYA list.

Whatever the reason, a noteworthy number of adult authors in both mainstream and even more so in genre fiction are writing for the teen market, where they keep company with Hiaasen. They have proliferated on BBYA lists, especially since 2002. Like Hiaasen, many are contributors of more than one book to the lists. The 2002 BBYA list included *The Amazing Maurice and His Educated Rodents* by the very clever and prolific science fiction and fantasy writer Terry Pratchett, along with fantasy writer Sharon Shinn's *Summers at Castle Auburn*. In addition to Hiaasen's *Hoot,* the 2003 BBYA list included Julia Alvarez's *Before We Were Free,* Clive Barker's *Abarat,* Neil Gaiman's *Coraline,* Ann Halam's *Dr. Franklin's Island* (Ms. Halam writes adult works under Gwyneth Jones), and Joyce Carol Oates's *Big Mouth and Ugly Girl.* Nina Kiriki Hoffman's *A Stir of Bones,* Terry Pratchett's *Wee Free Men,* and Timothy Zahn's *Dragon and Thief: A Dragonback Adventure* made the 2004 BBYA list. The 2005 list featured yet another from Terry Pratchett, *A Hat Full of Sky,* along with Charles de Lint's *The Blue Girl,* Sharon Shinn's *The Safe-Keeper's Secret,* and Scott Westerfeld's *So Yesterday.* And the 2006 list includes Ann Halam's *Siberia,* Alison McGhee's *All Rivers Flow to the Sea,* Rick Riordan's *The Lightning Thief,* and Scott Westerfeld's *Peeps* and *Uglies.*

Along with adult market authors writing for teens are authors perhaps not so easily categorized but who come to the world of teen literature from other literary traditions and unique artistic and academic backgrounds. Perhaps not so broadly seen on BBYA lists, they are nonetheless important, and if not truly a trend are still worthy of a brief mention. Adam Rapp, whose first book for teens, *Missing the Piano,* appeared on the 1995 BBYA list and heralded additional appearances for *33 Snowfish* in 2004 and in 2005 for *Under the Wolf, under the Dog,* is also an accomplished playwright whose works are produced in prominent theaters. Allan Stratton is an accomplished Canadian playwright with two BBYA teen novels: *Leslie's Journal,* in 2002, and, in 2005, *Chanda's Secrets,* which was also a 2005 Printz Honor book. Julius Lester is a man who wears many hats, including lecturer, radio show host and producer, professor of African American, Near Eastern, and Judaic studies, musician and photographer, and writer, among others. His ethnically reimagined, narrative retelling of *Othello* made the 1996 BBYA list, and his teen novel *Day of Tears: A Novel in Dialogue* appeared on the 2006 BBYA list and won the 2006 Coretta Scott King author award.

It is important to note that although the more prominent trend shows adult authors writing books for upper middle grades and older teens, not all adult market authors who write for teens are writing at the higher end. Hiaasen's teen books are for the younger set, or "tween" market, receiving fifth- through eighth-grade reading recommendations from reviewers. Also at the younger end are Rick Riordan's *The Lightning Thief* and Neil Gaiman's *Coraline,* both recommended by reviewers for fifth- through eighth- or ninth-grade readers.

The "Feminization" of Teen Literature

A 2004 article in *Locus Online* takes a look at turn-of-the-millennium publishing trends in relation to the science fiction and fantasy genres. Cynthia Ward, the article's author, notes that a "significant millennial trend" in the publishing industry at large "is the 'feminization' of the fiction readership." She specifically notes women's current "dominance" in the mystery and romance genres, and mentions as well the incredible advances publishers are giving to authors of chick lit (Ward 2004, 2). Although more than likely referring to the older end of the Millennial generation, Ward's "feminization" is also strongly evidenced in literature for those Millennials still in adolescence and is quite visible in the BBYA lists of the past several years. There is a significant trend in recent years toward books written for girls and young women in all stages of their teenage years and even beyond, featuring female characters both teenaged and adult with whom, despite subject or genre, they can identify. Books featuring strong, intelligent, courageous, quirky, artistic, determined, scrappy, wily, independent, resilient, witty females dominate not only fiction but nonfiction on recent BBYA lists.

A good half of the biographies on BBYA lists since 2000 feature exceptional women of strength and courage, from civil rights and social activists to competitive athletes, from artists and musicians to political figures and survivors of social and political cruelty. Among others are biographies of Babe Didrikson Zaharias, Dorothea Lange, Clara Schumann, Margaret Bourke-White, Ida B. Wells, Helen Keller, Prudence Crandall, Marian Anderson, Mary Church Terrell, and Louise Bourgeois. Equally compelling are the stories of ordinary women who faced great hardship in one form or another, personal or societal, and lived to tell the tale, including Andie Dominick's *Needles: A Memoir of Growing Up with Diabetes* (2000), Eleanor Ramrath Garner's *Eleanor's Story: An American Girl in Hitler's Germany* (2000), Adeline Yen Mah's *Chinese Cinderella: The True Story of an Unwanted Daughter* (2000), Irene Gut Opdyke's *In My Hands: Memories of a Holocaust Rescuer* (2000), Lori Gottlieb's *Stick Figure: A Diary of My Former Self* (2001), Loung Ung's *First They Killed My Father: A Daughter of Cambodia Remembers* (2001), Marjane Satrapi's *Persepolis* tales (2004 and 2005) and Tonya Bolden's *Maritcha: A Nineteenth-Century American Girl* (2006).

A number of nonfiction books look at women's roles in history and at women's rights issues. Recent BBYA lists have seen books about significant women in the nineteenth-century expansion to the American West, World War II army nurses, and influential twentieth-century American female musicians. As for women's rights, a strong showing of books exploring more than one facet of the long-term equality movement is represented on BBYA lists since 2000, including Catherine Gourley's *Good Girl Work: Factories, Sweatshops, and How Women Changed Their Role in the American Workforce* (2000), Martha E. Kendall's *Failure Is Impossible! The History of American Women's Rights* (2002), Ann Bausum's *With Courage and Cloth: Winning the Fight for a Woman's Right to Vote* (2005), and Karen Blumenthal's *Let Me Play: The Story of Title IX; The Law That Changed the Future of Girls in America* (2006). A handful simply look at the lives of adolescent girls and adult women in the modern world, including Tina Schwager and Michele Schuerger's *Gutsy Girls: Young Women Who Dare* (2000), *Things I Have to Tell You: Poems and Writing by Teenage Girls* (2002), edited by Betsy Franco, *Yell-oh Girls! Emerging Voices Explore Culture, Identity, and Growing Up Asian American* (2002), edited by Vickie Nam, and Valérie Zenatti's *When I Was a Soldier: A Memoir* (2006).

As for fiction, even a brief look at the BBYA lists since 2000 shows an abundance of books, both mainstream and in the genres, that feature strong or strong-in-the-making female protagonists. Many of these stories—be they contemporary realistic "problem" novels, historical fiction, mystery, fantasy, or science fiction—spotlight psychologically and emotionally invested protagonists who face internal and external obstacles and are given the opportunity to learn and grow even if their obstacles are not always surmountable. Strength is not always measured by triumph in these books, nor is it limited to any standard definition. At times the measure of success is simply a new awareness or understanding despite a difficult situation; at other times, it may be little more than survival.

It is probably safe to say, however, that the majority of female protagonists in the current literature do triumph. Today's teen literature has given rise to a new sort of young woman, one whose time among the cinders only serves to toughen her up and motivate her toward her goals. In many cases, secondary female characters that either complement or provide contrast for the story's lead play essential roles in these stories. The voices of these young women are more thoughtful, arch, serious, feisty, despairing, droll, angry, exuberant, and overall well-articulated than ever before in teen literature: they are carefully crafted, fully realized, individual literary characters.

A significant number of the books on BBYA lists since 2000 that feature young women and their concerns are seen in the contemporary realism genre. Female teens today face many of the same issues as they did in the past—self-image and self-esteem, social situations both ordinary and extreme, family matters, also both ordinary and extreme, romantic attachments and disappointments, educational goals—but the difference in the current literature often hinges on how these adolescent females perceive and handle those issues. Characters are often more focused, more resolute, more action-oriented, more resigned, and in the end, more in control—even if it takes awhile to get there—than ever before. In looking for examples from the BBYA lists to share, 115 contemporary realism books featuring young women of this description were readily identified. This accounts for 20 percent of the 577 total books of all genres and subjects, fiction and nonfiction, on BBYA lists since 2000. Suffice it to say, this trend is strong. Many of these books can be found among the themed lists section of this book.

Recent BBYA lists do contain some chick lit books as they are more commercially defined—with wryly self-deprecating or sardonically ebullient female characters that speak in a cheeky or ironic style and are engaged, if not in high jinks, in situations that may stretch credibility—such as Louise Rennison's *Angus, Thongs, and Full-Frontal Snogging: Confessions of Georgia Nicolson* (2001), Meg Cabot's *The Princess Diaries* (2001), Ann Brashares's *The Sisterhood of the Traveling Pants* (2002), and Susan Juby's *Alice, I Think* (2006). Many other books featuring ultimately indomitable female protagonists with chick lit–like voices, even if more plausible, weighty, and less stylized to lesser or greater degrees, include Sarah Dessen's *Keeping the Moon* (2000) and *This Lullaby* (2003), Karen Romano Young's *The Beetle and Me: A Love Story* (2000), Joan Bauer's *Hope Was Here* (2001), Ellen Wittlinger's *Zigzag* (2004), Tanuja Desai Hidier's *Born Confused* (2003), Carolyn Mackler's *The Earth, My Butt, and Other Big, Round Things* (2004), Nancy Osa's *Cuba 15* (2004), and Melina Marchetta's *Saving Francesca* (2005).

Even when female characters share the spotlight with other players, or play a supporting role, they are multidimensional and compelling, even serving at times as critical catalysts, if sometimes inadvertently, for primary characters. In Julie Anne Peters's *Define Normal* (2001), the black-lipsticked, pierced Jazz Luther provides straitlaced Antonia with an opportunity to more accurately see into herself. Gary D. Schmidt's Lizzie, among the most lovely of characters in recent teen fiction, not only offers Turner Buckminster an exceptional friendship but serves as his life teacher and mentor in *Lizzie Bright and the Buckminster Boy* (2005). The wildly whacked-out Colleen Minou in Ron Koertge's *Stoner and Spaz* (2003) allows Ben Bancroft, a young man afflicted with cerebral palsy, a shot at love. Matt Donaghy finds his only support in the bad-tempered Ursula Riggs after he makes a joke at his high school that has dire consequences in Joyce Carol Oates's *Big Mouth and Ugly Girl* (2003). Jen, an "Innovator," joins forces with the "Trendsetter," Hunter, to solve a pop culture mystery involving the most incredible shoes ever designed in Scott Westerfeld's *So Yesterday* (2005). Without Alaska Young in John Green's *Looking for Alaska* (2006), Miles "Pudge" Halter would not fall in love, experience great loss, and meet his "Great Perhaps." Metal Head Sam Markus needs the conventional and straight-shooting Melissa to understand what it is to love the wrong person in Christopher Krovatin's *Heavy Metal and You* (2006).

Although young women's issues are broadly explored in contemporary realism, they are also addressed in historical fiction. The BBYA lists of the past seven years show a strong trend in historical fiction featuring female protagonists whose stories are told from a uniquely female perspective. Some of these tales directly tackle issues women face in particular times and places; others simply tell tales of young women living and moving through their historical times in ways that reach young women in the here and now.

Fictionalized stories about real female royal and political figures are noteworthy on BBYA lists since 2000 and include books like Tracy Barrett's *Anna of Byzantium* (2000), based on the life of Anna Comnena (1083–1153), who unsuccessfully attempted to gain her usurped throne; Carolyn Meyer's *Mary, Bloody Mary* (2000); Jane Yolen and Robert Harris's *Queen's Own Fool* (2001), featuring two Marys—Mary Tudor and Mary Stuart—cousins often confused with one another; Rebecca Tingle's *The Edge on the Sword* (2002) and *Far Traveler* (2006), respectively featuring Aethelflaed, the teenage daughter of Alfred the Great, the West Saxon king in the late 800s, and Aethelflaed's teenage daughter Aelfwyn; and Jane Yolen and Robert Harris's *Girl in a Cage* (2003), which tells the story of Marjorie, the only daughter of Robert the Bruce, king of Scotland.

Among the BBYA lists' sassier, more resolute, and in some cases more rambunctious female characters—adventurers and swashbucklers who squarely face or even flaunt the societal mores of their times—are characters like Jennifer L. Holm's Jane in *Boston Jane: An Adventure* (2002), the title characters in Celia Rees's *Pirates! The True and Remarkable Stories of Minerva Sharpe and Nancy Kington, Female Pirates* (2004), and Jacky Faber in L. A. Meyer's *Bloody Jack: Being an Account of the Curious Adventures of Mary "Jacky" Faber, Ship's Boy* (2004) and *Curse of the Blue Tattoo: Being an Account of the Misadventures of Jacky Faber, Midshipman and Fine Lady* (2005). Another recent trend in teen fiction may be female pirate stories with titles of awe-inspiring length.

Historical characters of a less adventurous but perhaps equally plucky, exuberant, and even courageous nature include Marthe Jocelyn's Mable from *Mable Riley: A Reliable Record of Humdrum, Peril, and Romance* (2005), Faith from Trudy Krisher's *Uncommon Faith* (2004), and Melinda from Mary C. Sheppard's *Seven for a Secret* (2003). If not exactly plucky or exuberant, sixteen-year-old Mattie Gokey from Jennifer Donnelly's outstanding historical work *A Northern Light* (2004) is certainly courageous.

More somber in tone and content are books from the past several years of BBYA lists that feature female protagonists coping with a variety of difficult life situations, both personal and societal. Jerrie Oughton's *Perfect Family* (2001) tells the story of fifteen-year-old Welcome O'Neal, a small-town girl in 1955 North Carolina who gets pregnant after falling for an irresponsible older boy and is forced to make difficult decisions. A timeless concern for young women, teen pregnancy is also explored in *The Minister's Daughter* (2006) by Julie Hearn, a story that features several young women, among them the desperately duplicitous fifteen-year-old Grace, a Puritan minister's daughter pregnant out of wedlock in the perilous mid-1600s. Stories of young women dealing with less personal family matters are also found on BBYA lists since 2000, including Patricia Santana's *Motorcycle Ride on the Sea of Tranquility* (2003) and Linda Holeman's *Search of the Moon King's Daughter* (2003). These two books share in common profound sibling relationships between their main female protagonists and beloved brothers. In the first, fourteen-year-old Yoli Sahagun faces one of the tragedies of the Vietnam War when her brother, Chuy, returns home from his tour of duty in 1969 a broken man. In the second, fifteen-year-old Emmaline searches tirelessly for her brother in 1830s London when her laudanum-addicted mother sells her deaf younger brother into service as a chimney sweep.

A handful of historical fiction stories from recent BBYA lists feature young women who are by their nature and not just their actions different, set apart, and who must interact with the world from positions of disadvantage. Lensey Namioka's *Ties That Bind, Ties That Break* (2000) shares the story of Ailin, a young woman in 1911 China who cannot abide by the old traditions of foot binding and of societal subjugation of women, and who suffers extreme social censure for her choices. Randall Beth Platt's *The Likes of Me* (2001) relates fourteen-year-old Cordelia's plight as a half-white, half-

Chinese albino girl of exceedingly peculiar appearance neglected by a distant and angry father in a 1918 Washington State lumber camp, and who must find her own place in the world and make human connections to survive. Mary Nuttall, a fourteen-year-old healer in Celia Rees's *Witch Child* (2002), would be persecuted as a witch were her unique skills and capabilities to be revealed in the isolated and religiously zealous Massachusetts colony where she lives.

Books featuring young women who face great hardship in various time periods are prevalent on recent BBYA lists. In *Torn Thread* (2001), Anne Isaacs explores the suffering of two Polish Jews, Eva and her sister Rachel, in a Nazi labor camp during World War II. Patricia Reilly Giff renders the tremendous anguish and deprivation the poor Irish experienced during the Great Potato Famine in *Nory Ryan's Song* (2001). Several BBYA books are especially noteworthy for their depictions of American historical experiences through young female protagonists. Through teenaged Anna Maria Weems in *Stealing Freedom* (2000), author Elisa Carbone shows the tremendous misery black slave families experienced when they were torn apart and sold to different masters, as well as the endless efforts of abolitionists and the grueling road to freedom. In *Fever 1793* (2001), Laurie Halse Anderson re-creates the catastrophic Yellow Fever epidemic in Philadelphia through sixteen-year-old Mattie Cook and her fight for survival. Pam Muñoz Ryan tells the story of Esperanza Ortega, a privileged Mexican teen forced to flee her country and work in a California migrant camp during the Depression years, in *Esperanza Rising* (2001). Rose Nolan is forced to go it on her own and care for her younger sister in early twentieth-century New York City after her brother is turned away for health reasons at Ellis Island and must be returned to Ireland in Mary Jane Auch's *Ashes of Roses* (2003).

The fantasy genre is an area in which teenage girls are clearly center stage. Be it high fantasy, urban fantasy, dark fantasy, genre-blended fantasy, or any other of the many fantasy subgenres, female protagonists are making an increasingly strong showing. Omitting story collections, of the novel-length fantasy books that made BBYA lists since 2000, 60 percent feature female protagonists either as the sole primary character or sharing the spotlight with other characters, compared with 40 percent featuring male protagonists. As in contemporary realism and historical fiction, the young women who populate fantasy works are equally strong, intelligent, courageous, quirky, artistic, determined, scrappy, wily, independent, resilient, and witty—just in uniquely imaginative surroundings and with fantastical challenges.

International Authorship

An increasing number of teen books by international authors are being published in the United States for American teens, especially in fiction. BBYA lists since 2000 include a large number of books by authors from the United Kingdom, Canada, Australia, and New Zealand, and a handful of authors from other European and non-European countries.

From the United Kingdom come lauded authors of contemporary and literary fiction such as David Almond, Kevin Brooks, Melvin Burgess, and Gillian Cross. The United Kingdom's historical fiction authors are well represented on recent BBYA lists and include Theresa Breslin, Aidan Chambers, Adele Geras, Julie Hearn, James Heneghan, Geraldine McCaughrean, Nicola Morgan, Michael Morpurgo, Celia Rees, Ann Turnbull, and Eleanor Updale. Science fiction and fantasy writers from the United Kingdom make a strong showing, including Herbie Brennan, David Clement-Davies, Catherine Fisher, Ann Halam, Michael Lawrence, Terry Pratchett, Philip Pullman, J. K. Rowling, Jonathan Stroud, and Chris Wooding. Neil Gaiman, although British, lives near Minneapolis, so we'll count him with the Americans. And, of course, there is the immensely popular spy-adventure writer, Anthony Horowitz, with his teenage British spy, Alex Rider.

From our Canadian neighbors comes a wonderful array of BBYA books by skilled writers for teens. Authors of contemporary and literary fiction include Martha Brooks, Deborah Ellis, Gayle Friesen, Deborah Froese, Katherine Holubitsky, the prolific and inimitable Gordon Korman, Martine Leavitt, Graham McNamee, Allan Stratton, Teresa Toten, Diane Tullson, and Tim Wynne-Jones. Linda Holeman, Iain Lawrence, and Rebecca Tingle (she's an American raising her family in Canada) are honored on BBYA lists since 2000 for their historical fiction works. In science fiction and fantasy are Charles de Lint with his first book published for teens, *The Blue Girl* (2005), Janet McNaughton for her retelling of the Tam Lin legend in *An Earthly Knight* (2005), Kenneth Oppel with his award-winning fantasy adventure stories featuring the young Matt Cruse, *Airborn* (2005) and *Skybreaker* (2006), and Arthur Slade for his Depression-era Saskatchewan horror story, *Dust* (2004).

Although the American market has long had a strong relationship with children's and teen authors from the British Isles, authors from Australia and New Zealand are more recent arrivals to the literary party. Beginning in the 1990s with authors like John Marsden, Garth Nix, and Wendy Orr, an ever-increasing number of Aussies and Kiwis are entering the American market and receiving great acclaim for their exceptional literary skills. Acknowledged on recent BBYA lists are contemporary fiction writers such as Anna Fienberg, Sonya Hartnett, Melina Marchetta, Jaclyn Moriarty, and Markus Zusak. Joining them from the science fiction and fantasy genres are Lian Hearn (a pseudonym for Gillian Rubenstein), Sherryl Jordan, short story writer Margo Lanagan, and Justine Larbalestier.

A small gathering of European, South African, and Israeli authors round out the international showing on BBYA lists since 2000, most in the past two to three years. Ineke Holtwijk, a Dutch newspaper correspondent and author based in Brazil, is acknowledged on the 2000 BBYA List for her novel, *Asphalt Angels,* which tells the horrific story of a child living on the streets of Rio de Janeiro. German author Benjamin Lebert is recognized on the 2001 BBYA list for *Crazy,* written when he was fifteen, a boarding school coming-of-age story published in the United States three years after its original publication in Germany. A year later, South African author Beverley Naidoo (who now makes her home in England) made the 2002 BBYA list after branching out from several books set in her childhood country with *The Other Side of Truth,* a story of siblings who, after fleeing the political dangers of a corrupt Nigerian regime, find themselves alone in London. Naidoo followed this with the 2004 BBYA book *Out of Bounds: Seven Stories of Conflict and Hope,* a collection of South African apartheid stories set between 1948 and 2000. David Chotjewitz's *Daniel Half Human, and the Good Nazi,* a 2005 BBYA book originally published in Germany, is a horrifying story of two young German men joined as blood brothers at the dawn of the Nazi rise to power, until one finds out he's half-Jewish, and thus only half-human.

Four books on the 2006 BBYA list are by international authors. Josef Holub's *An Innocent Soldier,* translated from the German, features Adam, a hapless farmhand pressed into service in Napoleon's Grande Armée just before its march to Russia to fight the Czar's troops, and who along the way to makes friends with the young and equally ill-equipped officer he's assigned to serve. Belgian author Geert Spillebeen penned in *Kipling's Choice* the fictionalized story of John Kipling, Rudyard Kipling's son, who, to fulfill his father's wishes, allows himself to be enlisted into military service during World War I despite his poor eyesight. German author Lilli Thal wrote the gritty tale of a country betrayed and a young prince forced to train as a court jester for a rival king in *Mimus.* Of American origin, Pnina Moed Kass immigrated to Israel, where she has made her home for almost forty years. In *Real Time,* she tells through multiple narrators the preceding hours and aftermath of a suicide bombing on a Jerusalem bus.

New and Noteworthy Literary Forms

Any librarian who has been even a bit truant in the regular weeding of his or her teen collection will not have any difficulty picking out older titles on shelves with little more than a cursory glance. In recent years the teen publishing industry has given teen literature, both fiction and nonfiction, a complete physical makeover to more successfully appeal to contemporary teens. Gone are the days of sensitively drawn teens with fluffy hair and big glasses in front of a bank of lockers with their arms wrapped around their knees, gazing contemplatively off into the distance. Good-bye 1980s!

Good-bye 1990s, for that matter. Cover images are more sophisticated, sleek, creative, artistically innovative, and consumer savvy. Sure, there are those clinker covers still out there that bring a dismayed sigh to librarians' lips and are looked at balefully by even the most diehard of teen readers, but they are becoming fewer and farther between. Successful teen books that end up published in more than one format, notably in the fiction categories, may come out with different cover concepts for the trade or mass market editions to appeal even more broadly.

And inside these slick books for teens are a range of new and creative literary forms that tell their stories in unique ways, including some very long stories, either in larger single volumes or told across a number of books in duets, trilogies, and even longer series. Not to be overlooked is the newer and highly popular graphic novel format, which also finds a place of standing in current teen literature.

LITERARY FORMS IN FICTION

Fiction is the area in which the most innovative literary forms are evident on BBYA lists, with high-appeal, high-quality representatives of larger trends in the marketplace. Along with traditionally narrated novels and short story collections are stories told in verse or in the form of diaries or letters, stories written in script, stories composed using more than one literary form, and stories told through dual/multiple perspectives.

Verse fiction is the most ubiquitous of these literary forms on BBYA lists since 2000. Some verse fiction is narrative in nature, telling a story from beginning to end. Works of this sort are commonly referred to as verse novels, or novels in verse. Other works are less linear or cohesive, more suggestive, fragmented, and poetic, offering vignettes or brief pieces, sometimes from multiple perspectives, and that together add up to a complete work.

Contemporary verse fiction covers as many topics as narrative fiction, from family and personal issues to high school life to coming of age. Sonya Sones is an author worth noting, with three verse fiction works on BBYA lists since 2000: *Stop Pretending: What Happened When My Big Sister Went Crazy* (2000), *What My Mother Doesn't Know* (2002), and *One of Those Hideous Books Where the Mother Dies* (2005). Virginia Euwer Wolff's *True Believer*, the long-awaited follow-up to *Make Lemonade* (1994), was recognized on the 2002 BBYA list and also received a 2002 Printz Honor acknowledgment. In addition to appearing on the 2004 BBYA list, Helen Frost received a 2004 Printz Honor award for *Keesha's House*, a verse work that shares, through sestinas and sonnets, the voices of teens who, like Keesha herself, find a safe place in a house belonging to Joe, a caring and sympathetic man to teens in trouble. Authors of more traditional narrative formats who have successfully written in verse form and have been acknowledged on BBYA lists include Ron Koertge, Nikki Grimes, Cynthia Rylant, and David Levithan.

Though recent BBYA lists reflect that verse fiction is predominant in general rather than genre fiction categories, there is some historical fiction in verse recognized on BBYA lists. In 2005, Allan Wolf's *New Found Land,* written in verse and other literary forms, and Paul B. Janeczko's *Worlds Afire* made the BBYA list. Nikki Grimes's *Dark Sons* was a 2006 BBYA book told in free-verse narratives that alternate between modern New York City and biblical times.

Stories told in the form of diary or journal entries or as letters are also evident on BBYA lists as a more recent trend in teen fiction. Teen voices expressed as though they are writing for and even to the reader or to their fictional peers carry a particular immediacy and intimacy, allowing teen readers to feel they are inside the minds and hearts of these books' characters. Diary-style and epistolary voices allow authors more opportunity to express themselves outside the standards of fiction and lend characters a greater range of informal expression than is typical of standard narratives, even including the ubiquitous first-person narrative. The characters that voice these sorts of works are often unreliable, and this can be stimulating for readers, who are put in a position to know more than, or perhaps even know better than, the characters they are reading about.

Noteworthy in the diary and journal format are books like Louise Rennison's *Angus, Thongs, and Full-Frontal Snogging: Confessions of Georgia Nicolson* (2001), the humorous diary of a clever and acerbic British teen à la Bridget Jones, who experiences teen life in all its misery and glory, particularly through her crush on Robbie, the Sex God. The journal entries of Canadian teen Alice McLeod, the eponymous narrator of Susan Juby's *Alice, I Think* (2004), demonstrate that British chick lit–inspired teen voices are not alone in their hilarity and wit. In historical fiction, Marthe Jocelyn's *Mable Riley: A Reliable Record of Humdrum, Peril, and Romance* (2005) tells its story through the diary entries of an indomitable fourteen-year-old Canadian girl who, after relocating with her teacher sister to a small town, becomes involved with suffragettes. Setting a more somber tone are books like Allan Stratton's *Leslie's Journal* (2002), a dark and painful story that reveals Leslie's dysfunctional family life and abusive relationship with her boyfriend through her tenth-grade journal assignment. Adam Rapp exposes profound family trauma and extreme personal pain through Steve Nugent's writings from a therapeutic institution for troubled teens in *Under the Wolf, under the Dog* (2005).

Interestingly, three of the epistolary novels on BBYA lists since 2000 are adult market titles, including the highly lauded and highly discussed *The Perks of Being a Wallflower* (2000) by Stephen Chbosky, Brendan Halpin's *Donorboy* (2005), and Kalisha Buckhanon's *Upstate* (2006). All three books feature teenage protagonists, but the voices of Chbosky's and Buckhanon's protagonists in particular are central to their stories, and there was much debate about the appropriate market for those two books. Both books were thought to be at least as publishable as teen titles, if not more so. Perhaps to prove the point, *Upstate* was honored as a 2005 Alex Award title for its high potential appeal to teen readers, as was *Donorboy,* a story about the relationship between a teenager who has lost her lesbian parents and her sperm-donor father.

As Sonya Sones is notable for verse fiction, Jaclyn Moriarty is notable for epistolary fiction. Two of Moriarty's books have made BBYA lists in a four-year span: *Feeling Sorry for Celia* (2002) and *The Year of Secret Assignments* (2005). Lighthearted fare, these books feature Australian teens with a good measure of humor. Not limited to contemporary realism, epistolary fiction can be found in other genres, such as Patricia C. Wrede and Caroline Stevermer's historical fantasy genre blender book *Sorcery and Cecelia, or The Enchanted Chocolate Pot* (2004).

Many authors for teens are writing books in a combination of literary forms—narrative sections juxtaposed against verse or script, peppered between sections of monologue or dialogue. Predominantly in script form with passages of poetry recited by Elva, the elderly nursing home roommate of the spinally injured sixteen-year-old Courtney, is Paul Fleischman's *Mind's Eye* (2000). A master of experimental formats, Fleischman also contributed *Seek* to the BBYA lists (2002), a mix of many forms, including radio transcript, dialogue, poetry, narrative, and essay, that together make up a high school senior's memoir assignment. Sixteen-year-old Steve Harmon's experiences in prison while awaiting his trial for murder are told through both diary entries and the movie screenplay he is writing of the legal proceedings in Walter Dean Myers's *Monster,* a 2000 BBYA book and Printz Award winner. Through poems and dialogue, Mel Glenn tells the story of high school senior Laura Li's downward spiral toward suicide in *Split Image: A Story in Poems* (2001). The stories of four generations of young women who inhabit a Nebraska farm are told through a combination of narrative, diary entries, and letters in Dianne E. Gray's *Holding Up the Earth* (2001).

Very recent works using multiple literary forms include Eireann Corrigan's *Splintering* (2005), a tale that explores through verse and dual first-person narrative the family dynamics that follow a traumatic event, and Lynne Rae Perkins's *Criss Cross* (2006), which explores through poetry (including haiku), narrative, and question-and-answer formats the crossroads of life for fourteen-year-olds Debbie and Hector. *Criss Cross* also received the 2006 Newbery Medal. The largest slave auction in American history, which took place in Savannah, Georgia, in 1859, is the subject of Julius Lester's historical novel *Day of Tears* (2006), told through narrative, dialogue, and multiple voices.

The science fiction and fantasy genres also include a few works using multiple literary forms. Jonathan Stroud takes advantage of standard third-person narrative, first-person perspective (of the five-thousand-year-old djinni, Bartimaeus), and metatext (an additional layer of writing that remarks on what has already been written or expressed, as when Bartimaeus provides asides in subscript on his own narrative) in *The Amulet of Samarkand* (2004) and *The Golem's Eye* (2005), the first two books of his Bartimaeus trilogy. L. J. Adlington's *The Diary of Pelly D* (2006), a disturbing and provocative dystopian science fiction book that, through third-person narrative and diary entries, accompanies Toni V as he reads the diary of Pelly D, a girl who before a recent war lived a life of privilege in City Five.

A discussion of innovative formats, or literary forms, leads naturally to a look at narrative voice, or fictional perspective. The large majority of the teen fiction found on BBYA lists in the past seven years is written as first-person narrative, followed by the usual suspect, the third-person narrative. It is worth taking a look, however, at the increasing number of books written from multiple perspectives. For clarity's sake, it's important to differentiate between multiple first-person perspectives and a mere change of focus among multiple characters during the course of a story told in the third person. Multiple perspectives here mean that the author is writing in the first-person voice of more than one individual. It is worth noting that many of the books written in multiple literary forms also include multiple first-person narratives.

Examples of books with dual first-person perspectives seen on recent BBYA lists include Laura and Tom McNeal's *Crooked* and Miriam Bat-Ami's *Two Suns in the Sky,* both on the 2000 list; Mary Logue's *Dancing with an Alien* (2001); Adam Rapp's *33 Snowfish,* Susanna Vance's *Deep,* and Richard Peck's *The River between Us* from the 2004 list; Eireann Corrigan's *Splintering* (2005); and Paul Volponi's *Black and White* (2006). Even more common are books written with anywhere from three to more than ten perspectives. The 2001 BBYA list includes multiple-perspective stories like *The Girls* by Amy Goldman Koss, *Split Image* by Mel Glenn, and *What's in a Name* by Ellen Wittlinger, followed by Adele Geras's *Troy* in 2002. Trudy Krisher's *Uncommon Faith* and Edith Pattou's *East,* both from the 2004 BBYA list, are also told using several voices. The 2005 BBYA saw the addition of three more such books: Allan Wolf's *New Found Land,* Kathleen Jeffrie Johnson's *A Fast and Brutal Wing,* and Jacqueline Woodson's *Behind You.* Julius Lester's *Day of Tears: A Novel in Dialogue* and Justine Larbalestier's *Magic or Madness,* from the 2006 list, are also notable for their multiple perspectives.

David Chotjewitz's *Daniel Half Human, and the Good Nazi,* a 2005 BBYA book, stands out not only for its multiple viewpoints but also for its use of more than one narrative perspective for the same character. Julie Hearn's *The Minister's Daughter* (2006) is noteworthy for interchanging third-person present tense and first-person past tense as the story shuttles between 1645 and 1692.

It is not a trend by any means, but the very rare and very challenging second-person narrative is present in two titles on the 2002 BBYA list and is worth a mention while discussing perspectives in teen literature. The second-person narrative uses the "you" viewpoint, usually written in the command, or imperative, form and addressed to the narrator. In this form is Chris Lynch's *Freewill,* which is also a 2002 Printz Honor book, and A. M. Jenkins's *Damage.* In the first, the unique wood sculptures of a troubled high school teen are found near dead teenagers, bringing Will, the sculptor, under suspicion. In the second, seventeen-year-old Austin Reid, a high school senior who seems to have it all, battles profound depression. An infrequently used and often strident literary technique, the second-person narrative is perhaps especially suited to the telling of particularly difficult or peculiar stories.

LITERARY FORMS IN NONFICTION

The nonfiction books found on BBYA lists continue to improve in physical layout, with exceptional production quality. These books come in many sizes and shapes, tend to be printed on thick, slick paper with glossy photographs and artistic illustrations, and are designed to entice teens to the true tales of the real world, both current and past. Along with contemporary nonfiction in hipper, edgier packaging are high-interest stories about days gone by. Dry, dusty textbooks are no longer the only means to history for teen readers. Although at only a handful of titles poetry collections have not had a strong presence on recent BBYA lists, poetry has found its place among the narrative form in sharing the real world with teens.

Although there are only a few nonfiction books in verse on BBYA lists, those few pack a real punch. On the 2001 BBYA list, Ann Turner's *Learning to Swim: A Memoir* tells in verse the story of six-year-old Annie's sexual molestation at the hands of an older boy who terrifies her into keeping the secret. Marilyn Nelson combines verse and biography in *Carver: A Life in Poems,* a BBYA title from 2002 that introduces young readers to the great and highly driven African American inventor and botanist. Among its numerous appearances on many prestigious literary lists, this book received both a Newbery and Coretta Scott King honor in 2002 and was a National Book Award finalist in 2001. It is not in the least surprising that Ms. Nelson, Connecticut's poet laureate, has also received praise and multiple distinctions for *A Wreath for Emmett Till,* which, in addition to being a 2006 BBYA book and on multiple literary "best" lists, it is a Coretta Scott King Honor book and a Michael L. Printz Honor book. This incredible work, told in the form of a heroic crown of fifteen linked sonnets, speaks of the 1955 Mississippi lynching of fourteen-year-old African American Emmett Till for allegedly whistling at a white woman.

BOOK LENGTH

Peter D. Sieruta, in a 2005 article in *Horn Book Magazine* called "10 Things that Piss Me Off!" lists at number two the current trend toward "supersizing" in children's and teen novels. Whether for good or, as Sieruta feels, for ill, and whether written for the younger or older set, books for teens are getting longer. Perhaps this has been precipitated by the incredible and ever-expanding lengths of the Harry Potter books, which have proven to be worth the challenge for both children and teens and which demonstrate that young people can and will read books of potentially daunting length. Authors, both teen market and adult, may also be playing a role here, by offering increasingly mature content with complex themes and using sophisticated plotting and in-depth characterization that take many more pages than the heretofore average teen novel to successfully craft. Whatever the case may be, teen books seem to be, on average, in the words of Sieruta, "slouching toward four hundred" (Sieruta 2005, 224–225).

Regarding general fiction, Sieruta is right. A notable number of these books exceed 300 pages. As for fantasy, about which Sieruta sardonically pleads, "And let's not even talk about those @#&@#$ fantasy novels," (224) books in this genre are not slouching at all! Among the lengthiest books to appear on BBYA lists are, of course, the Harry Potter series, the heftiest of which is *Harry Potter and the Order of the Phoenix* (2004), coming in at 870 pages in the first American edition. The remaining Harry Potter books appearing on BBYA lists range from 312 pages up to 734 pages. Other titans of fantasy on recent BBYA lists include the final volume in Philip Pullman's His Dark Materials trilogy, *The Amber Spyglass* (2002), with 518 densely packed pages; the first and second books in Jonathan Stroud's Bartimaeus trilogy, with *The Amulet of Samarkand* (2004) at 462 pages and *The Golem's Eye* (2005) at 562 pages; Libba Bray's *A Great and Terrible Beauty* (2004) and *Rebel Angels* (2006), taking 403 and 548 pages, respectively, to unfold; Edith Pattou's *East* (2004) and Stephenie Meyer's *Twilight* (2006), tying at 498 pages each; Garth Nix's *Lirael, Daughter of the Clayr* (2002), which almost meets its 1997 BBYA predecessor, *Sabriel,* at 486 pages; and Nancy Farmer's Norse fantasy quest *The Sea of Trolls* (2005), at 459 pages.

SERIES/SEQUELS AND COMPANION NOVELS

Another noteworthy trend on BBYA lists is the increasing presence of a fairly traditional format: serial stories, or sequels, and companion novels, or stories that share worlds if not always characters. These books are differentiated from those commercial series that typically feature a dozen or more books, usually by multiple authors. Serial stories/sequels and companion novels tend to be more literary and are written by individual authors carrying characters in a serial story arc across more than one book or placing new characters in existing literary worlds. These books take the form of pairs, trilogies, tetralogies, and beyond. Many such books have found their way onto BBYA lists, especially in the science fiction, fantasy, and adventure genres.

The majority of the series books and companion novels on BBYA lists date from the year 2000. A small handful of series and companion books are present on BBYA lists between 1994 and 2000, though, and some of the post-2000 books have prequels on BBYA lists from the late 1990s. But just because a title in a series or a companion novel makes it onto a BBYA list does not mean other titles in the group will necessarily make the list. Only those books that each year's BBYA Committee deem worthy on their own merits, without also considering books from any other publication year, make the list. An example here is J. K. Rowling's *Harry Potter and the Goblet of Fire*. This fourth book in the Harry Potter series is the only volume to date that has not made a BBYA list.

Companion novels on BBYA lists since 2000 include Holly Black's *Tithe* (2003) and *Valiant* (2006), Dia Calhoun's *Firegold* (2000) and *White Midnight* (2004), E. L. Konigsburg's *Silent to the Bone* (2001) and *The Outcasts of 19 Schuyler Place* (2005), Gerald Morris's *The Squire, His Knight, and His Lady* (2000) and *The Savage Damsel and the Dwarf* (2001), both in the Squire's Tales series, and Rebecca Tingle's *The Edge on the Sword* (2002) and *Far Traveler* (2006).

Series/sequels are quite common on recent BBYA lists. Forty-one books by twenty authors are on BBYA lists in the last decade, most of them since 2000. Of these, only four books by two authors were published for the adult market—Orson Scott Card's *Ender's Shadow* (2000) and *Shadow of the Hegemon* (2002) and Marjane Satrapi's *Persepolis: The Story of a Childhood* (2004) and *Persepolis 2: The Story of a Return* (2005). The majority are in the science fiction and fantasy genres, followed by historical fiction then contemporary realism.

Leading the way in science fiction and fantasy are Garth Nix's *Sabriel* (1997) and *Lirael* (2002); Kenneth Oppel's *Airborn* (2005) and *Skybreaker* (2006); Terry Pratchett's *The Wee Free Men* (2004) and *A Hat Full of Sky* (2005); Philip Pullman's *The Golden Compass* (1997), *The Subtle Knife* (1998), and *The Amber Spyglass* (2002); Philip Reeve's *Mortal Engines* (2004) and *Predator's Gold* (2005), the first two books in the Hungry City Chronicles; all but the fourth book of J. K. Rowling's Harry Potter series (1999–2006); the first two books of Jonathan Stroud's Bartimaeus trilogy,

The Amulet of Samarkand (2004) and *The Golem's Eye* (2005); and Libba Bray's historical fantasies, *A Great and Terrible Beauty* (2004) and *Rebel Angels* (2006). First titles in the science fiction and fantasy genres that may see sequels or companions on future BBYA lists include Lian Hearn's *Across the Nightingale Floor* (2004); Catherine Fisher's *The Oracle Betrayed* (2005), the first book in the Oracle Prophecies; Joseph Delaney's *Revenge of the Witch* (2006), first in the Last Apprentice series; Justine Larbalestier's *Magic or Madness* (2006), the first in a proposed trilogy; and Rick Riordan's *The Lightning Thief* (2006), book 1 in the Percy Jackson and the Olympians series.

Historical books in series on recent BBYA lists include Gary Blackwood's *The Shakespeare Stealer* (1999) and *Shakespeare's Scribe* (2001); Iain Lawrence's *The Wreckers* (1999) and *The Smugglers* (2000) in his High Seas trilogy; L. A. Meyer's *Bloody Jack* (2004) and *Curse of the Blue Tattoo* (2005); Richard Peck's *A Long Way from Chicago* (1999) and *A Year down Yonder* (2001); and Francisco Jimenez's *The Circuit: Stories from the Life of a Migrant Child* (1999) and *Breaking Through* (2002).

Last but not least are Virginia Euwer Wolff's *Make Lemonade* (1994) and *True Believer* (2002) and Jacqueline Woodson's *If You Come Softly* (1999) and *Behind You* (2005), in the contemporary realism genre.

GRAPHIC NOVELS

Graphic novels, currently experiencing an incredible surge of popularity with all ages, made a first appearance on the 1999 BBYA list with Katherine Arnoldi's *The Amazing True Story of a Teenage Single Mom,* setting the stage for an additional sixteen graphic novels to find their way to BBYA lists between 2000 and 2006. With the exception of a very few, graphic novel publishers seem to ignore ages or markets. Those graphic novels selected for BBYA lists run the gamut of artistic styles, subjects, and genres and, although not marketed for any particular age range, tend to be fairly sophisticated.

The sixteen graphic novels on the past seven years of BBYA lists cover a broad range of both real and fictional subject matter: traditional superheroes and super villains, murder mysteries and teen sleuthing, adventurers and travelers, sibling relationships and spiritual questing, futuristic interpretations of the Old West and of Manhattan, childhood memoirs set during the Iranian Revolution, anti-Semitism and Russian propaganda, the Warsaw Ghetto Uprising, communism in North Korea, and AIDS. Fiction and nonfiction titles are equally well represented, with a balance of nine and seven titles, respectively.

Perhaps surprisingly, none of the graphic novels on BBYA lists are manga, the fastest-growing publishing trend in America and the category that is thought to be largely responsible for the popularity of the modern graphic novel with the Millennial generation. Why might this be? Manga are the rapidly produced commercial series of the graphic novel world. The equivalent in general fiction might well be the *Gossip Girl* and *A-List* novels and series like *The Mediator* or *Charmed*. Manga are common on Quick Picks for Reluctant Young Adult Readers lists, but they don't tend to match the charge of the BBYA Committee any more than the current commercial fiction series for teens.

Content Trends

General marketplace and format trends in teen literature are fascinating to follow, especially in the dynamic, booming teen publishing market today. Equally fascinating, though, are trends that go beyond the authors, intended audiences, and packaging. What is going on *inside* these books? A great and varied deal, as a matter of fact. Teen literature has become as diverse as there are real subjects to write about and stories to be imagined. Current content trends do occur within this broad range of incredibly diverse literature, though, and many are evident in recent BBYA lists.

CONTEMPORARY REALISTIC FICTION

With their reasonably clear literary boundaries, trends in nonfiction and genre fiction categories are fairly easy to identify. It is a greater challenge to identify content trends in general fiction, particularly over the broad range of works represented on the past seven years of BBYA lists. The 2000–2006 BBYA lists include 577 books total, 241 of which, or 42 percent, are in the general fiction category, otherwise known as contemporary realistic fiction. It makes sense for such a large group, given the incredible diversity in subject and treatment, to limit discussion of trends to a few obvious standouts that encompass comparatively larger numbers of books.

Evident in this decade's BBYA lists are strong trends toward books that address teen internal life, teen family life, and teen social life, notably the teen ethnic experience. These books look at both extremes of contemporary teen life, from light, humor-filled tales of the ordinary daily life of adolescents to dark and painful stories of challenge and abuse.

As for the latter, there is no doubt that the "problem novel" is alive and well, but it is arguable that in most cases it has matured from its simplistic, single-focused literary beginnings into a more subtle and complex literature. No longer merely a vehicle for sharing an obvious message about a single problem, populated by characters and carried by a story arc that support that message and little else, problem novels have on the whole become something entirely different in current teen literature. Increasingly common are books that feature more than one story line peopled with multiple and complicated characters of all ages from any number of backgrounds who face problems for which there may be no ready answers. Perhaps this trend reflects a more complex society and adolescent experience. Perhaps it is a natural progression or evolution of a literature that has simply grown up. As a sign of this evolution, some contemporary problem novels turn to heretofore-unimagined genres. One example is Nina Kiriki Hoffman's fantasy work, *A Stir of Bones* (2004), which features a teen girl tormented by her father's manipulative abuse of her mother and who finds succor with a ghost in a self-aware house.

Teen Internal Life

Books that focus on teen internal life represent a significant trend in current teen fiction. Such stories are generally told from the perspective of the central character or characters. They are often, if not always, first-person narratives. Though the focus of the story is the inner state, the basis for the story tends to be an external situation or circumstance. Much of the teen literature in this subgenre of contemporary realism is of a darker, more disturbing nature; the external circumstances or realities to which a teen reacts are generally not pleasant, and most of these books could be described as "problem" novels.

Although these books run the gamut of subjects, strong among them are books about various forms of abuse, both self-abuse and abuse at the hands of others, and books about a range of physical and psychological challenges experienced by teens. Hard on their heels are a larger number of books about loss, grief, and recovery.

Not all books in this subgenre of contemporary realism, however, are dire in tone. There has been a significant trend toward teen books about personal identity, self-image, and self-acceptance that take a bold, affirmative stance. Such books feature teens who seek for and discover a sense of self, or matter-of-factly and openly proclaim sometimes long-hidden truths about their identity. This is especially evident in current gay and lesbian fiction for teens.

Sexual Abuse

Books about sexual abuse are prominent in BBYA lists of the past seven years, and most are from the victim's perspective. Laurie Halse Anderson's *Speak* (2000), about a teen girl unable to speak about her rape at an end-of-summer party and the toll it takes on her during the following school year, remains immensely popular years after it was published. Other books that treat the sexual abuse of teen girls include Lori Aurelia Williams's *When Kambia Elaine Flew in from Neptune* (2001), Rita Williams-Garcia's *Every Time a Rainbow Dies* (2002), and Amanda Davis's *Wonder When You'll Miss Me* (2004). Ron Koertge's *Margaux with an X* (2005) is also worth a mention. Although the story does not directly address sexual abuse, it does look at a teen girl's damage from childhood when her father paid a gambling debt by allowing his then-ten-year-old daughter to be photographed in her underwear.

Girls are not the only victims of sexual abuse in teen literature. The 2000 BBYA list includes Catherine Atkins's *When Jeff Comes Home,* a painful story of a young man's re-entry into his family unit after being dropped on their doorstep by his kidnapper and sexual abuser of two and a half years. Kathleen Jeffrie Johnson tells the story of sixteen-year-old Grady, a boy violently raped by adult men and so damaged by the experience he is barely able to eat or speak, in *Target* (2004). Jennifer Richard Jacobson's *Stained* (2006) focuses on the search for a teen boy who has disappeared from his community because of a sexual relationship with his priest.

Although most books dealing with sexual abuse are from the perspective of the victim, Chris Lynch's *Inexcusable* (2006) is the exception. Its primary character date rapes his childhood friend and initially tries to excuse the act like he has with all his previous bad behaviors.

Physical Abuse

Other forms of physical abuse besides sexual are also explored in teen literature and are found on BBYA lists. Again, most stories are told from the victim's point of view. The 2000 BBYA list includes Graham McNamee's *Hate You,* a story featuring the seventeen-year-old Alice, a songwriter and would-be singer had her father not choked her in an uncontrolled rage and permanently damaged her vocal cords. David Klass's *You Don't Know Me* (2002) features a teen protagonist who is beaten by his mother's boyfriend while she avoids the situation. Teresa Toten deals with multiple issues in *The Game* (2003), with a focus on the root of teenager Dani's current and serious problems, namely, her physically abusive father and her guilt at leaving her sister behind with him. And worth yet another mention is Nina Kiriki Hoffman's *A Stir of Bones* (2004), a genre blender that features a teenage girl attempting some escape from a father who beats her mother to exert control on his daughter.

Sarah Dessen's *Dreamland* (2001) puts young Caitlin together with a very appealing boy, one Rogerson Biscoe, who is a wonderful distraction from her family problems until he begins to harm her. In Allan Stratton's *Leslie's Journal* (2002) the abusive physical and sexual behaviors of Leslie's boyfriend are revealed through her tenth-grade journal assignment. Like Chris Lynch's *Inexcusable,* Alex Flinn's *Breathing Underwater* (2002) tells its story of physical abuse from the perspective of the abuser. Flinn's sixteen-year-old protagonist Nick enters a program to address his violent tendencies after he beats up his girlfriend.

Last but certainly not least, and in a category of its own, is Adam Rapp's *33 Snowfish* (2004), a story that combines three profoundly abused and consequently criminal and abusive teens in a runaway road trip story.

Physical and Psychological Challenges

Stories involving physical and psychological challenges are another strong trend in books focusing on the internal lives of teens. In these stories, teens are either experiencing these challenges in their own lives or are coping with loved ones who are experiencing them. Physical challenges in teen literature seem to be a mix of illnesses, conditions, and accidents. Psychological challenges seem to focus predominantly on various forms of mental illness, from depression to schizophrenia and even to posttraumatic stress disorder.

Cancer is a regular subject in teen fiction, and many stories that either deal directly with cancer or arise from circumstances surrounding such an illness are found on recent BBYA lists. Joan Abelove's *Saying It Out Loud* and Diane Stanley's *A Time Apart* lead the way from the 2000 BBYA list, followed by Joan Bauer's *Hope Was Here* (2001), Carol Plum-Ucci's *What Happened to Lani Garver* (2003), Dorothea N. Buckingham's *Staring Down the Dragon* (2004), and Adam Rapp's *Under the Wolf, under the Dog* (2005). Physical injuries, conditions, and disabilities also make for strong teen literature. Notable BBYA books featuring characters with significant physical injuries include Paul Fleischman's *Mind's Eye* (2000) and Deborah Froese's *Out of the Fire* (2003). In the first, a sixteen-year-old girl deals with a paralyzing back injury from her hospital room; in the second, another sixteen-year-old girl is horribly burned at a bonfire. As for physical conditions that challenge teens, Terry Trueman's *Stuck in Neutral* (2001) and Ron Koertge's *Stoner and Spaz* (2003) feature primary characters with cerebral palsy, and Scott Johnson's *Safe at Second* (2000) and Iain Lawrence's *Ghost Boy* (2001) feature partial blindness by injury and by genetics. In Lawrence's story, the main character is also challenged by other aspects of albinism. Jean Ferris's *Of Sound Mind* (2002) tells the story of a boy whose life has been spent caring for his deaf parents.

There are a number of books on recent BBYA lists that deal with mental illnesses or challenges, faced both by teens and by those in teens' lives. Notable books with themes of depression include A. M. Jenkins's *Damage* (2002), E. R. Frank's *America* (2003), Melina Marchetta's *Saving Francesca* (2005), and Adam Rapp's *Under the Wolf, under the Dog* (2005). Stories on BBYA lists that treat other forms of mental illness include Sonya Sones's *Stop Pretending: What Happened When My Big Sister Went Crazy* (2000), Ruth White's *Memories of Summer* (2001), and Judith Ortiz Cofer's *The Meaning of Consuelo* (2004). Patricia Santana deals with a unique form of mental illness in *Motorcycle Ride on the Sea of Tranquility* (2003), in which a teenage girl's beloved brother returns mentally damaged from the Vietnam War.

Books about addiction and other self-destructive behaviors are a unique mixture of both physical and psychological challenges. On the 2006 BBYA list, Jake Coburn's *LoveSick* features an alcoholic teen and a bulimic teen.

Other books that treat alcoholism on BBYA lists since 2000 focus on teens dealing with alcoholic parents: S. L. Rottman's *Stetson* (2003), Sherri L. Smith's *Lucy the Giant* (2003), Jaye Murray's *Bottled Up* (2004), and Mary E. Pearson's *A Room on Lorelei Street* (2006). As for drug addiction, only a few books on the past seven years of BBYA lists treat the subject to any degree. In *Bottled Up,* the teen dealing with his alcoholic parent is doing so in part through a drug addiction of his own. Ron Koertge's *Stoner and Spaz,* mentioned already for its treatment of cerebral palsy, features another primary character who is drug addicted. Both of Adam Rapp's recent BBYA books, *33 Snowfish* (2004) and *Under the Wolf, under the Dog* (2005), also deal with substance abuse and addiction. Regarding other forms of self-destructive behavior, only a couple of books from recent BBYA lists stand out. Patricia McCormick's *Cut* (2002) tells the story of a girl who is so pressured by familial responsibility she begins to cut herself for release. Pete Hautman's *Sweetblood* (2004) explores Lucy's self-destructive responses to her diabetic condition.

Loss, Grief, and Recovery

Another meaningful trend in contemporary teen fiction is an influx of stories that delve into loss and its aftermath. Although there are books that deal with grief without a death, Martha Brooks's *True Confessions of a Heartless Girl* (2004) being an example, most do focus on death or include death following an accident or illness. Two short story collections from the 2002 BBYA list treat the subject of loss and death: Bruce Brooks's *All That Remains* and editor James Howe's *The Color of Absence: Twelve Stories about Loss and Hope* (2002).

The largest death theme on recent BBYA lists is by violence, whether intentional or otherwise. Because its companion book is on the 2005 BBYA list, it is well worth mentioning Jacqueline Woodson's *If You Come Softly* from the 1999 BBYA list, in which a young man is mistakenly shot and killed by the police. In her 2005 BBYA book, *Behind You,* Woodson beautifully and at times wrenchingly explores the grief that each person who loved this young man experiences following his death and how they attempt to recover through sometimes awkward reconnections with each other. Other books in this mode include Carolyn Coman's *Many Stones* (2001), in which a sixteen-year-old deals with the murder of her sister in South Africa; Alice Sebold's *The Lovely Bones* (2003), an adult market title narrated by a dead girl who was brutalized and murdered by a serial killer and who watches her family's grief process from the beyond; Joyce Maynard's *The Usual Rules* (2004), also an adult market title which features a teen girl dealing with the loss of her mother in the terrorist attacks on the World Trade Center; and Benjamin Alire Saenz's *Sammy and Juliana in Hollywood* (2005), a coming-of-age story that follows a young man in a 1969 New Mexico barrio who has lost his love interest to a violent death. Two stories treating death by drive-by shooting appear on the 2006 BBYA list: Walter Dean Myers's *Autobiography of My Dead Brother* and Sharon G. Flake's *Bang!*

Death resulting from illness is another theme in loss, grief, and recovery stories. From the 2000 BBYA list is Joan Abelove's *Saying It Out Loud,* about a girl coping with her mother's brain cancer and eventual death. Three books from the 2005 list feature deaths of family members from illness and the process of grief for their survivors, including Maureen Johnson's *The Key to the Golden Firebird* (father, heart attack), Adam Rapp's *Under the Wolf, under the Dog* (mother, cancer), and Sonya Sones's *One of Those Hideous Books Where the Mother Dies* (cancer).

Books for teens that treat sudden death by accident or by design (that is, by suicide) are yet another trend on recent BBYA lists. From the 2006 BBYA list come E. R. Frank's *Wrecked* and Alison McGhee's *All Rivers Flow to the Sea*. In the first, a teen girl survives an automobile accident that kills her brother's girlfriend in the other car. In the second, a teen girl's sister is left in a vegetative state, her life maintained solely by medical science, following an automobile accident in which both sisters were involved. Stories that look at the effects of suicide, either of peers or family members, include Kimberly Willis Holt's *Keeper of the Night* (2004), in which a teen's mother commits suicide; Adam Rapp's *Under the Wolf, under the Dog* (2005), in which the protagonist's brother commits suicide later in a story that also features the death of his mother to cancer; and John Green's *Looking for Alaska* (2006), which features a peer suicide. Tracy Mack's *Birdland* (2004) and Adele Griffin's *Where I Want to Be* (2006) tell stories about mysterious or just not clearly delineated deaths, the latter potentially being a suicide.

Self: Identity, Image, and Acceptance

Of great importance to teens at all stages of adolescence is the development of a positive sense of self, which does not often come smoothly and can exact a price. As the teen years are when an individual, separate identity and the early self of adulthood are being established, it comes as no surprise that a great number of books are published for teens that treat, in one way or another, themes of the self. Those that are most strongly reflected on recent BBYA lists include understanding self within family relationships, coming to terms with self through peers and romantic partners, accepting the physical self, and sexual orientation and identity. Of course, just about any book written for teens will deal to some degree with the self, but there are books that particularly stand out for their focus on and masterful handling of these themes.

Though books that center on teen family life will be explored in the next section, it is worth emphasizing here a few standouts that particularly emphasize identity issues: Cat Bauer's *Harley, Like a Person* (2001), in which a teen follows a strong hunch to unearth the biological father that has been hidden from her all her life; Sarah Weeks's *So B. It* (2005), in which a young teen seeks the family history her developmentally delayed mother cannot provide her; Meg Rosoff's Printz Award winner, *How I Live Now* (2005), in which an embittered teen finds home and identity with her English cousins during a military occupation; Alison McGhee's *All Rivers Flow to the Sea* (2006), featuring a teen who must redefine herself when her beloved sister enters a permanent vegetative state following an automobile accident; and Mary E. Pearson's *A Room on Lorelei Street* (2006), in which a self-destructive teen rents a room away from her alcoholic mother in an attempt to form a separate existence and identity. Also of note is Stephanie S. Tolan's *Surviving the Applewhites* (2003), in which a juvenile delinquent finds himself among the members of a wacky, creative home-schooled family.

Beyond family, relationships with peers, romantic partners, and larger society have a strong influence on teen identity. Books on BBYA lists in the past seven years that examine identity within friendships, romantic experiences, and the larger world include Gordon Korman's *Jake, Reinvented* (2004) and Sharon G. Flake's *Who Am I without Him? Short Stories about Girls and the Boys in Their Lives* (2005). In the first, a modern twist on *The Great Gatsby*, erstwhile nerd Jake Garrett reinvents himself to get the popular girl of his dreams. Told by a narrator who acknowledges the flimsy fabric of teen society, Jake's created identity leads to a fall and a lesson in being true to oneself. In the second, young African American teens define themselves and develop self-esteem in response to their desirability with members of the opposite sex. Two books from the 2006 BBYA list look at the impact love relationships have on identity. In Christopher Krovatin's *Heavy Metal and You,* a Metal Head finds out who he really is when he tries to be someone he isn't for a "straightedge" girlfriend. In Cecil Castellucci's *Boy Proof,* a purposefully isolated and eccentric teen girl discovers someone who sees through her public persona to the authentic person within. In Markus Zusak's *I Am the Messenger,* also a 2006 BBYA book, a socially disenfranchised teen cabby discovers himself when, following his heroic actions during a robbery, he begins to receive playing cards that lead him on philanthropic missions.

Body image, an essential and often painful aspect of adolescent identity, is regularly treated in teen literature. The 2000 BBYA list includes Sarah Dessen's *Keeping the Moon* and Kimberly Willis Holt's *When Zachary Beaver Came to Town.* Dessen's story features the slimmed-down Colie Sparks who, despite her healthy new body, still can't stand herself. Through their developing friendship with a 643-pound boy left alone in a trailer, Toby Wilson and his friend Cal come to larger understandings of life and themselves in Holt's story. Sherri L. Smith's *Lucy the Giant* (2003) features a young woman whose height makes it possible for her to pass as an adult and, by doing so, to find personal acceptance and deal with an alcoholic father to whom she remains invisible. Two books on the 2004 list, both of which were Printz Honor titles, address issues of physical difference and self-acceptance. K. L. Going's *Fat Kid Rules the World* is the story of Troy Billings, a nearly 300-pound kid who finds a sense of self through friendship and music. Carolyn Mackler's *The Earth, My Butt, and Other Big, Round Things* features Virginia Shreves, a teen girl who feels diminished not by an extreme physical difference, but by being average in a family of brilliant, accomplished, beautiful people. Virginia learns that beauty can be only skin-deep. Scrub Harbor, Massachusetts, is the setting for Ellen Wittlinger's 2001 BBYA book about identity, *What's in a Name,* in which related stories share the search for and challenges of identity for ten teens, framed by a larger story line in which the residents of the town are quarreling over its future identity.

Sexual Identity

As teens are growing into their adult bodies and experiencing the accompanying physical, psychological, and emotional shifts, their sexual identities take center stage and are of tantamount importance in their continuing development. Books for teens often include romantic elements of attraction and self-definition resulting from desirability to others (or the lack thereof), as well as sexual exploration and urge fulfillment for good or for ill. These stories necessarily treat identity to one degree or another as teens experience these aspects of adult life at the very beginning stages of their adult understanding. Because of their ubiquity at this stage in the development of teen literature, such themes are more a literary characteristic than they are a current trend. What does constitute a trend in teen literature are books that address sexual identities of and for gay, lesbian, bisexual, transgendered, and questioning teens (GLBTQ). This trend is by no means new, and professional literature is readily available for those who are interested in tracing the history of GLBTQ literature for teens, including a number of pieces by teen literary historian and author Michael Cart.

What is trendsetting over the past five to ten years is the slowly but surely increasing number of books that treat a broader range of sexual identities for teens and, perhaps more important, a change in the nature and delivery of the content. The nature of the content is not necessarily problematic, at least not beyond the normal challenges of emerging sexuality and individuation as they have been addressed in books about heterosexual teens all along. To treat a broader range of sexual identities no longer necessitates a somber tone and message-driven delivery. Such books vary as significantly in style and tone as any observable body of teen literature, from darkly serious to lighthearted. Particularly noteworthy is the much welcome trend that first appeared in

David Levithan's *Boy Meets Boy* (2004), in which the main character's homosexuality is simply a fact like any other unique characteristic an author might choose to explore when depicting complex adolescent human beings. The story does not focus on Paul's homosexual identity. Rather, its focus is Paul's romantic life in a near-utopian high school environment that is both wacky and tolerant. Paul's gayness is by no means incidental, but it is *normal*. And the story does not get hung up on his orientation; it is about much more. Few would dispute that *Boy Meets Boy* is as groundbreaking in teen literature as was Nancy Garden's *Annie on My Mind,* a BBYA book in 1982.

The BBYA lists since 2000 include eleven novels with GLBTQ themes. Of the total, seven feature gay male characters, three feature lesbian characters, and one features a transgendered character. No books on the list to date specifically explore bisexuality. In the majority of these books the main character or a significant supporting character is homosexual, although a small handful have protagonists who narrate and respond to characters who are homosexual or, in one case, transgendered. Examples of the latter include Ellen Wittlinger's *Hard Love* (2000), in which the main male character's love interest reveals to him she is a lesbian; Garret Freymann-Weyr's *My Heartbeat* (2003), in which a sister discovers her brother and his friend are gay; Julie Anne Peters's *Luna* (2005), in which a sister supports her brother, a physical male but a female in every other way, through the trauma of hiding his/her true nature; and Sonya Sones's *One of Those Hideous Books Where the Mother Dies* (2005), in which the main character suspects a strong supporting character of being gay. All these books and those mentioned below address sexual identity with varying degrees of attention and intensity.

Along with Levithan's *Boy Meets Boy*, Freymann-Weyr's *My Heartbeat,* and Sones's *One of Those Hideous Books Where the Mother Dies,* recent BBYA lists feature four more novels featuring gay male characters and themes. Jean Ferris's *Eight Seconds* (2002) features a young rodeo rider in the process of discovering his sexual orientation. Alex Sanchez's *Rainbow Boys* (2002) tells the stories of three high school students who are dealing with self, family, and society as young homosexual males. David Levithan's *The Realm of Possibility* (2005) is a verse novel written in twenty separate voices, beginning with Daniel, a young gay man and profound thinker who ponders his relationship with his boyfriend, Jed, as their first anniversary nears. Like *Boy Meets Boy,* David LaRochelle's *Absolutely, Positively Not* (2006) is told in a lighthearted fashion. Differing from Levithan's book, LaRochelle's, albeit humorously, treats a young man's initial denial of his sexual identity and ultimately unsuccessful attempt to transform himself into a stereotypical heterosexual male at a midwestern high school.

Two books in addition to *Hard Love* explore lesbianism and do so through their main protagonists rather than a strong supporting character. In Sara

Ryan's *Empress of the World* (2002), fifteen-year-old Nicola experiences first love with another girl at a summer institute. In Lauren Myracle's *Kissing Kate* (2004), sixteen-year-old Lissa and her longtime friend Kate kiss passionately at a party, eroding the friendship and causing Lissa to question her identity.

Teen Family Life

Although nearing the independence of adult life, most teens in modern American society are still strongly dependent on, influenced by, and, less pleasantly, easily damaged by family. Teen literature that treats family life in its many and varied forms and with equally varied issues is an especially noteworthy trend in recent years. The BBYA lists of the past seven years are full of books that focus on family life from the teen perspective. An examination of stories for teens that explore family life could easily be a book in itself, but suffice it to say here that two larger trends seem particularly observable on recent BBYA lists: families in crisis and the definition of family. Books about families in crisis include a number of themes, such as pregnancy, abortion, and adoption; neglect and abandonment by parents as well as general bad parenting; and trauma and its effects on families. As for the last theme, trauma ranges widely, from recent divorce to violence to death. Books that explore the definition of family treat such themes as the search for and adjustment to parents and other family members—those estranged from or no longer with the family unit for one reason or another, as well as biological parents who gave their children out for adoption; members of foster, adoptive, and nontraditional families; and teen parents.

Families in Crisis

Noteworthy books from recent BBYA lists that look at teen pregnancy and its consequences, including its impact on a family unit, are all from the 2001 BBYA list: Anna Fienberg's *Borrowed Light,* Jerrie Oughton's *Perfect Family,* and Louise Plummer's *A Dance for Three.* BBYA books that treat issues of neglect, abandonment, and general bad parenting seem to be particularly prevalent in the past three years. Manuel Luis Martinez's *Drift* starts the trend in 2004, followed in 2005 by Kimberly Newton Fusco's *Tending to Grace,* Angela Johnson's *Bird,* Ron Koertge's *Margaux with an X,* Kathe Koja's *The Blue Mirror,* and Martine Leavitt's *Heck, Superhero.* The trend continues in 2006 with Mary E. Pearson's *A Room on Lorelei Street* and Tim Wynne-Jones's *A Thief in the House of Memory.* This is not to say there have not been other noteworthy books with these themes prior to 2004, but the theme seems to have concentrated in the past few years. Standouts from prior years include Graham McNamee's *Hate You* (2000), Julie Anne Peters's *Define Normal* (2001), Paul Fleischman's *Seek* (2002), David Klass's *You Don't Know Me* (2002), Han Nolan's *Born Blue* (2002), and Susanna

Vance's *Sights* (2002), and, from 2003, S. L. Rottman's *Stetson* and Sherri L. Smith's *Lucy the Giant*.

Trauma and its effects on a family unit is a prominent and diverse trend in recent teen literature, demonstrated by such books early in the decade as Catherine Atkins's 2000 BBYA book *When Jeff Comes Home* (kidnapping and sexual abuse), Ellen Wittlinger's 2000 *Hard Love* (divorce), Carl Deuker's 2001 *Night Hoops* (divorce), Jacqueline Woodson's 2001 *Miracle's Boys* (death of a parent), and Lori Aurelia Williams's 2001 *When Kambia Elaine Flew in from Neptune* (runaway sibling). Books from the 2003 BBYA list include Iain Lawrence's *The Lightkeeper's Daughter* (death of a sibling) and Jacqueline Woodson's *Hush* (family in witness protection). The past three years of BBYA lists highlight books such as Carolyn Mackler's 2004 *The Earth, My Butt, and Other Big, Round Things* (sibling accused of date rape), Eireann Corrigan's 2005 *Splintering* (violent assault on family), and Allan Stratton's 2005 *Chanda's Secrets* (death of parents to AIDS).

Definition of Family

As society becomes ever more diverse and complex, family life bursts the seams of convention, manifests in myriad ways, and is reflected in the literature. Family units can be less constant and more fluid throughout young lives; the definition of what makes a family is broader and the family issues teens face are more varied and complex than ever before. By the teen years, young people are questioning the design and nature of their family units, sometimes rejecting what they are experiencing and seeking alternatives, other times searching for answers and meaning from within. Books that focus on teens in the context of their family lives generally address issues of identity in tandem, and can easily fit that theme as well.

Books that treat the search for, reunion with, introduction to, and adjustment to parents and other family members during the teen years, with varying degrees of success, are a notable trend. A striking number of these books focus on fathers, including Gayle Friesen's 2000 BBYA book *Janey's Girl* (search for information about father), Melina Marchetta's 2000 *Looking for Alibrandi* (introduction to heretofore absent father), Diane Stanley's 2000 *A Time Apart* (reunion with distant father), Cat Bauer's 2001 *Harley, Like a Person* (search for birth father), Rachel Cohn's 2003 *Gingerbread* (introduction to birth father), and Sonya Sones's 2005 *One of Those Hideous Books Where the Mother Dies* (new relationship with distant father). Also of note are S. L. Rottman's 2003 *Stetson* (reintroduction of sibling), Sarah Weeks's 2005 *So B. It* (search for family history), and David Levithan's 2006 *Are We There Yet?* (reconciliation of estranged brothers).

BBYA books that explore issues for teens who are members of foster, adoptive, or nontraditional families, although not a large trend, are worth a mention for their role in the larger trend in books that define family. On the 2001 list is Sharon Creech's *The Wanderer,* a story in which a young teen girl cannot bear to acknowledge that she hasn't always been with the family that adopted her three years ago. Patricia Reilly Giff's *Pictures of Hollis Woods* appeared on the 2003 list and follows Hollis after she runs away from a foster family that she loves, only to find guidance with an adult artist who helps her reconnect with her family unit. Meg Rosoff's *How I Live Now,* both a 2005 BBYA book and the winner of the 2005 Printz Award, features the angry and isolated young Daisy, who is sent away from her father and stepmother to cousins in England, with whom she finds a true sense of home and also romantic love.

Three outstanding books found on recent BBYA lists exemplify the theme of teens with children of their own who are either facing the decision to assume parental responsibility or are in the process of raising their children and are facing adult challenges at an adolescent stage of development. Two of the three feature young fathers, one a young mother. Margaret Bechard's *Hanging on to Max* appears on the 2003 BBYA list and tells the story of seventeen-year-old Max, who is trying to raise his baby on his own despite the wishes of the child's mother and the attitudes of his own father. On the 2004 list is Angela Johnson's exquisite *The First Part Last,* about sixteen-year-old Bobby, who, following the unexpected death of his girlfriend, must decide whether or not to keep his baby girl, Feather. *The First Part Last* won the 2004 Printz Award. *Spellbound,* by Janet McDonald, made the 2003 BBYA list and features young Raven, a single teen mother in the Brooklyn projects who is struggling to return to school so she can build a better life for her son.

Teen Social Life

Most contemporary realistic fiction deals with one or more aspects of teen social life—school life, friendships, romance, sports, and so on. Contemporary realism that is relevant and of interest to teens will necessarily include these and other aspects of teen social life, and their inclusion does not so much represent a trend as it reflects a standard. Many of the themed lists in this book showcase outstanding books from the past seven years of BBYA lists that focus on the more standard themes of teen social experience.

Ethnic Experience

One emergent literary trend that treats an aspect of teen social life is contemporary realistic fiction that explores the varied teen ethnic experience in America. Although clearly on the rise, these sorts of stories are not prolific on BBYA lists, as a significant body of multicultural literature for teens is simply not available yet from which to select "best" works. But those books that have made their way to BBYA lists represent more than ever before the evolving ethnic mix in America and a response from authors and publishers to find a place in that mix.

These stories not only examine the clash of "minority" and dominant cultures, many also introduce readers to an assortment of unique cultural backgrounds and life ways as seen through teen eyes, without an emphasize on larger societal conflict. Cultures with deep history in America, notably African America, make a stronger showing in teen literature than cultures newer to the American landscape, although there is a long way to go before a balanced and representative literary marketplace is achieved. It should be noted that there are many historical fiction and nonfiction books that highlight the challenges and triumphs of more established ethnic populations in America, but the trend discussed in this section is contemporary realistic fiction. Although the '60s, '70s, and '80s are certainly modern history, they are nonetheless history, especially to today's teens. For the purpose of the present discussion, otherwise notable books like Chris Lynch's *Gold Dust* (2001), Jaira Placide's *Fresh Girl* (2003), and Benjamin Alire Saenz's *Sammy and Juliana in Hollywood* (2005) are not considered contemporary.

Many of the contemporary stories of teen ethnic life deal with the unique challenges or conditions that teens and their families face as minorities in America. A number focus on the challenges of integrating traditional and contemporary lifestyles and points of view, especially between generations. Some address the mixed-race experience. Some treat the new immigrant experience. And virtually all address common and cross-cultural themes of adolescence.

From African America comes a broad range of rich and evocative stories, humorous and serious alike. A number of African American authors who write for teens and are found on recent BBYA lists are also recognized through children's and teen literature's highest awards for their extraordinary contributions. Walter Dean Myers and Angela Johnson each won the Printz Award, for *Monster* and *The First Part Last,* in 2000 and 2004, respectively. Myers holds the record for the highest number of books on BBYA lists in the past decade. In addition to *The First Part Last,* Johnson's *Bird* appears on the 2005 BBYA list. Christopher Paul Curtis was awarded the 2000 Newbery Medal for *Bud, Not Buddy,* which is also on the 2000 BBYA list. His *Bucking the Sarge* appeared on the 2005 BBYA list. Jacqueline Woodson is the recipient of the 2006 Margaret A. Edwards Award for lifetime achievement in young adult literature. Several of her works of fiction are present on recent BBYA lists, including *Miracle's Boys* (2001), *Hush* (2003), and *Behind You* (2005). Interestingly, the only other African American author to receive this award was Walter Dean Myers, twelve years earlier in 1994.

It is important to note that this decade's books reflecting the African American experience for teens are, like the current trend seen in literature with gay and lesbian themes, not solely a body of ethnic "problem" stories.

Recent BBYA lists include a number of wonderfully varied books by African American authors, those noted above as well as well-known authors such as Sharon G. Flake, Nikki Grimes, Janet McDonald, Lori Aurelia Williams, and Rita Williams-Garcia.

A small collection of contemporary realistic fiction representing other American ethnic groups has made its way to BBYA lists since 2000. From Hispanic America comes David Rice's *Crazy Loco* (2002), a collection of short stories that illuminate everyday Mexican American teen life in Texas's Rio Grande Valley. From the 2004 BBYA list come two books, *Drift* by Manual Luis Martinez and *Cuba 15* by Nancy Osa. In the first, sixteen-year-old Mexican American Robert tries to pull his family back together after his mother has a breakdown. In the latter, soon-to-be-fifteen-year-old Violet must accept her Cuban grandmother's desire for a traditional quinceañero, despite Violet's disconnection from this side of her ethnic heritage. An Na's 2002 BBYA list and Printz Award winner *A Step from Heaven* explores adaptation to life in America for Young Ju and her family when they immigrate to California from Korea.

New on the literary scene in both teen and adult literature are books that treat the Eastern Indian American and Middle Eastern American experience. Although this discussion has been limited to trends in teen literature, it is worth mentioning Vineeta Vijayaraghavan's *Motherland,* an adult market book that received acknowledgment for its quality and appeal to teens on the 2002 BBYA list. In it, teenage Maya is sent from her home in New York to spend the summer with her relatives in India and to be reintroduced to traditional ways when her parents find her behavior wayward. Tanuja Desai Hidier's *Born Confused* followed *Motherland* on the 2003 BBYA list and features Dimple, an Indian American girl living in New Jersey who finds she is torn between two cultures when her parents try to fix her up with an Indian boy. A unique and somber book for older teens appears on the 2006 BBYA list. In Tammar Stein's *Light Years,* a twenty-year-old Israeli, Maya, struggles to adjust to life in the United States and to accept the death of her boyfriend, who was killed in Israel by a suicide bomber.

Two contemporary realistic novels on current BBYA lists are noteworthy for presenting the clash of cultures in America and for delving into complex racial issues. In *Crossing Jordan* (2001), Adrian Fogelin explores extreme racial prejudice in a small town when a white girl and a black girl befriend each other. In *Black and White* (2006), Paul Volponi explores the profound societal imbalance and racial divide when Marcus, an African American, and his white friend, Eddie, are each treated differently by the law when they shoot a victim during a team robbery.

GENRE FICTION

Genre fiction is as popular with teens as it is with adult readers, and this is clearly evident on recent BBYA lists. Perhaps not quite as many genres are as robust in the teen market as they are in the adult market, which has a somewhat stronger audience for science fiction, mystery, and dark fantasy (the term used to describe any scary or dark story with a supernatural element). Giving adult genres a run for their money, though, are the teen fantasy, historical fiction, and adventure/survival genres, which are incredibly popular with teen readers. At the forefront is fantasy, a rich and diverse body of teen literature that has grown to a size that needs its own subgenres. Historical fiction is not far behind, with a range of exceptional books for teens set across all periods of American and world history. Not quite the genre giants of fantasy and historical fiction, but certainly quite respectable, are adventure and survival stories for teens, with individual stories crossing a considerable range of styles and subjects.

Although they are not the stars of the show, science fiction, mystery and thrillers, and dark fantasy do have their place in teen literature, and their numbers belie the fact that they are on the rise, offering some outstanding works that have received recent BBYA acknowledgment. For now, it is hard to say why these genres are comparatively underrepresented in teen literature. It could be that feelers into the market indicate they won't be successful with teen audiences and thus authors writing in these genres are not picked up, or are published in the adult market. It might be that very few authors are writing in these genres for the teen market. It is possible that the body of literature in the adult market in these genres is sufficiently attractive and accessible to teen readers that a separate teen-specific market has simply never evolved. It is also possible that these genres have yet to reach their peak in the teen market and will have their day in the future. On this last point, teen market mysteries (and also humorous fiction) may be worth keeping a particular eye on.

Although any genre could be examined for patterns or trends, a few of the genres represented on BBYA lists stand out for their obvious and in some cases heavily title-represented trends. The fantasy genre has more than one significant trend of note, and the science fiction and mystery genres, though they lend fewer titles to the lists, demonstrate trends worthy of discussion. Humorous fiction, though it may not be an official genre, is on the rise in teen literature, and many outstanding examples are present on BBYA lists. Also striking in teen genre literature and evident on recent BBYA lists is the trend toward genre blenders, or books that cross more than one fictional type or style.

Fantasy

Plain and simple, fantasy is a predominant trend in current teen literature. BBYA lists are loaded with outstanding books in the genre, and three of the 2006 BBYA Top Ten books are fantasy titles. Fantasy accounts for almost 15 percent of the 577 books on BBYA lists since 2000, the same share as nonfiction and exceeded only by general fiction. Along with the more select but outstanding science fiction books being published for teens, perhaps a strong indicator of teen fantasy's influence and respected status is the newly announced Andre Norton Award, created by the Science Fiction and Fantasy Writers of America to recognize exceptional fantasy or science fiction titles written for the teen market.

In the *Locus* article mentioned previously, Cynthia Ward reports that the "'feminization' of the fiction readership" has yet to be seen in the science fiction and fantasy genres (Ward 2004, 2). This may be the point of divergence between the older and younger Millennials, as it is not true in literature for teens. There is no doubt that in science fiction and fantasy literature for teens, young women are being courted quite successfully, and the BBYA lists are here to prove it. The past seven years of BBYA fantasy titles include forty-three that feature female protagonists, compared with twenty-nine featuring male protagonists.

Like contemporary realistic fiction, fantasy fiction is diverse in subject and treatment. It is not all witches and wizards and dragons, although there are a fair share of these. Not limited to realism, fantasy also tackles dark and difficult teen issues, albeit in alternative ways. Identity issues are prevalent in teen fantasy fiction as they are in all fantasy fiction, with young people on quests, often adventurous, to understand their unique selves and the nature of their contributions to the larger world—no matter how challenging the quest or unwanted the contribution.

On this point, fantasy can demonstrate a dark quality equal to that found in realistic problem novels. On the current BBYA lists are fantasy works that deal with abuse and suicide, like Nina Kiriki Hoffman's *A Stir of Bones* (2004); racial discrimination is explored in Dia Calhoun's *Firegold* (2000) and Susan Vaught's *Stormwitch* (2006); social difference and bullying features in Jean Thesman's *The Other Ones* (2000); painful family secrets and identity are explored in Rita Murphy's *Night Flying* (2001); Joyce McDonald's *Shades of Simon Gray* (2002) and Kathleen Jeffrie Johnson's *A Fast and Brutal Wing* (2005) feature profoundly troubled teens; death and the grief process are treated in Michael Lawrence's *A Crack in the Line* (2005). There are even a few fantasies featuring kidnappings, as in Nancy Farmer's *The Sea of Trolls* (2005), Clare B. Dunkle's *The Hollow Kingdom* (2005), and Chris Wooding's *Poison* (2006).

Unlike realistic fiction, fantasy need not subscribe to convention and is as unlimited in its treatment of issues as its authors have the imaginative powers to manifest. Some might argue that the fantastical settings and creatures found in fantasy books dilute life's real issues. Reading about a sibling kidnapped by a goblin or faeries does not, for some, have the same impact as reading about a real-world kidnapping. For others, the genre's fantastical nature serves to highlight and make more profound any issue by removing it from reality and casting it into a unique setting.

If fantasy in general is a strong current trend in teen literature, retellings and reimaginings of fairy tales, myths, legends, and religious stories are the genre's most noteworthy subgenre. At twenty-eight titles, retellings and reimaginings account for 34 percent of the fantasy books found on BBYA lists since 2000. In the not too distant past, a retelling generally meant that a well-known fairy tale from the European tradition was twisted a bit, or told using a different setting or time period than its original. Not so now. In addition to retellings of these European standards, and books based on those standards, are new takes—entire reimaginings—of not only fairy tales but myths, legends, and religious stories from many cultures across many time periods.

Books on recent BBYA lists based on the long collectively built world of faerie include Holly Black's gothic urban fantasies *Tithe* (2003) and *Valiant* (2006); Irish writer Herbie Brennan's *Faerie Wars* (2004); a work by the master of urban fantasy himself in his first book written for the teen market, Charles de Lint's *The Blue Girl* (2005); and Chris Wooding's *Poison* (2006). Books on 2000-plus BBYA lists that retell or reimagine individual fairy tales from the European tradition include Margaret Peterson Haddix's *Just Ella* (2000), based on the Cinderella story; the inimitable Terry Pratchett's *The Amazing Maurice and His Educated Rodents* (2002) and Donna Jo Napoli's *Breath* (2004), both based the Pied Piper of Hamelin story; Jean Ferris's *Once upon a Marigold* (2003), a humorous amalgam of many aspects of the fairy tale tradition; and Edith Pattou's *East* (2004), a retelling of the *East of the Sun, West of the Moon* story. Although not representatives of teen market fantasy, two adult market titles in the same vein are on recent BBYA lists and indicate the incredible popularity of books of this sort with teen readers: Juliet Marillier's *Daughter of the Forest* (2001), the first book in the Sevenwaters trilogy and based on the swan brothers fairy tale, and Charles de Lint's *Seven Wild Sisters* (2003).

Fairy tales are not the only sources for retellings and reimaginings. Myths, legends, and religious stories are also widely drawn upon in teen fantasy fiction. From classical antiquity and biblical times come Adele Geras's *Troy* (2002), a retelling of the Trojan War story; Catherine Fisher's *The Oracle Betrayed* (2005), loosely based in Greco-Roman theologies; Elsie V. Aidinoff's *The Garden* (2005), a retelling of the biblical Adam and Eve story; Clare B. Dunkle's *The Hollow Kingdom* (2005), influenced by the Greek myth of Persephone and Hades (and billed by reviewers as rich in the Beauty and the Beast theme); Rick Riordan's *The Lightning Thief* (2006), based on Greek mythology; and Nikki Grimes's *Dark Sons* (2006), a verse novel that alternates between modern New York City and the biblical tale of Abraham and Ishmael. From the adult publishing market comes Christopher Moore's *Lamb: The Gospel according to Biff, Christ's Childhood Pal* (2003), a lighthearted satire of the life of Christ.

From Middle Ages tales and legends come Gerald Morris's *The Squire, His Knight, and His Lady* (2000) and *The Savage Damsel and the Dwarf* (2001), both from his Squire's Tales series, with the first built on the Arthurian tales of Sir Gawain and the Green Knight, and the second on a lesser tale from Sir Thomas Malory's *Le Morte d'Arthur;* Jane Yolen's *Sword of the Rightful King: A Novel of King Arthur* (2004); and Janet McNaughton's *An Earthly Knight* (2005), which reinterprets the Tam Lin story set in twelfth-century Scotland. Also drawing on the Middle Ages is Nancy Farmer's *The Sea of Trolls* (2005), based on Norse mythology. Add to the mix the short story collection from editors Ellen Datlow and Terri Windling, *The Green Man: Tales from the Mythic Forest* (2003). Drawing on an era just after the Middle Ages is Grace Tiffany's *Ariel* (2006), a creative retelling of Shakespeare's *The Tempest.*

Influenced by the Middle East and Asia are works like Jonathan Stroud's *The Amulet of Samarkand* (2004) and *The Golem's Eye* (2005), the first two books in the Bartimaeus trilogy, which, though it is set in an alternate England, features an ancient and belligerent djinni; Lian Hearn's *Across the Nightingale Floor* (2004); L. G. Bass's *Sign of the Qin* (2005); and Donna Jo Napoli's *Bound* (2005). Napoli's book is a unique hybrid of Chinese myth and the Cinderella fairy tale. Susan Vaught's *Stormwitch* (2006) brings the influence of Africa and the Caribbean to teen fantasy fiction through Haitian-born Ruba and her Dahomey ancestry and their supernatural powers. From the adult market is Neil Gaiman's *Anansi Boys* (2006), a highly clever and engrossing reimagining of the African trickster/spider god, Anansi.

Another subgenre doing quite well in teen fantasy fiction of late is the dark fantasy or dark supernatural subgenre. In addition to the fantasy "problem" novels mentioned above are other books that focus on the darker aspects of the human psyche and are packaged in the supernatural or fantastic. Add the macabre, and from 2003 comes Neil Gaiman's highly creepy *Coraline.* Vampires are of lasting popularity in dark fantasy, and on recent BBYA lists are Stephenie Meyer's *Twilight* (2006) and Scott Westerfeld's *Peeps* (2006). To demonstrate that vampires come in all sorts of fictional packages: *Twilight* is a leisurely paced rural romance involving a human female and a very appealing male vampire; *Peeps* is a gritty, urban, science-based tale featuring a Texas transplant to Manhattan who, infected with vampirism during a sexual encounter, has the good fortune not to develop it in its full and very unbecoming form and dedicates himself to its eradication. His self-enforced celibacy to prevent passing the disease on is challenged, inevitably, by a female love interest. Not a teen market title but worth a mention is well-known teen author Robin McKinley's first foray into adult fiction with *Sunshine* (2005), which features a magically awakening human female and a charismatic vampire named Constantine. Chained together by a nefarious group of vampire toughs, they make their escape and prepare for a final showdown. Ghosts can also come in different shades (pun intended), as is evident in Laura Whitcomb's *A Certain Slant of Light* (2006). Also a strong contender as a fantasy "problem" novel, this is a complex, mature story of two sad and troubled teen ghosts who find solace and eventually profound love in each other while occupying bodies of the living.

Several short story collections recognized on BBYA lists are supernaturally dark. Vivian Vande Velde's *Being Dead* (2002) explores various aspects of dying and being dead, replete with a number of ghosts. The title story in Nancy Etchemendy's *Cat in Glass, and Other Tales of the Unnatural* (2003), which features a murderous cat sculpture that terrifies its owner, leads the way for seven more tales of horror. Deborah Noyes edited an outstanding collection on the 2005 BBYA list, *Gothic! Ten Original Dark Tales,* by well-known authors—many for teens—including M. T. Anderson, Neil Gaiman, Garth Nix, and Vivian Vande Velde. Margo Lanagan's original and often dark collection *Black Juice* (2006) was recognized for its literary quality and impact as a 2006 Printz Honor book.

A final notable trend in fantasy seen on BBYA lists is the altered history subgenre. Unlike science fiction's alternate histories, which rewrite historical time periods, events, and peoples with results that broadly differ from what actually occurred, altered history uses a time period and setting from a real and recognizable past in which to place a fully fantastic tale. Sherryl Jordan's *The Hunting of the Last Dragon* (2003) is set in fourteenth-century England and also includes as a main protagonist a noblewoman from China's Hangchow. Lian Hearn's *Across the Nightingale Floor* (2004) is set in medieval Japan. Clare B. Dunkle's *The Hollow Kingdom* (2005) takes place in nineteenth-century England. Joining Dunkle is quite a list of Victorian era–inspired fantasies, including Libba Bray's *A Great and Terrible Beauty* (2004) and *Rebel Angels* (2006), Patricia C. Wrede and Caroline Stevermer's *Sorcery and Cecelia, or The Enchanted Chocolate Pot* (2004), Kenneth Oppel's *Airborn* (2005) and *Skybreaker* (2006), and Chris Wooding's *The Haunting of Alaizabel Cray* (2005).

Science Fiction

As mentioned above, the teen market science fiction genre is not as significant as its closest literary cousin, fantasy. BBYA lists since 2000 recognize twenty-eight science fiction titles, approximately 5 percent of the fiction total. Despite their smaller showing, a significant trend in the genre was immediately apparent among these titles. A quarter of these recent BBYA science fiction titles are dystopian.

Dystopian stories are those that use fully imagined societies, or real societies modified and/or deteriorated, possibly advanced in time, often profoundly oppressive in some way or another, to explore faulty social systems and cultural practices and thus highlight the flaws and perils of existing societies. Some dystopian fiction is quite dire in tone and content, whereas some is more satirical, cleverly pointing out societal foibles not unlike a court jester mocking his royalty. Dystopian fiction provides teens an opportunity to consider established and arguably dangerous social systems, especially their own, through a fictional creation peopled with teens like them. These sorts of books may be of particular appeal to adolescents, who are prone to imagining the extreme by nature, and who, armed with some understanding of the difficulties and complexities faced by the modern world, are perhaps especially prone to fearing for their futures.

To the 2000 BBYA list, veteran science fiction writer Neal Shusterman contributed *Downsiders,* in which fourteen-year-old Talon, a Downsider living in a separate and secret society in subterranean New York City, accidentally meets Lindsay, a girl of the same age who lives Topside in the townhouse Talon happens to be searching to find medicine for his ailing sister. Rodman Philbrick's 2001 BBYA book *The Last Book in the Universe* is a relatively slight but incredibly powerful tale that explores the Earth in a postapocalyptic future, one in which a very few privileged people live in an Eden-like protected territory while the rest starve among the rubble in concrete boxes under petty and violent gang leaders. The 2003 list welcomed two of the most lauded science fiction works for teens in recent history: M. T. Anderson's *Feed* and Nancy Farmer's multiple-award-winning *The House of the Scorpion.* The first describes a future society whose members are hardwired to the corporate media "feed" from babyhood and spend their lives jacked into an addictive and opiating consumer culture of epic and insidious proportions. The second describes a future American/Mexican border country called Opium, which is controlled by El Patron, a 140-year-old dictator who, in addition to harvesting opium, harvests lobotomized, cloned humans to replace his deteriorating body parts. Joss Whedon's *Fray,* a graphic novel set in a future Manhattan, takes dystopian fiction into a new format for the BBYA list in 2005.

In 2006 an additional three dystopian stories made it to the BBYA list. L. J. Adlington's *The Diary of Pelly D* takes place on a world colonized by rival genetic clans. In it, a worker for the dominant clan finds and reads the diary of a young woman that describes her fall from social privilege when a self-proclaimed superior genetic clan assumes power. Ann Halam's *Siberia* features thirteen-year-old Sloe, who lives with her mother in a political prisoner camp in an icebound future where most mammals have become extinct. After being tricked into betraying her mother, a scientist working to reestablish lost species, Sloe takes on her mother's role. Scott Westerfeld's *Uglies,* the first book in the popular Uglies trilogy, depicts a future in which, at sixteen years of age, all young people must have an operation that molds them to an accepted model of beauty. Tally, still an Ugly, looks forward to her operation until she is given an opportunity to think differently by a friend who intends to reject it.

Mysteries and Thrillers

Non-serial mysteries and thrillers for teens are surprisingly rare compared to other genres, and those that make BBYA lists are even rarer. Since 2000, only eleven titles with library cataloging that in any way describes them as mystery or detective stories have made their way to BBYA lists. Interestingly, an easy half of the titles are strong representatives of other genres as well, making many of these mysteries for teens more a blended genre than a distinct genre of its own. Most feature teen sleuths, but not all.

The majority of the mysteries on BBYA lists are murder mysteries, and whether they follow a formula or not, and aside from a few lighter exceptions, they tend to be works of some intensity. Marsha Qualey, an established writer of murder mysteries for teens, contributed *Close to a Killer* to the 2000 BBYA list. While working for her ex-con mother at a hair salon staffed entirely by convicted murderers making new starts in life, Barrie Dupree attempts to exonerate that staff when two of their clients are found murdered. A master of mystery and suspense, Nancy Werlin has two mysteries on BBYA lists since 2000 to accompany her taut and disturbing 1999 BBYA title, *The Killer's Cousin.* One of these, *Black Mirror* (2002), is a murder mystery that features teenager Frances Leventhal, compelled to find the truth behind her brother's death from a heroin overdose at an elite prep school.

Robert Cormier's posthumously published *The Rag and Bone Shop* (2002) is not billed as a mystery but is certainly a thriller with a murder element, featuring a twelve-year-old boy who, suspected of the murder of a seven-year-old girl, is torturously interrogated by a professional interrogator who can't stop even when he realizes the boy is innocent. Of a similar sort is Jennifer Donnelly's *A Northern Light* (2004), historical fiction to which an element of murder is added when Mattie, the main protagonist, realizes the love letters she holds may shed light on the death of the young woman who left them in her care. Graham McNamee's *Acceleration* (2004) is a murder mystery with a slight twist: seventeen-year-old Duncan finds the diary of a potential serial killer in the Toronto subway's lost-and-found department and, to assuage personal guilt from an earlier failure to act, sets out to find the murderer before he strikes.

Murder mysteries that cross genres and formats are also present on recent BBYA lists. From 2000 is Vivian Vande Velde's *Never Trust a Dead Man,* a historical mystery that contains strong elements of fantasy and humor. In it, seventeen-year-old Selwyn is sealed in a cave alongside the corpse of Farold, the young man he has been accused of murdering. When Elswyth, a witch, visits him and offers to assist him in exchange for his service, he accepts. Farold is resurrected, inhabits the body of a bat, and the two young men set out to find the real killer, bickering all the way. Jason Little's graphic novel *Shutterbug Follies* is also a murder mystery with a humorous bent. A 2004 BBYA book, it features eighteen-year-old Bee, a photo lab assistant in New York who, after examining a picture of a naked female corpse that crosses her path, starts sleuthing and finds herself deeply enmeshed in a bona fide mystery.

BBYA lists do contain some mysteries that do not revolve around murder but delve into other sorts of crimes or mysterious events and actions. These include Dorothy and Thomas Hoobler's historical jewel theft mystery *The Ghost in the Tokaido Inn* (2000); Gillian Cross's taut, contemporary gang/stalker thriller, *Tightrope* (2001); Hilari Bell's genre-blending *A Matter of Profit* (2002), in which a young warrior is given the chance to escape his fate by hunting down a would-be assassin; and Nancy Werlin's *Double Helix* (2005), a bioethics and genetic engineering mystery. Finally, there is Gregory Galloway's *As Simple as Snow* (2006), an adult market title that could easily have been published for the teen market. This unique story, about a young man who connects with a very unusual young woman who then goes missing, joins him in his search for clues to her disappearance.

Humorous Fiction

The many literary genres, subgenres, and blended genres in teen literature stand in contrast to the unfortunately limited public perception that books for teens, when they are not about wealthy mean girls doing drugs and having sex in urban locales, are horrifically bleak and filled with depths of despair. In addition to the commercial juggernauts and "problem" novels and across what is a rich and varied array of mainstream and genre fiction books are those told in a humorous voice or tone, even if the underlying story or content is at times quite serious. BBYA lists since 2000 show a developing trend in humorous fiction, both in the teen and adult markets. Regardless of the genre, time period, or subject they treat, these books are imaginative and clever works eliciting responses from light amusement to laugh-out-loud hilarity.

In addition to the books with wry, witty chick lit voices mentioned earlier, the BBYA lists include some wonderful humorous works in mainstream fiction. Gordon Korman contributed *Son of the Mob* to the 2003 list, a charming story told by Vince Luca, the son of a mob leader who falls for the daughter of the FBI agent who is after Vince's father. Also on the 2003 list are Randy Powell's *Three Clams and an Oyster* and Carl Hiaasen's *Hoot.* In the first, a four-man flag football team makes the decision to replace one of its members with (gasp) a girl. In the second, as much a mystery as mainstream fiction, a new kid at school becomes wrapped up with an odd cast of characters in trying to save the tiny burrowing owls living on the site of the next Mother Paula's All-American Pancake House. The 2005 BBYA list saw the addition of Christopher Paul Curtis's *Bucking the Sarge,* a simultaneously humorous and ethical tale pitting Luther T. Farrell against his tough, slumlord mother, otherwise known as the Sarge. Carl Hiaasen returned to the 2006 BBYA list with *Flush,* another fun environmental story in which two children attempt to vindicate their father when he claims a casino boat is dumping raw sewage into the Florida waterways. Also on the 2006 list are David LaRochelle's *Absolutely, Positively Not* and David Lubar's *Sleeping Freshmen Never Lie.* The former, which won the 2005 Sid Fleischman Humor Award, features sixteen-year-old Steve DeNarski, who in a doomed attempt to deny he's gay, heads hardcore into heterosexual male territory and behavior. The latter follows Scott Hudson as he amusingly shares the highs and lows of his freshman year in high school.

Richard Peck has had a strong presence on recent BBYA lists, most notably for his Newbery Medal winner and historical fiction book, *A Year down Yonder* (2001), the sequel to *A Long Way from Chicago* (1999; a Newbery Honor book) and again featuring the inimitably gruff and hilarious Grandma Dowdel. In *Fair Weather* (2002), Peck brings a small-town family to the 1893 World's Columbian Exposition in Chicago, with delightful results. On the 2005 list, Peck was again recognized for *The Teacher's Funeral: A Comedy in Three Parts.* Set in 1904 rural Indiana, this book relates the madcap events that occur when the local school teacher dies and is replaced by the young male narrator's older sister. Also combining humor with historical fiction is Gennifer Choldenko's Newbery Honor book and 2004 Sid Fleischman Humor Award winner, *Al Capone Does My Shirts* (2005), a story that despite being set in 1935 at Alcatraz Island's famous federal prison and featuring a story line about an autistic sibling is told with warmth and humor.

In 2002, the great fantasy humorist Terry Pratchett entered the BBYA scene with his teen story *The Amazing Maurice and His Educated Rodents,* featuring the titular Maurice, a criminally minded cat, as well as a group of smart rats and a "stupid-looking kid" named Keith, who together concoct a

Pied Piper scam. Pratchett followed this up with two more teen books that have appeared on BBYA lists and which are also set in Discworld, the home of numerous adult market novels by Pratchett. *The Wee Free Men* (2004) begins the brilliantly witty Tiffany Aching adventures, featuring the now-beloved and quite ill-behaved little blue men of the fairy world in partnership with a young witch in the making. In it, Tiffany and the Wee Free Men take on the Fairy Queen, who has made off with Tiffany's very sticky and not so lovable little brother, Wentworth. In *A Hat Full of Sky* (2005), Tiffany and her little blue men return to battle a "hiver," an entity that takes control of Tiffany's brain and requires her rescue by the Wee Free Men and sundry witches.

Also an exceptional writer of fantasy and with more than one appearance on recent BBYA lists is Jonathan Stroud. The first two books in his Bartimaeus trilogy appear on the 2004 and 2005 lists, *The Amulet of Samarkand* and *The Golem's Eye.* Elaborate, densely written stories with serious matters to address and much at stake, these books also contain great wit. The djinni Bartimaeus provides the first-person narrative for alternating sections of the text and shows himself to be a clever, arch, acerbic, and somehow simultaneously good-hearted being who inspires in the reader everything from an amused smile to genuine laughter. Another fun story, also influenced by the ancient world and its stories, is Rick Riordan's action-packed *The Lightning Thief* (2006), told by its twelve-year-old protagonist as he comes to understand he is the son of Poseidon and a mortal woman. A rare thing in teen literature, Margaret Bechard has contributed a humorous science fiction story to the 2006 BBYA list. In *Spacer and Rat,* Jack, a space boy or Spacer, and Kit, a "rat" (a dirty word Spacers have for allegedly freeloading Earth children), end up working together to protect a sentient bot.

Other books found on BBYA lists that incorporate or even feature humor are from the adult market, starting with Christopher Moore's *Lamb: The Gospel according to Biff, Christ's Childhood Pal* (2003). The 2005 BBYA list includes a number of humorous adult market titles, among them Joshua Braff's *The Unthinkable Thoughts of Jacob Green,* Brendan Halpin's *Donorboy,* and Neil Gaiman's *Anansi Boys,* followed by A. Lee Martinez's *Gil's All Fright Diner* in 2006. Halpin, Gaiman, and Martinez all received Alex Award recognition for these works in 2005 and 2006.

Genre Blenders

As literature for teens continues to mature and expand, it becomes ever more challenging to sort it into clearly defined subjects or categories. Although many books are clearly in one literary camp or another, an increasing number come with ensemble casts of characters scattered across multiple and complex story lines and do not feel obliged to stick to one time period or even in accepted reality. Contemporary and historical fiction blend with fantasy and science fiction, science fiction and fantasy blend with each other, historical fiction blends with mystery, mystery blends with humor, and so forth.

Historical fiction and fantasy blends are particularly remarkable, and recent BBYA lists include books like Patricia C. Wrede and Caroline Stevermer's *Sorcery and Cecelia, or The Enchanted Chocolate Pot* (2004), which inhabits nineteenth-century England with wizardry and magic; Libba Bray's *A Great and Terrible Beauty* (2004) and *Rebel Angels* (2006), enlivening Victorian British society with mysticism, magic, and journeys to other realms; Lian Hearn's *Across the Nightingale Floor*, which imparts magic to medieval Japan; and *Stormwitch*, Susan Vaught's contribution to the 2006 BBYA list, which uniquely melds a Haitian immigrant story with African spiritual magic amidst the turmoil and events of 1969 America, including racism, the civil rights movement, and Hurricane Camille.

The BBYA lists since 2000 include a small selection of time travel stories that take the reader back and forth between contemporary reality and another time period, usually via a mystical or fantastical agent. Arvella Whitmore's *Trapped between the Lash and the Gun* (2000) sends back in time a contemporary street kid trying in the middle of a gang initiation to share the hardships of his slave ancestor on a plantation. Susan Cooper sends a contemporary young actor back in time to Shakespeare's England and the Globe Theatre in 1599 in *King of Shadows* (2000). Young Tom Mullen falls through a hole in a construction site in 1974 and finds himself in 1847 Ireland during the Potato Famine in James Heneghan's *The Grave* (2002).

Other genre blenders of note include Vivian Vande Velde's *Never Trust a Dead Man* (2000), a fantasy, mystery, and humorous fiction blend; Gary Blackwood's alternate history—a standard subgenre in adult fiction—in *The Year of the Hangman* (2003), in which he explores what might have happened had the British won the Revolutionary War; Timothy Zahn's *Dragon and Thief: A Dragonback Adventure* (2004), which blends science fiction and fantasy; and Alison Goodman's *Singing the Dogstar Blues* (2004), a veritable kitchen sink of genres including contemporary realism, science fiction, humorous fiction, mystery, and adventure.

NONFICTION

Trends in fiction tend to be more dramatic than in nonfiction, perhaps for the obvious reason that fiction is created and nonfiction is documented. That said, the trends most readily identified in nonfiction are in presentation rather than content. As mentioned earlier, nonfiction's physical formats are improving. It seems clear that the publishing industry has come to understand that nonfiction needs to be as attractively published as fiction to entice young readers. The true stuff is as compelling and fascinating as the imagined, but writing that is bland at best and impenetrable at worst has in the past placed nonfiction for teens in the same class as school textbooks. Fortunately, the quality of writing has also been improving over a fairly long period of time, with recent BBYA lists reflecting some superb nonfiction authorship.

Even if only 20 percent of the titles on BBYA lists in the past seven years are nonfiction (including biography and poetry), those relatively few books are truly exceptional representatives of the market.

Biography, autobiography, and memoir lead the way in nonfiction. Additional subjects that are predominant in BBYA lists since 2000 include American history, world history and current events, true stories of adventure and survival, the sciences, and social issues with, as mentioned earlier, an emphasis on women's issues. Also worth noting are books of poetry and the arts and a small collection of books featuring real-world teen voices. A quick look at the largest nonfiction category—biography, autobiography, and memoir—reveals some interesting subject trends.

Biography, Autobiography, and Memoir

Forty-five biographies, autobiographies, and memoirs appear on the past seven years of BBYA lists, and these are quite nicely balanced between male and female life experiences and along a broad range of time periods. Though they are a small percentage of all the books on BBYA lists, these biographical works show clear trends. The majority of these books are about Americans, with a focus on African Americans, especially civil rights activists. Only a handful feature Europeans, and two look at the lives of Chinese individuals. Biographies about artists and entertainers and about remarkable African Americans together account for half the total. Following these, famous sports figures are reasonably well represented. Particularly noteworthy among these biographies (and which is also witnessed in general nonfiction and, as discussed at length above, all genres of fiction) are works about strong women who overcome societal prejudices and limitations to reach personal and societal goals.

In the arts are biographies of photographers Margaret Bourke-White and Dorothea Lange; artists Vincent van Gogh, Louise Bourgeois, and Andy Warhol; and musicians Clara Schumann, Woody Guthrie, Marian Anderson, and John Lennon. Entertainers include tap master Savion Glover, escape artist Harry Houdini, and the Booth brothers. As for the literary arts, three autobiographies of authors for teens made BBYA lists since 2000, by Chris Crutcher, Jack Gantos, and Walter Dean Myers.

Biographies of African Americans in science, sports, the arts, and United States history focus both on personal accomplishments and on the incredibly adverse social circumstances in which these exceptional men and women excelled. The great scientist, educator, and social activist George Washington Carver is uniquely honored in verse by Marilyn Nelson. The lives of civil rights activists Ida B. Wells and Mary Church Terrell are chronicled, as is the personal experience with racism and fight for integration of Maritcha Remond Lyons. Sharon Robinson, Jackie Robinson's daughter, looks at the famous ball player's life as legendary sports figure, father, and civil rights activist. Walter Dean Myers shares the life of Muhammad Ali, a boxer, Black Muslim, and conscientious objector during the Vietnam War. Antwone Fisher's co-written memoir, since made into a movie, tells the personal story of a young African American man abused from early childhood and lost in the Cleveland foster care system, who through the Navy found a home and a future.

In addition to books about Jackie Robinson and Muhammad Ali are other biographies of sports figures, including Babe Didrikson Zaharias—one of those strong women—and Bruce Lee, as well as a co-written memoir featuring Lance Armstrong. Beyond those already mentioned, recent BBYA titles that present strong women to a teen audience include books featuring the women of World War II, from army nurses to Holocaust rescuers; remarkable women of the American West; female singers who influenced musical history; an unwanted Chinese daughter who withstood tremendous social and psychological abuse to succeed in her life; and women with significant physical problems who worked to overcome them. Along with a biography of Helen Keller are contemporary memoirs that look at life with diabetes and anorexia nervosa.

CONCLUSION

There can be no doubt that teen literature is in a truly remarkable period of growth and change. From its literary beginnings thirty-plus years ago, this literature for young people has increased in volume, variety, quality, breadth, and depth. It keeps closer pace with trends in teen life and provides an ever-clearer reflection of the needs, interests, and overall characteristics of its intended readership. Will this surge last? This is an important question, and one that only time will tell. What is certain is that the work of professional organizations that read, evaluate, select, and highlight exemplary works from this expanding literary body, like the Best Books for Young Adults Committee, can only help to showcase its incredible diversity and quality and contribute to its healthy future.

SOURCES CONSULTED

Aronson, Marc. 2005. "Getting Over the Rainbow Party: What's Really Going On in the World of Teenagers and Reading." *Publishers Weekly,* August 15.

Beatty, Sally. 2005. "Publishers Rolling Out Books for Teens with Heavy Themes." *Pittsburgh Post-Gazette,* June 24. http://www.post-gazette.com/pg/05175/528029 .stm.

Cart, Michael. 2004. "Carte Blanche: What Is Young-Adult Literature?" *Booklist* (December 15): 734.

Carter, Betty. 2000. *Best Books for Young Adults.* 2nd ed. Chicago: American Library Association, Young Adult Library Services Association.

Corbett, Sue. 2005. "Why YA and Why Not: Blurring the Line between Traditionally Distinct Markets." *Publishers Weekly,* September 5, 30–31.

Horn, Caroline. 2005. "Those Difficult Years: How Can Retailers and Publishers Make the Most of the Complex Teen Market?" *Bookseller,* February 18.

Magazine Publishers of America. 2004. *Teen Market Profile.* New York: Mediamark Research Inc. http://www.magazine.org/content/files/teenprofile04.pdf.

Packaged Facts. 2002. "By 2006, U.S. Teens Can Buy and Sell Russia." Press release, July 22. http://www.marketresearch.com/product/display.asp?productid=746398.

Rosen, Judith. 2005. "As If! Marketing to Older Teens." *Publishers Weekly,* July 18.

———. 2002. "Tapping the Teen Market: Publishers and Booksellers Target This Spend-Happy but Elusive Audience." *Publishers Weekly,* July 22.

Schwartz, Nomi. 2004. "Kid's Book Talk: Megan Tingley Books." *Bookselling This Week* (American Booksellers Association), October 28. http://news.bookweb.org/ features/2987.html.

Sieruta, Peter D. 2005. "Ten Things That Piss Me Off!" *Horn Book Magazine,* March/April, 223–230.

Taylor, Elizabeth. 2005. "Carl Hiaasen Tones Down Murder, Mayhem for Younger Set." *Ottawa Citizen,* December 29.

Ward, Cynthia. 2004. "Manga: Another SF/F Trend Missed by SF/F?" *Locus Online,* June 2. http://www.locusmag.com/2004/Reviews/06Ward_Manga.html.

Themed Lists

The books in the following themed lists were selected from the 2000–2006 BBYA lists and include standard and well-loved genres and themes, as well as select special themes that are representative of recent literary trends in both content and format and that may prove difficult to build through library catalogs or other online databases. All books included in these lists were in print and readily available in 2006. Although some books appear on more than one list, every attempt was made to include as broad a selection of books as possible across the lists. Each list contains twenty titles; emerging trends that do not yet represent a large enough body of work to fill a twenty-title list are not included here. If more than twenty titles were available in a genre or theme, inclusion was based on each book's reception in professional reviewing sources. Most lists are fiction, some are exclusively nonfiction, and a handful of lists include both fiction and nonfiction selections as are appropriate to their themes. In these lists, nonfiction books are noted. Thanks in large part to the explosion in teen publishing in the recent past, the introductory text found at the beginning of each list in the second edition of this book has been sacrificed to provide room for more annotated titles. The lists are primarily designed as readers' advisory tools for direct teen use and include annotations written to appeal to young people. They can, of course, serve secondarily as tools for the adults who help teens make meaningful reading connections.

ABUSE: PHYSICAL AND PSYCHOLOGICAL

Adichie, Chimamanda Ngozi. *Purple Hibiscus*. When Kambili and her brother get the chance to leave their cruel home in Nigeria to visit their Auntie Ifeoma, they find laughter, love, freedom, and hope.

Anderson, Laurie Halse. *Speak*. After Melinda Sordino calls the police and breaks up an end-of-summer party, she retreats behind a wall of misery and silence, unable to speak about what happened to her there.

Atkins, Catherine. *When Jeff Comes Home*. After two and a half years with his kidnapper and sexual abuser, Jeff is deposited back on his family's doorstep and finds the ordinary world excruciating and his anger overwhelming.

Davis, Amanda. *Wonder When You'll Miss Me*. Fifteen-year-old Faith is gang-raped by high schools boys, and after a huge weight loss and treatment for attempted suicide, she still can't shake the fat, angry girl inside.

Dessen, Sarah. *Dreamland*. Rogerson Biscoe, a sexy, fast-driving, pot-dealing boy, is a great way for Caitlin to rebel against her parents—until he begins to punch her.

Flinn, Alex. *Breathing Underwater*. Sixteen-year-old Nick Andreas is sentenced to a family violence program after he beats up his girlfriend, and through his daily journal explores the reasons for his actions.

Frank, E. R. *Friction*. Twelve-year-old Alex is happy at her school until a troubled and overly mature new girl arrives and begins to confuse Alex with her rumors and dark innuendos.

Hoffman, Nina Kiriki. *A Stir of Bones*. A fourteen-year-old girl with a cruel and manipulative father who beats her mother finds both friendship and healing with the ghost of a suicidal boy in a self-aware house.

Jacobson, Jennifer Richard. *Stained*. When her teenage neighbor goes missing, Joss joins the search to find him, only to discover he has left because of a sexual relationship with their church's priest.

Johnson, Kathleen Jeffrie. *Target*. Sixteen-year-old Grady, violently raped by two men and now almost incapable of speaking and eating, meets three unique teens in his new school who just might be good for him.

Klass, David. *You Don't Know Me*. John is certain no one knows him, especially his mom, because if she did, why would she look the other way while her boyfriend beats him up?

Koertge, Ron. *Margaux with an X.* The beautiful Margaux makes an unexpected friend in Danny, an unappealing boy who loves animals and helps her deal with her father's horrible betrayal when she was a little girl.

Konigsburg, E. L. *Silent to the Bone.* Connor tries to discover just what his best friend, Branwell, won't say while he sits mute in juvenile detention after being accused of dropping his own baby sister.

Lynch, Chris. *Inexcusable.* At first, high school senior Keir has an excuse for all his bad behaviors, including the date rape of his childhood friend, Gigi.

McNamee, Graham. *Hate You.* Alice, a seventeen-year-old songwriter, has to deal with how much she hates her father, who years ago choked her in a rage and permanently damaged her vocal cords.

Rapp, Adam. *33 Snowfish.* In a frigid Illinois winter, three horribly abused runaways, one of whom has murdered his parents and stolen his own baby brother, steal a car and hit the road.

Stratton, Allan. *Leslie's Journal.* Leslie bares her anger, frustration, and fear in her tenth-grade journal assignment, especially about Jason, her handsome but cruel boyfriend who sexually exploits and hits her.

Toten, Teresa. *The Game.* When Dani attempts suicide, she is sent to Riverwood Clinic, where through new friendships and therapy she confronts her father's abuse and reveals the "game" she played with her sister.

Williams, Lori Aurelia. *When Kambia Elaine Flew in from Neptune.* Twelve-year-old Shayla Dubois has a strange friend next door named Kambia who tells the wildest stories that Shayla comes to suspect mask a terrible truth.

Williams-Garcia, Rita. *Every Time a Rainbow Dies.* Sixteen-year-old Thulani helps a young woman after she is raped on the street, and through their connection comes to an understanding of the pain in his own life.

AMERICAN HISTORICAL FICTION

Anderson, Laurie Halse. *Fever 1793*. When the yellow fever comes to Philadelphia in August 1793, fourteen-year-old Mattie Cook is left alone to fight for her survival in a city ravaged by the horrible disease.

Auch, Mary Jane. *Ashes of Roses*. Irish immigrant Rose Nolan finds 1911 New York a difficult place to survive, especially when the Triangle Shirtwaist Factory where she works is destroyed by fire and 146 lives are lost.

Carbone, Elisa. *Stealing Freedom*. Ann Maria Weems, the only person in her family not yet free from slavery, determines to free herself with the help of the Underground Railroad in the 1850s. Based on a true story.

Crowe, Chris. *Mississippi Trial, 1955*. When fourteen-year-old African American Emmett Till is murdered in Mississippi by racists who do not pay for their crime, his white friend Hiram's eyes are opened to humanity's dark side. Based on a true story.

Hobbs, Will. *Jason's Gold*. Fifteen-year-old Jason and King, the husky dog he rescues, travel 5,000 miles north into the harsh Yukon Territory to strike it rich in the 1890s Alaska Gold Rush.

Holm, Jennifer L. *Boston Jane: An Adventure*. A proper young lady heads west to join her betrothed in Washington Territory in the mid-1800s, to find only Chinook Indians and filthy adventurers when she gets there.

Krisher, Trudy. *Uncommon Faith*. Ten different townspeople describe life in Millbrook, Massachusetts, in 1837 and 1838, including Faith, a teen who stands up for what she believes is right in a time when most women didn't.

Les Becquets, Diane. *The Stones of Mourning Creek*. In 1966 Alabama, Francie Grove, a white girl, and Ruthie Taylor, an African American girl, are tormented by their ugly, racist town just for being friends.

Lester, Julius. *Day of Tears: A Novel in Dialogue*. Many voices, white and black, recount the terrible day in 1859 when Pierce Butler held the largest slave auction in history to pay off his gambling debts. Based on a true story.

Levine, Gail Carson. *Dave at Night*. A young orphan sneaks out of the miserable Hebrew Home for Boys and finds magic in the New York jazz world during the Harlem Renaissance in 1926.

Peck, Richard. *A Year down Yonder*. Fifteen-year-old Chicagoan Mary Alice spends the summer of 1937 in a small Illinois town with her tough, wily, and hilarious Grandma Dowdel.

Rees, Celia. *Witch Child*. After Mary Newbury's grandmother is hanged for witchcraft in 1659 England, a mysterious benefactor helps Mary escape the same fate by sending her to the New World disguised as a Puritan.

Ryan, Pam Muñoz. *Esperanza Rising*. Tragedy forces Esperanza, a privileged girl from a wealthy Mexican ranching family, to learn a new life as a poor migrant field worker in California during the Great Depression.

Santana, Patricia. *Motorcycle Ride on the Sea of Tranquility*. Yolanda is excited to have her favorite brother, Chuy, back from the Vietnam War, until she discovers he is not the same person he was before he left.

Schmidt, Gary D. *Lizzie Bright and the Buckminster Boy*. In 1911 Maine, Turner, the new minister's son, and Lizzie, a girl from a nearby island community of former slaves, become friends despite the town's plan to rid the area of Lizzie's people.

Schwartz, Virginia Frances. *Send One Angel Down*. Because of her great beauty, Eliza, the blue-eyed, light-skinned daughter of the cotton plantation's master and a slave, will be sold as a "breeder" or prostitute unless the master's plan is stopped.

Taylor, Mildred D. *The Land*. The son of a white man and a black woman and torn between two worlds, Paul Logan is forced to choose his own direction in life at the close of the Civil War years.

Townley, Roderick. *Sky*. In 1959 New York, the piano-playing, jazz-loving Alec Schuyler finds the understanding and connection he doesn't have with his father when he meets a famous blind jazz pianist.

Weaver, Will. *Full Service*. When Paul, a conservative Christian teen, takes a job at a gas station in the summer of 1965, he is exposed to a weird and wonderful world of temptation.

Wolf, Allan. *New Found Land*. Fourteen different voices from the Corps of Discovery, including the dog, narrate the adventures of the 1804–1806 Lewis and Clark expedition to the Pacific Coast and back.

CHALLENGES: PHYSICAL AND PSYCHOLOGICAL

Buckingham, Dorothea N. *Staring Down the Dragon*. After surgery and treatment, Rell is cancer free and can go back to Kailua High School, but the doctor never told her she was cured forever.

Coburn, Jake. *LoveSick*. Ted, an alcoholic whose drinking destroyed his sports career, is bribed by a stranger to spy on Erica, a bulimic rich girl, which brings the two addicts together.

Cofer, Judith Ortiz. *The Meaning of Consuelo*. The dutiful Consuelo has to deal with parents who each have very different values, while also looking after her younger sister, who is becoming more and more mentally imbalanced.

Ferris, Jean. *Of Sound Mind*. Theo's whole life has been spent taking care of his deaf parents, which becomes an even greater burden when his father has a stroke and his mother falls apart.

Fleischman, Paul. *Mind's Eye*. Sixteen-year-old Courtney lies paralyzed in a hospital room with two old women, one of whom distracts her from her misery by helping her take an imaginary trip to Italy.

Frank, E. R. *America*. Born to a crack addict, stuck in the foster care system, moved around and sexually abused, America is finally getting the psychological care he needs after trying to kill himself.

Froese, Deborah. *Out of the Fire*. While she is partying with her new boyfriend and his friends who are much cooler than hers, Dayle is seriously burned when a boy uses gasoline to start a bonfire.

Hautman, Pete. *Sweetblood*. Lucy's diabetes controls her life, and after getting in trouble for writing a paper claiming the vampires of the past were really just untreated diabetics, she begins to self-destruct.

Jenkins, A. M. *Damage*. Austin is a handsome football player of almost legendary skill who has a stunning girlfriend and a great mom, but who is so depressed he might as well just die.

Johnson, Scott. *Safe at Second*. Paulie tries to get Todd, his best friend and a high school star pitcher, back on the mound when Todd loses both an eye and his chance at the majors.

Koertge, Ron. *Stoner and Spaz*. Ben has cerebral palsy and figures no one wants to deal with him, until he meets Colleen, a drug addict who falls asleep on his shoulder during a movie.

Lawrence, Iain. *Ghost Boy*. Harold, a tall, thin, almost blind albino called "Ghost Boy" by his tormentors, joins the circus to escape the misery and isolation of his small-town life.

Marchetta, Melina. *Saving Francesca.* Francesca has a lot to deal with between being one of the first girls to go to a previously all-boy Catholic school and having a totally depressed mother.

McCormick, Patricia. *Cut.* Callie is so worn out by having to take responsibility for her parents and her asthmatic younger brother that she starts cutting herself to release the pressure.

Rapp, Adam. *Under the Wolf, under the Dog.* Steve's therapy journal exposes the horrific family story that led to his severe depression, drug abuse, and current life in a facility for troubled teens.

Santana, Patricia. *Motorcycle Ride on the Sea of Tranquility.* Yolanda is excited to have her favorite brother, Chuy, back from the Vietnam War, until she discovers he is not the same person he was before he left.

Sones, Sonya. *Stop Pretending: What Happened When My Big Sister Went Crazy.* Cookie's older sister has a nervous breakdown and is institutionalized, leaving Cookie and her parents alone to deal with the pain it brings to their lives.

Trueman, Terry. *Stuck in Neutral.* Shawn can't move, can't talk, and can't even blink because of his severe cerebral palsy, which also means he can't let anyone know he suspects his father is plotting to kill him.

Weeks, Sarah. *So B. It.* So B. It, Heidi's mother, is a seriously mentally disabled woman who knows only twenty-three words and can't tell Heidi where she comes from and who she is.

White, Ruth. *Memories of Summer.* In 1955, Lyric and her father do everything they can to help Lyric's older sister, Summer, as she spirals deeper and deeper into schizophrenia.

FAMILY IN CRISIS

Cohn, Rachel. *Gingerbread*. Cyd discovers no one in her family is perfect when her mom and stepdad send her to her biological father in New York, a man she's only met once in sixteen years.

Corrigan, Eireann. *Splintering*. Crazy on PCP, a man with a machete attacks fifteen-year-old Paulie's family in their home, causing them all intense physical and psychological trauma.

Fienberg, Anna. *Borrowed Light*. Callisto's parents don't pay any attention to her unless she fails to care for her little brother, Jeremy, so she can't go to them when she finds out she's pregnant.

Fusco, Kimberly Newton. *Tending to Grace*. Cornelia's mother abandons her at Great-Aunt Agatha's cottage in the woods, leaving the older woman to deal with a lonely, withdrawn girl with a terrible stutter.

Johnson, Angela. *Bird*. Thirteen-year-old Bird runs away from home to Alabama to find Cecil, the stepfather who abandoned her family, and hides out at the farm owned by Cecil's cousin hoping to find Cecil there.

Koja, Kathe. *The Blue Mirror*. To escape her alcoholic mother, Maggy hangs out at a café called the Blue Mirror, there to meet Cole, a mysterious and attractive street teen who isn't what he seems at first.

Lawrence, Iain. *The Lightkeeper's Daughter*. Now the single mother of a two-year-old, seventeen-year-old Elizabeth returns home to Lizzie Island and a family filled with guilt over the drowning death of her brother.

Leavitt, Martine. *Heck, Superhero*. A young homeless boy abandoned by his mother and living alone on the streets finds comfort in his artwork and in imagining himself as a superhero.

Mackler, Carolyn. *The Earth, My Butt, and Other Big, Round Things*. Virginia's self-image issues seem small when her perfect brother date rapes a girl at college and her perfect family has to face the fact that it isn't so perfect after all.

Martinez, Manuel Luis. *Drift*. Sixteen-year-old Mexican American Robert Lomos wants to reunite his family after his mother breaks down, takes his baby brother away with her, and leaves him with his stern grandmother.

Nolan, Han. *Born Blue*. The daughter of a heroin-addicted mother, Janie holds tight to her dream to become a legendary blues singer even as she's moved between one horrible foster home and another.

Oughton, Jerrie. *Perfect Family*. When fifteen-year-old Welcome's older sister runs away to Hollywood and Welcome gets pregnant, her 1950s North Carolina family is shaken to its foundation, leaving Welcome to make a painful decision.

Plummer, Louise. *A Dance for Three*. Hannah's father is dead, her mother won't leave the house, and when she tells her boyfriend she's pregnant he slugs her and then cheats on her, sending Hannah toward a mental breakdown.

Sebold, Alice. *The Lovely Bones*. Susie Salmon watches her friends and family from heaven, and just as they cannot move on after her death, she cannot help but mourn her too-short time on earth.

Stratton, Allan. *Chanda's Secrets*. When sixteen-year-old Chanda's baby sister dies of AIDS, she is only the first in the family to fall to the disease in an African village that denies the presence of the terrifying epidemic.

Williams, Lori Aurelia. *When Kambia Elaine Flew in from Neptune*. Shayla Dubois's older sister has run away, leaving Shayla and her mother angry, sad, and worried, while Shayla also has worries about a strange new friend next door.

Wittlinger, Ellen. 2004. *Zigzag*. The angry and immature Robin accompanies her grieving aunt and cousins on a road trip that might end up in Phoenix, where her father and his new family live.

Woodson, Jacqueline. *Hush*. When Toswiah's father testifies against two white cops who killed a black teenager, it forces the family into the federal witness protection program, where they all suffer identity crises.

Woodson, Jacqueline. *Miracle's Boys*. After their beloved mother dies, thirteen-year-old Lafayette watches his tormented oldest brother accept the heavy burden of family responsibility and his angry middle brother turn to a life of crime.

Wynne-Jones, Tim. *A Thief in the House of Memory*. When a man is found dead in the family home Declan's mother disappeared from six years ago, Declan revisits old memories and searches for answers with his father and his mother's best friend.

FAMILY REDEFINED

Bauer, Cat. *Harley, Like a Person.* Harley is miserable at home and is convinced she must have been adopted, which motivates her to find her biological father.

Bechard, Margaret. *Hanging on to Max.* Sam is a seventeen-year-old single father who refused to give up his baby despite the mother's wishes, and who is trying to raise Max on his own.

Creech, Sharon. *The Wanderer.* Sophie is sailing across the ocean with the family she was adopted into three years ago, but she refuses to acknowledge that she hasn't always been with them.

Curtis, Christopher Paul. *Bud, Not Buddy.* During the Great Depression in Michigan, ten-year-old Bud runs away from an orphanage in search of his long-lost father and ends up with some old Jazz cats.

Fleischman, Paul. *Seek.* Paul has to write his autobiography for school and makes it into a radio play filled with all the sounds and voices in his past, except for the voice of the father who abandoned him.

Friesen, Gayle. *Janey's Girl.* When Claire's mother takes her to the small town she grew up in, Claire learns why her mother hated her grandfather and finds out the truth about her own father.

Giff, Patricia Reilly. *Pictures of Hollis Woods.* Hollis Woods has run away from the foster family she loves, but through a kind and forgetful artist who takes her in, finds her way back home.

Halpin, Brendan. *Donorboy.* When her lesbian mothers are killed in a poultry truck accident, fourteen-year-old Rosalind has to live with the sperm-donor dad she's never met and who is definitely not father material.

Haruf, Kent. *Plainsong.* A father raising his sons alone, a pregnant teenager kicked out by her mother, and two lonely old bachelors together find that families can be forged of love and preference.

Johnson, Angela. *The First Part Last.* When Nia suffers brain damage after having their baby, sixteen-year-old Bobby becomes a single father who has some big decisions to make.

Levithan, David. *Are We There Yet?* Two brothers who have grown apart are sent to Italy by parents who hope to reconcile them, but once there, a girl that both brothers want gets in the way.

Marchetta, Melina. *Looking for Alibrandi*. Raised by her single mother, Josie is a poor ethnic student on scholarship at her Catholic girls' school and, even harder, is faced with meeting the father who never knew about her.

McDonald, Janet. *Spellbound*. Once a promising student, Raven is now a young mother in the Brooklyn projects who has to start anew to build a better life for herself and her son.

Powell, Randy. *Tribute to Another Dead Rock Star*. Three years after Grady's heavy-metal rock star mom overdosed on drugs, he has to decide whether he can fit in to his mentally handicapped half-brother's family.

Rosoff, Meg. *How I Live Now*. When Daisy is sent to her cousins in England, she finds true love and a family worth fighting for as an invading military force occupies the country.

Rottman, S. L. *Stetson*. Seventeen-year-old Stetson has to deal with the troubled younger sister he never knew he had when she shows up to live with him and their angry, alcoholic father.

Sones, Sonya. *One of Those Hideous Books Where the Mother Dies*. After Ruby's mother dies, she has to move from Boston to California to live with Whip Logan, her super-rich, very famous movie star father, whom she absolutely loathes.

Stanley, Diane. *A Time Apart*. When Jennie's mother is diagnosed with breast cancer and faces uncomfortable treatment, Jennie is sent to stay with her father in a re-created Iron Age village in England.

Vijayaraghavan, Vineeta. *Motherland*. Maya is sent to India against her will to stay with relatives for the summer but begins to grow close to her traditional grandmother and appreciate her cultural heritage.

Weeks, Sarah. *So B. It*. Heidi travels from Nevada to New York to try to find out what her mentally disabled mother can't tell her: where she came from and who she is.

FANTASY: DARK AND LIGHT

Bell, Hilari. *The Goblin Wood*. When Makenna's mother is put to death for sorcery, the young hedgewitch joins forces with the goblins in the forest to fight the Hierarchy who took her mother from her.

Bray, Libba. *A Great and Terrible Beauty* and *Rebel Angels*. Gemma returns to England from India and is enrolled in a girls' academy after her mother dies, there to experience visions that take her and her friends between worlds to rebuild the mysterious Order.

Calhoun, Dia. *Aria of the Sea*. Cerinth, a talented healer, rejects her path to join Winward's prestigious School of Royal Dancers, only to find she can no longer hear the song of the Sea Maid, Aria.

Clement-Davies, David. *Fire Bringer*. Rannoch, a fawn born with the mark of an oak leaf on his forehead, is destined to become the hero foretold in the Prophecy and secure his herd's future.

Delaney, Joseph. *Revenge of the Witch,* Last Apprentice series, book 1. Tom Ward, the seventh son of a seventh son, accidentally frees a horrible witch while apprenticed to the Spook, a man who protects people against malevolent beings.

Dunkle, Clare B. *The Hollow Kingdom,* Hollow Kingdom trilogy, book 1. When Kate and Emily are orphaned and move to the isolated estate they are to inherit, the King of the Goblins chooses Kate for his bride.

Fisher, Catherine. *The Oracle Betrayed,* Oracle Prophecies, book 1. Mirany, a young woman who serves the Oracle in a place reminiscent of Greece and Egypt, must with the aid of unlikely friends find the Archon, the true god on earth.

Gaiman, Neil. *Coraline*. Behind the locked drawing room door is a flat almost like Coraline's own, with alternate black button-eyed parents who have a terrible desire to keep Coraline with them forever.

Gruber, Michael. *The Witch's Boy*. Lump, an ugly foundling, is raised by a well-meaning witch and her magical creatures, only to betray his makeshift family before finding out what really matters to him.

Jordan, Sherryl. *Secret Sacrament*. Gabriel, a Navoran healer, is drawn to the plains-dwelling Shinali, a people the Navorans intend to destroy and for whom Gabriel is destined to make a great sacrifice.

Lanagan, Margo. *Black Juice*. This hauntingly strange collection of ten fantasy short stories sometimes teeters on the edge of reality and at other times delves deep into disturbing other worlds.

Larbalestier, Justine. *Magic or Madness*. After her mother goes insane and she's sent to live with her frightening grandmother, Reason finds a key to a magical door that transports her from the Australian bush to New York City.

Noyes, Deborah, ed. *Gothic! Ten Original Dark Tales*. Well-known authors for teens, including M. T. Anderson, Garth Nix, and Celia Rees, test the boundaries of the gothic tradition with stories both frightening and funny.

Oppel, Kenneth. *Airborn* and *Skybreaker*. Matt Cruse starts as a cabin boy on the luxury airship *Aurora,* which floats across an alternate Earth, and after many swashbuckling adventures is accepted as a student at a prestigious airship academy where new intrigues unfold.

Pierce, Tamora. *Trickster's Choice,* Daughter of the Lioness, book 1. When sixteen-year-old Aly gets mad at her parents and takes off to cool down, she is kidnapped by pirates and sold as a slave to an exiled royal family on the Copper Islands.

Pratchett, Terry. *The Wee Free Men* and *A Hat Full of Sky*. The young witch Tiffany Aching first meets the Wee Free Men—little blue warriors with great big attitudes—when her little brother disappears into Fairyland, to find they've become her guardians for life.

Shinn, Sharon. *The Safe-Keeper's Secret.* Fiona knows she will be a Safe-Keeper just like her mother, the person all the villagers tell their secrets to, until her mother tells Fiona a secret that changes everything.

Vaught, Susan. *Stormwitch*. Even though Ruba Cleo has moved from Haiti to Mississippi, she remembers her Dahomey heritage and the magic of her people, especially when faced with racism and the threat of violence.

Whitcomb, Laura. *A Certain Slant of Light*. Helen and James, two ghosts who inhabit the bodies of modern teens, learn about each other's original lives and fall in love.

Wooding, Chris. *The Haunting of Alaizabel Cray*. In an alternate Victorian London, Thaniel, a wych-hunter, encounters Alaizabel Cray, a young woman possessed by the spirit of an evil wych, whom Thaniel vows to rescue.

FRIENDSHIP

Brashares, Ann. *The Sisterhood of the Traveling Pants*. Four friends going different directions for the summer share a magical pair of pants that fit the wearer perfectly despite their different body types.

Desai Hidier, Tanuja. *Born Confused*. When she helps her blond-haired, blue-eyed best friend, Gwyn, to become attractive to an Indian boy, Indian American Dimple falls for him herself.

Going, K. L. *Fat Kid Rules the World*. Three-hundred-pound Troy Billings thinks about killing himself but makes a different choice when the homeless guitar god Curt McCrae befriends him.

Hautman, Pete. *Invisible*. A tragic secret is gradually revealed about two unlikely friends: a disturbed loner, Dougie Hanson, and a popular athlete, Andy Morrow.

Johnson, Kathleen Jeffrie. *Target*. Sixteen-year-old Grady, violently raped by two men and now almost incapable of speaking and eating, meets three unique teens in his new school who just might be good for him.

Johnson, Scott. *Safe at Second*. Paulie tries to get Todd, his best friend and a high school star pitcher, back on the mound when Todd loses both an eye and his chance at the majors.

Koertge, Ron. *Stoner and Spaz*. Ben has cerebral palsy and figures no one wants to deal with him, until he meets Colleen, a drug addict who falls asleep on his shoulder during a movie.

Les Becquets, Diane. *The Stones of Mourning Creek*. In 1966 Alabama, Francie Grove, a white girl, and Ruthie Taylor, an African American girl, are tormented by their ugly, racist town just for being friends.

Lynch, Chris. *Gold Dust*. Richard makes friends with Napoleon, a Dominican transfer student and one of the only black students at his Boston Catholic school in 1975, and tries to interest him in baseball.

McDonald, Janet. *Spellbound*. Raven is a young African American mother and a high school dropout in a Brooklyn ghetto who wants to get back on track with her life, starting with winning a spelling bee.

Oates, Joyce Carol. *Big Mouth and Ugly Girl*. Ursula Riggs is the only person to help Matt Donaghy when he is falsely accused of threatening to blow up the school, beginning a friendship and maybe even more.

Perkins, Lynne Rae. *Criss Cross.* Through dialogue, poetry, questions and answers, and prose, the stories of fourteen-year-olds Debbie, Hector, and their friends unfold as they each reach important turning points in their lives.

Peters, Julie Anne. *Define Normal.* Nerdy honor student Antonia is surprised to find out that even though she's the peer counselor, Jazz, a black lipstick-wearing punk girl, has guidance to give her, too.

Plum-Ucci, Carol. *What Happened to Lani Garver.* The popular but troubled Claire is intrigued by the social outcast the rest of her friends are tormenting, a strange boy named Lani who might be more than he seems.

Powell, Randy. *Three Clams and an Oyster.* Three longtime friends must face their differences when the search for a fourth player for their flag football team ends with Rachel, a girl who can play a mean game.

Schmidt, Gary D. *Lizzie Bright and the Buckminster Boy.* In 1911 Maine, Turner, the new minister's son, and Lizzie, a girl from a nearby island community of former slaves, become friends despite the town's plan to rid the area of Lizzie's people.

Shusterman, Neal. *The Schwa Was Here.* Calvin Schwa has an amazing ability to seem invisible, to go virtually unnoticed, and his new pal Antsy Bonano concocts a scheme to profit from "the Schwa Effect."

Volponi, Paul. *Black and White.* When basketball players and best friends Eddie and Marcus get caught after their third robbery, the justice system treats them differently because one is white and one is black.

Wittlinger, Ellen. *Hard Love.* When John meets Marisol, the author of his favorite zine, he falls in love but settles for friendship when Marisol reveals to him why that is the only option.

Wittlinger, Ellen. *Sandpiper.* Known as the local slut, feeling shut out by her soon-to-be new stepfamily, and being stalked by an old boyfriend, Sandpiper desperately needs the friendship "the Walker" offers her.

HUMOR

Bechard, Margaret. *Spacer and Rat.* Jack, a space-dwelling "spacer," and Kit, an earth-dwelling "rat," find they have more in common than they think when they come together to protect Waldo, a sentient and highly illegal robot.

Braff, Joshua. *The Unthinkable Thoughts of Jacob Green.* Jacob uses "unthinkable thoughts" to insulate him from his father's tyranny in this coming-of-age story set in 1970s New Jersey.

Choldenko, Gennifer. *Al Capone Does My Shirts.* Moose's dad is a security guard on Alcatraz, a position that Moose uses to full advantage when the warden's daughter begins selling the laundry services of its most famous inmate, Al Capone.

Curtis, Christopher Paul. *Bucking the Sarge.* Luther's mother, "the Sarge," is the cruelest slumlord in Flint, Michigan, and when Luther discovers the full extent of her treachery, he must choose between doing what she wants and doing the right thing.

Fleischman, Paul. *Zap.* Pick up the remote control and "zap" between seven different plays in this audience participation satire of theater conventions.

Gaiman, Neil. *Anansi Boys.* When Fat Charlie's father dies, his long-lost brother turns up and steals his fiancée, which is not the most shocking thing that will happen to Fat Charlie.

Halpin, Brendan. *Donorboy.* When Rosalind's two moms are killed in a tragic run-in with a Turducken, she moves in with her donor father, Sean, who has no clue how to raise a teenage daughter.

Hiaasen, Carl. *Hoot.* When construction for a Mother Paula's All-American Pancake House begins on top of a burrow of endangered owls, it is up to Roy and his friends to stop the bulldozers.

Horvath, Polly. *The Canning Season.* At first, Ratchet feels wretched and unloved when her mother leaves her for the summer in the care of her eccentric great-aunts, Tilly and Penpen.

Korman, Gordon. *Son of the Mob.* Tony's dad runs the local "vending machine" business, and Kendra is the daughter of the FBI agent sworn to bring Tony's mob boss father to justice. Can their love survive?

LaRochelle, David. *Absolutely, Positively Not.* Steven is absolutely, positively *not* gay, and he sets out to prove it by hanging with the guys and dating girls, but he absolutely, positively cannot convince himself.

Lubar, David. *Sleeping Freshmen Never Lie*. Scott writes a survival manual for his unborn brother filled with advice on how to make it through the freshman year in high school.

Martinez, A. Lee. *Gil's All Fright Diner*. Duke and Earl, a werewolf and a vampire, fend off a zombie attack at Loretta's diner and there uncover the plot of a teenage witch to take over the world.

Moore, Christopher. *Lamb: The Gospel according to Biff, Christ's Childhood Pal*. Biff tells the story of his best friend, Josh, who was destined for a special place in human history.

Peck, Richard. *Fair Weather*. Rosie is a girl who has never strayed much from her family's farm until Aunt Euterpe decides to take her family to the 1893 Chicago World's Fair.

Powell, Randy. *Three Clams and an Oyster*. Three longtime friends must face their differences when the search for a fourth player for their flag football team ends with Rachel, a girl who can play a mean game.

Pratchett, Terry. *The Wee Free Men*. The Wee Free Men, the fiercest and foulest former inhabitants of Fairyland, just may be the only hope for Tiffany, a young witch whose brother has been kidnapped by the icy Fairy Queen.

Rennison, Louise. *Angus, Thongs, and Full-Frontal Snogging: Confessions of Georgia Nicolson*. Georgia tries everything to win the attentions of Robbie the "Sex God" and control her evil cat, Angus, in this British girl's humor-filled diary.

Tolan, Stephanie S. *Surviving the Applewhites*. The Applewhites are the most artistic and zany family Jake Semple has ever met, and their home school is the only place left that will take him in.

Young, Karen Romano. *The Beetle and Me: A Love Story*. There is no greater love than that between a girl and her car, or so thinks Daisy, whose object of affection is a 1957 Volkswagen Beetle.

IDENTITY, IMAGE, AND ACCEPTANCE

Bauer, Cat. *Harley, Like a Person.* Harley is miserable at home and is convinced she must have been adopted, which motivates her to find her biological father.

Castellucci, Cecil. *Boy Proof.* Victoria has a shaved head and calls herself Egg after a favorite sci-fi movie character to hide her true self, until a new boy at school helps her to open up.

Dessen, Sarah. *Keeping the Moon.* It takes an eccentric aunt and two waitresses at the Last Chance Café to help Colie realize she's really okay after she loses a lot of weight but still hates herself.

Ferris, Jean. *Eight Seconds.* While at bull-riding rodeo camp, eighteen-year-old John comes to realize that, like his new friend, Kit, he is gay in a world with little tolerance for differences.

Flake, Sharon G. *Who Am I without Him? Short Stories about Girls and the Boys in Their Lives.* Short stories about ten black teens explore how young people base their sense of self-worth on how attractive they are to members of the opposite sex.

Freymann-Weyr, Garret. *My Heartbeat.* When she asks about it, Ellen's brother, Link, is unwilling to admit that he and his best friend James share a romantic relationship, putting Ellen in the middle of their estrangement.

Going, K. L. *Fat Kid Rules the World.* Three-hundred-pound Troy Billings thinks about killing himself but makes a different choice when the homeless guitar god Curt McCrae asks Troy to drum for his band.

Holt, Kimberly Willis. *When Zachary Beaver Came to Town.* Tobey learns a lot about himself when he and his friend Cal befriend a 643-pound sideshow boy, Zachary, after he is abandoned by his guardian and left alone in his trailer.

Korman, Gordon. *Jake, Reinvented.* In this retelling of *The Great Gatsby,* Jake transforms himself from a nerd into a cool partier to attract the attention of the beautiful Didi, whom he used to tutor in math.

Krovatin, Christopher. *Heavy Metal and You.* Metal Head Sam Markus falls for a preppy girl, who at first seems like a dream come true but then tries to turn him into something he's not.

Mackler, Carolyn. *The Earth, My Butt, and Other Big, Round Things.* Virginia feels overweight and totally average among her beautiful and accomplished family but discovers that appearances can be deceptive and it is what's inside that really counts.

McGhee, Alison. *All Rivers Flow to the Sea*. Rose has to navigate her grief and find out who she is without her sister, Ivy, who lies in a permanent vegetative state following an automobile accident.

Myracle, Lauren. *Kissing Kate*. When her best friend, Kate, passionately kisses her at a party one night and then pretends it never happened, Lissa is left to find out what it means by herself.

Pearson, Mary E. *A Room on Lorelei Street*. To escape her alcoholic mother's neediness, seventeen-year-old Zoe rents a room on Lorelei Street but has hard lessons to learn about being on her own.

Peters, Julie Anne. *Luna*. Regan struggles to have a life of her own while helping her brother, Liam, deal with his life as a girl born into a boy's body.

Smith, Sherri L. *Lucy the Giant*. The largest girl in her school, Lucy passes as an adult to work on a commercial fishing boat so she can escape her neglectful, alcoholic father and become her own person.

Tolan, Stephanie S. *Surviving the Applewhites*. The juvenile delinquent Jake discovers things about himself that he never knew while at the Applewhite's eccentric home school.

Weeks, Sarah. *So B. It*. Heidi's mother is a seriously mentally disabled woman who knows only twenty-three words, leaving Heidi on her own to find out where she comes from and who she is.

Wittlinger, Ellen. *What's in a Name*. Ten different teens share their search for identity and self-understanding in Scrub Harbor, a town experiencing its own sort of identity crisis.

Zusak, Markus. *I Am the Messenger*. Teen cabbie Ed Kennedy finds himself changed when he inadvertently stops a bank robbery and starts receiving playing cards in the mail with the addresses of people who need help.

LOSS, GRIEF, AND RECOVERY

Abelove, Joan. *Saying It Out Loud.* Mindy's mother is alive but is not the same person after her brain surgery, and now Mindy and her father are left to work out their difficult relationship alone.

Brooks, Bruce. *All That Remains.* Three teens in three different stories react to the deaths of their loved ones in very unique ways.

Brooks, Martha. *True Confessions of a Heartless Girl.* A small town is rocked by the arrival of Noreen, a pregnant teenager in a stolen truck who brings both good and bad luck to the people who help her.

Coman, Carolyn. *Many Stones.* Berry travels to South Africa with her estranged father to attend her sister's memorial service, where they learn about forgiveness from people long used to suffering.

Flake, Sharon G. *Bang!* Mann's father draws inspiration from African initiation rites and leaves him in the wilderness in hopes that he will overcome the grief he feels about his brother's death.

Frank, E. R. *Wrecked.* Anna was the other driver in an accident that left her brother's girlfriend dead, and must fight her way through the anger, fear, and anxiety that tear at her.

Green, John. *Looking for Alaska.* Miles divides his memories into before and after the death of Alaska, a girl he comes to love at his exclusive boarding school.

Griffin, Adele. *Where I Want to Be.* Sisters Jane and Lily could not be more different: Jane is troubled and Lily is carefree, Jane is lonely and Lily is popular, Jane is dead and Lily is alive.

Holt, Kimberly Willis. *Keeper of the Night.* Isabel works so hard to keep her family together after her mother's suicide that she does not see it is she who is falling apart.

Howe, James, ed. *The Color of Absence: Twelve Stories about Loss and Hope.* Everyone experiences loss a little differently. Here, twelve authors tell original stories of pain and recovery.

Johnson, Maureen. *The Key to the Golden Firebird.* After the death of their beloved father, the Gold sisters hope the key to their father's Pontiac Firebird will unlock the grief that holds their hearts.

Mack, Tracy. *Birdland.* Jed is making a documentary about his New York neighborhood to help him overcome the guilt he feels after the death of his brother from insulin shock.

Maynard, Joyce. *The Usual Rules.* One day, Wendy's mother goes to work and does not come home, leaving Wendy behind to navigate the emotional rubble left by September 11th.

McGhee, Alison. *All Rivers Flow to the Sea*. Ivy goes to the Gorge with boys to feel something, anything, after the accident that leaves her sister in a vegetative coma.

Myers, Walter Dean. *Autobiography of My Dead Brother*. Sketches and comics illustrate the story of Rise and Jesse, two "blood brothers" on different paths in Harlem.

Rapp, Adam. *Under the Wolf, under the Dog*. Steve chronicles the events that led to his commitment to an institution for troubled teens: his mother's cancer death, his brother's suicide, and his own breakdown.

Saenz, Benjamin Alire. *Sammy and Juliana in Hollywood*. Sammy deals with first love, death, family, friendship, and war in the Hollywood barrio of Las Cruces, New Mexico, in the 1960s.

Sebold, Alice. 2003. *The Lovely Bones*. Susie Salmon watches her friends and family from heaven, and just as they cannot move on after her death, she cannot help but mourn her too-short time on earth.

Sones, Sonya. *One of Those Hideous Books Where the Mother Dies*. Ruby's super-famous father wants nothing more than a relationship with her after the sudden death of her mother, a relationship Ruby wants no part of.

Woodson, Jacqueline. *Behind You*. Ellie grieves the loss of her beloved Jeremiah in this sequel to Woodson's *If You Come Softly*, while "Miah" watches her and his friends face their futures without him.

LOVE AND ROMANCE

Bat-Ami, Miriam. *Two Suns in the Sky*. An American Catholic girl and a Yugoslavian Jewish boy who survived the Holocaust defy her father when they fall in love through the fence of a New York refugee camp in 1944.

Buckhanon, Kalisha. *Upstate*. When seventeen-year-old Antonio is sent upstate to serve a ten-year prison sentence for a crime he may not have committed, he and his girlfriend, Natasha, communicate through letters.

Castellucci, Cecil. *Boy Proof*. Victoria has a shaved head and calls herself Egg after a favorite sci-fi movie character to hide her true self, until a new boy at school helps her to open up.

Dessen, Sarah. *This Lullaby*. Her famous romance novelist mother's four and soon to be five marriages have made Remy a skeptic when it comes to love and romance, but rock singer Dexter just might change her mind.

Frank, Hillary. *Better Than Running at Night*. Ellie's first semester at the prestigious New England School of Art is about more than art when she meets Nate and does things with him she's never done before.

Johnson, Maureen. *13 Little Blue Envelopes*. When seventeen-year-old Ginny's Aunt Peg dies, she leaves Ginny $1,000 and instructions to buy a plane ticket to London, where she begins a great adventure and meets Keith.

Korman, Gordon. *Son of the Mob*. Tony's dad runs the local "vending machine" business, and Kendra is the daughter of the FBI agent sworn to bring Tony's mob boss father to justice. Can their love survive?

Krovatin, Christopher. *Heavy Metal and You*. Metal Head Sam Markus falls for a preppy girl, who at first seems like a dream come true but then tries to turn him into something he's not.

Levithan, David. *Boy Meets Boy*. Paul meets Noah, falls for Noah, gets Noah, loses Noah, and sets out to get Noah back after he's caught in a kiss with his old boyfriend, Kyle.

McNeal, Laura, and Tom McNeal. *Crooked*. Amos and Clara, both dealing with family problems, find comfort with each other and fall in love, only to be tormented by bullies when Amos catches them vandalizing mailboxes.

Meyer, Stephenie. *Twilight*. Bella, the clumsy, self-deprecating new girl in gloomy Forks, Washington, falls for her lab partner, Edward—a beautiful and talented vampire.

Nelson, Blake. *Rock Star, Superstar.* When bass player Pete's band gets signed, his relationship with his girlfriend, Margaret, is challenged by the different directions they are heading.

Randle, Kristen D. *Breaking Rank.* When Casey starts tutoring Thomas Fairbairn, a member of a reclusive group called the Clan, they have to break through barriers to work with each other, finding understanding and even love.

Ryan, Sara. *Empress of the World.* At a summer institute for gifted students, Nicola and Battle fall for each other, but the two young women have trouble understanding just what their attraction means.

Sones, Sonya. *What My Mother Doesn't Know.* Ninth-grader Sophie's life with her disconnected father and soap opera–addicted mother, her two best friends, her sexy boyfriend, Dylan, and her many additional crushes, is told through free-verse poems.

Turnbull, Ann. *No Shame, No Fear.* In the 1600s, a Quaker girl and Anglican boy must hide their love for each other during a time when the Quakers are being heavily persecuted by the British government.

Weaver, Beth Nixon. *Rooster.* Fifteen-year-old Kady wants nothing more than to be with her new, rich boyfriend in 1960s Florida, distracting her from her job watching over Rooster, the brain-damaged boy who lives next door.

Whitcomb, Laura. *A Certain Slant of Light.* Helen and James, two ghosts who inhabit the bodies of modern teens, learn about each other's original lives and fall in love.

Wittlinger, Ellen. *Hard Love.* When John meets Marisol, the author of his favorite zine, he falls in love but settles for friendship when Marisol reveals to him why that is the only option.

Young, Karen Romano. *The Beetle and Me: A Love Story.* There is no greater love than that between a girl and her car, or so thinks Daisy, who may find another object of affection along with her 1957 Volkswagen Beetle.

FICTION

MYSTERY AND CRIME

Bell, Hilari. *A Matter of Profit*. When his people invade the T'Chin Empire and install their own court, Ahvren must uncover a plot to assassinate the emperor with the help of a strange scholar.

Cormier, Robert. *The Rag and Bone Shop*. When his seven-year-old neighbor is murdered, Jason wants to do all he can to help solve the crime, not knowing that the police officer in charge believes Jason is the murderer.

Cross, Gillian. *Tightrope*. When she "tags" a grocery store with graffiti, the loner Ashley comes to the attention of a local gang leader who draws her in, only to reveal a terrifying agenda.

Donnelly, Jennifer. *A Northern Light*. The murder of a woman at a hotel in upstate New York in 1906 helps Mattie to make tough decisions about the direction of her own life.

Flinn, Alex. *Nothing to Lose*. When his mother is accused of murdering his abusive stepfather, Michael leaves the carnival he ran away to and heads home to help, revealing a deep secret.

Galloway, Gregory. *As Simple as Snow*. A high school boy who has fallen in love with a strange girl seeks to solve the mystery when she suddenly disappears in the dead of winter.

Giles, Gail. *Shattering Glass*. Murder is the result when Rob, the most popular boy in his high school, decides to show his power by making over the school's outcast, who has an agenda of his own.

Haddon, Mark. *The Curious Incident of the Dog in the Night-Time*. When the neighbor's poodle, Wellington, is killed with a garden fork, autistic teen Christopher Boone determines to solve the crime using the methods of Sherlock Holmes.

Hoobler, Dorothy, and Thomas Hoobler. *The Ghost in the Tokaido Inn*. Judge Ooka hires fourteen-year-old Seikei to help him solve the crime when a powerful samurai's jewel goes missing at the Tokaido Inn in eighteenth-century Japan.

Korman, Gordon. *Son of the Mob*. Tony's dad runs the local "vending machine" business, and Kendra is the daughter of the FBI agent sworn to bring Tony's mob boss father to justice. Can their love survive?

Little, Jason. *Shutterbug Follies*. After developing pictures of a naked corpse, Bee, a perky Manhattan photo lab technician, sets out to find out who committed the crime in this graphic novel.

McDonald, Joyce. *Shades of Simon Gray*. Strange things happen while Simon lies in a coma after he runs his car into a famous local tree, revealing secrets from the past and the present.

McNamee, Graham. *Acceleration*. Duncan's summer job in the Toronto subway's lost-and-found department brings a frightening journal to his attention and prompts him to seek out its owner before a killing spree begins.

Myers, Walter Dean. *Monster*. Sixteen-year-old Steve Harmon writes as a film script the court proceedings of his own trial as the lookout for a robbery that ended in the murder of a Harlem drugstore owner.

Plum-Ucci, Carol. *The Body of Christopher Creed*. When the school's worst misfit disappears, the popular Torey Adams can't stop thinking about it and bands together with two unlikely partners to track down the missing teen.

Qualey, Marsha. *Close to a Killer*. When two suburbanites are murdered, the town suspects sixteen-year-old Barrie's mother, recently released from fifteen years in prison, and her staff of ex-cons at the Killer Looks hair salon.

Sebold, Alice. *The Lovely Bones*. After fourteen-year-old Susie is lured to a secluded spot and murdered by a serial killer, she watches her family from heaven and waits for her murder to be discovered.

Updale, Eleanor. *Montmorency: Thief, Liar, Gentleman?* When a Victorian-era thief lies broken after a great fall, a surgeon puts him back together, giving him the opportunity to build a new life as a mysterious gentleman.

Vande Velde, Vivian. *Never Trust a Dead Man*. After the villagers seal Selwyn in a cave with the corpse of Farold, whom they believe he killed, a witch frees him and reanimates Farold so they can find the real murderer.

Werlin, Nancy. *Black Mirror*. After her brother commits suicide, Frances joins the charitable organization with which he was so heavily involved to look for answers, and finds things are not as they seem.

RETELLINGS: OLD STORIES MADE NEW

Aidinoff, Elsie V. *The Garden.* Eve befriends the Serpent, who shows her the world outside of Eden, where Adam and their Creator do not understand her sensitive and perceptive nature.

Black, Holly. *Tithe: A Modern Faerie Tale.* Kaye, the teenage daughter of a rocker mom, navigates between the world of Faerie and New Jersey, exploring a new love interest and seeking a friend stolen by the Faerie Court.

de Lint, Charles. *The Blue Girl.* When Imogene moves to a new town, she befriends Maxine, a fellow outsider, and Adrian, a ghost who haunts their school, and together they try to stop a band of malicious fairies.

Farmer, Nancy. *The Sea of Trolls.* Jack and his sister Lucy are destined for adventures with trolls, giant spiders, and even dragons when they are kidnapped by Olaf One-Brow, the captain of a Viking ship.

Ferris, Jean. *Once upon a Marigold.* Christian attempts to rescue the Princess Marigold from the clutches of her evil mother in this humorous story which draws from many classic fairy tale conventions.

Gaiman, Neil. *Anansi Boys.* When Fat Charlie's father dies, his long-lost brother turns up and steals his fiancée, which is not the most shocking thing that will happen to Fat Charlie.

Geras, Adele. *Troy.* Homer's *Iliad* is brought to vivid life in this retelling of the classic story of warring humans and the Greek gods who love them.

Marillier, Juliette. *Daughter of the Forest,* Sevenwaters trilogy, book 1. Only Sorcha can save her brothers from an avian fate by weaving them shirts that will transform them from swans back into the human sons of Lord Colum, an Irish chieftain.

Meyer, Stephenie. *Twilight.* Bella, the clumsy, self-deprecating new girl in gloomy Forks, Washington, falls for her lab partner, Edward—a beautiful and talented vampire.

Moore, Christopher. *Lamb: The Gospel according to Biff, Christ's Childhood Pal.* Biff tells the story of his best friend, Josh, who was destined for a special place in human history.

Morris, Gerald. *The Squire, His Knight, and His Lady* and *The Savage Damsel and the Dwarf,* Squire's Tales, books 2 and 3. The adventures of King Arthur's court are retold from the perspectives of lesser characters in these two humorous stories of chivalrous derring-do.

Napoli, Donna Jo. *Bound*. Xing Xing seeks to heal her sister from foot binding in this Chinese reinterpretation of the Cinderella story.

Pattou, Edith. *East*. Rose agrees to go with the White Bear when he offers her family a way out of poverty, but only her love can rescue him from the curse of a wicked Troll Queen.

Pratchett, Terry. *The Amazing Maurice and His Educated Rodents*. The cat Maurice and his clever rats have the Pied Piper act down, but danger awaits when they take their scam to the Discworld town of Bad Blintz.

Riordan, Rick. *The Lightning Thief*, Percy Jackson and the Olympians, book 1. Perseus Jackson, son of Poseidon, leaves a Long Island summer camp for the offspring of humans and gods to recover Zeus's stolen lightning bolt.

Skurzynski, Gloria. *Spider's Voice*. The mute "Spider" serves as the go-between for his master Abelard and Abelard's lovely young pupil Eloise.

Stroud, Jonathan. *The Amulet of Samarkand* and *The Golem's Eye*, Bartimaeus trilogy, books 1 and 2. Bartimaeus is the djinni-with-an-attitude who reluctantly serves the precocious magician Nathaniel in a world where magic is power.

Tiffany, Grace. *Ariel*. The world of William Shakespeare's *The Tempest* is reimagined in this story of Ariel, a wood spirit who inhabits an enchanted island.

Westerfeld, Scott. *Peeps*. An agent of a secret organization that hunts and rescues Peeps, "parasite positives" that infect their victims with vampirism, Cal discovers a much greater danger lurking under New York's streets.

Yolen, Jane. *Sword of the Rightful King*. Arthur can barely hold his kingdom together, but Merlinnus has a plan to convince the people of his rightful rule, one that involves a sword embedded in stone.

FICTION

SCIENCE FICTION

Adlington, L. J. *The Diary of Pelly D*. While drilling through the ruins of a city, Toni V finds the diary of Pelly D, a spoiled rich girl whose genetic family becomes a target for extermination.

Anderson, M. T. *Feed*. Titus is a privileged teen in a consumer-centered future whose relationship with a perceptive girl is complicated when she has problems with her "feed," the brain implant that links her to the world.

Barker, Clive. *Abarat*. Candy Quackenbush finds herself in the middle of a power struggle when she magically travels from her home in Chickentown, USA, to the island kingdom of Abarat.

Bechard, Margaret. *Spacer and Rat*. Jack, a space-dwelling "spacer," and Kit, an earth-dwelling "rat," find they have more in common than they think when they combine to protect Waldo, a sentient and highly illegal robot.

Bell, Hilari. *A Matter of Profit*. When his people invade the T'Chin Empire and install their own court, Ahvren must uncover a plot to assassinate the emperor with the help of a strange scholar.

Card, Orson Scott. *Ender's Shadow* and *Shadow of the Hegemon*. In this parallel story to *Ender's Game*, a superintelligent student at the Battle School is repeatedly tested, first in the battle with the Buggers and then in a struggle for world dominance.

Clements, Andrew. *Things Not Seen*. The only person who can see the newly invisible Bobby is a blind girl named Alicia. Will they remain friends if Bobby can never be "seen" again?

Cooper, Susan. *King of Shadows*. Two productions of *A Midsummer Night's Dream* are separated in time by 400 years but linked by Nat, a teen actor who wakes to find himself in the company of William Shakespeare.

Farmer, Nancy. *The House of the Scorpion*. Matt's life changes for the better, and then for the worse, when he is moved into the household of the druglord ruler of Opium, of whom Matt is an unwitting clone.

Gilmore, Kate. *The Exchange Student*. Daria's family hosts Fen, an exchange student from the planet Chela, but it is her mother's job as zookeeper that fascinates the animal-loving Fen.

Goodman, Alison. *Singing the Dogstar Blues*. Joss is the unwilling study partner of Mavkel, the first alien to enroll in her elite school, where students learn to time travel.

Halam, Ann. *Siberia*. When Sloe's mother disappears from the arctic wasteland that was once the European continent, Sloe must brave the wilds to bring the seeds of five animal species to safety.

Lowachee, Karin. *Burndive*. When Ryan's starship captain father makes unpopular political decisions, the teen celebrity becomes the target of assassins and must cooperate with the father he dislikes in the midst of an interstellar war.

Lubar, David. *Hidden Talents*. Edgeview Alternative School is not the end of the road that Martin and his misfit friends thought it was: it is place where they can explore their hidden "talents."

Philbrick, Rodman. *The Last Book in the Universe*. Spaz, an epileptic prevented from experiencing the virtual reality used to escape a bleak existence after the Big Shake, meets the book-loving Ryter and embarks on a quest to save his sister.

Reeve, Philip. *Mortal Engines* and *Predator's Gold*, Hungry City Chronicles, books 1 and 2. Tom and Hester fight for their survival when they are ejected from London, a colossal mobile city that rolls across the barren landscape seeking smaller towns to consume.

Shusterman, Neal. *Downsiders*. In the Downside, the world that exists beneath New York City, Talon breaks all the rules when he falls in love with Lindsay, a Topsider from above.

Vande Velde, Vivian. *Heir Apparent*. Giannine's fight to survive in a virtual reality world becomes real when a group of protesters break into the computer system while she is still attached to it.

Westerfeld, Scott. *Uglies*, Uglies trilogy, book 1. In Tally's world, you are Ugly until an operation on your sixteenth birthday turns you Pretty, but when Tally's best friend refuses the operation, she leads Tally to a settlement of renegade objectors.

Zahn, Timothy. *Dragon and Thief: A Dragonback Adventure*. Jack, a thief, becomes the unlikely host of Draycos, a dragon warrior symbiote, and together they attempt to clear Jack's name and save Draycos's race.

FICTION

SHORT STORIES

Appelt, Kathi. *Kissing Tennessee and Other Stories from the Stardust Dance*. Interrelated short stories, some serious and some lighthearted, follow individual students as they prepare for the eighth-grade Stardust Dance at Dogwood Junior High School.

Armstrong, Jennifer, ed. *Shattered: Stories of Children and War*. Wars affect people, sometimes directly, and these twelve short stories reveal the effects on young people as troops and battles march around the globe.

Cart, Michael, ed. *Love and Sex: Ten Stories of Truth*. The title says it all: ten stories by well-known authors for teens take a straightforward look at young love in all its forms, from gentle romance to the boldly sexual.

Cart, Michael, comp. *Tomorrowland: Ten Stories about the Future*. Ten well-known authors for teens, including the editor himself, write diverse and imaginative stories on "visions of times to come."

Datlow, Ellen, and Terri Windling, eds. *The Green Man: Tales from the Mythic Forest*. Fifteen stories and three poems make up this collection based on the ancient myth of the Green Man, an elemental spirit and protector of the wild world.

Etchemendy, Nancy. *Cat in Glass, and Other Tales of the Unnatural*. The title story, in which a terrifying cat sculpture commits grisly murders, is only the first of eight creepy and suspenseful stories for readers who love the dark side.

Flake, Sharon G. *Who Am I without Him? Short Stories about Girls and the Boys in Their Lives*. Short stories about ten black teens explore how young people base their sense of self-worth on how attractive they are to members of the opposite sex.

Gallo, Donald R., ed. *On the Fringe*. Teenage outsiders, outcasts, misfits, loners, geeks, nerds, and any others who aren't "in" are the subjects of these eleven short stories by famous authors for teens.

Hoffman, Alice. *Local Girls*. Fifteen related stories about four family members—Gretel, her mother, her best friend, and her mother's cousin—all come together to paint a picture of Gretel's teen years.

Howe, James, ed. *The Color of Absence: Twelve Stories about Loss and Hope*. Everyone experiences loss a little differently. Here, twelve authors tell original stories of pain and recovery.

Lanagan, Margo. *Black Juice*. This hauntingly strange collection of ten fantasy short stories sometimes teeters on the edge of reality and at other times delves deep into disturbing other worlds.

Mercado, Nancy E., ed. *Every Man for Himself: Ten Short Stories about Being a Guy*. What it's like to by a guy and what makes a boy into a man are the themes of this collection of ten short stories by male authors who write for teens.

Myers, Walter Dean. *145th Street: Short Stories*. Ten short stories filled with colorful characters, their tragedies and triumphs, and their connections with each other reveal the rich and diverse ethnic fabric of Harlem.

Naidoo, Beverley. *Out of Bounds: Seven Stories of Conflict and Hope*. Apartheid between 1948 and 2000 is the backdrop for this collection of stories told by a variety of young people living with the horror of South Africa's racially oppressive government.

November, Sharyn, ed. *Firebirds Rising: An Anthology of Original Science Fiction and Fantasy*. These sixteen inventive short stories by highly regarded fantasy and science fiction writers include Nancy Farmer, Diana Wynn Jones, Garth Nix, Patricia McKillip, and many more.

Noyes, Deborah, ed. *Gothic! Ten Original Dark Tales*. Well-known authors for teens, including M. T. Anderson, Garth Nix, and Celia Rees, test the boundaries of the gothic tradition with stories both frightening and funny.

Rice, David. *Crazy Loco: Stories*. Nine short stories share the lives of Mexican American teens who are growing up and dealing with each other and with their families in Texas's Rio Grande Valley.

Van Pelt, James. *Strangers and Beggars: Stories*. Seventeen dark and creepy science fiction and horror stories with upbeat endings are divided into four sections: Teaching, Love, Death and Time.

Vande Velde, Vivian. *Being Dead: Stories*. Like the title says, the seven stories in this spine-chilling collection, more than a few of which have unexpected and shocking endings, are all about death in its many forms.

STORIES CREATIVELY TOLD

Abelove, Joan. *Saying It Out Loud.* Through journal entries and flashbacks, sixteen-year-old Mindy describes the painful month when her mother was dying of a brain tumor and her father was growing ever more distant.

Adlington, L. J. *The Diary of Pelly D.* When Toni V finds a girl's diary sealed up in a battered old can in the war-torn rubble of City Five, he defies the authorities and begins to read.

Buckhanon, Kalisha. *Upstate.* When seventeen-year-old Antonio is sent upstate to serve a ten-year prison sentence for a crime he may not have committed, he and his girlfriend, Natasha, communicate through letters.

Chbosky, Stephen. *The Perks of Being a Wallflower.* As expressed through letters to an unknown friend, a smart, shy high school freshman and "wallflower" makes new friends, experiences a breakdown, and through therapy faces pain from his past.

Fleischman, Paul. *Mind's Eye.* In this tale told in dialogue, a spine-injured teenage girl and an old woman who share a room in a nursing home take an imaginary trip together to Italy using an old travel guide.

Fleischman, Paul. *Seek.* High school senior Rob writes his autobiography as a radio play and through monologues and dialogues describes the people who matter to him most, including his absent father.

Frost, Helen. *Keesha's House.* Sestinas and sonnets tell the stories of Keesha and other troubled teens who have found a home with Joe, a kind adult who gives them a safe place to be.

Grimes, Nikki. *Dark Sons.* Parallel stories of the troubles between fathers and teenage sons are told in verse, Ishmael's story set in biblical times and Sam's story set in modern times.

Halpin, Brendan. *Donorboy.* Fourteen-year-old Rosalind's new life with her sperm-donor father is told through journal entries and e-mail messages after her lesbian parents are killed in a freak accident.

Juby, Susan. *Alice, I Think.* Alice humorously shares her experiences through journal entries when, on her therapist's suggestion, she enrolls in the public high school after being home-schooled all her life by weird parents.

Koertge, Ron. *The Brimstone Journals.* The journal entries of fifteen unique seniors at Branston "Brimstone" High School reveal both their individual problems and the complexities of modern high school life.

Lester, Julius. *Day of Tears: A Novel in Dialogue*. Voices young and old, including slaves, slave owners, and even the slave auctioneer, tell the terrible story of the 1859 Savannah slave auction, the largest ever held in America.

Levithan, David. *The Realm of Possibility*. Connected poems in a variety of styles share the experiences of twenty different teenagers dealing with their own lives and life within the high school community.

Moriarty, Jaclyn. *The Year of Secret Assignments*. Three girls from a snobby school are paired as pen pals with three boys from a rival "lowlife" school and, through their communications, find more reasons to like each other than not.

Myers, Walter Dean. *Monster*. Sixteen-year-old Steve Harmon writes as a film script the court proceedings of his own trial as the lookout for a robbery that ended in the murder of a Harlem drugstore owner.

Perkins, Lynne Rae. *Criss Cross*. Through dialogue, poetry, questions and answers, and prose, the stories of fourteen-year-olds Debbie, Hector, and their friends unfold as they each reach important turning points in their lives.

Rennison, Louise. *Angus, Thongs, and Full-Frontal Snogging*. Fourteen-year-old British teen Georgia humorously shares a year in her life through her diary, including her exasperating family, her homicidal cat, and her crush on Robbie, the Sex God.

Sones, Sonya. *What My Mother Doesn't Know*. Ninth-grader Sophie's life with her disconnected father and soap opera–addicted mother, her two best friends, her sexy boyfriend, Dylan, and her many additional crushes, is told through free-verse poems.

Stratton, Allan. *Leslie's Journal*. Tenth-grader Leslie has to keep a journal for a school assignment and in it reveals her relationship with a devious older boy who exploits and abuses her.

Wolff, Virginia Euwer. *True Believer*. In verse, fifteen-year-old LaVaughn shares life's pains and joys through lost friendships, a first crush on the wrong boy, personal faith, academic success, and dreams of life beyond the projects.

THE TEEN SOCIAL EXPERIENCE

Anderson, Laurie Halse. *Speak.* Melinda cannot speak about the night she decided to call the cops on a high school party, and no one wants to speak to her afterwards.

Appelt, Kathi. *Kissing Tennessee and Other Stories from the Stardust Dance.* Interrelated short stories, some serious and some lighthearted, follow individual students as they prepare for the eighth-grade Stardust Dance at Dogwood Junior High School.

Coburn, Jake. *Prep.* Kris drags Nick, a former graffiti artist, into a gangland world to save her younger brother Danny from a string of bad choices.

Giles, Gail. *Shattering Glass.* Young Steward cannot accept the guilt he feels for creating and then shattering Simon Glass, the nerd in his high school circle.

Green, John. *Looking for Alaska.* Pudge has never had friends like the ones he makes at boarding school, but it is a girl named Alaska who breaks his heart.

Jenkins, A. M. *Out of Order.* Colt's whole world feels like it's coming down around him until he chooses to raise his grades with the help of a green-haired tutor named Corinne.

Koertge, Ron. *The Brimstone Journals.* Boyd is making a list of all of the people he resents in his senior class without realizing that he is not the only future graduate with problems.

Koja, Kathe. *Buddha Boy.* When Justin meets "Buddha Boy" Jinsen, he wants nothing to do with his peace-loving, artistic classmate.

Korman, Gordon. *Jake, Reinvented.* F. Scott Fitzgerald's *The Great Gatsby* is rewritten in this modern story of Jake Garrett, a teen who transforms himself from nerd to the coolest boy in town.

Koss, Amy Goldman. *The Girls.* Maya wakes up to find herself excluded from her middle school clique: was it Candace who orchestrated Maya's fall?

Lebert, Benjamin. *Crazy.* In this autobiographical novel, Benni wants to experience everything he can, despite being paralyzed and socially awkward.

Levithan, David. *Boy Meets Boy.* Imagine a world where a drag queen can be the captain of the football team and where when a boy meets a boy and falls in love it is no big deal.

Levithan, David. *The Realm of Possibility.* Girls and boys fall in and out of love in this series of poems about students in a suburban New Jersey high school.

Lubar, David. *Sleeping Freshmen Never Lie*. Scott wants to be sure his brother does not have a hard time in his freshman year in high school, so he keeps a diary telling him how to behave.

Marchetta, Melina. *Saving Francesca*. When her mother suffers a lengthy depression it colors every part of Francesca's life, including her new friendship with Will, an arrogant prefect in her mostly boys school.

McNeal, Laura, and Tom McNeal. *Crooked*. Clara and Amos struggle with their romantic relationship while facing parent problems and the threat of the Tripp brothers, the craziest delinquents in school.

Oates, Joyce Carol. *Big Mouth and Ugly Girl*. Matt's big mouth always gets him in trouble, and now the only person who believes he did not threaten their school with violence is Ursula, the "Ugly Girl."

Plum-Ucci, Carol. *What Happened to Lani Garver*. The popular but troubled Claire is intrigued by the social outcast the rest of her friends are tormenting, a strange boy named Lani who might be more than he seems.

Shusterman, Neal. *The Schwa Was Here*. Calvin Schwa has an amazing ability to seem invisible, to go virtually unnoticed, and his new pal Antsy Bonano concocts a scheme to profit from "the Schwa Effect."

Spinelli, Jerry. *Stargirl*. Stargirl tries to change the hearts and minds of Mica High's students, especially Leo, who must choose between his love for her and his own desire to conform.

WORLD HISTORICAL FICTION

Almond, David. *The Fire-Eaters*. In 1962 on the eve of the Cuban Missile Crisis, Bobby gains new understanding about family, friends, and love in his small town on the coast of Northern England.

Barrett, Tracy. *Anna of Byzantium*. In eleventh-century Constantinople, Anna Comnena is a Byzantine princess destined to inherit the throne and become the next emperor, until her underhanded brother steals her birthright.

Blackwood, Gary. *Shakespeare's Scribe*. When the plague reaches London in 1602 and its theatres are closed, Widge goes on the road with Shakespeare's players and is challenged by a rival apprentice actor.

Chevalier, Tracy. *Girl with a Pearl Earring*. In seventeenth-century Holland, young Griet takes a job as maid in the household of the famous artist Vermeer and becomes impassioned by both the artist and his art.

Giff, Patricia Reilly. *Nory Ryan's Song*. The tragedy of the Irish Potato Famine is told through the experiences of twelve-year-old Nory, a poor girl left alone to care for herself and her younger brother.

Hearn, Julie. *The Minister's Daughter*. When the minister's daughter gets pregnant in 1645 England, she and her sister accuse the town's midwife of witchcraft when the midwife refuses to end the pregnancy.

Holeman, Linda. *Search of the Moon King's Daughter*. When Emma's laudanum-addicted mother sells her little brother into service as a chimney sweep in 1830s England, Emma sets off for London to rescue him.

Jocelyn, Marthe. *Mable Riley: A Reliable Record of Humdrum, Peril, and Romance*. In 1901 Ontario, Mable keeps a diary of her "humdrum" life and writes a romance, but finds that life is really pretty exciting and real romance is better than what she made up.

Jordan, Sherryl. *The Raging Quiet*. Marnie, an outsider in a superstitious village, discovers that the young man the villagers say is insane is merely deaf, and she sets out to communicate with him.

McCaughrean, Geraldine. *The Kite Rider*. When Haoyou's father dies of fright during a forced kite ride to test the winds in thirteenth-century China, Haoyou learns to ride the kites to protect himself and his mother.

Meyer, Carolyn. *Mary, Bloody Mary*. The teen years of Mary Tudor, Henry VIII's eldest daughter, reveal how she came to be known as Bloody Mary during her brief reign as queen of England in the mid-sixteenth century.

Meyer, L. A. *Bloody Jack: Being an Account of the Curious Adventures of Mary "Jacky" Faber, Ship's Boy.* Left an orphan during the 1797 plague in London, Mary takes over the identity of an orphan gang leader when he dies and becomes a ship's boy on the high seas.

Morgan, Nicola. *Fleshmarket.* In 1800s Edinburgh, Scotland, young Eddie vows to take revenge on the surgeon he believes killed his mother, leading him into a dark life delivering dead bodies for medical experimentation.

Namioka, Lensey. *Ties That Bind, Ties That Break.* In 1911 China, Ailin is the first girl in her family to refuse to have her feet bound, leading her on a heartbreaking but ultimately triumphant new course in life.

Park, Linda Sue. *A Single Shard.* An orphan learns the potter's trade in twelfth-century Korea, leading him to make the difficult journey to the royal court to present his work, which by the end is only a single remaining shard.

Rees, Celia. *Pirates! The True and Remarkable Adventures of Minerva Sharpe and Nancy Kington, Female Pirates.* Nancy Kington and her half-sister Minerva Sharpe find a safe haven with Jamaican pirates in the 1700s when they flee their father's sugar plantation in the wake of unfortunate events.

Sheppard, Mary C. *Seven for a Secret.* In the 1960s, three cousins begin to explore the world beyond their small, isolated Newfoundland community the summer before their senior year.

Skurzynski, Gloria. *Spider's Voice.* The mute "Spider" serves as the go-between for his master Abelard and Abelard's lovely young pupil Eloise in twelfth-century Paris.

Thal, Lilli. *Mimus.* Twelve-year-old Prince Florin of Moltovia must act the jester in the court of King Theodo of Vinland or his father, locked in Vinland's dungeons, will be put to death.

Turnbull, Ann. *No Shame, No Fear.* In the 1600s, a Quaker girl and Anglican boy must hide their love for each other during a time when the Quakers are being heavily persecuted by the British government.

THE WORLD IN CONFLICT

Alvarez, Julia. *Before We Were Free.* Anita's relatives flee the family compound for America, leaving her puzzled until she realizes what life is like under the Dominican dictator Trujillo.

Armstrong, Jennifer, ed. *Shattered: Stories of Children and War.* Wars affect people, sometimes directly, and these twelve short stories reveal the effects on young people as troops and battles march around the globe.

Bagdasarian, Adam. *Forgotten Fire.* Join young Vahan Kenderian in 1915 as he sees his family and way of life destroyed by a government that chooses to systematically rid Turkey of all Armenians by massacring them.

Breslin, Theresa. *Remembrance.* Social classes dissolve during World War I, and five teens whose paths might not have crossed in their small Scottish village find themselves united by their support for—or against—the war.

Bruchac, Joseph. *Code Talker: A Novel about the Navajo Marines of World War Two.* Though forbidden to speak his native tongue while at an Anglo boarding school, Ned's Navajo language becomes critical to America's success during World War II.

Chotjewitz, David. *Daniel Half Human, and the Good Nazi.* Furious to learn he can't join the Hitler Youth because he's half-Jewish, Daniel watches as his friend Armin moves up through the ranks, but later notices Armin has removed his distinctive SS tattoos.

Holub, Josef. *An Innocent Soldier.* Orphaned farmhand Adam finds himself a soldier in Napoleon's disastrous campaign against Russia, contending with a brutal sergeant, hunger, and dysentery.

Kass, Pnina Moed. *Real Time.* Aboard a bus journeying to a kibbutz near Jerusalem, three people find their lives upended when a Palestinian teen launches a suicide bomb attack hoping to bring glory and financial gain to his family.

Lawrence, Iain. *B for Buster.* Lying about his age, Kak joins the Canadian Air Force and becomes a wireless operator on night bombing raids over Germany, where the terror of his first flight drives away thoughts of heroism.

Morpurgo, Michael. *Private Peaceful.* Following his brother into battle in World War I, Tommo tells of the one time Charlie disobeyed their hateful sergeant, and the fatal consequences he now faces.

Naidoo, Beverley. *The Other Side of Truth.* Forced to become refugees after their mother's assassination in Nigeria, Sade and her brother Femi become tangled in bureaucratic red tape when they seek asylum in England.

Park, Linda Sue. *When My Name Was Keoko*. Living under Japanese rule in 1940s South Korea, Sun-hee and her family are ordered to give up their Korean heritage, including their birth names.

Peck, Richard. *The River between Us*. A visit to Howard Leland Hutchings's relatives in Illinois reveals the mystery of his grandmother's birth, a secret hidden since the Civil War.

Salisbury, Graham. *Eyes of the Emperor*. Sixteen-year-old Japanese American Eddie Okubo lies about his age to enlist in the U.S. Army during World War II but encounters cruelty and prejudice from his fellow soldiers.

Spillebeen, Geert. *Kipling's Choice*. In an ironic twist, Rudyard Kipling's help in obtaining a commission for his nearsighted son to join the Irish Guards in World War I results in John's death in his very first battle.

Spinelli, Jerry. *Milkweed*. At first, young, orphaned Misha thinks the shiny boots and beetle-like tanks of the Nazi soldiers are impressive, but he quickly discovers their real purpose in 1930s Warsaw.

Staples, Suzanne Fisher. *Under the Persimmon Tree*. Losing her family to the Taliban and an American air raid, now-mute Najmah flees Afghanistan for a Pakistan refugee camp where she finds sanctuary and friendship with an American teacher.

Stein, Tammar. *Light Years*. Believing she might have been responsible for her boyfriend's death in a Tel Aviv suicide bombing, Maya Laor, an Israeli freshman at the University of Virginia, is unable to release her grief.

Tingle, Rebecca. *The Edge on the Sword* and *Far Traveler*. Wyn, unlike her military strategist mother, Aethelflaed, cannot accept her arranged marriage, so she runs away, dresses like a bard, and falls in love with a king.

Yolen, Jane, and Robert J. Harris. *Girl in a Cage*. Marjorie, the daughter of the newly crowned king of Scotland, is captured by England's King Edward and displayed in an iron cage, where she devises her own ways of waging war.

ADVENTURE AND SURVIVAL

Alexander, Caroline. *The* Endurance: *Shackleton's Legendary Antarctic Expedition.* Explorer Ernest Shackleton's ship, the *Endurance,* became trapped in Antarctic ice and was slowly crushed, forcing his crew to live exposed for twenty months in the coldest place on earth. Nonfiction.

Anderson, Laurie Halse. *Fever 1793.* A deadly epidemic sweeps Philadelphia in 1793, and although Mattie and her grandfather flee to the country, they may not be able to outrun the fever's attack.

Bartoletti, Susan Campbell. *Black Potatoes: The Story of the Great Irish Famine, 1845–1850.* Between 1845 and 1850, a fungus destroyed Ireland's potato crops that over six million laborers depended on for work and for food, causing mass starvation, disease, and death. Nonfiction.

Calabro, Marian. *The Perilous Journey of the Donner Party.* Told through the eyes of young Virginia Reed is the gruesome story of the 1846 wagon train that got stuck for too long in the Sierra Nevada mountains during a terrible winter. Nonfiction.

Fama, Elizabeth. *Overboard.* With a young Muslim boy, fourteen-year-old Emily spends seventeen grueling hours in the ocean trying to stay alive after the ferry she was on sinks near Sumatra. Based on a true story.

Halam, Ann. *Dr. Franklin's Island.* When their plane crashes on a small island, three out of fifty British science students bound for Ecuador survive, only to be captured and experimented on by a mad scientist.

Holm, Jennifer L. *Boston Jane: An Adventure.* Jane has turned herself into a fine young lady with impeccable manners, only to find no use for them when she travels west to rugged Washington Territory in the 1850s.

Horowitz, Anthony. *Eagle Strike.* The teenage spy must use all his skills and gadgets to stop his archrival from executing operation "Eagle Strike," a horrific plan conceived by a madman to destroy the world.

Johnson, Maureen. *13 Little Blue Envelopes.* When seventeen-year-old Ginny's Aunt Peg dies, she leaves Ginny $1,000, instructions to buy a plane ticket to London, and thirteen little blue envelopes with messages inside.

Lawrence, Iain. *The Smugglers.* In the nineteenth century, sixteen-year-old John Spencer is traveling aboard the *Dragon,* his father's new schooner, when it becomes clear the captain and crew are not who they first appeared.

Marrin, Albert. *Terror of the Spanish Main: Sir Henry Morgan and His Buccaneers*. The Englishman Henry Morgan was the wily leader of a group of filthy, violent, and brutal men called buccaneers who plundered and pillaged on sea and on land. Nonfiction.

Maurer, Richard. *The Wild Colorado: The True Adventures of Fred Dellenbaugh, Age 17, on the Second Powell Expedition into the Grand Canyon*. Teenager Fred Dellenbaugh joined Powell's adventurous sixteenth-month journey down the Colorado River and through the Grand Canyon, along the way becoming its primary artistic chronicler. Nonfiction.

Meyer, L. A. *Bloody Jack: Being an Account of the Curious Adventures of Mary "Jacky" Faber, Ship's Boy*. When the leader of Mary's orphan street gang is killed, Mary puts on his clothing, calls herself "Jacky," and joins the Royal Navy as a ship's boy on a pirate-hunting vessel in the 1700s.

Murphy, Jim. *An American Plague: The True and Terrifying Story of the Yellow Fever Epidemic of 1793*. The fever, which began one particularly sweltering summer with just the right conditions and tiny disease-carrying mosquitoes, in the end left 10 percent of Philadelphia's population dead. Nonfiction.

Oppel, Kenneth. *Airborn*. When the cabin boy aboard a luxury airship saves an old man floating unconscious in a nearby balloon, he's drawn into an adventure involving mystical creatures and air pirates.

Philbrick, Nathaniel. *Revenge of the Whale: The True Story of the Whaleship* Essex. In 1820, the whaleship *Essex* was rammed and sunk by a sixty-ton sperm whale, forcing the crew to abandon ship in three small lifeboats in the middle of the Pacific Ocean. Nonfiction.

Rees, Celia. *Pirates! The True and Remarkable Adventures of Minerva Sharpe and Nancy Kington, Female Pirates*. On her family's Jamaican sugar plantation, Nancy uncovers family secrets, sinister plots, and ugly cruelties that force her and a young house slave to hide among pirates.

Thal, Lili. *Mimus*. In the Middle Ages, Prince Florin of Moltovia is forced to become a jester in the court of his archenemy, King Theodo of Vinland, to save his father's life.

Tullson, Diane. *Red Sea*. Libby deliberately causes her mother and stepfather to set sail on the Red Sea without their traveling group, resulting in injury and death, and only Libby is able to make things right.

Wolf, Allan. *New Found Land*. The 1804 Lewis and Clark cross-country expedition to discover the Northwest Passage and find access to the Pacific Ocean is told in fourteen different voices, including that of Captain Lewis's dog.

THE AMERICAN ETHNIC EXPERIENCE

Desai Hidier, Tanuja. *Born Confused.* Dimple is torn between being an Indian and being an American living in New Jersey, and at first rejects a boy her traditional parents find to be a suitable match for her.

Flake, Sharon G. *Bang!* When Mann's younger brother is killed in a drive-by shooting, his father decides to toughen Mann up with some activities based on African coming-of-age rituals, only making things worse.

Gaskins, Pearl Fuyo, ed. *What Are You? Voices of Mixed-Race Young People.* Through interviews, essays, and poems, forty teenagers and young adults from a broad range of ethnic backgrounds talk about what it's like to grow up mixed-race in America. Nonfiction.

Grimes, Nikki. *Bronx Masquerade.* A group of inner-city high school teens express their personal and ethnic realities through poetry at Open Mike Friday in Mr. Ward's English class.

Hewett, Lorri. *Dancer.* Stephanie is not white and willowy, but she's an excellent ballet dancer who wants to follow her dream, and finds inspiration with Miss Winnie, a retired African American dancer.

Jimenez, Francisco. *Breaking Through.* Panchito and his family are deported back to Mexico but find a way to legally return to California, where they make their home and work toward a better future.

Lynch, Chris. *Gold Dust.* Richard makes friends with Napoleon, a Dominican transfer student and one of the only black students at his Boston Catholic school in 1975, and tries to interest him in baseball.

Martinez, Manuel Luis. *Drift.* Sixteen-year-old Mexican American Robert Lomos wants to reunite his family after his mother breaks down, takes his baby brother away with her, and leaves him with his stern grandmother.

McDonald, Janet. *Spellbound.* Raven is a young African American mother and a high school dropout in a Brooklyn ghetto who wants to get back on track with her life, starting with winning a spelling bee.

Myers, Walter Dean. *145th Street: Short Stories.* Ten short stories filled with colorful characters, their tragedies and triumphs, and their connections with each other reveal the rich and diverse ethnic fabric of Harlem.

Na, An. *A Step from Heaven.* Things don't go so well when Young Ju's family moves from Korea to America, but strangely, life might get better after her father's drinking and brutality force Young Ju to act.

Nam, Vicki, ed. *Yell-oh Girls! Emerging Voices Explore Culture, Identity, and Growing Up Asian American.* Eighty stories, essays, poems, and letters written by teen and young adult women describe what it's like to be Asian American and part of two distinct cultures. Nonfiction.

Osa, Nancy. *Cuba 15.* Violet looks Polish, doesn't speak much Spanish, and grew up in Chicago, but her Cuban grandmother wants her to have a big quinceañero—the traditional Latina coming-of-age party—anyway.

Placide, Jaira. *Fresh Girl.* Mardi is having a hard time in Brooklyn after fleeing Haiti during a bloody coup, but even harder are the terrible memories of what happened to her there.

Porter, Connie. *Imani All Mine.* Even though baby Imani is the result of rape, her fifteen-year-old mother loves her and wants a bright future for them both in their inner-city black neighborhood.

Rice, David. *Crazy Loco: Stories.* Nine short stories share the lives of Mexican American teens who are growing up and dealing with each other and with their families in Texas's Rio Grande Valley.

Saenz, Benjamin Alire. *Sammy and Juliana in Hollywood.* Sammy deals with first love, death, family, friendship, and war in the Hollywood barrio of Las Cruces, New Mexico, in the 1960s.

Stein, Tammar. *Light Years.* Even though Maya is now in college in the United States, she can't forget her former life in Israel or her boyfriend there, who was killed by a suicide bomber.

Vijayaraghavan, Vineeta. *Motherland.* When her parents decide she is behaving improperly, Maya has to leave her New York home and spend the summer in India with traditional relatives who will straighten her out.

Wolff, Virginia Euwer. *True Believer.* In this verse story, fifteen-year-old LaVaughn experiences life's pains and joys through lost friendships, a first crush on the wrong boy, personal faith, academic success, and dreams of life beyond the projects.

SOCIAL AND ENVIRONMENTAL ISSUES AND ACTIVISM

Auch, Mary Jane. *Ashes of Roses.* Irish immigrant Rose Nolan finds 1911 New York a difficult place to survive, especially when the Triangle Shirtwaist Factory where she works is destroyed by fire and 146 lives are lost.

Bardi, Abby. *The Book of Fred.* When Mary, a fundamentalist cult member, is placed in a foster home after her parents are convicted of neglect, it's a shock for her and for the family that takes her in.

Bartoletti, Susan Campbell. *Kids on Strike!* The author shows how children barely survived the horrible working conditions in factories, mills, and mines during the Industrial Revolution and discusses the social movements that arose to protect them. Nonfiction.

Bauer, Joan. *Hope Was Here.* When Hope and her Aunt Addy take charge of a diner in rural Wisconsin, Hope finds herself caught up in an intense political race for the town's mayor when she's not serving food.

Freese, Barbara. *Coal: A Human History.* An environmental attorney traces the history of the human use of coal, a substance that provides warmth but causes great harm to people and to the environment. Nonfiction.

Hampton, Wilborn. *Meltdown: A Race against Nuclear Disaster at Three Mile Island: A Reporter's Story.* An experienced journalist followed the harrowing events at Three Mile Island in 1979 when the nuclear power plant near Harrisburg, Pennsylvania, almost melted down. Nonfiction.

Hiaasen, Carl. *Hoot.* When construction for a Mother Paula's All-American Pancake House begins on top of a burrow of endangered owls, it is up to Roy and his friends to stop the bulldozers.

Holtwijk, Ineke. *Asphalt Angels.* Alex, a thirteen-year-old runaway, lands on the streets of Rio de Janeiro, Brazil, and falls in with a group of homeless youth who call themselves the Asphalt Angels.

Hoose, Phillip. *The Race to Save the Lord God Bird.* As people tore down the woodlands of the southeastern United States to sell timber and to build homes and businesses, they unknowingly destroyed the ivory-billed woodpecker's home.

Jimenez, Francisco. *Breaking Through.* Panchito and his family are deported back to Mexico but find a way to legally return to California, where they make their home and work toward a better future.

Konigsburg, E. L. *The Outcasts of 19 Schuyler Place*. While staying with her great uncles one summer, twelve-year-old Rose vows to protect their life's work—two unique and giant scrap metal towers—from demolition.

Leavitt, Martine. *Heck, Superhero*. A young homeless boy abandoned by his mother and living alone on the streets finds comfort in his artwork and in imagining himself as a superhero.

Lynch, Jim. *The Highest Tide*. When Miles O'Malley finds a giant squid dead on the tidal flats near home, it results in a rush of people who distress the fragile environment they claim to value.

Nelson, Peter. *Left for Dead: A Young Man's Search for Justice for the USS* Indianapolis. Half a century after the event, sixth-grader Hunter Scott spent six years proving that the captain was unfairly blamed when the USS *Indianapolis* was sunk by the Japanese at the end of World War II. Nonfiction.

Partridge, Elizabeth. *Restless Spirit: The Life and Work of Dorothea Lange*. The life of the independent and talented portrait photographer and social reformist is told along with sixty of her most moving photographs of people who suffered great hardship. Nonfiction.

Ryan, Pam Muñoz. *Esperanza Rising*. Tragedy forces Esperanza, a privileged girl from a wealthy Mexican ranching family, to learn a new life as a poor migrant field worker in California during the Great Depression.

Savage, Deborah. *Summer Hawk*. An aspiring journalist, Taylor finds the subject for her summer research project when she rescues an abandoned young red-tailed hawk and connects with the director of a raptor rehabilitation center.

Strasser, Todd. *Can't Get There from Here*. Maybe lives on the streets of New York with a group of homeless teens who, no matter how hard they try to care for each other, are dying one by one.

Stratton, Allan. *Chanda's Secrets*. When sixteen-year-old Chanda's baby sister dies of AIDS, she is only the first in the family to fall ill in an African village that denies the presence of the terrifying epidemic.

Tashjian, Janet. *The Gospel according to Larry*. Josh Swenson creates an alter ego named Larry to run an anti-consumerism website that becomes so popular, Josh can no longer remain anonymous and has to face his critics.

SPORTS AND COMPETITION

Bachrach, Susan D. *The Nazi Olympics: Berlin 1936*. The 1936 Summer Olympics in Berlin allowed the Nazi Party to promote an agenda of Aryan supremacy and anti-Semitism, forcing other nations to reconsider participation in the games. Nonfiction.

Blumenthal, Karen. *Let Me Play: The Story of Title IX; The Law That Changed the Future of Girls in America*. Blumenthal tells the story of Title IX, the 1972 law that gave American girls the same right to an education as boys, and the unwavering people who fought for it. Nonfiction.

Colton, Larry. *Counting Coup: A True Story of Basketball and Honor on the Little Big Horn*. Larry Colton shares his time on the Crow Reservation with the Hardin High School Girls Basketball Team and their star player, Sharon LaForge. Nonfiction.

Crutcher, Chris. *Whale Talk*. An outstanding athlete who won't play competitive sports, T.J. changes his mind when asked to form his own swim team and he sees a chance to challenge the school's sports bully.

Deuker, Carl. *Night Hoops*. Nick Abbott is certain he'll make the basketball team but is surprised when his no-good neighbor, Trent Dawson, also makes it and is someone worth getting to know.

Freedman, Russell. *Babe Didrikson Zaharias: The Making of a Champion*. One of the greatest female athletes of the twentieth century and a multiple medal winner in the 1932 Olympics faced many challenges as a woman in the male-dominated sports world. Nonfiction.

Hewett, Lorri. *Dancer*. Stephanie is not white and willowy, but she's an excellent ballet dancer who wants to follow her dream, and finds inspiration with Miss Winnie, a retired African American dancer.

Johnson, Scott. *Safe at Second*. Paulie tries to get Todd, his best friend and a high school star pitcher, back on the mound when Todd loses both an eye and his chance at the majors.

Karr, Kathleen. *The Boxer*. To care for his mother and five brothers, fifteen-year-old Johnny boxes illegally to earn a little extra cash after his long hours each day in an 1885 New York sweatshop.

King, Daniel. *Chess: From First Moves to Checkmate*. An International Chess Master explains the game of chess with the help of colorful imagery, from its ancient history to its individual pieces and game play. Nonfiction.

Lynch, Chris. *Gold Dust*. Richard makes friends with Napoleon, a Dominican transfer student and one of the only black students at his Boston Catholic school in 1975, and tries to interest him in baseball.

Myers, Walter Dean. *The Greatest: Muhammad Ali*. One of the most famous heavyweight boxers of all time aggressively defended his unpopular choices as a Black Muslim and as a conscientious objector during the Vietnam War. Nonfiction.

Paulsen, Gary. *How Angel Peterson Got His Name: And Other Outrageous Tales about Extreme Sports*. Based on memories of his Minnesota childhood, the author shares short stories that illustrate the 1950s version of extreme sports including bear wrestling, kite riding, and speed skiing. Nonfiction.

Peet, Mal. *Keeper*. A reporter listens while El Gato, the famous goalkeeper responsible for winning the World Cup, tells the strange story of his childhood in the South American rainforest.

Peña, Matt de la. *Ball Don't Lie*. The skinny white seventeen-year-old Stick lives to play basketball at Los Angeles's Lincoln Park basketball court and hopes for a college scholarship, but needs to face his horrific past first.

Powell, Randy. *Three Clams and an Oyster*. Three longtime friends must face their differences when the search for a fourth player for their flag football team ends with Rachel, a girl who can play a mean game.

Robinson, Sharon. *Promises to Keep: How Jackie Robinson Changed America*. Jackie Robinson's daughter shares the story of her father's childhood, his involvement in civil rights, and his role as the first African American baseball player in the major leagues. Nonfiction.

Tocher, Timothy. *Chief Sunrise, John McGraw, and Me*. When Hank Cobb runs away from his abusive father to play baseball, he meets a pitcher named Chief Sunrise, and the two set off to try out for the New York Giants.

Wallace, Rich. *Playing without the Ball*. When he's cut from the basketball team, Jay McLeod, a high school senior who lives alone above the bar where he works, joins a YMCA church league and leads it to victory.

Zusak, Markus. *Fighting Ruben Wolfe*. Two working-class brothers in England sign up as boxers with a local promoter to bring money to their family, feel a sense of purpose, and have a little respect.

BIOGRAPHY, AUTOBIOGRAPHY, AND MEMOIR

Bolden, Tonya. *Maritcha: A Nineteenth-Century American Girl.* A free black woman born before the Civil War fought for her right to be the first person of color to go to high school in New York.

Crutcher, Chris. *King of the Mild Frontier: An Ill-Advised Autobiography.* The well-known author of books for teens shares both the funny and painful stories of his childhood and teen years growing up in Cascade, Idaho.

Fleming, Candace. *Ben Franklin's Almanac: Being a True Account of the Good Gentleman's Life.* In this book, Benjamin Franklin's life is organized into pieces that, put together, describe his long career as one of America's most talented and unique statesmen and scientists.

Fradin, Dennis Brindell, and Judith Bloom Fradin. *Ida B. Wells: Mother of the Civil Rights Movement.* An ex-slave and hard-hitting journalist who despised racial inequality fought for black women's right to vote and campaigned to put an end to the brutal practice of lynching.

Freedman, Russell. *Babe Didrikson Zaharias: The Making of a Champion.* In an era when women were not welcome in sports, Babe became one of the most famous female athletes of the twentieth century.

Gantos, Jack. *Hole in My Life.* When this author of books for children and teens was nineteen, he spent a year in prison for smuggling drugs, and while there turned himself around.

Giblin, James Cross. *Good Brother, Bad Brother: The Story of Edwin Booth and John Wilkes Booth.* During the Civil War years upright Edwin supported the North, and bad boy John supported the South so passionately that it drove him to kill President Abraham Lincoln.

Hickam, Homer H., Jr. *Rocket Boys: A Memoir.* Homer fell in love with rockets as a teenager and started making his own, leading him to a long career as a prominent NASA engineer.

Lalicki, Tom. *Spellbinder: The Life of Harry Houdini.* The life of the world's most famous escape artist and magician is told from his birth in 1874 through his incredible rise to fame performing amazing and death-defying stunts.

Mah, Adeline Yen. *Chinese Cinderella: The True Story of an Unwanted Daughter.* Wu Mie is held responsible for her mother's death and lives a sad and lonely young life as an outcast in her own family in China in the 1940s.

Marrin, Albert. *George Washington and the Founding of a Nation*. The real, complex, and fascinating life of the first president of the United States is separated from legend in this biography that focuses on Washington's military and political careers.

Myers, Walter Dean. *Bad Boy: A Memoir*. One of the best-known authors of books for teens shares his struggles as an African American juvenile delinquent growing up in Harlem who loved to read.

Myers, Walter Dean. *The Greatest: Muhammad Ali*. One of the most famous heavyweight boxers of all time aggressively defended his unpopular choices as a Black Muslim and as a conscientious objector during the Vietnam War.

Nelson, Marilyn. *Carver: A Life in Poems*. Poems and photographs tell the life story of George Washington Carver, the extraordinary African American botanist, inventor, and teacher who researched crops and helped black farmers.

Opdyke, Irene Gut. *In My Hands: Memories of a Holocaust Rescuer*. Seventeen-year-old Irene suffers terribly when Germany invades Poland in 1939 but still finds the strength to help the Jewish people who are suffering even more than her.

Partridge, Elizabeth. *John Lennon: All I Want Is the Truth*. The life of the troubled musical genius is told from his birth to his fame in the Beatles, from his marriage to Yoko Ono to his murder in 1980.

Robinson, Sharon. *Promises to Keep: How Jackie Robinson Changed America*. Jackie Robinson's daughter shares the story of her father's childhood, his involvement in civil rights, and his role as the first African American baseball player in the major leagues.

Rubin, Susan Goldman. *Margaret Bourke-White: Her Pictures Were Her Life*. Margaret Bourke-White made a name for herself as a wartime photojournalist who left a chronicle of truth in a time when it was difficult for women to build careers.

Sis, Peter. *The Tree of Life: A Book Depicting the Life of Charles Darwin, Naturalist, Geologist, and Thinker*. This creative biography full of visual images explores the life of the great scientist and author from his early childhood onward, including his work aboard the science ship *Beagle*.

Zenatti, Valérie. *When I Was a Soldier: A Memoir*. Translated from French, this memoir shares Valérie's experiences both as a typical teenager and as a soldier in the Israeli Army between 1988 and 1990.

EXCEPTIONAL WOMEN

Bausum, Ann. *With Courage and Cloth: Winning the Fight for a Woman's Right to Vote*. Between 1906 and 1920, two groups of tough, determined women laid it all on the line at both state and federal levels to achieve voting rights for American women.

Blumenthal, Karen. *Let Me Play: The Story of Title IX; The Law That Changed the Future of Girls in America*. Blumenthal tells the story of Title IX, the 1972 law that gave American girls the same right to an education as boys, and the un-wavering people who fought for it.

Bolden, Tonya. *Maritcha: A Nineteenth-Century American Girl*. Maritcha was born a free black in Manhattan in the 1800s but couldn't attend the only high school in town because of her color, until she fought for her rights.

Fleming, Candace. *Our Eleanor: A Scrapbook Look at Eleanor Roosevelt's Remarkable Life*. Full of images, clippings, letters, and diary excerpts, this biography looks at the life of one of America's most active, controversial, and famous first ladies.

Fradin, Dennis Brindell, and Judith Bloom Fradin. *Fight On! Mary Church Terrell's Battle for Integration*. Born to slaves in 1863, Mary Church Terrell became one of the most active figures in civil rights and rights for women, fighting for equality into her nineties.

Fradin, Dennis Brindell, and Judith Bloom Fradin. *Ida B. Wells: Mother of the Civil Rights Movement*. Deeply opposed to racial inequality, this former slave and tough activist dedicated her life to halting violence against blacks and demanding equal rights.

Freedman, Russell. *Babe Didrikson Zaharias: The Making of a Champion*. One of the greatest female athletes of the twentieth century and a multiple medal winner in the 1932 Olympics faced many challenges as a woman in the male-dominated sports world.

Freedman, Russell. *The Voice That Challenged a Nation: Marian Anderson and the Struggle for Equal Rights*. In 1939 one of the most talented singers in America, when denied the right to sing at Constitution Hall because she was black, sang instead to an audience of 75,000 at the Lincoln Memorial.

Gourley, Catherine. *Good Girl Work: Factories, Sweatshops, and How Women Changed Their Role in the American Workforce*. In the late nineteenth and early twentieth centuries, girls and women worked long hours in miserable conditions for very little pay, until they decided to organize and make some changes.

Greenberg, Jan, and Sandra Jordan. *Runaway Girl: The Artist Louise Bourgeois.* The first female sculptor to have a retrospective at the Museum of Modern Art, this controversial artist with a troubled background broke barriers for women in the arts.

Jurmain, Suzanne. *The Forbidden Schoolhouse: The True and Dramatic Story of Prudence Crandall and Her Students.* In 1831, when Prudence Crandall opened a school for African American girls in Connecticut, both she and her students had to remain courageous in the face of extreme prejudice and resistance.

Kendall, Martha E. *Failure Is Impossible! The History of American Women's Rights.* From the Puritans to the present, from the colonies to current times, the author traces the history of American women's issues and their fight for equal rights.

Kuhn, Betsy. *Angels of Mercy: The Army Nurses of World War II.* Dozens of the almost 60,000 women who served as Army nurses during World War II share stories both grim and humorous from their years caring for American soldiers.

Lawlor, Laurie. *Helen Keller: Rebellious Spirit.* Born in 1880 and both blind and deaf before she was two years old, Helen overcame her disabilities to become a strong, humorous woman with passionate social and political beliefs.

Opdyke, Irene Gut. *In My Hands: Memories of a Holocaust Rescuer.* Irene was forced to work for the German Army when it invaded Poland in World War II, but despite her own suffering, she risked her life to help her persecuted Jewish neighbors.

Orgill, Roxane. *Shout, Sister, Shout! Ten Girl Singers Who Shaped a Century.* A famous singer who took charge of her life and career is profiled for each decade since 1900, including greats like Judy Garland, Joan Baez, Madonna, and Lucinda Williams.

Partridge, Elizabeth. *Restless Spirit: The Life and Work of Dorothea Lange.* The life of the independent and talented portrait photographer and social reformist is told along with sixty of her most moving photographs of people who suffered great hardship.

Reich, Susanna. *Clara Schumann: Piano Virtuoso.* Through illustrations, photographs, and personal letters, the life of the child prodigy, composer, and performer, who also supported an equally famous husband and raised a large family, is told.

Rubin, Susan Goldman. *Margaret Bourke-White: Her Pictures Were Her Life.* The first female photojournalist in America risked her life all over the world during World War II, the Korean War, India's Great Migration, and South African apartheid to get her famous images.

Schwager, Tina, and Michele Schuerger. *Gutsy Girls: Young Women Who Dare.* Twenty-five young women between fourteen and twenty-four years of age who showed courage and strength in meeting their goals, for themselves and to help others, are featured with photographs.

FASCINATING TRUE STORIES

Allison, Anthony. *Hear These Voices: Youth at the Edge of the Millennium.* Eighteen teens reveal how they've triumphed over devastating situations including prostitution, drugs, and homelessness.

Armstrong, Jennifer. *Shipwreck at the Bottom of the World: The Extraordinary True Story of Shackleton and the* Endurance. While attempting a 1914 trans-Antarctic expedition, Sir Ernest Shackleton's ship becomes ice-bound and the crew abandons her, forced to face the Antarctic winter without any hope of rescue.

Capuzzo, Michael. *Close to Shore: The Terrifying Shark Attacks of 1916.* Just as beachgoers began to embrace the notion of ocean swimming, a rogue white shark attacked and killed four swimmers, creating havoc and hysteria along the Jersey shore.

Deem, James M. *Bodies from the Ash: Life and Death in Ancient Pompeii.* Almost 2,000 years after the sudden tragedy, photos of plaster casts of the Pompeii citizens reveal their death throes as they tried to escape the body-encasing flows of lava from erupting Mount Vesuvius.

Dendy, Leslie, and Mel Boring. *Guinea Pig Scientists: Bold Self-Experimenters in Science and Medicine.* Inoculating against tropical diseases, testing the effect of very hot saunas on the body, or inhaling laughing gas are just a few of the scientists' dangerous self-experiments.

Dominick, Andie. *Needles: A Memoir of Growing Up with Diabetes.* It takes the death of her older sister Denise, also a diabetic, for Andie to accept the necessity of regular insulin shots and change her reckless lifestyle.

Farrell, Jeanette. *Invisible Allies: Microbes That Shape Our Lives.* Invisible microbes, first seen under a microscope in the 1600s, are indispensable not only in food production but also in its digestion and decomposition.

Fleischman, John. *Phineas Gage: A Gruesome but True Story about Brain Science.* While setting explosives, Gage accidentally shoots a thirteen-pound iron rod through his brain, leaving him alive but impaired, and leading doctors to an understanding of personality and brain function.

Gaskins, Pearl Fuyo, ed. *What Are You? Voices of Mixed-Race Young People.* Which box do you check for nationality? These forty-five teens reveal what they share in common, but, more important, their uniqueness, in this collection of poetry, essays, and interviews.

Gottlieb, Lori. *Stick Figure: A Diary of My Former Self*. This reflective memoir was written twenty years after Lori decided at the age of eleven that she was too fat.

Hampton, Wilborn. *September 11, 2001: Attack on New York City*. The actions of a guide dog, the mayor, a hijacker, and selected New Yorkers reveal the human element of the attack on New York City's World Trade Center.

Lee, Bruce, selected and edited by John Little. *Bruce Lee: The Celebrated Life of the Golden Dragon*. Photos spanning Lee's childhood to his 1973 death accompany his thoughts on martial arts, family, and acting in this work based on the documentary film *In His Own Words*.

Mattison, Chris. *Snake*. Facts and folklore, accompanied by incredible photos of the coloration and patterns of twelve snakes, make this the perfect browsing book for herpetology lovers.

Murphy, Jim. *Blizzard! The Storm that Changed America*. The Great Blizzard of 1888 left more than snow and disaster behind, as it also led to emergency planning, underground transportation, and better weather forecasting.

Nelson, Peter. *Left for Dead: A Young Man's Search for Justice for the USS* Indianapolis. A chance remark in the movie *Jaws* piques eleven-year-old Hunter Scott's curiosity about the wrongful court-martial of the captain of the USS *Indianapolis*, sunk during World War II.

Owen, David. *Hidden Evidence: Forty True Crimes and How Forensic Science Helped Solve Them*. Gruesome photos highlight the use of forensic science in catching murderers, determining the authenticity of documents, and even preventing the recurrence of some tragedies.

Philbrick, Nathaniel. *Revenge of the Whale: The True Story of the Whaleship* Essex. In the 1820s a sperm whale attacks and destroys a Nantucket whaling ship, forcing the crew into life rafts and giving author Herman Melville the idea for *Moby Dick*'s final scene.

Roach, Mary. *Stiff: The Curious Lives of Human Cadavers*. Bet you didn't know that cadavers are used as crash-test dummies, to determine decay rates for body decomposition, or to provide transplant organs for the living.

Silverstein, Ken. *The Radioactive Boy Scout: The True Story of a Boy and His Backyard Nuclear Reactor*. Eagle Scout David Hahn manages to avoid discovery by teachers, parents, and Department of Energy officials as he builds a crude nuclear reactor in his backyard.

Steer, Dugald A., ed. *Dr. Ernest Drake's Dragonology: The Complete Book of Dragons*. Everything you would ever want to know about dragons, from their anatomy and physiology to suggestions for tracking, taming, and flying them, are found in this special book.

THE WORLD IN CONFLICT: PAST AND PRESENT

Akbar, Said Hyder, and Susan Burton. *Come Back to Afghanistan: A California Teenager's Story*. The twenty-year-old immigrant to America shares three summers spent back in his native Afghanistan after the fall of the Taliban, the brutal government that forced his family's flight to another country.

Allen, Thomas B. *George Washington, Spymaster: How the Americans Outspied the British and Won the Revolutionary War*. Espionage is not a modern invention: General George Washington was the mastermind behind a network of spies that played a major role in helping the colonies win the Revolutionary War.

Bartoletti, Susan Campbell. *Hitler Youth: Growing Up in Hitler's Shadow*. Seven million young people were members of the Hitler Youth, a Nazi youth organization that used Germany's children to promote the Third Reich's agendas and policies of extermination.

Cooper, Michael L. *Fighting for Honor: Japanese Americans and World War II*. After Japan bombed Pearl Harbor, many Japanese American men joined the military to prove their loyalty despite the shameful way the U.S. government treated them.

Delisle, Guy. *Pyongyang: A Journey in North Korea*. This graphic work documents the three months in 2001 that a French cartoonist spent in North Korea, the last remaining totalitarian Communist country.

Eisner, Will. *The Plot: The Secret Story of the Protocols of the Elders of Zion*. A false document that claimed the Jews intended to take over the world was created by Russians as propaganda in the nineteenth century and is the subject of this graphic work.

Frank, Mitch. *Understanding the Holy Land: Answering Questions about the Israeli-Palestinian Conflict*. Through questions and answers, this book sheds light on the complex issues between Israel and Palestine that continue to inspire hatred and violence to this very day.

Freedman, Russell. *Give Me Liberty! The Story of the Declaration of Independence*. Beginning with the Boston Tea Party and following through to its creation and acceptance by the founding fathers, this book chronicles the development of the colonies' Declaration of Independence from British control.

Garner, Eleanor Ramrath. *Eleanor's Story: An American Girl in Hitler's Germany*. When Eleanor's father accepted a job offer in Germany, the family had no idea that World War II was about to begin and they would not see America again for seven frightening years.

Hampton, Wilborn. *September 11, 2001: Attack on New York City.* A *New York Times* editor tracks the events of 9/11 through the experiences of ordinary people immediately affected when the Towers collapsed.

Kubert, Joe. *Yossel, April 19, 1943: A Story of the Warsaw Ghetto Uprising.* The famous comic artist graphically explores what could have happened if his Polish family hadn't immigrated to America and he had been a teenager in the Warsaw Ghetto Uprising.

Levine, Ellen. *Darkness over Denmark: The Danish Resistance and the Rescue of the Jews.* The Danes resisted Hitler's extermination of Jews despite Germany's occupation of Denmark during World War II and heroically sought ways to rescue them from the horrors of the Third Reich.

McPherson, James M. *Fields of Fury: The American Civil War. Maps,* photographs, paintings, and time lines accompany this introduction to the Civil War, which took as many American lives as all other wars combined up through the Vietnamese Conflict.

Murphy, Jim. *Inside the Alamo.* The author explains what led to and happened during the famous two-week siege in 1836 when a group of Anglo settlers took a stand inside the Alamo against the Mexican general, Santa Ana.

Nelson, Peter. *Left for Dead: A Young Man's Search for Justice for the USS* Indianapolis. Half a century after the event, sixth-grader Hunter Scott spent six years proving that the captain was unfairly blamed when the USS *Indianapolis* was sunk by the Japanese at the end of World War II.

O'Donnell, Joe. *Japan 1945: A U.S. Marine's Photographs from Ground Zero.* In September 1945, the twenty-three-year-old military photographer documented the impact of the atomic bomb drops on Japan and also took personal photographs, revealed here for the first time.

Rall, Ted. *To Afghanistan and Back: A Graphic Travelogue.* An editorial cartoonist who traveled to Afghanistan during the recent American bombing campaign to document its effects on ordinary people shares what he experienced in this graphic journal.

Satrapi, Marjane. *Persepolis: The Story of a Childhood* and *Persepolis 2: The Story of a Return.* In a graphic format, Satrapi shares her childhood during the Islamic Revolution in Iran and the Iran-Iraq War, her high school years in Vienna, and her return to Iran.

Ung, Loung. *First They Killed My Father: A Daughter of Cambodia Remembers.* Loung Ung's life as the privileged daughter of a ranking government official in Cambodia was destroyed when the brutal Khmer Rouge regime took power in 1975.

Van Der Vat, Dan. *D-Day: The Greatest Invasion; A People's History.* This illustrated book provides an overview of the massive Allied assault at the beaches of Normandy on June 6, 1945, that paved the way to freeing Europe from German occupation.

PART II

Best Books for Young Adults Selections

1966–2007

The Books
by Author

Entries are arranged alphabetically by author's last name. Dates are dates of publication. "F" and "NF" indicate fiction and nonfiction, respectively.

Aaron, Henry, and Lonnie Wheeler. *I Had a Hammer: The Hank Aaron Story.* HarperCollins, 1991. **NF**
Henry Aaron, the man who broke Babe Ruth's home-run record, found that his accomplishments brought cheers from some but unleashed ugly racial hatred in others.

Abdul-Jabbar, Kareem, and Mignon McCarthy. *Kareem.* Random House, 1990. **NF**
Action and day-to-day routine are combined in Abdul-Jabbar's quiet reflections in a behind-the-scenes look at his last year in professional basketball.

Abel, Elie. *Missile Crisis.* Lippincott, 1966. **NF**
President Kennedy's decisive action during the 1962 nuclear confrontation between Russia and the United States over missile sites in Cuba is chronicled.

Abelove, Joan. *Go and Come Back.* DK Ink, 1998. **F**
Young Alicia wonders why the two white women have come to her Peruvian village since they hoard their liquor, value work over partying, and don't have a clue about marriage or sex.

———. *Saying It Out Loud.* DK, 1999. **F**
Sixteen-year-old Mindy must deal with her mother's impending death and her father's refusal to see her as anything but her mother's little girl.

Abercrombie, Barbara. *Run for Your Life.* Morrow, 1984. **F**
Writing a mystery that climaxes with a marathon while training for a similar contest, Sarah finds herself in a race with death as her fiction becomes reality.

Adams, Douglas. *The Hitchhiker's Guide to the Galaxy.* Harmony, 1980. **F**
The hilarious journey of Arthur Dent and his friend Ford Prefect, a space hitchhiker, who escape from Earth seconds before it is demolished and travel to a variety of galactic civilizations while gathering information for a hitchhiker's guidebook.

Adams, Douglas, and Mark Carwardine. *Last Chance to See.* Harmony, 1991. **NF**
Adams, author of the Hitchhiker's trilogy, and zoologist Carwardine embark on a personal journey filled with humor, irony, and frustrations as they attempt to observe some of Earth's exotic endangered species.

Adams, Richard. *Watership Down.* Macmillan, 1974. **F**
Follow the epic Tolkienesque adventures of Fiver, Hazel, and a ragtag lapin band. Rabbits will never seem the same again.

Adichie, Chimamanda Ngozi. *Purple Hibiscus.* Algonquin, 2003. **F**
While his Nigerian community sees him as a devout Christian and highly respected man, Kambili's fanatically religious father has always privately demanded perfection of his family and doled out brutal punishment.

Adler, Bill, et al. *Growing Up Black.* Morrow, 1968. **NF**
Violence, hatred, and degradation have marked the childhood of 19 black Americans from the days of slavery to today's ghettos. A new edition edited by Jay David was published in 1992.

Adler, C. S. *The Shell Lady's Daughter.* Coward-McCann, 1983. **F**

Kelly, living in Florida with her disapproving grandmother and senile grandfather because of her mother's nervous breakdown, must decide whether her mother's needs or her own struggle for independence comes first.

Adlington, L. J. *The Diary of Pelly D.* Greenwillow, 2005. **F**

While working on a demolition crew after the war, Toni V finds the diary of Pelly D buried in an empty water can. The more he reads of the diary, the more he begins to question what he has believed his whole life.

Adoff, Arnold, ed. *Celebrations: A New Anthology of Black American Poetry.* Follett, 1977. **NF**

This outstanding compilation of poems by 85 black poets, familiar and new, is a celebration of black life as reflected in diverse themes, including "The Idea of Ancestry," "The Southern Road," "Young Soul," and "Make Music with Your Life."

———. *Slow Dance: Heart Break Blues.* Lothrop, 1995. **NF**

Sparkling explosions of soul, this collection of contemporary poems captures the essence of teen experience.

Agard, John, comp. *Life Doesn't Frighten Me at All.* Holt, 1990. **NF**

A stimulating collection of poetry by writers from all over the world, from unknowns to Bob Marley and Maya Angelou.

Aidinoff, Elsie V. *The Garden.* HarperTempest, 2004. **F**

In an alternate Eden after the creation of the first human beings, God tutors Adam while Eve is left in the care of the Serpent.

Akbar, Said Hyder, and Susan Burton. *Come Back to Afghanistan: A California Teenager's Story.* Bloomsbury, 2005. **NF**

California teen Hyder describes three summers he spent in Afghanistan with his father, an exile who returned after the fall of the Taliban to help rebuild his country as a presidential spokesman and provincial governor.

Alabiso, Vincent, et al., eds. *Flash! The Associated Press Covers the World.* Abrams, 1998. **NF**

This tribute to the fearless men and women who have put their lives on the line for 150 years to bring us information and photographs of worldwide events is both moving and exciting.

Alcock, Vivien. *Singer to the Sea God.* Delacorte, 1993. **F**

Marooned on a mysterious island, Phaidon must confront the ancient gods and monsters that he and his uncle have always scorned.

Alder, Elizabeth. *The King's Shadow.* Farrar, Straus & Giroux, 1995. **F**

Despite having had his tongue cut out while watching his father's murder, Evyn rises from serfdom to become the king's foster son.

Aldridge, James. *A Sporting Proposition.* Little, Brown, 1973. **F**

A poor teenage boy and the town's richest girl are pitted against each other for the ownership of a pony.

Alexander, Caroline. *The* Endurance: *Shackleton's Legendary Antarctic Expedition.* Knopf, 1998. **NF**

How do 28 men survive two years stranded in the Antarctic Ocean? It takes guts, luck, and an incredible leader.

Alexander, Lloyd. *The Beggar Queen.* Dutton, 1984. **F**

As the kingdom of Westmark is torn by brutal civil strife, Theo must balance his personal and political responsibilities and face the monster in himself.

———. *The Iron Ring.* Dutton, 1997. **F**

There's high adventure in this quest for honor, as young King Tamar loses everything in a dice game and enters a battle between good and evil while trying to resolve his debt.

———. *The Kestrel.* Dutton, 1982. **F**

In this sequel to *Westmark,* Theo, along with his revolutionary friends, helps Mickie, now the queen, to victory when Westmark is invaded by the neighboring country.

———. *Westmark.* Dutton, 1981. **F**

Forced to leave town because of a murder he thinks he committed, Theo becomes involved with a medicine showman, a dwarf, and a beautiful girl—and with Cabbarus, who is influencing the king against him.

Ali, Muhammad, and Richard Durham. *The Greatest: My Own Story.* Random House, 1975. **NF**

Heavyweight boxing champ and outrageous poet, Muhammad Ali reveals the man behind the gloves.

Allen, Maury. *Jackie Robinson: A Life Remembered.* Watts, 1987. **NF**
A compassionate biography/oral history of the first black pro baseball player, who demonstrated competitiveness and courage.

Allen, Terry, ed. *The Whispering Wind: Poetry by Young American Indians.* Doubleday, 1972. **NF**
The wind whispers and the heart soars with the eagle in these brief, moving poems on loneliness, love, and the search for self.

Allen, Thomas B. *George Washington, Spymaster: How the Americans Outspied the British and Won the Revolutionary War.* National Geographic, 2004. **NF**
Who knew our most famous founding father was a colonial James Bond? This book features Washington in a little known but incredibly important role as the mastermind behind an intricate network of Patriot spies during the Revolutionary War.

Allison, Anthony. *Hear These Voices: Youth at the Edge of the Millennium.* Dutton, 1999. **NF**
Unflinchingly honest glimpses into the lives of at-risk youth from around the world are paired with compelling black-and-white portraits.

Almond, David. *Clay.* Delacorte, 2006. **F**
In a novel steeped in religious symbolism, the strange new kid Stephen convinces Davie to create a giant golem who will obey his command to kill the local bully.

————. *The Fire-Eaters.* Delacorte, 2004. **F**
During the intense Cuban Missile Crisis of 1962, Bobby Burns walks a tightrope between faith and fear as he struggles with a sadistic school master, his father's mysterious illness, and the overwhelming events of a world poised on the brink of destruction.

————. *Kit's Wilderness.* Delacorte, 2000. **F**
Kit finds ghostly young coal miners in the abandoned mines of Stoneygate when he plays the game of Death with the roughneck John Askew.

Alvarez, Julia. *Before We Were Free.* Knopf, 2002. **F**
Twelve-year-old Anita de le Torres's increasing physical maturation is matched by an increasing social awareness, not only of the boys around her but also of the mounting danger to her family, active opponents of the Dominican dictator Trujillo.

————. *In the Time of the Butterflies.* Algonquin, 1994. **F**
Dede and her three sisters, "Las Mariposas," turn from being interested in hair ribbons to gunrunning and acts of political sabotage against the despotic Dominican Republic dictator, Trujillo.

Amos, James. *The Memorial: A Novel of the Vietnam War.* Crown, 1989. **F**
Standing in front of the Vietnam War Memorial, Marine Lt. Jakes vividly recalls the horrors leading to its creation.

Amosov, Nikolai. *The Open Heart.* Simon & Schuster, 1967. **NF**
Life and death drama fills this absorbing personal diary of two days and nights in the life of a compassionate Russian heart surgeon.

Anastos, Phillip, and Chris French. *Illegal: Seeking the American Dream.* Rizzoli, 1991. **NF**
Expressions of bleak desperation and tentative hope are captured in photographs of "illegal aliens" crossing the Rio Grande and searching for a better life in America.

Anderson, Joan, and George Ancona. *The American Family Farm.* Harcourt Brace Jovanovich, 1989. **NF**
Focusing on three separate families from Massachusetts, Georgia, and Iowa, this photo-essay examines the typical joys and struggles of running the small family farm.

Anderson, Laurie Halse. *Catalyst.* Viking, 2002. **F**
Kate Malone, the preacher's daughter, learns there is more to life than her obsession about getting into MIT when she becomes involved with her tragedy-stricken neighbors.

————. *Fever 1793.* Simon & Schuster, 2000. **F**
Sixteen-year-old Matilda survives the 1793 yellow fever epidemic in Philadelphia and learns important lessons of perseverance and self-reliance.

————. *Speak.* Farrar, Straus & Giroux, 1999. **F**
Melinda is shunned by her friends when they don't understand the reason she called the police during a party.

Anderson, M. T. *The Astonishing Life of Octavian Nothing, Traitor to the Nation, Volume 1: The Pox Party.* Candlewick, 2006. **F**
He was raised as an experiment and considered a piece of property. Now that revolution has come to America, will Octavian find freedom?

————. *Feed.* Candlewick, 2002. **F**
Titus and Violet are teenagers in a future society where corporations define the lives and lifestyles of Americans, and where it has become common for prosperous parents to implant their newborn children with Feed: mini-computers with wireless Internet connections.

Anderson, Rachel. *The Bus People.* Holt, 1992. **F**
Six heart-wrenching, interconnected stories tell about the disabled children who ride Bertram's bus to their special school.

Anderson, Scott. *Distant Fires.* Pfeifer-Hamilton, 1990. **NF**
Risking both life and sense of humor, two young men re-create Eric Severeid's 1930 portage and canoe trip over 1,700 miles from the tip of Lake Superior to the shores of Hudson Bay.

Andronik, Catherine M. *Quest for a King: Searching for the Real King Arthur.* Atheneum, 1989. **NF**
Andronik unravels the mysteries of King Arthur's life and places the legends in historical and geographical perspective.

Angell, Judie. *One-Way to Ansonia.* Bradbury, 1985. **F**
At the turn of the century, Rose and her siblings emigrate from Russia to New York, where—with great determination—they fight to succeed in their new environment.

Angelou, Maya. *All God's Children Need Traveling Shoes.* Franklin Library, 1986. **NF**
The experience of finding a "home" where she has never lived before becomes the catalyst for insights about African and American blackness for this astute and celebrated author.

———. *Gather Together in My Name.* Random House, 1974. **NF**
This sequel to *I Know Why the Caged Bird Sings* continues the moving autobiography of a dauntless young woman forced to undertake a variety of jobs to support herself and her infant son.

———. *I Know Why the Caged Bird Sings.* Random House, 1970. **NF**
This remarkable, poetic, and frank autobiography of a black girl who grew up in Arkansas, St. Louis, and San Francisco is for mature readers.

———. *Singin' and Swingin' and Gettin' Merry Like Christmas.* Random House, 1976. **NF**
Angelou continues her autobiography, telling of her brief marriage, her efforts to raise her young son, and her beginning successes in show business.

Anonymous. *Go Ask Alice.* Prentice-Hall, 1971. **F**
The painful diary of a young girl when she accidentally falls into the contemporary drug scene.

Ansa, Tina McElroy. *Baby of the Family.* Harcourt Brace Jovanovich, 1989. **F**
Lena is special, not only because she is the baby of her middle-class African American family but also because of the supernatural gifts she received at birth.

Anson, Jay. *The Amityville Horror.* Prentice-Hall, 1977. **NF**
Bone-chilling cold, poltergeist activity, nauseating stench, unnatural noise, and green slime are only a few of the manifestations that terrify a family in their new home. Is this story a hoax or not?

Anson, Robert Sam. *Best Intentions: The Education and Killing of Edmund Perry.* Random House, 1987. **NF**
This is the gripping story of events surrounding the death of black prep school student Edmund Perry at the hands of an undercover cop.

Anthony, Piers. *On a Pale Horse.* Ballantine, 1983. **F**
During his attempted suicide, Zane kills Death and thereafter must do Death's job of collecting souls.

Appel, Allen. *Till the End of Time.* Doubleday, 1990. **F**
Transported back to the time of the bombing of Pearl Harbor, Alex Balfour uses his knowledge of contemporary history to try to stop the bombing of Hiroshima and Nagasaki.

———. *Time after Time.* Carroll & Graf, 1985. **F**
After traveling through time to 1917 Russia, Alex wonders if he should change history or simply escape.

Appelt, Kathi. *Just People, and Other Poems for Young Readers; and Paper/Pen/Poem: A Young Writer's Way to Begin.* Absey, 1997. **NF**
Want to write your own original poetry? These poems and commentaries on them can help you get started.

———. *Kissing Tennessee, and Other Stories from the Stardust Dance.* Harcourt, 2000. **F**
A collection of stories reveal the lives of the unique kids that attended the Stardust Dance held in their middle school gym.

Archer, Jeffrey. *Not a Penny More, Not a Penny Less.* Doubleday, 1976. **F**
Discovering they have been conned by a fast-talking promoter, four strangers get together to recover their million dollars.

Archer, Jules. *The Incredible Sixties: The Stormy Years That Changed America.* Harcourt Brace Jovanovich, 1986. **NF**
Archer's thematic overview of the 1960s presents the important historical, political, and social events and personalities of the period.

Armor, John, and Peter Wright. *Manzanar.* Times Books, 1988. **NF**
The tragic internment of Japanese Americans during World War II at one California relocation center is documented through Armor's evocative words and Ansel Adams's photos.

Armstrong, Charlotte. *The Gift Shop.* Coward-McCann, 1967. **F**
An exciting mystery in which Jean Cunliffe helps Harry Fairchild find and save a kidnapped child threatened with death.

Armstrong, Jennifer, ed. *Shattered: Stories of Children and War.* Knopf, 2002. **F**
The shattering effects of war on children are described in 12 short stories by authors both familiar and new.

———. *Shipwreck at the Bottom of the World: The Extraordinary True Story of Shackleton and the* Endurance. Crown, 1998. **NF**
The amazing, true-life adventure of the Antarctic explorer Ernest Shackleton is highlighted.

———. *Steal Away.* Orchard, 1992. **F**
During a dangerous escape to the north, orphaned Susannah and her unwanted gift slave, Bethlehem, form a lifelong friendship.

Armstrong, Lance, and Sally Jenkins. *It's Not about the Bike: My Journey Back to Life.* Putnam, 2000. **NF**
Olympian Lance Armstrong shares his life before and after his struggle against cancer and as a world-famous cyclist.

Arnoldi, Katherine. *The Amazing True Story of a Teenage Single Mom.* Hyperion, 1998. **NF**
The remarkable story of a teen mom's struggle to support and educate herself comes across well in this true-to-life graphic novel.

Arnosky, Jim. *Flies in the Water, Fish in the Air: A Personal Introduction to Fly Fishing.* Lothrop, 1986. **NF**
Author, illustrator, and trout fisherman Arnosky shares his knowledge of fly-fishing, his intimate acquaintance with water, and his love of nature.

Arrick, Fran. *God's Radar.* Bradbury, 1983. **F**
Roxie and her family, newcomers in a small town in Georgia, are seduced by religious neighbors into joining a fundamentalist church, and Roxie must make decisions, some of them against the tide.

———. *Steffie Can't Come Out to Play.* Bradbury, 1978. **F**
When naive 14-year-old Steffie runs away to New York to be a model, she meets Favor and becomes one of his prostitutes before a concerned cop intervenes.

———. *What You Don't Know Can Kill You.* Bantam, 1992. **F**
Ellen's agenda is exciting—graduation, college, lots of romance, and marriage. If it weren't for this "bug," everything would be perfect, but Ellen is HIV-positive.

Arter, Jim. *Gruel and Unusual Punishment.* Delacorte, 1991. **F**
Always in trouble, Arnold jokes his way through school to hide the pain of repeating seventh grade, being friendless and fatherless and protecting a mother others consider crazy.

Ash, Brian, ed. *The Visual Encyclopedia of Science Fiction.* Harmony, 1977. **NF**
A visually appealing compendium of SF info contains views on major themes by notable writers, a history of the genre, notes on fandom, science fiction art, movie tie-ins, and much more.

Ashabranner, Brent. *Always to Remember: The Story of the Vietnam Veterans Memorial.* Dodd, Mead, 1988. **NF**
The story of Vietnam veteran Jan C. Scruggs's struggle to build a national monument honoring Americans who died or are missing in the Vietnam War.

———. *To Live in Two Worlds: American Indian Youth Today.* Dodd, Mead, 1984. **NF**
Through words and photographs, young Native American men and women talk about their lives, on and off the reservation, and their hopes for the future.

Ashe, Arthur, and Arnold Rampersad. *Days of Grace: A Memoir.* Knopf, 1993. **NF**
Ashe's memoir reveals why he was considered a champion—both on and off the tennis court.

Asimov, Isaac. *Fantastic Voyage.* Houghton Mifflin, 1966. **F**
How a miniaturized submarine carrying a team of doctors travels through the blood stream of a brilliant scientist in order to save his life.

Asimov, Isaac, et al., eds. *Creations: The Quest for Origins in Story and Science.* Crown, 1983. **NF**
Speculations on the creation of the universe and its parts in fiction, scientific observation, and religious belief are described clearly.

Atkin, S. Beth. *Voices from the Fields: Children of Migrant Farmworkers Tell Their Stories.* Joy Street, 1993. **NF**
Photos and poetry accompany personal stories of the everyday problems, hopes, and dreams of Latino migrant young people, ages 9 to 18.

———. *Voices from the Streets: Young Former Gang Members Tell Their Stories.* Little, Brown, 1996. **NF**

This is a collection of raw, unedited interviews with former gang members.

Atkins, Catherine. *When Jeff Comes Home.* Putnam, 1999. **F**

Jeff's kidnapper releases him after two and a half years, and there is much speculation about the abuse he endured.

Atwood, Ann. *Haiku-Vision in Poetry and Photography.* Scribner, 1977. **NF**

The fusion of seeing and feeling is an experience of the spirit in an exquisitely illustrated book of haiku poetry and photography.

Atwood, Margaret. *The Handmaid's Tale.* Houghton Mifflin, 1986. **F**

Offred, a handmaid living in a near-future time, endures life in a society in which women able to bear children are used for procreation.

Auch, Mary Jane. *Ashes of Roses.* Holt, 2002. **F**

Sixteen-year-old Irish immigrant Rose Nolan survives the breakup of her family on Ellis Island, an uncomfortable stay with resentful relatives, and a sweatshop owner's roving hands before finally landing a choice job in New York City's Triangle Shirtwaist Factory.

Auel, Jean M. *The Clan of the Cave Bear.* Crown, 1980. **F**

A Cro-Magnon girl-child, adopted by a tribe of Neanderthals, struggles to subdue her strong feminine creativity while growing up in their mystical and instinctive male-dominated society.

Avi. *Beyond the Western Sea, Book One: The Escape from Home.* Orchard, 1996. **F**

Driven from their Irish home and struggling to get to America, Maura and Patrick become trapped in the slimy slums of Liverpool.

———. *Blue Heron.* Bradbury, 1992. **F**

A solitary blue heron becomes a symbol of strength and peace for 13-year-old Maggie when she discovers a troubling change has come over her father and his new family.

———. *The Fighting Ground.* Lippincott, 1984. **F**

Jonathon sees his dream of heroic battle turn to a nightmare when he is captured by Hessian soldiers during the American Revolution.

———. *Nothing but the Truth.* Orchard, 1991. **F**

It's against regulations to hum the national anthem in school. Philip decides to disobey the rule, and the whole nation watches what happens.

———. *The True Confessions of Charlotte Doyle.* Orchard, 1990. **F**

The only passenger on a ship sailing from England to America in 1832, Charlotte finds herself accused of murder as she becomes involved in a plot to overthrow the villainous captain.

———. *Wolf Rider: A Tale of Terror.* Bradbury, 1986. **F**

When 15-year-old Andy gets a crank call from a man claiming to have murdered a woman, his life turns into a psychological nightmare.

Ayer, Eleanor H., et al. *Parallel Journeys.* Atheneum, 1995. **NF**

Looking back at their teen years, Helen Waterford, a concentration camp survivor, and Alfons Heck, who was an enthusiastic member of the Hitler Youth Group, tell about their experiences during the Third Reich.

Bach, Alice. *Waiting for Johnny Miracle.* Harper & Row, 1980. **F**

Twins Becky and Theo Maitland do everything together, but when cancer strikes Becky, they know that life will never be the same again in this sensitive portrait of a family in crisis.

Bach, Richard. *Biplane.* Harper & Row, 1966. **NF**

Trading in his modern plane for a 1929 open cockpit biplane, the writer makes a hazardous cross-country flight from North Carolina to California.

Bachman, Richard. *The Long Walk.* Signet, 1979. **F**

Of the 100 boys who begin a grueling marathon walk, 99 will die—and one will have his every wish granted. Or will he?

Bachrach, Susan D. *The Nazi Olympics: Berlin 1936.* Little, Brown, 2000. **NF**

A history of the 1936 Olympic Games held in Berlin exposes the "Aryans only" and anti-Semitic stance of the Nazi Party and how the rest of the world responded.

———. *Tell Them We Remember: The Story of the Holocaust.* Little, Brown, 1994. **NF**

The story of the Holocaust is told clearly and dramatically.

Bacon, Katherine Jay. *Shadow and Light.* Margaret K. McElderry, 1987. **F**

During a summer at her beloved grandmother's farm in Vermont, 15-year-old Emma learns to cope with her grandmother's dying.

Bagdasarian, Adam. *Forgotten Fire.* DK, 2000. **F**
This teen's account of the Armenian Massacres from 1915 to 1918 are based on the life of the author's great-uncle.

Bagley, Desmond. *Landslide.* Doubleday, 1967. **F**
Amnesiac Bob Boyd struggles to find out who he really is in this adventure and suspense novel.

———. *The Vivero Letter.* Doubleday, 1968. **F**
The discovery of a 16th-century golden plate leads to murder and an ancient Mayan city in Quintana Roo.

Balducci, Carolyn. *Is There a Life after Graduation, Henry Birnbaum?* Houghton Mifflin, 1971. **F**
Henry Birnbaum and David Schoen, best friends in Queens, enroll in separate colleges and find life away from home almost overwhelmingly complicated by women and activists.

Baldwin, J., ed. *Whole Earth Ecolog: The Best of Environmental Tools and Ideas.* Harmony, 1990. **NF**
A browser's delight, this catalog of the best ecological books, information, processes, tools, and ideas allows individuals to make an environmental difference.

Baldwin, James. *If Beale Street Could Talk.* Dial, 1974. **F**
A young black couple, separated by his unjust imprisonment, are bolstered by their love for each other and the determination of her loyal family.

Ball, John. *The Cool Cottontail.* Harper & Row, 1966. **F**
Virgil Tibbs, the African American detective of *In the Heat of the Night,* is assigned to a case involving a murder committed in a nudist colony.

———. *Johnny Get Your Gun.* Little, Brown, 1969. **F**
Detective Virgil Tibbs is called into a case involving nine-year-old Johnny McGuire, who sets out to murder a schoolmate for breaking his transistor radio, but shoots a popular teenager instead.

Ballard, J. G. *Empire of the Sun.* Simon & Schuster, 1984. **F**
Eleven-year-old Jim's orderly life in 1939 Shanghai turns into a nightmare when the Japanese attack, separate him from his family, and imprison him for three years.

Banfield, Susan. *The Rights of Man, The Reign of Terror: The Story of the French Revolution.* Lippincott, 1989. **NF**
Do the ends justify the means? The French Revolution in all its glory and terror is chronicled in fascinating detail.

Banks, Lynne Reid. *Dark Quartet: The Story of the Brontës.* Delacorte, 1976. **F**
The brilliant but tortured lives of the Brontës are presented in a biographical novel that is as dramatic as *Wuthering Heights* or *Jane Eyre.*

———. *The Writing on the Wall.* Harper & Row, 1981. **F**
Tracy is bicycling through Holland with her "punk" boyfriend when she innocently becomes involved in drug smuggling.

Banks, Russell. *Rule of the Bone.* HarperCollins, 1995. **F**
Fourteen-year-old runaway Chappie becomes known as "Bone" during an adventurous year full of pot, travel, danger, and new friends.

Bardi, Abby. *The Book of Fred.* Washington Square, 2001. **F**
How do the lives of 15-year-old Heather, her mother, and her uncle change when Mary Fred Anderson, a teen raised in a fundamentalist commune, is placed in their home as a foster child?

Barjavel, Rene. *The Ice People.* Morrow, 1971. **F**
In a cryogenic vault under the polar ice cap an international team of scientists discovers a man and a woman who are 900,000 years old.

Barker, Clive. *Abarat.* HarperCollins, 2002. **F**
Candy Quackenbush leaves her home in Chickentown, Minnesota, and enters the magical world of Abarat, where the wicked Lord Carrion pursues her.

Barker, S. Omar. *Little World Apart.* Doubleday, 1966. **F**
Two brothers find excitement and adventure while growing up on a small cattle ranch in New Mexico.

Barlowe, Wayne Douglas, and Ian Summers. *Barlowe's Guide to Extraterrestrials.* Workman, 1979. **NF**
Have you ever wondered what a Puppeteer or a Vegan Mother Thing looks like? How Pegulas move or Polarians reproduce? This fascinating and meticulously detailed, illustrated guide to great science fiction aliens can tell you all that and more.

Barrett, Tracy. *Anna of Byzantium.* Delacorte, 1999. **F**
This historical novel is based on the life of an 11th-century Byzantine princess whose ascendancy to the throne is threatened by family rivalries and palace intrigue.

Barron, T. A. *The Lost Years of Merlin.* Philomel, 1996. **F**

Emrys, a young boy who washes ashore with no memory, travels to the mythical land of Fincayra to discover his true parentage and destiny.

Bartoletti, Susan Campbell. *Black Potatoes: The Story of the Great Irish Famine, 1845–1850.* Houghton Mifflin, 2001. **NF**

This is a detailed account of the rapid onset of the Great Irish Famine of 1845–1850 and its devastating, long-lasting effect on the Irish people.

————. *Growing Up in Coal Country.* Houghton Mifflin, 1996. **NF**

The harsh life of immigrant workers in the Pennsylvania coal mines is vividly brought to life in this haunting photo-essay.

————. *Hitler Youth: Growing Up in Hitler's Shadow.* Scholastic, 2005. **NF**

"I begin with the young . . . What material! With them I can make a new world." Adolf Hitler exploited the idealism of millions of Germany's young people to fuel his master plan for global domination.

————. *Kids on Strike!* Houghton Mifflin, 1999. **NF**

This book takes a look at the working world of children from the 1830s through the turn of the last century, and the conditions that drove them to go on strike.

Bass, L. G. *Sign of the Qin.* Hyperion, 2004. **F**

Dangers abound in this magical epic martial arts fantasy that follows Prince Zong, the Starlord, and his mother, Silver Lotus, the First Consort, after their separate escapes from the dangerous and corrupt Emperor Han.

Bat-Ami, Miriam. *Two Suns in the Sky.* Front Street, 1999. **F**

Chris and Adam meet at the Emergency Refugee Shelter in Oswego, New York, in 1944. A friendship forms but faces barriers of language, religion, and family.

Bauer, Cat. *Harley, Like a Person.* Winslow, 2000. **F**

When an artistic, 14-year-old, straight-A student believes she must have been adopted, her search for her identity tears her world apart.

Bauer, Joan. *Hope Was Here.* Putnam, 2000. **F**

Sixteen-year-old Hope and her aunt move from Brooklyn to Mulhoney, Wisconsin, to run a diner, where they become involved with the owner's political campaign to oust the town's corrupt mayor.

————. *Rules of the Road.* Putnam, 1998. **F**

Seventeen-year-old Jenna's job at crusty Mrs. Gladstone's shoe store leads to her driving Mrs. Gladstone across the country to Texas to prevent a company takeover.

————. *Thwonk.* Delacorte, 1995. **F**

Teen photographer A.J. is the lucky—or is it unlucky?—recipient of a visitation from Jonathan, a wily Cupid who pierces the heart of the high-school hunk, bringing him to A.J. on his knees.

Bauer, Marion Dane, ed. *Am I Blue? Coming Out from the Silence.* HarperCollins, 1994. **F**

Sixteen short stories, told from gay and lesbian perspectives by popular young adult authors, explore pride, individuality, and struggle.

Bauer, Steven. *Satyrday: A Fable.* Berkley, 1980. **F**

Evil Owl's attempt to rule the world requires that Matthew, a satyr, and Dairn, a boy, try to save the moon and all creatures.

Bausum, Ann. *Freedom Riders: John Lewis and Jim Zwerg on the Front Lines of the Civil Rights Movement.* National Geographic, 2006. **NF**

Though Lewis and Zwerg were of different races, their lives became entwined as their activism helped end segregation.

————. *With Courage and Cloth: Winning the Fight for a Woman's Right to Vote.* National Geographic, 2004. **NF**

The long, arduous, and sometimes violent struggle for a woman's right to vote is told in this engaging narrative.

Beake, Lesley. *Song of Be.* Holt, 1993. **F**

In newly independent Namibia, teenager Be despairs of finding her place in the new political culture, which seems to be destroying the traditional way of life of her San people.

Beattie, Owen, and John Geiger. *Buried in Ice.* Scholastic, 1992. **NF**

The story of Owen Beattie's discovery of the remains of Sir John Franklin's doomed 1845 expedition through the Northwest Passage is dramatic and exciting.

Bechard, Margaret. *Hanging on to Max.* Roaring Brook, 2002. **F**

Teen father Sam juggles the care of his 11-month-old son, Max, against his best hopes for both their futures.

————. *Spacer and Rat.* Roaring Brook, 2005. **F**

Jack is all set to leave Freedom Station for a new job on Liberty when an "Earthie Rat" and her "bot" endanger not only his plans but also his life.

Beck, Calvin Thomas. *Heroes of the Horrors.* Collier, 1975. NF

All those movie monster favorites—Karloff, Lugosi, Chaney, and Price—are here in a splendid brew of photos and text.

Beckett, Sister Wendy. *My Favorite Things: 75 Works of Art from Around the World.* Abrams, 1999. NF

Sister Wendy Beckett introduces 75 works of art from around the world through short essays and lavish illustrations.

Begay, Shonto. *Navajo: Visions and Voices across the Mesa.* Scholastic, 1995. NF

Begay portrays both the traditional and the contemporary worlds of the Navajo people through his beautiful poetry, stories, and paintings.

Begley, Kathleen A. *Deadline.* Putnam, 1977. NF

The experiences of a young newspaper reporter, whose personal and professional lives become intertwined when, for example, she celebrates her birthday in a police station, and when she writes her own mother's obituary.

Bell, Clare. *Ratha and Thistle-Chaser.* Margaret K. McElderry, 1990. F

Ratha's encounter with outsider Thistle-Chaser reunites her with her forgotten past as her tribe of intelligent cats fights for survival during a severe drought.

———. *Ratha's Creature.* Atheneum, 1983. F

Ratha, born into a society of intelligent prehistoric felines, is banished from the Clan, rescued by an unnamed male cat, and helps the Clan when she learns to tame fire.

Bell, David. *A Time to Be Born.* Morrow, 1975. NF

A two-pound "preemie" and a newborn addict are only two of the many babies that Dr. Bell, a young pediatrician, cares for and also deeply cares about.

Bell, Hilari. *The Goblin Wood.* HarperCollins, 2003. F

A young hedgewitch, a disgraced but honorable knight, and myriad goblins are at the center of events in a magical world at war.

———. *A Matter of Profit.* HarperCollins, 2001. F

The Vivitare have conquered most of the peaceful T'chin Confederacy, but Ahvren questions the victory as he tries to trace an assassination plot in time to prevent it.

Bell, Ruth. *Changing Bodies, Changing Lives: A Book for Teens on Sex and Relationships.* Random House, 1980. NF

Here's everything you want to know about teenage sexuality, presented in an honest, explicit manner, inspired by *Our Bodies, Ourselves* and written by some of the same people.

Benanav, Michael. *Men of Salt: Crossing the Sahara on the Caravan of White Gold.* Lyons, 2006. NF

On a 40-day odyssey through the Sahara on a camel caravan to the salt mines, an American journalist experiences the amazing resolve and fascinating traditions of a nearly extinct culture.

Benchley, Nathaniel. *Bright Candles: A Novel of the Danish Resistance.* Harper & Row, 1974. F

Two teenagers turn from pranks to sabotage in this tense story of a people pushed to their limits by the tyranny of the Nazi regime in Denmark.

Benedict, Helen. *Safe, Strong, and Streetwise.* Joy Street, 1987. NF

Both men and women can learn how to protect themselves from sexual assault.

Bennett, Cherie. *Life in the Fat Lane.* Delacorte, 1998. F

Shallow, self-centered, thin homecoming queen Laura's life is turned upside down when she inexplicably starts to pile on pound after pound after pound.

Bennett, James. *Dakota Dream.* Scholastic, 1994. F

Floyd (or Charly Black Crow, as he prefers to be called) runs away from his group home to seek his destiny as a member of the Dakota tribe.

———. *I Can Hear the Mourning Dove.* Houghton Mifflin, 1990. F

Struggling to recover from her father's death and her own suicide attempt, Grace meets rebellious Luke, a fellow patient and her first real friend.

———. *The Squared Circle.* Scholastic, 1995. F

Sonny lives for basketball until his college program becomes the subject of an NCAA investigation and he begins to question his family, his coaches, and his life.

Berg, Elizabeth. *Durable Goods.* Random House, 1993. F

After their mother's death, Katie and her older sister struggle to establish a workable relationship with their harsh father on a Texas military base.

———. *Joy School.* Random House, 1997. **F**
Teenage Katie deals with the complexities of an unstable home when she falls in love with a young married man.

Bernstein, Sara Tuvel. *The Seamstress: A Memoir of Survival.* Putnam, 1997. **NF**
A powerful and engrossing story of 12-year-old Sara Tuvel's lifesaving decision to walk out of her classroom in war-torn Romania and into a new life.

Berry, James. *Ajeemah and His Son.* Harper Collins, 1992. **F**
Snatched by African slave traders, Ajeemah and his soon-to-be-married son, Atu, are shipped to Jamaica, where, though separated, they never accept their status as slaves or give up their desire for freedom.

Berry, Liz. *The China Garden.* Farrar, Straus & Giroux, 1996. **F**
Seventeen-year-old Londoner Clare spends a summer in Ravensmere, where she and handsome biker Mark find themselves enmeshed in a labyrinth of magic.

Bess, Clayton. *Tracks.* Houghton Mifflin, 1986. **F**
Eleven-year-old Blue Roan persuades his older brother to take him on the rails in Depression-era Oklahoma, where their adventures range from vicious attacks by a hobo to an almost fatal encounter with the KKK.

Bickham, Jack M. *Katie, Kelly, and Heck.* Doubleday, 1973. **F**
A lady, a tough guy, and a kid clash in this funny, fast-moving tale set in a rough, raw frontier town of the 1880s.

Bing, Leon. *Do or Die.* HarperCollins, 1991. **NF**
A bone-chilling account of gang-banging in which Bing lets Crips and Bloods, infamous rival Los Angeles gangs, speak for themselves.

Bird, Eugenie. *Fairie-ality: The Fashion Collection from the House of Ellwand.* Candlewick, 2002. **F**
What will the fairies be wearing this season: calla lilies and rose-petal dresses, gerbera daisy bell-bottoms, or snakeskin bikinis? This fashion catalog for the wee folks will set trends.

Birmingham, John. *Our Time Is Now: Notes from the High School Underground.* Praeger, 1970. **NF**
In this stinging anthology uncensored high school students speak out about the injustices in the schools and in America, the home of the not-so-brave, and of changes needed now.

Bitton-Jackson, Livia. *I Have Lived a Thousand Years: Growing Up in the Holocaust.* Simon & Schuster, 1997. **NF**
Thirteen when she and her family were sent to Auschwitz, Bitton-Jackson vividly describes the horrors they faced.

Black, Holly. *Tithe: A Modern Faerie Tale.* Simon & Schuster, 2002. **F**
Kaye never imagined that saving the life of the impossibly gorgeous Roiben would bring her to the attention of the Unseelie court as the intended sacrifice for the tithe.

———. *Valiant: A Modern Tale of Faerie.* Simon & Schuster, 2005. **F**
After catching her boyfriend cheating on her with her own mother, Valerie runs away from home and slides into a seductively magical world full of betrayal and honor.

Blackwood, Gary. *The Shakespeare Stealer.* Dutton, 1998. **F**
Widge, an orphan in Elizabethan England, is forced to use his talent for transcribing shorthand to steal Mr. Shakespeare's *Hamlet* for a rival theater company.

———. *Shakespeare's Scribe.* Dutton, 2000. **F**
When the plague in London closes Shakespeare's Globe Theatre in 1602, the bard and his troupe of players—including the young actor, Widge—take to the road, playing in small towns not yet menaced by disease.

———. *The Year of the Hangman.* Dutton, 2002. **F**
In an alternate history set in 1777, a rowdy English teen encounters the remnants of the unsuccessful American Revolution when he is exiled to the Colonies.

Blais, Madeleine. *In These Girls, Hope Is a Muscle.* Atlantic Monthly, 1995. **NF**
The Amherst Lady Hurricanes have always been good but never quite good enough to go to the girl's basketball championship—one season, though, things are different.

Blake, Jeanne. *Risky Times: How to Be AIDS-Smart and Stay Healthy.* Workman, 1990. **NF**
The author and six teens bring you a book of facts on AIDS: how you get it, how you don't, and the decisions you must make for a healthy life.

Blankfort, Michael. *Take the A Train.* Dutton, 1978. **F**
After he becomes the protégé of black pimp and numbers man Mr. Gilboa, "Doc" Henshel, a 17-year-old white boy, learns some hard facts about life, love, and friendship on the electric streets of Harlem.

Bleier, Rocky, and Terry O'Neil. *Fighting Back.* Stein & Day, 1975. **NF**
Rocky Bleier tells how he overcame the battle wounds of Vietnam through rigid self-discipline to play in the Super Bowl.

Block, Francesca Lia. *Baby Be-Bop.* Harper Collins, 1995. **F**
Sixteen-year-old Dirk struggles to come to terms with being gay, fearful that family and friends will no longer love or accept him.

———. *Cherokee Bat and the Goat Guys.* HarperCollins, 1992. **F**
Cherokee and the Goat Guys rock band descend into the wild excess of the drug-rock-punk scene and need to be rescued by Native American Coyote's wise spiritual friendship.

———. *Missing Angel Juan.* HarperCollins, 1993. **F**
Witch Baby gets help from ghostly Grandpa Charlie Bat in her search for Angel Juan in New York City.

———. *Weetzie Bat.* Harper & Row, 1989. **F**
Lanky lizards! Punk teens Weetzie and Dirk search for love in a modern fairy tale that is funny, moving, and unlike any book you've read before.

Bloor, Edward. *Tangerine.* Harcourt Brace, 1997. **F**
Is Tangerine, Florida, like the Bermuda Triangle? A sinkhole swallows the middle school, lightning strikes repeatedly, underground fires burn endlessly—and all newcomer Paul Fisher wants to do is play soccer, despite his thick glasses, his parents' indifference, and his evil brother.

Blum, Joshua, et al., eds. *The United States of Poetry.* Abrams, 1996. **NF**
Contemporary poems are enhanced by outstanding photographs highlighting poets from Nobel laureates to rappers.

Blum, Ralph. *Old Glory and the Real-Time Freaks: A Children's Story and Patriotic Goodtime Book, with Maps.* Delacorte, 1972. **F**
Quintus Ells is encouraged by his grandfather to write, while stoned, a "map" of his 17th summer, describing his close relationships with family and friends for his future grandson.

———. *Simultaneous Man.* Little, Brown, 1970. **F**
American scientists replace a man's mind with the memory and personality of another in this chilling tale of U.S. and Russian intrigue.

Blum, Ralph, and Judy Blum. *Beyond Earth: Man's Contact with UFOs.* Bantam, 1974. **NF**
A rational account documents the UFO sightings of 1973—the objects, the terrified people who saw and/or were taken aboard them, and the stories they told afterward.

Blume, Judy. *Here's to You, Rachel Robinson.* Orchard, 1993. **F**
While dealing with her own adolescent angst, Rachel Robinson, a 13-year-old prodigy, must endure the return home of her rebellious brother, Charles, who has been expelled from boarding school.

———. *Letters to Judy: What Your Kids Wish They Could Tell You.* Putnam, 1986. **NF**
A popular author responds to a large variety of letters from many young fans who have confided in her.

———. *Tiger Eyes.* Bradbury, 1981. **F**
After her father's murder, Davey moves to Los Alamos, where she meets Wolf, a college boy whose father is dying of cancer.

Blumenthal, Karen. *Let Me Play: The Story of Title IX; The Law That Changed the Future of Girls in America.* Atheneum, 2005. **NF**
Only a few years ago, opportunities for women in male-dominated sports were extremely limited, but in 1972 Congress passed a momentous law called Title IX, which forever changed the lives of women nationwide.

Boas, Jacob, ed. *We Are Witnesses: Five Diaries of Teenagers Who Died in the Holocaust.* Holt, 1995. **NF**
The compelling and poignant diaries of five teenagers who died during the Holocaust tell their tragic, courageous stories.

Bober, Natalie S. *Abigail Adams: Witness to a Revolution.* Atheneum, 1995. **NF**
Romance, fame, and hard work are all facets of Abigail Adams's life in this vivid narrative of the American Revolution.

Bodanis, David. *Secret House: 24 Hours in the Strange and Unexpected World in Which We Spend Our Nights and Days.* Simon & Schuster, 1986. **NF**
The microbiological drama found within a house is explored from early morning to late evening.

Bode, Janet. *Beating the Odds: Stories of Unexpected Achievers.* Watts, 1991. **NF**
Racial discrimination, abuse, poverty, depression: teens and adults talk about dealing with the problems of life and making it in spite of them.

————. *Kids Having Kids: The Unwed Teenage Parent.* Watts, 1980. **F**

Sexual conduct, the health risks associated with teenage pregnancy, birth control, and the options open to unwed mothers are covered in this guide for pregnant teenagers as well as those in danger of becoming pregnant because of lack of information.

————. *New Kids on the Block: Oral Histories of Immigrant Teens.* Watts, 1989. **NF**

Eleven teenage immigrants reveal the trials, frustrations, and joys of making a new life in the United States after escaping poverty, repression, and even war in their native countries.

————. *The Voices of Rape.* Watts, 1990. **NF**

Date and stranger rape are explored through interviews with victims, perpetrators, and those involved in the medical and justice systems.

Bode, Janet, and Stan Mack. *Hard Time: A Real Life Look at Juvenile Crime and Violence.* Delacorte, 1996. **NF**

Hard-hitting stories from young people whose lives have been dramatically affected by crime and violence—as both victims and perpetrators.

————. *Heartbreak and Roses: Real-Life Stories of Troubled Love.* Delacorte, 1994. **NF**

In this eye-opening collection of narratives, teens talk about their troubled love relationships.

Bogle, Donald. *Brown Sugar: Eighty Years of America's Black Female Superstars.* Harmony, 1980. **NF**

In a dazzling and informative portrait, selected black female performers are presented as individuals and as important social symbols.

Boissard, Janice. *A Matter of Feeling.* Little, Brown, 1979. **F**

From the safety of her suburban Paris family home, 17-year-old French schoolgirl Pauline Moreau reaches out in a brief and tender love affair in a Parisian garret with 40-year-old artist Pierre.

Bolden, Tonya. *Maritcha: A Nineteenth-Century American Girl.* Abrams, 2005. **NF**

Maritcha Lyons, born in a free African American family in New York in 1843, led an amazing life, one directly influenced by pivotal events in American history. Her story provides a unique look at free blacks who struggled to live normal lives in the "free North."

————, ed. *33 Things Every Girl Should Know: Stories, Songs, Poems, and Smart Talk by 33 Extraordinary Women.* Crown, 1998. **NF**

In poems, short stories, letters, essays, and a comic strip, 33 prominent and successful women share words of wisdom for young women.

————. *Wake Up Our Souls: A Celebration of Black American Artists.* Abrams, 2004. **NF**

This book highlights influential and important 20th-century African American artists from periods including the Harlem Renaissance and contemporary times.

Bond, Nancy. *A Place to Come Back To.* Margaret K. McElderry, 1984. **F**

As Charlotte finds herself strongly attracted to one of her childhood friends, she discovers how difficult it is to give and receive love.

Bondoux, Anne-Laure. *The Killer's Tears.* Delacorte, 2006. **F**

When murderer Angel Allegria kills young Paolo's parents, the killer and the orphan embark together on a journey of rebirth and redemption.

Bonner, Cindy. *Lily.* Algonquin, 1992. **F**

When hardworking farm girl Lily DeLony falls in love with Marion, the youngest member of the outlaw Beatty gang, the town of McDade, Texas, is set on its ear.

————. *Looking after Lily.* Algonquin, 1994. **F**

It is 1884, and Lily is very young and very pregnant, and her outlaw husband is in a Texas jail.

Booher, Dianna Daniels. *Rape: What Would You Do If . . . ?* Messner, 1981. **NF**

These clear guidelines on how to judge a potential rape situation spell out specifics about what to do if a rape should occur.

Booth, Coe. *Tyrell.* Scholastic, 2006. **F**

Homeless teen Tyrell resists the pressures of the streets to keep his family together and maintain a relationship with "good girl" Novisha.

Bosse, Malcolm. *Captives of Time.* Delacorte, 1987. **F**

To escape not only plague but also the barbaric hordes that killed their parents, Anne and her mute brother make their way to their eccentric uncle in the city.

————. *The Examination.* Farrar, Straus & Giroux, 1994. **F**

Hong sacrifices everything to travel with his impractical, intelligent older brother Chen, protecting him from danger as they journey to the government examinations, with their promise of wealth and position.

Boston Women's Health Book Collective. *Our Bodies, Ourselves: A Book by and for Women, 2nd ed.* Simon & Schuster, 1976. **NF**

The 2005 edition of this classic handbook on the female body incorporates information on women's health and reproductive rights as well as new medical findings and up-to-date feminist perspectives.

Boulle, Pierre. *The Whale of the Victoria Cross.* Vanguard, 1983. **NF**
A blue whale, saved from killer orcas by a British destroyer bound for the Falkland Islands, becomes a friend to the entire fleet.

Bouton, Jim. *Ball Four: My Life and Hard Times Throwing the Knuckleball in the Big Leagues.* World, 1970. **NF**
Definitely not for hero worshippers, this is a lively, often funny but devastating account of the antics of baseball players, managers, and coaches by former big leaguer Bouton.

Bova, Ben. *The Multiple Man: A Novel of Suspense.* Bobbs-Merrill, 1976. **F**
President James J. Halliday has a top level security secret—several exact duplicates of himself have been mysteriously and secretly killed. Press secretary Meric Albano wants to know why.

———. *Welcome to Moonbase.* Ballantine, 1987. **F**
From lunar cuisine to low gravity football, this handbook introduces new employees to Moonbase, Inc.

Boyd, Malcolm. *Are You Running with Me, Jesus? Prayers.* Holt, Rinehart and Winston, 1965. **NF**
These are the provocative prayers of a former campus chaplain who is concerned with all facets of modern life.

Bradbury, Ray. *I Sing the Body Electric! Stories.* Knopf, 1969. **F**
In this collection of 18 stories the author writes of mechanical grandmothers and fourth-dimensional babies as well as the Irish Republican Army and Texas chicken farmers.

Bradford, Richard. *Red Sky at Morning.* Lippincott, 1968. **F**
Joshua Arnold, a wise, wry man-child, must cope with an absent father and a sherry-tippling mother and learn to live in a new town, make friends, and finish growing up.

Bradley, Bill. *Life on the Run.* Quadrangle, 1976. **NF**
Knicks veteran Bradley talks about the sport he loves, his teammates, and the pressures of professional basketball.

Bradley, Marion Zimmer. *Hawkmistress!* DAW, 1982. **F**
Forbidden to use her gift for communicating with animals and pushed by her father to marry a man she hates, Romilly MacAran flees to the hills of Darkover.

Bradshaw, Gillian. *The Beacon at Alexandria.* Houghton Mifflin, 1986. **F**
Charis flees ancient Ephesus disguised as a man to avoid an arranged marriage and makes her way to Alexandria to study medicine.

———. *Hawk of May.* Simon & Schuster, 1980. **F**
The war between good and evil is portrayed in this fantasy in which King Arthur's nephew, Gwalchmai, a reluctant warrior, first turns to his mother, an evil sorceress, for knowledge and power, then sets out to join King Arthur.

Braff, Joshua. *The Unthinkable Thoughts of Jacob Green.* Algonquin, 2004. **F**
Jacob Green tries to establish his identity in his seriously dysfunctional suburban Jewish family during the late 1970s and early 1980s.

Braithwaite, E. R. *Paid Servant.* McGraw-Hill, 1968. **NF**
Too white for an African American family, too black for a white family, four-year-old Roddy poses a problem for welfare officer Braithwaite, who tries desperately to find him a home.

Brancato, Robin F. *Come Alive at 505.* Knopf, 1980. **F**
Danny Fetzer copes with senior-year anxiety through his imaginary radio station WHUP, 505 on the dial, and through it becomes involved and obsessed with classmate Mimi.

———. *Sweet Bells Jangled Out of Tune.* Knopf, 1982. **F**
Everybody in Windsor laughs at Eva Dohrmann, the town eccentric—everybody but Ellen, her 15-year-old granddaughter.

———. *Winning.* Knopf, 1977. **F**
After sustaining a paralyzing injury in a high school football game, Gary Madden is forced to face the fact that he may never walk again.

Brandenburg, Jim. *An American Safari: Adventures on the North American Prairie.* Walker, 1995. **NF**
Prairie dogs, bison, and rattlesnakes are only a part of the endangered ecological treasures captured in Brandenburg's exquisite color photographs and memorable personal experiences.

———. *To the Top of the World: Adventures with Arctic Wolves.* Walker, 1993. **NF**
In a wildlife photo-documentary, Brandenburg enters the world of a wolf pack on Ellesmen Island and captures the animal's behaviors, personalities, and intelligence.

Branscum, Robbie. *The Girl.* Harper & Row, 1986. **F**
Though left in the exploitive care of their grand-mother, a girl and her siblings find strength in each other as well as hope in the dream of their mother's return.

Brashares, Ann. *The Sisterhood of the Traveling Pants.* Delacorte, 2001. **F**
Four lifelong high school friends and a magical pair of jeans take summer journeys of love, disappointment, and self-realization.

Bray, Libba. *A Great and Terrible Beauty.* Delacorte, 2003. **F**
In 1895 Victorian England, rebellious 16-year-old Gemma Doyle finds herself embroiled in a decades-old supernatural mystery at a stuffy finishing school that she is forced to attend following her mother's tragic death.

————. *Rebel Angels.* Delacorte, 2005. **F**
Gemma's act of breaking the runes has given magic to all. Does she have the strength and power to bind the magic and restore it to its rightful possessors, the Order?

Bredes, Don. *Hard Feelings.* Atheneum, 1977. **F**
Explicit in language and incident, this is 16-year-old Bernie Hergruter's story of growing up—confronting a class bully intent on hurting him, getting along with his family, and understanding his sexuality.

Brennan, Herbie. *Faerie Wars.* Bloomsbury, 2003. **F**
Henry Atherton, a teen from "our" world, and his octogenarian employer join forces with an animal-loving boy from the faerie world who is in "mortal" danger.

Brenner, Barbara, ed. *Voices: Poetry and Art from Around the World.* National Geographic, 2000. **NF**
This beautiful and powerful anthology of the universal language of poetry and art is organized by continent.

Brenner, Joseph H., et al. *Drugs and Youth: Medical, Psychiatric, and Legal Facts.* Liveright, 1970. **NF**
The authors give clinical studies and young drug users equal time in an objective, informative report.

Breslin, Theresa. *Remembrance.* Delacorte, 2002. **F**
The chaos and waste on the battlefields of World War I cause a comparable upheaval in the traditional ways of life in a tiny Scots village in this tender love-and-war story.

Bridgers, Sue Ellen. *All Together Now.* Knopf, 1979. **F**
Twelve-year-old Casey befriends 33-year-old retarded Dwayne and saves him from being sent to a home.

————. *Home before Dark.* Knopf, 1976. **F**
When her father takes his migrant family back to his childhood home in Florida, 14-year-old Stella Willis is determined to put down roots and never leave again.

————. *Notes for Another Life.* Knopf, 1981. **F**
Caught between their father's recurrent bouts with mental illness and their mother's career ambitions, teenagers Kevin and Wren attempt to preserve their fragile identities and relationships.

————. *Permanent Connections.* Harper & Row, 1987. **F**
While caring for an ill relative, Rob finds that spending his junior year in a rural town is living hell, until he meets equally unhappy Ellery.

————. *Sara Will.* Harper & Row, 1985. **F**
In a story of acceptance and coming-of-age, Sara Will's life is disrupted forever by the arrival of her brother-in-law, his unwed teenage niece, and her baby.

Briggs, Raymond. *When the Wind Blows.* Schocken, 1982. **F**
In this grim, cartoon-style satire an elderly British couple innocently—and futilely—tries to prepare for nuclear attack by following government directives.

Brin, David. *The Postman.* Bantam, 1985. **F**
Wearing the uniform of a long dead postman, Gordon Krantz travels among scattered communities in the western United States, struggling against survivalists and uniting people in a post-nuclear-holocaust America.

Brooks, Bruce. *All That Remains.* Atheneum, 2001. **F**
Three novellas highlight teens whose lives are affected in various ways by a death in the family.

————. *Midnight Hour Encores.* Harper & Row, 1986. **F**
Arrogant and musically gifted Sib and her father travel across the country so that she can audition for a musical genius and meet the "hippie" mother who deserted her at birth.

————. *The Moves Make the Man.* Harper & Row, 1984. **F**
As Jerome, a black athlete, shares his skills and interest in basketball with Bix, a white baseball player, their friendship grows and the game becomes a reflection of both their lives.

———. *No Kidding.* Harper & Row, 1989. **F**
In a not-too-distant future where alcoholism is rampant, 14-year-old Sam must decide the fate of his alcoholic mother and younger brother.

———. *On the Wing: The Life of Birds; From Feathers to Flight.* Scribner, 1989. **NF**
A companion to the PBS-TV series *Nature*, this beautifully written and illustrated book explores the life of birds—from feathers to flight.

———. *Predator!* Farrar, Straus & Giroux, 1991. **NF**
Stunning color photographs and a fascinating text illuminate the never-ending quest for food that faces all animals in the wild.

———. *What Hearts.* HarperCollins, 1992. **F**
Follow Asa from age 7 to age 12 as he learns how to appreciate his family.

Brooks, Earle, and Rhoda Brooks. *The Barrios of Manta: A Personal Account of the Peace Corps in Ecuador.* New American Library, 1965. **NF**
A young sales engineer and his schoolteacher wife describe their Peace Corps activities among the poverty-stricken people of Manta, Ecuador.

Brooks, Kevin. *Lucas.* Scholastic, 2003. **F**
Caitlin becomes isolated after befriending an attractive and mysterious newcomer who is hated by the other residents of Hale Island.

———. *The Road of the Dead.* Scholastic, 2006. **F**
Cole and his psychic brother Ruben journey to the ghostly moors of Dartmoor to discover the truth behind their sister's brutal murder.

Brooks, Martha. *Being with Henry.* Dorling Kindersley, 2000. **F**
Seventeen-year-old Laker Wyatt runs away from an unhappy home and is taken in by an elderly man who has family problems of his own.

———. *Bone Dance.* Orchard, 1997. **F**
When Alexandra inherits a log cabin in the wilderness from a father she never met, she goes there to make sense of their relationship—and meets Lonny.

———. *Traveling On into the Light, and Other Stories.* Orchard, 1994. **F**
In 11 short stories, readers meet teens, ranging from Laker, a throwaway dealing with his mother's rejection, to Sidonie and Kieran in their journey toward adulthood.

———. *True Confessions of a Heartless Girl.* Farrar, Straus & Giroux, 2003. **F**
After stealing her boyfriend's money and truck, newly pregnant Noreen lands in the small town of Pembina Lake and becomes a catalyst for change for the town's residents.

———. *Two Moons in August.* Joy Street, 1992. **F**
Surrounded by a family unable to come to terms with the death of her mother, Sidonie conquers her self-doubts and faces the fact that survival means accepting life with all its tragedies and triumphs.

Brooks, Polly Schoyer. *Beyond the Myth: The Story of Joan of Arc.* Lippincott, 1990. **NF**
Condemned as a witch but later canonized as a saint, young Joan, inspired by her love of France, leads her countrymen in their battle against the English.

Brooks, Terry. *Magic Kingdom for Sale—Sold!* Ballantine, 1986. **F**
In a funny fantasy adventure, disillusioned sorrowing widower Ben buys a magic kingdom for $1,000,000 only to find a run-down castle operated by a motley group of inept courtiers.

———. *The Sword of Shannara.* Ballantine, 1977. **F**
A small band of humans, elves, and dwarfs must face the armies of an evil sorcerer in order to reach the sword that can destroy him.

Brown, Dee. *Bury My Heart at Wounded Knee: An Indian History of the American West.* Holt, Rinehart and Winston, 1971. **NF**
Battle by battle, massacre by massacre, broken treaty by broken treaty, this is a documented, gripping chronicle of the Native American struggle from 1860 to 1890 against the white man.

———. *Creek Mary's Blood.* Franklin Library, 1980. **F**
They call her Creek Mary, a proud and beautiful daughter of a Muskogee chief and a leader among her people. The story of Creek Mary and her descendants, four generations of Native Americans, begins with Revolutionary War Georgia and ends with the 1905 White House.

Brown, Mary. *Pigs Don't Fly.* Baen, 1994. **F**
With the help of her magic unicorn-horn ring, Somerdai acquires a horse, a dog, a bird, a turtle, a handsome knight, and a flying pig on her quest to find home and happiness.

Brown, Michael H. *Laying Waste: The Poisoning of America by Toxic Chemicals.* Pantheon, 1980. **NF**
The dumping of industrial chemical waste creates a disaster at Love Canal, and the reporter who breaks the story warns that it can happen again.

Brown, Rita Mae. *Starting from Scratch: A Different Kind of Writer's Manual.* Bantam, 1988. **NF**
Unorthodox, funny, but very practical advice on how to write—plus the author's irreverent comments on life in general.

Brown, Turner, Jr. *Black Is.* Grove, 1969. **NF**
"Black is when somebody brings you home to lunch during Brotherhood Week—after dark" and other definitions of black not in the dictionary.

Bruchac, Joseph. *Code Talker: A Novel about the Navajo Marines of World War Two.* Dial, 2005. **F**
After years of mistreatment at white-run boarding schools, Ned Begay and other Navajo are enlisted by the army to develop an unbreakable code during World War II.

———. *Dawn Land.* Fulcrum, 1993. **F**
Young Hunter and his three faithful dog companions travel far to the West to save the Only People and his newly adopted family from the vicious Stone People.

Buck, Rinker. *Flight of Passage.* Hyperion, 1997. **NF**
In this true coming-of-age adventure, two teenage brothers pilot a Piper Cub from New York to San Diego.

Buckhanon, Kalisha. *Upstate.* St. Martin's, 2005. **F**
Young lovers Natasha and Antonio communicate via letters for nine years during his incarceration for the murder of his father.

Buckingham, Dorothea N. *Staring Down the Dragon.* Sydney, 2003. **F**
Rell is in remission from cancer but can't quite resume her normal life, feeling as though no one truly understands what she's been through or how the disease has changed her life.

Budhos, Marina. *Ask Me No Questions.* Atheneum, 2006. **F**
When their father is detained by U.S. Immigration, Nadira and Aisha must maintain an illusion of normality while they fight for his release.

Bull, Emma. *Finder: A Novel of the Borderlands.* TOR, 1994. **F**
A human living in the Borderlands fantasy world, Orient (known as the Finder) is asked by the police to use his talent for locating missing things and people in a murder investigation.

———. *War for the Oaks.* Ace, 1987. **F**
A mad phouka, the queen of the Faerie, and band leader Eddi McCandry battle the Dark Court's evil power, in a tale of rock music in Minneapolis.

Bunting, Eve. *If I Asked You, Would You Stay?* Lippincott, 1984. **F**
Crow and Valentine step tentatively out of their private worlds of hurt and loneliness toward one another.

———. *Jumping the Nail.* Harcourt Brace Jovanovich, 1991. **F**
Some teens see jumping off the Nail, a 90-foot cliff above the bottomless sea, as a way to prove their love for another, but Elisa jumps for a more sinister reason.

Burch, Jennings Michael. *They Cage the Animals at Night.* New American Library, 1984. **NF**
The author recalls the sometimes kind but often brutal treatment he received between ages 8 and 11 when he was placed in a series of institutions and foster homes by his mother, who was ill and could no longer care for him or his brothers.

Burchard, Sue. *The Statue of Liberty: Birth to Rebirth.* Harcourt Brace Jovanovich, 1985. **NF**
Packed full of facts and anecdotes about Miss Liberty, this book chronicles the statue's conception to its centennial reconstruction and plans for the future.

Burgess, Melvin. *Doing It.* Holt, 2004. **F**
Rude, crude, and obsessed with the needs of "Mr. Knobby Knobster," high school students Jonathon and his mates Dino and Ben provide an unflinching inside look at the terrors and delights of male sexuality.

———. *Smack.* Holt, 1998. **F**
English teens Tar and Gemma run away from home and into heroin's fearsome grip.

Burnford, Sheila. *Bel Ria.* Atlantic Monthly, 1977. **F**
How an abandoned but spunky circus dog, who lives through the Nazi takeover of France, shipboard life, and the bombing of England, affects the lives of those he encounters.

Burns, Olive Ann. *Cold Sassy Tree.* Ticknor & Fields, 1984. **F**
As his tiny rural Georgia hometown undergoes many changes in the year 1906, Will Tweedy survives family scandal, his first kiss, and being run over by a train.

Burt, Guy. *Sophie.* Ballantine, 2003. **F**
Mattie, now an adult, recounts his strange childhood with his hostage—his sister, Sophie.

Buss, Fran Leeper, and Daisy Cubias. *Journey of the Sparrows.* Lodestar, 1991. **F**
Maria makes the dangerous trip across the border to the United States, where jobs are scarce and she must evade immigration officers.

Busselle, Rebecca. *Bathing Ugly.* Orchard, 1988. **F**
When 13-year-old Betsy represents her cabin in their camp's beauty and ugly contests, her absurd behavior causes peers and adults to reevaluate their attitudes toward outward appearance.

Butler, Octavia E. *Parable of the Sower.* Four Walls Eight Windows, 1993. **F**
Armed with hope for the future and her unusual ability to feel the pain of others, 18-year-old Lauren leads a band of survivors north from the ruins of 2025 Los Angeles.

Butterworth, Emma Macalik. *As the Waltz Was Ending.* Four Winds, 1982. **NF**
The German occupation of Vienna interrupts a promising ballet career for Emma, and life becomes a desperate struggle to stay alive.

Butterworth, W. E. *Leroy and the Old Man.* Four Winds, 1980. **F**
After witnessing a gang mugging, LeRoy leaves his home in Chicago to live with his grandfather in Mississippi. When the victim dies, LeRoy must decide if he wants to continue to hide or if he should testify against the gang members.

Bykov, Vasil. *Pack of Wolves.* Crowell, 1981. **F**
Paralyzed with fear and betrayed by comrades, a wounded Russian partisan leads his small band through swamps in a terrifying escape from German soldiers.

Cable, Mary. *The Blizzard of '88.* Atheneum, 1988. **NF**
Shocked Easterners rally to survive the blizzard of 1888, considered one of the most serious natural disasters in American history.

Cabot, Meg. *The Princess Diaries.* Avon, 2000. **F**
When Mia is a freshman at a New York City high school, she learns that her father is a royal personage and that she is the heir to the throne of Genovia.

Cagin, Seth, and Philip Dray. *We Are Not Afraid: The Story of Goodman, Schwerner, and Chaney and the Civil Rights Campaign for Mississippi.* Macmillan, 1988. **NF**
Cagin describes the battle for civil rights in Mississippi—and the murders of three young activists, tragic casualties of that 1964 summer.

Calabro, Marian. *The Perilous Journey of the Donner Party.* Clarion, 1999. **NF**
This documentary tale of the famous Donner party and their tragic tale of survival places a special focus on the young people involved.

Calhoun, Dia. *Aria of the Sea.* Winslow, 2000. **F**
Since her mother's death, Aria has refused to use her talent for healing, but as one of the few "commoner" students at a royal school for dancers, she fails to feel the joy she expected her change in career to bring.

————. *Firegold.* Winslow, 1999. **F**
This fantasy adventure draws 12-year-old Jonathon into the mountainous land of the barbarous Dalriadas on a quest for his roots and a legendary golden apple.

————. *White Midnight.* Farrar, Straus & Giroux, 2003. **F**
Discounted as timid, ugly, and inconsequential by her community, Rose finds the inner strength to face her fears and the frightening "Thing" that lives in the Bighouse's attic so she can save her beloved Greengarden.

Callahan, Steven. *Adrift: Seventy-Six Days Lost at Sea.* Houghton Mifflin, 1986. **NF**
When his small sailboat sinks in the Atlantic, Steve Callahan spends 76 days in a five-foot inflatable raft, drifting 1,800 miles before rescue.

Calvert, Patricia. *The Snowbird.* Scribner, 1980. **F**
Orphaned 14-year-old Willie Bannerman and her brother, T.J., come to the Dakota Territory in 1883 to live with an aunt and uncle. With the help of Snowbird, a white mare, Willie begins to repair her life and discover her true strength.

————. *Yesterday's Daughter.* Scribner, 1986. **F**
Hurt and resentful, 16-year-old Leenie vows to shut her returning mother out of her life—until a brief romantic interlude opens her mind and heart.

Campbell, Eric. *The Place of Lions.* Harcourt Brace Jovanovich, 1991. **F**
After surviving a plane crash on the African Serengeti Plain, 14-year-old Chris sets off to find help for his father and the pilot, who are injured, and forges a magical relationship with an aging lion.

Campbell, Hope. *No More Trains to Tottenville.* McCall, 1971. **F**
When her mother "splits the scene" to India, Jane suddenly finds herself woman of the house and involved with a strange young man named Scorpio.

Campbell, R. Wright. *Where Pigeons Go to Die.* Rawson, 1978. **F**
While waiting for the overdue return of his racing pigeon Dickens, entered in a 600-mile competition, ten-year-old Hugh is forced to cope with the death of his beloved grandfather.

Cannon, A. E. *Amazing Gracie.* Delacorte, 1991. **F**
When her mother remarries, Gracie's life changes: she moves away from her best friend, gets a weird six-year-old stepbrother, and watches her mother sink into total depression.

————. *The Shadow Brothers.* Delacorte, 1990. **F**
Marcus discovers that change is the only constant in his life when his Navajo foster brother Henry begins a search for his Native American identity and the girl next door becomes more than a friend.

Capps, Benjamin. *A Woman of the People.* Duell, Sloan and Pearce, 1966. **F**
Captured by the Comanches as a child, Helen fights tribal customs until she falls in love with a young warrior.

Capuzzo, Michael. *Close to Shore: The Terrifying Shark Attacks of 1916.* Crown, 2003. **NF**
This book chronicles the mass hysteria that gripped the Jersey shore in 1916 and the voyage of the shark that caused it during a time before people truly understood this predator's danger.

Caras, Roger. *Mara Simba: The African Lion.* Holt, Rinehart and Winston, 1985. **F**
The birth, maturation, and death of an African lion are fictionalized against the larger landscape of Africa, its people, and their interdependency.

Carbone, Elisa. *Stealing Freedom.* Knopf, 1998. **F**
When a cruel slave master refuses to set her free, Ann Maria seeks escape to Canada on the Underground Railroad.

Card, Orson Scott. *Ender's Game.* TOR, 1985. **F**
Andrew "Ender" Wiggin, a young genius in Battle School, where he is training to fight the alien Buggers, has to put his skills to the ultimate test much sooner than he expected.

————. *Ender's Shadow.* TOR, 1999. **F**
Alien monsters threaten Earth's future. Will a tiny super-intelligent kid be able to lead his older comrades to victory?

————. *Pastwatch: The Redemption of Christopher Columbus.* TOR, 1996. **F**
To rid the world of slavery, three 23rd-century scientists travel back in time to change history—even though it means the extinction of themselves and their culture.

————. *Seventh Son.* TOR, 1987. **F**
Alvin, born seventh son of a seventh son, is destined for greatness, but something evil is trying to keep him from growing up.

————. *Shadow of the Hegemon.* TOR, 2001. **F**
Targeted for assassination, Bean escapes when the other Battle School kids are abducted from their recently united families, leaving Petra to spearhead the fight from captivity.

————. *Speaker for the Dead.* TOR, 1986. **F**
"Ender" Wiggin seeks a chance to redeem himself when Portuguese colonists on the planet Lusitania discover an intelligent species whose brutal customs threaten to start another war.

Carlson, Dale. *Girls Are Equal Too: The Women's Movement for Teenagers.* Atheneum, 1973. **NF**
How girls grow up, what is expected (and not expected) of them, how girls got where they are, and what they can do about it are all covered in this book for younger readers.

————. *The Mountain of Truth.* Atheneum, 1972. **F**
In a remote Tibetan lamasery Michael finds his mystic destiny, but his brother Peter finds only questions that haunt him the rest of his life.

Carlson, Lori M., ed. *American Eyes: New Asian-American Short Stories for Young Adults.* Holt, 1994. **F**
These ten memorable stories evoke the voices and visions of Asian American teens as they merge ancient traditions and American culture.

————, ed. *Cool Salsa: Bilingual Poems on Growing Up Latino in the United States.* Holt, 1994. **NF**
Party times, hard times, memories, and dreams come to life in these English, Spanish, and Spanglish poems by 29 Latino writers.

Carrighar, Sally. *Home to the Wilderness.* Houghton Mifflin, 1973. **NF**
An intimate, moving self-portrait of a famous naturalist who at the age of six learns to adjust to her mother's hatred and cruelty and eventually finds a home in the wilderness.

Carroll, Joyce Armstrong, and Edward E. Wilson, comps. *Poetry after Lunch: Poems to Read Aloud.* Absey, 1997. **NF**
This collection of poems offers attractive entries, some appealing to the eye, others to the ear, for pleasure reading aloud after lunch, or anytime.

Carson, Jo. *Stories I Ain't Told Nobody Yet: Selections from the People Pieces.* Orchard, 1989. **NF**
Haunting, funny, and full of folk wisdom and honesty, these powerful poems bring to life the colorful personalities and the lifestyle of the Appalachian region.

Cart, Michael, ed. *Love and Sex: Ten Stories of Truth.* Simon & Schuster, 2001. **F**
Ten highly original stories of love, lust, intimacy, and sex—gay, straight, questioning, and gender bending—make up this intriguing collection.

——. *My Father's Scar.* Simon & Schuster, 1996. **F**
In a series of flashbacks, Andy, now a college freshman entering a relationship with another man, recalls his lonely childhood in a homophobic community.

——, comp. *Tomorrowland: Ten Stories about the Future.* Scholastic, 1999. **F**
Ten popular authors of books craft a collection of futuristic short stories for teens.

Carter, Alden R. *Between a Rock and a Hard Place.* Scholastic, 1995. **F**
Stranded in the Minnesota wilderness, Mark and Randy have only each other to rely on.

——. *Bull Catcher.* Scholastic, 1996. **F**
"Bull" Larsen hopes to cap his high-school baseball career with a college scholarship and then a move to the pros, but, like his love life, Bull's baseball dreams don't turn out as expected.

——. *Growing Season.* Coward-McCann, 1984. **F**
During his senior year in high school, Rick Simon moves to the country to help his family realize their lifelong dream of owning a farm.

——. *Sheila's Dying.* Putnam, 1987. **F**
Basketball jock Jerry is planning to break up with his steady girl Sheila until he learns she is dying of cancer.

——. *Up Country.* Putnam, 1989. **F**
Sent to live with relatives in the country while his alcoholic mother receives treatment, city kid Carl faces a serious problem from the past.

——. *Wart, Son of Toad.* Pacer, 1985. **F**
Nicknamed "Wart" by the school jocks, Steve, son of the most disliked teacher in his school, is constantly in conflict with his father about his grades, his friends, and his love of auto mechanics.

Carter, Peter. *Borderlands.* Farrar, Straus & Giroux, 1990. **F**
Heroes, villains, cowboys, and common settlers populate a tale of the 1870s as 13-year-old Ben Curtis struggles to find his place in the vast frontier.

——. *Bury the Dead.* Farrar, Straus & Giroux, 1987. **F**
The lives of promising high jumper Erika and her family in East Berlin are tragically changed when her grandmother's long-gone brother suddenly appears from West Germany.

Cary, Lorene. *Black Ice.* Knopf, 1991. **NF**
As a black scholarship student in a formerly all-white private school, the author struggles with racism, her family's expectations, peer pressure, and her own idealism.

Caseley, Judith. *Kisses.* Knopf, 1990. **F**
Hannah is looking for answers: Why is her chest so flat? Why does everyone think she's a snob? Will anything ever turn out the way she wants?

——. *My Father, the Nutcase.* Knopf, 1992. **F**
Just when 15-year-old Zoe needs him the most, her father quits his job and leaves his family because he is clinically depressed.

Castaneda, Carlos. *Journey to Ixtlan: The Lessons of Don Juan.* Simon & Schuster, 1972. **NF**
The story of how the author became a "man of knowledge" through a long and arduous apprenticeship to the Yaqui Indian sorcerer, Don Juan Matus.

Castellucci, Cecil. *Boy Proof.* Candlewick, 2005. **F**
Victoria Denton ("Egg") hides behind her strange, self-created identity until she falls in love with an interesting new boy and learns to share her true self with others.

Cavagnaro, David, and Maggie Cavagnaro. *Almost Home.* American West, 1975. **NF**
Through an appealing combination of photographs and narrative, the author describes his down-to-earth harmony with nature.

Chadwick, Douglas H., and Joel Sartore. *The Company We Keep: America's Endangered Species.* National Geographic, 1996. **NF**
The world's endangered and threatened plants and animals are featured in stunning photographs and fascinating text.

Chambers, Aidan. *Dance on My Grave: A Life and Death in Four Parts.* Harper & Row, 1983. **F**
Hal, the romantic, and Barry, the cad, are lovers. When Barry is killed in a motorcycle accident, Hal cannot come to grips with his loss.

——. *Postcards from No Man's Land.* Dutton, 2002. **F**
Jacob's visit to the seductive city of Amsterdam reveals family secrets and new ideas about sexuality and death, as he learns of a passionate love story from his family's past and perhaps begins to create one of his own.

Chambers, Veronica. *Mama's Girl.* Riverhead, 1996. **NF**
This is an autobiography of a woman who learned to make peace with her mother on her journey from a troubled Brooklyn childhood to *Glamour* magazine editor.

Chang, Pang-Mei Natasha. *Bound Feet and Western Dress.* Doubleday, 1996. **NF**
This engrossing memoir, based on the life of the author's Chinese aunt, as told to the author during her own search for identity, is a tale of survival and struggle amid a sea of tradition.

Chbosky, Stephen. *The Perks of Being a Wallflower.* Pocket, 1999. **F**
This is the hilarious, heartbreaking tale of Charlie, a high school wallflower in full bloom.

Cherry, Mike. *On High Steel: The Education of an Ironworker.* Quadrangle, 1974. **NF**
An articulate ironworker discusses his lifestyle in an absorbing book about his trade and his co-workers.

Chester, Deborah. *The Sign of the Owl.* Four Winds, 1981. **F**
Wint must recapture his father's land from an evil uncle in this medieval tale.

Chestnut, J. L., Jr., and Julia Cass. *Black in Selma: The Uncommon Life of J. L. Chestnut, Jr.* Farrar, Straus & Giroux, 1990. **NF**
The life of J. L. Chestnut is detailed against the dramatic backdrop of the civil rights movement in his native Selma, Alabama.

Chetwin, Grace. *Collidescope.* Bradbury, 1990. **F**
When his space ship crashes on Earth, a highly advanced alien interferes in the lives of two teenagers living on the island of Manhattan during different centuries.

Chevalier, Tracy. *Girl with a Pearl Earring.* Dutton, 2000. **F**
In Holland in 1664, Griet leaves her family to become a maid in the household of the painter Vermeer, but the passion she inspires in him and the passion art inspires in her may end in sorrow.

Childers, Thomas. *Wings of Morning: The Story of the Last American Bomber Shot Down over Germany in World War II.* Addison-Wesley, 1995. **NF**
Howard Goodner was barely out of his teens when he flew on the last doomed bombing raid in the *Black Cat*. This riveting account describes the fears and bravery of young U.S. airmen in World War II.

Childress, Alice. *A Hero Ain't Nothin' but a Sandwich.* Coward, McCann & Geoghegan, 1973. **F**
Benjie, a 13-year-old in Harlem, cannot face the reality of his drug addiction or the realization that someone cares for him.

———. *Rainbow Jordan.* Coward, McCann & Geoghegan, 1981. **F**
Frequently abandoned and neglected by her young and carefree mother, 14-year-old Rainbow suffers—until she learns to accept love and compassion from others.

Childress, Mark. *V for Victor.* Knopf, 1989. **F**
Victor stumbles on a plot to land spies on the Alabama coast when his motorboat collides with a German U-boat sneaking into the harbor.

Chisholm, Shirley. *Unbought and Unbossed.* Houghton Mifflin, 1970. **F**
The first black woman to be elected to the U.S. Congress, Shirley Chisholm wins this unique distinction against the odds of her race and sex, and by being "unbought and unbossed."

Choi, Sook Nyul. *Year of Impossible Goodbyes.* Houghton Mifflin, 1991. **F**
A North Korean family barely survives the Japanese occupation during World War II only to find that after the war they must flee Russian Communists.

Choldenko, Gennifer. *Al Capone Does My Shirts.* Putnam, 2004. **F**
Twelve-year-old Moose Flanagan is dismayed and wary when his family moves to Alcatraz Island for his father's new job as a prison guard and so that his autistic sister Natalie may attend an exclusive special school.

Chotjewitz, David. *Daniel Half Human, and the Good Nazi.* Atheneum, 2004. **F**
When Daniel tells his parents that they cannot forbid him from joining the Hitler Youth, they reveal to him that he is half-Jewish and the Nazi Party will not allow him to join.

Christiansen, C. B. *I See the Moon.* Atheneum, 1994. **F**
Bitte, overjoyed to be an aunt, learns what true love is when her 15-year-old sister puts her baby up for adoption.

Claire, Keith. *The Otherwise Girl.* Holt, Rinehart and Winston, 1976. **F**
What can 15-year-old Matt do when he discovers that the beautiful redhead he befriends is really the ghost of a girl who drowned eight years before?

Clapp, Patricia. *Witches' Children: A Story of Salem.* Lothrop, 1982. **F**
A frightening tale of the Salem witchcraft trials, based on historical fact and told from the perspective of one of the ten "afflicted girls."

Clarke, Arthur C. *Imperial Earth*. Harcourt Brace Jovanovich, 1976. **F**
Find out what happens to Duncan Makenzie when he is sent from Titan, a moon of Saturn, to Earth's quincentennial celebration.

————. *Rendezvous with Rama*. Harcourt Brace Jovanovich, 1973. **F**
A brief encounter with an alien world, Rama, proves perilous and baffling to the humans who explore its mysteries.

Clarke, J. *The Heroic Life of Al Capsella*. Holt, 1990. **F**
Fourteen-year-old Al wants to be "like everyone else"—but with weird parents like his, he hasn't got a chance.

Cleary, Beverly. *A Girl from Yamhill: A Memoir*. Morrow, 1988. **NF**
An honest and humorous account of the Depression-era childhood and adolescence of Beverly Cleary in Oregon, where she encountered many of the same situations that teens do today.

Cleaver, Eldridge. *Soul on Ice*. McGraw-Hill, 1967. **NF**
In a collection of essays and open letters written while in prison, Eldridge Cleaver talks about the inner feelings and drives of the outraged black man in the United States today.

Clement-Davies, David. *Fire Bringer*. Dutton, 2000. **F**
Rannoch, a young red deer, discovers he is the changeling destined to fulfill the prophecy to defeat the evil Sgorr and reunite the Great Herd.

Clements, Andrew. *Things Not Seen*. Philomel, 2002. **F**
Fifteen-year-old Bobby Phillips wakes one morning to find that he is invisible.

Clements, Bruce. *Tom Loves Anna Loves Tom*. Farrar, Straus & Giroux, 1990. **F**
Tom and Anna find love at first sight and together face Anna's deepest secret.

Clifford, Francis. *The Naked Runner*. Coward-McCann, 1966. **F**
A former British intelligence agent has his Frankfurt vacation turned into a cold war nightmare.

Clinton, Catherine, ed. *I, Too, Sing America: Three Centuries of African-American Poetry*. Houghton Mifflin, 1998. **NF**
With informative narration and stunning art, this collection of African American poetry appeals to both the mind and the heart.

Clute, John. *Science Fiction: A Visual Encyclopedia*. Dorling Kindersley, 1995. **NF**
This beautifully illustrated exploration of science fiction is complete with themes, author profiles, television shows, and videos.

Coburn, Jake. *LoveSick*. Dutton, 2005. **F**
Crippled in a drunk driving accident, Ted loses his basketball scholarship, but a shocking offer to spy on a Manhattan princess brings another chance to attend college his way.

————. *Prep*. Dutton, 2003. **F**
Long after a tragedy caused Nick to abandon his Krylon cans and his crew, he is forced to dive back into the prep school gangster underworld in order to save the life of Danny, the brother of the girl Nick secretly loves.

Cofer, Judith Ortiz. *An Island Like You: Stories of the Barrio*. Orchard, 1995. **F**
Twelve beautifully written stories capture the pain and joy of teens growing up Puerto Rican in a New Jersey barrio.

————. *The Meaning of Consuelo*. Farrar, Straus & Giroux, 2003. **F**
In 1950s Puerto Rico, Consuelo struggles to understand her place in the world as her father embraces each technological advance and the wealth it might offer, her mother reaches for the past and the natural beauty of the island, her cousin begins to reveal his homosexuality, and her younger sister slips quietly into madness.

Cohen, Barbara. *Unicorns in the Rain*. Atheneum, 1980. **F**
Violence, pollution, and overcrowding have reached the point of no return. One family has built a large ship, an ark, and filled it with animals, and now it's starting to rain . . .

Cohen, Barbara, and Bahija Lovejoy. *Seven Daughters and Seven Sons*. Atheneum, 1982. **F**
In this retelling of a traditional Arabic tale, a poor merchant's daughter, disguised as a boy, makes a fortune and takes satisfying revenge on seven insulting male cousins.

Cohen, Susan, and Daniel Cohen. *A Six-Pack and a Fake I.D.: Teens Look at the Drinking Question*. Evans, 1986. **NF**
Here's an objective discussion of alcohol and its role in today's society of adults and young adults.

————. *When Someone You Know Is Gay*. Evans, 1989. **NF**
The authors describe what it's really like and what it means to be gay and include a list of books and videos for more information.

Cohn, Nik. *Rock from the Beginning.* Stein & Day, 1969. **NF**

If you dig rock, Nik Cohn gives it to you straight—the lowdown and feel of the now sounds from folk to protest to psychedelic, from Elvis to Dylan to the Jefferson Airplane and beyond.

Cohn, Rachel. *Gingerbread.* Simon & Schuster, 2002. **F**

When 16-year-old Cyd Charisse is sent to New York to stay with her biological father, she gets to know not only her older brother and the sister who calls her "Daddy's little indiscretion," but also herself.

Cohn, Rachel, and David Levithan. *Nick and Norah's Infinite Playlist.* Random House, 2006. **F**

When Nick asks a total stranger in a New York punk club to be his girlfriend for five minutes, a chaotic night of music and romance ensues.

Cole, Brock. *Celine.* Farrar, Straus & Giroux, 1989. **F**

Casualities of divorce, independent teenager Celine and her seven-year-old neighbor, Jake, share an interest in television and Jake's father.

———. *The Goats.* Farrar, Straus & Giroux, 1987. **F**

Stripped naked by fellow campers and left on a deserted island, social misfits Laura and Howie survive humiliation, natural dangers, and each other.

Cole, Ernest, and Thomas Flaherty. *House of Bondage.* Random House, 1967. **NF**

The oppression suffered by blacks in South Africa is compellingly reported in text and photographs.

Coleman, Lonnie. *Orphan Jim.* Doubleday, 1975. **F**

As if life in the Depression isn't hard enough, Trudy and her young brother choose to be "orphans" but avoid being sent to an orphans' home.

Coles, William E., Jr. *Another Kind of Monday.* Atheneum, 1996. **F**

Mark Bettors finds money and a note hidden between the pages of a Dickens novel inviting him to pick a female partner for a secret quest.

Collier, James Lincoln. *When the Stars Begin to Fall.* Delacorte, 1986. **F**

Angry that he's treated as "thieving trash," Harry decides to prove himself by exposing a local carpet factory's illegal polluting.

Collins, Larry, and Dominique Lapierre. *Or I'll Dress You in Mourning.* Simon & Schuster, 1968. **NF**

Manuel Benitez, an impoverished juvenile delinquent, fights tragedy and hunger to become the highest paid matador in the world and a symbol of the new Spain.

Collins, Max Allan. *The Dark City.* Bantam, 1987. **F**

After leaving Chicago, legendary gangbuster Eliot Ness goes to Cleveland to clean up a corrupt police force.

Colman, Penny. *Corpses, Coffins, and Crypts: A History of Burial.* Holt, 1997. **NF**

Colman's well-researched account of death and burial answers questions for the curious and satisfies a taste for the morbid.

———. *Rosie the Riveter: Women Working on the Home Front in World War II.* Crown, 1995. **NF**

More than 60 posters and photographs attractively depict working women during World War II.

Colton, Larry. *Counting Coup: A True Story of Basketball and Honor on the Little Big Horn.* Warner, 2000. **NF**

Sportswriter Larry Colton chronicles a season with the Hardin High School girls' basketball team as the players struggle with injuries, prejudice, and the dismal reality of life on the Crow Indian Reservation.

Coman, Carolyn, ed. *Body and Soul: Ten American Women.* Hill, 1988. **NF**

These personal narratives and photo-essays about unusual women, including Susan Butcher, two-time Iditarod winner, and "S&M businesswoman" Belle de Jour, portray lives of courage and perseverance.

———. *Many Stones.* Front Street, 2000. **F**

Berry travels to South Africa with her estranged father to attend her sister's memorial service, where they learn about forgiveness from people long used to suffering.

Comfort, Alex, and Jane Comfort. *Facts of Love: Living, Loving, and Growing Up.* Crown, 1979. **NF**

Birth control and respect for one's partner are stressed in a warm and readable guide to responsible sex for younger teens.

Conford, Ellen. *The Alfred G. Graebner Memorial High School Handbook of Rules and Regulations.* Little, Brown, 1976. **F**

These humorous episodes of a girl's first year in high school as she copes with every freshman's nightmare—the school's unbelievable official handbook of regulations.

Conly, Jane Leslie. *Crazy Lady!* HarperCollins, 1993. **F**

The neighborhood's "crazy lady" and her developmentally disabled son, Ronald, teach Vernon the true meaning of love.

———. *Trout Summer.* Holt, 1995. **F**

While spending the summer mostly on their own along a Maryland river, siblings Shana and Cody meet a grouchy old man who teaches them about boating and life and death.

Conot, Robert. *Rivers of Blood, Years of Darkness.* Bantam, 1967. **NF**

The violent events before, during, and after the 1965 Watts riots in Los Angeles are told in vivid on-the-scene detail.

Conover, Ted. *Rolling Nowhere.* Viking, 1984. **NF**

Ivy League Denverite Ted Conover drops out of his safe existence and experiences life as a railroad hobo, scavenging for food, hopping trains, and making friends with other hobos who help him realize what people have in common.

Conrad, Pam. *My Daniel.* Harper & Row, 1989. **F**

Years after treacherous and unscrupulous dinosaur hunters try to steal Daniel's discovery, Grandmother Julia reveals the exciting secrets of the now-famous bones.

———. *Prairie Songs.* Harper & Row, 1985. **F**

Louisa idealizes Emmeline, the local doctor's beautiful, cultured wife, who, unable to adjust to the harsh and lonely pioneer life on the bleak Nebraska prairie, goes mad.

———. *What I Did for Roman.* Harper & Row, 1987. **F**

Vulnerable Darcie becomes involved with a handsome, disturbed young man while working at the zoo.

Conrat, Maisie, and Richard Conrat. *Executive Order 9066: The Internment of 110,000 Japanese Americans.* California Historical Society, 1972. **NF**

A nation's paranoia is strikingly revealed in this photographic view of World War II concentration camps, American style.

Conway, Jill Ker. *The Road from Coorain.* Knopf, 1989. **NF**

Jill Ker Conway survives the physically harsh life of Australia's outback in the 1930s and becomes the first woman president of Smith College.

Cook, Karin. *What Girls Learn.* Pantheon, 1997. **F**

When two sisters go with their divorced mother from their southern home to live with their mother's boyfriend in the North, he becomes their caretaker after their mother's death.

Cook, Robin. *Coma.* Little, Brown, 1977. **F**

A young woman medical student discovers the horrifying truth—a black market in spare parts—about the rash of mysterious deaths of patients who have undergone surgery in a Boston hospital.

Cooney, Caroline B. *Don't Blame the Music.* Pacer, 1986. **F**

Susan's plans for an uneventful senior year are dashed when her older sister, Ashley, an embittered, failed rock musician, returns to cause her family anguish.

———. *Driver's Ed.* Delacorte, 1994. **F**

Guilt and fear permeate Remy and Morgan's new romance when a street-sign-stealing caper planned in driving class takes a deadly turn.

———. *Flight #116 Is Down.* Scholastic, 1992. **F**

A 747 crashes on the grounds of her family's estate, and 16-year-old Heidi, alone and terrified, pulls herself together to help rescue the survivors.

———. *The Voice on the Radio.* Delacorte, 1996. **F**

Janie is humiliated when her former loving boyfriend reopens old wounds by splashing her story on the airwaves while hosting a radio show.

———. *What Child Is This? A Christmas Story.* Delacorte, 1997. **F**

Several teens discover the true meaning of Christmas.

———. *Whatever Happened to Janie?* Delacorte, 1993. **F**

In this sequel to *The Face on the Milk Carton,* Janie's heartfelt decision leads her to leave her former parents and boyfriend to begin a new life with her "real" family.

Cooper, Henry S. F., Jr. *Thirteen: The Flight That Failed.* Dial, 1973. **NF**

This is a riveting minute-by-minute account of the intense efforts to save the ill-fated Apollo 13 and its precious three-man crew.

Cooper, J. California. *Family.* Doubleday, 1991. **F**

From beyond the grave, Clora narrates the story of her family as she watches her children emerge from slavery during the Civil War.

Cooper, Louise. *The Sleep of Stone.* Atheneum, 1991. **F**

Shapechanger Ghysla is jealous of Prince Anyr's fiancée and tries to take her place, with tragic results.

Cooper, Michael L. *Fighting for Honor: Japanese Americans and World War II.* Clarion, 2000. **NF**
The Japanese American experience at home and on the front lines is revealed in this thoughtful book about World War II.

Cooper, Susan. *King of Shadows.* Margaret K. McElderry, 1999. **F**
As a member of an all-boy acting company preparing to perform one of Shakespeare's plays in a replica of the original Globe Theatre, Nat is mysteriously transported to Elizabethan England and meets the famous playwright himself.

Corbett, Sara. *Venus to the Hoop: A Gold-Medal Year in Women's Basketball.* Doubleday, 1997. **NF**
This exciting book tells of the extraordinary young American athletes who won basketball gold at the Atlanta Olympics.

Corman, Avery. *Prized Possessions.* Simon & Schuster, 1991. **F**
Months after being raped during her first week in college, Elizabeth presses charges, precipitating a campus protest and her own healing.

Cormier, Robert. *After the First Death.* Pantheon, 1979. **F**
Ben tries unsuccessfully to balance his father's betrayal and his own failure after a busload of children is hijacked by a group of ruthless terrorists.

————. *The Bumblebee Flies Anyway.* Pantheon, 1983. **F**
In an experimental hospital for the terminally ill, his memory shattered by mind-altering drugs, 16-year-old Barney is told that he is the "control" and should not get involved with the dying; but he cannot stop himself from reaching out to others as he slowly discovers the truth about himself.

————. *The Chocolate War.* Pantheon, 1974. **F**
"Sweets" abound at Trinity High while a schoolmaster feasts on his students' fear—a bitter story of one student's resistance and the high price he pays.

————. *Fade.* Delacorte, 1988. **F**
One boy in each generation of the Moreaux family inherits the power—and the curse—of invisibility.

————. *Heroes.* Delacorte, 1998. **F**
Eighteen-year-old Francis returns home from World War II with his face blown off and a mission to murder the childhood hero he feels betrayed him.

————. *I Am the Cheese.* Knopf, 1977. **F**
A victim of amnesia, and under the influence of drugs administered by mysterious and unidentified questioners, teenager Adam searches through haunting memories that must not be recalled or revealed if he is to survive.

————. *In the Middle of the Night.* Delacorte, 1995. **F**
Sixteen-year-old Danny answers the phone and finds that a tragic accident 25 years earlier has set a dangerous chain of events in motion.

————. *The Rag and Bone Shop.* Delacorte, 2001. **F**
When 12-year-old Jason is questioned as a witness in a young girl's murder investigation, he doesn't realize that his interrogation in the hands of a skilled detective will become a matter of life and death.

————. *Tenderness.* Delacorte, 1997. **F**
Fifteen-year-old Lori loves 18-year-old serial killer Eric Poole.

————. *Tunes for Bears to Dance To.* Delacorte, 1992. **F**
Henry discovers evil when his bigoted boss manipulates him into betraying his friend, an elderly Holocaust survivor.

————. *We All Fall Down.* Delacorte, 1991. **F**
All is not peaceful in small-town Burnside—drunk teenagers trash a house, a young girl is flung down the stairs, a murderer is quietly planning revenge, and Jane Jerome falls in love with a lost soul.

Cornish, D. M. *Monster Blood Tattoo: Foundling.* Putnam, 2006. **F**
An orphan, sent to become a lamplighter in distant High Vesting, encounters fantastical creatures as he aids a beautiful monster slayer.

Corrigan, Eireann. *Splintering.* Scholastic, 2004. **F**
A family faces the aftermath of a brutal attack by a violent stranger.

Counter, S. Allen. *North Pole Legacy: Black, White, and Eskimo.* University of Massachusetts Press, 1991. **NF**
Counter's interest in black explorer Matthew Henson, who accompanied Robert E. Peary to the North Pole, triggers his search beyond the Arctic Circle for still living Eskimo descendants of both men.

Couper, Heather, and David Pelham. *The Universe: A Three-Dimensional Study.* Random House, 1985. **NF**
Through pop-ups and pull tabs, paper mechanics provide three-dimensional illustrations of the Big Bang, star birth, and star death.

Courlander, Harold. *The African.* Crown, 1967. **F**
Captured by slavers in a village raid, Wes Hunu survives the ocean crossing from Dahomey and life on a Georgia plantation, eventually escaping with the hope that somewhere in America there is a future for him.

Cousteau, Jacques-Yves, and Philippe Cousteau. *The Shark: Splendid Savage of the Sea.* Doubleday, 1970. **NF**
The Cousteaus present a world of beauty and danger as they study the shark and carry out research face to face with the most savage animal in the sea.

Cousteau, Jacques-Yves, and Philippe Diole. *Life and Death in a Coral Sea.* Doubleday, 1971. **NF**
The authors guide the reader through the beautiful coral jungles of the Red Sea and Indian Ocean, introducing their inhabitants along the way.

Coville, Bruce. *Oddly Enough.* Harcourt Brace, 1994. **F**
An angel, a unicorn, a vampire, and a werewolf are among the featured creatures in these nine funny, poignant, and riveting short stories.

Craig, John. *Chappie and Me.* Dodd, Mead, 1979. **F**
Wearing blackface in order to play with Chappie Johnson and His Colored All Stars in the summer of 1939, a young white Canadian boy gains understanding of what being black means.

Craig, Kit. *Gone.* Little, Brown, 1992. **F**
Mrs. Hale's children are sure she'll have breakfast ready, but where is she? She's been kidnapped by a pyromaniac who is about to reunite the family in a modern-day chamber of horrors. Someone will soon die.

Craven, Margaret. *I Heard the Owl Call My Name.* Doubleday, 1974. **F**
Native American beliefs and nature lore enhance the poignant story of a dying young minister who wins the Native Americans' respect and friendship while coming to terms with death.

Creech, Sharon. *Chasing Redbird.* HarperCollins, 1997. **F**
Zinny, at odds with her siblings, escapes the chaos by restoring a historic trail and unearths fascinating information about her family.

———. *The Wanderer.* HarperCollins, 2000. **F**
While sailing across the Atlantic Ocean in Uncle Dock's reconditioned sailboat, Sophie and Cody keep a detailed log of the perilous journey, both on the water and in their lives.

Crew, Linda. *Children of the River.* Delacorte, 1989. **F**
Sundara struggles with the conflict between her Cambodian heritage and her growing love for Jonathan.

Crichton, Michael. *The Andromeda Strain.* Knopf, 1969. **F**
Four scientists race against the clock to isolate a deadly microorganism from outer space which has killed all but two people in a small Arizona town.

———. *Electronic Life: How to Think about Computers.* Knopf, 1983. **NF**
In this informal introduction to computers and the information society, a best-selling author explains computer terminology and considers what computers can and cannot do.

———. *Jurassic Park.* Knopf, 1990. **F**
Dinosaurs created from fossilized DNA for a fabulous theme park are not supposed to be capable of breeding, but they do—and they're hungry.

———. *The Terminal Man.* Knopf, 1972. **F**
Terror spreads as a man wearing bandages, a bathrobe, and wires in his brain disappears from his hospital room.

———. *Timeline.* Knopf, 1999. **F**
Imagine you are a scientist and have discovered how to transport through time to the year 1357, when cruel lords, power-hungry abbots, scheming ladies, and fighting knights ruled.

Crispin, A. C. *Starbridge.* Ace, 1989. **F**
Mahree Burroughs discovers her talent for languages and diplomacy when, on a routine flight to Earth, Spaceship Desiree encounters intelligent beings from other planets.

Cross, Gillian. *Chartbreaker.* Holiday House, 1987. **F**
Love and rage permeate the story of Janis Mary "Finch," a British rock star who sings "like concentrated danger."

———. *On the Edge.* Holiday House, 1985. **F**
Tug, the son of a well-known British newswoman, is captured by terrorists in a story of relentless suspense.

———. *Tightrope.* Holiday House, 1999. **F**
While taking care of her sick mother and being an all-around "good girl," Ashley gets her thrills by secretly tagging neighborhood buildings until she is frightened by a stalker and seeks help from a neighborhood tough guy.

Crowe, Chris. *Getting Away with Murder: The True Story of the Emmett Till Case.* Phyllis Fogelman, 2003. **NF**

When Emmett Till, a 14-year-old black boy from Chicago visiting relatives in Money, Mississippi, violated the most serious tenet of white supremacy in the summer of 1955, his murder touched off the civil rights movement.

———. *Mississippi Trial, 1955.* Phyllis Fogelman, 2002. **F**

This gripping novel is based on the true story of 14-year-old Emmett Till, whose brutal lynching for whistling at a white woman helped to launch the civil rights movement.

Crutcher, Chris. *Athletic Shorts: Six Short Stories.* Greenwillow, 1991. **F**

Tales of love, death, bigotry, and heroism are of real people with the courage to stand up to a world that often puts them down.

———. *Chinese Handcuffs.* Greenwillow, 1989. **F**

A winning triathlete's need to understand his older brother's suicide is complicated by memories and daring challenges.

———. *The Crazy Horse Electric Game.* Greenwillow, 1987. **F**

Star athlete Willie Weaver's crippling accident forces him to leave his family and friends to rebuild his shattered life.

———. *Ironman.* Greenwillow, 1995. **F**

When he calls his teacher an asshole in class, Bo is forced to attend an anger management program, where he learns to deal with his real problem—his cruel father.

———. *King of the Mild Frontier: An Ill-Advised Autobiography.* Greenwillow, 2003. **NF**

The autobiography of the award-winning author of books for teens recounts hysterical vignettes from his childhood, profound yet simple truths that he learned along the way, and the path that led him to write honest and gritty books.

———. *Running Loose.* Greenwillow, 1983. **F**

Louie takes a stand against his coach and playing dirty football, falls in love, and loses his girlfriend in a fatal accident—all in his senior year.

———. *Staying Fat for Sarah Byrnes.* Greenwillow, 1993. **F**

When the horrific truth about Sarah's past is revealed, only her true friend Eric ("Moby") Calhoun can help her come to terms with her family and plan for her future.

———. *Stotan!* Greenwillow, 1986. **F**

A high school coach invites four members of his swim team to a week of rigorous training that tests their moral fiber as well as their physical stamina.

———. *Whale Talk.* Greenwillow, 2001. **F**

Mixed-race T.J. leads a high school swim team of nonconformists on a quest for a varsity letter jacket.

Culin, Charlotte. *Cages of Glass, Flowers of Time.* Bradbury, 1979. **F**

Abused by her mother (who in turn is still being beaten by her mother), 14-year-old Claire is afraid to trust anyone—until she meets kindness from some special friends.

Cullen, Brian. *What Niall Saw.* St. Martin's, 1986. **F**

The misspelled fragments in a seven-year-old Irish boy's diary after the Bomb offer a chilling testament to the end of the world.

Cummings, Priscilla. *Red Kayak.* Dutton, 2004. **F**

Brady, J.T., and Digger don't call out to the people in the red kayak as it heads out on a stormy morning, and Brady will regret it the rest of his life.

Currie, Elliott. *Dope and Trouble: Portraits of Delinquent Youth.* Pantheon, 1991. **NF**

This appeal to the social consciousness of America gives graphic and disturbing insight into the hopes and dreams of troubled teens.

Curtis, Christopher Paul. *Bucking the Sarge.* Wendy Lamb, 2004. **F**

Fifteen-year-old Luther T. Farrell has come to terms with the fact that his mother, "the Sarge," is a number one scam artist, and seeks a different sort of life for himself—even if it threatens to expose his mother's illegal dealings.

———. *Bud, Not Buddy.* Delacorte, 1999. **F**

On the road in search of his musician father, Bud learns about the joys and hardships of life during the Depression.

———. *The Watsons Go to Birmingham—1963.* Delacorte, 1995. **F**

Because Kenny Watson's older brother, Byron, is fast becoming a juvenile delinquent, the family drives from Detroit to Birmingham so Grandma can straighten him out.

Curtis, Edward S. *The Girl Who Married a Ghost, and Other Tales from the North American Indian.* Four Winds, 1978. **NF**

Ghost stories, trickster tales, and other pieces of authentic Native American folklore are combined with Edward Curtis's haunting photographs.

Curtis, Patricia. *Animal Rights: Stories of People Who Defend the Rights of Animals.* Four Winds, 1980. NF

The stories of seven imaginary people provide a thoughtful look at the rights of animals, ways in which they are abused, and what can be done to correct the abuse.

Cushman, Karen. *Catherine, Called Birdy.* Clarion, 1994. F

Fighting fleas, unsuitable suitors, and her mother's attempts to make a lady of her, Catherine writes in her diary about her frustrations with her life as a young noblewoman in medieval times.

———. *The Midwife's Apprentice.* Clarion, 1995. F

Beetle, a homeless girl, is found in a dung heap and apprenticed to the village midwife in this sensitive 14th-century tale set in England.

Cushman, Kathleen, and Montana Miller. *Circus Dreams: The Making of a Circus Artist.* Joy Street, 1990. NF

Follow Montana Miller through her first year at a circus school in France as she realizes her dream of becoming a trapeze artist.

D'Aguiar, Fred. *The Longest Memory.* Pantheon, 1994. F

A young slave's father misguidedly betrays his son's attempted escape in this painfully intimate view of the "peculiar institution" of slavery.

Dahl, Roald. *Boy: Tales of Childhood.* Farrar, Straus & Giroux, 1984. NF

A famous author recalls his struggle from school days to maturity in a humorous autobiography.

———. *Going Solo.* Farrar, Straus & Giroux, 1986. NF

Dahl's recollections become a collage of events from time spent in Africa to exciting flying experiences in Greece during World War II.

Dana, Barbara. *Necessary Parties.* Harper & Row, 1986. F

With the help of an offbeat lawyer/auto mechanic, 15-year-old Chris goes to court to fight his parents' divorce.

Dann, Patty. *Mermaids.* Ticknor & Fields, 1986. F

In this quietly bizarre story, 14-year-old Charlotte wants to become a saint—if only she can stop lusting after the gardener at the nearby convent.

Dash, Joan. *We Shall Not Be Moved: The Woman's Factory Strike of 1909.* Scholastic, 1996. NF

A lively picture of women in the New York garment industry rebelling against unfair conditions and organizing the first women's labor strike in the early 20th century is inspiring.

Datlow, Ellen, and Terri Windling, eds. *The Green Man: Tales from the Mythic Forest.* Viking, 2001. F

Eighteen stories and poems celebrate the pagan myth of the Green Man and other friendly and frightening fairy folk.

Davies, Hunter. *The Beatles: The Authorized Biography.* McGraw-Hill, 1968. NF

John, Paul, George and Ringo are seen as interesting, fallible human beings, each quite different from the others, each with his own history, hangups, and hopes.

Davis, Amanda. *Wonder When You'll Miss Me.* Morrow, 2003. F

When everything in her life spirals out of control, 16-year-old Faith/Annabelle runs away to the circus.

Davis, Daniel S. *Behind Barbed Wire: The Imprisonment of Japanese Americans during World War II.* Dutton, 1982. NF

An absorbing chronicle of an episode in American history when Japanese Americans were forcibly interned in "relocation" camps.

Davis, Jenny. *Checking on the Moon.* Orchard, 1991. F

Thirteen-year-old Cab spends the summer with her grandmother in a decaying neighborhood helping the area's despairing residents, and learning to rely on her own resourcefulness.

———. *Good-bye and Keep Cold.* Orchard, 1987. F

The death of Edda's father in a strip-mining accident unleashes inexplicable currents of love and hate that threaten the family's fragile survival.

Davis, Lindsey. *The Silver Pigs.* Crown, 1989. F

The murder of a senator's daughter forces Marcus Didius Falco (Bogey in a toga) to investigate a possible attempt to overthrow the emperor of ancient Rome.

Davis, Mildred. *Tell Them What's-Her-Name Called.* Random House, 1975. F

Three murders are all preceded by the same mysterious message—is it just coincidence?

Davis, Terry. *If Rock and Roll Were a Machine.* Delacorte, 1992. F

After a teacher humiliates Bert, motorcycles, writing, racquetball, and a few caring adults help him regain his devastated self-confidence.

———. *Vision Quest.* Viking, 1979. **F**
As he prepares himself for adulthood, 18-year-old Louden finds a special joy in competitive wrestling, in the uniqueness of the Columbia River, and in his live-in girlfriend, Carla.

de Hartog, Jan. *The Captain.* Atheneum, 1966. **F**
This is a gripping story of a Dutch tug boat captain facing personal conflict and awesome danger in the North Atlantic during World War II.

de Larrabeiti, Michael. *The Borribles.* Macmillan, 1978. **F**
The savage epic battle between the Borribles—strange children with pointed ears—and the Rumbles—intelligent ratlike creatures—is the focal point of an unusual, disconcerting fantasy set in London.

de Lint, Charles. *The Blue Girl.* Viking, 2004. **F**
Being temporarily blue-skinned hasn't helped brash, street-smart Imogene's status as her high school's social outcast, nor does it help her and her friends—real, dead, and imaginary—to defeat the soul-eating Anamithims.

———. *Seven Wild Sisters.* Subterranean, 2002. **F**
When one of seven red-haired sisters befriends a backwoods wise woman, she unwittingly draws all of them into a centuries-old feud between the bee fairies and 'sangmen in this modern fairy tale.

———. *Trader.* TOR, 1997. **F**
Max, a guitar maker, discovers he has lost his identity to another man and, determined to get it back, is drawn into a dream world where spirits are not what they seem.

De Veaux, Alexis. *Don't Explain: A Song of Billie Holiday.* Harper & Row, 1980. **NF**
The life of the incredibly gifted yet tragically insecure American jazz singer Billie Holiday, nicknamed "Lady Day," is told in this free verse "song."

de Vries, Anke. *Bruises.* Front Street, 1995. **F**
Although her teacher suspects the truth about Judith's frequent absences from school, Michael believes her tale of being attacked and offers his help, protection, and friendship.

Dear, William. *Dungeon Master: The Disappearance of James Dallas Egbert III.* Houghton Mifflin, 1984. **NF**
When computer genius James Dallas Egbert III disappears from Michigan State University in 1979, private investigator William Dear suspects that the fantasy world of Dungeons & Dragons has become too real for this 16-year-old.

Deaver, Julie Reece. *Say Goodnight, Gracie.* Harper & Row, 1988. **F**
Sharing a zany sense of humor and anxieties about their futures, Jimmy and Morgan are best friends on the brink of love when Jimmy is killed by a drunk driver, leaving Morgan to cope with the reality of death.

Decker, Sunny. *An Empty Spoon.* Harper & Row, 1969. **NF**
At a high school in Philadelphia's black ghetto, the school with the highest crime and dropout rates in the city, Sunny Decker, a young white college graduate, attempts to overcome the hostility and belligerence of her students.

Deem, James M. *Bodies from the Ash: Life and Death in Ancient Pompeii.* Houghton Mifflin, 2005. **NF**
A clear and intriguing explanation of the eruption of Vesuvius that destroyed Pompeii in AD 79 is presented in this thin volume.

Del Calzo, Nick, et al. *The Triumphant Spirit: Portraits and Stories of Holocaust Survivors, Their Messages of Hope and Compassion.* Triumphant Spirit, 1997. **NF**
Current photographs of Holocaust survivors, who have not only survived but have also thrived, accompany brief sketches of their lives from Hitler's ghettos and camps to today.

Del Rey, Lester. *Pstalemate.* Putnam, 1971. **F**
When engineer Harry Bronson discovers he has psi powers, he vows that he will not become insane like other telepaths.

Delaney, Joseph. *Revenge of the Witch.* Greenwillow, 2005. **F**
Thomas Ward, the seventh son of a seventh son with an aptitude for the supernatural, becomes an apprentice to the Spook, who has the important if feared job of ridding the countryside of pesky "ghouls, boggarts, and all manner of wicked beasties."

Delany, Sarah, and A. Elizabeth Delany. *Having Our Say: The Delany Sisters' First 100 Years.* Kodansha, 1993. **NF**
The colorful, thoughtful reminiscences of African American sisters Sadie and Bessie Delany (both more than 100 years old), recount their battles against racism and sexism in this remarkable oral history.

Delisle, Guy. *Pyongyang: A Journey in North Korea.* Drawn & Quarterly, 2005. **NF**
Guy Delisle, a French Canadian animator sent to North Korea to oversee a project, shares his experiences as a foreigner in communist North Korea in a simple, straightforward, and at times funny graphic novel.

Demas, Vida. *First Person, Singular.* Putnam, 1974. **F**
In a rambling diary-like letter to her psychiatrist Pam recounts her struggles to find herself despite an unstable family and her own feelings of inadequacy.

Dendy, Leslie, and Mel Boring. *Guinea Pig Scientists: Bold Self-Experimenters in Science and Medicine.* Holt, 2005. **NF**
These extraordinary and often disturbing stories feature ten people who cared so much about scientific exploration that they conducted experiments upon themselves to test their theories.

Denenberg, Barry. *An American Hero: The True Story of Charles A. Lindbergh.* Scholastic, 1996. **NF**
This is an honest look at the man whose solo transatlantic flight in 1927 captured the heart of the nation.

————. *Voices from Vietnam.* Scholastic, 1995. **NF**
Gripping descriptions by American men and women, Vietnamese citizens, and North Vietnamese soldiers convey what it was like to be in Vietnam during the war.

Derby, Pat. *Visiting Miss Pierce.* Farrar, Straus & Giroux, 1986. **F**
For a school social concerns class project, Barry Wilson, a shy, awkward ninth-grader, regularly visits Miss Pierce, an 83-year-old convalescent-hospital resident, and becomes intrigued by her tales of her older brother.

Derby, Pat, and Peter Beagle. *The Lady and Her Tiger.* Dutton, 1976. **NF**
You can train wild animals by love rather than force, and Pat Derby proves it. One of her favorites is Chauncey, the Lincoln-Mercury cougar.

Desai Hidier, Tanuja. *Born Confused.* Scholastic, 2002. **F**
In the summer before her senior year, 17-year-old Dimple is confused about her relationships with her family, her heritage, and her beautiful best friend.

Dessen, Sarah. *Dreamland.* Viking, 2000. **F**
After her sister runs away, Caitlin decides to forge her own identity and gets involved with a dramatic and mysterious guy who may not be good for her.

————. *Just Listen.* Viking, 2006. **F**
Being nice, never complaining, and avoiding conflict no longer work for Annabel Green. Can she listen to her own voice and speak up?

————. *Keeping the Moon.* Viking, 1999. **F**
Fifteen-year-old Colie has shed almost 50 pounds but still carries memories of the Fat Years, until one magical summer in a North Carolina beachside town.

————. *Someone Like You.* Viking, 1998. **F**
Halley's friendship with Scarlett changes during their junior year, after Scarlett's boyfriend dies, her pregnancy is revealed, and Halley experiences her own first serious relationship.

————. *That Summer.* Orchard, 1996. **F**
Fifteen-year-old Haven struggles through a summer in which her sister gets married, her father remarries, and her mother plans big changes in their lives.

————. *This Lullaby.* Viking, 2002. **F**
Made cynical by her romance-novelist mother's five failed marriages, Remy Starr is stunned to discover that her heart may not be made of stone when she reluctantly falls for quirky-cute Dexter the summer before she leaves for college.

Deuker, Carl. *Heart of a Champion.* Joy Street, 1993. **F**
Seth Barham tells the story of his friendship with Jimmy Winter, a gifted but troubled high school baseball star.

————. *Night Hoops.* Houghton Mifflin, 2000. **F**
Nick Abbott makes the varsity basketball team his sophomore year, but must hone his skills as a point guard while also learning to get along with Trent Dawson, his arrogant, brutish nemesis on the court.

————. *On the Devil's Court.* Joy Street, 1988. **F**
Seventeen-year-old Joe Faust must decide if it's worth selling his soul to the devil for one perfect season of basketball.

————. *Painting the Black.* Houghton Mifflin, 1997. **F**
While catching for Josh during pitching practice, Ryan decides to try out for the team but finds himself in an ethical dilemma when he discovers his friend has a serious flaw.

Dickinson, Peter. *AK.* Delacorte, 1992. **F**
Paul, an orphaned 12-year-old warrior in the Fifth Commando Unit of the NLA, fights for freedom in his African homeland, both with and without his AK-47 assault rifle.

————. *A Bone from a Dry Sea.* Delacorte, 1993. **F**
The bone Vinny finds on an archaeological dig in Africa is the same bone that Li, a thinker among her prehistoric sea ape people, wore as a sign of magical abilities.

———. *Eva.* Delacorte, 1989. **F**

After a violent auto accident, 13-year-old Eva wakes up in a hospital to find she must learn how to live as a chimpanzee.

———. *Tulku.* Dutton, 1979. **F**

Surviving a Boxer massacre of a Christian mission in China, 13-year-old Theodore accompanies an eccentric British plant collector and her guide-lover through danger-laden territory to Tibet and a Buddhist monastery.

Dickinson, Peter, and Wayne Anderson. *The Flight of Dragons.* Harper & Row, 1979. **NF**

Dragons aren't real . . . or are they? This carefully constructed and beautifully illustrated case for the existence of dragons will convince even the skeptics.

Dickson, Margaret. *Maddy's Song.* Houghton Mifflin, 1985. **F**

Sixteen and musically gifted, Maddy Dow is abused by a brutal father who is seemingly a model citizen in their community.

Dijk, Lutz Van. *Damned Strong Love: A True Story of Willi G. and Stefan K.* Holt, 1995. **F**

Based on a true event, this moving narrative tells the tragic story of a gay Polish teenager who falls in love with an occupying German soldier in 1941 and is tortured and imprisoned for the relationship.

Dixon, Paige. *May I Cross Your Golden River?* Atheneum, 1975. **F**

The rare, terminal disease which killed Lou Gehrig is also killing 18-year-old Jordan, but with his family's support he tries to lead a normal life.

Doherty, Berlie. *Dear Nobody.* Orchard, 1992. **F**

High school seniors Chris and Helen are ready for love, but not for its responsibilities, which include a baby.

———. *White Peak Farm.* Orchard, 1990. **F**

As a teenager on her family's isolated Derbyshire farm, Jeannie Tanner faces secrets, change and growing up.

Dolan, Edward F., Jr. *Adolf Hitler, a Portrait in Tyranny.* Dodd, Mead, 1981. **NF**

An examination of the man, what he stood for, and how he came to assume power.

———. *How to Leave Home—and Make Everybody Like It.* Dodd, Mead, 1977. **NF**

This is a guidebook for the young person longing to get away from home—how to tell the family, find a job, manage money, and locate a place to live.

Dolmetsch, Paul, and Gail Mauricette, eds. *Teens Talk about Alcohol and Alcoholism.* Doubleday, 1987. **NF**

Young people talk about how alcoholism affects their lives, families, and friends.

Dominick, Andie. *Needles: A Memoir of Growing Up with Diabetes.* Scribner, 1998. **NF**

This frank account of the needles that rule a young diabetic girl's existence is an unsparing story of a life transformed by disease.

Donnelly, Jennifer. *A Northern Light.* Harcourt, 2003. **F**

In upstate New York in 1906, against the background of a true and scandalous murder, Mattie Gokey fights her family and the societal constraints of the times to become her own person.

Donofrio, Beverly. *Riding in Cars with Boys: Confessions of a Bad Girl Who Makes Good.* Morrow, 1990. **NF**

Denied college, Beverly loses interest in everything but riding around, drinking, smoking, and rebelling against authority. After a divorce, she arrives in New York City with a young son and turns her life around.

Dorman, Michael. *Under 21: A Young People's Guide to Legal Rights.* Delacorte, 1970. **NF**

Legal advice for those under 21 is presented in a clear, straightforward manner on such subjects as dress, hairstyle, free speech, employment, driving, contracts, voting, criminal law, drug use, and parental problems.

Dorris, Michael. *The Window.* Hyperion, 1997. **F**

After being moved from one foster home to another, 11-year-old Rayona Taylor learns the importance of family when she's finally sent to live with relatives she doesn't know in Kentucky.

———. *A Yellow Raft in Blue Water.* Holt, 1987. **F**

Half-Native American, half-African American Rayona's agonizing search for her true self is told from a three-generation perspective—Rayona's, her mother's, and her grandmother's.

Dowdey, Landon, comp. *Journey to Freedom: A Casebook with Music.* Swallow, 1969. **NF**

From the Bible to the Beatles, material gathered from poetry, plays, folk songs, and spirituals is combined in a joyous statement on the brotherhood of man and the celebration of life.

Dragonwagon, Crescent, and Paul Zindel. *To Take a Dare.* Harper & Row, 1982. **F**

Thirteen-year-old Chrysta is already into drugs and sex when she runs away from home. After a couple of years on the road learning life the hard way, she meets several people who teach her about love, happiness and giving.

Draper, Sharon M. *Forged by Fire.* Atheneum, 1997. **F**

Gerald, who has struggled his entire life to survive in spite of his drug-addicted mother, now must protect his sister from an abusive stepfather.

———. *Tears of a Tiger.* Atheneum, 1994. **F**

High-school senior Andy Jackson is overcome by guilt after his best friend dies in an automobile accident that happened when Andy was driving drunk.

Dribben, Judith Strick. *A Girl Called Judith Strick.* Cowles, 1970. **NF**

Seventeen-year-old Judith Strick lures Germans into partisan traps, spies for the Polish underground, bamboozles and charms her German captors, and survives three prisons, including Auschwitz.

Drucker, Olga Levy. *Kindertransport.* Holt, 1992. **NF**

Drucker relates her six years as a child evacuee from Nazi Germany and her encounters with anti-Semitism while in foster care in England.

Duder, Tessa. *In Lane Three, Alex Archer.* Houghton Mifflin, 1989. **F**

Overcoming injuries, Alex competes with her rival for a spot on the New Zealand Olympic swim team.

Due, Linnea A. *High and Outside.* Harper & Row, 1980. **F**

Niki, the star pitcher on the girls softball team, has a drinking problem. Her catcher knows, her coach knows, but Niki won't admit it.

Dufresne, Frank. *My Way Was North.* Holt, Rinehart and Winston, 1966. **NF**

As a field agent for the U.S. Biological Survey, Dufresne spends 20 years in Alaska enjoying the frozen wastes, unusual animals, and individualistic people.

Duncan, Lois. *Chapters: My Growth as a Writer.* Little, Brown, 1982. **NF**

A popular author tells about her need and desire to be a writer from the time she was ten years old; examples of her early writing are used to demonstrate how life becomes fiction and to show how her career develops.

———. *Don't Look Behind You.* Delacorte, 1989. **F**

April's life changes forever when her family must disappear into the federal witness protection program after her father testifies against members of a drug ring.

———. *Killing Mr. Griffin.* Little, Brown, 1978. **F**

A group of high school students kidnaps a strict English teacher in order to get even with him—and what starts as a prank becomes a horror.

———. *Stranger with My Face.* Little, Brown, 1981. **F**

Will Laurie's evil twin sister, Lia, already experienced in astral projection, succeed in taking over Laurie's body and comfortable life?

———. *Who Killed My Daughter?* Delacorte, 1992. **NF**

Determined to find her daughter's murderer, author Lois Duncan seeks the aid of psychics and uncovers startling parallels to her YA novels.

Dunkle, Clare B. *The Hollow Kingdom.* Holt, 2003. **F**

Beautiful Kate agrees to marry the King of the Goblins in exchange for the safe return of her kidnapped sister.

Durán, Cheli, ed. *The Yellow Canary Whose Eye Is So Black.* Macmillan, 1977. **NF**

A rich bilingual collection of poems by more than 40 poets reflects the variegated tapestry of life in Latin America.

Durham, Marilyn. *The Man Who Loved Cat Dancing.* Harcourt Brace Jovanovich, 1972. **F**

A western, a relentless character study, a violent tragedy, but, most of all, this is a love story.

Durham, Michael S. *Powerful Days: The Civil Rights Photography of Charles Moore.* Stewart, Tabori & Chang, 1991. **NF**

Graphic black-and-white photographs by a noted photojournalist vividly document events of the civil rights movement.

Durkin, Barbara Wernecke. *Oh, You Dundalk Girls, Can't You Dance the Polka?* Morrow, 1984. **F**

Fat but smart and gutsy Beatrice (Bebe) Schmidt becomes one of the crowd in her 1950s suburb of Baltimore.

Durrell, Gerald. *Birds, Beasts, and Relatives.* Viking, 1969. **NF**

An owl in the attic, a bear in the parlor, an overweight sister with acne, and a brother who collects eccentric humans are part of the Durrell "menagerie" which invades Corfu for a season and occupies it for five years.

———. *Rosy Is My Relative.* Viking, 1968. **F**

Adrian Rookwhistle inherits Rosy, a lovable beer-drinking elephant, and on their journey through the English countryside to find a circus home for Rosy, their progress is marked by many disquieting occasions.

————. *Two in the Bush.* Viking, 1966. **NF**
A noted animal collector humorously relates his travels through New Zealand, Australia, and Malaysia to observe and photograph flying lizards, lyre birds, and other species close to extinction.

Durrell, Gerald, and Lee Durrell. *The Amateur Naturalist.* Knopf, 1983. **NF**
In 17 "nature walks" the authors guide both amateur and seasoned naturalists from the beaches to the woodlands, suggesting observations and experiments that do not intrude on the natural world.

Dyer, Daniel. *Jack London: A Biography.* Scholastic, 1997. **NF**
This exciting portrait of the author of *The Call of the Wild* focuses on London's true-life adventures riding the rails, dogsledding during the Yukon gold rush, and sailing the South Seas.

Eagan, Andrea Boroff. *Why Am I So Miserable If These Are the Best Years of My Life? A Survival Guide for the Young Woman.* Lippincott, 1976. **NF**
This is straight talk on women's anatomy, sex, and legal rights.

Eckert, Allan W. *Song of the Wild.* Little, Brown, 1980. **F**
The unusual gift of being able to project his mind inside other living creatures separates Caleb Erikson from other 14-year-olds and causes tension between his parents and himself.

Edelman, Bernard, ed. *Dear America: Letters Home from Vietnam.* Norton, 1985. **NF**
In their personal letters, soldiers and civilians reveal the pain, frustration, confusion, and anger that were part of their daily lives in Vietnam.

Edelman, Marian Wright. *The Measure of Our Success: A Letter to My Children and Yours.* Beacon, 1992. **NF**
A powerful mix of personal anecdote and moral conviction, Edelman's 25 lessons for life are an inspiration for everyone.

Edgerton, Clyde. *The Floatplane Notebooks.* Algonquin, 1988. **F**
The love and strength of the Copelands are portrayed generationally as they chronicle their adventures from a locked shed in rural Georgia.

Edmonds, Walter D. *The South African Quirt.* Little, Brown, 1985. **F**
Natty Dunston, a young boy on a New York farm, is unwilling to give up his own standards to adjust to his father's tyrannical demands.

Einstein, Charles, ed. *The Fireside Book of Baseball, 4th ed.* Simon & Schuster, 1987. **NF**
This collection of pictures, cartoons, history, and poetry in praise of "America's favorite pastime," is a treasury of works by many of America's most talented baseball writers and fans.

Eisen, Jonathan, ed. *Altamont: Death of Innocence in the Woodstock Nation.* Avon, 1970. **NF**
The Altamont Rock Festival was intended to be a West Coast Woodstock but instead became a disaster. The event is clearly examined in relation to its meaning for the future of the counterculture.

Eisner, Will. *The Plot: The Secret Story of the Protocols of the Elders of Zion.* Norton, 2005. **NF**
This graphic novel examines a historical treatise actually published in 1902 called "The Protocols of the Elders of Zion," a false pamphlet which fueled a surge of anti-Semitism that has been quoted by Hitler, Klansmen, and other defamation groups to support their cause.

Elder, Lauren, and Shirley Streshinsky. *And I Alone Survived.* Dutton, 1978. **NF**
The true story of a courageous young woman, who, as sole survivor of a plane crash in the High Sierras, spends a grueling ordeal in the mountains.

Elders, Joycelyn, and David Chanoff. *Joycelyn Elders, M.D.: From Sharecropper's Daughter to Surgeon General of the United States of America.* Morrow, 1996. **NF**
Overcoming poverty and prejudice in a small farm town in Arkansas, Elders succeeds in becoming a dedicated doctor, advocating for the poor, and serving as a controversial U.S. Surgeon General.

Eldred, Tim. *Grease Monkey: A Tale of Growing Up in Orbit.* TOR, 2006. **F**
In this hilarious graphic novel, a teenage spaceship mechanic learns to adjust to his crotchety new boss—who happens to be a gorilla.

Elfman, Blossom. *The Girls of Huntington House.* Houghton Mifflin, 1972. **F**
"What can you teach pregnant girls that they do not already know?" ask Blossom Elfman's friends when they learn she has accepted a teaching assignment in a school for unwed mothers.

————. *A House for Jonnie O.* Houghton Mifflin, 1976. **F**
Jonnie and her three friends—students at a school for pregnant unmarried teenagers—search for a "dream house" where they can be independent and support one another and their babies.

Ellis, Deborah. *Parvana's Journey.* Groundwood, 2002. **F**

After her father dies, 13-year-old Parvana, disguised as a boy, wanders alone through war-torn Afghanistan looking for her family who disappeared in the Taliban takeover, and forms a new family of abandoned children she meets along the way.

Ellison, Harlan. *Deathbird Stories: A Pantheon of Modern Gods.* Harper & Row, 1975. **F**

In these tales set in some future time, the objects and rites of man's worship are stretched to the limits of believability and horror.

Embury, Barbara, and Thomas D. Crouch. *The Dream Is Alive.* Harper & Row, 1990. **NF**

Based on three shuttle flights, with photographs taken on a 1984 mission, this photo-essay describes what takes place on a typical space flight.

Engle, Margarita. *The Poet Slave of Cuba: A Biography of Juan Francisco Manzano.* Holt, 2006. **NF**

This beautifully illustrated collection of linked poems explores the life of Juan, a brutally treated slave who nonetheless sees the world in unique and lyrical ways.

Epstein, Sam, and Beryl Epstein. *Kids in Court: The ACLU Defends Their Rights.* Four Winds, 1982. **NF**

Eleven case histories that involve the rights of young people who were defended by the American Civil Liberties Union during the 1950s and 1960s become precedents for many of today's court cases.

Esquivel, Laura. *Like Water for Chocolate: A Novel in Monthly Installments, with Recipes, Romances, and Home Remedies.* Doubleday, 1992. **F**

Tita's life and the food she cooks take a strange twist when her true love Pedro is forbidden her in this tale of magic, comedy, romance, and tragedy.

Etchemendy, Nancy. *Cat in Glass, and Other Tales of the Unnatural.* Cricket, 2002. **F**

These eight tales range from the supernatural to the unknown to the horrific.

Faber, Doris. *Love and Rivalry: Three Exceptional Pairs of Sisters.* Viking, 1983. **NF**

This narrative examines the relationships between Emily Dickinson, Charlotte Cushman, and Harriet Beecher Stowe and their respective sisters.

Fair, Ronald. *We Can't Breathe.* Harper & Row, 1972. **NF**

For Ernie Johnson, life in Chicago's black ghetto in the 1930s means roaches and rats, wine and grass, street games and violence, and even the "wow" of discovering a book.

Fall, Thomas. *The Ordeal of Running Standing.* McCall, 1970. **F**

Running Standing, a Kiowa, and his girl-wife, Crosses-the-River, marry for love but part—she to help her people, he to search for success in the white man's world, a choice which inevitably leads to his betrayal and death.

Fama, Elizabeth. *Overboard.* Cricket, 2002. **F**

While on a trip to visit her uncle, Emily escapes the sinking ferry and finds herself and a young, courageous Muslim boy adrift in the waters off the islands of Sumatra.

Fante, John. *1933 Was a Bad Year.* Black Sparrow, 1985. **F**

High school senior Dominic Molise dreams of making it in the major leagues as a pitcher and of making out with his best friend's sister, in this witty and poignant story set in the Depression.

Farmer, Nancy. *The Ear, the Eye, and the Arm.* Orchard, 1994. **F**

When General Matsika's three children are kidnapped after they leave the safety of their armed compound, their mother hires the best detective team available in 2194 Zimbabwe—the appropriately named mutant partners the Ear, the Eye, and the Arm.

———. *A Girl Named Disaster.* Orchard, 1996. **F**

When her family arranges her marriage to a cruel man with three wives, Nhamo escapes by canoe to seek a better future.

———. *The House of the Scorpion.* Atheneum, 2002. **F**

Matt is a clone, no better than an animal, but one who unlike the others has his brain left intact by order of El Patron. What could El Patron want from Matt?

———. *The Sea of Trolls.* Atheneum, 2004. **F**

When the Northmen invade Great Britain in 793, 11-year-old Jack and his 5-year-old sister, Lucy, are taken as slaves and are involved in a series of adventures with trolls, dragons, magic, and a very angry Berserker girl.

Farrell, Jeanette. *Invisible Allies: Microbes That Shape Our Lives.* Farrar, Straus & Giroux, 2005. **NF**

This lively examination of the beneficial and necessary microbes in our bodies traces a lunch consisting of a cheese sandwich and a chocolate bar from beginning to end.

——. *Invisible Enemies: Stories of Infectious Disease.* Farrar, Straus & Giroux, 1998. **NF**
This is a fascinating account of the behaviors, treatments, and control of seven deadly diseases and the scientists who tamed them.

Fast, Howard. *The Hessian.* Morrow, 1972. **F**
War is the awful villain and two boys are among the victims in this quiet, powerful novel of the American Revolution.

Feelings, Tom. *The Middle Passage: White Ships/ Black Cargo.* Dial, 1995. **NF**
Feelings's heartrending illustrations document the horrific journey of slaves from Africa to America.

——. *Soul Looks Back in Wonder.* Dial, 1993. **NF**
The poetry of 13 African Americans, including Maya Angelou and Langston Hughes, complement Feelings's beautiful illustrations.

Feinstein, John. *A Season on the Brink: A Year with Bob Knight and the Indiana Hoosiers.* Macmillan, 1986. **NF**
The 1985–86 season of controversial coach Bob Knight and the Indiana Hoosiers is chronicled in detail.

Feintuch, David. *Midshipman's Hope.* Warner, 1994. **F**
Through a series of freak accidents and tragic illnesses, 16-year-old Midshipman Nicholas Seafort finds himself in charge of the space vessel U.N.S. *Hibernia.*

Feldbaum, Carl B., and Ronald J. Bee. *Looking the Tiger in the Eye: Confronting the Nuclear Threat.* Harper & Row, 1988. **F**
This passionate and clear look at the atom bomb examines the way it has changed civilization—and, perhaps, will end it.

Ferazani, Larry. *Rescue Squad.* Morrow, 1974. **NF**
Being a member of a fire department rescue squad with all the joys and tragedies can lead to enormous emotional and physical costs.

Ferris, Jean. *Across the Grain.* Farrar, Straus & Giroux, 1990. **F**
Will is dragged from his beloved beach to live in the desert with his irresponsible older sister, where he adjusts with the help of new friends.

——. *Bad.* Farrar, Straus & Giroux, 1998. **F**
Sixteen-year-old Dallas spends six months in a girls' rehabilitation center.

——. *Eight Seconds.* Harcourt, 2000. **F**
John's 18th summer is complicated by his struggle to understand his feelings toward Kit, a star bull rider whom he meets at rodeo camp.

——. *Invincible Summer.* Farrar, Straus & Giroux, 1987. **F**
While hospitalized with leukemia, Robin and Rick fall in love.

——. *Love among the Walnuts.* Harcourt Brace, 1998. **F**
A chicken in a coma? Alexander Huntington-Ackerman can barely cope with the serious stuff, like his diabolical uncles who try to bump off his parents and steal the family fortune.

——. *Of Sound Mind.* Farrar, Straus & Giroux, 2001. **F**
High school senior Theo is tired of being the "ears" for his deaf parents, especially when it begins to interfere with his plans for college and the rest of his life.

——. *Once upon a Marigold.* Harcourt, 2002. **F**
Christian decides to leave his foster father, Ed the Troll, and his life in the forest in order to meet the princess he has observed through his telescope.

Ferris, Louanne. *I'm Done Crying.* Evans, 1969. **NF**
For Louanne Ferris it takes a strong determination to raise a family in a hopeless ghetto neighborhood; but it takes more than determination to survive as a nurse in the inhuman world of a ghetto hospital.

Ferris, Timothy, and Carolyn Zecca. *Spaceshots: The Beauty of Nature beyond Earth.* Pantheon, 1984. **NF**
Spectacular photographs (with textual explanation) taken from space picture Earth, the moon, and a variety of planets, stars, and galaxies.

Ferry, Charles. *Binge.* Daisy Hill, 1992. **F**
When his drunken joy ride kills several teenagers, 18-year-old Weldon must face the consequences.

——. *Raspberry One.* Houghton Mifflin, 1983. **F**
Two young men, both of whom fall in love before shipping out to the Pacific to fight the Japanese, return home changed and scarred by their war experiences.

Feuer, Elizabeth. *Paper Doll.* Farrar, Straus & Giroux, 1990. **F**
An amputee, Leslie has centered on becoming a concert violinist, but now her developing relationship with Jeff is forcing her to reevaluate her choices.

Fields, Jeff. *A Cry of Angels.* Atheneum, 1974. **F**
The antics, adventures, and friendships of an assorted bunch of misfits are woven into a compelling story of a man's capacity for cruelty and love.

Fienberg, Anna. *Borrowed Light.* Delacorte, 2000. **F**

Sixteen-year-old Callisto May, a student of astronomy, sees herself as a moon—a borrower of light rather than a source of it—and wonders how she can manage her family problems and her unexpected pregnancy.

Fine, Judylaine. *Afraid to Ask: A Book for Families to Share about Cancer.* Lothrop, 1986. **NF**

The terrifying subject of cancer is dispassionately explained in Fine's description of the causes, treatment, types, and emotional impact on victims and their families.

Fink, Ida. *A Scrap of Time, and Other Stories.* Pantheon, 1987. **F**

Unforgettable stories evoke the horrific time when Polish Jews wait and suffer while the Nazis destroy their lives.

Finnegan, William. *Crossing the Line: A Year in the Land of Apartheid.* Harper & Row, 1986. **NF**

While teaching in a "colored" high school in South Africa, Finnegan, a white Californian, witnessed extreme racial segregation and educational repression.

Finney, Jack. *Time and Again.* Simon & Schuster, 1970. **F**

As part of a top-secret government project, Simon Morley steps out of the 20th century to take up residence in the New York of 1882, where he becomes involved in blackmail and romance.

Fisher, Antwone Quenton, and Mim Eichler Rivas. *Finding Fish.* Morrow, 2001. **NF**

Once an abused foster child and a homeless teen, Antwone relates his struggle to attain successful manhood and find his lost family.

Fisher, Catherine. *The Oracle Betrayed.* Greenwillow, 2004. **F**

The Archon sacrifices himself to the scorpion to bring rain to his drought-stricken land, but not before warning shy Mirany, the new Bearer, that treachery and deceit are all around.

Flake, Sharon G. *Bang!* Hyperion, 2005. **F**

Mann, still mourning the senseless shooting of his younger brother, is left in the wilderness by his father in order to become a "man."

———. *The Skin I'm In.* Hyperion, 1998. **F**

Her extremely dark complexion makes 13-year-old Malleka the butt of jokes and an outcast—until her teacher shows her that she can accept herself.

———. *Who Am I without Him? Short Stories about Girls and the Boys in Their Lives.* Hyperion, 2004. **F**

Ten short stories focus on the sometimes-difficult relationships experienced by African American teen girls.

Flanigan, Sara. *Alice.* St. Martin's, 1988. **F**

A nearly deaf, epileptic teen who has been abused by her family, Alice blossoms after two young neighbors rescue her from a locked shed in rural Georgia.

Fleischman, John. *Phineas Gage: A Gruesome but True Story about Brain Science.* Houghton Mifflin, 2002. **NF**

In 1848 a tamping iron blasted through the head of Phineas Gage, foreman on a railroad construction gang, leaving him alive but mentally and emotionally changed, and providing new insights into the workings of the human brain.

Fleischman, Paul. *The Borning Room.* HarperCollins, 1991. **F**

Life and death, triumph and tragedy, occur throughout generations of an Ohio farm family in their "borning room."

———. *Bull Run.* HarperCollins, 1993. **F**

Sixteen individuals voice their hopes and fears in this interwoven collage of "snapshots" set during the first battle of the Civil War.

———. *Dateline: Troy.* Candlewick, 1996. **NF**

History comes full circle in a retelling of the Trojan War accompanied by newspaper clippings of current events that show how history does indeed repeat itself.

———. *Joyful Noise: Poems for Two Voices.* Harper & Row, 1988. **NF**

"Book Lice" and the other delightful two-voice poems in this collection are direct, rhythmic, and great for reading aloud.

———. *Mind's Eye.* Holt, 1999. **F**

Two unlikely roommates in a nursing home—one 16 and paralyzed, the other elderly and blind—use one another's imaginations to embark upon a virtual trip to Italy.

———. *Seedfolks.* HarperCollins, 1997. **F**

Urban neighbors splintered by race, economy, ethnicity, and age join hands in an empty lot to make a garden.

———. *Seek.* Cricket, 2001. **F**

The sounds of Rob's life—a radio DJ, Mexican soap operas, and his grandparents' storytelling—make up this compelling radio play.

———. *Whirligig.* Holt, 1998. **F**

After killing a girl when driving drunk, Brent Bishop learns a lot about himself and life when he's forced to pay for his crime by traveling to the four corners of the United States to build whirligigs in her memory.

———. *Zap.* Candlewick, 2005. **F**

Dead bodies, a sarcastic performance artist, an English country manor, bored Russians, Richard III, scheming writers, and artificial buttocks are just a few things found in this book comprising seven mini-plays within a play.

Fleischman, Sid. *The Abracadabra Kid: A Writer's Life.* Greenwillow, 1996. **NF**

From budding vaudevillian-type magician to popular writer of children's books—Fleischman describes his journey with humor and warmth.

———. *Escape! The Story of the Great Houdini.* Greenwillow, 2006. **NF**

A famous teen book author and fellow magician wrote this spellbinding biography of the amazing Harry Houdini.

Fleming, Candace. *Ben Franklin's Almanac: Being a True Account of the Good Gentleman's Life.* Atheneum, 2003. **NF**

Modeled on his own *Poor Richard's Almanac,* this is an original biography of the printer, writer, scientist, statesman, inventor, and the only founding father who signed all four of the documents that are the basis of our country today.

———. *Our Eleanor: A Scrapbook Look at Eleanor Roosevelt's Remarkable Life.* Atheneum, 2005. **NF**

This scrapbook-format biography of Eleanor Roosevelt covers her childhood, marriage, motherhood, and years as First Lady, highlighting her accomplishments as an astute politician, writer, social activist, delegate to the United Nations, and champion of those in need.

Fletcher, Susan. *Alphabet of Dreams.* Atheneum, 2006. **F**

Mitra sells her brother's ability to dream the future, leading them to one of the three magi as he seeks the birth of the king foretold in the stars.

———. *Flight of the Dragon Kyn.* Atheneum, 1993. **F**

In a story set in the same fantasy world as *Dragon's Milk,* 15-year-old Kara is being forced by the king to use her gift of calling birds to help him destroy the dragons who once saved her life.

———. *Shadow Spinner.* Atheneum, 1998. **F**

Crippled Marjan is brought in secret to the sultan's harem to replenish Scheherazade's supply of the tales she tells the sultan so that he won't have her killed.

Flinn, Alex. *Breathing Underwater.* HarperCollins, 2001. **F**

After Nick's girlfriend has a restraining order issued against him, he is forced to come to grips with his anger and low self-esteem.

———. *Nothing to Lose.* HarperTempest, 2004. **F**

What happened the night that Michael Daye joined the carny life? Now that his mother is on trial for murder, perhaps the truth will come out.

Fluek, Toby Knobel. *Memories of My Life in a Polish Village, 1930–1949.* Knopf, 1990. **NF**

Intimate drawings and paintings portray Jewish life in Poland in the years before, during, and after the Russian and German World War II occupations.

Fogelin, Adrian. *Crossing Jordan.* Peachtree, 2000. **F**

When African American Jemmie moves in next door, Cass's father is horrified and builds a fence separating the houses, but despite their families' prejudices, the girls form a friendship based on running and become the "chocolate milk" team.

Fogle, Bruce. *The Encyclopedia of the Cat.* DK, 1997. **NF**

This complete and colorful guide to the history, lore, and literature of cats includes many photos as well as tips on cat care.

Ford, Michael Thomas. *100 Questions and Answers about AIDS: A Guide for Young People.* Macmillan, 1992. **NF**

With reliable and up-to-date research, Ford presents candid and comprehensive answers to questions about AIDS.

———. *The Voices of AIDS: Twelve Unforgettable People Talk about How AIDS Has Changed Their Lives.* Morrow, 1995. **NF**

Men and women tell what it is like to be HIV-positive, to have AIDS, or to love someone confronting the disease.

Ford, Richard. *Quest for the Faradawn.* Delacorte, 1982. **F**

Nab, raised by forest animals from birth, begins a quest with Beth and several animal companions to save the world from destruction by mankind.

Forman, James D. *A Ballad for Hogskin Hill.* Farrar, Straus & Giroux, 1979. **F**
Deciding that big city life is not for him, David Kincaid returns to Kentucky, where he helps his father and grandfather do battle against a powerful coal company.

———. *Becca's Story.* Scribner, 1992. **F**
Becca can't decide which of her two beaus to choose—serious, secure Alex or exciting, unpredictable Charlie—but the Civil War takes away her choice.

Foster, Rory C. *Dr. Wildlife: The Crusade of a Northwoods Veterinarian.* Watts, 1985. **NF**
Founder of a hospital for orphaned or injured wild animals, Dr. Foster shows not only his reverence for animal life but also his struggles with the government to establish his practice.

Fox, Paula. *Monkey Island.* Orchard, 1991. **F**
Awakening in a welfare hotel to find his mother gone, 11-year-old Clay takes to the streets of New York City and finds shelter with two homeless men who help him survive.

———. *One-Eyed Cat.* Bradbury, 1984. **F**
Sneaking out one night, young Ned Wallace shoots the air rifle his father has forbidden him to use and shortly thereafter becomes guilt-ridden at the appearance of a one-eyed cat.

Fradin, Dennis Brindell. *Bound for the North Star: True Stories of Fugitive Slaves.* Clarion, 2000. **NF**
These are the stories of 15 fugitive slaves who escaped to the North via the Underground Railroad and other routes.

———. *The Planet Hunters: The Search for Other Worlds.* Margaret K. McElderry, 1997. **NF**
Are we alone in space? Explore the universe with those who have sought answers and contact since AD 100.

Fradin, Dennis Brindell, and Judith Bloom Fradin. *Fight On! Mary Church Terrell's Battle for Integration.* Clarion, 2003. **NF**
Mary Church Terrell was an indomitable fighter against all forms of discrimination who in her late 80s conducted a successful campaign to integrate D.C. restaurants and movie theaters.

———. *Ida B. Wells: Mother of the Civil Rights Movement.* Clarion, 2000. **NF**
Ida B. Wells, born a slave, was a ferocious fighter against lynching and an early leader in the fight for civil rights.

Fradin, Judith Bloom, and Dennis Brindell Fradin. *5,000 Miles to Freedom: Ellen and William Craft's Flight from Slavery.* National Geographic, 2006. **NF**
In this true story, a couple goes to extraordinary lengths to escape slavery, eventually helping others by sharing their experiences.

Francke, Linda Bird. *The Ambivalence of Abortion.* Random House, 1978. **NF**
Adults and teenagers, women and men, convey their honest feelings about the abortion experience and its effect on their lives.

Franco, Betsy, ed. *Things I Have to Tell You: Poems and Writing by Teenage Girls.* Candlewick, 2001. **NF**
This collection of stories and poems by teen girls reveals the truth about boyfriends, body image, and being female.

———, ed. *You Hear Me? Poems and Writing by Teenage Boys.* Candlewick, 2000. **NF**
Teenage guys tell it like they see it in this collection.

Frank, Anne. *The Diary of a Young Girl: The Definitive Edition.* Doubleday, 1995. **NF**
This new edition contains the complete diary—some of which was not published in the original work.

Frank, E. R. *America.* Atheneum, 2002. **F**
A young man named America gets "lost" in the social welfare system and, after a series of foster homes, hospitals, and suicide attempts, meets a caring psychiatrist who refuses to give up on him.

———. *Friction.* Atheneum, 2003. **F**
An innocent young girl's budding sexuality contributes to the terrible confusion—and ultimately to tragic consequences—when a new classmate begins an insidious campaign to portray their popular teacher as a pervert.

———. *Wrecked.* Atheneum, 2005. **F**
Sixteen-year-old Anna develops post-traumatic stress disorder after being in a car accident in which she feels responsible for killing her brother's girlfriend and seriously injuring her best friend.

Frank, Hillary. *Better Than Running at Night.* Houghton Mifflin, 2002. **F**
Native New Yorker Ellie Yelinsky's freshman year at art school turns into an unexpectedly strange and wonderful experience, as she "dances with the Devil" and learns that painting is more about craft than it is about angst.

Frank, Mitch. *Understanding the Holy Land: Answering Questions about the Israeli-Palestinian Conflict.* Viking, 2005. **NF**
Using a question-and-answer format, the complexities of the Israeli-Palestinian conflict are examined.

Fraustino, Lisa Rowe. *Ash.* Orchard, 1995. **F**
When Ash leaves for college, his younger brother, Wes, assumes that Ash will succeed brilliantly—but Ash suddenly becomes an odd stranger.

Frazier, Walt, and Ira Berkow. *Rockin' Steady: A Guide to Basketball and Cool.* Prentice-Hall, 1974. **NF**
"Clyde" explains how to get it all together and be cool on and off the basketball court.

Freedman, Russell. *Babe Didrikson Zaharias: The Making of a Champion.* Clarion, 1999. **NF**
This biography tells the story of one of the greatest female athletes of the century—Olympic gold medalist, basketball star, and championship golfer Babe Didrickson Zaharias.

———. *Eleanor Roosevelt: A Life of Discovery.* Clarion, 1993. **NF**
A compelling photo-biography of Eleanor Roosevelt relates the remarkable story of a shy, lonely girl who grows up to be a powerful force in the fight for world peace and equality and an inspiration to millions of people.

———. *Franklin Delano Roosevelt.* Clarion, 1990. **NF**
The complex and controversial life and times of FDR are revealed in Freedman's powerful photo-biography.

———. *Freedom Walkers: The Story of the Montgomery Bus Boycott.* Holiday House, 2006. **NF**
Through photos and eyewitness accounts, Freedman draws readers close to the dramatic 1955 Montgomery bus boycott and the ordinary people who participated.

———. *Give Me Liberty! The Story of the Declaration of Independence.* Holiday House, 2000. **NF**
From the night of the Boston Tea Party to July of 1776, events rolled forward which were to change the world and unite a nation.

———. *In Defense of Liberty: The Story of America's Bill of Rights.* Holiday House, 2003. **NF**
The first ten amendments to the U.S. Constitution listed the individual freedoms guaranteed Americans, but court cases and social changes have altered our understanding of these freedoms over the years.

———. *Indian Chiefs.* Holiday House, 1987. **NF**
Words and pictures tell the stories of six legendary Native American chiefs who are forced off their lands by westward expansion and the United States government.

———. *Indian Winter.* Holiday House, 1992. **NF**
Paintings by Karl Bodmer and journal entries by German prince Maximilian immerse you in their 1833–34 winter stay-over in Missouri River Indian country.

———. *Kids at Work: Lewis Hine and the Crusade against Child Labor.* Clarion, 1994. **NF**
Through the impressive photography of reformer-photographer Hine and direct writing, Freedman chronicles the state of child labor in early 20th-century America.

———. *The Life and Death of Crazy Horse.* Holiday House, 1996. **NF**
This vivid portrait of Crazy Horse and his times traces his development from a shy, sensitive young warrior to the brave Sioux leader at the Battle of Little Big Horn.

———. *Lincoln: A Photobiography.* Clarion, 1987. **NF**
This skillfully written, appealing overview of Lincoln's life from boyhood to death, is accompanied by carefully chosen photographs and prints.

———. *Martha Graham: A Dancer's Life.* Clarion, 1998. **NF**
An eloquent photo-biography of a woman who, after being told she was too old, too short, too heavy, and too plain to become a professional dancer, goes on to revolutionize the world of modern dance through determination and talent.

———. *The Voice That Challenged a Nation: Marian Anderson and the Struggle for Equal Rights.* Clarion, 2004. **NF**
This biography of the great singer Marian Anderson highlights her role in bringing the injustice of segregation in the arts to national awareness.

———. *The Wright Brothers: How They Invented the Airplane.* Holiday House, 1991. **NF**
Freedman tells the fascinating story of how two self-taught bicycle mechanics solve the problems that had baffled generations of scientists and engineers.

Freedman, Samuel G. *Small Victories: The Real World of a Teacher, Her Students, and Their High School.* Harper & Row, 1990. **NF**
The neglected students at Stewart Park High School in Manhattan and their caring teacher, Jessica Siegel, find a way to beat the odds and make a future.

Freeman, Suzanne. *The Cuckoo's Child.*
Greenwillow, 1996. **F**
In Beirut, Mia longed for a normal American life, but after her parents are lost at sea, she finds life in Tennessee a real challenge.

Freemantle, Brian. *Good-bye to an Old Friend.*
Putnam, 1973. **F**
A Russian space scientist appears to defect to England, but a British investigator, a scruffy and intelligent civil servant, has his doubts.

Freese, Barbara. *Coal: A Human History.*
Perseus, 2003. **NF**
The historic, scientific, economic, political, cultural, and literary aspects of coal are examined in this fascinating book that also highlights the current debates about energy consumption, developing nations, and global warming.

Fremon, Celeste. *Father Greg and the Homeboys: The Extraordinary Journey of Father Greg Boyle and His Work with the Latino Gangs of East L.A.* Hyperion, 1995. **NF**
Through his work with L.A. gang members, Father Greg proves that one person can make a difference.

French, Albert. *Billy.* Viking, 1993. **F**
In 1930 Mississippi, it is punishable by death for a black to kill a white, even if it is an accident—and even if the "killer" is only ten years old.

Fretz, Sada. *Going Vegetarian: A Guide for Teenagers.* Morrow, 1983. **NF**
This complete guide includes the reasons why people become vegetarians and how to plan a healthy, meatless diet, along with wonderful recipes.

Frey, Darcy. *The Last Shot: City Streets, Basketball Dreams.* Houghton Mifflin, 1994. **NF**
Journalist Frey follows the lives of four hoop stars of Abraham Lincoln High School as they pursue their dreams of athletic scholarships.

Freymann-Weyr, Garret. *My Heartbeat.*
Houghton Mifflin, 2002. **F**
Ellen's question about her brother's relationship with his best friend James changes everything in this tight, three-way friendship.

Friedman, Ina R. *The Other Victims: First-Person Stories of Non-Jews Persecuted by the Nazis.* Houghton Mifflin, 1990. **NF**
Would you be considered "unworthy of life"? Hitler's persecution extended beyond Jews; those often forgotten victims are remembered in these compelling first-person narratives.

Friedman, Myra. *Buried Alive: The Biography of Janis Joplin.* Morrow, 1973. **NF**
Janis Joplin, the legendary rock singer of the 1960s, has a passion for life but is also a tortured and driven woman.

Friedman, Philip. *Rage.* Atheneum, 1972. **F**
Dying, as is his son, from exposure to experimental nerve gas, Dan Logan uses the last reserves of his strength to take revenge.

Friel, Brian. *Philadelphia, Here I Come!* Farrar, Straus & Giroux, 1966. **NF**
Gar's last night at home, as dramatized in this contemporary play, exposes the lack of communication between generations.

Friesen, Gayle. *Janey's Girl.* Kids Can Press, 1998. **F**
On a trip to her mother's childhood home, 14-year-old Claire tries to discover the secrets that have isolated her and her mother from the family, especially from her father.

Froese, Deborah. *Out of the Fire.* Sumach, 2002. **F**
A careless moment at a teen bonfire party forces Dayle to reevaluate her values and her relationships with her friends and family.

Frost, Helen. *The Braid.* Farrar, Straus & Giroux, 2006. **F**
In tightly structured, braided poems, two sisters tell of their difficult separation when one leaves Scotland for a better life in Canada in the mid-1800s.

————. *Keesha's House.* Frances Foster, 2003. **F**
Joe, whose aunt took him into her house when he was young and in need, now owns that same house and helps others kids with their own problems in this story told through poetry.

Fuller, John G. *The Ghost of Flight 401.* Berkley, 1976. **NF**
Ghosts of crew members killed in the 1972 Eastern Airlines Everglades disaster haunt the crews and passengers of other flights.

————. *Incident at Exeter: The Story of Unidentified Flying Objects over America Today.* Putnam, 1966. **NF**
A journalist investigates unexplained UFO phenomena.

————. *The Poison That Fell from the Sky.* Random House, 1977. **NF**
Fuller dramatically reports the 1976 accident at a chemical factory that left a small Italian town permanently poisoned and its evacuated inhabitants physically and emotionally scarred.

Fusco, Kimberly Newton. *Tending to Grace.* Knopf, 2004. **F**
Cornelia Thornhill, silent because of a speech impediment, discovers she may have something to say when she is left with her Great-Aunt Agatha so her mother can head off to Vegas with a new boyfriend.

Fussell, Samuel Wilson. *Muscle: Confessions of an Unlikely Bodybuilder.* Poseidon, 1991. **F**
His muscles are like iron and ripple under the stage lights; steroids have made him perfect. But something is wrong!

Gaan, Margaret. *Little Sister.* Dodd, Mead, 1983. **F**
Little Sister, a third-generation Chinese American, visits Shanghai at the beginning of a revolution and learns about her family from family members.

Gaiman, Neil. *Anansi Boys.* Morrow, 2005. **F**
Everyone's parents are annoying—even when they're dead. Oh, and so are the gods.

———. *Coraline.* HarperCollins, 2002. **F**
One day, while exploring her family's new home, Coraline wanders down the wrong corridor.

———. *Stardust.* Avon, 1999. **F**
Tristan's quest for a fallen star brings him adventure, love, and encounters with a variety of magical creatures.

Gaiman, Neil, and Terry Pratchett. *Good Omens: The Nice and Accurate Prophecies of Agnes Nutter, Witch.* Workman, 1990. **F**
In this zany romp, living on Earth is so much fun that Crowley, the demon, and Aziraphale, the angel, disobey orders and team up to prevent the Apocalypse.

Gaines, Ernest J. *The Autobiography of Miss Jane Pittman.* Dial, 1971. **F**
Born a slave in Louisiana before the Civil War, Jane Pittman lives to witness the struggle in the 1960s for civil rights in this fictional autobiography that reflects the courage and fortitude of America's blacks.

———. *A Gathering of Old Men.* Knopf, 1983. **F**
When a white man is killed by an African American in Louisiana, more than a dozen aging black men and one young white woman each confess to the sheriff, each with a different long-standing motive.

———. *A Lesson before Dying.* Knopf, 1993. **F**
Jefferson, a black youth likened to a hog and sentenced to death for a crime he did not commit, must learn to regain his self-esteem and face death with dignity.

Gaines, William M., and Albert E. Feldstein, eds. *The Ridiculously Expensive MAD: A Collection of the Worst from 17 Years of MAD.* World, 1969. **NF**
MAD is 17 years old and this is a collection of the best of the worst from the magazine which takes on the Establishment with vigor and revels in its inanities.

Gale, Jay. *A Young Man's Guide to Sex.* Holt, Rinehart and Winston, 1984. **NF**
A comprehensive and explicit guide to sex and sexuality, written specifically for young men.

Gallagher, Hugh Gregory. *FDR's Splendid Deception.* Dodd, Mead, 1985. **NF**
New insights into Roosevelt's life are provided as Gallagher reveals the way in which FDR refused to admit or expose his physical handicap—paralysis resulting from polio.

Gallery, Daniel V. *Stand by-y-y to Start Engines.* Norton, 1966. **F**
Ensign Willie Wigglesworth is the ringleader of above-deck monkey-business in a series of salty anecdotes about life aboard the atomic carrier *Guadalcanal.*

Gallo, Donald R., ed. *No Easy Answers: Short Stories about Teenagers Making Tough Choices.* Delacorte, 1997. **F**
Teens face tough ethical and moral choices in this collection of 16 stories.

———, ed. *On the Fringe.* Dial, 2001. **F**
Eleven outstanding young adult authors contribute riveting stories as current as today's headlines.

———, ed. *Sixteen: Short Stories by Outstanding Writers for Young Adults.* Delacorte, 1984. **F**
School, friendship, family, and love are all found within this unusual collection of humorous and serious short stories.

———, ed. *Speaking for Ourselves: Autobiographical Sketches by Notable Authors of Books for Young Adults.* National Council of Teachers of English, 1990. **NF**
Popular young adult authors, from Lloyd Alexander to Paul Zindel, write brief sketches about their lives and work.

———, ed. *Visions: Nineteen Short Stories by Outstanding Writers for Young Adults.* Delacorte, 1987. **F**
Stories of youthful discoveries, among them, Richard Peck's "Shadows," in which an orphan learns about love, and Todd Strasser's "On the Bridge," in which Seth learns about betrayal from a friend.

Galloway, Gregory. *As Simple as Snow.* Putnam, 2005. **F**

High school student Anastasia Cayne disappears, leaving behind a neatly placed dress near a hole in the ice.

Galloway, Priscilla. *Truly Grim Tales.* Delacorte, 1995. **F**

Not for the faint of heart! Eight familiar fairy tales are twisted into sinister, macabre stories.

Gantos, Jack. *Hole in My Life.* Farrar, Straus & Giroux 2002. **NF**

This compelling story by the prize-winning author of books for children and teens describes how, as a teen himself, he helped smuggle hash and was sent to prison, where he did his time and decided on a different life for himself.

———. *The Love Curse of the Rumbaughs.* Farrar, Straus & Giroux, 2006. **F**

Loving your mother is a blessing; loving her so much you feel the need to perform taxidermy on her is a curse.

Garden, Nancy. *Annie on My Mind.* Farrar, Straus & Giroux, 1982. **F**

Lisa and Annie meet at New York's Metropolitan Museum of Art, fall in love, and then find that a public declaration is too threatening to their friends and relatives.

Garfield, Brian. *The Paladin.* Simon & Schuster, 1979. **F**

A 15-year-old boy, recruited by Winston Churchill to be his personal secret agent, is involved in murder, assassination, and sabotage on both sides of the front lines in this World War II novel.

———. *Recoil.* Morrow, 1977. **F**

With his government-manufactured cover blown and syndicate men closing in, a former star government witness decides to turn the tables on his pursuers.

Garland, Sherry. *Indio.* Harcourt Brace, 1995. **F**

Ipa-tah-chi survives an Apache raid on her pueblo. Later, on her wedding day, strange white-skinned men riding horses capture her. Can she escape?

———. *Shadow of the Dragon.* Harcourt Brace, 1993. **F**

Sixteen-year-old Danny Vo must resolve the conflict between his recently immigrated Vietnamese cousin, a Vietnamese gang, Danny's girlfriend, and her skinhead brother's gang.

———. *Song of the Buffalo Boy.* Harcourt Brace Jovanovich, 1992. **F**

Running away to Ho Chi Minh City with the boy she loves after being promised in marriage to a menacing old man, 17-year-old Loi tries to find out about her American soldier father.

Garner, Eleanor Ramrath. *Eleanor's Story: An American Girl in Hitler's Germany.* Peachtree, 1999. **NF**

Trapped in Germany for the duration of World War II, an American girl and her family endure the war's privations and terrors.

Gaskins, Pearl Fuyo, ed. *What Are You? Voices of Mixed Race Young People.* Holt, 1999. **NF**

Forty-five young people explore being mixed-race in essays and poems both lighthearted and bitter.

Gaylin, Willard. *In the Service of Their Country: War Resisters in Prison.* Viking, 1970. **NF**

Six imprisoned war resisters tell their stories in compelling case histories as recorded by Dr. Gaylin, a psychiatrist.

Gedge, Pauline. *Child of the Morning.* Dial, 1977. **F**

Reared by her Pharaoh father to assume his throne upon his death, Hatshepsut—a real historical figure—has to contend with her weak half-brother before she can realize her dream.

Gee, Maurice. *The Champion.* Simon & Schuster, 1993. **F**

The arrival of an African American soldier in a small New Zealand community during World War II changes the lives of 12-year-old Rex and his friends forever.

Gelman, Rita Golden. *Inside Nicaragua: Young People's Dreams and Fears.* Watts, 1988. **F**

The fear and danger surrounding the war between the Sandinistas and the contras are recorded through the lives of Nicaragua's youth.

Gerani, Gary, and Paul H. Schulman. *Fantastic Television.* Harmony, 1977. **NF**

This pictorial history of the best of 1950s and 1960s television serials and science fiction includes *Star Trek, Batman, The Twilight Zone,* and *Superman.*

Geras, Adele. *Troy.* Harcourt, 2001. **F**

Told from the point of view of the women of Troy, this modern version of the story portrays the last weeks of the Trojan War, complete with gods and goddesses who find ways to stir up trouble.

———. *Voyage.* Atheneum, 1983. **F**

A group of young Jewish immigrants share love, friendship, hope, and fears during their two-week voyage in steerage to America, the land of freedom.

Gibbons, Kaye. *Charms for an Easy Life.*
Putnam, 1993. **F**

In the years before and during World War II, Margaret comes of age with the help of a self-educated and highly successful doctor/grandmother and a mother in search of the perfect man.

———. *Ellen Foster.* Algonquin, 1987. **F**

After her mother's untimely death, young Ellen must survive despite her abusive father and other relatives who want no part of her.

Giblin, James Cross. *Charles A. Lindbergh: A Human Hero.* Clarion, 1997. **NF**

"Lucky Lindy" becomes an American hero when he makes the first nonstop transatlantic flight, but he falls into disgrace after being accused of sympathizing with the Nazis.

———. *Good Brother, Bad Brother: The Story of Edwin Booth and John Wilkes Booth.* Clarion, 2005. **NF**

This is the story of two brothers, Edwin Booth and John Wilkes Booth; both were famous actors, and one assassinated Abraham Lincoln.

———. *When Plague Strikes: The Black Death, Smallpox, AIDS.* HarperCollins, 1995. **NF**

This eye-opening account of three of humankind's most serious epidemics is told with compassion and depth.

Giddings, Robert. *The War Poets.* Orion, 1988. **NF**

The work of a variety of World War I poets, many of whom died in that conflict, is reinforced with illustrations, biographical notes, and a brief history of "the war to end all wars."

Gies, Miep, and Alison Leslie Gold. *Anne Frank Remembered: The Story of the Woman Who Helped to Hide the Frank Family.* Simon & Schuster, 1987. **NF**

The story of quiet personal courage by the woman who hid the Frank family and retrieved Anne's diary so that the world would never forget is itself unforgettable—and inspiring.

Giff, Patricia Reilly. *Nory Ryan's Song.* Delacorte, 2000. **F**

Twelve-year-old Nory fights to survive the potato famine with her family on the west coast of Ireland in the mid-1800s, resulting in a difficult choice between staying with the land she loves and going with her family to a better life in America.

———. *Pictures of Hollis Woods.* Wendy Lamb, 2002. **F**

An artistic foster child who has bounced from place to place seeks a real home and recalls the tragedy of the previous summer.

Giles, Gail. *Shattering Glass.* Roaring Brook, 2002. **F**

Rob, popular and used to getting his way, decides to make Simon Glass, the class geek, popular, but he doesn't count on the iron will beneath Simon's pushover exterior.

———. *What Happened to Cass McBride?* Little, Brown, 2006. **F**

In this taut, psychologically rich thriller Cass McBride and her tormentor, who has buried her alive, form a unique and surprising bond.

Gilman, Dorothy. *The Clairvoyant Countess.* Doubleday, 1975. **F**

Exotic Madame Karitska and her psychic powers help the police handle some of their more distressing dilemmas: robbery, murder, voodoo possession, and a missing person.

———. *The Unexpected Mrs. Pollifax.* Doubleday, 1966. **F**

Volunteering her services to the CIA the irrepressible Mrs. Pollifax accepts a job as courier to Mexico where her safe assignment suddenly becomes sinister.

Gilmore, Kate. *Enter Three Witches.* Houghton Mifflin, 1990. **F**

Sixteen-year-old Bren finds living with witches hard enough, but how can he prevent his girlfriend from discovering their existence?

———. *The Exchange Student.* Houghton Mifflin, 1999. **F**

The exchange student from another planet staying with Daria and her family shows an unusual interest in Daria's work with endangered species.

Gilstrap, John. *Nathan's Run.* HarperCollins, 1996. **F**

Having escaped from a juvenile detention center after killing a guard, 12-year-old Nathan is running for his life, searching for someone who will believe he really is a victim of circumstance.

Gingher, Marianne. *Bobby Rex's Greatest Hit.* Atheneum, 1986. **F**

A suggestive hit song by a small North Carolina town's heartthrob catapults its namesake, Pally Thompson, into the national limelight and passionate disavowal.

Giovanni, Nikki. *Gemini: An Extended Autobiographical Statement on My First Twenty-five Years of Being a Black Poet.* Bobbs-Merrill, 1972. **NF**

A dynamic young African American writer explores her life and times with the fierce intensity of a poet.

———. *My House: Poems.* Morrow, 1972. **NF**
A well-known African American author celebrates love in all its many facets with gentle, compelling immediacy.

———. *The Women and the Men.* Morrow, 1975. **NF**
Poems, from the heart and soul of a spirited young woman, that speak directly to the lives of young and old, women and men.

Girion, Barbara. *A Handful of Stars.* Scribner, 1981. **F**
Julie Meyers, 15, must learn to cope with epilepsy as her resentment mounts against the thoughtless cruelties of her family and friends.

———. *A Tangle of Roots.* Scribner, 1979. **F**
When her mother's unexpected death forces 16-year-old Beth Frankle to cope with grief and sorrow, her relationships with family and friends are affected.

Glass, Frankcina. *Marvin and Tige.* St. Martin's, 1977. **F**
Tige, an orphaned 11-year-old streetwise African American youth, and Marvin, a white alcoholic executive dropout, establish a friendship based on caring for and needing each other.

Glass, Linzi. *The Year the Gypsies Came.* Holt, 2006. **F**
Against the backdrop of anti-apartheid riots, a family of wanderers brings tragedy to a South African teen in this shattering story about lost innocence.

Glasser, Ronald J. *Ward 402.* Braziller, 1973. **NF**
While treating a child dying of leukemia, a young intern is forced to reexamine his attitudes and those of his colleagues toward their daily dealings with life and death.

Glenn, Mel. *Class Dismissed! High School Poems.* Clarion, 1982. **NF**
Glenn's poems, accompanied by photographs, mirror the agony and the ecstasy of high school as experienced by young people.

———. *Jump Ball: A Basketball Season in Poems.* Lodestar, 1997. **NF**
The rhythm of basketball permeates a series of poems that tell the story of the Tower High School team's winning season.

———. *My Friend's Got This Problem, Mr. Candler: High School Poems.* Clarion, 1991. **NF**
Poems both serious and funny express the thoughts and emotions of students and their families as they speak to a high school guidance counselor.

———. *Split Image: A Story in Poems.* HarperCollins, 2000. **F**
A story in poems about a young girl and her seemingly perfect life, told from the point of view of the people who thought they knew her.

———. *The Taking of Room 114: A Hostage Drama in Poems.* Lodestar, 1997. **NF**
First-person narrative poems focus on the last day of high school, when a distraught history teacher holds his seniors hostage.

———. *Who Killed Mr. Chippendale? A Mystery in Poems.* Lodestar, 1996. **NF**
A high-school English teacher's murder is witnessed, investigated, and solved in a series of clever poems.

Glover, Savion, and Bruce Weber. *Savion! My Life in Tap.* Morrow, 2000. **NF**
This colorful and inspiring biography chronicles the rise to fame of hugely talented, Tony Award–winning tapper Savion Glover.

Godden, Rumer. *Thursday's Children.* Viking, 1984. **F**
Neglected Doone Penny and his pampered older sister, Crystal, both strive to be the best in the competitive world of ballet.

Going, K. L. *Fat Kid Rules the World.* Putnam, 2003. **F**
Troy, struggling with obesity and depression, is rescued from a near suicide attempt by a chance encounter with a homeless teenage punk-rock icon who wants Troy to become a drummer for his new band.

———. *Saint Iggy.* Harcourt, 2006. **F**
Meth-damaged Iggy Corso faces many obstacles, including his expulsion from school, but he still yearns to make a difference.

Golden, Frederic. *The Trembling Earth: Probing and Predicting Quakes.* Scribner, 1983. **NF**
This clear and concise statement of knowledge concerning earthquakes is brief enough to be exciting but complete enough to cover the facts.

Goldman, E. M. *Getting Lincoln's Goat: An Elliot Armbruster Mystery.* Delacorte, 1995. **F**
When Lincoln High's beloved mascot—an old goat—disappears before the big football game, Elliot has the perfect opportunity to excel in a class assignment to learn about the world of private detectives.

Goldman, Peter, et al. *Charlie Company: What Vietnam Did to Us.* Morrow, 1983. **NF**
Men who served in Vietnam talk with poignancy, pain, and bitterness about their experiences.

Goldston, Robert. *Sinister Touches: The Secret War against Hitler.* Dial, 1982. **NF**
Dramatic accounts of covert activities and espionage during World War II read like a spy novel.

Goodall, Jane. *In the Shadow of Man.* Houghton Mifflin, 1971. **NF**
A young Englishwoman writes about the ten years she spent in Tanzania studying chimpanzees and describes with loving care each facet of their lives from birth to death.

Goodman, Alison. *Singing the Dogstar Blues.* Viking, 2002. **F**
Seventeen-year-old Joss consoles herself with her blues music as she faces an assassin, unruly demonstrators, a peevish professor, and intrusive high-tech security when she is selected as a partner by Mavkel, the first alien to study time travel at the Center for Neo-Historical Studies.

Gordon, Jacquie. *Give Me One Wish.* Norton, 1988. **F**
A mother tells the bittersweet story of the short life of her daughter Chris, who, despite being stricken with cystic fibrosis, eagerly participates in high school activities and in everything from slam dancing and trying pot to Christian fellowship.

Gordon, Ruth, ed. *Pierced by a Ray of Sun: Poems about the Times We Feel Alone.* HarperCollins, 1995. **NF**
In this unusually attractive anthology, world-famous poets reflect on the experience of feeling alone.

————, ed. *Under All Silences: Shades of Love; An Anthology of Poems.* Harper & Row, 1987. **NF**
From e. e. cummings and Sappho to Emily Dickinson and Yosan Akiko, this collection of poems celebrates the universal experience of love and passion.

Gordon, Sheila. *Waiting for the Rain.* Orchard, 1987. **F**
On a South African farm, Tengo, black, and Frikkie, white, forge a friendship that is later challenged by the injustices of apartheid.

Gordon, Sol, and Roger Conant. *You! The Psychology of Surviving and Enhancing Your Social Life, Love Life, Sex Life, School Life, Home Life, Work Life, Emotional Life, Creative Life, Spiritual Life, Style of Life, Life.* Quadrangle, 1975. **NF**
A positive, practical, lively approach to learning about "you." Comic book sections include "Ten Heavy Facts about Sex" and "Juice Use." Updated edition published as *The Teenage Survival Book* in 1981.

Gordon, Suzanne. *Off Balance: The Real World of Ballet.* Pantheon, 1983. **NF**
Behind the glittering facade of ballet lies a darker world of pain, rivalry, and exploitation.

Goro, Herb. *The Block.* Vintage, 1970. **NF**
The struggle for survival by young blacks in a decaying Bronx neighborhood is told in pictures and text to show the underlying pride and hope of people trapped in a hopeless situation.

Gottlieb, Lori. *Stick Figure: A Diary of My Former Self.* Simon & Schuster, 2000. **NF**
This diary chronicles one year in the life of a girl with anorexia.

Goulart, Ron. *What's Become of Screwloose? and Other Inquiries.* Scribner, 1971. **NF**
A computer turned author, a homicidal dishwasher, an evil pet dog who is also a cyborg, and a totally automated house are just four of the malign machines that populate these stories.

Gould, Steven. *Jumper.* TOR, 1992. **F**
Davy jumps for the first time when he escapes a beating by teleporting to the library. Now he's on the run from his alcoholic father, the police, and a secret government agency—but who can catch a jumper?

————. *Wildside.* TOR, 1996. **F**
Eighteen-year-old Charlie faces challenges and danger when he explores a pristine world he found on the other side of his barn door.

Gourley, Catherine. *Good Girl Work: Factories, Sweatshops, and How Women Changed Their Role in the American Workforce.* Millbrook, 1999. **NF**
This account of the industrial workforce of young girls and women in the 19th and early 20th centuries is often told in their own words.

Grace, Fran. *Branigan's Dog.* Bradbury, 1981. **F**
After the loss of his beloved dog, Casey Branigan is forced out of his self-imposed isolation and must confront the reason for his impulse to set fires.

Graham, Robin Lee, and Derek L. T. Gill. *Dove.* Harper & Row, 1972. **NF**
Setting out in his sloop *Dove* to encircle the globe, a 16-year-old boy finds adventure and romance.

Granatelli, Anthony. *They Call Me Mister 500.* Regnery, 1969. **NF**
Andy Granatelli, daring automobile racer and builder, tells how he made it through poverty and crashes to become a millionaire at age 30.

Grant, Cynthia D. *Mary Wolf.* Atheneum, 1995. F
Sixteen-year-old Mary longs for a normal life as her family travels the country aimlessly in their RV after her father loses his job.

————. *Phoenix Rising, or How to Survive Your Life.* Atheneum, 1989. F
Reading her sister Helen's diary of her yearlong bout with cancer helps Jenny cope with her feelings of pain and anger about Helen's death.

————. *Shadow Man.* Atheneum, 1992. F
Dead at 18, having wrapped his pickup around a tree while drunk, Gabriel McCloud is brought to "life" again through the first-person narratives of those who knew and loved him, including his pregnant girlfriend.

————. *Uncle Vampire.* Atheneum, 1993. F
Twins Carolyn and Honey have a family secret—there's a "vampire" in their midst.

Gratz, Alan. *Samurai Shortstop.* Dial, 2006. F
In 1890 Tokyo, 16-year-old Toyo uses traditional bushido training to improve his baseball game and comes to understand the place of samurai values in Japanese culture.

Gravelle, Karen, and Leslie Peterson. *Teenage Fathers.* Messner, 1992. NF
Thirteen teenage fathers talk about their parenthood with feelings that range from total alienation and irresponsibility to complete devotion to the children they have fathered.

Gray, Dianne E. *Holding Up the Earth.* Houghton Mifflin, 2000. F
Fourteen-year-old Hope visits her new foster mother's Nebraska farm and, through old letters, a diary, and stories, gets a vivid picture of the past in the voices of four girls her age who once lived there.

Gray, Martin, and Max Gallo. *For Those I Loved.* Little, Brown, 1972. NF
A Polish Jew survives the horrors of wartime Warsaw and a Nazi death camp only to be deprived of his well-earned peace and happiness by a cruel twist of fate.

Green, Connie Jordan. *The War at Home.* Margaret K. McElderry, 1989. F
Chauvinistic Virgil infuriates cousin Mattie when he comes to live with her family in Oak Ridge, Tennessee, during the secretive and security-ridden days of World War II.

Green, John. *An Abundance of Katherines.* Dutton, 2006. F
After the 19th girl named Katherine breaks his heart, Colin and his friend Hassan hit the road.

Can a mathematical formula help this former child prodigy find the new love of his life?

————. *Looking for Alaska.* Dutton, 2005. F
Miles is looking for the "Great Perhaps," and an Alabama boarding school offers the possibility of finding it, especially after he meets the captivating, unpredictable, and utterly alive Alaska.

Greenbaum, Dorothy, and Deidre S. Laiken. *Lovestrong: A Woman Doctor's True Story of Marriage and Medicine.* Times Books, 1984. NF
Dorothy Greenbaum, wife and mother, struggles to get through medical school and become a doctor.

Greenberg, Jan, ed. *Heart to Heart: New Poems Inspired by Twentieth Century American Art.* Abrams, 2001. NF
Poems written in response to various pieces of American art are brought together in this collection.

————. *No Dragons to Slay.* Farrar, Straus & Giroux, 1983. F
A high school soccer star afflicted with cancer finds the courage to fight back while working at an exciting archaeological dig.

Greenberg, Jan, and Sandra Jordan. *The American Eye: Eleven Artists of the Twentieth Century.* Delacorte, 1995. NF
Innovative and energetic images of 20th-century art are interwoven with biographies of artists and discussions of individual artworks.

————. *Andy Warhol: Prince of Pop.* Delacorte, 2004. NF
This biography of Andy Warhol illuminates his life and times, highlighting his impact on art and culture.

————. *Runaway Girl: The Artist Louise Bourgeois.* Abrams, 2003. NF
The French artist Louise Bourgeois, a woman ahead of her time, was known for her postmodern arachnid sculptures, her hemp and naturalistic material pieces, and her rebellious attitude.

————. *Vincent Van Gogh: Portrait of an Artist.* Delacorte, 2001. NF
This intriguing, colorful biography portrays the Dutch artist's troubled life.

Greenberg, Joanne. *The Far Side of Victory.* Holt, Rinehart and Winston, 1983. F
Paroled after being sentenced for "driving under the influence," Eric Gordon meets Helen, the woman whose husband and children were killed in the accident he caused.

———. *In This Sign*. Holt, Rinehart and Winston, 1970. **F**

The isolation and the often frenzied rage of the deaf in trying to cope in a hearing world are vividly portrayed in this story of Abel and Janice Ryder and their hearing daughter, Margaret.

———. *Of Such Small Differences*. Holt, 1988. **F**

Immersed in the world of 25-year-old blind and deaf John Moon, the reader experiences not only John's attempts to survive alone, but also the turmoil, passion, and love brought into his life by Leda, a sighted, hearing actress.

———. *Simple Gifts*. Holt, 1986. **F**

A simple poor family of engaging misfits turns their ranch into a place where visitors pay to sample "authentic" 1880s homestead life.

Greenburger, Ingrid. *A Private Treason: A German Memoir*. Little, Brown, 1973. **NF**

Rejecting Nazism completely, this gentile girl leaves her country and family and flees to France, where she falls in love with a young French Resistance worker.

Greene, Constance C. *The Love Letters of J. Timothy Owen*. Harper & Row, 1986. **F**

Tim thinks he will finally have a successful romance when he sends anonymous love letters, but the results are unexpected and discouraging.

Greene, Marilyn, and Gary Provost. *Finder: The True Story of a Private Investigator*. Crown, 1988. **NF**

The story of Marilyn Greene, no hard-boiled detective but a housewife who finds a career through years of search and rescue training, hard work, and caring.

Greenfeld, Josh, and Paul Mazursky. *Harry and Tonto*. Saturday Review Press, 1974. **F**

Forcibly evicted from his condemned apartment house, 72-year-old Harry and his marmalade cat, Tonto, set off on a hilarious cross-country jaunt to a new life in California.

Greenfield, Susan A., ed. *The Human Mind Explained: An Owner's Guide to the Mysteries of the Mind*. Holt, 1996. **NF**

The ultimate handbook of the brain—full-color graphics and clear explanations bring within reach an understanding of the most complex human system.

Gregory, Kristiana. *Earthquake at Dawn*. Harcourt Brace Jovanovich, 1992. **NF**

Experience being a survivor of one of the worst earthquakes in American history.

Gregory, Susan. *Hey, White Girl!* Norton, 1970. **NF**

Susan Gregory attends a black ghetto high school in her senior year and becomes more than another "whitey" in this rare and honest book.

Griffin, Adele. *Amandine*. Hyperion, 2001. **F**

Delia is the new girl at school, and at first Amandine seems like the perfect best friend . . . until things go terribly wrong.

———. *The Other Shepards*. Hyperion, 1998. **F**

Geneva and Holland Shepard must travel far from their Greenwich Village townhouse to dispel the ghosts of their older brothers and sister, who died nearly 20 years earlier.

———. *Sons of Liberty*. Hyperion, 1997. **F**

Thirteen-year-old Rock is torn about running away from his controlling father, but older brother Cliff sees flight as the only way to deal with those kooky, bizarre midnights working on the roof.

———. *Where I Want to Be*. Putnam, 2005. **F**

Jane and Lily have always been close despite their differences, but after Jane dies both must come to terms with their troubled relationship.

Grimes, Nikki. *Bronx Masquerade*. Dial, 2002. **F**

Eighteen inner-city teens in Mr. Ward's English class tell about their lives through text and poetry as they participate in weekly "Open Mike Fridays."

———. *Dark Sons*. Hyperion, 2005. **F**

In this free-verse novel, Sam, a modern-day African American teen, copes with the breakup of his parents' marriage and his changed relationship with his father. A parallel narrative explores the biblical story of Ishmael, son of Abraham, and his despair upon being replaced by Isaac.

Grisham, John. *The Pelican Brief*. Doubleday, 1992. **F**

When the wrong people find Darby Shaw's legal brief outlining her theory about who killed two Supreme Court justices, she must use all her wits to outrun them and save her own life.

Gruber, Michael. *The Witch's Boy*. HarperTempest, 2005. **F**

A witch who knows little about the practicalities of daily life finds a hideously ugly baby boy in the woods and raises him as her son.

Grunwald, Lisa. *Summer*. Knopf, 1985. **F**

Intimate summers with her artistic family on a Massachusetts island have always been perfect, but now Jennifer must bear her dying mother's last summer.

Guest, Judith. *Ordinary People.* Viking, 1976. **F**
Seventeen-year-old Conrad returns home from a mental institution, where he was sent after his brother's accidental death and his own ensuing suicide attempt. To begin a new life he must learn to accept himself and those close to him.

Guffy, Ossie, and Caryl Ledner. *Ossie: The Autobiography of a Black Woman.* Norton, 1971. **NF**
An African American woman, who is not famous, smart, or rich but just loves her children and wants the best she can get for them, tells a moving story.

Gurney, James. *Dinotopia: A Land Apart from Time.* Turner Publishing, 1992. **F**
A newly discovered, illustrated journal reveals life on the lost island of Dinotopia, where shipwrecked human survivors work and play in harmony with dinosaurs.

Guy, David. *Football Dreams.* Seaview, 1980. **F**
Dan Keith desperately wants to succeed as a high school football player—mostly to please and prove himself to his dying father.

———. *Second Brother.* New American Library, 1985. **F**
High school freshman Henry underestimates his own special talents in the shadows of his super-achieving older brother and his daredevil "Renaissance man" best friend.

Guy, Rosa. *The Disappearance.* Delacorte, 1979. **F**
Released from jail into the custody of the Aimsley family, Imamu Jones immediately becomes a prime suspect when Perk, their youngest daughter, disappears.

———. *Edith Jackson.* Viking, 1978. **F**
Though Edith fails in her struggle to hold her orphaned family of three younger sisters together and has an unhappy love affair, she eventually begins to discover her own identity.

———. *The Friends.* Holt, Rinehart and Winston, 1973. **F**
Rejected by her classmates because she "talks funny," Phyllisia Cathy, a young West Indian girl, is forced to become friends with poor, frazzled Edith, the only one who will accept her.

———. *The Music of Summer.* Delacorte, 1992. **F**
Spending the summer on Cape Cod, talented pianist Sara, who is ostracized by Cathy and her "light skinned" friends, overcomes racism with courage and the help of a new love.

———. *Ruby.* Viking, 1976. **F**
Ruby, daughter of a West Indian restaurant owner in Harlem, fights her loneliness by forming a relationship with the beautiful Daphne.

Habenstreit, Barbara. *"To My Brother Who Did a Crime . . .": Former Prisoners Tell Their Stories in Their Own Words.* Doubleday, 1973. **NF**
Taped interviews with prisoners who are allowed to enroll and live at Long Island University in a rehabilitation experiment reveal that some can make it and some cannot.

Haddix, Margaret Peterson. *Among the Hidden.* Simon & Schuster, 1998. **F**
After remaining hidden for 12 years because the population police want to eliminate all third children, Luke finally has hope for a future when he learns there are others like him.

———. *Don't You Dare Read This, Mrs. Dunphrey.* Simon & Schuster, 1996. **F**
Hoping that her teacher will keep her promise not to read her English journal, Tish reveals her growing anxiety, which begins with the return of her abusive father.

———. *Just Ella.* Simon & Schuster, 1999. **F**
After she realizes that her prince is not very charming, 15-year-old Cinderella seeks her freedom and independence to find her true love.

———. *Leaving Fishers.* Simon & Schuster, 1997. **F**
Dorry has just moved to Indianapolis and has no friends—until she joins a church group called "Fishers of Men." Soon she is no longer making her own decisions.

———. *Running Out of Time.* Simon & Schuster, 1995. **F**
Thirteen-year-old Jessie learns that she is not living in 1840 but in a historical demonstration village in 1995.

Haddon, Mark. *The Curious Incident of the Dog in the Night-Time.* Doubleday, 2003. **F**
Welcome to the world of a 15-year-old autistic teen who can solve quadratic equations in his head but can't bear to be touched or to eat foods that are touching on his plate.

Hahn, Mary Downing. *The Wind Blows Backward.* Clarion, 1993. **F**
High-school seniors Lauren and Spencer try to return to their innocent days of reading fantasies together, but fantasy worlds and Lauren's love cannot save Spencer from the insistent, disturbing memories of his father.

Hailey, Kendall. *The Day I Became an Autodidact, and the Advice, Adventures, and Acrimonies That Befell Me Thereafter.* Delacorte, 1988. **NF**
This journal records the joys and pitfalls of Kendall Hailey's life after she decided at 15 to graduate early and stay home to educate herself.

Halam, Ann. *Dr. Franklin's Island.* Wendy Lamb, 2002. **F**
While on their way to a special science camp in Ecuador, three teens find themselves the sole survivors of a plane wreck, or so they think. Little do they know that the island is home to a mad scientist just waiting for fresh young flesh to inject with animal genes.

———. *Siberia.* Wendy Lamb, 2005. **F**
Thirteen-year-old Sloe treks through a cold, dystopian wilderness full of thieves and outlaws in an attempt to find a safe haven for the DNA of genetically engineered lost animal species.

Halberstam, David. *The Amateurs.* Morrow, 1985. **NF**
By providing an in-depth look at the Olympic rowing team, Halberstam truly defines what is involved in "going for the gold."

Haley, Alex. *Roots.* Doubleday, 1976. **NF**
This poignant and powerful narrative tells the dramatic story of Kunta Kinte, snatched from freedom in Africa and brought by ship to America and slavery, and his descendants.

Hall, Barbara. *Dixie Storms.* Harcourt Brace Jovanovich, 1990. **F**
Spending all her 14 years in a small Virginia farming town, Dutch Peyton has found life to be pretty good until the drought-plagued summer when her sophisticated cousin Norma arrives and family secrets bring trouble.

———. *Fool's Hill.* Bantam, 1992. **F**
Summer is usually long, hot, and boring in Libby's small town, but when two new girls with a convertible move into the area, Libby discovers that excitement also brings frightening choices.

Hall, Elizabeth. *Possible Impossibilities: A Look at Parapsychology.* Houghton Mifflin, 1977. **NF**
This is a sensible look at what's possible and what's impossible about telepathy, clairvoyance, precognition, psychokinesis, and other psychic phenomena.

Hall, Lynn. *Flying Changes.* Harcourt Brace Jovanovich, 1991. **F**
The Kansas prairie sizzles as 17-year-old Denny faces the aftermath of her first love affair, her rodeo-rider father's crippling injury, and her mother's sudden reentry into her life.

———. *Just One Friend.* Scribner, 1985. **F**
Unattractive and slightly retarded, Dory is desperate for just one friend when she is mainstreamed—with tragic results—into a regular high school.

———. *Leaving.* Scribner, 1980. **F**
After graduation from high school, Roxanne believes it is time to leave her familiar home and family farm. A job in the big city may be her ticket to happiness—or is it?

———. *The Solitary.* Scribner, 1986. **F**
Unwilling to accept the support of others, Jane returns to her backwoods childhood home to become independent and self-reliant.

———. *Sticks and Stones.* Follett, 1972. **F**
Sixteen and a newcomer to tiny Buck Creek, Iowa, Tom Naylor suddenly realizes that the hostility of his fellow students and teachers is due to his friendship with Ward Alexander.

———. *Uphill All the Way.* Scribner, 1984. **F**
Callie, 17, learns that being a horseshoer is easier than helping a troubled delinquent friend.

Hallet, Jean-Pierre. *Congo Kitabu.* Random House, 1965. **NF**
Astounding adventures of a Belgian civil servant arise while working with the people and animals in the jungles of the Congo.

Halpin, Brendan. *Donorboy.* Villard, 2004. **F**
In this wryly humorous book, 14-year-old Rosalind Butterfield's life is shattered when her lesbian parents die in a freak accident and she is sent to live with her sperm-donor father.

Hamanaka, Sheila. *The Journey: Japanese Americans, Racism and Renewal.* Orchard, 1990. **NF**
Hamanaka's mural presents a capsule history of Japanese American oppression before and during World War II, and the slow healing after the war.

Hambly, Barbara. *Dragonsbane.* Ballantine, 1985. **F**
John, the Dragonsbane, fights the dreaded Black Dragon, but Jenny, a half-taught sorceress and mother of John's two sons, pays the price of the dragon's surrender.

———. *Stranger at the Wedding.* Ballantine, 1994. **F**
Journeyman wizard Kyra returns home to save her sister, Alix, from a sinister wizard's death spell and falls in love with her sister's betrothed.

———. *Those Who Hunt the Night*. Ballantine, 1988. **F**

The silent tombs of London's Highgate Cemetery and the gaiety of 1906 Paris are the settings when James Asher is forced to investigate the mystery of who is killing the vampires of London.

Hamilton, Eleanor. *Sex with Love: A Guide for Young People*. Beacon, 1978. **NF**

Candid and liberal, though advising some restraints, this sex handbook takes a positive approach to human sexuality.

Hamilton, Virginia. *Anthony Burns: The Defeat and Triumph of a Fugitive Slave*. Knopf, 1988. **NF**

Anthony Burns escapes from slavery only to be returned to it under the Fugitive Slave Law—until he regains his freedom through the efforts of the antislavery movement.

———. *Cousins*. Philomel, 1990. **F**

In trying to cope with her grandmother's aging and death, Cammy overlooks the terrifying knowledge that younger people die as well—in deaths that seem to have no reason.

———. *Her Stories: African American Folktales, Fairy Tales, and True Tales*. Blue Sky, 1995. **NF**

This feast of folktales and fairy tales about and by women is strikingly illustrated.

———. *In the Beginning: Creation Stories from Around the World*. Harcourt Brace Jovanovich, 1988. **NF**

A visually stunning treatment of creation myths, told by people from around the world, reminds us of the spirit and the vivid imagination of the human race.

———. *A Little Love*. Philomel, 1984. **F**

Sustained by the love of her boyfriend and her grandparents, Sheema searches for her father and discovers that, although she feels fat, insecure, and slow, she is strong and beautiful.

———. *M.C. Higgins, the Great*. Macmillan, 1974. **F**

M.C.'s illusions and fantasies of escaping the dreary hill country and its threats are shattered, but he gains new insights into his own future and that of his warm but tough family.

———. *The Magical Adventures of Pretty Pearl*. Harper & Row, 1983. **F**

The god-child Pretty Pearl meets the doomed hero John Henry when she joins a hidden community of African Americans who are closely in touch with a Cherokee band deep in the forests of Georgia during Reconstruction times.

———. *Sweet Whispers, Brother Rush*. Philomel, 1982. **F**

Fourteen-year-old Tree learns a lot about her family and the interconnections between their past and present tragedies from Brother Rush, her uncle's ghost.

Hamlin, Liz. *I Remember Valentine*. Dutton, 1987. **F**

A seriocomic view of the Depression through the eyes of an 11-year-old girl who learns about four-letter words and sex when she moves next door to an infamous family.

Hammer, Richard. *One Morning in the War: The Tragedy at Son My*. Coward-McCann, 1970. **NF**

Without attempting to condemn or excuse, the author presents carefully researched documentation of the 1968 Son My massacre and tries to understand why Americans sent to protect the Vietnamese should end up slaughtering them.

Hampton, Wilborn. *Meltdown: A Race against Nuclear Disaster at Three Mile Island; A Reporter's Story*. Candlewick, 2001. **NF**

This eyewitness account of the escalating Three Mile Island nuclear power plant disaster of 1979, told by a reporter, is placed in the context of other significant nuclear events.

———. *September 11, 2001: Attack on New York City*. Candlewick, 2003. **NF**

The terrorist attacks on the World Trade Center are told through the experiences of people closely involved with the tragedy, including survivors who escaped the falling towers, a man who lost his wife, firemen, the mayor, a perpetrator, and even the author.

Hanauer, Cathi. *My Sister's Bones*. Delacorte, 1996. **F**

When her beautiful, smart, and "practically perfect" sister returns from college refusing to eat or sleep, Billie knows that something is seriously wrong.

Hanckel, Frances, and John Cunningham. *A Way of Love, a Way of Life: A Young Person's Introduction to What It Means to Be Gay*. Lothrop, Lee & Shepard, 1979. **NF**

This positive guide to what being homosexual means—physically, emotionally, and socially—includes profiles of 12 diverse gay lives.

Hardman, Ric Lynden. *Sunshine Rider: The First Vegetarian Western*. Delacorte, 1998. **F**

On his first cattle drive, Wylie encounters a cast of colorful characters, adventures galore, and Roselle, a "cattalo" (a cross between a cow and a buffalo) that becomes his best friend.

Hardy, William M. *U.S.S.* Mudskipper: *The Submarine That Wrecked a Train.* Dodd, Mead, 1967. **F**
A psychopathic World War II submarine captain takes his crew on shore and blows up a tiny Japanese train to add one more trophy to his collection.

Harper, Hill. *Letters to a Young Brother: MANifest Your Destiny.* Penguin, 2006. **NF**
Through family stories, life experiences, and the words of some celebrity friends, actor Hill Harper provides guidance to young men facing difficult decisions.

Harris, Marilyn. *Hatter Fox.* Random House, 1973. **F**
Seventeen-year-old Hatter Fox, a spirited Navajo loner, is befriended by a young white doctor, Teague Summer, who never stops questioning his involvement with her.

Harris, Rosemary. *Zed.* Faber & Faber, 1982. **F**
Held hostage by a group of terrorists, Zed finds courage, cowardice, kindness, and cruelty in unexpected places and discovers his own strength.

Harrison, Sue. *Mother Earth, Father Sky.* Doubleday, 1990. **F**
Chagak, the only survivor of a brutal massacre, endures starvation, cold, and forced marriage as she struggles to find her father's family in prehistoric America.

Hartman, David, and Bernard Asbell. *White Coat, White Cane.* Playboy, 1978. **NF**
The true story of David Hartman, M.D., blind since the age of eight, whose only ambition was to become a doctor, is one of courage, ambition, and fortitude.

Hartnett, Sonya. *Stripes of the Sidestep Wolf.* Candlewick, 2005. **F**
Satchel O'Rye finishes work on possibly the very last job in his dying town, pushing him toward a whole new existence, while an animal long thought extinct returns to life. These two tales of endings and beginnings are at the heart of this beautifully told story.

———. *Surrender.* Candlewick, 2006. **F**
As 20-year-old Gabriel lies dying, he remembers his miserable childhood and the influence of his mysterious companion, Finnigan.

Haruf, Kent. *Plainsong.* Knopf, 1999. **F**
The lives of two young boys, two old farmers, and a pregnant teenager intersect in this deceptively simple story about family, love, and loyalty.

Haskins, James. *Black Dance in America: A History through Its People.* Crowell, 1990. **NF**
Haskins explores the development of African American dance from the forced dancing on slave ships through the era of music video.

———. *Black Music in America: A History through Its People.* Crowell, 1987. **NF**
Haskins demonstrates the unique place of Afro-American music in American culture.

———. *One More River to Cross: The Stories of Twelve Black Americans.* Scholastic, 1992. **NF**
Haskins presents the lives of 12 black Americans and their impact on American society.

Haskins, James, and Kathleen Benson. *The 60's Reader.* Viking Kestrel, 1988. **NF**
The authors describe in depth the major movements of the 1960s and how they changed the direction of American history.

Hathorn, Libby. *Thunderwith.* Little, Brown, 1991. **F**
Rejected after her mother's death by her father's new wife in the Australian outback, Laura seeks solace in a strange dog she discovers during a storm.

Haugaard, Erik Christian. *Chase Me, Catch Nobody!* Houghton Mifflin, 1980. **F**
Hitler's prewar Germany is the destination for a group of Danish schoolboys on holiday, among them 14-year-old Erik who, through the anti-Nazi underground, becomes involved in an adventure filled with intrigue and danger.

Hautman, Pete. *Godless.* Simon & Schuster, 2004. **F**
Sixteen-year-old Jason Bock, tired of the tedious "Teen Power Outreach" sessions he is forced to attend at his Catholic church, decides to create his own religion that involves worshipping the town's water tower as a god.

———. *Invisible.* Simon & Schuster, 2005. **F**
Seventeen-year-old Doug's teachers and parents think he is highly disturbed, and the kids at school find him creepy. Only his best friend Andy understands him, and together they harbor deep secrets that are eventually revealed in a most shocking way.

———. *Mr. Was.* Simon & Schuster, 1996. **F**
After witnessing his mother's brutal murder by his father, Jack Lund escapes through a mysterious attic door and finds himself 50 years in the past.

————. *Sweetblood.* Simon & Schuster, 2003. F
Sixteen-year-old Lucy comes to terms with her out-of-control diabetes by comparing her disease to blood-dependent vampirism and immersing herself in Goth culture.

Hautzig, Deborah. *Hey, Dollface.* Greenwillow, 1978. F
As Val and Chloe share their home and school experiences during one eventful year, Val becomes concerned that the relationship between the two girls is becoming something more than friendship.

Hay, Jacob, and John M. Keshishian. *Autopsy for a Cosmonaut.* Little, Brown, 1969. F
Sam Stonebreaker, M.D., is chosen by computer to be the first doctor in space and his assignment is to find out what killed the Russian cosmonauts in a marooned space vehicle.

Hayden, Torey L. *Ghost Girl: The True Story of a Child in Peril and the Teacher Who Saved Her.* Little, Brown, 1991. NF
Torey Hayden finds that eight-year-old Jadie's bizarre behavior is a result of sexual abuse and a satanic cult.

————. *Murphy's Boy.* Putnam, 1983. NF
Will therapist Torey Hayden be able to help 15-year-old Kevin, who is autistic and whose life has been filled with abuse and violence?

————. *One Child.* Putnam, 1980. NF
It's not easy to work with emotionally disturbed children when your youth and jeans mean more to the administration than your rapport with your class—but Torey Hayden manages it.

Hayes, Billy, and William Hoffer. *Midnight Express.* Dutton, 1977. NF
This is a graphic account of a young man's hellish captivity in a Turkish prison after his conviction on a drug charge, and his adventurous escape to freedom.

Hayes, Daniel. *Flyers.* Simon & Schuster, 1996. F
While shooting a horror film for a school project, Gabe and his friends see unusual sightings in their neighborhood that lead to more than a ghost.

————. *No Effect.* Godine, 1994. F
Tyler's adventures escalate in the eighth grade when he falls in love with his science teacher and becomes a fanatical member of the wrestling team.

————. *The Trouble with Lemons.* Godine, 1991. F
When Tyler and Lymie discover a body floating in the quarry where they are taking a forbidden midnight swim, they fear for their lives.

Hayes, Kent, and Alex Lazzarino. *Broken Promise.* Putnam, 1978. F
Abandoned by their parents en route to California, five children (the oldest 11 years old, the youngest 18 months old) learn to subsist on their own and to defy a juvenile court system that threatens to separate them.

Haynes, David. *Right by My Side.* New Rivers, 1993. F
Marshall's humor helps him through the difficult year in which his mother leaves and he finds he is attracting attention by being one of the only African Americans in his redneck high school.

Hayslip, Le Ly, and Jay Wurts. *When Heaven and Earth Changed Places: A Vietnamese Woman's Journey from War to Peace.* Doubleday, 1989. NF
The haunting memoir of a young Vietnamese girl is an account of the brutal Vietnam War and learning to forgive.

Head, Ann. *Mr. and Mrs. Bo Jo Jones.* Putnam, 1967. F
When July, 16 and pregnant, rushes into marriage with her high school steady, the two must cope with parental interference and personal problems.

Hearn, Julie. *The Minister's Daughter.* Atheneum, 2005. F
The fates of Nell, the healer's daughter and "merrybegot," and the minister's daughters, Grace and Patience, are intertwined when Grace accuses Nell and her grandmother of witchcraft.

Hearn, Lian. *Across the Nightingale Floor.* Riverhead, 2002. F
An adventure of epic proportions begins for Kateo when his village is slaughtered and Lord Otori, who somehow guesses his secret identity, rescues him.

Hearne, Betsy. *Love Lines: Poetry in Person.* Margaret K. McElderry, 1987. NF
Here are passionate, wryly humorous, and gently regretful lines about love in all its guises.

Hedgepeth, William, and Dennis Stock. *The Alternative: Communal Life in New America.* Macmillan, 1970. NF
Communes as a way of life for "quiet revolutionaries" who feel alienated from the established world and seek the humanness of man are pictured almost poetically in photographs and text.

Heidish, Marcy. *The Secret Annie Oakley.* New American Library, 1983. F
Told in flashback, this is a novelization of Annie Oakley's cruel and abused childhood.

Helfer, Ralph. *Modoc: The True Story of the Greatest Elephant That Ever Lived.* HarperCollins, 1997. **NF**
The fascinating story of the bond between a circus elephant and the boy who grew up with her is told with love, affection, and admiration.

Hellman, Peter. *The Auschwitz Album: A Book Based upon an Album Discovered by a Concentration Camp Survivor, Lili Meier.* Random House, 1981. **NF**
A powerful visual presentation of the extermination process at Auschwitz is viewed through candid photographs of its victims.

Helms, Tom. *Against All Odds.* Crowell, 1978. **NF**
Twice paralyzed by accidents, Tom Helms fought back—not only against his body but against the attitudes of the physically whole.

Helprin, Mark. *Swan Lake.* Houghton Mifflin, 1989. **F**
A totally new and surprising version of a famous ballet, this is a timeless and awesomely beautiful book.

Henderson, Zenna. *Holding Wonder.* Doubleday, 1971. **F**
Some of these 20 science fiction tales deal with "The People," but others treat more mundane subjects such as murder and almost all take place in the author's favorite arena—the classroom.

Hendry, Frances Mary. *Quest for a Maid.* Farrar, Straus & Giroux, 1990. **F**
Young Meg is pitted against political forces and her sister's powerful sorcery when she is chosen to be companion to the Maid of Norway on her journey to Scotland to ascend to the throne.

Heneghan, James. *The Grave.* Farrar, Straus & Giroux, 2000. **F**
A 13-year-old Irish orphan's life is changed forever when he is drawn into the past through a construction site that reveals a mass grave.

Henkes, Kevin. *Olive's Ocean.* Greenwillow, 2003. **F**
When Martha's classmate Olive is killed in a hit-and-run accident, Martha sets out to accomplish the things that Olive never had the chance to do.

Henry, Sue. *Murder on the Iditarod Trail.* Atlantic Monthly, 1991. **F**
Money, dogs, and reputation are at stake during the intense competition of the Iditarod. As mushers are murdered, state trooper Jensen looks at the race with new eyes.

Hentoff, Nat. *American Heroes: In and Out of School.* Delacorte, 1987. **NF**
First Amendment rights become part of everyday lives when students and other ordinary people resist infringements on basic freedoms.

————. *Does This School Have Capital Punishment?* Delacorte, 1981. **F**
While fighting false charges for possessing dope, Sam makes friends with a famous black jazz trumpeter.

Herbert, Frank. *Soul Catcher.* Putnam, 1972. **F**
Transformed into a mystical spirit named Katsuk, a young Native American sets out to avenge the injustices suffered by his people by performing a ritual murder.

Hermes, Patricia. *A Solitary Secret.* Harcourt Brace Jovanovich, 1985. **F**
Abandoned by her mother, a lonely and frightened 14-year-old girl becomes the victim of her father's sexual abuse.

Herring, Robert. *Hub.* Viking, 1981. **F**
In this story reminiscent of *Huckleberry Finn*, flood waters trap Hub and Hitesy on an island with a man they saw commit a murder.

Herriot, James. *All Things Bright and Beautiful.* St. Martin's, 1974. **NF**
This completely captivating continuation of *All Creatures Great and Small* relates episodes in the life of a veterinarian and the human and animal characters he encounters.

Hersh, Gizelle, and Peggy Mann. *"Gizelle, Save the Children!"* Everest, 1980. **NF**
Gizelle Hersh, inspired by her mother's parting words, attempts to save her three younger sisters and a brother from death in the Auschwitz concentration camp at the close of World War II.

Herzog, Arthur. *The Swarm.* Simon & Schuster, 1974. **F**
Killer bees, moving up from South America, terrorize citizens and baffle scientists who are trying to prevent a national disaster.

Hesse, Karen. *Letters from Rifka.* Holt, 1992. **F**
In letters to her cousin, 12-year-old Rifka describes what happens when she flees to the United States with her family to escape religious persecution in Russia.

————. *The Music of Dolphins.* Scholastic, 1996. **F**
Lost at sea at age four, Mila was fostered by dolphins. Now, 13 years later, she is found and returned to "civilization."

————. *Out of the Dust.* Scholastic, 1997. **F**

In a story told through simple, elegant poetry, 15-year-old Billie Jo fights to hold on to her dreams in the face of family tragedy and the crushing hardships of the dust-bowl years in Oklahoma.

————. *Phoenix Rising.* Holt, 1994. **F**

After losing almost everyone who matters to her, Nyle does not want to get to know 15-year-old Ezra, who has taken refuge in the back bedroom after a nuclear accident.

Hesser, Terry Spencer. *Kissing Doorknobs.* Delacorte, 1998. **F**

Tara struggles to live with her obsessive-compulsive behavior, but before her condition is diagnosed, her relationships with family and friends begin to crumble.

Hewett, Lorri. *Dancer.* Dutton, 1999. **F**

Hurt by her parents' doubts about her future as a dancer, 16-year-old Stephanie finds an older dancer (with a handsome and talented nephew) to act as her mentor.

Heyerdahl, Thor. *The Ra Expeditions.* Doubleday, 1971. **NF**

The spirit of *Kon-Tiki* lives on in the author's dramatic tale of crossing the Atlantic by papyrus reed boat to prove that the ancient Egyptians beat Columbus.

Heyman, Anita. *Exit from Home.* Crown, 1977. **F**

Opposing the demands of a dictatorial father, the oldest son of a Jewish family in czarist Russia follows his own commitment to social revolution.

Hiaasen, Carl. *Flush.* Knopf, 2005. **F**

This is the story of what happens after Paine Underwood pulls the plug on the *Coral Queen,* gets arrested for the act, and spurs his family and community to take action.

————. *Hoot.* Knopf, 2002. **F**

New to Florida and to Trace Middle School, Ray Eberhardt is at the mercy of the local bully but intrigued by a strange kid whose passion for the local wildlife leads them both into a crusade against a new pancake shop that will displace a colony of burrowing owls.

Hickam, Homer H., Jr. *Rocket Boys: A Memoir.* Delacorte, 1998. **NF**

Teenage Homer is fascinated with rockets after the launching of Sputnik. This is the story of his adolescence in 1957 Coalwood, West Virginia, as he and his buddies build their own rockets.

Higa, Tomiko. *The Girl with the White Flag: An Inspiring Tale of Love and Courage in War Time.* Kodansha, 1991. **NF**

Higa recounts her harrowing childhood ordeal wandering Okinawa alone at the end of the war.

Higgins, Jack. *The Eagle Has Landed.* Holt, Rinehart and Winston, 1975. **F**

In a small English town, a reporter uncovers the hidden grave of German soldiers and a suspenseful story of a Nazi plot to kidnap Churchill.

Highwater, Jamake. *Anpao: An American Indian Odyssey.* Lippincott, 1977. **NF**

Native American legends are combined in the story of Anpao's love for a girl promised to the Sun and of his search to find proof of the Sun's agreement to let him marry her.

————. *The Ceremony of Innocence.* Harper & Row, 1985. **F**

In the early 19th-century Northwest, Amana, a Blackfoot Indian, strives to survive in a white world that refuses to accept her friendship with a French-Cree prostitute and causes Amana's daughter to lose her pride in the culture of her people.

————. *Legend Days.* Harper & Row, 1984. **F**

Amana struggles to maintain her heritage even as she witnesses the disintegration of her Native American civilization as a result of famine, disease, and the encroaching presence of white settlers.

Hill, Ernest. *A Life for a Life.* Simon & Schuster, 1998. **F**

In a desperate attempt to save his little brother's life, 15-year-old D'Ray kills a young man, but is ultimately given a second chance by the victim's father.

Hill, Susan. *The Woman in Black.* Godine, 1986. **F**

An old-fashioned ghost story of quiet horror is set on the desolate English moors.

Hillerman, Tony. *The Blessing Way.* Harper & Row, 1970. **F**

Navajo detective Joe Leaphorn must solve the riddle of a mysterious death and an Indian spirit, part wolf, part man, who is frightening the people on a lonely reservation.

————. *Dance Hall of the Dead.* Harper & Row, 1973. **F**

When Navajo policeman Lt. Joe Leaphorn is called upon to investigate the murder of the young fire god he becomes involved in the world of Zuni religious beliefs.

————. *A Thief of Time*. Harper & Row, 1988. **F**
The disappearance of an anthropologist propels Navajo tribal policemen Jim Chee and Joe Leaphorn into mysteries of ancient cultures and modern murders.

Hinton, S. E. *Rumble Fish*. Delacorte, 1975. **F**
Brothers, caught in an environment of violence, are as incapable of changing their behavior as are the fighting fish who battle to their death.

————. *Taming the Star Runner*. Delacorte, 1988. **F**
Travis attacks his stepfather and is sent to live with his uncle Ken on a ranch, where he learns how to make friends and how to deal with his inner conflicts.

————. *Tex*. Delacorte, 1979. **F**
The life of easygoing Tex is complicated by his older brother's serious outlook and the frequent absences of his father. Simply surviving becomes a real challenge.

————. *That Was Then, This Is Now*. Viking, 1971. **F**
In this sequel to *The Outsiders,* Bryon and Mark at 16 are still inseparable, but Bryon is beginning to care about people while Mark continues to hot-wire cars, steal, and do things for kicks.

Hirshey, Gerri. *Nowhere to Run: The Story of Soul Music*. Times Books, 1984. **NF**
Interviews with the artists who produced the music that exploded in the 1960s are interwoven with research results and personal recollections to capture the beat of soul, from Motown to James Brown.

Hite, Sid. *It's Nothing to a Mountain*. Holt, 1994. **F**
Stunned by their parents' deaths in a fiery car crash, Lisette and Riley find both healing and a very special guardian angel at their grandparents' home in the Blue Ridge Mountains.

Ho, Minfong. *Rice without Rain*. Lothrop, Lee & Shepard, 1990. **F**
From changes in her rural village to the student protests in Bangkok, events propel 17-year-old Jinda toward choices that she must make about her own life.

Hobbs, Valerie. *How Far Would You Have Gotten If I Hadn't Called You Back?* Orchard, 1995. **F**
After moving to California in the 1950s, Bron is lonely—until she discovers danger, drag racing, and two boys, J.C. and Will, one of whom she truly loves.

Hobbs, Will. *Beardance*. Atheneum, 1993. **F**
Cloyd, a Ute teen, spends the winter helping two orphaned grizzly cubs survive, in this sequel to *Bearstone.*

————. *Bearstone*. Atheneum, 1989. **F**
Coming to terms with his Native American heritage, Cloyd learns to accept himself in a battle for survival in the mountains of Colorado.

————. *The Big Wander*. Atheneum, 1992. **F**
In this compelling adventure story, Clay goes on his "big wander" through Arizona's canyon country in search of his missing uncle.

————. *Downriver*. Atheneum, 1991. **F**
Fifteen-year-old Jesse and other rebellious teenage members of a wilderness survival team abandon their adult leader, steal his van and rafts, and run the dangerous whitewaters of the Grand Canyon.

————. *Far North*. Morrow, 1996. **F**
Stranded in the Canadian wilderness, two boys endure a brutal subarctic winter of bear, wolf, and moose attacks while they repeatedly struggle to escape.

————. *Jason's Gold*. Morrow, 1999. **F**
Fifteen-year-old Jason endures severe wilderness hardships and meets many colorful characters after he joins the rush to Alaska to find gold and his prospector brother.

————. *The Maze*. Morrow, 1998. **F**
Fourteen-year-old detention-center escapee Rick finds refuge in Utah's canyon country, where he meets condor preservationist Lon, who becomes both mentor and father figure to him.

Hockenberry, John. *Moving Violations: War Zones, Wheelchairs, and Declarations of Independence*. Hyperion, 1995. **NF**
This fearless journalist takes you along to experience war, chaos, and romance, as he covers the world from his wheelchair.

Hodge, Merle. *For the Life of Laetitia*. Farrar, Straus & Giroux, 1993. **F**
Twelve-year-old Laetitia's life changes drastically when she has to leave her loving extended family in a Caribbean village and move in with her abusive father while she attends high school on a government scholarship.

Hodges, Margaret. *Making a Difference: The Story of an American Family*. Scribner, 1989. **NF**
Hodges tells the extraordinary story of the Sherwoods, a family whose belief in social responsibility effected changes in women's rights, politics, medicine, and conservation.

Hoffman, Alice. *At Risk.* Putnam, 1988. **F**
When 11-year-old Amanda Farrell is diagnosed as having AIDS, her family, friends, and neighbors react in unexpected ways, in spite of their best intentions.

———. *Incantation.* Little, Brown, 2006. **F**
Secrets are dangerous during the Spanish Inquisition—especially if you are secretly Jewish.

———. *Local Girls.* Putnam, 1999. **F**
Gretel deals with life's joys and heartaches in this series of interconnected short stories.

———. *Turtle Moon.* Franklin Library, 1992. **F**
Keith Rosen, the meanest boy in Verity, Florida, runs away, steals a baby, and does other peculiar things, none of which are very strange—considering that it is May and the time of the Turtle Moon.

Hoffman, Nina Kiriki. *A Stir of Bones.* Viking, 2003. **F**
Fourteen-year-old Susan Backstrom may be perfect in every way, but she's also hiding a perfectly horrible secret that only three new friends, a lovestruck ghost, and a helpful haunted house can help her face.

Hogan, James P. *Bug Park.* Baen, 1997. **F**
Teenagers Kevin and Taki, who have created the interactive computer game Bug Park, must use the game and their impressive computer skills to save Kevin's father from a murder plot.

Hogan, William. *The Quartzsite Trip.* Atheneum, 1980. **F**
P. J. Cooper takes 36 Los Angeles high school seniors into the Arizona desert to discover who and why and how, and to learn that the Great Equalizer cannot always be ignored.

Holeman, Linda. *Search of the Moon King's Daughter.* Tundra, 2002. **F**
When Emmaline's mother sells her little brother to a master sweep to get money for the opium that kills her pain, Emmaline must find him before it is too late.

Holland, Isabelle. *The Man without a Face.* Lippincott, 1972. **F**
Not much affection has come Charles's way until the summer he is 14, when he meets McLeod and learns that love has many facets.

———. *Of Love and Death and Other Journeys.* Lippincott, 1975. **F**
The death of her lovable, easy-going mother forces 15-year-old Meg to adjust to a new life with the father she had resented but never known.

Holliday, Laurel, ed. *Heart Songs: The Intimate Diaries of Young Girls.* Bluestocking, 1978. **NF**
Spanning several centuries and different countries, the writings of these ten young girls reflect the same joys and fears of approaching womanhood as those experienced by young women today.

Hollinger, Carol. *Mai Pen Rai Means Never Mind.* Houghton Mifflin, 1965. **NF**
A foreign-service wife becomes a university teacher in Bangkok, crashes head-on with the unfamiliar customs of the Thai people but soon succumbs completely to their charm.

Holm, Jennifer L. *Boston Jane: An Adventure.* HarperCollins, 2001. **F**
A graduate of a young ladies' academy, 16-year-old Jane is forced to forget all her etiquette training when she takes a voyage to meet her fiancé.

Holman, Felice. *Slake's Limbo.* Scribner, 1974. **F**
A loser and loner picked on by everyone, Slake finds refuge in a subway which becomes his home for 121 days.

———. *The Wild Children.* Scribner, 1983. **F**
Overlooked in the arrest of his family, Eric runs with the outlawed and homeless children trying to survive in the bleak aftermath of the Bolshevik Revolution.

Holt, Kimberly Willis. *Keeper of the Night.* Holt, 2003. **F**
Isabel and her family try to survive and heal after her mother's suicide in Guam.

———. *My Louisiana Sky.* Holt, 1998. **F**
In rural 1950s Louisiana, Tiger Ann must balance her shame at having mentally slow parents against the changes brought on by complicated family secrets and responsibility.

———. *When Zachary Beaver Came to Town.* Holt, 1999. **F**
The summer of 1971 is pretty dull until Zachary Beaver, the fattest boy in the world, arrives and best friends Toby and Cal befriend him.

Holtwijk, Ineke. *Asphalt Angels.* Front Street, 1999. **F**
When a crime gone wrong breaks up his Rio gang, Alex must choose between a life on the streets and the safety of the shelter.

Holub, Josef. *An Innocent Soldier.* Arthur A. Levine, 2005. **F**
Conscripted in place of a farmer's son, farmhand Adam joins Napoleon's 1811 march on Russia, first serving and then becoming friends with a highborn lieutenant as they help each other survive the slog to Moscow and retreat home.

Holubitsky, Katherine. *Alone at Ninety Foot.* Orca, 1999. **F**

Fourteen-year-old Pam grieves for her mother, who committed suicide.

Homes, A. M. *Jack.* Macmillan, 1989. **F**

Still dealing with his parents' divorce and a wacko friend, 15-year-old Jack is hit with another bombshell—his father's revelation that he's gay.

Honeycutt, Natalie. *Ask Me Something Easy.* Orchard, 1991. **F**

Addie feels like an outsider as her older sister, Dinah, and their angry mother cling to each other following her parents' divorce.

Hoobler, Dorothy, and Thomas Hoobler. *The Ghost in the Tokaido Inn.* Philomel, 1999. **F**

The son of a merchant who longs to become a samurai gets an opportunity to sample the samurai lifestyle when a mysterious jewel theft causes the shogun to request his help in solving the crime.

Hoose, Phillip. *The Race to Save the Lord God Bird.* Farrar, Straus & Giroux, 2004. **NF**

The story of the ivory-billed woodpecker's demise is the centerpiece for a book about extinction and the impacts of humankind upon the Earth.

———. *We Were There, Too! Young People in U.S. History.* Farrar, Straus & Giroux, 2001. **NF**

The stories of more than 70 people from diverse cultures who were present at or played a role in important events in U.S. history are featured.

Hoover, H. M. *Another Heaven, Another Earth.* Viking, 1981. **F**

Survivors of an unsuccessful attempt at colonization must choose between primitive life on a doomed planet or returning to a mechanized, crowded Earth.

———. *The Dawn Palace: The Story of Medea.* Dutton, 1988. **F**

Denied her inheritance of Dawn Palace, Medea marries Jason and helps him secure the Golden Fleece, only to endure the dissolution of their marriage and the murder of her children.

Hopkins, Lee Bennett. *Been to Yesterdays: Poems of a Life.* Wordsong/Boyds Mills, 1995. **NF**

Hopkins's autobiographical poems capture his teenage feelings, experiences, and aspirations as he deals with his parents' divorce, his grandmother's death, and his hopes to become a writer.

Hopkinson, Deborah. *Up before Daybreak: Cotton and People in America.* Scholastic, 2006. **NF**

Oral histories and archival photographs enrich the story of King Cotton, deepening readers' understanding of the place of an iconic crop in American history.

Horan, James D. *The New Vigilantes.* Crown, 1975. **F**

Eight Vietnam veterans released from prison camp return to the United States to find justice a travesty. They decide to take the law into their own hands.

Horner, John R., and James Gorman. *Digging Dinosaurs.* Workman, 1988. **NF**

The discovery of a baby dinosaur's bones during a six-year dig in Montana results in a revolutionary theory about cold-blooded creatures.

Horowitz, Anthony. *Eagle Strike.* Philomel, 2004. **F**

Teenage British spy Alex Rider is back in an all-new addictive adventure that includes a reunion with an old enemy, a celebrity madman, and a near-fatal rendezvous with destiny aboard the famous presidential Air Force One!

Horrigan, Kevin. *The Right Kind of Heroes: Coach Bob Shannon and the East St. Louis Flyers.* Algonquin, 1992. **NF**

Coach Bob Shannon of the East St. Louis Flyers isn't the easiest guy to play football for. But whoever said anything in East St. Louis was easy?

Horvath, Polly. *The Canning Season.* Farrar, Straus & Giroux, 2003. **F**

When her mother sends her off to spend the summer with her twin aunts, PenPen and Tilly, Ratchet Clark is surprised to find a real home with them.

Horwitz, Elinor Lander. *Madness, Magic, and Medicine: The Treatment and Mistreatment of the Mentally Ill.* Lippincott, 1977. **NF**

How mentally ill people have been treated from ancient times to the present is a bizarre, tragic, and inhumane chapter of history.

Hotchner, A. E. *Looking for Miracles: A Memoir about Loving.* Harper & Row, 1975. **F**

Results are hilarious and poignant when Aaron masquerades as an experienced camp counselor to get himself and his younger brother into a summer camp.

Hotze, Sollace. *Acquainted with the Night.* Clarion, 1992. **F**

During a Maine island summer, 17-year-old Molly and her cousin Caleb, wounded in Vietnam, resist their romantic feelings for each other as they help a ghost find peace.

———. *A Circle Unbroken.* Clarion, 1988. **F**

Recaptured by her father after living with Sioux Indians for seven years, Rachel faces prejudice and needs great courage to find happiness.

Hough, John T., Jr. *A Peck of Salt: A Year in the Ghetto.* Little, Brown, 1970. **NF**
A very personal, moving story of a young white VISTA volunteer and his honorable failure to help black junior high school students in Detroit.

Houriet, Robert. *Getting Back Together.* Coward, McCann & Geoghegan, 1971. **NF**
The rambling odyssey of one man who sets out to discover whether "the simple life" can be found in the more stable communes and communities throughout the country. For mature readers.

Houston, James. *Ghost Fox.* Harcourt Brace Jovanovich, 1977. **F**
Kidnapped by the Abnaki Indians in colonial times, 16-year-old Sarah Wells gradually adopts the Abnaki way of life and must eventually choose between it and returning to the life from which she was taken.

———. *The White Dawn: An Eskimo Saga.* Harcourt Brace Jovanovich, 1971. **F**
Based on a real incident in the 1890s, three lost white whalers are rescued by Eskimos and taken into their community where the lack of appreciation for and understanding of Eskimo tradition leads to tragedy.

Howard, Jane. *Please Touch: A Guided Tour of the Human Potential Movement.* McGraw-Hill, 1970. **NF**
A *Life* magazine writer subjects herself to many forms of encounter group and sensitivity-training programs before making this shrewd and delightfully witty assessment.

Howe, James, ed. *The Color of Absence: Twelve Stories about Loss and Hope.* Atheneum, 2001. **F**
Twelve stories explore the theme of loss—losing family members, friends, pets, and innocence—and the possibilities for healing and hope.

———. *The Watcher.* Atheneum, 1997. **F**
A lonely, troubled girl lives in an elaborate fantasy world.

Howe, Norma. *The Adventures of Blue Avenger.* Holt, 1999. **F**
Sixteen-year-old David Schumacher becomes a comic book hero and takes on real life as the Blue Avenger in this hilariously funny and original novel.

Howker, Janni. *Badger on the Barge, and Other Stories.* Greenwillow, 1984. **F**
In each of five beautiful stories, a young person encounters an older stranger who helps to shed light on the problem each is posed.

———. *Isaac Campion.* Greenwillow, 1986. **F**
The death of his older brother forces young Isaac to assume the entire burden of working on his vicious father's horse farm in turn-of-the-century England.

Hubner, John. *Last Chance in Texas: The Redemption of Criminal Youth.* Random House, 2005. **NF**
This heartrending but ultimately hopeful look at a Texas program for violent teen offenders offers an unblinking view of the juvenile justice system.

Hudson, Jan. *Dawn Rider.* Philomel, 1990. **F**
Though she has hidden her early morning encounters with her Blackfoot tribe's first horse, 16-year-old Kit's riding experience proves vital during battle.

———. *Sweetgrass.* Philomel, 1989. **F**
A 15-year-old Blackfoot girl of the 1830s must prove herself a capable woman before she can marry Eagle Sun.

Huffaker, Clair. *The Cowboy and the Cossack.* Trident, 1973. **F**
Confronted by nearly insurmountable odds—including a Tartar raid—15 American cowboys with a Cossack escort drive 500 cattle across several thousand miles of Russian wilderness in 1880.

Hughes, Langston. *The Block: Poems.* Viking, 1995. **NF**
Selections from Hughes's poetry match Bearden's rich six-panel collage "The Block," portraying a Harlem neighborhood.

Hughes, Monica. *Hunter in the Dark.* Atheneum, 1983. **F**
In this rites-of-passage novel, Mike, a 15-year-old leukemia patient, comes to terms with his illness during a solitary camping trip.

———. *The Keeper of the Isis Light.* Atheneum, 1981. **F**
Never having seen another human, Olwen does not know how different she is until Earth settlers come to Isis and she falls in love.

Human Rights in China. *Children of the Dragon: The Story of Tiananmen Square.* Collier, 1990. **NF**
Never before published photographs and words of student activists vividly re-create the 1989 Tiananmen Square massacre.

Hunt, Scott. *Twice Told: Original Stories Inspired by Original Art.* Dutton, 2006. **F**
Pairs of authors respond to nine original drawings with strikingly divergent short stories.

Hunter, Kristin. *The Survivors.* Scribner, 1975. **F**
Each is a survivor—Miss Lena, independent businesswoman, and B.J., a tough, appealing street kid—but they learn that they need each other.

Hunter, Mollie. *Cat, Herself.* Harper & Row, 1985. **F**
Cat finds ways to blend an old Scottish "on the road" lifestyle with her own needs.

Hurwin, Davida Wills. *A Time for Dancing.* Little, Brown, 1995. **F**
Seventeen-year-old best friends Juliana and Samantha share a passion for dance, for life, and for each other—then Jules is diagnosed with cancer and must travel a path Sam cannot follow.

Huth, Angela. *Land Girls.* St. Martin's, 1996. **F**
Three young city women find romance, true love, and danger in 1941 when they volunteer to help the war effort by working as farm laborers.

Huygen, Wil, and Rien Poortvliet. *Gnomes.* Abrams, 1977. **NF**
Everything anyone ever wanted to know about gnomes, plus colorful illustrations identifying these unusual little creatures.

Hyde, Catherine Ryan. *Pay It Forward.* Simon & Schuster, 1999. **F**
Twelve-year-old Trevor McKinney accepts the challenge his teacher gives the class to come up with a plan to change the world for the better and put that plan into action.

Ingold, Jeanette. *The Window.* Harcourt Brace, 1996. **F**
Blinded by the accident that took her mother's life, 15-year-old Mandy finds an unexpected trip back in time is the key to helping her cope.

Inouye, Daniel K., and Lawrence Elliott. *Journey to Washington.* Prentice-Hall, 1967. **NF**
This exciting and inspiring autobiography is about the first Japanese American to become a U.S. senator.

Ipswitch, Elaine. *Scott Was Here.* Delacorte, 1979. **NF**
In a moving record of personal and family courage, Ipswitch tells the story of her son Scott, whose battle with Hodgkin's disease ended with his death at the age of 15.

Irwin, Hadley. *Abby, My Love.* Margaret K. McElderry, 1985. **F**
Chip loves Abby and can't understand why she keeps him at a distance, until she reveals that she has been sexually abused by her father.

————. *What about Grandma?* Margaret K. McElderry, 1982. **F**
When Grandmother Wyn refuses to stay in a nursing home, 16-year-old Rhys and her mother spend the summer with her. It is a time of conflict, discovery, and Rhys's first love affair.

Isaacs, Anne. *Torn Thread.* Scholastic, 2000. **F**
"Whenever you can, ask yourself which choice might keep you and Rachel alive for one more hour." These are the words of wisdom spoken to Eva by her father when she and her sister were sent to a Nazi work camp in 1943, where they endured the horrors of the Holocaust and fought daily for that "one more hour."

Isaacson, Philip M. *A Short Walk around the Pyramids and through the World of Art.* Knopf, 1993. **NF**
Unique examples of cars and radios, along with traditional art forms, beautifully and simply introduce that intangible something that makes a work of art.

Ives, John. *Fear in a Handful of Dust.* Dutton, 1978. **F**
Four kidnapped psychiatrists, one a woman, manage to survive the rigors and horrors of the desert after being left to die by a psychotic killer.

Jacobs, Anita. *Where Has Deedie Wooster Been All These Years?* Delacorte, 1981. **F**
Because her English teacher has faith in her, Deedie blossoms, finds herself, and realizes that she no longer needs to beg for her mother's love.

Jacobson, Jennifer Richard. *Stained.* Atheneum, 2005. **F**
Why did Gabe suddenly disappear? Can Jocelyn put the pieces together and make it safe for his return, or are they all forever stained?

Jacobson, Sid, and Ernie Colón. *The 9/11 Report: A Graphic Adaptation.* Hill & Wang, 2006. **NF**
This concise graphic novel re-creation of the government's official report conveys the horror of 9/11 and looks at how it happened.

Jacopetti, Alexandra. *Native Funk and Flash: An Emerging Folk Art.* Scrimshaw, 1974. **NF**
Beautiful color photos with brief text describe functional, unique lovingly hand-decorated objects: clothes, puzzles, furniture, and fine embroidery.

Jacot, Michael. *The Last Butterfly.* Bobbs-Merrill, 1974. **F**
A half-Jewish clown is forced to entertain Jewish children at Terezin. When the International Red Cross team departs, children board carefully concealed cattle trains. Destination: Auschwitz.

Jacques, Brian. *Redwall.* Philomel, 1986. **F**
With the help of animal allies, peace-loving mice defend their medieval abbey when it is beseiged by Cluny the Scourge and his fierce band of rats.

Jaffe, Rona. *Mazes and Monsters.* Delacorte, 1981. **F**
Fantasy becomes terrifyingly real when four college students discover underground caverns near their campus and one of them confuses game strategy with reality.

James, J. Alison. *Sing for a Gentle Rain.* Atheneum, 1990. **F**
Disturbing dreams pull James into the past where a lonely Native American girl and the timeless mystery of the Anasazi beckon.

James, P. D. *An Unsuitable Job for a Woman.* Scribner, 1973. **F**
When Cordelia Gray, slight but savvy, inherits a shabby detective agency after the suicide of her partner, her first case involves the apparently motiveless suicide of a Cambridge student.

Janeczko, Paul B. *Brickyard Summer: Poems.* Orchard, 1989. **NF**
These poems set in a New England mill town evoke the feelings of growing up during the summer between eighth and ninth grades.

——, ed. *Don't Forget to Fly: A Cycle of Modern Poems.* Bradbury, 1981. **NF**
A panorama of modern poems, by a variety of poets, span the range of human experience.

——, ed. *Going Over to Your Place: Poems for Each Other.* Bradbury, 1987. **NF**
These contemporary poems tease the emotions of each of us.

——, ed. *Looking for Your Name: A Collection of Contemporary Poems.* Orchard, 1993. **NF**
More than 100 poems representing the conflicts of contemporary life cover such topics as AIDS, war, gun control, and unemployment, and evoke anger, distrust, and many other emotions.

——, ed. *The Music of What Happens: Poems That Tell Stories.* Orchard, 1988. **NF**
Poems that are stories—and stories that are poems—tell of ghosts and lovers, triumph and tragedy.

——, ed. *The Place My Words Are Looking For: What Poets Say About and Through Their Work.* Bradbury, 1990. **NF**
Writers share their poems and give insights into their craft and life.

——, ed. *Pocket Poems: Selected for a Journey.* Bradbury, 1985. **NF**
A pocket-size collection of 120 short modern poems by some 80 poets ranges from "Song against Broccoli" to "An Elegy."

——, ed. *Poetspeak: In Their Work, about Their Work.* Bradbury, 1983. **NF**
Sixty-two living North American poets select and comment on their works for a teenage audience.

——. *Stardust Hotel: Poems.* Orchard, 1993. **NF**
Fourteen-year-old Leary experiences loss and love in these poems that bring his friends, enemies, and acquaintances to life.

——, ed. *Strings: A Gathering of Family Poems.* Bradbury, 1984. **NF**
More than 70 modern poets present a multifaceted view of families and their special relationships—husbands, wives, parents, children, etc.—in a 127-poem anthology.

——. *Worlds Afire.* Candlewick, 2004. **NF**
On July 6, 1944, 167 people were killed and more than 500 were injured when the circus they were attending in Hartford, Connecticut, caught fire. Read about the before, during, and after of this true event through haunting poetry.

Jansen, Hanna. *Over a Thousand Hills I Walk with You.* Lerner, 2006. **F**
Based on the experiences of the author's adopted daughter, a survivor of the Rwandan genocide, this story provides a heart-wrenching perspective on the horrors of a modern holocaust.

Jaramillo, Ann. *La Línea.* Roaring Brook, 2006. **F**
Mexican teen Miguel crosses *la línea* to join his parents in the United States, a journey full of danger and hardship.

Jenkins, A. M. *Damage.* HarperCollins, 2001. **F**
Football star and high school senior Austin clings to a relationship with beautiful, sexy Heather in the hopes that she will be his salvation.

——. *Out of Order.* HarperCollins, 2003. **F**
High school sophomore Colt Trammel struggles to maintain his macho image despite problems with both his girlfriend and his class work.

Jenkins, Peter. *A Walk across America.* Morrow, 1979. **NF**
The author begins his 1500-mile hike from New York to Louisiana with disdain for American lifestyles and ends it with a feeling of expectation and discovery.

Jenner, Bruce, and Phillip Finch. *Decathlon Challenge: Bruce Jenner's Story.* Prentice-Hall, 1977. **NF**
The 1976 American Olympic champion's story tells of his rigorous training and the many ups and downs he experienced before winning the decathlon gold medal.

Jennings, Peter, and Todd Brewster. *The Century for Young People.* Doubleday, 1999. **NF**
This tribute to the past 100 years focuses on the lives of ordinary people who witnessed historic events. Adapted from the bestselling adult version, with stunning photographs.

Jiang, Ji-li. *Red Scarf Girl: A Memoir of the Cultural Revolution.* HarperCollins, 1997. **NF**
Ji-li Jiang's quiet, prosperous way of life is destroyed during the turmoil and tragedy of the Chinese Cultural Revolution.

Jimenez, Francisco. *Breaking Through.* Houghton Mifflin, 2001. **F**
When 14-year-old Francisco returns to California after being adopted, his hard work and inner strength bring him success.

————. *The Circuit: Stories from the Life of a Migrant Child.* University of New Mexico Press, 1997. **F**
Panchito dreams of living in a world without constant uprooting from migrant camps and schools, a world in which a compassionate teacher might help him learn and grow.

Jocelyn, Marthe. *Mable Riley: A Reliable Record of Humdrum, Peril, and Romance.* Candlewick, 2004. **F**
Mable Riley dreams of grand adventures when she and her sister leave their home and board with a farm family in turn-of-the-last-century Ontario.

Johnson, Angela. *Bird.* Dial, 2004. **F**
Thirteen-year-old Bird runs away from her home in Ohio in hopes of retrieving her departed stepfather, Cecil.

————. *The First Part Last.* Simon & Schuster, 2003. **F**
The story of teenage father Bobby Morris is told, alternating between the past and his present life in New York City raising his daughter, Feather.

————. *Heaven.* Simon & Schuster, 1998. **F**
Young Marley's idyllic life in the small town of Heaven, Ohio, is suddenly disrupted when she discovers that her mother and father are not her real parents.

————. *Toning the Sweep.* Orchard, 1993. **F**
Emmie and her mother have come to the desert to dismantle her dying grandmother's house, but the trip proves to be a healing process for these two strong women.

Johnson, Earvin "Magic." *What You Can Do to Avoid AIDS.* Times Books, 1992. **NF**
Facts, questions, answers and interviews make up a thorough teen guide to AIDS.

Johnson, Harriet McBryde. *Accidents of Nature.* Holt, 2006. **F**
Jean has lived her life as the poster child for cerebral palsy. When she meets Sara at a summer camp for teens with disabilities, she becomes aware of the politics of the differently abled community.

Johnson, Kathleen Jeffrie. *A Fast and Brutal Wing.* Roaring Brook, 2004. **F**
Emmet and Niki may or may not be brother and sister shape shifters implicated in the disappearance of a local celebrity, who may or may not be dead.

————. *Target.* Roaring Brook, 2003. **F**
Grady struggles through his senior year haunted by the memory of the gang rape that nearly destroyed him.

Johnson, LouAnne. *Making Waves: A Woman in This Man's Navy.* St. Martin's, 1986. **NF**
This bittersweet, raunchy, and eye-opening look at one woman's military experience in today's navy sprints from recruiting promises, through basic training, to a hitch overseas.

Johnson, Maureen. *Devilish.* Razorbill, 2006. **F**
Jane, the smartest girl at St. Teresa's Preparatory School for Girls, has a fight on her hands when a cupcake-eating demon buys the soul of her best friend.

————. *The Key to the Golden Firebird.* HarperCollins, 2004. **F**
A year after their father dies from a heart attack in his prized 1967 Firebird, the three Gold sisters try to cope with their grief and get their lives back to normal.

————. *13 Little Blue Envelopes.* HarperCollins, 2005. **F**
The 13 blue envelopes Ginny receives from her Aunt Peg will take her through Europe and change her life.

Johnson, Scott. *One of the Boys.* Atheneum, 1992. **F**
Being part of the in-crowd is fun for Eric, until his new friend Marty's pranks become serious and criminal.

———. *Safe at Second*. Philomel, 1999. **F**
Todd Bannister, star high school pitcher, must cope with big changes when a line drive causes him to lose sight in one eye.

Johnston, Jennifer. *How Many Miles to Babylon?* Doubleday, 1974. **F**
A friendship between two young Englishmen from different social classes continues despite parental objection and leads to tragedy.

Jones, Adrienne. *The Hawks of Chelney*. Harper & Row, 1978. **F**
Siri, a wild young outcast who takes refuge near the hawks that obsess him, incurs the wrath of superstitious villagers who fear his difference and blame the birds for their empty fishing nets.

Jones, Diana Wynne. *Archer's Goon*. Greenwillow, 1984. **F**
A menacing, oversized Goon joins Howard's unusual family and refuses to leave until Howard's father has met the demands of his unrelenting master.

———. *Castle in the Air*. Greenwillow, 1991. **F**
Abdullah is whisked away to a magic kingdom when he falls asleep on a magic carpet he has just bought, but is he really sleeping?

———. *The Homeward Bounders*. Greenwillow, 1981. **F**
When Jamie discovers a group of specters warring with real people, he is condemned to wander the outer boundaries forever.

———. *Howl's Moving Castle*. Greenwillow, 1986. **F**
When a witch turns 17-year-old Sophie into an old woman, Sophie goes to live with the feared wizard Howl in his castle and becomes embroiled in the zany events that lead to her happiness.

———. *A Sudden Wild Magic*. Morrow, 1992. **F**
The good witches of Earth band together to stop the magicians of Arth from stealing Earth's technology and creating disasters.

Jones, Douglas C. *Gone the Dreams and Dancing*. Holt, Rinehart and Winston, 1984. **F**
Defeated but not beaten, the Comanche chief Kwahadi bargains with the whites to achieve a place for his people without betraying their past.

Jones, K. Maurice. *Say It Loud! The Story of Rap Music*. Millbrook, 1994. **NF**
Full-color illustrations accompany the lively story of the history, personalities, and social significance of rap—as well as the controversies that swirl around it.

Jordan, June. *His Own Where*. Crowell, 1971. **F**
Refusing to be trapped by the hopelessness of life in a black ghetto, 16-year-old Buddy Rivers escapes with his girl Angela to a deserted cemetery shed, in this short, honest, and poignant inner city love story for mature readers.

———, ed. *Soulscript: Afro-American Poetry*. Doubleday, 1970. **NF**
The black experience seen through the prism of poetry—some poems are angry and bitter, others are eerie and enigmatic; some lash out reflexively; others brood philosophically.

Jordan, Robert. *The Eye of the World*. TOR, 1990. **F**
Three teenagers take on a classic fantasy quest in this epic struggle between good and evil.

Jordan, Sherryl. *The Hunting of the Last Dragon*. HarperCollins, 2002. **F**
When Jude becomes the sole survivor of his village after a dragon attack, he finds himself becoming friends and unlikely allies with Jing-Wei, the "freak" in a sideshow, in a quest that could kill them both.

———. *The Raging Quiet*. Simon & Schuster, 1999. **F**
Newlywed Marnie defies threats from an entire village to befriend Raver, a mad boy she calls Raven.

———. *Secret Sacrament*. HarperCollins, 2000. **F**
After Gabriel witnesses a terrible crime against a Shinali woman, he becomes disenchanted with the rulers of the Navoran Empire and is determined to become a healer at the Citadel.

———. *Winter of Fire*. Scholastic, 1992. **F**
Elsha, saved from death on her 16th birthday when the Firelord chooses her as his Handmaiden, challenges centuries of social standards in her dark, frozen world.

———. *Wolf-Woman*. Houghton Mifflin, 1994. **F**
Sixteen-year-old Tanith must make a choice between the love of a young man and the call of the wolves who raised her until age three.

Juby, Susan. *Alice, I Think*. HarperTempest, 2003. **F**
Not many girls have given a counselor a breakdown at the age of 15, but hopefully Alice Macleod has nowhere else in her small town to go but up.

Jurmain, Suzanne. *The Forbidden Schoolhouse: The True and Dramatic Story of Prudence Crandall and Her Students.* Houghton Mifflin, 2005. **NF**

This is the inspiring true story of Prudence Crandall, a white woman who opened a school for African American girls in Canterbury, Connecticut, in 1833 despite vicious opposition.

Kalergis, Mary Motley. *Seen and Heard: Teenagers Talk about Their Lives.* Stewart, Tabori & Chang, 1998. **NF**

A cross-section of American teens talk candidly about their lives and viewpoints.

Kaplan, Helen Singer. *Making Sense of Sex: The New Facts about Sex and Love for Young People.* Simon & Schuster, 1979. **NF**

Addressing older teens, a leading sex therapist provides knowledgeable and detailed information, including some of the latest scientific findings, on human sexual functioning.

Karr, Kathleen. *The Boxer.* Farrar, Straus & Giroux, 2000. **F**

Having learned how to box while in prison, 15-year-old Johnny sets out to discover whether he can make a decent living as a fighter in late-19th-century New York City.

Kass, Pnina Moed. *Real Time.* Clarion, 2004. **F**

Thomas Wanninger feigns interest in gardening as his motivation for wanting to work on the kibbutz. This modern German teen really wants to discover whether or not his grandfather was a Nazi war criminal.

Katz, Jon. *Geeks: How Two Lost Boys Rode the Internet Out of Idaho.* Villard, 2000. **NF**

Trapped in rural Idaho, two 19-year-old self-proclaimed geeks use their computer skills to land jobs, an apartment, and new lives in Chicago.

Katz, William Loren. *Breaking the Chains: African-American Slave Resistance.* Atheneum, 1990. **NF**

The myth that black slaves wore their chains quietly is shattered by this account of how slaves actually fought for their freedom before, during, and after the Civil War.

Kavaler, Lucy. *Freezing Point: Cold as a Matter of Life and Death.* John Day, 1970. **NF**

Cold, once considered an enemy, is revealed as one of man's greatest allies when utilized in such areas as diet, medicine, and research to defer death.

Kaye, Geraldine. *Someone Else's Baby.* Hyperion, 1992. **F**

Terry, 17, single, and pregnant, tells the truth in her journal as she fights to do what's right.

Kaysen, Susanna. *Girl, Interrupted.* Turtle Bay, 1993. **NF**

A successful author who spent two of her adolescent years as a patient in a mental institution shares her harrowing experiences.

Kazimiroff, Theodore L. *The Last Algonquin.* Walker, 1982. **NF**

Joe Two Trees, an Algonquin Native American orphaned at age 13, first tries to make his way in the hostile white man's world, but finally returns to a traditional lifestyle.

Keane, John. *Sherlock Bones, Tracer of Missing Pets.* Lippincott, 1979. **NF**

Pet detective Keane describes his funny, sad, and suspenseful true adventures tracking down lost and stolen pets with his sidekick Paco, an old English sheep dog.

Keillor, Garrison, and Jenny Lind Nilsson. *The Sandy Bottom Orchestra.* Hyperion, 1996. **F**

Fourteen-year-old Rachel finds comfort in her violin while living with eccentric parents in a small town.

Kellogg, Marjorie. *Tell Me That You Love Me, Junie Moon.* Farrar, Straus & Giroux, 1968. **F**

Junie Moon, an acid-scarred girl, Warren, a paraplegic, and Arthur, who is suffering from a progressive neurological disease, decide to leave the hospital and set up housekeeping together.

Kelly, Gary F. *Learning about Sex: The Contemporary Guide for Young Adults.* Barron's Educational Series, 1977. **NF**

This is a down-to-earth, nonjudgmental discussion of values, relationships, love, and sex.

Kelton, Elmer. *Cloudy in the West.* TOR, 1997. **F**

When 12-year-old Joey flees his East Texas farm to escape the deadly intentions of his stepmother and her lover, he finds adventure and danger in the company of outlaws and his wastrel cousin.

Kendall, Martha E. *Failure Is Impossible! The History of American Women's Rights.* Lerner, 2001. **NF**

A brief but lively account of the struggles for equality and opportunity faced and won by American women throughout our country's history.

Kennedy, William P. *Toy Soldiers.* St. Martin's, 1988. **F**

When Arab terrorists take over an exclusive American boarding school in Rome, they face an implacable foe—high school student Billy Tepper, practical joker and computer whiz.

Kerner, Elizabeth. *Song in the Silence: The Tale of Lanen Kaelar.* TOR, 1997. **F**
Vibrant young Lanen Kaelar is compelled to leave the farm on which she was raised to seek out the awe-inspiring dragons that she's dreamed of since childhood.

Kerr, M. E. *Deliver Us from Evie.* HarperCollins, 1994. **F**
Parr has much to contend with—his small-town farm life, his emerging and raging hormones, and his older sister's lesbianism.

———. *Fell.* Harper & Row, 1987. **F**
Being paid $20,000 to impersonate another boy at a private school seems like child's play to John Fell, until he has to cope with the Sevens, a mysterious club that dominates the entire school.

———. *Gentlehands.* Harper & Row, 1978. **F**
Buddy's world is turned upside down when he falls in love and then, catastrophically, when he discovers that his refined and cultured grandfather is a notorious Nazi war criminal.

———. *I Stay near You: 1 Story in 3.* Harper & Row, 1985. **F**
Family members fall in love, cope with sudden death, and survive numerous separations in linked stories that follow three generations from the big-band 1940s to the hard-rock 1980s.

———. *Is That You, Miss Blue?* Harper & Row, 1975. **F**
There are ups and downs in the lives of three teenage girls in a boarding school, where the unforgettable Miss Blue is "the best teacher" in spite of her unusual habits.

———. *Little Little.* Harper & Row, 1981. **F**
Teenage dwarfs Little Little La Belle and Sidney Cinnamon try to find romance in spite of a mother's matchmaking.

———. *Me, Me, Me, Me, Me: Not a Novel.* Harper & Row, 1983. **NF**
A series of autobiographical anecdotes from Kerr's youth relate to their use in her novels.

———. *Night Kites.* Harper & Row, 1986. **F**
Seventeen-year-old Jim's relationships with his family and friends change when his older brother reveals he has AIDS.

Kessler, Cristina. *No Condition Is Permanent.* Philomel, 2000. **F**
When Jodie's anthropologist mother decides they are moving to Sierra Leone, Jodie is worried about finding friends, until she meets Khadi, a village girl who will soon be joining the mysterious "Secret Society."

Ketchum, Liza. *Into a New Country: Eight Remarkable Women of the West.* Little, Brown, 2000. **NF**
Eight women who made fascinating contributions to the history of the American West are profiled in this book that includes photos and illustrations.

Kibuishi, Kazu. *Daisy Kutter: The Last Train.* Viper Comics, 2005. **F**
Daisy Kutter is a reformed bandit in a strange wild west town where robots and cell phones are as common as corrupt poker games and shotguns. Her reform is short-lived as she tries to pull off the ultimate heist and maintain a relationship with her ex-partner and lover, who is now the sheriff.

Kidd, Sue Monk. *The Secret Life of Bees.* Viking, 2002. **F**
In the summer of 1964, 14-year-old motherless Lily Owens breaks her black caretaker, Rosaleen, out of jail and they run off to find a home with the beekeeping Calendar Sisters of Tiburon, South Carolina.

Kilworth, Garry. *The Foxes of Firstdark.* Doubleday, 1990. **F**
Human encroachment makes survival in Trinity Woods a struggle for O-ha the she-fox, her mate and her kits.

Kim, Richard E. *Lost Names: Scenes from a Korean Boyhood.* Praeger, 1970. **NF**
A famous Korean writer tells what it was like to grow up during the oppressive Japanese regime of the 1930s and '40s.

Kimble, Bo. *For You, Hank: The Story of Hank Gathers and Bo Kimble.* Delacorte, 1992. **NF**
Bo and Hank are inseparable friends and teammates who know that basketball is the road up, but Hank is in trouble—then dead, and all of Bo's memories lead to the same question—why?

Kincaid, Jamaica. *Annie John.* Farrar, Straus & Giroux, 1985. **F**
Growing up on the island of Antigua, Annie changes from happy child to defiant teenager in a fiercely painful separation from her strong, loving mother.

Kincaid, Nanci. *Crossing Blood.* Putnam, 1992. **F**
In the 1960s South, Lucy Conyers is fascinated by the people in the house across the way, and especially by Skippy, the handsome, clever son of their black maid—a fascination that is not only forbidden but dangerous.

Kindl, Patrice. *Owl in Love.* Houghton Mifflin, 1993. **F**

Girl by day, owl by night, 14-year-old Owl Tycho finds life is complicated—not only by a crush on her science teacher, but also by the presence of a deranged boy in the woods.

——. *The Woman in the Wall.* Houghton Mifflin, 1997. **F**

Painfully and obsessively shy, Anna comes of age in a world of her own, which she builds within the walls of her family's Victorian house.

King, Coretta Scott. *My Life with Martin Luther King, Jr.* Holt, Rinehart and Winston, 1969. **NF**

With dignity and emotion, Coretta Scott King tells her story of being black, of devotion to the movement, and of marriage to the man who said, "I have a dream."

King, Daniel. *Chess: From First Moves to Checkmate.* Kingfisher, 2000. **NF**

This attractive introduction to the game of chess combines easy to understand explanations with stunning computer graphics.

King, Laurie R. *The Beekeeper's Apprentice, or On the Segregation of the Queen.* St. Martin's, 1994. **F**

Sherlock Holmes meets an intellectual equal, 15-year-old Mary Russell, who challenges him to investigate yet another case.

King, Stephen. *Firestarter.* Viking, 1980. **F**

Eight-year-old Charlie can set things on fire just by looking at them, but will she use her awesome power against The Shop, the secret government agency pursuing her and her father?

——. *The Girl Who Loved Tom Gordon.* Scribner, 1999. **F**

Lost in the woods for nine days, a resourceful young girl survives by her wits and imagined help from baseball hero Tom Gordon.

——. *Night Shift.* Doubleday, 1978. **F**

The author of *Carrie* serves up a horrifying collection of short stories packed with vampires, bogeymen, a cellar full of rats, and a fatal can of beer.

Kingsolver, Barbara. *Animal Dreams.* HarperCollins, 1990. **F**

When Codi returns after 14 years to the small Arizona town of her childhood, she finds a new career, a cause to fight for, and a man to love again.

——. *The Bean Trees.* Harper & Row, 1988. **F**

Attempting to break away from her harsh life in Appalachia, Taylor Greer finds herself in a small Oklahoma town, with a new name, a new life, and strangest of all, a new Cherokee baby girl whom she names Turtle.

Kisor, Henry. *What's That Pig Outdoors? A Memoir of Deafness.* Hill & Wang, 1990. **NF**

The autobiography of a Chicago journalist who, though deaf, never lets it prevent him from doing what he wants.

Kittredge, Mary. *Teens with AIDS Speak Out.* Messner, 1991. **NF**

In the most important fight of their lives, teenagers confront past and current behaviors as they tell their AIDS stories.

Klass, David. *Danger Zone.* Scholastic, 1996. **F**

The thrill of playing international basketball for the American high-school dream team becomes more than a series of games as Jim faces prejudice and politics.

——. *Wrestling with Honor.* Lodestar, 1989. **F**

Ron Woods's anticipation of a championship wrestling season is complicated when he fails a drug test and refuses to take another.

——. *You Don't Know Me.* Frances Foster, 2001. **F**

A 14-year-old boy from a small town defends himself against an abusive home life, outcast status at school, and being a social misfit by living outside of himself.

Klass, Perri. *A Not Entirely Benign Procedure: Four Years as a Medical Student.* Putnam, 1987. **NF**

A young woman wittily describes her four years at Harvard Medical School.

Klass, Sheila Solomon. *Page Four.* Scribner, 1986. **F**

When his father deserts the family, David channels his feelings of confused betrayal into his college application essay.

Klause, Annette Curtis. *Blood and Chocolate.* Delacorte, 1997. **F**

Beautiful teenage werewolf Vivian falls in love with Aiden, a human—a meat-boy—and longs to share her secret with him.

——. *The Silver Kiss.* Delacorte, 1990. **F**

Feeling alienated from everyone during her mother's terminal illness, Zoë comes under the spell of Simon, a vampire doomed to live until he avenges the death of his mother 300 years earlier.

Klein, Norma. *No More Saturday Nights.* Knopf, 1988. **F**

Seventeen-year-old Tim's life is turned upside down when he decides to raise his baby alone while attending college.

Knowles, John. *Peace Breaks Out*. Holt, Rinehart and Winston, 1981. **F**
Returning to teach at Devon School after World War II, Pete Hallam finds violence and tragedy among his students.

Knox, Elizabeth. *Dreamhunter: Book One of the Dreamhunter Duet*. Farrar, Straus & Giroux, 2006. **F**
In a world where dreams can be harvested, 16-year-old Laura uses her dream-catching ability to expose intrigue and government corruption.

Knudson, R. R., and May Swenson, eds. *American Sports Poems*. Orchard, 1988. **NF**
Representing a wide variety of sports, from skateboarding to baseball, this treasury of nearly 200 poems conveys the vigor of American sports and their heroes and heroines.

Koebner, Linda. *Zoo Book: The Evolution of Wildlife Conservation Centers*. TOR, 1994. **NF**
Complemented by handsome photographs, an inside in-depth look at the inner workings of a modern-day zoo examines the changing role of the zoo community as it reorients itself into a global conservation leader.

Koehn, Ilse. *Mischling, Second Degree: My Childhood in Nazi Germany*. Greenwillow, 1977. **NF**
A young woman grows up in Nazi Germany, not knowing that she is part Jewish.

———. *Tilla*. Greenwillow, 1981. **F**
Two young German survivors of World War II, Tilla and Rolf, flee to Berlin and slowly attempt to create a new life in the occupied, war-torn city.

Koertge, Ron. *The Arizona Kid*. Joy Street, 1988. **F**
Working one summer at a racetrack, living with his gay uncle, and falling madly in love make wimpy, short, tenth-grader Billy Kennedy more self-confident and wiser in the ways of the world.

———. *The Boy in the Moon*. Joy Street, 1990. **F**
Senior year changes everything for Nick, who copes with acne, love, and changing relationships while pondering the meaning of his essay "Who Am I?"

———. *The Brimstone Journals*. Candlewick, 2001. **F**
In short poems, 15 students from Branston High School (known by the students as "Brimstone") write about their problems, their plans, and the fears that connect them all.

———. *The Harmony Arms*. Joy Street, 1992. **F**
Gabriel struggles to survive the culture shock he suffers when he moves from small-town Bradleyville to Los Angeles.

———. *Margaux with an X*. Candlewick, 2004. **F**
Margaux "with an X," a beautiful ice queen, can have any boy she wants until she meets Danny Riley, school outcast.

———. *Stoner and Spaz*. Candlewick, 2002. **F**
What happens when a 16-year-old guy with cerebral palsy and a sarcastic wit falls in love with a drugged-out girl with tattoos?

———. *Tiger, Tiger Burning Bright*. Orchard, 1994. **F**
Afraid that his mother will send his beloved but senile grandfather to a nursing home, Jesse tries to cover for the old man when he insists he has spotted tiger tracks in the nearby California hills.

———. *Where the Kissing Never Stops*. Atlantic Monthly, 1986. **F**
In a warmly humorous first-person narrative, 17-year-old Walker deals with his father's death, his mother's new job as a stripper, and his attraction to Rachel.

Kogan, Judith. *Nothing but the Best: The Struggle for Perfection at the Juilliard School*. Random House, 1987. **NF**
A profile of the Juilliard School reveals the ecstasy and disappointment of the exceptional musicians, singers, and others who study there.

Kohner, Hanna, and Walter Kohner. *Hanna and Walter: A Love Story*. Random House, 1984. **NF**
Separated by the Nazi invasion of Czechoslovakia, Walter Kohner goes to America and Hanna Bloch to Holland. At the end of the war, learning that Hanna is still alive after enduring concentration camps and her husband's death, Walter searches throughout Europe until they are finally reunited.

Koja, Kathe. *The Blue Mirror*. Farrar, Straus & Giroux, 2004. **F**
The Blue Mirror cafe serves as Maggy's escape from her alcoholic mother and her introduction to the destructive, abusive world of Cole, an enigmatic homeless teen.

———. *Buddha Boy*. Frances Foster, 2003. **F**
Justin is shaken from his safe little niche at school when he meets Jinsen, an unusual new student who will only smile at the abuse he experiences from the school's predators.

Koller, Jackie French. *The Falcon.* Atheneum, 1998. **F**
Seventeen-year-old Luke attempts death-defying adventures while trying to hide the truth about how he lost his eye.

————. *The Primrose Way.* Harcourt Brace Jovanovich, 1992. **F**
In 17th-century America, 16-year-old Rebekah Hall defies her missionary father's beliefs and embraces the gentle ways of the Pawtuckets—especially the wise and handsome Mishannock.

Komunyakaa, Yusef. *Dien Cai Dau.* Wesleyan University Press, 1988. **NF**
In these powerful poems, Komunyakaa remembers the agony of the Vietnam War.

Konecky, Edith. *Allegra Maud Goldman.* Harper & Row, 1976. **F**
A sensitive, funny, and at times sad story of a precocious, strong-minded girl's struggle to find her identity while growing up in Brooklyn during the 1930s.

Konigsburg, E. L. *Father's Arcane Daughter.* Atheneum, 1976. **F**
Overprotected children of wealthy parents get a chance to grow up normally because of the efforts of their mysterious half sister.

————. *The Outcasts of 19 Schuyler Place.* Atheneum, 2004. **F**
Rescued from summer camp bullies by her Old World grand-uncles, Margaret Rose Kane spends a transformative month lodging at their unusual home.

————. *Silent to the Bone.* Atheneum, 2000. **F**
Thirteen-year-old Branwell becomes unable to speak when his family's au pair accuses him of hurting his baby stepsister.

Koontz, Dean R. *Watchers.* Putnam, 1987. **F**
Travis takes in a very special golden retriever that is being stalked by The Outsider, a hideous, evil monster.

Kopay, David, and Perry Deane Young. *The David Kopay Story: An Extraordinary Self-Revelation.* Arbor House, 1977. **NF**
A pro football player candidly relates his agonizing journey in coming to terms with his homosexuality and making public his sexual preference.

Korman, Gordon. *Jake, Reinvented.* Hyperion, 2003. **F**
A mysterious new high school student, who instantly becomes the center of the social scene and a star on the football team, harbors secrets from his past that threaten to topple the new identity he's constructed for himself.

————. *Losing Joe's Place.* Scholastic, 1990. **F**
Convinced his older brother Joe is the "coolest," Jason has been looking forward to spending an unchaperoned summer with two friends in Joe's apartment, but he doesn't figure on his brother's best friend, 300-pound Rootbeer, moving in, too.

————. *A Semester in the Life of a Garbage Bag.* Scholastic, 1987. **F**
Will Sean's sabotage of the school's solar power plant thwart Raymond's hilarious schemes to earn a trip to a Greek island?

————. *Son of Interflux.* Scholastic, 1986. **F**
It's hilarious and improbable, this tale of high school students who challenge Interflux, a major corporation.

————. *Son of the Mob.* Hyperion, 2002. **F**
This is the ultimate Romeo and Juliet tale: the son of a mobster falls in love with the daughter of an FBI agent. Communication is a problem when your girlfriend's dad is the agent in charge of bugging your house.

Korschunow, Irina. *A Night in Distant Motion.* Godine, 1983. **F**
Regine questions her loyalty to the Nazi party after she meets Jan, a Polish prisoner considered "subhuman." Only then does she begin to notice the injustice and horror, the muted rebellion and fear of the people around her.

Koss, Amy Goldman. *The Girls.* Dial, 2000. **F**
Five girls in a middle school clique reveal how their manipulative leader exerts control over the group.

————. *Side Effects.* Roaring Brook, 2006. **F**
Fourteen-year-old Izzy's life changes when she is diagnosed with lymphoma.

Kotlowitz, Alex. *There Are No Children Here: The Story of Two Boys Growing Up in the Other America.* Doubleday, 1991. **NF**
This searing portrait of life in Chicago's public housing projects depicts the love and the terror in the lives of two brothers.

Kovic, Ron. *Born on the Fourth of July.* McGraw-Hill, 1976. **NF**
Beginning with the battle that leaves him paralyzed from the chest down, Kovic tells of his struggle to reenter American society—a struggle which leads him to become a leading antiwar activist.

Kozol, Jonathan. *Amazing Grace: The Lives of Children and the Conscience of a Nation.* Crown, 1995. **NF**
Amid violence, AIDS, and terrible poverty, people keep hope alive in the South Bronx.

————. *Rachel and Her Children: Homeless Families in America*. Crown, 1988. **NF**

Kozol's look at families living on the streets challenges everyone who takes the word "home" for granted.

Krakauer, Jon. *Into the Wild*. Villard, 1996. **NF**

Leaving a comfortable life behind for an adventurous one, Chris McCandless dies on a poorly planned hike in the Alaskan wilderness.

————. *Into Thin Air: A Personal Account of the Mount Everest Disaster*. Villard, 1997. **NF**

Courage, cowardice, foolishness, and great adventure marked the 1996 rival expeditions' efforts to reach the summit of Everest when everything went terribly wrong.

Kramer, Jerry. *Instant Replay: The Green Bay Diary of Jerry Kramer*. World, 1968. **NF**

In this day-by-day account, the physical wear and tear on the field and the business deals off it are equally important to this Green Bay Packers guard.

Krech, Bob. *Rebound*. Marshall Cavendish, 2006. **F**

Most Polish guys go out for wrestling, but basketball is in Ray's blood. He knows his game, but can he make the squad?

Krementz, Jill. *How It Feels to Be Adopted*. Knopf, 1982. **NF**

Kids from 8 to 16 share their feelings about being adopted.

————. *How It Feels to Fight for Your Life*. Joy Street, 1989. **NF**

Fourteen courageous young people suffering from life-threatening illnesses talk about what it's like to live with constant pain.

————. *How It Feels When a Parent Dies*. Knopf, 1981. **NF**

Feeling lonely, frightened, and betrayed by death, 18 young people talk candidly about the continuation of their lives after losing a parent.

Krents, Harold. *To Race the Wind: An Autobiography*. Putnam, 1972. **NF**

He is totally blind, but Harold and his parents determine that he will not be limited by his blindness.

Krisher, Trudy. *Kinship*. Delacorte, 1997. **F**

Fifteen-year-old Pert longs for a permanently stable home, which she believes she will have if her absentee father returns. Then "Daddy" comes home.

————. *Spite Fences*. Delacorte, 1994. **F**

It is the summer of 1960 in Kinship, Georgia, and living is not so easy for 13-year-old Maggie after the civil rights movement comes to town.

————. *Uncommon Faith*. Holiday House, 2003. **F**

The livery fire in 1837 was only the beginning of the changes in Millbrook, Massachusetts, when young people who felt invisible began to question the established authority, to compare the status of women to the status of slaves, and to object to them both.

Krizmanic, Judy. *The Teen's Vegetarian Cookbook*. Viking, 1999. **NF**

This collection of recipes for the new or veteran teen vegetarian includes quotes, insanely easy recipes, and a "Build Your Own" section.

Kropp, Lloyd. *Greencastle and the Denizens of the Sacred Crypt*. Freundlich, 1986. **F**

The difficulties faced by a bright, awkward high school student are captured in this haunting 1950s coming-of-age novel.

Krovatin, Christopher. *Heavy Metal and You*. Scholastic, 2005. **F**

Sam likes his life LOUD until a "straightedge" girl starts whispering to him and tempts him away from drugs, alcohol, and tobacco. But can she turn down the volume?

Kubert, Joe. *Yossel, April 19, 1943: A Story of the Warsaw Ghetto Uprising*. ibooks, 2003. **NF**

With rough pencil sketches, 15-year-old Yossel chronicles the horrifying events of the Holocaust in the Warsaw Ghetto, culminating in the ill-fated uprising.

Kuhn, Betsy. *Angels of Mercy: The Army Nurses of World War II*. Atheneum, 1999. **NF**

See the war through the eyes of World War II army nurses who brought medical skills to the hospitals and courage and cheer to the soldiers.

Kuklin, Susan. *After a Suicide: Young People Speak Up*. Putnam, 1994. **NF**

Friends and family members of suicide victims and survivors themselves share their experiences and feelings in this thought-provoking collection of essays.

————. *Fighting Back: What Some People Are Doing about AIDS*. Putnam, 1988. **NF**

A moving look—in words and inspired photographs—at a team of volunteers fighting the war against AIDS by offering practical and emotional support to patients.

————. *Reaching for Dreams: A Ballet from Rehearsal to Opening Night.* Lothrop, Lee & Shepard, 1987. **NF**

Kuklin details the activities and emotions of the choreographer and dancers involved in Alvin Ailey's production of the ballet *Speeds.*

————. *What Do I Do Now? Talking about Teenage Pregnancy.* Putnam, 1991. **NF**

"I can't believe how frightened I am," admits one young woman in this collection of honest interviews with pregnant teenagers, expectant fathers, and those who care for them.

Kullman, Harry. *The Battle Horse.* Bradbury, 1981. **F**

A modern-day joust, played in the magnificent style of Ivanhoe, goes astray when a young contender is compelled to beat a mysterious black knight.

Kunen, James S. *The Strawberry Statement: Notes of a College Revolutionary.* Random House, 1969. **NF**

An ex-varsity crew member at Columbia joins the 1968 confrontation over the university's indifference to war, racism, and poverty and records the struggle on the spot.

Kuper, Jack. *Child of the Holocaust.* Doubleday, 1968. **NF**

Jankel, a young Jewish boy, escapes Nazi persecution (in Poland) by posing as a Christian. When the war ends he begins a harrowing odyssey to find his family and his faith.

Kurtis, Bill. *Bill Kurtis on Assignment.* Rand McNally, 1983. **F**

Danger, intrigue, power, and compassion are fact, not fiction, as CBS news-anchor Kurtis presents sensitive, on-the-scene investigative reports of Agent Orange, Vietnam, the Iranian hostages, and the plight of Amerasian children.

Kuznetsov, Anatoly. *Babi Yar.* Dial, 1967. **F**

The German occupation of Kiev in 1941 is seen through the eyes of a Ukranian boy who witnesses Nazi barbarity and the mysterious disappearance of thousands of the city's Jews.

Lackey, Mercedes. *Arrows of the Queen.* DAW, 1987. **F**

Discovered by a telepathic steed, Talia, a misfit in her society, is taken to be educated as herald to the queen.

————. *The Lark and the Wren.* Baen, 1992. **F**

No risk is too daunting for 14-year-old Rune, daughter of a tavern wench, as she pursues her dream of joining the Bardic Guild.

Laird, Christa. *But Can the Phoenix Sing?* Greenwillow, 1995. **F**

In a letter to his stepson, Misha Edelman describes the heroism and horrors he witnessed when, after losing his family to the Nazis, he becomes a fighter in the Polish Resistance during World War II.

Laird, Elizabeth. *Kiss the Dust.* Dutton, 1992. **F**

It's Iraq, and Tara's family are Kurds. "He" has put out the word, and they must flee for their lives.

————. *Loving Ben.* Delacorte, 1989. **F**

When Ann's hydrocephalic brother Ben is born, she finds herself overcome with ambivalent emotions—love, embarrassment, anger, and eventually acceptance.

Lalicki, Tom. *Spellbinder: The Life of Harry Houdini.* Holiday House, 2000. **NF**

The life of the world-famous escape artist is told through vivid descriptions of his feats and what it took to pull off his world of magic and entertainment.

Lamb, Wendy, ed. *Meeting the Winter Bike Rider, and Other Prize Winning Plays.* Dell, 1986. **NF**

A wide range of topics and moods is explored by playwrights ages 10 to 18 in eight compelling works performed at the Young Playwrights Festival in New York.

Lanagan, Margo. *Black Juice.* EOS 2005. **F**

Ten stories from Down Under explore the darkness and the light of the human spirit.

————. *White Time.* EOS 2006. **F**

From a tale about a horny ant to one about a time travel internship, these ten mind-stretching stories are as bizarre as they are touching.

Lane, Dakota. *Johnny Voodoo.* Delacorte, 1996. **F**

Taken with her brother to rural south Louisiana by their father after their mother's death, 15-year-old Deidre searches for friendship, true love, and a place to belong.

Langone, John. *AIDS: The Facts.* Little, Brown, 1988. **NF**

By an experienced science writer, this comprehensive, understandable, and well-researched study presents a nonjudgmental overview of knowledge about AIDS.

Lanier, Shannon, and Jane Feldman, eds. *Jefferson's Children: The Story of One American Family.* Random House, 2000. **NF**

A journey across the country and through the ages reunites the two branches of the Jefferson family, one black, the other white.

Lanker, Brian. *I Dream a World: Portraits of Black Women Who Changed America.* Stewart, Tabori & Chang, 1989. NF
Photographs and text highlight the strength of black women who have prevailed in the face of adversity and prejudice.

Lansens, Lori. *The Girls.* Little, Brown, 2006. F
Ruby and Rose are conjoined twins who reveal the secrets, struggles, and dreams of their remarkable lives.

Lantz, Frances. *Someone to Love.* Avon, 1997. F
In letters to her soon-to-be-adopted sibling, Sara explains how, defying her parents, she becomes friends with the birth mother, Iris, and ruins everything.

Larbalestier, Justine. *Magic or Madness.* Razorbill, 2005. F
When 15-year-old Reason's mother suffers a mental breakdown, Reason is sent to live with the grandmother she never really knew. Her grandmother turns out to be a witch, who shows Reason that magic is real, runs in her genes, and exacts a terrible price.

LaRochelle, David. *Absolutely, Positively Not.* Arthur A. Levine, 2005. F
Steven has noticed that his new health teacher, Mr. Bowman, is extremely handsome, but he still tries to convince himself that he's not gay in this hilarious coming out story.

Larrick, Nancy, ed. *Crazy to Be Alive in Such a Strange World: Poems about People.* Evans, 1977. NF
Tinged with humor and irony, a collection of poems written by both well- and little-known poets about people of varied backgrounds and ages.

Larson, Gary. *The PreHistory of The Far Side: A 10th Anniversary Exhibit.* Andrews and McMeel, 1989. NF
In cartoons and words not for the "humorously squeamish," Larson describes his life as *The Far Side*'s creator.

———. *There's a Hair in My Dirt! A Worm's Story.* HarperCollins, 1998. NF
Cartoonist Larson reminds us that though nature is pretty, it's just waiting to eat us.

Larson, Kirby. *Hattie Big Sky.* Delacorte, 2006. F
In 1918, 16-year-old Hattie Brooks runs a 400-acre Montana farm, faces threats from wolves, and fights prejudice and loneliness.

Lasky, Kathryn. *Beyond the Burning Time.* Blue Sky, 1994. F
In this shocking story, Mary Chase fights to save her mother from being executed as a witch in 1692 Salem.

———. *Beyond the Divide.* Macmillan, 1983. F
Meribah runs away to join her father on a trek to California—and ends up surviving alone in the Sierra Nevada mountains.

———. *Pageant.* Four Winds, 1986. F
Sarah's years at an exclusive high school are full of self-awareness, humor, and conflict with the teachers.

———. *Prank.* Macmillan, 1984. F
While trying to determine her future plans, Birdie Flynn confronts her brother about his involvement in vandalizing a synagogue.

Lat. *Kampung Boy.* Roaring Brook, 2006. F
Lat's Malaysian village comes alive in this graphic novel, which shows a picture of life in a 1950s Muslim kampung at a time when Western influences threaten his familiar world.

Lauber, Patricia. *Seeing Earth from Space.* Orchard, 1990. NF
Lauber's photo-essay shows how scientists use various photographic methods to study the Earth.

———. *Summer of Fire: Yellowstone 1988.* Orchard, 1991. NF
In an account enhanced by stunning photographs, Lauber clearly describes the effects, both positive and negative, of the awesome fires that roared through our oldest national park in 1988.

Laure, Jason, and Ettagale Laure. *South Africa: Coming of Age under Apartheid.* Farrar, Straus & Giroux, 1980. NF
Eight young people talk about their lives and their aspirations in a country where color rules one's place in society. Photographs depict lifestyles unique to each.

Lavallee, David. *Event 1000.* Holt, Rinehart and Winston, 1971. F
A nuclear-powered submarine is marooned in over 1200 feet of water, 160 miles from New York City, where for over a month the rescue team fights political and business interests to get an outmoded diving bell altered to rescue the trapped men below.

Lavender, Bee. *Lessons in Taxidermy.* Akashic/ Punk Planet, 2005. **NF**
Pushed around "like putty" by legions of doctors surgically attacking almost every body part at one time or another, Bee Lavender survived a childhood and adolescence battling multiple cancers and other diseases by relying on a family where "the women hit back" and by honing her own unique sense of humor.

Lawlor, Laurie. *Helen Keller: Rebellious Spirit.* Holiday House, 2001. **NF**
Helen Keller's life, including her fun-loving nature, romance, and strong political views, is the focus of this biography.

———. *Shadow Catcher: The Life and Work of Edward S. Curtis.* Walker, 1994. **NF**
Curtis's passion for documenting the lives of Native Americans through photographs and narrative claims 30 years of his life and nearly impoverishes him.

Lawrence, Iain. *B for Buster.* Delacorte, 2004. **F**
Sixteen-year-old Kak illegally enlists in the Canadian Air Force in 1943 and experiences the horrors of war as he battles his fear of flying in the bombing raids over Germany.

———. *Ghost Boy.* Delacorte, 2000. **F**
Constantly taunted by everyone in his small prairie town because of his strange white hair and ghostly pale skin, Harold runs away and joins a down-on-its-luck traveling circus, where he meets a host of characters who will change his life.

———. *The Lightkeeper's Daughter.* Delacorte, 2002. **F**
A teenage mother tries to reconcile with her lighthouse-keeping parents, despite her feeling that it was their remote and lonely lifestyle that led to her brother's death.

———. *The Smugglers.* Delacorte, 1999. **F**
An 18th-century merchant's son encounters a world of high adventure when he sets out on a sea voyage aboard the star-crossed schooner *Dragon.*

———. *The Wreckers.* Delacorte, 1998. **F**
Eighteenth-century Cornwall provides an eerie backdrop for this heart-pounding mystery full of nautical adventure and with a 14-year-old hero.

Lawrence, Louise. *Calling B for Butterfly.* Harper & Row, 1982. **F**
Six young survivors of a destroyed starliner must depend on their own wits, a fragile radio link, and a mysterious alien presence.

———. *Children of the Dust.* Harper & Row, 1985. **F**
Three generations of the same family represent the two human factions—those who mutated due to exposure to the nuclear holocaust and those who were sheltered.

Lawrence, Michael. *A Crack in the Line.* Greenwillow, 2004. **F**
Sixteen-year-old Alaric stumbles into a parallel universe in which his dead mother still lives, and he discovers that his room is occupied by Naia, a girl who looks just like him.

Lawson, Don. *The United States in the Vietnam War.* Crowell, 1981. **NF**
Lawson traces U.S. involvement beginning with the use of advisors through the fall of Saigon and the final peace treaty.

Lawson, Donna. *Mother Nature's Beauty Cupboard.* Crowell, 1973. **NF**
Strawberries and avocados are just two foods that you can turn into natural and inexpensive beauty aids that are fun to make.

Laxalt, Robert. *Dust Devils.* University of Nevada Press, 1997. **F**
This is an Old West coming-of-age novella with bronco riding, horse rustling, Native American wisdom, and the desert landscape.

Le Guin, Ursula K. *The Beginning Place.* Harper & Row, 1980. **F**
Irena and Hugh each follow a hidden path to Tembreabrezi, a fantasy place, where they struggle to save their friends and make peace with the real world.

———. *The Dispossessed: An Ambiguous Utopia.* Harper & Row, 1974. **F**
Shevek, the Dispossessed, a brilliant but politically naive scientist, attempts to establish interplanetary relations between two disparate societies, neither of which shares his utopian dream.

———. *Very Far Away from Anywhere Else.* Atheneum, 1976. **F**
In a brief and unique Le Guin story, Owen and Natalie, two gifted 17-year-olds, find friendship and love by sharing their dreams: one to be a scientist, the other, a musician.

Leavitt, Martine. *The Dollmage.* Red Deer, 2001. **F**
The Dollmage, wise woman of Seekvalley, predicts the birthday of her successor, a day on which two girls are born, leading her to make a decision that will affect all of the lives in the valley.

————. *Heck, Superhero*. Front Street, 2004. **F**
Participate in 96 critical hours in the life of an artistic 13-year-old who has channeled a lifetime of chronic neglect by his severely depressed mother into his role as a caregiver and doer of good deeds.

Lebert, Benjamin. *Crazy*. Knopf, 2000. **F**
Sent to a boarding school to turn his grades around and to spare him from seeing his parents' marriage fall apart, 16-year-old Benni, partially paralyzed on his left side, falls in with a group of misfits who are eager to fill their youth with thrills.

Leder, Jane Mersky. *Dead Serious: A Book for Teenagers about Teenage Suicide*. Atheneum, 1987. **NF**
What to do and not to do for friends and parents of those who are considering suicide is discussed with sensitivity and good sense.

Lee, Bruce, ed. John Little. *Bruce Lee: The Celebrated Life of the Golden Dragon*. Tuttle, 2000. **NF**
This biography of the martial arts legend includes never-before-published photos as well as Lee's writings about his childhood, his family, and his stardom.

Lee, Marie G. *Necessary Roughness*. Harper Collins, 1996. **F**
For Chan, it's football, and for his twin sister, Young, it's her flute, as the two try to adapt to small-town Minnesota life after moving from L.A. Where does their Korean heritage fit in?

Lee, Mildred. *Fog*. Seabury, 1972. **F**
In October Luke Sawyer's life is going great; in December everything in his comfortable world starts to fall apart.

————. *The People Therein*. Clarion, 1980. **F**
A turn-of-the-century love story set in southern Appalachia joins together Lanthy, resigned to life without marriage because she is crippled, and Drew, a botanist who comes to the Great Smoky Mountains from Boston to cure his fondness for alcohol.

Lee, Tanith. *Black Unicorn*. Atheneum, 1991. **F**
Bored with her lonely life as the no-talent daughter of a quirky sorceress, Tanaquil reconstructs a unicorn and, when it comes to life, takes off for adventure.

————. *Red as Blood, or Tales from the Sisters Grimmer*. DAW, 1983. **F**
These bizarre and chilling new twists to old fairy tales are told by a master fantasy writer.

Leekley, Sheryle, and John Leekley. *Moments: The Pulitzer Prize Photographs*. Crown, 1978. **NF**
Dramatic, prizewinning photographs from 1942 to the 1970s illuminate small everyday human happenings and make important historical events come alive again.

Leffland, Ella. *Rumors of Peace*. Harper & Row, 1979. **F**
Growing up in California, a young girl finds the anxieties of childhood and adolescence complicated by the turmoil of World War II.

LeFlore, Ron, and Jim Hawkins. *Breakout: From Prison to the Big Leagues*. Harper & Row, 1978. **NF**
A former thief, drug addict, and ex-con recalls the people and events that led him from the prison baseball team to the Detroit Tigers and the All-Star game.

Lehrman, Robert. *Juggling*. Harper & Row, 1982. **F**
In this touching novel, affluent high school student Howie Berger not only suffers the agonies of first love but also is frustrated as he tries to become an accepted member of an all-Jewish-immigrant soccer team.

Leitner, Isabella. *Fragments of Isabella: A Memoir of Auschwitz*. Crowell, 1978. **NF**
The strength of the human spirit and the passionate will to survive the degradation and death of Auschwitz are portrayed with searing intensity through Leitner's fragmented memories.

LeMieux, A. C. *The TV Guidance Counselor*. Morrow, 1993. **F**
After his parents' bitter divorce, 16-year-old Michael becomes obsessed with photography but soon learns he can't hide his pain behind a camera.

L'Engle, Madeleine. *Many Waters*. Farrar, Straus & Giroux, 1986. **F**
Intruding in their father's lab, twins Sandy and Dennys are flung across time to a desert where Noah's family lives among mythical creatures.

LeRoy, Gen. *Cold Feet*. Harper & Row, 1979. **F**
Attempting to give her life new direction, Geneva draws away from family and school and becomes involved in a gambling ring . . . disguised as a boy!

Les Becquets, Diane. *The Stones of Mourning Creek*. Winslow, 2001. **F**
Francie's grief over her mother's mysterious death is eased by her growing friendship with an African American teen and her family.

Leslie, Robert Franklin. *The Bears and I: Raising Three Cubs in the North Woods.* Dutton, 1968. **NF**

While panning for gold in Canada the author is "adopted" by three orphan bear cubs whom he has to teach to find food, recognize danger, and share his cabin.

Lester, Julius. *Day of Tears: A Novel in Dialogue.* Hyperion, 2005. **F**

After being sold in the largest slave auction in American history, Emma and Joe agonize over whether to try to escape or remain chattel in this fact-based novel told almost entirely in dialogue.

————. *From Slave Ship to Freedom Road.* Dial, 1998. **NF**

This stunning combination of art and prose brings alive the effects of slavery on all humanity.

————. *Othello.* Scholastic, 1995. **F**

A powerful, accessible retelling of Shakespeare's story of doomed love and jealousy, with an unusual twist, speaks to us across racial lines and through the centuries.

————. *Search for the New Land: History as Subjective Experience.* Dial, 1969. **NF**

Combining autobiography, contemporary history, and "found" poetry, a sensitive black militant reveals the frustrations of his life, the sickness in American society, and a revolutionary hope for the future.

————. *This Strange New Feeling.* Dial, 1982. **F**

Three black slave couples reach freedom by different paths, but all experience an emancipation made richer by their dangerous struggle.

Levenkron, Steven. *The Best Little Girl in the World.* Contemporary, 1978. **F**

Obsessive dieting and bizarre rituals with food are symptoms of Francesca's battle with anorexia nervosa, a disorder that afflicts one out of every 300 teenage girls.

————. *The Luckiest Girl in the World.* Scribner, 1997. **F**

Fifteen-year-old figure skater Katie Roskova inflicts pain on herself when she can't manage her feelings about her absent father, her overbearing mother, the pressures of her sport, and her school life.

LeVert, John. *The Flight of the Cassowary.* Atlantic Monthly, 1986. **F**

More and more obsessed with the animal characteristics of people, 16-year-old Paul—bright, normal, and athletic—comes to believe that he can fly.

Levin, Betty. *Brother Moose.* Greenwillow, 1990. **F**

Survival takes on new meaning for orphans Louisa and Nell, as they trek through the Maine woods with an old Native American and his grandson.

Levin, Ira. *The Boys from Brazil.* Random House, 1976. **F**

Nazis living in Brazil have an ingenious plot for establishing a Fourth Reich.

Levine, Ellen. *Darkness over Denmark: The Danish Resistance and the Rescue of the Jews.* Holiday House, 2000. **NF**

The events in Denmark during World War II as the Danes risked their lives to protect and rescue Jews from the Nazis are retold in this gripping book.

————. *Freedom's Children: Young Civil Rights Activists Tell Their Own Stories.* Putnam, 1993. **NF**

Here is a thought-provoking collection of oral histories from 30 African Americans who were teenagers in the 1950s and 1960s and were involved in the desegregation effort and civil rights movement.

Levine, Gail Carson. *Dave at Night.* HarperCollins, 1999. **F**

When Dave is sent to the Hebrew Home for boys, he sneaks out at night and is welcomed into the music- and culture-filled world of the Harlem Renaissance.

————. *Ella Enchanted.* HarperCollins, 1997. **F**

Imagine this: Cinderella's real problem isn't her cruel stepmother and stepsisters, it's just that she cannot refuse a direct command from anyone!

Levit, Rose. *Ellen: A Short Life Long Remembered.* Chronicle, 1974. **NF**

Told at 15 that she has cancer, Ellen for two years finds the inner strength to live each day as fully as she can.

Levithan, David. *Are We There Yet?* Knopf, 2005. **F**

Brothers Elijah and Danny travel through Italy together even though they feel that they have nothing in common, which they may not, until they meet Julia.

————. *Boy Meets Boy.* Knopf, 2003. **F**

"Gay boy" Paul finds himself on an emotional rollercoaster as he tries to establish a new relationship with Noah while at the same time caring for Kyle.

————. *The Realm of Possibility*. Knopf, 2004. F
This novel in verse presents 20 distinctive yet interwoven stories by high school students who share defining pieces of their lives in a variety of poetic forms.

Levitin, Sonia. *Escape from Egypt*. Little, Brown, 1994. F
Miracles, plagues, and love are only part of what two teens—Jesse, a Hebrew slave, and Jennat, a half-Egyptian, half-Syrian girl—confront in this retelling of the biblical story of the Exodus.

————. *Return*. Atheneum, 1987. F
Desta, an Ethiopian Jew, and her family make a courageous and tragic journey across Ethiopia to Israel with the help of Operation Moses.

————. *Silver Days*. Atheneum, 1989. F
Escaping from Nazi Germany, the Platts struggle to find a home in America and pursue their own dreams.

Levitt, Leonard. *African Season*. Simon & Schuster, 1967. NF
A swinging Peace Corps Volunteer in Tanganyika quickly became "broo," meaning brother, to the villagers.

Levoy, Myron. *Pictures of Adam*. Harper & Row, 1986. F
Though 14-year-old camera bug Lisa is drawn to class misfit Adam, she is dismayed when he claims to be an alien from the planet Vega-X.

————. *A Shadow Like a Leopard*. Harper & Row, 1981. F
Ramon Santiago, a street punk and gifted poet, forms an unlikely friendship with an elderly artist, and each helps the other face his private fears.

Levy, Marilyn. *Run for Your Life*. Houghton Mifflin, 1996. F
A group of girls from a ghetto turn their lives around by running track.

Liang, Heng, and Judith Shapiro. *Son of the Revolution*. Knopf, 1983. NF
Liang Heng recounts his growing up during the Chinese Cultural Revolution, which fractured his family and changed his life.

Libby, Bill, and Vida Blue. *Vida: His Own Story*. Prentice-Hall, 1972. NF
Baseball pitcher Vida Blue tells what it feels like to achieve instant stardom and then be expected to produce miracles on the field every day.

Lieberman, E. James, and Ellen Peck. *Sex and Birth Control: A Guide for the Young*. Crowell, 1973. NF
Mature, responsible sexual behavior is the cornerstone of a candid, comprehensive handbook offering facts about sex and sexual relationships.

Lindall, Edward. *Northward the Coast*. Morrow, 1966. F
Having agreed to hide two political refugees, hard-boiled Lang Bowman takes them across the Australian wasteland with the police in pursuit.

Lipsyte, Robert. *Brave*. HarperCollins, 1991. F
Sonny Bear, half-white and half-Moscondaga Indian, wants to be a boxer but has difficulty controlling his anger until he meets Alfred Brooks, a New York City cop and former contender.

————. *One Fat Summer*. Harper & Row, 1977. F
Overweight Bobby Marks confronts the ridicule of friends and sheds his excess pounds, in a comical story of his last fat summer.

Lisle, Janet Taylor. *Black Duck*. Philomel, 2006. F
While researching a newspaper article about a mysterious 1929 event, 14-year-old David uncovers secrets surrounding the deaths of three bootleggers on the rum-running vessel the *Black Duck*.

————. *Sirens and Spies*. Bradbury, 1985. F
Fourteen-year-old Elsie feels betrayed when she discovers that her beloved violin teacher, Miss Fitch, has a dark and painful secret she has been hiding since her girlhood in World War II France.

Little, Jason. *Shutterbug Follies*. Doubleday Graphic Novels, 2002. F
Bee's job as a one-hour photo lab technician leads her into a bizarre murder mystery involving an art photographer's grisly subjects.

Littlefield, Bill. *Champions: Stories of Ten Remarkable Athletes*. Little, Brown, 1993. NF
The accomplishments and contributions of ten extraordinary athletes, from both genders and many cultural backgrounds, are explored through moving essays and evocative full-color paintings.

Llewellyn, Chris. *Fragments from the Fire: The Triangle Shirtwaist Company Fire of March 25, 1911*. Viking, 1987. NF
This slim volume of poetry tells the story of the young women who died when fire destroyed the Triangle Shirtwaist Factory.

Llywelyn, Morgan. *The Horse Goddess.* Houghton Mifflin, 1982. **F**
A young Celtic woman and a savage warrior journey throughout the ancient world pursued by a Druid priest, the horrible Shapechanger.

Lobel, Anita. *No Pretty Pictures: A Child of War.* Greenwillow, 1998. **NF**
A moving account of the award-winning illustrator's childhood in Nazi-occupied Poland, her imprisonment in a series of concentration camps, and her life after the war as a displaced person in Sweden.

Lockley, Ronald. *Seal-Woman.* Bradbury, 1975. **F**
Truth and fantasy blend in this haunting story of an Irish girl who becomes a princess of the seals and of the man she chooses as her prince.

Logan, Jane. *The Very Nearest Room.* Scribner, 1973. **F**
Fifteen-year-old Lee Kramer's life is bounded by family—a hardworking doctor father, boy-crazy younger sister, frail younger brother, and, especially, her dying mother.

Logue, Mary. *Dancing with an Alien.* Harper Collins, 2000. **F**
After a virus kills all the females on his planet, Branko falls in love with an Earth girl and wants her to return with him to his planet.

London, Mel. *Getting into Film.* Ballantine, 1977. **NF**
An award-winning filmmaker shares the "inside dope" on career opportunities in all aspects of the film industry.

Lopes, Sal, ed. *The Wall: Images and Offerings from the Vietnam Veterans Memorial.* Collins, 1987. **NF**
Images of peace, war, and remembrance are evoked in this photo-essay about the healing force of the Vietnam Veterans Memorial.

Lopez, Barry. *Arctic Dreams: Imagination and Desire in a Northern Landscape.* Scribner, 1986. **NF**
This is an enchanting and challenging account of the animals, people, geology, and history of the Arctic.

Lopez, Steve. *Third and Indiana.* Viking, 1994. **F**
Fourteen-year-old Gabriel runs away from home to protect his mother when he realizes that the boss of his drug-selling gang is crazy and murderous.

Lord, Bette Bao. *Legacies: A Chinese Mosaic.* Knopf, 1990. **NF**
These unique portraits of life in China during the past 40 years form an affecting picture of events that led to Tiananmen Square.

Lord, Walter. *Incredible Victory.* Harper & Row, 1967. **NF**
The crucial World War II Battle of Midway is stirringly re-created from both the American and Japanese points of view.

Lowachee, Karin. *Burndive.* Warner, 2003. **F**
Ryan Azarcon is drawn into an interstellar war when his famous family is targeted by assassins.

Lowenfels, Walter, ed. *The Writing on the Wall: 108 American Poems of Protest.* Doubleday, 1969. **NF**
Martyrdom, inhumanity, war, and death confront the conscience of the reader in this anthology of protest poetry.

Lowry, Lois. *The Giver.* Houghton Mifflin, 1993. **F**
When he turns 12, Jonas is given his life assignment from the committee of elders—to become the receiver of memories from far-past times—and discovers the horrible secret that his society has hidden for the "safety and happiness" of its citizens.

Lubar, David. *Hidden Talents.* TOR, 1999. **F**
Edgeview Alternative School is for losers, but when Martin arrives he discovers that some talents can be used to make losers into winners.

————. *Sleeping Freshmen Never Lie.* Dutton, 2005. **F**
In a series of humorous diary entries, ninth-grader Scott offers a list of dos and don'ts to his unborn sibling on surviving freshman year of high school.

Lueders, Edward, and Primus St. John, comps. *Zero Makes Me Hungry: A Collection of Poems for Today.* Lothrop, Lee & Shepard, 1976. **NF**
Poems in a contemporary vein are excitingly presented with eye-catching modern graphics.

Lund, Doris. *Eric.* Lippincott, 1974. **NF**
Told, at 17, that he has leukemia, Eric crowds his dreams for the future—college, sports, love—into the short time he has left.

Lydon, Michael. *Rock Folk: Portraits from the Rock 'n' Roll Pantheon.* Dial, 1971. **NF**
These sketches bring to life the personality, lifestyle, and music of rock stars Chuck Berry, Carl Perkins, B. B. King, Smokey Robinson, Janis Joplin, The Grateful Dead, and The Rolling Stones.

Lynch, Chris. *Freewill.* HarperCollins, 2001. **F**
Why are you carving statues, Will? Do you think it's causing the suicides? Are you doing it of your own free will? Will you ever know?

———. *Gold Dust*. HarperCollins, 2000. **F**
Richard believes that learning to love baseball will help a black Caribbean boy fit in to a racially charged Boston neighborhood in the 1970s.

———. *Gypsy Davey*. HarperCollins, 1994. **F**
Learning about love, life, and growing up, Davey challenges our perceptions of a mentally disabled teenager.

———. *Iceman*. HarperCollins, 1994. **F**
Eric plays hockey with a savage intensity, hoping that this only link to his father will improve their troubled relationship.

———. *Inexcusable*. Atheneum, 2005. **F**
High school senior and football star Keir Sarafina says, "I hate it when people I love condemn me," but has Keir done something inexcusable to Gigi Boudakian?

———. *Shadow Boxer*. HarperCollins, 1993. **F**
Lynch writes about the love between two brothers, their dead father, and the sport that killed him.

———. *Slot Machine*. HarperCollins, 1995. **F**
Elvin and his two best friends are sent to a summer camp for incoming freshmen at a Catholic boys' high school. Will short, round Elvin fit the slots the good fathers are trying to jam him into?

Lynch, Jim. *The Highest Tide*. Bloomsbury, 2005. **F**
Miles O'Malley discovers peculiar sea life in a cove of Puget Sound.

Lynch, Scott. *The Lies of Locke Lamora*. Bantam, 2006. **F**
In this fantasy caper, professional thief Locke Lamora has long preyed on the nobles of Camorr; now, someone unexpected is preying on him.

Lynd, Alice. *We Won't Go: Personal Accounts of War Objectors*. Beacon, 1968. **NF**
Told with utter sincerity, these are the personal accounts of Vietnam protesters.

Lynn, Elizabeth A. *Sardonyx Net*. Putnam, 1981. **F**
Star captain Dana Ikoro becomes Rhani Yago's slave, bodyguard, and lover, as well as her pilot, after he is convicted of smuggling dorazine.

Lyons, Mary E. *Letters from a Slave Girl: The Story of Harriet Jacobs*. Scribner, 1992. **F**
Through letters to family and friends, Harriet Jacobs describes her life as a young slave girl in North Carolina and her daring escape to freedom.

———. *Sorrow's Kitchen: The Life and Folklore of Zora Neale Hurston*. Scribner, 1990. **NF**
A biography of Zora Neale Hurston who, wanting to preserve the cultural heritage of black Ameri-cans, achieves fame and triumph through her stories and plays, only to die poor and, until recently, almost forgotten.

Maas, Peter. *Rescuer*. Harper & Row, 1967. **NF**
Charles Momsen utilizes his previously untried diving bell and succeeds in rescuing 33 men entombed in the sunken submarine *Squalus*.

———. *Serpico*. Viking, 1973. **NF**
Believing cops should be honest, New York policeman Frank Serpico attempts to get action from the top against corrupt fellow officers.

Macaulay, David. *Motel of the Mysteries*. Houghton Mifflin, 1979. **NF**
"Plastic is forever" is an illustrated catalog of the wonderful things discovered by archaeologists in the year 4022, when they excavate the ruins of the Toot 'n' C'mon Motel.

———. *The Way Things Work*. Houghton Mifflin, 1988. **NF**
Little woolly mammoths help you learn everything you always wanted to know about machines and how they work.

MacCracken, Mary. *A Circle of Children*. Lippincott, 1974. **NF**
Involving herself in a school for emotionally disturbed children, Mary MacCracken learns that these children can be helped through the love, trust, and compassion of those who teach them.

———. *Lovey: A Very Special Child*. Lippincott, 1976. **NF**
A profoundly disturbed child, Hannah is trapped in the prison of her emotions until a gifted teacher helps her break free.

MacInnes, Helen. *The Salzburg Connection*. Harcourt, Brace & World, 1968. **F**
Tension mounts steadily as Bill Mathison, a young attorney sojourning in the Alps, finds himself facing a dangerous group of international agents.

Mack, Tracy. *Birdland*. Scholastic, 2003. **F**
Jed's East Village video documentary and the people he meets help him deal with his grief over the recent death of his brother, Zeke, a poet and jazz fan.

Mackay, Donald A. *The Building of Manhattan*. Harper & Row, 1987. **NF**
Ever wonder how the Empire State Building was built, how the New York subway works, or what happened to the farmland on Manhattan Island? Mackay explains it all.

MacKinnon, Bernie. *The Meantime.* Houghton Mifflin, 1984. **F**

Told through the eyes of their son, this is the story of a middle-class black family living in a white suburb and facing the hostility of neighbors and schoolmates.

Mackler, Carolyn. *The Earth, My Butt, and Other Big, Round Things.* Candlewick, 2003. **F**

Fifteen-year-old Virginia Shreves learns how to manage her weight, the wandering hands of Froggy Welsh the Fourth, and an accusation of date rape against her perfect older brother.

MacLachlan, Patricia. *Baby.* Delacorte, 1993. **F**

Left on the doorstep—but only for temporary care—baby Sophie forces Larkin's family to deal with their own unresolved tragedy.

———. *Journey.* Delacorte, 1991. **F**

Journey's grandparents find a way to restore his family to him after his mother abandons him and his sister.

MacLaine, Shirley. *You Can Get There from Here.* Norton, 1975. **NF**

Invited to visit the People's Republic of China, the author and a group of American women were not prepared for what they saw and learned.

MacLean, Alistair. *Circus.* Doubleday, 1975. **F**

It takes a five-man circus act with a psychic tightrope artist to get in and out of an East European prison safely.

———. *When Eight Bells Toll.* Doubleday, 1966. **F**

Philip Calvert, a ruthless agent for Britain's secret service, outwits a gang of modern pirates operating on the Irish Sea.

MacLean, John. *Mac.* Houghton Mifflin, 1987. **F**

Mac's world, which centers on sports, school, and girls, crumbles when he is molested by a physician—and he tries to act as if it never happened.

MacLeish, Roderick. *The First Book of Eppe: An American Romance.* Random House, 1980. **F**

Sherborne Eppe, a lovable bungler, reentering the world after seven years in an "insane asylum," encounters several opportunities to do good as he flees from his mother, searches for his father, and tries to find himself.

Macy, Sue. *A Whole New Ball Game: The Story of the All-American Girls Professional Baseball League.* Holt, 1993. **NF**

From 1943 to 1954, the United States had a professional women's baseball league that "packed 'em in" and inspires this noteworthy chapter of American sports history.

———. *Winning Ways: A Photohistory of American Women in Sports.* Holt, 1996. **NF**

Macy's social and photographic history treats women's sports in the United States—from the 1800s, when even bicycle riding was unacceptable, to the mid-1990s.

Madaras, Lynda. *Lynda Madaras Talks to Teens about AIDS: An Essential Guide for Parents, Teachers, and Young People.* Newmarket, 1988. **NF**

The curious, worried, or scared will find information, help, and hope in this honest look at how AIDS affects teens today.

Madaras, Lynda, and Area Madaras. *What's Happening to My Body? A Growing Up Guide for Mothers and Daughters.* Newmarket, 1983. **NF**

This illustrated guide discusses body images, body changes, menstruation, puberty in boys, and sexuality, emphasizing the importance of liking and knowing one's own body. An updated edition was published in 2007, and a version for boys is also available.

Magorian, Michelle. *Back Home.* Harper & Row, 1984. **F**

When Virginia (Rusty) Dickinson returns to England after being evacuated to America during World War II, she feels lonely and alienated until she and her mother grow toward mutual understanding and acceptance.

———. *Good Night, Mr. Tom.* Harper & Row, 1981. **F**

A badly battered and frightened young boy evacuated from London during World War II fills an empty void in the heart of a dour old man.

———. *Not a Swan.* HarperCollins, 1992. **F**

Spending an unchaperoned summer in a seaside English town during World War II, three sisters discover their lives will never be the same.

Magubane, Peter. *Black Child.* Knopf, 1982. **NF**

The sad, harsh realities of life in South Africa are sensitively revealed in photographs of children's faces.

Maguire, Gregory. *I Feel Like the Morning Star.* Harper & Row, 1989. **F**

Pioneer Colony's three dissidents—Ella, Mort, and Sorb—plot to escape their underground post–nuclear holocaust community.

Mah, Adeline Yen. *Chinese Cinderella: The True Story of an Unwanted Daughter.* Delacorte, 1999. **NF**

Adapted from her adult book *Falling Leaves*, Mah's autobiography for young readers is the heartbreaking story of her struggle with her stepmother.

Mahy, Margaret. *The Catalogue of the Universe.* Margaret K. McElderry, 1986. **F**
Angela's search for the father she has never met leads to a surprising new relationship with her best friend, Tycho Potter.

———. *The Changeover: A Supernatural Romance.* Margaret K. McElderry, 1984. **F**
With the help of an older boy who loves her, Laura "changes over" into a witch to fight the evil forces that are attacking her little brother.

———. *Memory.* Margaret K. McElderry, 1988. **F**
After a wild, drunken night seeking the truth behind his confused memories of his sister's death, teenage Jonny meets Sophie, an old woman who has lost her memory but has retained her zest for life.

———. *The Tricksters.* Margaret K. McElderry, 1986. **F**
Three strangers from nowhere are catalysts in the lives of Harry and her family when reality and fantasy merge to expose unexpected secrets.

Maiorano, Robert. *Worlds Apart: The Autobiography of a Dancer from Brooklyn.* Coward, McCann & Geoghegan, 1980. **NF**
A soloist with the New York City Ballet recounts his first 16 years by presenting the two contrasting worlds in which he grew up—the tough streets of Brooklyn and the demanding and exciting world of ballet.

Manchester, William. *One Brief Shining Moment: Remembering Kennedy.* Little, Brown, 1983. **NF**
Twenty years after John F. Kennedy's assassination, friends, family, and associates offer sentimental, yet candid reminiscences in words and pictures.

Mandela, Winnie. *Part of My Soul Went with Him.* Norton, 1985. **NF**
Battered but unyielding, Winnie Mandela reveals brutal facts about apartheid through her personal account of life in South Africa.

Manry, Robert. *Tinkerbelle.* Harper & Row, 1966. **NF**
A copy editor of the *Cleveland Plain Dealer* realizes a lifelong goal when he sails his 13-1/2 foot sloop across the Atlantic alone.

Marchetta, Melina. *Looking for Alibrandi.* Orchard, 1999. **F**
Australian high school senior Josie must contend with boy problems, getting admitted to university and law school, and the knowledge that she is an illegitimate child.

———. *Saving Francesca.* Knopf, 2004. **F**
Francesca is dealing with her classes, her friends, and the complications that arise from being one of 30 girls in a school with 750 guys, while also searching for a way to help bring her mother back from a breakdown.

Margolies, Marjorie, and Ruth Gruber. *They Came to Stay.* Coward, McCann & Geoghegan, 1976. **NF**
The heartwarming story of how a single woman adopted two daughters—one Korean and the other Vietnamese—and the problems they had until the three strangers became a family.

Marillier, Juliet. *Daughter of the Forest.* TOR, 2000. **F**
Twelve-year-old Sorcha faces a nearly impossible task as she works to rescue her six brothers from their stepmother's magic spell.

Marlette, Doug. *In Your Face: A Cartoonist at Work.* Houghton Mifflin, 1991. **NF**
Kudzu creator and political cartoonist Doug Marlette describes—in words and art—his sometimes offbeat life.

Marrin, Albert. *Commander-in-Chief Abraham Lincoln and the Civil War.* Dutton, 1997. **NF**
Marrin vividly portrays Lincoln as a self-educated, inexperienced politician, who finds himself leading the North's armed forces through one of the greatest tragedies in U.S. history.

———. *George Washington and the Founding of a Nation.* Dutton, 2001. **NF**
This information-packed biography makes Washington a real person and reveals the hard road he and his contemporaries traveled in the formation of our country.

———. *Sitting Bull and His World.* Dutton, 2000. **NF**
Explore the life and times of Sitting Bull and the time line of events in the West.

———. *Terror of the Spanish Main: Sir Henry Morgan and His Buccaneers.* Dutton, 1999. **NF**
Buccaneer Henry Morgan's 17th-century life is like an action movie filled with vivid images of ruthless campaigns, punishments, and raw adventure.

———. *Unconditional Surrender: U. S. Grant and the Civil War.* Atheneum, 1994. **NF**
In addition to pointing out the many ironies in Grant's life and his pivotal role in the Civil War, Marrin portrays a soldier's life, early medical services, and battle tactics.

————. *Virginia's General: Robert E. Lee and the Civil War*. Atheneum, 1994. **NF**

Marrin's spirited biography shows how Lee, though opposed to slavery and secession, felt compelled by his honor to take up arms for his home state of Virginia—and in doing so changed the course of history.

Marsden, John. *Letters from the Inside*. Houghton Mifflin, 1994. **F**

With each letter, teenage pen pals Tracey and Mandy share personal experiences, each fearing the future—then Tracey's letters come back stamped "Return to Sender."

————. *So Much to Tell You*. Joy Street, 1989. **F**

In her diary, Marina, a young Australian girl locked in a self-imposed silence, reveals her deepest feelings and the family problems that led to her muteness.

————. *Tomorrow, When the War Began*. Houghton Mifflin, 1995. **F**

When they return from a wilderness camping trip, Ellie and her friends are shocked to discover Australia has been invaded and soon find fighting and surviving have become their way of life.

Marsh, Dave. *Born to Run: The Bruce Springsteen Story*. Dolphin, 1979. **NF**

This illustrated biography of a rock star traces his beginnings in Asbury Park, N.J., to the top of the rock and roll charts.

Marshall, Kathryn. *In the Combat Zone: An Oral History of American Women in Vietnam, 1966–1975*. Little, Brown, 1987. **NF**

Dramatic, thoughtful, often tragic accounts by a few of the thousands of women who served in Vietnam and, years later, tell a story few people know about.

Martin, Valerie. *Mary Reilly*. Doubleday, 1990. **F**

Intrigued by the mysterious Dr. Jekyll, housemaid Mary Reilly finds life taking a different twist as she learns more about his late-night prowling in Victorian England.

Martinez, A. Lee. *Gil's All Fright Diner*. TOR, 2005. **F**

When Earl, a vampire, and his werewolf buddy, Duke, pull up to Rockwood's only diner in their out-of-gas pickup, they find themselves uniquely suited to stop Armageddon.

Martinez, Manuel Luis. *Drift*. Picador, 2003. **F**

Set adrift by his family, 16-year-old Robert Lomos tries to put his life together but keeps screwing up, with only his iron-willed Grams to truly believe in him.

Marzollo, Jean. *Halfway down Paddy Lane*. Dial, 1981. **F**

Kate experiences a drastic change in lifestyle when she is transported back in time to 1850 as the daughter of an Irish immigrant family that lives and works in a New England mill town.

Mason, Bobbie Ann. *In Country*. Harper & Row, 1985. **F**

On a pilgrimage to the Vietnam War Memorial in Washington, D.C., Sam, a recent high school graduate, tries to understand the strange behavior of her uncle Emmett and the death of the father she never knew, both victims of the Vietnam War.

Mason, Robert. *Chickenhawk*. Viking, 1983. **F**

The account of an American helicopter pilot in Vietnam who recalls his military training, the horror of Vietnam combat, and the pain of coming home.

Mastoon, Adam. *The Shared Heart: Portraits and Stories Celebrating Lesbian, Gay, and Bisexual Young People*. Morrow, 1997. **NF**

Thirty-nine young people pose for the camera and tell about their struggles, heartaches, fear, joys, and triumphs growing up gay.

Matas, Carol. *After the War*. Simon & Schuster, 1996. **F**

Met with hatred and violence when she returns home from a concentration camp, Ruth joins with other Jews who are trying to make their way to Palestine.

Matcheck, Diane. *The Sacrifice*. Farrar, Straus & Giroux, 1998. **F**

A 15-year-old Apsaalooka girl overcomes the objections of her family and her tribe as she tries to become a warrior, a hunter, and the "Great One" prophesied at the birth of her and her twin brother.

Mather, Melissa. *One Summer in Between*. Harper & Row, 1967. **F**

Harriet Brown, an African American college student working temporarily for a white family in Vermont, is shocked when she recognizes her own prejudice.

Mathis, Sharon Bell. *Listen for the Fig Tree*. Viking, 1974. **F**

In spite of her blindness and an alcoholic mother, Muffin, with the help of a kind neighbor, celebrates Kwanza and is able to face the future.

————. *Teacup Full of Roses*. Viking, 1972. **F**

Into the lives of a middle-class African American family reach the tragedies of drugs, demolished dreams, and sudden death.

Matsubara, Hisako. *Cranes at Dusk.* Dial, 1985. **F**

Like her defeated country of Japan, ten-year-old Saya faces painful readjustments after World War II, as her mother, who can neither abandon tradition nor accept changes, attempts to turn Saya against her wise and progressive father.

Matthew, Christopher. *The Long-Haired Boy.* Atheneum, 1980. **F**

War, self-pity, endless skin grafts, and long hospitalizations face Hugh Fleming, a young British fighter pilot, as he learns about life and finds a purpose for living.

Mattison, Chris. *Snake.* DK, 1999. **NF**

The evolution, anatomy, and behavior of snakes are portrayed through excellent illustrations and interesting descriptions.

Maurer, Richard. *The Wild Colorado: The True Adventures of Fred Dellenbaugh, Age 17, on the Second Powell Expedition into the Grand Canyon.* Crown, 1999. **NF**

This is the exciting true adventure of the teen who made the first sketches of the Grand Canyon ever on the 1869 Exploratory Expedition.

Maxwell, Robin. *The Secret Diary of Anne Boleyn.* Arcade, 1997. **F**

Elizabeth, England's monarch, receives her mother's secret diary and becomes acquainted with a mother she has never known.

Mayhar, Ardath. *Soul-Singer of Tyrnos.* Atheneum, 1981. **F**

Though only a novice at singing souls, Yeleeve becomes the singer chosen to help combat the great evil threatening to overpower the land.

Maynard, Joyce. *Looking Back: A Chronicle of Growing Up Old in the Sixties.* Doubleday, 1973. **NF**

Writing at age 18, the author takes a nostalgic look back at what it was like to grow up in middle-class, white America in the 1960s.

———. *The Usual Rules.* St. Martin's, 2003. **F**

Thirteen-year-old Wendy tries to pick up the pieces of her shattered life after her beloved mother, an executive secretary, dies in the World Trade Center on September 11, 2001.

Mazer, Anne, ed. *Working Days: Stories about Teenagers and Work.* Persea, 1997. **F**

Fifteen short stories about teenagers finding their way in the world of work.

Mazer, Harry. *The Girl of His Dreams.* Crowell, 1987. **F**

Runner Willis Pierce has to reconcile his fantasy about the "girl of his dreams" with reality when he meets Sophie, a girl who makes the world a less lonely place.

———. *I Love You, Stupid!* Crowell, 1981. **F**

Marcus Rosenbloom wants to love a girl but isn't sure he knows how—until he meets Wendy Barrett.

———. *The Last Mission.* Delacorte, 1979. **F**

When 15-year-old Jack Raab lies his way into becoming a tail gunner during World War II, he has no idea of the terrifying experiences that await him.

———. *The War on Villa Street.* Delacorte, 1978. **F**

Thirteen-year-old Willis, who has turned to running as an escape from an unhappy home, coaches a retarded boy in athletics, an experience that helps both gain self-respect.

———. *When the Phone Rang.* Scholastic, 1985. **F**

When their parents are killed in an air crash, Billy, Lori, and their older college-age brother, Kevin, struggle against adults and among themselves to avoid separating the family.

———. *Who Is Eddie Leonard?* Delacorte, 1993. **F**

Orphaned by the death of his grandmother, 15-year-old Eddie convinces himself that he is the boy whose face is on a poster at the post office, but can he convince the Diaz family that he is their missing Jason?

Mazer, Harry, and Norma Fox Mazer. *The Solid Gold Kid.* Delacorte, 1977. **F**

When five teenagers accept a ride from strangers, they become the victims of a kidnap plot and experience six horror-filled days that change their lives.

Mazer, Norma Fox. *After the Rain.* Morrow, 1987. **F**

Rachel tells the story of her growing understanding of her 83-year-old grandfather, a cantankerous old man she finds hard to love and almost impossible to like.

———. *Dear Bill, Remember Me? and Other Stories.* Delacorte, 1976. **F**

Eight short stories, all featuring strong female characters, range from a sensitive portrayal of an 18-year-old dying from cancer to the tale of a turn-of-the-century immigrant girl who defies tradition by getting an education and not getting married.

———. *Downtown*. Morrow, 1984. F
When his mother reappears after eight years, Pete Connors, son of antiwar activists who have been hiding, must reconcile his desire for normalcy with a realization of his parents' ideals and acts.

———. *Out of Control*. Morrow, 1993. F
After Rollo joins his friends in assaulting the artistic loner Valerie, he begins to understand what it means to be violated.

———. *Silver*. Morrow, 1988. F
When 14-year-old Sarabeth Silver transfers to a new school, she is thrilled to find herself a part of the in crowd, until she becomes privy to an awful secret.

———. *Someone to Love*. Delacorte, 1983. F
When Nina and Mitch fall in love, it seems only natural for them to live together until Nina finishes college.

———. *Up in Seth's Room: A Love Story*. Delacorte, 1979. F
Though Finn's parents forbid her relationship with 19-year-old Seth, the two develop a real attachment that helps them understand more about themselves and each other.

———. *When She Was Good*. Arthur A. Levine, 1997. F
Seventeen-year-old Em remembers what it was like living with her emotionally disturbed, abusive sister, Pamela.

McCaffrey, Anne. *Dragonsinger*. Atheneum, 1977. F
With the help of Master-harper, Menolly and her fire lizards overcome the prejudice against a woman's becoming a harper on the planet Pern.

———. *Pegasus in Flight*. Ballantine, 1990. F
In a future where the psychically talented are both exploited and shunned, quadriplegic Peter and slum-kid Tirla join forces to build a new space station and infiltrate a child-smuggling ring.

McCall, Nathan. *Makes Me Wanna Holler: A Young Black Man in America*. Random House, 1994. NF
McCall remembers his journey from a working-class African American neighborhood to prison to a prestigious position on the *Washington Post*.

McCammon, Robert R. *Boy's Life*. Pocket, 1991. F
Cory and his dad find a corpse handcuffed to the steering wheel of a sunken car and decide to search for the killer.

McCants, William D. *Much Ado about Prom Night*. Harcourt Brace, 1995. F
Honor student Becca Singleton, embroiled in a battle to save peer counseling from being shut down by the school board, worries about getting a date for the prom.

McCartney, Linda. *Linda's Pictures: A Collection of Photographs*. Knopf, 1976. NF
Large-size color photographs of the Beatles—especially McCartney and family—and other rock groups by Paul's photographer-wife provide a unique look at them.

McCaughrean, Geraldine. *The Kite Rider*. HarperCollins, 2002. F
Danger lurks everywhere in 13th-century China as Haoyou rescues his grieving mother from an evil potential second husband, an action which forces him to join a traveling circus in the perilous role of the Kite Rider.

———. *The Pirate's Son*. Scholastic, 1998. F
Imagine living your fantasy of sailing off to exotic Madagascar with pirates: 14-year-old Nathan Gull does just that but not always with the wished-for results.

McClafferty, Carla Killough. *Something Out of Nothing: Marie Curie and Radium*. Farrar, Straus & Giroux, 2006. NF
Marie Curie, the first woman to win the Nobel Prize, was also the first person to win it twice. This biography explores Curie's achievements in an era when women scientists struggled for recognition.

McConnell, Joan. *Ballet as Body Language*. Harper & Row, 1977. NF
A vivid and realistic introduction to the behind-the-scenes sweat and pain—as well as the onstage glamor—of ballet.

McCorkle, Jill. *Ferris Beach*. Algonquin, 1990. F
Katie Burns is caught in the conflict between the conventional life of her family and the daring, romantic lives of her beautiful cousin Angela and her lively neighbor, Mo Rhodes.

McCormick, Patricia. *Cut*. Front Street, 2000. F
Thirteen-year-old Callie, confined to a treatment facility for self-mutilation, gradually begins to take time to understand some of the reasons behind her behavior.

———. *Sold*. Hyperion, 2006. F
In this startling, frank novel in free verse, a 13-year-old Nepalese girl is sold into prostitution by her stepfather after a monsoon leaves her family destitute.

McCullough, Frances, ed. *Earth, Air, Fire, and Water: Poems.* Harper & Row, 1989. F

What is a poem? This revised edition of a memorable collection of poems by 125 poets from all over the world may change your definition of poetry in surprising and intriguing ways.

————, ed. *Love Is Like the Lion's Tooth: An Anthology of Love Poems.* Harper & Row, 1984. NF

Passion, not romance, is the theme of this diverse anthology of love poems from various times and places.

McDonald, Janet. *Spellbound.* Frances Foster, 2001. F

Raven feels trapped at home with her baby until her sister suggests that she compete in a spelling bee to win a college scholarship.

McDonald, Joyce. *Shades of Simon Gray.* Delacorte, 2001. F

Was the terrible crash that put Simon Gray into a coma really an accident, or was he simply wishing to end the guilt he felt when his illegal computer project failed?

————. *Swallowing Stones.* Delacorte, 1997. F

Depression, guilt, and fear plague Michael's dreams after a stray bullet from his rifle kills a man.

McFarlane, Milton C. *Cudjoe of Jamaica: Pioneer for Black Freedom in the New World.* R. Enslow, 1977. NF

This is a retelling of the story of General Cudjoe, who led the proud Maroons of Jamaica in their successful 18th-century fight against enslavement by the British.

McGhee, Alison. *All Rivers Flow to the Sea.* Candlewick, 2005. F

It's always been Rose and Ivy, until that fateful night when an accident separates the sisters into two realities: one skirting a stupefying grief, the other dependent on the mechanized breathing of a ventilator.

McGuire, Paula. *It Won't Happen to Me: Teenagers Talk about Pregnancy.* Delacorte, 1983. NF

Interviews with 15 young women who have faced unwanted pregnancies.

McIntyre, Vonda N. *Dreamsnake.* Houghton Mifflin, 1978. F

Snake, a young healer in a dangerous post-holocaust world, undertakes an arduous search for a replacement for Grass, the slain dreamsnake vital to her profession.

McKee, Tim, ed. *No More Strangers Now: Young Voices from a New South Africa.* DK, 1998. NF

Twelve South African teenagers share their experiences of life under and since apartheid, as well as their hopes for the future of their country and themselves.

McKibben, Bill. *The End of Nature.* Random House, 1989. NF

McKibben explores and explains the environmental cataclysms and global climate changes facing planet Earth.

McKillip, Patricia A. *Fool's Run.* Warner, 1987. F

Masked musician the Queen of Hearts and her band entertain in an orbiting prison and create an intergalactic emergency.

McKinley, Robin. *Beauty: A Retelling of the Story of Beauty and the Beast.* Harper & Row, 1978. F

Fantasy and romance are beautifully blended in an evocative, much-expanded version of the classic fairy tale.

————. *The Blue Sword.* Greenwillow, 1982. F

Harry Crewe, bored with her dull and sheltered life, finds new magic, love, and her destiny as a woman warrior when kidnapped by a handsome king who has mysterious powers.

————. *Deerskin.* Ace, 1993. F

Charles Perrault's fairy tale "Donkeyskin," the story of a king who rapes his own daughter, is re-created here in the unforgettable adventure of Princess Lissar, whose faithful dog Ash helps her escape the obsessive love of her father.

————. *The Hero and the Crown.* Greenwillow, 1985. F

Struggling to become a dragon killer, Aerin almost dies subduing the Black Dragon—only to face the evil mage, Agsded.

————. *The Outlaws of Sherwood.* Greenwillow, 1988. F

In a retelling that transcends the centuries, Newbery medalist Robin McKinley gives readers a lively, romantic new version of Robin Hood and his merry band.

————. *Rose Daughter.* Greenwillow, 1997. F

Beauty, who possesses the gift of growing roses, is compelled to stay at the Beast's castle and help him bring his magnificent garden, the heart of his magical kingdom, back to life.

———. *Sunshine*. Berkley, 2003. **F**
Sunshine is chained to the wall of an abandoned ballroom and left to be devoured by the ballroom's other prisoner, a vampire, who instead asks her to help him escape.

McKissack, Patricia C., and Fredrick L. McKissack. *Rebels against Slavery: American Slave Revolts*. Scholastic, 1996. **NF**
Exciting profiles of heroic men and women tell accounts of those who rebelled against slavery in North America.

———. *Red-Tail Angels: The Story of the Tuskegee Airmen of World War II*. Walker, 1995. **NF**
A fascinating, well-illustrated history of African American pilots tells of their integral role in World War II.

———. *Sojourner Truth: Ain't I a Woman?* Scholastic, 1992. **NF**
A slave for the first 30 years of her life, Sojourner Truth achieves freedom and becomes an eloquent orator for the abolition of slavery and the emancipation of women—in spite of never learning to read or write.

———. *Young, Black, and Determined: A Biography of Lorraine Hansberry*. Holiday House, 1998. **NF**
A lively biography of the young black playwright who achieved success and recognition for her contribution to the arts and her hard work as a civil rights activist.

McLaren, Clemence. *Inside the Walls of Troy: A Novel of the Women Who Lived the Trojan War*. Atheneum, 1996. **F**
The beautiful Helen and the prophetess Cassandra describe, from their respective viewpoints, the events that led to the great Trojan War.

McNamee, Graham. *Acceleration*. Wendy Lamb, 2003. **F**
While working a summer job in the Lost and Found Office of the Toronto Transit Commission, Duncan discovers a journal containing a man's plans to murder women.

———. *Hate You*. Delacorte, 1999. **F**
Seventeen-year-old Alice has spent most of her life writing songs to deal with her anger toward the abusive father who damaged her vocal cords.

McNaughton, Janet. *An Earthly Knight*. HarperCollins, 2004. **F**
In 1162, Jenny finds herself in the dutiful role of eldest daughter when her older sister runs away with a dangerous suitor, leaving Jenny torn between her father's marriage wishes for her and her growing love for the mysterious Tam Lim.

McNeal, Laura, and Tom McNeal. *Crooked*. Knopf, 1999. **F**
Ninth-graders Clara and Amos find their lives turned upside down by family, bullies, and each other.

McPherson, James M. *Fields of Fury: The American Civil War*. Atheneum, 2002. **NF**
Event by event, a noted Civil War historian chronicles for younger readers the deadliest conflict the United States ever fought, providing battle descriptions, personal stories, biographies of the most important players, clear maps, and illustrations from paintings, photographs, other historical documents.

McWhorter, Diane. *A Dream of Freedom: The Civil Rights Movement from 1954 to 1968*. Scholastic, 2004. **NF**
This handsome volume summarizes and explains the key years of the civil rights movement, featuring major players as well as lesser known heroes and heroines.

Mead, Alice. *Adem's Cross*. Farrar, Straus & Giroux, 1996. **F**
Fourteen-year-old Adem endures the horrors of war in the former Yugoslavia until forced to flee for his life.

Meltzer, Milton. *Ain't Gonna Study War No More: The Story of America's Peace Seekers*. Harper & Row, 1985. **NF**
A lively account of the individuals and groups that have protested against the wars in which the United States has been involved—people convinced that there are peaceful solutions to conflict.

———, ed. *The American Revolutionaries: A History in Their Own Words, 1750–1800*. Crowell, 1987. **NF**
Letters, journals, etc., provide the personal views of people living in a turbulent time.

———. *Benjamin Franklin: The New American*. Watts, 1988. **NF**
This biography is the life story of an American original—a self-made man of many interests and talents and one of the revolutionaries who bucked the establishment to found a new country.

———. *Columbus and the World around Him*. Watts, 1990. **NF**
Meltzer's "no holds barred" biography of Columbus details the explorer's voyages in search of Asia and describes the tragic impact of the Spaniards upon the Native Americans.

———. *Never to Forget: The Jews of the Holocaust.* Harper & Row, 1976. **NF**

Based on diaries, letters, songs, and history books, this is a moving account of Jewish suffering in Nazi Germany before and during World War II.

———. *Rescue: The Story of How Gentiles Saved Jews in the Holocaust.* Harper & Row, 1988. **NF**

In an account of individuals who risked their own lives to save thousands of others during the Holocaust, Meltzer shows the quiet but impressive courage of those who chose to stand firm in the face of monstrous evil.

———, ed. *Voices from the Civil War: A Documentary History of the Great American Conflict.* Crowell, 1989. **NF**

Details and excerpts from letters, diaries, and other primary sources make the Civil War come alive through the voices of those who fought, died and survived its ravages.

Mercado, Nancy E., ed. *Every Man for Himself: Ten Short Stories about Being a Guy.* Dial, 2005. **F**

Ten short stories explore what it means to be a man.

Meriwether, Louise. *Daddy Was a Number Runner.* Prentice-Hall, 1970. **F**

Francie, a 12-year-old black girl, faces the daily hazards of life in the Harlem of the 1930s.

Merrick, Monte. *Shelter.* Hyperion, 1993. **F**

Nelson, a teen saddled with the care of his three-year-old sister, inadvertently discovers what his life is missing when his friends con him into investigating the disappearance of a developmentally disabled man from the neighborhood.

Messing, Shep, and David Hirshey. *The Education of an American Soccer Player.* Dodd, Mead, 1978. **NF**

One of the North American Soccer League's great goalies, Messing relates anecdotes about his Bronx childhood, Harvard education, participation in the Munich Olympics, and career with the New York Cosmos.

Meyer, Carolyn. *C.C. Poindexter.* Atheneum, 1978. **F**

In this zany story, C.C. (Cynthia Charlotte) Poindexter, who at age 15 is 6'1" and still growing, tells how she coped with her own problems and with family conflicts during one chaotic summer.

———. *The Center: From a Troubled Past to a New Life.* Margaret K. McElderry, 1979. **F**

David, who smokes marijuana, pops pills, cuts school, and steals, is sent to the Center, where teenagers help each other.

———. *Denny's Tapes.* Margaret K. McElderry, 1987. **F**

Rejected by his stepfather, Dennis goes across the country in search of his real father, detouring to visit both his grandmothers, from whom he learns about his biracial heritage.

———. *Drummers of Jericho.* Harcourt Brace, 1995. **F**

Jewish Panzit Trujillo challenges the traditions of her new community when she questions the high school marching band's use of a Christian symbol and hymns.

———. *Gideon's People.* Harcourt Brace, 1996. **F**

When Isaac, an Orthodox Jew, is injured and taken in by Gideon's Amish family, the two teenagers must learn about each other's culture.

———. *Jubilee Journey.* Harcourt Brace, 1997. **F**

Young biracial Emily is shocked out of her feelings of comfort as she discovers she needs to come to terms with her racial identity when she visits her African American family in Texas.

———. *Mary, Bloody Mary.* Harcourt Brace, 1999. **F**

Young Mary Tudor fights to retain her rights as heir to the English throne when Anne Boleyn turns Mary's father against her.

———. *Voices of South Africa: Growing Up in a Troubled Land.* Harcourt Brace Jovanovich, 1986. **NF**

Meyer recounts her journey to South Africa in a moving record of life in that beautiful and violent country.

———. *Where the Broken Heart Still Beats: The Story of Cynthia Ann Parker.* Harcourt Brace Jovanovich, 1992. **F**

Discovered and forced to return to her own family in 1836, 24 years after her capture by Comanche Indians, Cynthia Ann Parker is tragically unable to adjust to life away from the tribe that she now claims as her own.

———. *White Lilacs.* Harcourt Brace Jovanovich, 1993. **F**

Rose Lee Jefferson, 12, and her family have always lived in Freedom, the "Negro" community in Denton, Texas, until the white folks decide to turn Freedom into a municipal park.

Meyer, L. A. *Bloody Jack: Being an Account of the Curious Adventures of Mary "Jacky" Faber, Ship's Boy.* Harcourt, 2002. **F**

Reduced to begging and thievery on the streets of London, Mary transforms herself into Jacky Faber, ship's boy on the British warship *Dolphin*.

————. *Curse of the Blue Tattoo: Being an Account of the Misadventures of Jacky Faber, Midshipman and Fine Lady.* Harcourt, 2004. F

Jacky Faber, ship's boy and aspiring fine lady, is unceremoniously dropped off in Boston by the HMS *Dolphin* crew to attend the Lawson Peabody School for Young Girls, where she encounters more sharks than she could ever meet at sea!

Meyer, Stephenie. *Twilight.* Little, Brown, 2005. F

Bella's move to rainy Forks, Washington, is the most boring move she will ever make, until she meets Edward, the vampire love of her life.

Michaels, Barbara. *Ammie, Come Home.* Meredith, 1968. F

A ghost that never quite materializes and the spirit of "Ammie" Campbell haunt an old Georgetown house, threatening the lives of its occupants.

————. *Be Buried in the Rain.* Atheneum, 1985. F

Medical student Julie Newcomb rediscovers love as well as the terrors of her childhood when she goes to care for her sinister grandmother in a southern mansion that is—perhaps—haunted.

————. *The Dark on the Other Side.* Dodd, Mead, 1970. F

Writer Michael Collins does not believe in supernatural powers until he too sees the savage black dog that is driving Linda Randolph to the brink of insanity.

————. *Witch.* Dodd, Mead, 1973. F

Ellen's beautiful house, rumored to be haunted by a witch and her cat, changes from a refuge to a prison as she tries to understand the strange and threatening events that crowd around her.

Michelson, Maureen R., ed. *Women and Work: Photographs and Personal Writings.* NewSage, 1986. NF

Handsome black-and-white photographs together with women's personal testimonies capture the depth and breadth of American working women.

Mickle, Shelley Fraser. *The Queen of October.* Algonquin, 1989. F

Sent to her grandparents while her parents contemplate divorce, Sally comes to terms with herself and her life in a story set in the 1950s.

Mikaelsen, Ben. *Petey.* Hyperion, 1998. F

Born in 1905 and mistakenly diagnosed as an idiot, young Petey is sent to an insane asylum, where, 60 years later, his life is drastically changed by a teenage boy.

————. *Touching Spirit Bear.* HarperCollins, 2001. F

After angry Cole attacks another boy, he agrees to a Circle Justice sentence of banishment to a remote island, where he encounters a mystical spirit bear.

Miller, E. Ethelbert, ed. *In Search of Color Everywhere: A Collection of African-American Poetry.* Stewart, Tabori & Chang, 1994. NF

From spirituals to rap, these works by famous poets are a presentation to delight.

Miller, Frances A. *The Truth Trap.* Dutton, 1980. F

Mathew McKendrick is 15 and a nonconformist. When their parents are killed in an automobile accident, he and his nine-year-old deaf sister Kathie run away to Los Angeles where he finds himself unjustly accused of murder.

Miller, Jim, ed. *The Rolling Stone Illustrated History of Rock and Roll.* Rolling Stone, 1976. NF

In-depth portraits illustrate the most important movers of rock and roll, from the 1950s to the 1970s. A new edition was published in 1980.

Miller, Jim Wayne. *Newfound.* Orchard, 1989. F

Newfound Creek in Tennessee is home to teenager Robert Wells and his extended family in this haunting story of what it is really like to grow up in Appalachia.

Miller, Jonathan, and David Pelham. *The Facts of Life: Three-Dimensional, Movable Illustrations Show the Development of a Baby from Conception to Birth.* Viking, 1984. NF

Six three-dimensional, movable models illustrate the human reproductive system and fetal development from conception to birth.

Miller, Kirsten. *Kiki Strike: Inside the Shadow City.* Bloomsbury, 2006. F

Beneath the streets of New York, menacing gangsters, killer princesses, and Girl Scouts gone bad embark upon a wild adventure.

Miller, Mary Beth. *Aimee.* Dutton, 2002. F

How well do you think you'd cope if your best friend made sure you were the only witness to her suicide, you weren't allowed contact with any of the rest of your tight-knit group of friends, and everyone believed that you must have helped her kill herself, or perhaps even murdered her?

Mills, Judie. *John F. Kennedy.* Watts, 1988. NF

This biography reveals President John F. Kennedy's failures and faults as well as his moral courage and political successes.

Mitchell, David. *Black Swan Green.* Random House, 2006. **F**

In this darkly humorous novel, Jason's stammering terrorizes him, making silence preferable to humiliation.

Moeri, Louise. *The Forty-third War.* Houghton Mifflin, 1989. **F**

Forced to join a Central American army, 12-year-old Uno learns firsthand about soldiering and war.

Mohr, Nicholasa. *In Nueva York.* Dial, 1977. **F**

Interrelated stories of love, friendship, and the struggle to survive show the tragic and comic sides of life in a Puerto Rican community on New York's Lower East Side.

Mojtabai, A. G. *The 400 Eels of Sigmund Freud.* Simon & Schuster, 1976. **F**

Summer at a scientific community for gifted teenagers ends in tragedy for Isaiah, the rebel among them, who prefers music to science.

Moll, Richard. *The Public Ivys: A Guide to America's Best Public Undergraduate Colleges and Universities.* Viking, 1985. **NF**

Assuming that some state-supported colleges offer programs equivalent to those of the higher-priced Ivy League, Moll's thoughtful evaluations of the "public ivys" are right on target.

Monk, Lorraine. *Photographs That Changed the World: The Camera as Witness, the Photograph as Evidence.* Doubleday, 1989. **NF**

Fifty-one memorable photographs, with short essays that explore their enduring meaning.

Montalbano, William D., and Carl Hiaasen. *A Death in China.* Atheneum, 1984. **F**

Romance and murder lead a former Vietnam Special Forces officer on spectacular chases through thousands of clay soldiers who guard a Chinese emperor's tomb at Xi'an—where he finds clues to the mysterious death of his friend.

Montandon, Pat. *The Intruders.* Coward, McCann & Geoghegan, 1975. **NF**

A San Francisco television star becomes perplexed and terrified by the intrusion of unexplained violence into her glamorous hilltop home.

Montgomery, Sy. *Walking with the Great Apes: Jane Goodall, Dian Fossey, Birute Galdikas.* Houghton Mifflin, 1991. **NF**

These are the fascinating stories of three intrepid women who leave civilization to study and share the lives of primates.

Moody, Anne. *Coming of Age in Mississippi.* Dial, 1968. **NF**

This is what it's like to grow up poor and black in Mississippi; although flawed by the Southern racial system, Anne Moody refuses to be broken by it.

Moody, Raymond A., Jr. *Life after Life: The Investigation of a Phenomenon—Survival of Bodily Health.* Stackpole, 1976. **NF**

What is it like to die? Here are speculations by Dr. Moody and reports on interviews with people who had clinically died but lived to relate their comforting near-death experiences.

Moore, Christopher. *Lamb: The Gospel according to Biff, Christ's Childhood Pal.* Morrow, 2002. **F**

What would Jesus do? At age six? Thirteen? Eighteen? Restoring lizards to life and hanging out with Biff and Maggie are only a couple of His activities.

Moore, Gilbert. *A Special Rage.* Harper & Row, 1971. **NF**

A black *Life* reporter assigned to the Huey Newton trial in 1968 writes convincingly of Oakland ghetto conditions, Newton's background, the Panthers, and the trial.

Moore, Martha. *Under the Mermaid Angel.* Delacorte, 1995. **F**

Much to her mother's dismay, 13-year-old Jesse's new best friend is the 30-year-old tattoo-sporting waitress who lives in the trailer next door, but helping Roxanne solve her problems helps Jesse get a grip on her own.

Morgan, Nicola. *Fleshmarket.* Delacorte, 2004. **F**

Traumatized by the sounds of his mother's breast surgery in a 19th-century theatre of surgeons in Edinburgh, Scotland, young Robbie Anderson tries to uncover the true nature of the head surgeon and learn all about medicine.

Mori, Kyoko. *One Bird.* Holt, 1995. **F**

After she is abandoned by her mother, who is hurt by her husband's infidelities, 15-year-old Megumi struggles to find hope, love, and a sense of home.

————. *Shizuko's Daughter.* Holt, 1993. **F**

In the years following her mother's suicide, Yuki develops an inner strength in coping with her distant father, her resentful stepmother, and her haunting, painful memories.

Moriarty, Jaclyn. *Feeling Sorry for Celia.* St. Martin's, 2001. **F**
Elizabeth's life as an Australian teen is revealed through notes from imaginary organizations such as the Cold Hard Truth Association, and from Post-it notes from her mom and letters to a local pen pal.

———. *The Year of Secret Assignments.* Arthur A. Levine, 2004. **F**
Best friends Lydia, Emily, and Cassie's pen pal project with boys from a rival high school results in hilarious high jinks, including out-of-control pranks, identity theft, and a perfect act of sweet, sweet revenge.

Morpurgo, Michael. *Private Peaceful.* Scholastic, 2004. **F**
Fifteen-year-old Tommy Peaceful and his older brother Charlie enlist in the British army and are sent to fight in the trenches in France after their noble landlord offers them a choice between joining up or having the family evicted from their home.

———. *Waiting for Anya.* Viking, 1991. **F**
In World War II France, young Jo helps Benjamin hide Jewish children from the Germans and conduct them over the mountains to safety in Spain.

———. *The War of Jenkins' Ear.* Philomel, 1995. **F**
Convinced that Christopher is the Son of God, Toby watches as miracles unfold at his English boarding school.

Morris, Gerald. *The Savage Damsel and the Dwarf.* Houghton Mifflin, 2000. **F**
A feisty young woman journeys to King Arthur's court to find a knight to rescue her beautiful older sister; she is joined in her quest by a clever dwarf and a bold kitchen knave, neither of whom is what he seems.

———. *The Squire, His Knight, and His Lady.* Houghton Mifflin, 1999. **F**
When resourceful Squire Terrence and brave Sir Gawain go off to challenge the Green Knight, they face trials and dangers as well as the clever Lady Eileen.

Morrison, Lillian, ed. *Rhythm Road: Poems to Move To.* Lothrop, Lee & Shepard, 1988. **NF**
The essence of motion is captured in this collection of poetry by classic and contemporary writers.

Mosher, Richard. *Zazoo.* Clarion, 2001. **F**
From the moment Zazoo sees the handsome young man on the black bicycle, her life is changed forever, with never-before-explored questions about her own past and that of her beloved Grand-Pierre.

Mowry, Jess. *Way Past Cool.* Farrar, Straus & Giroux, 1992. **F**
Struggling to survive the streets of Oakland, California, 13-year-old Gordon and his gang of "friends" join forces with a neighboring gang to run the local drug dealer off their turf but are hindered rather than helped by the police.

Murdock, Catherine Gilbert. *Dairy Queen.* Houghton Mifflin, 2006. **F**
Running her family's dairy farm and fulfilling others' expectations makes D.J. feel like a cow, until she finds herself training the rival school's quarterback.

Murphy, Barbara Beasley, and Judie Wolkoff. *Ace Hits the Big Time.* Delacorte, 1981. **F**
A black eye patch and a dragon-emblazoned jacket help transform Horace Hobart into "Ace"—gang member, movie star, and cool guy.

Murphy, Jim. *An American Plague: The True and Terrifying Story of the Yellow Fever Epidemic of 1793.* Clarion, 2003. **NF**
During its disastrous course, the yellow fever epidemic of 1793 disrupted the federal government, divided the medical establishment, and destroyed the lives of thousands of Philadelphians.

———. *Blizzard! The Storm That Changed America.* Scholastic, 2000. **NF**
Based on newspaper articles and personal accounts, this chronicle of the blizzard of 1888 vividly portrays how the Northeast was crippled by snow for three days.

———. *The Boys' War: Confederate and Union Soldiers Talk about the Civil War.* Clarion, 1990. **NF**
Riveting photographs, diaries, and painfully honest letters tell the little-known story of hundreds of thousands of boys who fought in the Civil War.

———. *Death Run.* Clarion, 1982. **F**
Four high school boys try to evade the police after a malicious prank accidentally causes the death of a fellow student.

———. *The Great Fire.* Scholastic, 1995. **NF**
The terrible Chicago Fire of 1871 is seen from the viewpoints of eyewitnesses and illustrated with period drawings in Murphy's vivid look at the famous disaster.

———. *Inside the Alamo.* Delacorte, 2003. **NF**
In February 1836, General Santa Anna and his Mexican army massacred most of the men holed up in the Alamo Mission who were defending the newly formed territory of Texas from Santa Anna's attempts to reclaim it for Mexico.

————. *The Long Road to Gettysburg.* Clarion, 1992. NF
The personal journals of two young soldiers, one from each side, illuminate the events leading up to this pivotal battle, the bloody fighting, and the aftermath.

Murphy, Pat. *The City, Not Long After.* Doubleday, 1989. F
Following a devastating plague, a teenage girl leads the surviving residents of San Francisco, all artists and dreamers, against an invasion by a cruel despot.

Murphy, Rita. *Night Flying.* Delacorte, 2000. F
The relationships in this strong, unique family of women threaten to destroy them, but when Georgia turns 16, events occur that may have the power to bring them together.

Murphy, Sean. *Off Road.* Oni, 2005. F
While off-roading, three self-described tough guys get stuck midstream in this hilarious graphic novel.

Murray, Jaye. *Bottled Up.* Dial, 2003. F
Pip gets his kicks by drinking, smoking, cutting class, and generally getting in lots of trouble, until the school principal gets involved and Pip is forced to come to terms with what he's doing and the impact it has on his six-year-old brother.

Murrow, Liza Ketchum. *Fire in the Heart.* Holiday House, 1989. F
Molly realizes that to reunite her family she must uncover the secret surrounding her mother's death.

Myers, Walter Dean. *Autobiography of My Dead Brother.* HarperTempest, 2005. F
Jesse examines his life and the lives of those around him in words and art.

————. *Bad Boy: A Memoir.* HarperCollins, 2001. NF
In a memoir that is funny, heart wrenching, and unforgettable, Myers tells the story of his childhood in Harlem.

————. *Fallen Angels.* Scholastic, 1988. F
Seventeen-year-old Richie Perry's stint in Vietnam brings home to him the agony and futility of war as he learns to kill and watches his comrades die.

————. *The Glory Field.* Scholastic, 1994. F
From slavery to the present, the Lewis family clings to its piece of South Carolina land, despite adversity, discrimination, and family problems.

————. *The Greatest: Muhammad Ali.* Scholastic, 2001. NF
This moving biography of the greatest boxer who ever lived includes his unpopular political views, his fallibility, and his generous spirit.

————. *Harlem: A Poem.* Scholastic, 1997. NF
The sights and sounds of Harlem are vividly portrayed in this striking volume of colorful illustrations and melodious verse.

————. *Here in Harlem: Poems in Many Voices.* Holiday House, 2004. NF
The hopes, dreams, and disappointments of the African American community in Harlem are explored in verse and vintage photographs.

————. *Hoops.* Delacorte, 1981. F
Lonnie and the rest of his Harlem ghetto basketball team learn the fine art of playing and winning like pros from Cal, who once was one.

————. *The Legend of Tarik.* Viking, 1981. F
Having witnessed the annihilation of his West African family and tribesmen at the hands of El Muerte, young Tarik seeks justice after proving himself worthy.

————. *Malcolm X: By Any Means Necessary.* Scholastic, 1993. NF
This is a biography of a complex, intelligent man whose philosophy and beliefs still resonate today.

————. *Monster.* HarperCollins, 1999. F
In this riveting courtroom drama, Steve Harmon recounts his trial for murder in the form of a movie script.

————. *The Mouse Rap.* Harper & Row, 1990. F
Fourteen-year-old rapper Mouse, his ace Styx and other friends search for money hidden by a 1930s gangland leader, finding friendship and romance along the way.

————. *Now Is Your Time! The African-American Struggle for Freedom.* HarperCollins, 1991. NF
Blending well-known facts, obscure incidents, and his own family stories into a telling of African American history, Myers brings the past to life.

————. *145th Street: Short Stories.* Delacorte, 2000. F
This collection of short stories reveals life on a block in Harlem.

————. *One More River to Cross: An African American Photograph Album.* Harcourt Brace, 1995. NF
A celebration of the African American through carefully selected photographs of famous and unknown people and minimal text.

————. *The Righteous Revenge of Artemis Bonner.* HarperCollins, 1992. F
Wanting to recover his Uncle Ugly Ned's lost fortune for his widowed aunt, Artemis tracks evil Catfish Grimes through the Old West in a chase that turns into a wild, hilarious romp.

————. *Scorpions*. Harper & Row, 1988. **F**
Jamal's ability to be a good student and to live up to his father's expectations are challenged by his role as a gang leader.

————. *Slam!* Scholastic, 1996. **F**
"Slam" Harris is a talented basketball player whose dreams of fame and fortune in the NBA can come true—if he can control his anger.

————. *Somewhere in the Darkness*. Scholastic, 1992. **F**
Jimmy is shocked when an unexpected visitor turns out to be his father, who has been in prison for eight years and now wants Jimmy to drive with him to Chicago.

————. *Street Love*. HarperTempest, 2006. **F**
College-bound basketball star Damien, whose story is told in spoken word rhythms, defies the expectations of his family and friends when he falls hard for troubled Junice.

————. *The Young Landlords*. Viking, 1979. **F**
In an amusing story, Paul, his girlfriend Gloria, and their friends inadvertently become landlords of a slum apartment building inhabited by some unusual tenants.

Myracle, Lauren. *Kissing Kate*. Dutton, 2003. **F**
A brief, intimate episode between two longtime high school girlfriends results in an unbridgeable rift when they react in radically different ways to what happens between them at a party—a shared kiss.

Na, An. *A Step from Heaven*. Front Street, 2001. **F**
One Korean family's struggle to find its way in America is seen through the eyes of young Ju Park, from her earliest memories through the end of high school.

————. *Wait for Me*. Putnam, 2006. **F**
Mina lies about grades to fulfill the expectations of her Korean mother; she lies about boys and sex; and eventually she lies so much that she has trouble remembering who she is.

Naar, Jon. *Design for a Livable Planet: How You Can Help Clean Up the Environment*. Perennial, 1990. **NF**
In an environmental handbook for the 1990s, Naar explains the causes and effects of pollution, offering practical solutions for individuals and groups.

Nabokov, Peter, ed. *Native American Testimony: An Anthology of Indian and White Relations; First Encounter to Dispossession*. Crowell, 1978. **NF**
Authentic illustrations, photographs, and historical documents provide insight into Native American and white relationships through the 19th century.

Nader, Ralph. *Unsafe at Any Speed: The Designed-In Dangers of the American Automobile*. Grossman, 1965. **NF**
Nader exposes "the designed-in dangers of the American automobile."

Naidoo, Beverley. *Chain of Fire*. Lippincott, 1990. **F**
The South African government uses psychological abuse and physical brutality to force Naledi and others to relocate to a desolate township.

————. *The Other Side of Truth*. HarperCollins, 2001. **F**
Sade flees Nigeria for London with her younger brother after her mother is assassinated, leading to a difficult journey of victimization and fraud as they seek to be reunited with their family.

————. *Out of Bounds: Seven Stories of Conflict and Hope*. HarperCollins, 2003. **F**
Seven short stories set in South Africa between 1948 and 2000 chronicle the collapse of South African apartheid through individual experiences.

Nam, Vickie, ed. *Yell-oh Girls! Emerging Voices Explore Culture, Identity, and Growing Up Asian American*. Quill, 2001. **NF**
Young women of Asian descent detail their experiences of growing up in America.

Namioka, Lensey. *Island of Ogres*. Harper & Row, 1989. **F**
An out-of-work samurai has to solve the mystery of an island's ogres before a political plot to free the deposed ruler is successful.

————. *Ties That Bind, Ties That Break*. Delacorte, 1999. **F**
A wealthy Chinese girl tells of the changes the Chinese Revolution brought to her family, her hard-fought battle to escape traditional foot-binding, and her ultimate flight to America.

————. *Village of the Vampire Cat*. Delacorte, 1981. **F**
Two young masterless samurai solve the mystery of the vampire cat that has been terrorizing the villagers.

Napoli, Donna Jo. *Bound.* Atheneum, 2004. **F**
In this retelling of the Cinderella story, 14-year-old Xing Xing is resigned to a life of servitude to her ungrateful stepmother and sickly stepsister, until, with the help of an extraordinary fish, she finds the strength to decide her own fate.

———. *Breath.* Atheneum, 2003. **F**
In the late 1200s in rat-infested Hameln, Germany, a young boy with a terrible disease meets the piper and rats take the blame for everything.

———. *The Magic Circle.* Dutton, 1993. **F**
When the Ugly One succumbs to the demons' trickery and is changed from good sorceress to evil witch, she flees to a remote forest, but her destiny lies in the arrival of two children, Hansel and Gretel.

———. *Sirena.* Scholastic, 1998. **F**
With sexuality and innocence, the mermaid Sirena enchants her Greek sailor, only to find that passion may not bind the two together for eternity.

———. *Song of the Magdalene.* Scholastic, 1996. **F**
Napoli tells a haunting story of Mary Magdalene's youth and the tragic romance that may have led to her biblical downfall.

———. *Stones in Water.* Dutton, 1997. **F**
Abducted by Nazis from a movie house near his home in Venice, Roberto finds himself a slave laborer in German work camps, until he escapes in the frozen Ukraine and struggles to return home.

Naughton, Jim. *My Brother Stealing Second.* Harper & Row, 1989. **F**
Grief-stricken Bobby, coming to terms with his brother's death, is devastated to learn the truth about the fatal accident.

Naylor, Phyllis Reynolds. *The Keeper.* Atheneum, 1986. **F**
His father's mental illness paralyzes the entire family, forcing Nick to make an agonizing decision.

———. *Outrageously Alice.* Atheneum, 1997. **F**
The irrepressible Alice, now in eighth grade, suffers an identity crisis that leads to outrageous experiments with her appearance and behavior.

———. *Send No Blessings.* Atheneum, 1990. **F**
A proposal from Harless Prather looks like the best escape from the cramped trailer 16-year-old Beth shares with her family, but she fears marriage will ultimately end her dreams of a better life.

———. *A String of Chances.* Atheneum, 1982. **F**
When she goes to spend the summer with her less religiously oriented cousin and her husband, 16-year-old Evie Hutchins is confronted with an unexpected tragedy that turns her life around.

———. *Unexpected Pleasures.* Putnam, 1986. **F**
A heartwarming romance between a 32-year-old Tidewater, Maryland, bridge worker and a 16-year-old girl fleeing a shiftless family.

———. *The Year of the Gopher.* Atheneum, 1987. **F**
Fed up with college-application writing and parental nagging, George Richards opts for a blue-collar job.

Naythons, Matthew. *Sarajevo: A Portrait of the Siege.* Warner, 1994. **NF**
Shocking, stark black-and-white photographs taken during the 1992–1993 war portray the suffering in Sarajevo, providing an unforgettable message about the horrors of war.

Nelson, Blake. *Rock Star, Superstar.* Viking, 2004. **F**
Sixteen-year-old bass player Peter learns bittersweet lessons of life, love, and rock and roll during his sophomore and junior years of high school playing with the underground band the Tiny Masters of Today.

Nelson, Marilyn. *Carver: A Life in Poems.* Front Street, 2001. **NF**
This biography in poems illuminates George Washington Carver's gentle spirit, artistic sensibility, generosity, and faith in addition to his skills as a scientist and inventor.

———. *Fortune's Bones: The Manumission Requiem.* Front Street, 2004. **NF**
A stunning mix of powerful poetry and history honors Fortune, a slave whose body was dissected and rendered after his death and whose skeleton was studied by his master and put on display in a museum.

———. *A Wreath for Emmett Till.* Houghton Mifflin, 2005. **NF**
In a heartbreaking collection, a "heroic crown of sonnets," the death of 14-year-old Emmett Till is placed in historic and poetic context.

Nelson, Peter. *Left for Dead: A Young Man's Search for Justice for the USS* Indianapolis. Delacorte, 2002. **NF**
The USS *Indianapolis* was sunk by a Japanese submarine in the last days of World War II. Over fifty years later, a teen works with the survivors of the disaster to clear the name of the ship's captain, who was wrongly court-martialed for the tragedy.

Nelson, Theresa. *And One for All.* Orchard, 1989. **F**
The time is 1967, and young men are struggling to make it to college to avoid the Vietnam War—except for Wing, whose decision affects his whole family.

———. *The Beggars' Ride.* Orchard, 1992. **F**
Fleeing an alcoholic mother and a sexually abusive stepfather, Clare joins a gang of young runaways in Atlantic City and learns to survive by depending on this new family.

———. *Earthshine.* Orchard, 1994. **F**
Twelve-year-old Slim must face the truth that her beloved, irreplaceable father is dying from AIDS.

Newth, Mette. *The Abduction.* Farrar, Straus & Giroux, 1989. **F**
An Inuit woman, kidnapped by brutal whalers, finds friendship and understanding from her Norwegian jailer, Christine.

———. *The Dark Light.* Farrar, Straus & Giroux, 1998. **F**
Tora must leave her village in 19th-century Norway when she contracts leprosy. At the hospital, where she endures the cruelty of a fellow patient, she struggles to learn to read the Bible so she can realize God's plan.

Newton, Suzanne. *I Will Call It Georgie's Blues.* Viking, 1983. **F**
In music, Neil has a secret escape from the dark tensions beneath his family's smooth public facade—but the strain pushes his little brother Georgie over the edge of sanity.

Ngor, Haing, and Roger Warner. *A Cambodian Odyssey.* Macmillan, 1987. **NF**
Cambodian doctor Haing Ngor chronicles the destruction of his homeland and family under the brutal rule of the Khmer Rouge.

Nicholls, Peter, ed. *The Science in Science Fiction.* Knopf, 1983. **NF**
Presenting the scientific basis for many of the "what ifs" raised in science fiction—from Jules Verne's submarines to extraterrestrials—Nicholls weaves fact and fiction into a fascinating account.

Nichols, Michael. *The Great Apes: Between Two Worlds.* National Geographic, 1993. **NF**
Descriptions of the lives of chimps, gorillas, and orangutans—so humanlike, yet disappearing because of us—are accompanied by stunning, full-color photographs that bring the reader into their worlds.

Nicholson, Joy. *The Tribes of Palos Verdes.* St. Martin's, 1997. **F**
Fourteen-year-old Medina Mason wants to surf away from her parents' bitter divorce, the pretty, tan girls who hate her, and her twin brother's slow self-destruction.

Nicol, C. W. *The White Shaman.* Little, Brown, 1979. **F**
A young student undergoes a spiritual rebirth as he discovers a mystical kinship with the Inuit or Eskimo people of northern Canada.

Niven, Larry, and Jerry Pournelle. *The Mote in God's Eye.* Simon & Schuster, 1974. **F**
Who will win out in man's first extragalactic contact with an alien civilization, totally different in life and culture but equal in technology, cunning, and suspicion?

Nix, Garth. *Lirael, Daughter of the Clayr.* HarperCollins, 2001. **F**
Lirael becomes a librarian in the vast warren of a library that not only houses books but also guards monstrous dangers and an arcane magic. She uses the magic to conjure up the Disreputable Dog, who accompanies her on a quest when the dead start warring with the living.

———. *Sabriel.* HarperCollins, 1995. **F**
Sabriel makes a desperate quest through the Gates of Death to free her necromancer father from the strengthening powers of the spirits of the dead.

———. *Shade's Children.* HarperCollins, 1997. **F**
The few remaining human children must find and destroy the "Grand Projector" in order to release themselves from the mutant rulers of Earth.

Nolan, Han. *Born Blue.* Harcourt, 2001. **F**
Abandoned as a toddler by her addicted mother, Janie/Leshaya finds a friend in foster brother Harmon and solace in singing like the soulful ladies of jazz and the blues.

———. *Dancing on the Edge.* Harcourt Brace, 1997. **F**
After her psychic grandmother tells her that her father has melted, Miracle McCloy, obsessed with finding him, sets out in search of self and the truth.

Nolen, William A. *The Making of a Surgeon.* Random House, 1970. **NF**
An account of a young surgeon's training at New York's Bellevue Hospital is told with wit and honesty.

Nomberg-Przytyk, Sara. *Auschwitz: True Tales from a Grotesque Land.* University of North Carolina Press, 1985. **NF**

Forced to work for Dr. Josef Mengele as a teenage hospital attendant at Auschwitz during World War II, the author gives a firsthand account of the cruel medical experiments that left nearly 500,000 Jews dead.

Noonan, Michael. *McKenzie's Boots.* Orchard, 1988. **F**

Getting into the Australian army by lying about his age, 16-year-old Rod McKenzie finds himself alone, unarmed, and face-to-face with the enemy in the person of soldier and butterfly collector Hiroshi Ohara.

Norman, David, and Angela Milner. *Dinosaur.* Knopf, 1989. **F**

Representative of the outstanding Eyewitness series, this account traces the history of dinosaurs through photographs, other illustrations, and text.

North, James. *Freedom Rising.* Macmillan, 1985. **NF**

A young white journalist's 25,000-mile clandestine travels through southern Africa reveal the daily reality of apartheid.

November, Sharyn, ed. *Firebirds: An Anthology of Original Fantasy and Science Fiction.* Penguin, 2003. **F**

A broad range of science fiction and fantasy stories showcases major authors of the genre, including heavy hitters like Lloyd Alexander, Nancy Springer, and Garth Nix, with all new original stories.

————, ed. *Firebirds Rising: An Anthology of Original Science Fiction and Fantasy.* Penguin, 2006. **F**

Teens from different worlds and times populate these 16 short stories, which are as wildly inventive as they are relevant.

Noyes, Deborah, ed. *Gothic! Ten Original Dark Tales.* Candlewick, 2004. **F**

Ten gifted authors create short gothic tales that thrill and chill.

————. *One Kingdom: Our Lives with Animals; The Human-Animal Bond in Myth, History, Science, and Story.* Houghton Mifflin, 2006. **NF**

Seamlessly incorporating the scientific process, this pictorial exploration of the human-animal bond blends myth and history while raising provocative questions.

Nye, Naomi Shihab. *Habibi.* Simon & Schuster, 1997. **F**

Fourteen-year-old Palestinian American Liyana Abboud must learn to fit into a new world and understand the political conflicts when her family moves from St. Louis to Jerusalem.

————. *19 Varieties of Gazelle: Poems of the Middle East.* Greenwillow, 2002. **NF**

Nye, the daughter of Palestinian and German American parents, grew up around the world and offers poetry from this unique perspective, including stories of the Middle East through the eyes of an American child, as well as stories of America through the eyes of Middle Easterners.

————, ed. *The Space between Our Footsteps: Poems and Paintings from the Middle East.* Simon & Schuster, 1998. **NF**

Heartfelt poems from the Middle East are paired with equally beautiful art reproductions in a collection that captures the imagination.

————, ed. *The Tree Is Older Than You Are: A Bilingual Gathering of Poems and Stories from Mexico with Paintings by Mexican Artists.* Simon & Schuster, 1995. **NF**

Modern and ancient Mexican poetry, prose, and paintings come vividly alive in this lavish anthology.

————. *What Have You Lost?* Greenwillow, 1999. **NF**

From gloves to spouses, losses both petty and tragic are explored in this contemporary collection of poems and portraits that will speak to the reader's heart.

Nye, Naomi Shihab, and Paul B. Janeczko, eds. *I Feel a Little Jumpy around You: A Book of Her Poems and His Poems Collected in Pairs.* Simon & Schuster, 1996. **NF**

In this anthology of thought-provoking poems, male and female writers view life from a gender perspective.

Oates, Joyce Carol. *Big Mouth and Ugly Girl.* HarperTempest, 2002. **F**

What are the consequences when high school junior Matt Donaghy jokingly threatens to blow up the school during lunch one day?

O'Brien, Robert C. *A Report from Group 17.* Atheneum, 1972. **F**

A strange zoo in the Russian embassy, an ex-Nazi biologist, and a missing 12-year-old girl—it is Fergus's job to find out how they all fit together.

————. *Z for Zachariah*. Atheneum, 1975. **F**
In a peaceful valley, two survivors of an atomic holocaust are brought together—one a self-sufficient young girl, the other a killer bent on killing again.

O'Brien, Tim. *If I Die in a Combat Zone, Box Me Up and Ship Me Home.* Delacorte, 1973. **NF**
This introspective memoir of a foot soldier in Vietnam is a perceptive statement on courage, cowardice, and morality in war.

————. *The Things They Carried.* Franklin Library, 1990. **F**
In these candid short stories based on O'Brien's Vietnam experiences, pictures, heartaches, dreams, and terror are among the things soldiers in Vietnam carry.

O'Donnell, Joe. *Japan 1945: A U.S. Marine's Photographs from Ground Zero.* Vanderbilt University Press, 2005. **NF**
The absolute devastation of Ground Zero in Japan is portrayed with a camera's unflinching eye through a series of photographs taken shortly after the bombings of Hiroshima and Nagasaki.

O'Donohoe, Nick. *The Magic and the Healing.* Ace, 1994. **F**
B. J. Vaughan and other veterinary students participate in an internship that crosses beyond science and enters the magical realm of mythical creatures.

Okimoto, Jean Davies. *Jason's Women.* Atlantic Monthly, 1986. **F**
Jason fights his "wimpy tendencies" by getting a hot date through a newspaper ad and by working for a feisty old woman running for mayor.

Okutoro, Lydia Omolola. *Quiet Storm: Voices of Young Black Poets.* Hyperion, 1999. **NF**
Young black people from around the world express themselves, their cultures, and their heritages in a moving collection of original poetry.

O'Leary, Brian. *The Making of an Ex-Astronaut.* Houghton Mifflin, 1970. **NF**
A NASA "dropout" tells about his seven months as an astronaut and why he was the first scientist to resign.

Olsen, Jack. *Black Is Best: The Riddle of Cassius Clay.* Putnam, 1967. **NF**
A sportswriter describes the controversial career of Cassius Clay and tells why the great fighter believes that "black is best."

————. *Night of the Grizzlies.* Putnam, 1969. **NF**
On the night of August 12, 1967, grizzlies attack a campground in Glacier National Park—a violent and inevitable clash between a vanishing species and the humans invading its territory.

Oneal, Zibby. *A Formal Feeling.* Viking, 1982. **F**
A year after the death of her mother, Anne Cameron gradually comes to terms with their past relationship while adjusting to a new life with her stepmother.

————. *In Summer Light.* Viking Kestrel, 1985. **F**
Reluctantly returning to her island home to recuperate from mono, Kate hates the dominance and power her famous artist father holds over her, but her love for graduate art student Ian Jackson helps her grow to understand her father and herself.

————. *The Language of Goldfish.* Viking, 1980. **F**
Afraid of growing up, 13-year-old Carrie Stokes suffers a mental breakdown when she retreats to the happy childhood world where life is uncomplicated and unthreatening.

Opdyke, Irene Gut. *In My Hands: Memories of a Holocaust Rescuer.* Knopf, 1999. **NF**
A Catholic girl forced to work as a housekeeper to a German officer in occupied Poland risks her life to hide and rescue Jewish workers during World War II.

Oppel, Kenneth. *Airborn.* EOS, 2004. **F**
More at home on the *Aurora*, the airship on which he serves, than on land, Matt Cruse, along with a young traveler named Kate, must battle pirates and strange winged creatures when his airship is damaged and forced to land on an uncharted island.

————. *Skybreaker.* EOS, 2006. **F**
As a first-year student at the Airship Academy, Matt Cruse is part of the crew on a training stint that sights the *Hyperion*, a legendary ship that never reached its destination and is reputed to be carrying great treasure.

Orgill, Roxane. *Shout, Sister, Shout! Ten Girl Singers Who Shaped a Century.* Margaret K. McElderry, 2001. **NF**
This collective musical biography of female singers spans the decades of the 20th century.

Orlev, Uri. *The Man from the Other Side.* Houghton Mifflin, 1991. **F**
Knowing the way through the sewers, Marek leads a Polish Jew, who wants to die among Jews, back to the doomed Warsaw Ghetto.

Orr, Wendy. *Peeling the Onion.* Holiday House, 1997. **F**
Anna struggles to recover her health and her life after a car accident shatters her body and leaves her brain damaged.

Osa, Nancy. *Cuba 15*. Delacorte, 2003. **F**
Fifteen-year-old Violet Paz is struggling to understand her Cuban heritage while her Abuela plans her quinceañero and she gathers great material for her speech team performances from her crazy family.

Oughton, Jerrie. *Perfect Family*. Houghton Mifflin, 2000. **F**
Welcome is 15 years old and living in a conservative North Carolina small town when she finds herself pregnant—not by the boy of her dreams, but by a longtime friend.

——. *The War in Georgia*. Houghton Mifflin, 1997. **F**
Orphaned Shanta Cola Morgan must reconcile her feelings of loss and confusion about not being part of a "real" family in a small southern town during World War II.

Ousseimi, Maria. *Caught in the Crossfire: Growing Up in a War Zone*. Walker, 1995. **NF**
Interviews and haunting photographs document the experiences of young people growing up in war-torn areas in Lebanon, Bosnia-Herzegovina, Mozambique, El Salvador, and Washington, D.C.

Owen, David. *Hidden Evidence: Forty True Crimes and How Forensic Science Helped Solve Them*. Firefly, 2000. **NF**
The evolution of forensic science and crime investigation is detailed in this study that includes famous cases including Jack the Ripper, presidential assassinations, and recent serial killers.

Page, Thomas. *The Hephaestus Plague*. Putnam, 1973. **F**
An eccentric entomologist, charged with finding a way to destroy flame-throwing roaches, develops an affinity for them and breeds them while others work to save the East Coast from the destructive insects.

Page, Tim. *NAM*. Knopf, 1983. **NF**
UPI photographer Tim Page utilizes the photo-essay to demonstrate the reality and the horror found on the front lines of the Vietnam conflict.

Palmer, David R. *Emergence*. Bantam, 1984. **F**
Heroic deeds become the daily routine for 11-year-old Candy Smith-Foster who, as a member of a new human species, begins a trek with her pet macaw, Terry D., across an American landscape scarred by bionuclear war.

Palmer, Laura. *Shrapnel in the Heart: Letters and Remembrances from the Vietnam Veterans Memorial*. Random House, 1987. **NF**
Who can forget those who died in 'Nam? Not the buddies, sweethearts, families, and friends who leave remembrances at the Vietnam Memorial in Washington.

Panzer, Nora, ed. *Celebrate America: In Poetry and Art*. Hyperion, 1994. **NF**
Join in this celebration of the American way of life through this rich multicultural collection of poetry and art.

Parini, Jay. *Patch Boys*. Holt, 1986. **F**
In a small Pennsylvania mining town in the 1920s, 15-year-old Sammy di Cantini learns about maturity and friendship and takes on responsibility when his brother is killed in a miners' protest.

Park, Linda Sue. *A Single Shard*. Clarion, 2001. **F**
In 12th-century Korea, 13-year-old orphan Tree-ear becomes an apprentice to a maker of celadon pottery through unexpected paths.

——. *When My Name Was Keoko*. Clarion, 2002. **F**
In 1940 when the Japanese rulers of Korea decreed that all Koreans must take Japanese names, Kim Sun-hee's official name changed, but she did not lose her Korean identity or her patriotism, which grew as the war came far too close to home.

Park, Ruth. *Playing Beatie Bow*. Atheneum, 1982. **F**
When she is transported backward in time, Abigail must survive in 19th-century Australia while struggling to return home.

Parker, Jeff. *The Interman*. Octopus, 2003. **F**
Now that the government that created him has decided Van Meach, a perfect war machine and assassin, is too dangerous to live, they are finding their prototype has become far more successful than they ever hoped.

Parks, David. *GI Diary*. Harper & Row, 1968. **NF**
A frank diary of a young African American draftee's service in the army, during which he experiences a rough year in boot camp and a grim tour of Vietnam.

Parks, Gordon. *Born Black*. Lippincott, 1971. **NF**
The celebrated author-photographer interviews Malcolm X, Muhammed Ali, Eldridge Cleaver, and other black notables and concludes with the statement: "America is still a racist nation. It has not learned much from the turbulent decade just passed."

——. *A Choice of Weapons*. Harper & Row, 1966. **NF**
With love, dignity, and hard work, *Life* photographer Gordon Parks wins his battle against the debasement of poverty and racial discrimination.

————. *Voices in the Mirror: An Autobiography.* Doubleday, 1990. **NF**

Breaking one racial barrier after another to rise above a life of bitter poverty, this celebrated black filmmaker, photographer, and Renaissance man expands our views of life's possibilities.

Parks, Rosa, and Jim Haskins. *Rosa Parks: My Story.* Dial, 1992. **NF**

Rosa Parks tells in her own words what it is like to defy the system and, in the process, become a symbol of freedom for African Americans.

Parnall, Peter. *The Daywatchers.* Macmillan, 1984. **NF**

This is a beautifully illustrated, nontechnical narrative of Parnall's observations of and experiences with various birds of prey.

Partridge, Elizabeth. *John Lennon: All I Want Is the Truth.* Viking, 2005. **NF**

This telling photo-biographical account of John Lennon, the man who sought truth through music, traces Lennon's life from birth to his remarkable career with the Beatles, to his love of Yoko Ono, to his untimely death.

————. *Restless Spirit: The Life and Work of Dorothea Lange.* Viking, 1998. **NF**

This beautiful photo-biography features the life and works of one of the most notable photographers of the 20th century.

————. *This Land Was Made for You and Me: The Life and Songs of Woody Guthrie.* Viking, 2002. **NF**

The tragic life story of the rambling folk singer Woody Guthrie, author of "This Land Is Your Land," is told in this biography for young readers.

Pascal, Francine. *My First Love and Other Disasters.* Viking, 1979. **F**

Fifteen-year-old Victoria humorously describes the summer of her first love, when she comes to realize that there's more to real affection than outward appearances.

Paschen, Elise, and Neil Neches, eds. *Poetry in Motion: 100 Poems from the Subways and Buses.* Norton, 1996. **NF**

A rich mix of short poems and excerpts of longer poems that are used on New York City's subways and buses.

Patent, Dorothy Hinshaw. *The Quest for Artificial Intelligence.* Harcourt Brace Jovanovich, 1986. **NF**

Patent examines the nature of intelligence and traces attempts to make machines duplicate such human behavior.

Paterson, Katherine. *Jacob Have I Loved.* Crowell, 1980. **F**

While growing up among the "water people" on an island off the coast of eastern Maryland during the 1940s, Louise searches for her identity and fights the jealousy she feels toward her talented, fragile, and beautiful twin sister.

————. *Jip: His Story.* Lodestar, 1996. **F**

Unclaimed after falling off a wagon, Jip is sent to a poor farm, where he discovers, in 1855, that his life is in jeopardy because his past is unexpectedly uncovered.

————. *Lyddie.* Lodestar, 1991. **F**

Unable to pay off the debt on the family farm, feisty, single-minded Lyddie survives the dangers of the textile mills in 1840s Massachusetts, determined not to forfeit her dreams.

Paton Walsh, Jill. *A Parcel of Patterns.* Farrar, Straus & Giroux, 1983. **F**

Vividly and dramatically, Mall Percival writes in her journal of the tragic events that befell her and the other villagers of Eyam during the disastrous plague of the 1660s in England.

Patterson, Sarah. *The Distant Summer.* Simon & Schuster, 1976. **F**

Set in England during World War II, this is the story of 17-year-old Kate who is courted by two young fliers—a sensitive, serious Englishman and a happy-go-lucky American.

Pattou, Edith. *East.* Harcourt, 2003. **F**

Rose agrees to travel far from her home on the back of the mysterious White Bear, a journey that leads her "East of the Sun and West of the Moon" on an adventure she never imagined.

Paulsen, Gary. *The Beet Fields: Memories of a Sixteenth Summer.* Delacorte, 2000. **F**

Gary Paulsen tells the story of his 16th summer, when he ran away from home to experience life by working in the beet fields, encountering death, helping an old woman on her farm, and working in a carnival for two brothers.

————. *The Cookcamp.* Orchard, 1991. **F**

What would cause a mother to pin a note to her five-year-old son's jacket, put him on a train, and send him far away to live in the north woods?

————. *The Crossing.* Orchard, 1987. **F**

An alcoholic army sergeant and a homeless Mexican orphan come together in an unlikely friendship.

————. *Dancing Carl.* Bradbury, 1983. **F**

Carl comes to McKinley, Minnesota, in the winter, drunk and maybe crazy, but he soon holds the attention of the entire town with his power and strange dance.

———. *Dogsong.* Bradbury, 1985. **F**
Fourteen-year-old Russell, an Eskimo boy, borrows a neighbor's sled and dog team for a 1,400-mile journey, encounters a mammoth from earlier times and a pregnant girl from the present, and discovers his own relationship to his Eskimo culture.

———. *Harris and Me: A Summer Remembered.* Harcourt Brace, 1993. **F**
The narrator and his cousin share adventures—often with both painful and hilarious results—in this short, action-packed story of one summer spent on a farm.

———. *The Haymeadow.* Delacorte, 1992. **F**
This survival story pits John, only 14, against 6,000 sheep, four dogs, two horses, and uncooperative Mother Nature.

———. *How Angel Peterson Got His Name, and Other Outrageous Tales about Extreme Sports.* Wendy Lamb, 2003. **NF**
Gary Paulsen relates a series of bizarre and daredevil feats attempted by his friends during their childhood in Minnesota.

———. *The Island.* Orchard, 1988. **F**
The island in the middle of Sucker Lake gives 15-year-old Wil Newton the opportunity to discover himself and the harmony of nature.

———. *The Monument.* Delacorte, 1991. **F**
Rocky, a mixed-race teen, has her life changed by the unusual artist who comes to her small town to design a war memorial.

———. *Nightjohn.* Delacorte, 1993. **F**
Nightjohn, a free black man, returns to the South to secretly teach slaves to read, igniting a desire for learning in the heart of 12-year-old Sarny.

———. *Puppies, Dogs, and Blue Northers: Reflections on Being Raised by a Pack of Sled Dogs.* Harcourt Brace, 1996. **NF**
In an exciting narrative, experienced sled-dog racer Paulsen tells the story of his beloved dog Cookie and her pups.

———. *The Schernoff Discoveries.* Delacorte, 1997. **F**
Everybody knows a Harold Schernoff—the nerd, the geek. In this laugh-out-loud tale, Harold and his buddy team up for everything—from scientifically retrieving golf balls to designing that first kiss.

———. *Soldier's Heart: A Novel of the Civil War.* Delacorte, 1998. **F**
After facing the reality of fighting in the Civil War, Charlie realizes that war is hell on earth—both mentally and physically.

———. *Tracker.* Bradbury, 1984. **F**
The dramatic journey of an orphan, John, who, in tracking a deer through the Minnesota wilderness, comes to terms with his grandfather's approaching death.

———. *The Voyage of the Frog.* Orchard, 1989. **F**
Lost at sea without a radio, David fights for survival in his small sailboat during a fierce storm.

———. *The Winter Room.* Orchard, 1989. **F**
Seated around a cozy fire in "the winter room," Elton and his brother Wayne challenge the truth of Uncle David's almost mythological stories about death and survival during his earlier life in Norway.

———. *Winterdance: The Fine Madness of Running the Iditarod.* Harcourt Brace, 1994. **NF**
Vividly bringing to life the Alaskan Iditarod, a dogsled race requiring intensive training, skill, endurance, and the ability to survive subzero temperatures, Paulsen highlights the dogs who made it possible for him to make it to the finish line.

———. *Woodsong.* Bradbury, 1990. **NF**
Through his dogsledding adventures in the Minnesota wilderness where there are wolves, deep snow, and minus-30-degree temperatures, the author comes to understand nature's ways and harrowing surprises.

Pausewang, Gudrun. *The Final Journey.* Viking, 1996. **F**
Horrid images emerge in this story of the two days a young girl spends on a railway car on her way to a concentration camp.

Pearson, Mary E. *A Room on Lorelei Street.* Holt, 2005. **F**
A bed in a room doesn't seem like much, but when you are 17 and your alcoholic mother can't even remember to pay rent and you deal, deal, deal with it, the room on Lorelei Street seems like heaven—if you can only figure out how to pay for it.

Peck, Richard. *Are You in the House Alone?* Viking, 1976. **F**
After receiving a series of threatening notes, Gail Osburne is raped by one of the richest and most popular boys in her school—but nobody believes her story.

———. *Close Enough to Touch.* Delacorte, 1981. **F**
How do you recover from your girlfriend's sudden death? Matt's solution is Margaret, who helps change his pain into love.

———. *Fair Weather*. Dial, 2001. **F**

Rosie's family is invited by Aunt Euterpe to attend the 1893 World's Columbian Exposition in Chicago, and her unpredictable grandfather decides to come along.

———. *Father Figure*. Viking, 1978. **F**

The security that Jim Atwater finds in his role as surrogate father to his eight-year-old brother is threatened when, after their mother's suicide, the boys are packed off to spend the summer with their father, who had long ago abandoned them.

———. *Ghosts I Have Been*. Viking, 1977. **F**

In a hilarious sequel to *The Ghost Belonged to Me,* Alexander Armsworth meets his match in Blossom Culp, whose wits and psychic powers save the day.

———. *The Last Safe Place on Earth*. Delacorte, 1995. **F**

Todd, 15, thinks he's found the perfect girl in Laura, his little sister's babysitter—then he sees the effect that Laura's fundamentalist beliefs are having on his sister.

———. *A Long Way from Chicago*. Dial, 1998. **F**

Grandma Dowdel creates more fun and surprises for Joe and Mary Alice during their summer visits to her small Illinois town.

———. *Princess Ashley*. Delacorte, 1987. **F**

"New girl" Chelsea must decide what price she is willing to pay to win popular Ashley Packard's acceptance.

———. *Remembering the Good Times*. Delacorte, 1985. **F**

Meeting at a time of change in their lives, Kate, Buck, and Trav develop a special friendship—but even their mutual caring can't keep the gap from widening or avert the tragedy of Trav's suicide.

———. *Representing Super Doll*. Viking, 1974. **F**

Darlene Hoffmeister, beautiful but dumb Miss Hybrid Seed Corn, sets out on the Beauty Contest Road and runs into some unexpected traffic.

———. *The River between Us*. Dial, 2003. **F**

In 1916, Howard Leland Hutchings travels to his father's ancestral home in southern Illinois and meets Tilly, who tells him the story of his father's kin during the Civil War era.

———. *Strays Like Us*. Dial, 1998. **F**

Uprooted once again and dumped on her great-aunt, Molly learns that the world is full of strays and that all towns have secrets.

———. *The Teacher's Funeral: A Comedy in Three Parts*. Dial, 2004. **F**

When mean ole Myrt Arbuckle hauls off and dies, 15-year-old Russell Culver thinks he is finally done with school forever—until his older sister becomes the new teacher.

———. *A Year down Yonder*. Dial, 2000. **F**

Mary Alice, reluctant to spend a year with her feisty grandmother in a "hick" town during the Recession, finds there are many lessons to be learned from her—some hilarious.

Peck, Robert Newton. *A Day No Pigs Would Die*. Knopf, 1972. **F**

Through his relationship with his hardworking father, 12-year-old Rob learns to cope with the harshness of Shaker life and emerges a mature individual.

Peet, Mal. *Keeper*. Candlewick, 2005. **F**

Holding the World Cup as he talks, "El Gato," the great goalie, describes his early life in a remote South American village, the secret soccer field hewn from the jungle, and the mysterious figure he knows only as the Keeper who trained him.

Pei, Lowry. *Family Resemblances*. Random House, 1986. **F**

Visiting her unconventional aunt, 15-year-old Karen becomes aware of the complexities of adult relationships and also experiences a love affair of her own.

Pelé, and Robert L. Fish. *My Life and the Beautiful Game: The Autobiography of Pelé*. Doubleday, 1977. **NF**

An intimate and touching autobiography of the world's most famous soccer player on the eve of his retirement from "the beautiful game."

Peña, Matt de la. *Ball Don't Lie*. Delacorte, 2005. **F**

Seventeen-year-old Sticky, foster care victim and talented basketball player, overcomes his tough upbringing with the support of his girlfriend and the older hoopsters at the local gym.

Penman, Sharon Kay. *The Queen's Man: A Medieval Mystery*. Holt, 1996. **F**

Young Justin de Quincey finds himself in a viper's nest of murderous nobles and false allies when the queen chooses him to discover the truth about her son, who's gone missing on his return from the Crusades.

Pennebaker, Ruth. *Don't Think Twice*. Holt, 1996. **F**

Pregnant and living in a home for unwed mothers, 17-year-old Anne believes that once she puts her baby up for adoption, life will get back to normal.

Perkins, Lynne Rae. *Criss Cross.* Greenwillow, 2005. F
Criss Cross is a radio show that Debbie, Hector, and others listen to in the car, and it is a symbol in this unique book for how beautiful and tenuous love and other connections can be.

Pershall, Mary K. *You Take the High Road.* Dial, 1990. F
Samantha is delighted to have a new baby brother, but suddenly her life is torn apart when the baby is killed in a tragic accident.

Peters, Ellis. *Black Is the Colour of My True-Love's Heart.* Morrow, 1967. F
A folk song festival in rural England goes awry when a thwarted romance erupts into violence and murder.

Peters, Julie Anne. *Define Normal.* Little, Brown, 2000. F
When she agrees to peer counsel Jasmine at their middle school, Antonia never dreams that this girl with the black lipstick and pierced eyebrow will end up helping her deal with the serious problems she faces at home.

———. *Luna.* Little, Brown, 2004. F
Luna, like her namesake the moon, can only come out at night. What happens when she decides to show herself in the light of day, changing Liam into Luna before his family's very eyes?

Petersen, P. J. *Nobody Else Can Walk It for You.* Delacorte, 1982. F
Eighteen-year-old Laura desperately tries to lead a group of young backpackers to safety as they are pursued by three threatening motorcyclists through isolated mountainous country.

———. *Would You Settle for Improbable?* Delacorte, 1981. F
Just released from juvenile hall, Arnold is befriended by a student teacher and some of his ninth-grade classmates, with unexpected results.

Petty, Richard. *King of the Road.* Macmillan, 1977. NF
An American race car driver and his family share their team spirit in a winning photographic documentary.

Pevsner, Stella. *How Could You Do It, Diane?* Clarion, 1989. F
Bethany struggles to understand why her pretty, popular sister committed suicide.

Peyton, K. M. *Prove Yourself a Hero.* Collins+World, 1978. F
After being released by kidnappers, 16-year-old Jonathan feels guilty for having acted like a coward and for having cost his family the ransom money.

Pfeffer, Susan Beth. *About David.* Delacorte, 1980. F
When Lynn finds out that David, whom she has known since childhood, has murdered his adoptive parents and killed himself, she must confront new feelings about him before she can recover from this loss.

———. *Family of Strangers.* Bantam, 1992. F
Abby feels so alone and unloved that she attempts suicide. It takes a sympathetic therapist to help her recover from the damage done by her family of strangers.

———. *Life as We Knew It.* Harcourt, 2006. F
In her journal, 16-year-old Miranda records the catastrophes that occur after a meteor strikes the moon and alters its course, causing tsunamis, volcanic eruptions, and escalating chaos.

———. *The Year without Michael.* Bantam, 1987. F
The unexplained disappearance of a high school student throws his family into a state of uncertainty and agony.

Philbrick, Nathaniel. *Revenge of the Whale: The True Story of the Whaleship* Essex. Putnam, 2002. NF
This is a detailed account of the 1820 voyage of the whaleship *Essex*, which was attacked and sunk by a sperm whale.

Philbrick, Rodman. *Freak the Mighty.* Blue Sky, 1993. F
Separately, hulking Max and tiny Freak are each missing something, but together they are the adventure-prone "Freak the Mighty."

———. *The Last Book in the Universe.* Blue Sky, 2000. F
In this futuristic urban dystopia, an epileptic boy, together with an old man and an orphan, travels over hostile turf to visit his sister before she dies.

Philip, Neil, ed. *In a Sacred Manner I Live: Native American Wisdom.* Clarion, 1997. NF
Prayers, poems, essays, and photographs portray the deep spirituality of Native American life in this visually handsome volume.

———, ed. *War and the Pity of War.* Clarion, 1998. NF
Ranging from ancient Rome to modern-day Bosnia, this unforgettable collection of poems illustrates both the heroism and the horror of war.

Phipson, Joan. *Hit and Run.* Margaret K. McElderry, 1985. F
After stealing a Ferrari and running from an accident, 16-year-old Roland has to decide whether or not to abandon the injured constable who has followed him into the Australian bush.

Pierce, Meredith Ann. *The Dark-angel.* Atlantic Monthly, 1982. **F**
Although both fascinated and repelled by the vampyre, Aeriel tries to save her mistress and the other vampyre brides.

———. *The Pearl of the Soul of the World.* Joy Street, 1990. **F**
In the conclusion of the Darkangel trilogy, Aeriel must carry the Pearl of the Soul of the World to the witch Irrylath, who seeks to destroy her.

———. *Treasure at the Heart of the Tanglewood.* Viking, 2001. **F**
When amnesiac Hannah defies a wizard and allows the healing flora that grows in her tresses to go unplucked, she and her talking animal companions set out on a trek that brings a change of seasons back to the world.

———. *The Woman Who Loved Reindeer.* Atlantic Monthly, 1985. **F**
The daimon child that her sister-in-law brings Caribou to rear in the cold lands of the North grows into her unearthly companion and helps Caribou serve as the leader of her people.

Pierce, Ruth I. *Single and Pregnant.* Beacon, 1970. **NF**
Here is a blunt, cautionary, never judgmental discussion by a social worker on the medical, financial, and social problems facing the single, young, and pregnant.

Pierce, Tamora. *The Emperor Mage.* Atheneum, 1995. **F**
Fifteen-year-old Daine uses her animal communication skills to help avert a war for her country.

———. *Squire.* Random House, 2001. **F**
Keladry of Mendalin, now 14 years old and a squire to a kindly knight, faces challenges in the field and in her first romance as she anticipates her final ordeal in the frightening magic chamber.

———. *Terrier.* Random House, 2006. **F**
Raised in the slums, trained to the law-keeping force, and armed with the ability to hear the voices of the dead, Beka Cooper is determined to save the people of the Lower City.

———. *Trickster's Choice.* Random House, 2003. **F**
When Aly decides to avoid her famous warrior mother, she never dreams that slavers will capture her, but it gives her the opportunity to prove that she has all the makings of the spy she wants to become.

Pinkwater, Jill. *Buffalo Brenda.* Macmillan, 1989. **F**
The outrageous team of India Ink Teidlebaum and Brenda Tuna take on their high school and its cliques.

Placide, Jaira. *Fresh Girl.* Wendy Lamb, 2002. **F**
Fourteen-year-old Mardi's sunlit childhood in Haiti disappeared in the violence that forced President Aristide and thousands of other Haitians into exile in America ten years ago, and it takes a long time for Mardi to admit to her family in Brooklyn just how traumatic her escape was.

Plath, Sylvia. *The Bell Jar.* Harper & Row, 1971. **F**
During a queer, sultry summer in New York, Esther Greenwood works as a junior editor on *Mademoiselle,* quarrels with her mother and boyfriend, and is gradually aware of her descent into madness.

Platt, Kin. *Headman.* Greenwillow, 1975. **F**
Owen's desperate fight for survival through the streets of Los Angeles, in a "rehabilitative" youth camp, and as "headman" of a gang is told in swift, sharp, and realistic street language.

Platt, Randall Beth. *The Likes of Me.* Delacorte, 2000. **F**
In 1918, the half-Chinese albino Cordelia runs away from the Pacific Northwest logging town where she lives with her father and stepmother to begin a career as a sideshow act in a Seattle carnival.

Plimpton, George. *Paper Lion.* Harper & Row, 1966. **NF**
A writer-by-trade plays the part of a rookie quarterback with the Detroit Lions in order to write this entertaining inside view of pro football.

Plummer, Louise. *A Dance for Three.* Delacorte, 2000. **F**
When 15-year-old Hannah becomes pregnant and her rich, popular boyfriend claims he is not responsible, Hannah and her mother must face the problems they have refused to admit before.

———. *My Name Is Sus5an Smith. The 5 Is Silent.* Delacorte, 1991. **F**
When Susan leaves her small town to study art in Boston, she loses her illusions of life and love but rediscovers herself and her independence.

Plum-Ucci, Carol. *The Body of Christopher Creed.* Harcourt, 2000. **F**
Class freak Christopher Creed is missing. What happened, and why does only one person really want to know?

————. *What Happened to Lani Garver.* Harcourt, 2002. F

Claire McKenzie is haunted by her brief relationship with Lani Garver, a newcomer to her close island community who changed her life.

Pohl, Frederik. *Man Plus.* Random House, 1976. F

To survive without mechanical help on the surface of Mars, Roger Torraway must become a biological monster and yet stay sane until he reaches his destination.

Pollack, Dale. *Skywalking: The Life and Films of George Lucas.* Harmony, 1983. NF

This is all about the man who created such spectacular movies as *Star Wars* and *Raiders of the Lost Ark.*

Popham, Melinda Worth. *Skywater.* Graywolf, 1990. F

Brand X never intended to be a savior, and indeed most of his fellow coyotes never reach their destination. But their quest for the unpolluted water source Skywater leads to a deeper understanding of their desert world.

Porte, Barbara Ann. *Something Terrible Happened.* Orchard, 1994. F

The happy and quiet life that Gillian has with her mother and grandmother begins to unravel when her mother is diagnosed with AIDS.

Porter, Connie. *Imani All Mine.* Houghton Mifflin, 1999. F

As an inner-city mom, Tasha struggles to attend school, realize her dreams of a better life, and rise above tragedy.

Porter, Tracey. *Treasures in the Dust.* HarperCollins, 1997. F

The friendship between Annie and Violet survives Dust Bowl Oklahoma through the letters they write after Violet's family leaves to look for work in California.

Portis, Charles. *True Grit.* Simon & Schuster, 1968. F

With her papa's pistol tied to her saddle horn and a supersized ration of audacity, 14-year-old Mattie Ross sets out to avenge her father's murder.

Portman, Frank. *King Dork.* Delacorte, 2006. F

While creating outrageous album covers and trying to name his band, 14-year-old Tom grapples with his father's death.

Portola Institute. *The Last Whole Earth Catalog: Access to Tools.* Random House, 1971. NF

This supercatalog, a kind of counterculture *Consumer Reports,* lists everything from papoose-packs to Moog synthesizers and all items are "useful as tools, relevant to independent education, high quality or low cost, and easily available by mail."

Postman, Neil, and Charles Weingartner. *The Soft Revolution: A Student Handbook for Turning Schools Around.* Delacorte, 1971. NF

Here is a treatise on how students can change their schools without violence through innovative suggestions, persuasion, and gentle manipulation.

Potok, Chaim. *The Chosen.* Simon & Schuster, 1967. F

Two Jewish boys growing to manhood in Brooklyn discover that differences can strengthen friendship and understanding.

————. *My Name Is Asher Lev.* Knopf, 1972. F

Asher Lev is an ordinary Jewish boy from Brooklyn until his passion and genius for painting create a furor in the art world and alienate him from the parents he loves.

————. *The Promise.* Knopf, 1969. F

In this sequel to *The Chosen,* rabbinical student Reuven confronts his dogmatic teacher, and his friend Danny undertakes his first case as a clinical psychologist, one requiring a drastic, experimental treatment.

————. *Zebra, and Other Stories.* Knopf, 1998. F

In this collection of short stories, Zebra, Isabel, and other teens struggle to find themselves while confronting the rules and regulations of the adult world.

Powell, Randy. *Dean Duffy.* Farrar, Straus & Giroux, 1995. F

At 15, Dean Duffy had it all and pitched for a world championship Little League team until he hit a slump. Now, at 18, he is trying to decide where to go with his life.

————. *Is Kissing a Girl Who Smokes Like Licking an Ashtray?* Farrar, Straus & Giroux, 1992. F

Eighteen-year-old Biff looks 14, and he gets tongue-tied around girls, so he can't speak to Tommie, whom he's loved for two years. But, look out! He's about to meet Heidi, and his life will never be the same again.

————. *Three Clams and an Oyster.* Farrar, Straus & Giroux, 2002. F

Three members of a flag football team search for a fourth teammate over a weekend during which they confront their attitudes about friendship, girls, and their shared past.

————. *Tribute to Another Dead Rock Star.* Farrar, Straus & Giroux, 1999. F
Fifteen-year-old Grandy Grennan wades through emotional troughs and peaks of humor during a visit to Seattle to attend a tribute to his mother, a dead rock star.

Power, Susan. *The Grass Dancer.* Putnam, 1994. F
A multigenerational story about a Sioux family begins with the love of Ghost Horse and Red Dress and ends in the 1980s with Charlene Thunder, who falls in love with Harley Wind Soldier, a grass dancer.

Powers, John R. *Do Black Patent-Leather Shoes Really Reflect Up? A Fictionalized Memoir.* Regnery, 1975. F
Doing battle with an army of pimples, being a teenager, and spending four years in a South Side Chicago high school far exceed Eddie's worst fears.

————. *The Unoriginal Sinner and the Ice-Cream God.* Contemporary, 1977. F
The irreverently humorous adventures and misadventures of Tim Conroy, a Catholic teenager growing up on Chicago's South Side.

Powers, Thomas. *Diana: The Making of a Terrorist.* Houghton Mifflin, 1971. NF
This is an examination of the tragic forces in the life of Weatherwoman Diana Oughton that led her from a comfortable, wealthy home to a commitment to revolution and finally to her death in a "bomb factory" town house explosion in 1970.

Pratchett, Terry. *The Amazing Maurice and His Educated Rodents.* HarperCollins, 2001. F
All those stories about plagues and rats and magic pipers make great advance publicity for Maurice, the talking cat, and his rat acquaintances when they roll into town to scam yet another gullible bunch.

————. *A Hat Full of Sky.* HarperCollins, 2004. F
When Tiffany Aching leaves the Chalk and her Wee Free Men to become a witch-in-training, she does not know that she will soon need their help to battle an invisible foe.

————. *The Wee Free Men.* HarperCollins, 2003. F
Armed with an iron frying pan, Tiffany Aching and the Wee Free Men set off to rescue her little brother, one of many young people kidnapped by the Queen of Fairyland.

————. *Wintersmith.* HarperTempest, 2006. F
Waily, waily, waily! In this Discworld novel, witch-in-training Tiffany Aching accidentally attracts the attention of the Wintersmith, imperiling her family and requiring the expertise of the Wee Free Men.

Preston, Douglas, and Lincoln Child. *Relic.* TOR, 1995. F
A PhD candidate knows something monstrous is living in the American Museum of Natural History but cannot convince the PR person to delay the opening of a new exhibit. The gruesome results will keep you up all night reading.

Preston, Richard. *The Hot Zone.* Random House, 1994. NF
Follow the terrifying history of the deadly Ebola virus and its journey from Zaire in Africa to Reston, Virginia.

Price, Charlie. *Dead Connection.* Roaring Brook, 2006. F
Murray enjoys listening to the voices of the dead—until a missing cheerleader begs him to help solve the mystery of her death.

Prince, Alison. *The Turkey's Nest.* Morrow, 1980. F
Eighteen-year-old Kate rejects the father of her unborn child for the security of her aunt's farm in Suffolk. There she comes to terms with herself and her future.

Pringle, Terry. *A Fine Time to Leave Me.* Algonquin, 1989. F
Chris and Lori experience ups and downs, joys and ordeals, as they discover the hard realities of marriage.

————. *The Preacher's Boy.* Algonquin, 1988. F
The community keeps an eagle eye on Michael's blossoming romance with Amy as her career and his first college year complicate his struggles for a better relationship with his father.

Prochnik, Leon. *Endings: Death, Glorious and Otherwise, as Faced by Ten Outstanding Figures of Our Time.* Crown, 1980. NF
Exploration of the lives and often unusual deaths of ten fascinating people, from Freud and Houdini to Isadora Duncan and Malcolm X.

Psihoyos, Louie, and John Knoebber. *Hunting Dinosaurs.* Random House, 1994. NF
With beautiful photographs and a zany sense of humor, Psihoyos and Knoebber impart the adventure of digging for fossils the world over.

Pullman, Philip. *The Amber Spyglass.* Knopf, 2000. F
In this third and final installment of Pullman's His Dark Materials series, Lyra and Will are reunited, visit the underworld, and pursue the puzzle of Dust.

————. *The Broken Bridge.* Knopf, 1992. **F**
During her 16th summer, Ginny must come to terms with a brother she never knew she had, secrets her father won't share with her, and a tale of a long-ago kidnapping.

————. *The Golden Compass.* Knopf, 1996. **F**
With the aid of friends, witches, and armored polar bears, 12-year-old Lyra fights the evil that is stealing children and conducting horrible experiments on them.

————. *The Ruby in the Smoke.* Knopf, 1985. **F**
Sally, 16 and an orphan, must find her way through a maze of 19th-century villains to claim her inheritance and her independence.

————. *Shadow in the North.* Knopf, 1988. **F**
In an attempt to protect a client's investment, Sally Lockhart, a financial consultant in 19th-century London, comes up against an evil, rich industrialist who seeks to win her by any means.

————. *The Subtle Knife.* Knopf, 1997. **F**
Will and Lyra are pulled into a parallel world, where they must fight the shadowy specters, as angels and witches aid them in their quest for the truth about dust.

————. *The Tiger in the Well.* Knopf, 1990. **F**
Did Sally Lockhart marry Arthur Parrish? Sally's certain that she didn't, but his legal evidence proves the contrary. What protection does Sally have against the evil forces that are threatening her?

Purdy, Anne, and Robert Specht. *Tisha: The Story of a Young Teacher in the Alaska Wilderness.* St. Martin's, 1976. **NF**
True account of a young girl who goes to Chicken, Alaska, in 1927 and is beset by all the problems of frontier living and prejudice.

Qualey, Marsha. *Close to a Killer.* Delacorte, 1999. **F**
When customers connected to her mom's beauty shop begin turning up dead, 17-year-old Barrie wonders if her ex-con mom and her prison buddy cosmetologists are serving up more than haircuts.

————. *Come In from the Cold.* Houghton Mifflin, 1994. **F**
Jeff and Maud, two 17-year-olds whose families have suffered personal tragedies caused by the Vietnam conflict, find comfort and love when they meet during the 1969 antiwar movement.

————. *Just Like That.* Dial, 2005. **F**
Could 18-year-old Hanna have prevented the deaths of two teens? Her realization that everything can change in an instant causes her to reevaluate her life and relationships as she keeps her guilty secret.

————. *Revolutions of the Heart.* Houghton Mifflin, 1993. **F**
Seventeen-year-old Cory is caught between her Native American boyfriend and her older brother's prejudices, as native spearfishing in northern Wisconsin tears their little town apart.

Quarles, Heather. *A Door Near Here.* Delacorte, 1998. **F**
Caring for her alcoholic mother and her three younger siblings almost overwhelms 15-year-old Katherine as she tries to keep her family's plight a secret from her father, her teachers, her neighbors, and the authorities.

Rall, Ted. *To Afghanistan and Back: A Graphic Travelogue.* Nantier, Beall, Minoustchine, 2002. **NF**
Syndicated cartoonist and columnist Ted Rall shares the details of his fascinating and dangerous 2001 trip to Afghanistan, along with his liberal political views, in this graphic travelogue.

Ramati, Alexander. *And the Violins Stopped Playing: A Story of the Gypsy Holocaust.* Watts, 1986. **NF**
Based on a young survivor's account, this gripping story tells of the Nazi massacre of the Gypsies during World War II.

Randle, Kristen D. *Breaking Rank.* Morrow, 1999. **F**
Popular, 17-year-old Casey learns about trust, friendship, and love when she begins tutoring Baby, a member of a nonconformist society called the Clan.

————. *The Only Alien on the Planet.* Scholastic, 1995. **F**
Moving to the East Coast, high school senior Ginny becomes friends with a boy who never speaks and uncovers his dark secret.

Rapp, Adam. *Missing the Piano.* Viking, 1994. **F**
Initially thrilled when his younger sister wins a role in the national tour of *Les Miserables,* Mike Tegroff finds his enthusiasm waning when he discovers that he is being sent to a military academy while his mother and sister travel.

————. *33 Snowfish.* Candlewick, 2003. **F**
Boobie, Curl, and Custis are on the run with Boobie's baby brother in tow as they each attempt to escape their demons and cling to one another in their darkest hours.

———. *Under the Wolf, under the Dog.* Candlewick, 2004. **F**

High school student Steve Nugent reveals the sad and gruesome family tragedies that led to his life at a facility for troubled teens.

Rappaport, Doreen. *American Women: Their Lives in Their Words.* Crowell, 1990. **NF**

The vital and changing roles women have played in American history from colonial times to the present are vividly portrayed through their diaries, letters, and photos.

Rather, Dan, and Mickey Herskowitz. *The Camera Never Blinks: Adventures of a TV Journalist.* Morrow, 1977. **NF**

This controversial autobiography is by one of the best known and most respected TV newscasters.

Ray, Delia. *A Nation Torn: The Story of How the Civil War Began.* Lodestar, 1990. **NF**

An accessible, well-illustrated account of pre-Civil War events relates the way they lead to the fateful firing on Fort Sumter.

Read, Piers Paul. *Alive: The Story of the Andes Survivors.* Lippincott, 1974. **NF**

A compassionate account of 16 young rugby players who survive a plane crash in the Andes and live for ten weeks on faith, finally choosing to use the bodies of their dead comrades for sustenance.

Reader, Dennis J. *Coming Back Alive.* Random House, 1981. **F**

Because Bridget's parents are dead and Dylan is in conflict with his, the two seek refuge in the rugged Trinity Mountains and in each other.

Reaver, Chap. *A Little Bit Dead.* Delacorte, 1992. **F**

After Reece saves Shanti from being lynched, information from a dance hall girl saves Reece from the marshal and his posse.

Reed, Kit. *The Ballad of T. Rantula.* Little, Brown, 1979. **F**

Because his mother has left his father and his best friend is committing suicide by not eating, Futch hides in the monstrous alter ego of T. Rantula.

Rees, Celia. *Pirates! The True and Remarkable Adventures of Minerva Sharpe and Nancy Kington, Female Pirates.* Bloomsbury, 2003. **F**

In the 1720s, dire circumstances propel two girls— a wealthy merchant's daughter from England and her father's Jamaican slave—into a life of piracy.

———. *Witch Child.* Candlewick, 2001. **F**

In 1659, having watched her grandmother hang from the gallows as a witch and having fled to the New World, Mary Newbury keeps a journal of her experiences there with the same intolerance that killed her grandmother.

Reese, Lyn, et al., eds. *I'm on My Way Running: Women Speak on Coming of Age.* Avon, 1983. **NF**

Young women come of age in autobiography, poetry, fiction, and anthropological accounts from around the world.

Reeve, Philip. *Mortal Engines.* EOS, 2003. **F**

In a future so bleak that cities travel on huge tank-like tracks hunting and consuming smaller towns, teens uncover a diabolical plan to reconstruct the very weapons that destroyed civilization.

———. *Predator's Gold.* EOS, 2004. **F**

In a futuristic world where wheeled cities devour other cities, lovers Hester and Tom are pursued by a terrorist group as they shelter on a traction city attempting to find the "Dead Continent" of America.

Reich, Susanna. *Clara Schumann: Piano Virtuoso.* Clarion, 1999. **NF**

This biography features the extraordinary piano virtuoso who was the devoted wife of Robert Schumann, a mother to eight children, and a composer in her own right.

Reidelbach, Maria. *Completely Mad: A History of the Comic Book and Magazine.* Little, Brown, 1991. **NF**

MAD magazine is funny and offensive. No wonder teens love it and parents hate it! Read all about it in this illustrated history.

Reinhardt, Dana. *A Brief Chapter in My Impossible Life.* Wendy Lamb, 2006. **F**

Encouraged by her supportive adoptive family, Simone reaches out to her birth mother and finds unexpected blessings, including a new appreciation for her Jewish heritage.

Reiss, Kathryn. *Time Windows.* Harcourt Brace Jovanovich, 1991. **F**

Moving into a mysterious old house, Miranda finds that she can see the horrifying things that happened there in the past; but can she do anything now to change history?

Rendell, Ruth. *The Crocodile Bird.* Crown, 1993. **F**

Liza has lived a completely sheltered life with her obsessive mother on a remote English estate, but when her mother is arrested for murder, Liza is forced to flee, totally unprepared for the real world.

———. *Heartstones.* Harper & Row, 1987. **F**

A victim of anorexia and bonded to her father, teenage Elvira leads her family to total destruction.

Rennison, Louise. *Angus, Thongs, and Full-Frontal Snogging: Confessions of Georgia Nicolson.* HarperCollins, 2000. **F**

This yearlong comic romp with Georgia shows her flipping from soaring joys to bottomless angst.

Renvoizé, Jean. *A Wild Thing.* Atlantic Monthly, 1971. **F**

Morag, a foster child, runs away to the isolated wilderness of the Scottish mountains, where she is happy for a time but soon realizes that no one can survive alone.

Reuter, Bjarne. *The Boys from St. Petri.* Dutton, 1994. **F**

When the Germans occupy Denmark during World War II, a group of teenage boys escalate their pranks to a series of increasingly dangerous resistance missions.

Reynolds, Marilyn. *Detour for Emmy.* Morning Glory, 1993. **F**

Fifteen-year-old Emmy, an A student with college ambitions, must put her life on hold when she becomes pregnant and decides to keep her baby.

————. *Too Soon for Jeff.* Morning Glory, 1994. **F**

Jeff's plans for the future, which include college, debate, and girls, but not his high-school girlfriend Christy, come crashing down when she has his baby.

Reynolds, Marjorie. *The Starlite Drive-In.* Morrow, 1997. **F**

Thirteen-year-old Callie falls hard for the romantic drifter who disrupts the lives of her lonely mother and bitter father.

Rhodes, Richard. *Farm: A Year in the Life of an American Farmer.* Simon & Schuster, 1989. **NF**

Here's everything you didn't think you needed to know about the real life of a family earning its livelihood from the land.

Rice, David. *Crazy Loco: Stories.* Dial, 2001. **F**

This collection features tales from Chicano life in small-town Texas that are both poignant and hilarious.

Rice, Robert. *The Last Pendragon.* Walker, 1991. **F**

Sir Bedwyr disobeys Arthur's dying wish and hides the sword Caliburn instead of returning it to the lake, but when he returns to help Arthur's grandson fight the Saxons, the sword has disappeared.

Richards, Arlene Kramer, and Irene Willis. *What to Do If You or Someone You Know Is under 18 and Pregnant.* Lothrop, Lee & Shepard, 1983. **NF**

This is information for teens on all aspects of pregnancy, including single parenting, adoption, abortion, marriage, and infant care.

Riddles, Libby, and Tim Jones. *Race across Alaska: First Woman to Win the Iditarod Tells Her Story.* Stackpole, 1988. **NF**

A true tale recounts how Libby Riddles overcomes all odds to become the first woman to win the Iditarod.

Ridgway, John, and Chay Blyth. *A Fighting Chance.* Lippincott, 1967. **NF**

Two young British paratroopers undertake a harrowing voyage across the Atlantic in a 20-foot row boat.

Riley, Jocelyn. *Only My Mouth Is Smiling.* Morrow, 1982. **F**

Merle desperately tries to hide her mother's mental illness from the whole world and especially from her own family.

Rinaldi, Ann. *An Acquaintance with Darkness.* Harcourt Brace, 1997. **F**

After her mother's death, 14-year-old Emily Pigbrush must go to live with her uncle, a doctor she suspects is a grave robber.

————. *A Break with Charity: A Story about the Salem Witch Trials.* Harcourt Brace Jovanovich, 1992. **F**

Susanna, fearful for the safety of her family, keeps silent about the motives of her friends who are accusing the Salem townspeople of witchcraft.

————. *Hang a Thousand Trees with Ribbons: The Story of Phillis Wheatley.* Harcourt Brace, 1996. **F**

Kidnapped in Senegal in 1761 and sold into slavery in America, Phillis Wheatley becomes educated and well-known for her poetry, only to face a struggle to fit into a white man's world.

————. *In My Father's House.* Scholastic, 1993. **F**

During the Civil War, Oscie watches her Southern way of life disappear forever.

————. *The Last Silk Dress.* Holiday House, 1988. **F**

As teenage Susan Chilmark champions the Confederate cause by collecting the last silk dresses in Richmond to build a hot air balloon, she examines her loyalty to family, friends, and country.

————. *Time Enough for Drums.* Holiday House, 1986. **F**

Fifteen-year-old Jemima, torn by her growing love for a supposed Tory sympathizer during the American Revolution, matures through her father's murder and her brothers' fight for independence.

————. *Wolf by the Ears.* Scholastic, 1991. **F**
Harriet Hemings, rumored to be Thomas Jefferson's daughter, faces the choice of passing as white or remaining a slave in the sheltered but restricted life at Monticello.

Riordan, Rick. *The Lightning Thief.* Hyperion, 2005. **F**
After dyslexic teen Percy Jackson vaporizes his algebra teacher and is attacked by the Minotaur, he discovers that he is not who he thought he was!

Ritter, John H. *Choosing Up Sides.* Philomel, 1998. **F**
Luke's preacher father believes that left-handedness is a sign of the devil, and Luke's love of baseball, especially his left-handed pitching, leads to a family tragedy.

Ritter, Lawrence S. *The Babe: A Life in Pictures.* Ticknor & Fields, 1988. **NF**
The life of Babe Ruth, the orphan who became the greatest legend in baseball history, is captured in this photo-biography.

Rivers, Glenn, and Bruce Brooks. *Those Who Love the Game: Glenn "Doc" Rivers on Life in the NBA and Elsewhere.* Holt, 1993. **NF**
Doc Rivers tells it like it is—his life, his family, his teammates and coaches, and above all, how he lives and plays the game of basketball.

Roach, Mary. *Stiff: The Curious Lives of Human Cadavers.* Norton, 2003. **NF**
This book explores the afterlife of human cadavers, with a humorous yet touching look at how scientists utilize every precious element of the human body.

Roberson, Jennifer. *Lady of the Forest.* Zebra, 1992. **F**
Maid Marian is the lady in this romantic retelling of the Robin Hood legend.

Robertson, Dougal. *Survive the Savage Sea.* Praeger, 1973. **NF**
Having survived the wreck of their boat by killer whales, the Robertson family and a friend face an incredible 38-day battle for life in a secondhand raft, 1,000 miles from land.

Robertson, James I., Jr. *"Civil War!": America Becomes One Nation.* Knopf, 1992. **NF**
A vivid portrayal of the Civil War shows the way it was on both the battlefield and the home front.

————. *Robert E. Lee: Virginian Soldier, American Citizen.* Atheneum, 2005. **NF**
Dashing Robert E. Lee was Abraham Lincoln's choice to lead the Union, but Lee's devotion to Virginia changed the course of U.S. history. This fascinating biography explores a remarkable life.

Robeson, Susan. *The Whole World in His Hands: A Pictorial Biography of Paul Robeson.* Citadel, 1981. **NF**
A memoir of a brilliant, talented and controversial black singer is lovingly told in words and pictures by his granddaughter.

Robinson, Sharon. *Promises to Keep: How Jackie Robinson Changed America.* Scholastic, 2004. **NF**
Jackie Robinson's daughter shares her views of her father's baseball career, family life, and political activism with beautiful photographs and handwritten correspondence.

Robinson, Spider. *Callahan's Crosstime Saloon.* R. Enslow, 1978. **F**
The misfits of Earth and elsewhere who belly up to Callahan's bar have lived some of the wildest and funniest stories in the galaxies.

Rochelle, Belinda, ed. *Words with Wings: A Treasury of African-American Poetry and Art.* HarperCollins, 2001. **NF**
This treasury tells the story of the African American experience through an arresting compilation of 20 poems and 20 works of art by African Americans.

Rochman, Hazel, ed. *Somehow Tenderness Survives: Stories of Southern Africa.* Harper & Row, 1988. **F**
Ten short stories and autobiographical sketches by both whites and blacks from southern Africa reveal how it is to grow up under apartheid.

Rochman, Hazel, and Darlene Z. McCampbell, eds. *Bearing Witness: Stories of the Holocaust.* Orchard, 1995. **NF**
Twenty-four selections confront the Holocaust with intensity and realism, wrestling art and meaning from the unspeakable.

————, eds. *Leaving Home: Stories.* HarperCollins, 1997. **F**
Leaving whatever one considers "home" can cause many emotions, as experienced in this collection of short stories, poems, and essays.

————, eds. *Who Do You Think You Are? Stories of Friends and Enemies.* Joy Street, 1993. **F**
These 16 thought-provoking stories and autobiographical excerpts tell about friends and enemies.

Rodowsky, Colby. *Hannah in Between.* Farrar, Straus & Giroux, 1994. **F**
Hannah is caught between childhood and adult responsibilities as she desperately tries to keep her mother's alcoholism a secret.

————. *Julie's Daughter*. Farrar, Straus & Giroux, 1985. F

Slug meets the mother who deserted her when she was a baby and finally learns to accept the past.

Rogasky, Barbara. *Smoke and Ashes: The Story of the Holocaust*. Holiday House, 1988. NF

Photographs and a graphic text trace the annihilation of the Jews before and during World War II.

Rol, Ruud van der, and Rian Verhoeven. *Anne Frank, beyond the Diary: A Photographic Remembrance*. Viking, 1993. NF

The combination of family photos, biographical sketches of Anne Frank and others in the "secret annex," with brief essays identifying stages of the Holocaust lets readers begin to know the real Anne.

Rose, Louise Blecher. *The Launching of Barbara Fabrikant*. McKay, 1974. F

A witty, empathetic, and earthy first-person story about the freshman college year of the overweight daughter of a rabbi.

Rosoff, Meg. *How I Live Now*. Wendy Lamb, 2004. F

Fifteen-year-old Daisy finds her whole world turned upside down when she travels to England to stay with relatives, falls in love, and is caught up in a devastating war.

————. *Just in Case*. Wendy Lamb, 2006. F

After David rescues his baby brother from a near-tragic occurrence, the 15-year-old struggles to re-invent himself and change his destiny.

Ross, Stewart. *Shakespeare and Macbeth: The Story behind the Play*. Viking, 1994. NF

Both Shakespeare's England and the exciting story behind the bard's most bloody play are illuminated in Ross's vivid account.

Rosten, Leo. *A Most Private Intrigue*. Atheneum, 1967. F

A sophisticated and intriguing novel in which former espionage agent Peter Galton attempts to bring three important scientists out of Russia.

Rostkowski, Margaret I. *After the Dancing Days*. Harper & Row, 1986. F

Thirteen-year-old Annie befriends hideously disfigured Andrew, a World War I veteran.

Rothenberg, Mira. *Children with Emerald Eyes: Histories of Extraordinary Boys and Girls*. Dial, 1977. NF

Heartrending case histories of autistic and schizophrenic children are told by a psychologist who works closely with them.

Rottman, S. L. *Head above Water*. Peachtree, 1999. F

High school junior Skye Johnson is responsible for a lot around the home, including her Down syndrome brother, Sunny, but she thinks life might be getting better when a football star begins to pursue her.

————. *Hero*. Peachtree, 1997. F

Sean, an angry 15-year-old from an abusive home, learns that he can take control of his own life while doing community service on a farm owned by an old man.

————. *Stetson*. Viking, 2002. F

Stetson has learned to survive a drunken, negligent father by fending for himself, working at the salvage yard, and devoting his free time to rebuilding his car—until a sister he didn't know he had turns up and turns his life upside down.

Roueche, Berton. *Feral*. Harper & Row, 1974. F

What happens to a fictional, rural Long Island community when stray cats turn wild and terrorize the town's residents?

Rowling, J. K. *Harry Potter and the Chamber of Secrets*. Arthur A. Levine, 1999. F

Harry Potter's training as a wizard continues with more magical adventures in his second year at Hogwarts.

————. *Harry Potter and the Half-Blood Prince*. Arthur A. Levine, 2005. F

In the sixth book in the series, Harry is more contrary and less trusting, yet also a leader who wants revenge against He Who Shall Not Be Named, sending him on a series of dark adventures to accomplish his goal.

————. *Harry Potter and the Order of the Phoenix*. Arthur A. Levine, 2003. F

Harry Potter, in his fifth year at Hogwarts, is snappier and moodier than ever and is also haunted by dreams that foreshadow a terrifying secret.

————. *Harry Potter and the Prisoner of Azkaban*. Arthur A. Levine, 1999. F

Harry's third year at Hogwarts is packed with adventure, mystery, and a dangerous new enemy.

————. *Harry Potter and the Sorcerer's Stone*. Arthur A. Levine, 1998. F

With only a lightning-bolt scar on his forehead as a clue to his true identity, Harry Potter, by a twist of fate, leaves his unloving foster family for a life of wizardry and celebrity.

Roybal, Laura. *Billy.* Houghton Mifflin, 1994. **F**
A confused 16-year-old, who had been kidnapped at age 10, must decide whether he is Billy Melendez, a New Mexico cowboy from a rural community, or Will Campbell, a middle-class midwesterner.

Rubin, Susan Goldman. *Margaret Bourke-White: Her Pictures Were Her Life.* Abrams, 1999. **NF**
Determined, dedicated, and brilliant, White pursued photography in a time when most women did not have careers and men dominated the world of business and art.

Ruby, Lois. *Arriving at a Place You've Never Left.* Dial, 1977. **F**
Seven moving short stories deal with such personal crises as coping with a mother's nervous breakdown; being 17, pregnant, and unmarried; and facing anti-Semitism.

———. *Miriam's Well.* Scholastic, 1993. **F**
When Miriam is diagnosed with bone cancer, her life hangs in the balance while advocates of her religion, which prohibits medical treatment, battle doctors and lawyers.

Ruskin, Cindy. *The Quilt: Stories from the NAMES Project.* Pocket, 1988. **NF**
The lovers, friends, and relatives of the thousands who have died from AIDS express their love and loss in handcrafted 3-by-6-foot panels sewn into an enormous memorial quilt.

Russell, Bill, and William McSweeny. *Go Up for Glory.* Coward-McCann, 1966. **NF**
The Boston Celtics' superstar recounts the highlights of his career and gives his opinions on subjects ranging from coaches to civil rights in an outspoken autobiography.

Ryan, Cornelius. *The Last Battle.* Simon & Schuster, 1966. **NF**
This is an exciting day-by-day chronicle, based on eye-witness accounts, of the twenty-one days prior to the fall of Berlin in 1945.

Ryan, Joan. *Little Girls in Pretty Boxes: The Making and Breaking of Elite Gymnasts and Figure Skaters.* Doubleday, 1995. **NF**
You'll never look at Olympic champion gymnasts and figure skaters in the same way after reading this startling expose of how young female athletes suffer physically and psychologically for their gold.

Ryan, Pam Muñoz. *Esperanza Rising.* Scholastic, 2000. **F**
Esperanza and her mother are forced to leave their life of wealth and privilege in Mexico to work in the labor camps of Southern California, where they must adapt to harsh circumstances on the eve of the Great Depression.

Ryan, Sara. *Empress of the World.* Viking, 2001. **F**
Nicola meets a group of new friends while studying archaeology at a summer institute for gifted high school students, and her attraction to Battle leads to her first experience of love and heartbreak.

Ryden, Hope. *God's Dog.* Coward, McCann & Geoghegan, 1975. **NF**
A naturalist's two-year field study of coyotes results in a compassionate plea for changes in our attitudes toward these misunderstood creatures.

Ryerson, Eric. *When Your Parent Drinks Too Much: A Book for Teenagers.* Facts on File, 1985. **NF**
In addition to letting young adults know they are not alone, Ryerson provides hope: "You can't control your parent's drinking, but you can make changes that will make your life better."

Rylant, Cynthia. *A Couple of Kooks, and Other Stories about Love.* Orchard, 1990. **F**
Many faces of love are found in these short stories—from love for an unborn child to romantic love and love that can never be reciprocated.

———. *A Fine White Dust.* Bradbury, 1986. **F**
When the traveling preacher comes to town, Peter's religious beliefs find a focus—but is running away with the preacher the answer to Peter's needs?

———. *God Went to Beauty School.* HarperCollins, 2003. **F**
This funny yet thoughtful collection of poems presents an alternative view of God.

———. *Kindness.* Orchard, 1988. **F**
Chip must cope with many conflicting emotions when his mother reveals that she is pregnant and refuses to name the father.

———. *Missing May.* Orchard, 1992. **F**
After the death of her beloved Aunt May, Summer is afraid that she will also lose her Uncle Ob to his grief, but a quirky boy and the remembrance of May's extraordinary love help them to heal and to reaffirm life.

———. *Soda Jerk.* Orchard, 1990. **F**
In poetic observations, a young drug store soda jerk in a small Virginia town comments on the people and activity around him.

———. *Something Permanent.* Harcourt Brace, 1994. **NF**
Rylant reinterprets Walker Evans's well-known Depression-era photographs in poetry that is as unforgettable as that extraordinary time in history.

Sachar, Louis. *Holes.* Farrar, Straus & Giroux, 1998. F
Stanley Yelnats is sentenced to Camp Green Lake, where he finds a treasure and puts an end to a long-running curse on his family.

Sachs, Marilyn. *The Fat Girl.* Dutton, 1984. F
Jeff Lyons is obsessed with creating a new person out of an unhappy fat girl, but loses control of the situation when the girl begins to think for herself.

Sáenz, Benjamin Alire. *Sammy and Juliana in Hollywood.* Cinco Puntos, 2004. F
In the 1960s, Sammy dreams of getting away from the barrio and going to college, but when the girl he loves is tragically killed, his grief nearly overwhelms him.

Sagan, Carl. *Cosmos.* Random House, 1980. NF
Based on the PBS series, this chronicle of the life of our galactic backyard includes history, science, astronomy, and philosophy in a format that can be enjoyed in bits and pieces or from cover to cover.

Salassi, Otto R. *Jimmy D., Sidewinder, and Me.* Greenwillow, 1987. F
In jail, 15-year-old Dumas Monk is writing—on the judge's orders—the story of how he became a pool hustler and a murderer.

Saleh, Dennis. *Rock Art: The Golden Age of Record Album Covers.* Ballantine, 1978. NF
Printed in full color from original negatives, this is a lavish collection of the best rock album covers from the preceding decade.

Salisbury, Graham. *Blue Skin of the Sea.* Delacorte, 1992. F
In a series of 11 stories, Sonny Mendoza faces fear, love, and challenges as he comes of age in a small Hawaiian fishing village.

———. *Eyes of the Emperor.* Wendy Lamb, 2005. F
To make his father proud, 16-year-old Eddy Okubo lies about his age and joins the U.S. army in Honolulu in 1941, just before the bombing of Pearl Harbor—a time when young Japanese American men will train experimental K-9 units to hunt the Japanese during World War II.

———. *Jungle Dogs.* Delacorte, 1998. F
While growing up in Hawaii, James "Boy" Regis learns some tough lessons about courage and respect when he faces his darkest fears.

———. *Lord of the Deep.* Delacorte, 2001. F
Thirteen-year-old Mikey learns some hard truths about life and honor during three fateful days aboard his stepfather's deep-sea fishing boat off Hawaii.

———. *Under the Blood-Red Sun.* Delacorte, 1994. F
Tomi, a Japanese American teen living in Hawaii, must become the man of his family when his father and grandfather are interned after the bombing of Pearl Harbor.

Sallis, Susan. *Only Love.* Harper & Row, 1980. F
The adversity of a wheelchair existence does not overwhelm Fran, and the knowledge that she is dying leads her to live each day to the fullest with humor, adventure, and love. Fran's love affair with Lucas, another wheelchair occupant at Thornton Hall, is full of surprises.

Salzman, Mark. *Iron and Silk.* Random House, 1986. NF
A young Yale graduate describes his two years in China teaching English to medical students, perfecting his Chinese, and studying martial arts with a master.

———. *Lost in Place: Growing Up Absurd in Suburbia.* Random House, 1995. NF
Growing up in the Connecticut suburbs is not easy for a wanna-be kung fu expert and wandering Zen monk.

Samson, Joan. *The Auctioneer.* Simon & Schuster, 1975. F
What begins as a harmless Saturday pastime turns sinister when the auctioneering stranger in town becomes its most influential and evil citizen.

Samuels, Gertrude. *Run, Shelley, Run!* Crowell, 1974. F
Runaway Shelley, a victim of family neglect and juvenile injustice, finally gets the help she needs through the concern of a sympathetic judge and the intercession of a kind neighbor.

Sanchez, Alex. *Rainbow Boys.* Simon & Schuster, 2001. F
Three very different high school boys deal with the issues involved in being gay: coming out to parents and friends, self-acceptance, the art of forming relationships, health-related issues, and the dangers of exploitation.

Sanders, Dori. *Clover.* Algonquin, 1990. F
When her father is killed in an automobile accident in rural South Carolina, ten-year-old Clover is left to be reared by her white stepmother within the black community.

Sanders, Scott R. *Bad Man Ballad.* Bradbury, 1986. F
In the early 1800s, two unlikely partners, a backwoods boy and a Philadelphia lawyer, go in search of a frontier "bigfoot" who has been accused of murder.

Sanderson, Ivan T. *Uninvited Visitors: A Biologist Looks at UFO's.* Cowles, 1967. **NF**
Using exacting scientific methodology, the author delves deep into such problems as what UFOs could be, where they might come from, when they started coming, and what they would want from us.

Sandler, Martin W. *The Story of American Photography: An Illustrated History for Young People.* Little, Brown, 1979. **NF**
From daguerreotypes to Polaroids, this illustrated history tells the story of the men and women who shaped the course of a major art and industry.

Santana, Patricia. *Motorcycle Ride on the Sea of Tranquility.* University of New Mexico Press, 2002. **F**
When 14-year-old Yolanda Sahagun's favorite brother returns from Vietnam in the spring of 1969, things are different and keep on changing.

Santiago, Danny. *Famous All Over Town.* Simon & Schuster, 1983. **F**
Chato, a young Mexican American growing up in a Los Angeles barrio, has an IQ of 135 but gets bad grades in school because his first loyalty is to his family and gang.

Santoli, Al, ed. *Everything We Had: An Oral History of the Vietnam War.* Random House, 1981. **NF**
Thirty-three veterans of the Vietnam war recount its impact on their lives one decade later.

Sargent, Pamela. *Earthseed.* Harper & Row, 1983. **F**
Ship has created and raised a generation of Earth children as it carries them through space toward a new planet where they must survive alone without Ship's care.

————, ed. *Women of Wonder: Science Fiction Stories by Women about Women.* Vintage, 1975. **F**
These exceptional stories show that science fiction is no longer a field completely reserved for men.

Satrapi, Marjane. *Persepolis: The Story of a Childhood.* Pantheon, 2003. **F**
Marjane, the daughter of radical Marxists, grows up in Iran during the time of its revolution and subsequent war with Iraq.

————. *Persepolis 2: The Story of a Return.* Pantheon, 2004. **NF**
Marjane Satrapi continues where she left off in her first graphic novel, *Persepolis,* living in Vienna and enduring the hardships of being an Iranian citizen in a Western country.

Saul, John. *Creature.* Bantam, 1989. **F**
Seemingly perfect Silverdale hides a horrible secret brought to light only when the coach's boys begin turning into monsters—both on and off the football field.

Savage, Candace. *Cowgirls.* Ten Speed, 1996. **NF**
From real life to reel life, this photo-history tells the story of sharpshooting women who settled the American West and rode the rodeo circuit from Wyoming to Madison Square Garden.

Savage, Deborah. *Kotuku.* Houghton Mifflin, 2002. **F**
Seventeen-year-old Wim Thorpe resists caring after the loss of her best friend, but an attractive New Zealand historian investigating Maori connections to her hometown looks exactly like a benevolent tattooed apparition who may be showing her the way to her own truth.

————. *Summer Hawk.* Houghton Mifflin, 1999. **F**
While spending the summer in rural Pennsylvania with her father, city girl Taylor becomes involved with a local raptor rehabilitation center after she and a classmate find an injured hawk.

Savage, Georgia. *The House Tibet.* Graywolf, 1991. **F**
After she is raped by her father, Vicky and her autistic younger brother run away, learn survival skills from street kids in an Australian beach town, and are befriended by some unusual people.

Say, Allen. *The Ink-Keeper's Apprentice.* Harper & Row, 1979. **F**
Living on his own in post-World War II Tokyo, 13-year-old Kiyoi begins a new life when he becomes an apprentice to a famous cartoonist.

Sayres, Meghan Nuttall. *Anahita's Woven Riddle.* Abrams, 2006. **F**
In early 20th-century Iran, a headstrong girl convinces her father that she will marry the suitor who can guess the riddle woven into her wedding carpet.

Scaduto, Anthony. *Bob Dylan.* Grosset & Dunlap, 1972. **NF**
What makes Dylan tick—from his early days in Hibbing, Minnesota, to his later silent stance—is told in this story of the complicated man.

Schaap, Dick. *Turned On.* New American Library, 1967. **NF**
At 19 Celeste Crenshaw is dead of an overdose of drugs, and her wealthy, socially prominent boyfriend is on his way to prison.

Schami, Rafik. *A Hand Full of Stars.* Dutton, 1990. **F**

A young teenage boy in modern Damascus faces career choices, political ferment, and romance.

Schell, Jonathan. *The Fate of the Earth.* Knopf, 1982. **NF**

The possibility of human extinction from nuclear disaster is discussed in this frightening, and important, book.

Schliff, Ken. *Passing Go.* Dodd, Mead, 1972. **F**

A curious blend of the real and surreal, this is an 18-year-old boy's day-by-day account of four bleak months in a mental hospital.

Schmidt, Gary D. *Lizzie Bright and the Buckminster Boy.* Clarion, 2004. **F**

Turner's family moves to Phippsburg, Maine, in 1912, a time when the town's white leaders seek to eliminate a nearby island community founded by former slaves in hopes of attracting tourism.

———. *The Sin Eater.* Lodestar, 1996. **F**

When Cole hears stories of the mysterious "Sin Eater," he sets out to solve the mystery, making many self-discoveries along the way.

Schmidt, Thomas, and Jeremy Schmidt. *The Saga of Lewis and Clark: Into the Uncharted West.* DK, 1999. **NF**

Lavish illustrations spark this version of the famed journey into the American West to find a route to the Pacific.

Scholl, Hans, and Sophie Scholl. *At the Heart of the White Rose: Letters and Diaries of Hans and Sophie Scholl.* Harper & Row, 1987. **NF**

The personal writings of a brother and sister beheaded by the Nazis for their opposition to the Hitler terror are poignant and passionate.

Schrier, Eric W., and William F. Allman, eds. *Newton at the Bat: The Science in Sports.* Scribner, 1984. **NF**

From Schrier's sports column in *Science 84* magazine, these essays survey the part that physics, physiology, and aerodynamics play in baseball, Frisbee, skiing, sailing, and many other sports.

Schulke, Flip, ed. *Martin Luther King, Jr.: A Documentary, Montgomery to Memphis.* Norton, 1976. **NF**

Striking pictures and text graphically recapitulate the entire civil rights movement through the story of Dr. King's struggle to fulfill his dream.

Schulman, Audrey. *The Cage.* Algonquin, 1994. **F**

When she is chosen to join an expedition to photograph polar bears from behind the thin bars of a tiny metal cage, Beryl's courage is tested to the limit.

Schulz, Charles M. *Peanuts Treasury.* Holt, Rinehart and Winston, 1968. **F**

Lucy, the natural-born fussbudget turned amateur psychiatrist, Charlie Brown, much maligned but dedicated manager of the world's most defeated baseball team, and Snoopy, the only dog in existence with a split personality, devise their own inimitable philosophies to cope with life's adversities.

Schwager, Tina, and Michele Schuerger. *Gutsy Girls: Young Women Who Dare.* Free Spirit, 1999. **NF**

Autobiographical sketches share the lives of young women who skydive, drag race, and climb mountains, among other daring activities.

Schwartz, Virginia Frances. *Send One Angel Down.* Holiday House, 2000. **F**

A young slave tries to protect his younger cousin from the hardships of slavery.

Schwarz-Bart, Andre. *A Woman Named Solitude.* Atheneum, 1973. **F**

Understated and suffused with imagery and irony, this is the tale of a beautiful mulatto slave girl who is eventually driven into a zombie-like state of madness.

Schwarzenegger, Arnold, and Douglas Kent Hall. *Arnold: The Education of a Bodybuilder.* Simon & Schuster, 1977. **NF**

The six-time winner of the Mr. Olympia title and star of *Pumping Iron* recounts his life and presents a program for successful body building.

Scieszka, Jon, and Lane Smith. *Math Curse.* Viking, 1995. **F**

Math can be a real curse when you begin to think of everything as a math problem.

———. *The Stinky Cheese Man, and Other Fairly Stupid Tales.* Viking, 1992. **F**

This is a wickedly hysterical parody of childhood stories, complete with wild illustrations and a "surgeon general's warning."

Scoppettone, Sandra. *Happy Endings Are All Alike.* Harper & Row, 1978. **F**

Traditional values are questioned and love is tested when Jaret is raped by a disturbed boy and everyone learns of her lesbian relationship with Peggy.

———. *Trying Hard to Hear You.* Harper & Row, 1974. **F**

Sixteen-year-old Camilla recalls the tumultuous summer of 1973 when her best friend, Jeff, and Phil, the boy she has a crush on, fall in love with each other.

Scortia, Thomas N., and Frank G. Robinson. *The Prometheus Crisis.* Doubleday, 1975. **F**
Did human error, sabotage, or carelessness cause the final breaking point at the nuclear power station Prometheus?

Seagle, Steven T. *It's a Bird.* DC Comics, 2004. **NF**
A comic writer named Steve is unable to accept the job of a lifetime—to write a Superman story—because the problems in his past continue to haunt him in the present.

Searls, Hank. *Sounding.* Ballantine, 1982. **F**
As the old sperm whale seeks his former pod, a disabled Russian submarine teeters on a reef; perhaps the ancient cetacean hope that man can communicate will come true.

Sebestyen, Ouida. *Far from Home.* Atlantic Monthly, 1980. **F**
After the death of his mother, 14-year-old Salty follows the words in a note his mother left him to find a home for himself and his elderly grandmother, and begins to learn about love and family.

———. *IOU's.* Atlantic Monthly, 1982. **F**
Stowe Garrett is torn between the loyalty and love he feels for his mother and his longing to break free and experiment with life.

———. *Words by Heart.* Atlantic Monthly, 1979. **F**
Lena learns what it means to be black in a white world, but, helped by her brave father, she also learns how to be a real person.

Sebold, Alice. *The Lovely Bones.* Little, Brown, 2002. **F**
With wisdom and compassion, 14-year-old Susie Salmon narrates the story of her brutal murder and glowing afterlife as she watches her family and friends grapple with the hole her death has left in their lives.

Sedgwick, Marcus. *The Foreshadowing.* Wendy Lamb, 2006. **F**
During World War I, Sasha poses as a nurse and travels to France to save her brother from the fate she has foreseen for him.

Seed, Suzanne. *Fine Trades.* Follett, 1979. **NF**
In photographs and words, ten craftspersons explain their trades—ranging from violin making to bookbinding—and tell of the personal satisfaction they get from their work.

Segal, Erich. *Love Story.* Harper & Row, 1970. **F**
Oliver Barrett IV, a rich, cocky Harvard senior, and Jennie Cavilleri, a poor and serious Radcliffe music type, discover they are made for each other in this funny but touching love story.

Selvadurai, Shyam. *Swimming in the Monsoon Sea.* Tundra, 2005. **F**
Against the backdrop of a sultry Sri Lankan summer, 14-year-old Amrith makes discoveries about both his family's past and his own sexuality when his Canadian cousin visits.

Senn, Steve. *A Circle in the Sea.* Atheneum, 1981. **F**
After wearing a special ring, Robin dreams that she is the dolphin Breee. In fact, her mind actually inhabits the body of Breee, who is involved in the fight against those who are destroying the seas with pollution.

Severin, Tim. *The Sindbad Voyage.* Putnam, 1983. **NF**
In a hand-sewn boat, Severin follows the trading routes, attributed to Sinbad, to China by way of the Indian Ocean.

———. *The Ulysses Voyage: Sea Search for the Odyssey.* Dutton, 1988. **NF**
Severin tells how he and a crew of scholars and adventurers sailed the Mediterranean in a Bronze Age–style galley in an attempt to follow the path of Ulysses and identify sites made famous by Homer.

Shannon, George. *Unlived Affections.* Harper & Row, 1989. **F**
Discovering a box of old letters, Willie learns the truth about his parents' relationship.

Sharpe, Roger C. *Pinball!* Dutton, 1977. **NF**
For players and lovers of the pinball machine, here's a vicarious experience enlivened by full-page color photos of the real thing.

Shaw, Arnold. *The World of Soul: Black America's Contribution to the Pop Music Scene.* Cowles, 1970. **NF**
The brothers and sisters of soul—Otis Redding, James Brown and Aretha Franklin—are all here in this full story of blues and R & B.

Sheehan, Carolyn, and Edmund Sheehan. *Magnifi-Cat.* Doubleday, 1972. **F**
When a cat appears at the gates of heaven with an extraordinary halo, the whole computerized admissions process grinds to a halt.

Sheehan, Susan. *Ten Vietnamese.* Knopf, 1967. **NF**
Revealing interviews with men and women represent a cross section of the Vietnamese people, including the Viet Cong.

Sheldon, Mary. *Perhaps I'll Dream of Darkness.* Random House, 1981. **F**
Effie is dead now, and her sister Susan, through her diary, asks why. The answer lies with David Angel, the self-destructive rock star whom Effie idolized.

Sheppard, Mary C. *Seven for a Secret.* Groundwood, 2001. **F**

Fifteen-year-old cousins Melinda, Kate, and Rebecca face the decisions that will determine their futures in a remote Newfoundland community in the 1960s.

Sherman, D. R. *Brothers of the Sea.* Little, Brown, 1966. **F**

This simple and moving tale is about a fisherman's son whose friendship with a dolphin leads to tragedy.

————. *Lion's Paw.* Doubleday, 1975. **F**

An obsessed white hunter, a young Bushman, and a crippled lion confront one another in the conflict for survival.

Sherman, Josepha. *Child of Faerie, Child of Earth.* Walker, 1992. **F**

Percinet, the son of the queen of Faerie, is in love with a mortal girl, but can she accept his love and the presence of magic in her life?

Shevelev, Raphael, and Karine Schomer. *Liberating the Ghosts: Photographs and Text from the March of the Living with Excerpts from the Writings of Participants.* LensWork, 1996. **NF**

Photographs and memories from the March of the Living, the [1994] journey of Holocaust survivors and 5,000 teenagers from 40 countries.

Shilts, Randy. *And the Band Played On: Politics, People, and the AIDS Epidemic.* St. Martin's, 1987. **NF**

The shocking story of the failure of the U.S. government, the medical establishment, and the American people themselves to face the devastating modern AIDS plague is both tragic and frightening.

Shinn, Sharon. *The Safe-Keeper's Secret.* Viking, 2004. **F**

A foundling is raised with the Safe-Keeper's own baby, forcing the two as they grow older to come to terms with who they are and who they might become.

————. *Summers at Castle Auburn.* Ace, 2001. **F**

As the years pass, Coriel, a nobleman's illegitimate daughter, spends her summers at the castle and becomes aware of the dark intrigues that surround the royalty.

Shoup, Barbara. *Stranded in Harmony.* Hyperion, 1997. **F**

How can Lucas, a high-school senior, loosen the grip of his parents, his girlfriend, and his best friend, all of whom want him to live up to their expectations?

————. *Wish You Were Here.* Hyperion, 1994. **F**

Jax experiences life's highs and lows during his senior year when he falls in love and also has to deal with his father's near-fatal accident and his best friend's running away.

Shreve, Susan. *Masquerade.* Knopf, 1980. **F**

After their father is arrested for embezzlement and their mother has a nervous breakdown, the Walker family—especially 17-year-old Rebecca—must learn to cope with the disturbing truth and begin to sort out their lives.

Shusterman, Neal. *The Dark Side of Nowhere.* Little, Brown, 1997. **F**

Feeling trapped and bored in his normal, peaceful hometown, Jason slowly learns that he and most of the townspeople are aliens.

————. *Downsiders.* Simon & Schuster, 1999. **F**

Lindsay meets Talon and discovers his world, which evolved from the subway built in New York in 1867, and the two friends experience the clash of their cultures.

————. *The Schwa Was Here.* Dutton, 2004. **F**

When Antsy Bonano realizes that his friend Calvin Schwa is functionally invisible, they decide to use this "Schwa Effect" to make some big bucks. Their plan works wonderfully until they are caught in loony Old Man Crawley's apartment.

————. *What Daddy Did.* Little, Brown, 1991. **F**

After the murder of his mother, Preston must find a way to face, and even forgive, his father—the man who killed her.

Sieruta, Peter D. *Heartbeats, and Other Stories.* Harper & Row, 1989. **F**

Depicting joy and pain, love and sorrow, family conflicts and relationships, these nine short stories feature teenagers dealing with life's problems and issues.

Silverberg, Robert. *Lord Valentine's Castle.* Harper & Row, 1980. **F**

Joining a troupe of itinerant jugglers, young Valentine gathers a motley, many-specied party of supporters and journeys across the continent of Majipoor to regain his rightful throne.

Silverstein, Ken. *The Radioactive Boy Scout: The True Story of a Boy and His Backyard Nuclear Reactor.* Random House, 2004. **NF**

Science geek David Hahn's obsession with nuclear energy results in the unsupervised creation of a radioactive device with the potential to spark an environmental disaster in his community.

Silvey, Anita, ed. *Help Wanted: Short Stories about Young People Working.* Little, Brown, 1997. **F**
This diverse collection of stories by Michael Dorris, Ray Bradbury, Vivien Alcock, and nine others shows just how momentous a first job can be.

Simak, Clifford D. *Enchanted Pilgrimage.* Berkley, 1975. **F**
This is a strange, enchanting, allegorical journey in a world where elves, gnomes, and goblins are as normal as bacon and eggs.

————. *The Werewolf Principle.* Putnam, 1967. **F**
Strange adventure follows when Andrew Blake is found frozen in a space capsule and is brought back to Earth after 200 years.

Simon, Neil. *Brighton Beach Memoirs.* Random House, 1984. **NF**
Sex and baseball are the primary preoccupations of 15-year-old Eugene, in this play about lower middle-class Jewish family life in New York City during the Depression.

————. *Lost in Yonkers.* Random House, 1991. **NF**
Two young brothers rely on their sense of humor when they are sent to live with their fearsome, irascible grandmother during World War II.

Simon, Nissa. *Don't Worry, You're Normal: A Teenager's Guide to Self-Health.* Crowell, 1982. **NF**
This brief but thorough guide answers many questions about physical and psychological changes occurring during the teen years.

Sinclair, April. *Coffee Will Make You Black.* Hyperion, 1994. **F**
Stevie, a young African American girl growing up in the late 1950s, struggles—humorously—to make sense of the adult world she is entering.

Singer, Marilyn. *The Course of True Love Never Did Run Smooth.* Harper & Row, 1983. **F**
While acting the role of love-sick Helena in a high school production of *A Midsummer Night's Dream,* Becky is infatuated with the handsome lead, until she discovers that she loves her long-time friend Nemi.

Sis, Peter. *The Tree of Life: A Book Depicting the Life of Charles Darwin, Naturalist, Geologist, and Thinker.* Farrar, Straus & Giroux, 2003. **F**
The 19th-century scientist who sailed around the world and wrote a book that changed it is featured through illustrations and material from his own diaries.

Skurzynski, Gloria. *Manwolf.* Clarion, 1981. **F**
Adam's heritage as the son of a masked knight and a serf in medieval Poland results in some unearthly tendencies and the need to turn to Kasia, the witch, for survival and true identity.

————. *Spider's Voice.* Atheneum, 1999. **F**
This medieval thriller features Aran, a mute boy who escapes a horrific fate by helping the famous lovers Heloise and Abelard.

————. *The Tempering.* Clarion, 1983. **F**
Karl faces a decision to stay in school or go to work in a Pennsylvania steel mill, in the early 20th century.

————. *Virtual War.* Simon & Schuster, 1997. **F**
In this quick read, genetically engineered soldiers prepare for a virtual war. Even in cyberspace, adolescents rebel and there are FLKs (funny-looking kids).

Slade, Arthur. *Dust.* Wendy Lamb, 2003. **F**
Eleven-year-old Robert is the only person in his small Saskatchewan town who remains impervious enough to the dazzling visitor and his promise of a rainmaking machine to wonder where all the town's missing people have gone.

Sleator, William. *The Boy Who Reversed Himself.* Dutton, 1986. **F**
How strange is Omar? Laura's question is answered when her high school friend takes her into the fourth dimension.

————. *Duplicate.* Dutton, 1988. **F**
When David needs to be in two places at once, he duplicates himself with a machine he picked up on the beach—and finds his life in danger.

————. *House of Stairs.* Dutton, 1974. **F**
Five 16-year-old orphans find themselves alone in an experimental nightmare where stairs and landings stretch as far as the eye can see and a weird red light trains them to dance for their food.

————. *Interstellar Pig.* Dutton, 1984. **F**
Barney's strange new neighbors invite him to play a bizarre board game called Interstellar Pig, which actually spans the universe and can destroy worlds.

————. *Oddballs: Stories.* Dutton, 1993. **F**
Growing up as part of an unusual family isn't so bad when everyone is an oddball.

————. *Singularity.* Dutton, 1985. **F**
Rivalry between 16-year-old twins Barry and Harry Krasner intensifies after their discovery of a foreboding playhouse leads them to the gateway of a universe that accelerates time's passage 3,600-fold and may unleash a monster.

———. *Strange Attractors*. Dutton, 1990. F
With a time travel phaser in his pocket and no memory of how it got there, Max must determine where it belongs without sending himself into oblivion.

Slepian, Jan. *The Night of the Bozos*. Dutton, 1983. F
George, a teenage electronic musician, and his young uncle see their lives change when they meet a strange carnival girl and the Bozo, the clown who dares passersby to knock him into a tub of water.

Slesar, Henry. *The Thing at the Door*. Random House, 1974. F
Haunted by memories of her mother's suicide when she was a child, Gail Gunnison at 26 is driven to the edge of suicide by strange events.

Smelcer, John. *The Trap*. Holt, 2006. F
In the Alaskan wilderness, Grandfather Albert attempts to escape one of his own steel-jawed traps; back in their village, Johnny worries about his grandfather's safety while pondering his own future.

Smith, Dennis. *Report from Engine Co. 82*. McCall, 1972. NF
On crowded, angry city streets, firemen respond when no one else does—to fire alarms, heart attacks, childbirth, and mob violence.

Smith, K. *Skeeter*. Houghton Mifflin, 1989. F
Hoping to enhance their hunting skills, two boys stumble on the best hunting terrain while trespassing on the property of an ornery black man.

Smith, Kevin. *Green Arrow: Quiver*. DC Comics, 2002. F
Oliver Queen, a.k.a. The Green Arrow, comes back to life, reunites with his old superhero pals, and unravels the mystery of his resurrection.

Smith, Martin Cruz. *Nightwing*. Norton, 1977. F
A young Hopi Indian searches desperately for the cave of the vampire bats that have swarmed into the Southwest, bringing the threat of bubonic plague.

Smith, Mary-Ann Tirone. *The Book of Phoebe*. Doubleday, 1985. F
In a novel that is at once hilarious and moving, Yale senior Phoebe goes to Paris to have her illegitimate baby, finds a man who loves her, and tells him a bizarre story from her adolescence—the time she and a friend held Grant's tomb hostage.

———. *Lament for a Silver-Eyed Woman*. Morrow, 1987. F
After a carefree stint as Peace Corps volunteers in Cameroon, Mattie's and Jo's friendship is destroyed by Jo's life-threatening involvement with tragic victims of the Mideast conflict.

Smith, Robert Kimmel. *Jane's House*. Morrow, 1982. F
When Paul Klein remarries after his wife's sudden death, Hilary, 16, and Bobby, 10, reluctantly accept bright, independent, businesswoman Ruth.

Smith, Rukshana. *Sumitra's Story*. Coward-McCann, 1983. F
Sumitra, an East Indian girl, is torn between her traditional home, loving but repressive, and English society, which offers freedom as well as prejudice.

Smith, Sherri L. *Lucy the Giant*. Delacorte, 2002. F
Lucy escapes her life with a drunken father by posing as an adult and gaining work on a commercial crabbing boat on the Bering Sea, where she finds a family of a different sort.

Smith, W. Eugene, and Aileen M. Smith. *Minamata*. Holt, Rinehart and Winston, 1975. NF
Using their cameras, the Smiths have recorded the horrors of industrial pollution that has killed or disabled more than 800 people in a Japanese town.

Smith, Wayne. *Thor*. St. Martin's, 1992. F
It isn't easy being the German shepherd Thor when the family needs protection from a visitor—who happens to be a werewolf.

Snyder, Zilpha Keatley. *A Fabulous Creature*. Atheneum, 1981. F
James Fielding almost causes the death of a magnificent stag he has gentled.

———. *Libby on Wednesday*. Delacorte, 1990. F
Membership in the small class of Future Writers of America helps previously home-educated Libby overcome the shock of entering eighth grade in public school.

Sones, Sonya. *One of Those Hideous Books Where the Mother Dies*. Simon & Schuster, 2004. F
After her mother dies of cancer, Ruby is forced to move to "Cali-phony-a" to live with her father, the famous movie star Whip Logan.

———. *Stop Pretending: What Happened When My Big Sister Went Crazy*. HarperCollins, 1999. F
Told in verse, this emotional novel tells what can happen when a sister has a nervous breakdown.

————. *What My Mother Doesn't Know.* Simon & Schuster, 2001. **F**

Writing in free verse, Sophie describes her first experiences with boyfriends, love, and other hazards in her search for Mr. Right.

Sorrentino, Joseph N. *Up from Never.* Prentice-Hall, 1971. **NF**

The son of a street sweeper, Joe Sorrentino tells of his youth in Brooklyn in the 1940s and of his journey from street punk to Harvard graduate.

Soto, Gary. *Baseball in April, and Other Stories.* Harcourt Brace Jovanovich, 1990. **F**

These short stories reflect the funny and touching side of growing up Latino in Fresno, California, including one about Gilbert, who decides to emulate a character in a popular movie by finding a karate teacher and becoming an expert.

————. *Buried Onions.* Harcourt Brace, 1997. **F**

Mexican American Eddie tries desperately to escape his violence-infested life in Fresno, California.

Southall, Ivan. *The Long Night Watch.* Farrar, Straus & Giroux, 1984. **F**

During World War II a young sentry fails in his duty, and causes the death of all but a few of the religious refugees on an isolated island in the South Pacific.

Southerland, Ellease. *Let the Lion Eat Straw.* Scribner, 1979. **F**

Choosing marriage over a musical career that promises escape from the poverty she has always known, Abeba Williams fights to achieve a decent life for her husband and children.

Southgate, Martha. *Another Way to Dance.* Delacorte, 1996. **F**

Being selected for the School of American Ballet is a dream come true for African American Vicki—until she encounters racism and disappointment in meeting her dancing idol.

Speare, Elizabeth George. *The Sign of the Beaver.* Houghton Mifflin, 1983. **F**

A proud, resourceful Native American boy deigns to help Matt survive the raw Maine wilderness winter when he is left alone to guard the newly built cabin.

Spiegelman, Art. *Maus: A Survivor's Tale.* Pantheon, 1986. **NF**

In a comic book of revolutionary graphic design, a cartoonist juxtaposes his frustration with his father's insensitivity today and his father's desperate struggle to stay alive 40 years earlier during the Holocaust.

————. *Maus II: A Survivor's Tale; And Here My Troubles Began.* Pantheon, 1991. **NF**

This graphic novel, the sequel to *Maus,* re-creates Vladek and Anja's agonizing struggles to survive in the concentration camp.

Spielman, Ed. *The Mighty Atom: The Life and Times of Joseph L. Greenstein.* Viking, 1979. **NF**

This biography relates the story of the amazing Yosselle (Joe) Greenstein, born in 1893 in a Jewish ghetto in Poland, an asthmatic and sickly child, who trains himself to become the world's strongest man.

Spillebeen, Geert. *Kipling's Choice.* Houghton Mifflin, 2005. **F**

John Kipling, son of the famous writer Rudyard Kipling, joins the British army in World War I with help from his father.

Spinelli, Jerry. *Crash.* Knopf, 1996. **F**

Self-centered John "Crash" Coogan has always had everything go his way, but after years of teasing Penn, Crash must choose between right and wrong.

————. *Knots in My Yo-Yo String: The Autobiography of a Kid.* Knopf, 1998. **NF**

A popular author relates this rollicking account of his first 16 years—before he even liked to read.

————. *Maniac Magee.* Little, Brown, 1990. **F**

"Maniac, Maniac he's so cool." The orphan Jeffrey Lionel Magee blitzes into the town of Two Mills and changes it forever.

————. *Milkweed.* Knopf, 2003. **F**

A resourceful orphan steals to survive the horrors of the Warsaw Ghetto in Nazi-occupied Poland.

————. *Stargirl.* Knopf, 2000. **F**

The eccentric new student, Stargirl, sees life differently than any of the students at Mica High School, and her nonconformist behavior changes her classmates and their perceptions of what it costs to be popular.

————. *There's a Girl in My Hammerlock.* Simon & Schuster, 1991. **F**

Whoever heard of a girl on a wrestling team? She might get hurt; besides, it's embarrassing and dumb!

Springer, Nancy. *I Am Mordred: A Tale from Camelot.* Philomel, 1998. **F**

Mordred struggles to escape a fate that will lead him to kill his own father.

————. *Toughing It.* Harcourt Brace, 1994. **F**
After witnessing his older brother's senseless murder, 16-year-old Tuff leaves home in shocked anger, determined to find the killer—but finds a father instead.

St. George, Judith. *In the Line of Fire: Presidents' Lives at Stake.* Holiday House, 1999. **NF**
The author re-creates the four U.S. presidential assassinations of Lincoln, Garfield, McKinley, and Kennedy and explores their impact on our country and the world.

Stahler, David, Jr. *Doppelganger.* HarperCollins, 2006. **F**
After murdering a popular athlete and possessing his body, a shape-shifting killer becomes embroiled in his victim's troubled life.

Stanley, Diane. *A Time Apart.* Morrow, 1999. **F**
While her mother undergoes treatment for cancer, 13-year-old Ginny goes to live with her father in England, where she stays in a reconstruction of an Iron Age village.

Staples, Suzanne Fisher. *Dangerous Skies.* Farrar, Straus & Giroux, 1996. **F**
In the back creeks of Chesapeake Bay, Buck discovers a dead body, and nothing is ever the same when his best friend, Tunes, becomes the primary murder suspect.

————. *Haveli.* Knopf, 1993. **F**
A young woman struggles against the strictures of her rigid culture to find freedom for herself and her small daughter in modern-day Pakistan.

————. *Shabanu: Daughter of the Wind.* Knopf, 1989. **F**
Torn between allegiance to her family and her growing independence and strength, Shabanu tells the story of her life as a member of a nomadic tribe in the Pakistani desert.

————. *Under the Persimmon Tree.* Farrar, Straus & Giroux, 2005. **F**
Najmah, an Afghan girl who witnesses her mother's and brother's deaths in an air raid and her father's and older brother's conscription by the Taliban, finds refuge in Pakistan with an American Muslim teacher.

Stassen, Jean-Philippe. *Deogratias, a Tale of Rwanda.* Roaring Brook, 2006. **F**
Deogratias, a Hutu boy, desperately clings to his humanity and his love for Benina, a Tutsi girl, in this unsettling graphic novel depicting the Rwandan genocide.

Steer, Dugald A., ed. *Dr. Ernest Drake's Dragonology: The Complete Book of Dragons.* Candlewick, 2003. **F**
Dragonologists both amateur and academic will hail Dr. Drake's lavishly illustrated guide, which includes dragon classification, dragon anatomy, helpful riddles for outwitting the European genus, and a list of essential equipment for the serious scientist.

Steffan, Joseph. *Honor Bound: A Gay American Fights for the Right to Serve His Country.* Villard, 1992. **NF**
Revealing he is gay two weeks before his Annapolis graduation, all-American boy Joe Steffan is discharged and begins to fight for the right to serve his country.

Steger, Will, and Jon Bowermaster. *Over the Top of the World: Explorer Will Steger's Trek across the Arctic.* Scholastic, 1997. **NF**
The account of Steger's breathtaking 1995 Arctic adventure includes dazzling photos and details of human and canine party members.

Stein, Tammar. *Light Years.* Knopf, 2005. **F**
Maya Laor comes to Virginia to escape the tragic Tel Aviv bombing that killed her boyfriend and for which she feels responsible—but even that may not be far enough to escape from the grief and pain.

Steinberg, Jacques. *The Gatekeepers: Inside the Admissions Process of a Premier College.* Viking, 2002. **NF**
This behind-the-scenes look at the college admissions process is written by the national education correspondent for the *New York Times*, who shadows an admissions officer at Wesleyan through a year's work.

Steinem, Gloria. *Outrageous Acts and Everyday Rebellions.* Holt, Rinehart and Winston, 1983. **NF**
The founder and editor of *MS.* magazine writes about her life and work and discusses politics, pornography, and literature from a feminist point of view.

Sterling, Dorothy, ed. *We Are Your Sisters: Black Women in the Nineteenth Century.* Norton, 1984. **NF**
This documents the history of African American women in the 19th century, based on transcripts of interviews with former slaves, memoirs, letters, and other primary sources.

Stevenson, Florence. *The Curse of the Concul-
    lens.* World, 1970. **F**
Beautiful, 18-year-old Lucinda Ayers longs to be
a governess, but she gets more than she bargained
for when she obtains a position with an eccentric
Irish family that comes complete with a castle,
ghosts, and werewolves.

Stevermer, Caroline. *River Rats.* Harcourt Brace
    Jovanovich, 1992. **F**
Tomcat and his teenage friends try to survive after
a nuclear holocaust by taking over a Mississippi
riverboat, but their lives are endangered when killers come after the boat.

Stewart, Fred Mustard. *The Mephisto Waltz.*
    Coward-McCann, 1969. **F**
A dead, diabolical genius inhabits the body of
Myles Clarkson, concert pianist; only Myles's
wife suspects what has happened but she has no
proof.

Stewart, Mary. *The Crystal Cave.* Morrow,
    1970. **F**
Merlin, the base-born son of royalty in 5th-century
Britain, uses magic to outwit his enemies until he
sets the stage for the birth of Arthur, the future
king.

———. *The Hollow Hills.* Morrow, 1973. **F**
In this sequel to *The Crystal Cave,* Merlin con-
ceals and grooms the child Arthur until the time
of his coronation.

Stoehr, Shelley. *Crosses.* Delacorte, 1991. **F**
Nancy loves cutting herself; the bloody designs
and scars are "cool." Then there are always alcohol and other drugs—all thanks to Katie, the best
teacher at school.

Stoll, Cliff. *The Cuckoo's Egg: Tracking a Spy
    through the Maze of Computer Espionage.*
    Doubleday, 1989. **NF**
A young astrophysicist turns detective as he embarks on the trail of an elusive computer hacker
who has managed to break into top-secret government and military data banks.

Stolz, Mary. *Cezanne Pinto: A Memoir.* Knopf,
    1994. **F**
As an old man, Cezanne relives his experiences as
a slave, a stable hand in Canada, and a Texas cowboy during the late 1800s.

Stone, Bruce. *Half Nelson, Full Nelson.* Harper
    & Row, 1985. **F**
Nelson Gato tells how he faked the kidnapping of
his little sister and her friend in an effort to bring
about a reconciliation between his wrestler father
and his mother, who could no longer stand life in
a tacky Florida trailer park.

Strasser, Todd. *Can't Get There from Here.*
    Simon & Schuster, 2004. **F**
A teen named Maybe and her tribe of fellow home-
less teens try to survive the winter on the streets in
Manhattan.

———. *Friends till the End.* Delacorte, 1981. **F**
David thinks he has problems—with soccer, his
girlfriend, parents, and college plans—until he
meets Howie, the new guy in school, who has leukemia.

———. *Rock 'n' Roll Nights.* Delacorte, 1982. **F**
Determined to make it to the top in rock music,
Gary Specter plays lead guitar and sings with his
group almost every night.

Stratton, Allan. *Chanda's Secrets.* Annick, 2004. **F**
Sixteen-year-old Chanda loves school and dreams
of a life beyond her family's poverty, but following
her baby sister's death she must fight to conquer
her fears and keep her dreams alive in the face of
Africa's AIDS epidemic.

———. *Leslie's Journal.* Annick, 2000. **F**
Using her English journal, Leslie records her life as
it spins out of control.

Strauss, Gwen. *Trail of Stones.* Knopf, 1990. **F**
These dark and dramatic retellings of fairy tales
in poetic monologues are accompanied by equally
stark drawings.

Strieber, Whitley. *Wolf of Shadows.* Knopf/Sierra
    Club, 1985. **F**
In their attempt to survive after a nuclear war, a
woman and her daughter join and learn from a
wolf pack led by Wolf of Shadows.

Stroud, Jonathan. *The Amulet of Samarkand.*
    Hyperion, 2003. **F**
A brilliant, self-taught young magician aims to
take revenge by conjuring up a powerful djinni
named Bartimaeus and commanding him to steal
the Amulet of Samarkand from Simon Lovelace, a
magician who cruelly humiliated him.

———. *The Golem's Eye.* Hyperion, 2004. **F**
Nathaniel, a talented and ambitious 14-year-old
magician, summons Bartimaeus, the sarcastic and
irreverent djinni from *The Amulet of Samarkand,*
yet another time to help him destroy a hideous
golem that is attacking London.

Sturtevant, Katherine. *A True and Faithful
    Narrative.* Farrar, Straus & Giroux, 2006. **F**
In 17th-century London, women don't write—
except for Meg, who disobeys her father to pen
the story of a young merchant kidnapped by pirates and enslaved in Algiers.

Styron, William. *The Confessions of Nat Turner.* Random House, 1967. **F**
While awaiting execution, the instigator of the 1831 slave rebellion in Virginia reconstructs the agonizing events that led to insurrection and murder.

Sullivan, Charles, ed. *Children of Promise: African-American Literature and Art for Young People.* Abrams, 1991. **NF**
A choice sampling of art and literature conveys the image of African Americans over the past 200 years.

————, ed. *Imaginary Animals: Poetry and Art for Young People.* Abrams, 1996. **NF**
Meet talking cats, purple cows, "long-legety" beasties, wicked dragons, and other fantastic creatures in this beautifully illustrated book of incredible poetry.

Sullivan, Jack, ed. *The Penguin Encyclopedia of Horror and the Supernatural.* Viking, 1986. **NF**
Surpassing the typical reference book, this collection of articles leads the reader from Stephen King to *The Birds* to Prokofiev.

Sullivan, Tom, and Derek Gill. *If You Could See What I Hear.* Harper & Row, 1975. **NF**
Tom Sullivan refuses to let blindness interfere with school or sports, his marriage, his career, or his life.

Summers, Ian, ed. *Tomorrow and Beyond: Masterpieces of Science Fiction Art.* Workman, 1978. **NF**
A magical mystery tour through the imaginative images used to illustrate speculative fiction is surprising and fascinating.

Sussman, Alan N. *The Rights of Young People: The Basic ACLU Guide to a Young Person's Rights.* Avon, 1977. **NF**
This legal bible for those less than age 18 states what the law allows and what it prohibits, emphasizing differences in state laws and offering advice on legal defense.

Sutcliff, Rosemary. *Black Ships before Troy: The Story of the Iliad.* Delacorte, 1993. **NF**
Helen of Troy is stolen from her husband by her lover Paris—and the Trojan War begins!

————. *The Road to Camlann.* Dutton, 1982. **F**
King Arthur strives to preserve the Round Table as Mordred plots against him and gossip about Lancelot and Guinivere intensifies.

Sutton, Roger. *Hearing Us Out: Voices from the Gay and Lesbian Community.* Little, Brown, 1994. **NF**
Documenting a wide range of experience, 15 gay and lesbian individuals narrate their joys and struggles to be who they are.

Swanson, Walter S. J. *Deepwood.* Little, Brown, 1981. **F**
A young man's desire for sexual fulfillment and personal freedom challenges his moral values and his devoted relationship to an older woman.

Swarthout, Glendon. *Bless the Beasts and Children.* Doubleday, 1970. **F**
Five misfits in an Arizona boys' camp sneak out on a daring escapade to save a herd of buffaloes from bloodthirsty gun-toting tourists.

Sweeney, Joyce. *Center Line.* Delacorte, 1984. **F**
Fearing for their safety, five teenage brothers steal their abusive, alcoholic father's car and run away from home.

————. *Shadow.* Delacorte, 1994. **F**
Shadow died a year earlier, but Sarah still senses her beloved cat's presence, which is fortunate because she has started dreaming about blood, violence, and broken glass, and needs all the help she can get.

————. *The Spirit Window.* Delacorte, 1998. **F**
Miranda must convince her father that love—be it for family or for wild creatures—is more important than money, when she tries to save her grandmother's bird sanctuary.

————. *The Tiger Orchard.* Delacorte, 1993. **F**
Zach comes face-to-face with his dreams when he discovers that his father, who his mother claimed was dead, is alive and then decides to meet him.

Switzer, Ellen. *How Democracy Failed.* Atheneum, 1975. **NF**
Personal reminiscences of Germany under Hitler from people who were then only teenagers make plain how he came to power.

Szabo, Joseph. *Almost Grown.* Harmony, 1978. **NF**
Provocative photographs and telling poems written by teenagers themselves express the concerns and feelings, the highs and the lows, of kids who are "almost grown."

Szulc, Tad. *The Bombs of Palomares.* Viking, 1967. **NF**
Four H-bombs lost over Spain in 1966 create potentially explosive social and political situations.

Talbert, Marc. *Dead Birds Singing.* Little, Brown, 1985. F

Left alone because of a tragic accident, Matt must face the reality of losing the last of his family—his mother and sister—and cope with his feelings for the drunken driver who killed them.

Tamar, Erika. *Fair Game.* Harcourt Brace, 1993. F

Cara, a mentally challenged teen, claims she was sexually assaulted by a group of athletes from her school, but the boys swear she was a willing participant.

Tan, Amy. *The Joy Luck Club.* Putnam, 1989. F

Chinese American daughters find conflict, love, and connection with their mothers, who are haunted by their early lives in China.

Tang, Xiyang. *Living Treasures: An Odyssey through China's Extraordinary Nature Reserves.* Bantam, 1987. NF

A beautifully photographed description of China's wildlife and landscapes is testament to its stunning natural reserves.

Tapert, Annette, ed. *Lines of Battle: Letters from American Servicemen, 1941–1945.* Times Books, 1987. NF

Letters from the battle lines of World War II convey a sense of adventure, loneliness, and tragedy.

Tashjian, Janet. *The Gospel according to Larry.* Holt, 2001. F

Things spiral out of control for Josh, a loner who masquerades as "Larry" to promote anti-consumerism on his anonymous website.

Tate, Sonsyrea. *Little X: Growing Up in the Nation of Islam.* Harper San Francisco, 1997. NF

Sonsyrea, who was raised in a Nation of Islam family, honestly describes life in the strict religious community.

Taylor, Clark. *The House That Crack Built.* Chronicle, 1992. F

Following the same pattern as the children's nursery rhyme, this bleak picture book shows the strung-out addicts, the crack lord's mansion, and the hungry baby of a crack addict.

Taylor, David. *Zoo Vet: Adventures of a Wild Animal Doctor.* Lippincott, 1977. NF

An authority on treating wild animals describes unusual cases from his veterinary practice around the world.

Taylor, Gordon Rattray. *Biological Time Bomb.* World, 1968. NF

The biological revolution is at hand and in the offing are memory-erasing drugs, choice of sex in offspring, reconstructed organisms, and the indefinite postponement of death.

Taylor, Mildred D. *The Land.* Phyllis Fogelman, 2001. F

In this prequel to the Newbery Medal winner *Roll of Thunder, Hear My Cry*, Cassie Logan's grandfather, Paul Edward, tells of his heartbreaking but ultimately triumphant struggle to acquire the land that would become the Logan family legacy.

———. *Let the Circle Be Unbroken.* Dial, 1981. F

In this sequel to *Roll of Thunder, Hear My Cry*, the Logan family survives the Depression, a murder trial, and the jailing of a son.

———. *The Road to Memphis.* Dial, 1990. F

On the eve of World War II, Cassie Logan is finishing high school and dreaming of college when a violent racial incident forces her to help a good friend escape to the north.

Taylor, Theodore. *The Bomb.* Harcourt Brace, 1995. F

Teenage Sorry will do anything to stop the Americans from using his island home for nuclear testing.

———. *Sniper.* Harcourt Brace Jovanovich, 1989. F

A gunman begins killing the big cats the week Ben, 15, is left in charge of the family's animal preserve.

———. *Timothy of the Cay.* Harcourt Brace, 1993. F

In alternating chapters, this compelling prequel-sequel to *The Cay* outlines the lives of Timothy Gumbs before he meets 12-year-old Philip on the cay and of Philip immediately after his rescue from the cay.

———. *The Weirdo.* Harcourt Brace Jovanovich, 1991. F

Disfigured in a plane crash and called Weirdo by the locals, Chip seeks refuge in the swamp with his recovering alcoholic artist father. There he befriends Samantha, and the two teens find themselves threatened by murderous bear poachers.

Taylor, Yuval, ed. *Growing Up in Slavery: Stories of Young Slaves as Told by Themselves.* Lawrence Hill, 2005. NF

This intense collection of ten American slave narratives is sobering and brutal, but also speaks to the triumph of the spirit and the determination to be free.

Teague, Bob. *Letters to a Black Boy.* Walker, 1968. NF

A former college football star (now a New York television newscaster) voices the frustrations of being considered a black man rather than an individual.

Teitz, Joyce. *What's a Nice Girl Like You Doing in a Place Like This?* Coward, McCann & Geoghegan, 1972. **NF**
Women talk candidly about their careers and ambitions, their challenges and dreams.

Telander, Rick. *Heaven Is a Playground.* St. Martin's, 1976. **NF**
The inspirational story of the dreams, hopes, and frustrations of talented African American urban youths whose love of basketball is their lifeline to the future.

Temple, Frances. *Grab Hands and Run.* Orchard, 1993. **F**
When his father, a political revolutionary in El Salvador, "disappears" one day, Felipe's mother is forced to "grab hands and run" with the children on a dangerous journey north to Canada.

———. *The Ramsay Scallop.* Orchard, 1994. **F**
Betrothed, though they barely know each other, 14-year-old Elenor and 18-year-old Thomas are sent by their castle priest on a pilgrimage from their English village through France to Spain in 1299.

Tepper, Sheri S. *Beauty.* Doubleday, 1991. **F**
In this modern retelling of the fairy tale, Beauty avoids the sleeping spell and trips through time into different worlds, searching for beauty and love.

Terkel, Studs. *American Dreams, Lost and Found.* Pantheon, 1980. **NF**
Sharing their innermost hopes and dreams through interviews with Studs Terkel is a cross section of Americans ranging from celebrities such as Joan Crawford, Bill Veeck, and Coleman Young to steelworker Ed Sadlowski and 16-year-old Linda Haas.

———. *"The Good War": An Oral History of World War Two.* Pantheon, 1984. **NF**
This vibrant Second World War oral history offers wonderfully readable tales that are alive, spontaneous, and personal as Americans from all walks of life recall their involvement and participation.

Terris, Susan. *Nell's Quilt.* Farrar, Straus & Giroux, 1987. **F**
Not knowing how to resist her parents' plans for her marriage, Nell stitches her lost dreams of college and independence into a quilt—all the while literally wasting away.

Terry, Douglas. *The Last Texas Hero.* Doubleday, 1982. **F**
A humorous, bawdy, and explicit look at life as a college freshman and all-American football hero, told in the inspiring words of Homer Jones.

Terry, Wallace, ed. *Bloods: An Oral History of the Vietnam War by Black Veterans.* Random House, 1984. **NF**
From their own perspectives, 20 black soldiers give graphically detailed accounts of the Vietnam War and its emotional aftereffects on themselves, their families, and their friends.

Testa, Maria. *Dancing Pink Flamingos, and Other Stories.* Lerner, 1995. **F**
In these ten urban short stories, teens of various ethnicities strive to find hope in a world of crime and violence.

Tevis, Walter. *The Queen's Gambit.* Random House, 1983. **F**
In the orphanage where she lives Beth learns the game of chess, beginning an obsession that takes her all the way to the top.

Thal, Lilli. *Mimus.* Annick, 2005. **F**
A prince must play at being a jester as he strives to rescue his imprisoned father.

Tharp, Tim. *Knights of the Hill Country.* Knopf, 2006. **F**
High school football star Hampton Green believes that his buddy Blaine started him toward a better future, but how far should he go out of loyalty to his friend?

Thesman, Jean. *The Ornament Tree.* Houghton Mifflin, 1996. **F**
Moving in with two progressive aunts who own a Seattle boardinghouse, Bonnie must seek her identity against the tumultuous backdrop of labor riots, women's suffrage, and the temperance movement.

———. *The Other Ones.* Viking, 1999. **F**
Bridget struggles through the miseries of high school without using her "special gifts," feeling that they will make her appear even more different than she already is.

———. *The Rain Catchers.* Houghton Mifflin, 1991. **F**
Abandoned by her mother and growing up in a household of women, Grayling, at 14, must deal with love, death, and her relationship with her mother.

————. *When the Road Ends*. Houghton Mifflin, 1992. **F**

Can four abandoned strangers—a 12-year-old, a teenager, a silent child, and a brain-injured woman —come together as a loving family?

Thimmesh, Catherine. *Team Moon: How 400,000 People Landed Apollo 11 on the Moon.* Houghton Mifflin, 2006. **NF**

Suspenseful and packed with little-known facts, this exploration of the Apollo 11 mission captures the dedication of the people behind the scenes.

Thomas, Jane Resh. *Behind the Mask: The Life of Queen Elizabeth I.* Clarion, 1998. **NF**

This spirited, authentic picture of Elizabeth I is a historical account of a woman who overcomes vast odds to become one of the most important and influential people in history.

Thomas, Joyce Carol. *Marked by Fire.* Avon, 1982. **F**

When tragedy strikes Abby, her proud black rural Oklahoma community gathers around to protect and save her from all harm.

Thomas, Kurt, and Kent Hannon. *Kurt Thomas on Gymnastics.* Simon & Schuster, 1980. **NF**

This portrayal of Kurt Thomas's life provides an insight into the world of men's gymnastics—the training, dedication, and lifestyle necessary to reach the level of Olympic competition.

Thomas, Lewis. *The Youngest Science: Notes of a Medicine Watcher.* Viking, 1983. **NF**

These autobiographical musings by the author of *Lives of a Cell* appeal because of their "celebration and a warning about the nature of man and the future of life on our planet."

Thomas, Rob. *Doing Time: Notes from the Undergrad.* Simon & Schuster, 1997. **F**

Ten high school students doing mandatory community service in order to graduate give ten different voices and viewpoints to the enterprise.

————. *Rats Saw God.* Simon & Schuster, 1996. **F**

"Troubled teen" Steve York reflects on his life and his relationship with his famous father.

Thomas, Velma Maia. *Lest We Forget: The Passage from Africa to Slavery and Emancipation.* Crown, 1997. **NF**

Artifacts from the black Holocaust exhibit are used to create a three-dimensional interactive history of slavery in America.

Thompson, Craig. *Blankets.* Top Shelf, 2003. **F**

This autobiographical graphic novel depicts the life of the author, illuminating the trials and tribu-

lations of being an outcast, attending a zealous bible camp, and meeting the girl of his dreams.

Thompson, Estelle. *Hunter in the Dark.* Walker, 1979. **F**

The only witness to the kidnapping of a child who is later murdered, blind teacher Philip Blair determines to find the criminal.

Thompson, Jean. *The House of Tomorrow.* Harper & Row, 1967. **NF**

In a home for unwed mothers, Jean overcomes despair and faces many decisions about her future and that of her unborn child.

Thompson, Joyce. *Conscience Place.* Doubleday, 1984. **F**

The Place, an idyllic, protected secret settlement for the mutant offspring of nuclear-energy workers, has come to the attention of scientists who want to use its inhabitants for experimentation.

Thompson, Julian F. *A Band of Angels.* Scholastic, 1986. **F**

Unaware that government agents are pursuing them with the intent to kill, five teenagers camp in the wilderness to plan a crusade against nuclear war.

Thornton, Yvonne S., and Jo Coudert. *The Ditchdigger's Daughters: A Black Family's Astonishing Success Story.* Carol, 1995. **NF**

Dr. Yvonne Thornton tells the story of her 1950s upbringing by her father, a poor African American man who raises five daughters to succeed in a world that prefers them invisible.

Tiburzi, Bonnie. *Takeoff! The Story of America's First Woman Pilot for a Major Airline.* Crown, 1984. **NF**

In this autobiography, the first woman pilot for a major U.S. airline shares her love of flying and tells of her challenging and often frustrating climb to success.

Tidyman, Ernest. *Dummy.* Little, Brown, 1974. **NF**

What defense does an illiterate deaf-mute African American have against a murder charge? His deaf lawyer must contend not only with his client's inability to communicate but also with an unfeeling court system and circumstantial evidence.

Tiffany, Grace. *Ariel.* HarperCollins, 2005. **F**

Behind Shakespeare's *Tempest* is the mysterious figure of Ariel and her story of dreams, lies, and madness.

Tillage, Leon. *Leon's Story.* Farrar, Straus & Giroux, 1997. NF

Tillage tells the story of his life as the son of a southern sharecropper killed by the KKK, and of the changes brought about by the civil rights movement.

Tingle, Rebecca. *The Edge on the Sword.* Putnam, 2001. F

In 9th-century Britain, 15-year-old Aethlflaed, daughter of King Alfred, finds she must assume new responsibilities—including betrothal to her father's ally—to strengthen their kingdom against Danish invaders.

———. *Far Traveler.* Putnam, 2005. F

After the sudden death of her mother, 16-year-old Aelfwyn disguises herself as a bard to escape marriage to an older man allied with the king.

Tocher, Timothy. *Chief Sunrise, John McGraw, and Me.* Cricket, 2004. F

Escaping his abusive father, 15-year-old Hank Cobb joins Chief Sunrise, an "immortal in the making," in a journey to meet John McGraw and try out for the 1919 New York Giants baseball team.

Tolan, Stephanie S. *Surviving the Applewhites.* HarperCollins, 2002. F

Troublemaker Jake Semple is sent to live with his grandfather after being kicked out of several schools. Once there, it is no problem getting kicked out of Traybridge Middle School, but the Applewhites' Creative Academy is another story.

Tomey, Ingrid. *Nobody Else Has to Know.* Delacorte, 1999. F

A high school track star struggles to remember the auto accident that ended his season as a runner. Can he trust his grandfather's version of the crash, or is his grandpa trying to shield him from the truth?

Torchia, Joseph. *The Kryptonite Kid.* Holt, Rinehart and Winston, 1979. F

Jerry's letters to his hero, Superman, reveal his sinking into insanity and his discovery of who Superman really is.

Toten, Teresa. *The Game.* Red Deer, 2001. F

When Dani wakes up in a psychiatric hospital, she doesn't remember the events leading up to her attempted suicide—she only remembers the game that she and her sister played and which masks a terrifying reality.

Townley, Roderick. *Sky.* Atheneum, 2004. F

Sky, a 15-year-old jazz musician, is forced to come to terms with his overbearing father and struggles to find himself in 1958 Manhattan.

Townsend, John Rowe. *Good Night, Prof, Dear.* Lippincott, 1971. F

Seventeen-year-old Graham Hollis, unhappy with himself and his home life, runs off with Lynn, a waitress, and finds her a surprising but beautiful person.

Townsend, Sue. *The Adrian Mole Diaries.* Grove, 1986. F

In cryptically funny entries, teenager Adrian worries incessantly about his problems—acne, his parents' separation, sexual urges, and much more.

Trevor, Elleston. *The Theta Syndrome.* Doubleday, 1977. F

"For God's sake help me" is the desperate telepathic cry of a young woman deep in a coma prolonged by her fear of another attempt on her life.

Trudeau, G. B. *The Doonesbury Chronicles.* Holt, Rinehart and Winston, 1975. NF

No one can feel the pulse of the world like Garry Trudeau, whose satirical look at the 1960s and early 1970s is a real delight.

———. *Doonesbury's Greatest Hits.* Holt, Rinehart and Winston, 1978. NF

Washington politics, student activists, talking to plants, and relations between the United States and China are among the popular cartoonist's targets.

Trueman, Terry. *Inside Out.* HarperTempest, 2003. F

While waiting for his mom in a coffee shop, 16-year-old Zach, who suffers from adolescent-onset schizophrenia, becomes the voice of reason when a foiled robbery by armed teens turns into a hostage situation.

———. *Stuck in Neutral.* HarperCollins, 2000. F

Fourteen-year-old Shawn suffers from a debilitating disease and thinks his father may be planning to kill him.

Trull, Patti. *On with My Life.* Putnam, 1983. NF

A courageous young cancer victim at 15, Patti Trull loses her leg despite numerous treatments and surgery but finds hope as an occupational therapist for other young victims.

Tullson, Diane. *Red Sea.* Orca, 2005. F

Fourteen-year-old Libby is purposely late to the launch of their group sailing trip, leaving her family to sail alone. After encountering pirates and a fierce storm, Libby's stepfather is dead and her mother is seriously injured, leaving Libby on her own to save her mother and herself.

Turnbull, Ann. *No Shame, No Fear.* Candlewick, 2004. F

In 1662 Britain, as violent intolerance of the Quaker religion mounts, a 15-year-old Quaker girl and the well-educated son of a prosperous and respected Anglican businessman fall in love.

Turner, Ann. *Learning to Swim: A Memoir.* Scholastic, 2000. NF

A series of poems convey the feelings of a young girl whose sense of joy and security at the family's summer home is shattered when an older boy who lives nearby sexually abuses her.

———. *A Lion's Hunger: Poems of First Love.* Marshall Cavendish, 1998. NF

Turner's series of poems expresses the emotions of a young girl falling in and out of love for the first time.

Turner, Megan Whalen. *The King of Attolia.* Greenwillow, 2006. F

Eugenides must convince his new queen, his court, and his subjects of his ability to rule, despite his disreputable past as a liar and a thief.

———. *The Thief.* Greenwillow, 1996. F

Gen prides himself on being a master thief and is delighted to be rescued from prison under the condition that he steal a precious item from a long-lost temple.

Turnley, David C., and Alan Cowell. *Why Are They Weeping? South Africans under Apartheid.* Stewart, Tabori & Chang, 1988. NF

One hundred color photographs vividly show the brutal conflict in a troubled and beautiful land.

Tyler, Anne. *A Slipping-Down Life.* Knopf, 1970. F

The story of fat, plain Evie Decker's romance and marriage to a rock singer and their slipping-down life together.

Uchida, Yoshiko. *The Invisible Thread.* Messner, 1991. NF

The author describes growing up in Berkeley as a second-generation Japanese American and her family's humiliating experience in Utah internment camps during World War II.

Uhlman, Fred. *Reunion.* Farrar, Straus & Giroux, 1977. F

Thirty years later, the Jewish narrator recalls his doomed friendship with the son of a nobleman in Nazi Germany. A poignant and provocative novella.

Ung, Loung. *First They Killed My Father: A Daughter of Cambodia Remembers.* Harper Collins, 2000. NF

This memoir of a young girl shows how lives and families were torn apart by the Khmer Rouge regime in Cambodia.

Unger, Zac. *Working Fire: The Making of an Accidental Fireman.* Penguin, 2004. NF

A young rookie provides a behind-the-firehouse-doors look at what it's like to fight fire in a big city.

Updale, Eleanor. *Montmorency: Thief, Liar, Gentleman?* Orchard, 2003. F

Montmorency, a petty thief in Victorian England, is badly injured and caught by the police, but his time recuperating in jail is the beginning of a whole new life for "prisoner #493."

Ure, Jean. *Plague.* Harcourt Brace Jovanovich, 1991. F

Returning to London from a wilderness camping trip, Fran finds her family and friends dead from a plague that has engulfed the city.

———. *See You Thursday.* Delacorte, 1981. F

Marianne, a 16-year-old British schoolgirl, helps her family's boarder, Abe, a 24-year-old blind music teacher, achieve independence as their friendship grows into love.

Van Der Vat, Dan. *D-Day: The Greatest Invasion; A People's History.* Bloomsbury, 2003. NF

Van Der Vat offers a visually stunning overview of the pivotal invasion of Europe that changed the course of World War II.

Van Devanter, Lynda, and Christopher Morgan. *Home before Morning: The Story of an Army Nurse in Vietnam.* Beaufort, 1983. NF

Lt. Lynda Van Devanter recounts her experiences as an army surgical nurse in Vietnam and the stress after coming home.

Van Leeuwen, Jean. *Seems Like This Road Goes on Forever.* Dial, 1979. F

Guided by an empathetic psychologist, the 17-year-old daughter of a fundamentalist minister learns to separate her needs from the expectations of her remote, domineering parents.

Van Pelt, James. *Strangers and Beggars: Stories.* Fairwood, 2002. F

A giant spider that encapsulates a student and a teacher in its web, a kid who has always felt he was an alien and really is, and an endless trip in awful traffic that even death can't stop are just a few of the stories in this collection.

Van Raven, Pieter. *The Great Man's Secret.* Scribner, 1989. **F**
Jerry, a 14-year-old student reporter, is sent to interview reclusive writer Paul Bernard and discovers not only Bernard's secret, but also those hidden within himself and others.

———. *Pickle and Price.* Scribner, 1990. **F**
Pickle, the son of a white prison farm supervisor, and Price, a newly released African American convict Pickle has befriended, travel across America.

Vance, Susanna. *Deep.* Delacorte, 2003. **F**
The spoiled 13-year-old Birdie Sidwell and the solemn, seafaring 17-year-old Morgan become unlikely allies when they both come in contact with a ruthless, utterly charming modern pirate.

———. *Sights.* Delacorte, 2001. **F**
Baby Girl has the gift of seeing the future, and she and her beautiful mother make a new life amid the characters in small-town Cot.

Vande Velde, Vivian. *Being Dead: Stories.* Harcourt, 2001. **F**
Unquiet souls haunt these seven stories that chill the mind of the reader.

———. *Companions of the Night.* Harcourt Brace, 1995. **F**
Is Ethan really just an innocent college student kidnapped by vampire-hunting crazies? Sixteen-year-old Kerry, who saves him and loves him, finds that the allure of the vampire is alive and well.

———. *Heir Apparent.* Harcourt, 2002. **F**
Trapped in a virtual reality game by religious agitators who have stormed the video arcade and damaged the sensitive equipment, 14-year-old Giannine isn't just playing to win, she's playing for her life!

———. *Never Trust a Dead Man.* Harcourt Brace, 1999. **F**
Selwyn may not have liked Farold, his rival for Anora's affection, but he certainly didn't kill him, and now he must rely on the dead man's spirit to help him prove his innocence.

Vare, Ethlie Ann, and Greg Ptacek. *Mothers of Invention: From the Bra to the Bomb; Forgotten Women and Their Unforgettable Ideas.* Morrow, 1988. **NF**
Vare presents and praises the often ignored accomplishments of women in areas that include nuclear physics and the invention of the cotton gin.

Vaughan, Brian K. *Runaways.* Marvel, 2006. **F**
Six teenagers discover that their parents are supervillains, and after deciding to turn them in, they fight for both their own survival and an end to the evil of which they were born.

Vaught, Susan. *Stormwitch.* Bloomsbury, 2005. **F**
Ruba, a teenager in Mississippi in 1969, struggles to deal with civil rights and Hurricane Camille using the voodoo skills her Haitian grandmother taught her.

———. *Trigger.* Bloomsbury, 2006. **F**
After blowing a hole in his head with a gun and suffering severe brain damage, Jersey Hatch sets out to discover why he did it.

Vick, Helen Hughes. *Walker of Time.* Harbinger, 1993. **F**
Walker, a 15-year-old Hopi, is thrust abruptly back in time to the last days of the ancient, cliff-dwelling Sinagua people, where he finds enmity, friendship, and family.

Vijayaraghavan, Vineeta. *Motherland.* Soho, 2001. **F**
Even though Maya was born in India, she is all-American, until her parents send her to visit her grandmother for the summer and she rediscovers her homeland, receives an offer of marriage, and uncovers a family secret.

Vinge, Joan D. *Psion.* Delacorte, 1982. **F**
In the year 2417, a poor orphan, taken from the slums to participate in a dangerous experiment, soon finds that his extraordinary telepathic powers endanger his life.

Vizzini, Ned. *It's Kind of a Funny Story.* Hyperion, 2006. **F**
Suicidal Craig, overwhelmed by academic pressures, ends up in the adult psych ward, where he encounters a hilarious cast of characters while moving toward recovery.

Voigt, Cynthia. *Elske.* Atheneum, 1999. **F**
A sage young woman becomes the helpmate and companion to a headstrong princess who seeks the throne she has been denied.

———. *Izzy, Willy-Nilly.* Atheneum, 1986. **F**
Who are your real friends? Izzy struggles to rethink her friendships after losing a leg in a car crash.

———. *On Fortune's Wheel.* Atheneum, 1990. **F**
Fourteen-year-old Birle's impulsive attempt to stop a stranger from stealing a boat leads to romance and adventure with a young runaway lord.

———. *The Runner.* Atheneum, 1985. **F**
Bullet, a 17-year-old cross-country runner, finds that compromise is sometimes necessary if an athlete is going to be the best.

———. *A Solitary Blue.* Atheneum, 1983. **F**
Jeff Green's mother leaves home when he is only seven, and when she shows up in his life again Jeff learns some hard lessons about loving and caring.

————. *Sons from Afar.* Atheneum, 1987. **F**
Dicey's brothers, on the brink of growing up, search for the father who deserted them as infants—and find unforeseen truths.

————. *Tell Me If the Lovers Are Losers.* Atheneum, 1982. **F**
Three college roommates—each very different, but gifted—clash and come together as they learn values from one another.

————. *When She Hollers.* Scholastic, 1994. **F**
Tish takes a knife and her destiny in hand on the day she decides to stop her father from sexually abusing her.

Volavková, Hana, ed. *I Never Saw Another Butterfly: Children's Drawings and Poems from Terezin Concentration Camp, 1942–1944, 2nd ed.* Schocken, 1993. **NF**
Through the agony and hope expressed in the poems and drawings of the children of Terezin, the reader sees the sheer hell experienced by the 15,000 children under age 15 who passed through the Terezin Concentration Camp between 1942 and 1944.

Volponi, Paul. *Black and White.* Viking, 2005. **F**
Life looks good for Marcus (a.k.a. Black) and Eddie (a.k.a. White), best friends and co-players on their high school basketball team. Then an armed robbery goes terribly wrong and changes everything.

————. *Rooftop.* Viking, 2006. **F**
There are no easy answers for his family or for their African American community after Clay witnesses the shooting of his cousin by a police officer.

Von Canon, Claudia. *The Inheritance.* Houghton Mifflin, 1983. **F**
A young medical student faces the horrors of the Inquisition in 16th-century Spain.

Vonnegut, Kurt. *Jailbird.* Franklin Library, 1979. **F**
Harvard, the New Deal, the Holocaust, World War II, Watergate, two prison terms, and a giant conglomerate—Walter Starbuck, who tries to live by the Sermon on the Mount, experiences them all. Shall the meek inherit the earth? Perhaps on a short-term basis.

Vonnegut, Mark. *The Eden Express.* Praeger, 1975. **NF**
Kurt Vonnegut's son reflects on his life in the counterculture and his battle with schizophrenia.

Vrettos, Adrienne Maria. *Skin.* Margaret K. McElderry, 2006. **F**
After his sister starves herself to death, 14-year-old Donnie reflects upon her illness and its devastating effects on the family.

Wagenheim, Kal. *Clemente!* Praeger, 1973. **NF**
The tragic death of Roberto Clemente, well known as a great baseball player, reveals the depths of his commitment and his concern for others.

Wagoner, David. *The Road to Many a Wonder.* Farrar, Straus & Giroux, 1974. **F**
Setting out with his wheelbarrow to seek his fortune in western gold fields, Ike Bender marries a high-spirited young woman, and together they travel roads which do indeed lead to many a wonder.

Waid, Mark, et al. *Superman: Birthright.* DC Comics, 2004. **F**
The origin of Superman is updated in this graphic novel.

Wain, John. *The Free Zone Starts Here.* Delacorte, 1982. **F**
After his younger sister is killed in a plane crash, 17-year-old Paul Waterford flies to Lisbon for a memorial service and finally gives up his escapist private world after a disturbing night in Lisbon makes him aware of his own imperfections.

Walker, Alice. *In Search of Our Mothers' Gardens: Womanist Prose.* Harcourt Brace Jovanovich, 1983. **NF**
Thirty-five essays examine Walker's development as a human being, writer, and woman.

Walker, Kate. *Peter.* Houghton Mifflin, 1993. **F**
Outwardly, 15-year-old Peter lives by the rough-playing, rough-talking rules of his dirt-bike crowd, but inside he questions this male image as well as his own sexuality.

Walker, Margaret. *Jubilee.* Houghton Mifflin, 1966. **F**
Life at the time of the Civil War as experienced by Vyry, daughter of a slave and the white plantation owner.

Wallace, Duncan R. *The Mountebank.* Houghton Mifflin, 1972. **F**
Lee, who wants to be a writer, is drawn to Nonno, the prankster, as they enter prep school together.

Wallace, Rich. *Playing without the Ball.* Knopf, 2000. **F**
Jay McLeod, who lives alone above a bar and works in the kitchen to help pay his rent, joins the church basketball team and discovers friendship in various forms as the season progresses.

————. *Wrestling Sturbridge.* Knopf, 1996. **F**
Living in Sturbridge, Pennsylvania, where wrestling is king, high-school senior Benny must compete against his best friend for a spot on the team.

Wallin, Luke. *The Redneck Poacher's Son.* Bradbury, 1981. **F**

The son of a redneck poacher in an Alabama swamp, Jesse hates—perhaps enough to kill—his father, whom he blames for his mother's death.

Walsh, John, and Robert Gannon. *Time Is Short and the Water Rises.* Dutton, 1967. **NF**

Subtitled "Operation Gwamba: The story of the rescue of 10,000 animals from certain death in a South American rain forest."

Walsh, M. M. B. *The Four-Colored Hoop.* Putnam, 1976. **F**

Surviving the cruelty of the reservation, Mildred Shoot-Eagle becomes a feared mystic and medicine woman and revenges herself on the white man.

Walter, Virginia. *Making Up Megaboy.* DK Ink, 1998. **F**

Why would a quiet kid who likes to draw kill a man after school one day?

Watkins, Yoko Kawashima. *My Brother, My Sister, and I.* Bradbury, 1994. **F**

After escaping war-torn Korea in 1947, Yoko and her brother and sister return to face harsh prejudice in Japan, struggling for survival after their mother's death as they await the return of their missing father.

Watson, James D. *Double Helix: A Personal Account of the Discovery of the Structure of DNA.* Atheneum, 1968. **NF**

A young scientist gives an inside view of how he and a colleague, pursuing fame and the Nobel Prize, manage to discover the structure of DNA, the molecule of heredity.

Watson, Larry. *Montana 1948.* Milkweed, 1993. **F**

The summer he is 12 David watches as his family and small town are shattered by scandal and tragedy.

Watson, Lyall. *The Dreams of Dragons: Riddles of Natural History.* Morrow, 1987. **NF**

Random numbers, movement of water, chance, and the pulse of the earth are among the subjects of essays that extol the magic and wonder of science and the world.

Weaver, Beth Nixon. *Rooster.* Winslow, 2001. **F**

Frustrated with all her responsibilities, which include taking care of the senile grandmother of a mentally handicapped neighbor, Kady becomes enamored with the wealthy, popular, and unscrupulous Jon.

Weaver, Will. *Farm Team.* HarperCollins, 1995. **F**

Billy is left in charge of the family farm when his dad is sent to prison, and so begins the "farm team," a ragtag group of local baseball players who try to whip the town team in the big game.

———. *Full Service.* Farrar, Straus & Giroux, 2005. **F**

When 16-year-old farm boy Paul Sutton takes a job at the full-service Shell station in town, he sees the town and its inhabitants through new eyes.

———. *Hard Ball.* HarperCollins, 1998. **F**

When Billy and King's rivalry extends beyond the baseball field to a fight over a girl, a coach comes up with an unusual solution.

———. *Striking Out.* HarperCollins, 1993. **F**

Five years after his brother's death, Billy discovers baseball can be an escape from his grim farm life.

Webb, Sheyann, and Rachel West Nelson. *Selma, Lord, Selma: Girlhood Memories of the Civil-Rights Days.* University of Alabama Press, 1980. **F**

In this recollection of the events of 1965 in Selma, Alabama, Sheyann, 8, and Rachel, 9, face nightsticks, dogs, and mounted police, alongside Dr. Martin Luther King Jr. and the other adults who fight to achieve the right to vote.

Weeks, Sarah. *So B. It.* HarperCollins, 2004. **F**

Twelve-year-old Heidi, whose severely mentally disabled mother cannot tell her what she needs to know, embarks on a journey to discover the truth of her mother's and her own past.

Weiss, Ann E. *Who's to Know? Information, the Media, and Public Awareness.* Houghton Mifflin, 1990. **NF**

Putting the public's right to know in historical perspective, Weiss illustrates how business, advertising, special interest groups, politics, and the media shape and manipulate the news and information Americans receive.

Wells, Evelyn. *I Am Thinking of Kelda.* Doubleday, 1974. **F**

Kelda's story moves from New York sweatshops to a pioneer farm in Kansas and finally to California, where she is captivated by a new entertainment called "movies."

Wells, Ken. *Meely LaBauve.* Random House, 2000. **F**

Fifteen-year-old Meely has adventures with bullies, a crooked cop, alligators, and an exploding cow in Louisiana's Catahoula Bayou.

Wells, Rosemary. *Through the Hidden Door.* Dial, 1987. **F**

A bullied prep school student discovers his inner strengths as he helps the school misfit excavate a mysterious ruin.

———. *When No One Was Looking.* Dial, 1980. F

Fourteen-year-old Kathy thrives on pressure to become a tennis star until the death, possibly murder, of a competitor forces her to question her ambition and her future.

Welter, John. *I Want to Buy a Vowel.* Algonquin, 1996. F

Guatemalan Alfredo learns what limited English he knows from TV commercials and Wheel of Fortune as he searches for the American dream.

Werlin, Nancy. *Black Mirror.* Dial, 2001. F

While she comes to terms with her mixed heritage, Frances tries to uncover the secrets at her boarding school that may explain the real reason for her brother's death.

———. *Double Helix.* Dial, 2004. F

Haunted by too many unanswered questions, Eli Samuels finds they all seem to lead to the world-famous transgeneticist Quincy Wyatt, a man whose eerie familiarity masks a chilling truth.

———. *The Killer's Cousin.* Delacorte, 1998. F

After David is acquitted of murder and moves in with his aunt and uncle, he finds his new home to be less safe and secure than he'd hoped.

———. *The Rules of Survival.* Dial, 2006. F

When Matthew and his younger sisters witness a man confronting an abusive parent, they think they may have found a hero who will save them from their vicious mother.

Wersba, Barbara. *The Carnival in My Mind.* Harper & Row, 1982. F

Harvey Beaumont is 14, five feet tall, and in love for the first time—with a 20-year-old, six-foot-tall, would-be actress.

———. *The Country of the Heart.* Atheneum, 1975. F

A brief, poignant romance between a dying older woman who is a famous poet and a young man who aspires to be a writer.

———. *Run Softly, Go Fast.* Atheneum, 1970. F

This is the story, written in diary form, of 19-year-old David Marks and his attempt to reconcile his love-hate relationship with his father.

———. *Tunes for a Small Harmonica.* Harper & Row, 1976. F

Sixteen-year-old J. F. McAllister, a constant source of worry to everyone, masters the harmonica and then uses her talents to help her poetry teacher, with whom she is in love.

———. *Whistle Me Home.* Holt, 1997. F

Tomboy Noli and TJ are friends and almost a couple, and Noli is totally shocked when she discovers that TJ is gay.

West, Jessamyn. *Massacre at Fall Creek.* Harcourt Brace Jovanovich, 1975. F

Seventeen-year-old Hannah Cape is only one of the people affected by the first trial (in 1824) of white men accused of murdering Native Americans.

Westall, Robert. *The Devil on the Road.* Greenwillow, 1979. F

In a time fantasy set in 1970s England, John Webster travels from a barn with strange symbols and an unusual cat to a trial 300 years in the past, where he fights to save a young woman sentenced to die for being a witch.

———. *Futuretrack 5.* Greenwillow, 1983. F

This is the story of Henry Kitson, one of a small group responsible for keeping the highly computerized, manipulative, 21st-century British society functioning, and Keri, the London bike-riding champion of Futuretrack 5.

———. *Gulf.* Scholastic, 1992. F

During the Gulf War, Tom grapples with his sense of guilt when his brother is possessed by the spirit of an Iraqi solder and committed to a mental institution.

———. *The Kingdom by the Sea.* Farrar, Straus & Giroux, 1991. F

It's 1942, and Harry has just become a war orphan. Will he and the stray dog he takes up with be able to survive on their own?

———. *Stormsearch.* Farrar, Straus & Giroux, 1992. F

Tim's summer vacation turns into a quest when an antique model ship, washed up on the beach after a terrible storm, brings with it secrets of love and death.

———. *The Wind Eye.* Greenwillow, 1977. F

The members of a professor's family are transported, via an old boat said to have belonged to St. Cuthbert, back into medieval times—where the not altogether friendly monk touches each of their lives.

———. *Yaxley's Cat.* Scholastic, 1992. F

Renting the wrong vacation cottage proves to be an almost fatal mistake for a mother and two teenagers, especially after a stray cat moves in and starts digging around in the garden.

Westerfeld, Scott. *Peeps.* Razorbill, 2005. F

College freshman Cal comes to New York, spends a night with a beautiful girl, and becomes a carrier. Now everyone he kisses develops a craving for meat, an aversion to sunlight, and incredible strength.

————. *So Yesterday.* Razorbill, 2004. **F**
When Hunter Braque, a "Cool Hunter," meets Jen Jones, an "Innovator," the pair unwittingly falls into a secret scheme to rock the foundations of a multinational shoe manufacturer.

————. *Uglies.* Simon & Schuster, 2005. **F**
Tally can't wait for her 16th birthday and the surgery that will transform her into a "pretty," because if everyone is beautiful, everything is perfect—right?

Wetherby, Terry, ed. *Conversations: Working Women Talk about Doing a "Man's Job."* Les Femmes, 1977. **NF**
Twenty-two women talk about their experiences in such traditionally male-dominated jobs as welder, carpenter, butcher, grain elevator operator, and chairperson of the board.

Wharton, William. *Birdy.* Knopf, 1979. **F**
In a V.A. hospital, Birdy is prompted by his friend Al to review his bird-obsessed youth, and discovers freedom without flight.

————. *A Midnight Clear.* Knopf, 1982. **F**
A group of unseasoned teenage soldiers standing guard in an old chalet in the Ardennes Forest in December 1944 experience first hand the irony and tragedy of war when they desperately try to set up peaceful communications with a similar group of Germans.

Whedon, Joss. *Fray.* Dark Horse, 2003. **F**
In the distant future, Fray, a thief making a living in the slum that was once Manhattan, discovers her destiny is to kill the monsters that are at war with mankind.

Whelan, Gloria. *Homeless Bird.* HarperCollins, 2000. **F**
In modern India, 13-year-old Koly is forced into an arranged marriage with a dying boy, becomes a teenage widow, and finds herself abandoned by her mother-in-law in a strange city where she must make a life for herself or die.

Whipple, Dorothy V. *Is the Grass Greener? Answers to Questions about Drugs.* Luce, 1971. **NF**
In question-and-answer form, a physician reports with total objectivity on the facts about drugs of all kinds, the laws, the uses, and the ways to confront the problem.

Whitcomb, Laura. *A Certain Slant of Light.* Houghton Mifflin, 2005. **F**
Helen has been a ghost for 130 years, gently and anonymously haunting various hosts until the day when a boy in a classroom lets her know that he can actually see her.

White, Ellen Emerson. *Long Live the Queen.* Scholastic, 1989. **F**
Abducted by terrorists, Megan, the president's daughter, realizes her survival is completely up to her.

————. *The Road Home.* Scholastic, 1995. **F**
Lt. Rebecca Phillips, who served as a combat nurse in Vietnam, comes to terms with what she experienced there as she tries to readjust to life in the United States.

White, Robb. *Deathwatch.* Doubleday, 1972. **F**
Ben's hunting expedition for bighorn sheep becomes a deathwatch in the desert—with hope of survival 45 miles away!

White, Ruth. *Belle Prater's Boy.* Farrar, Straus & Giroux, 1996. **F**
What really happened to the parents of 12-year-old Gypsy and her cousin Woodrow?

————. *Memories of Summer.* Farrar, Straus & Giroux, 2000. **F**
In 1955, 13-year-old Lyric finds her whole life changing when her family moves from the hills of Virginia to a town in Michigan and her older sister Summer begins descending into mental illness.

————. *Weeping Willow.* Farrar, Straus & Giroux, 1992. **F**
Life in idyllic 1950s Virginia is difficult for Tiny Lambert as she struggles to emerge whole from her stepfather's brutal attention.

White, Ryan, and Ann Marie Cunningham. *Ryan White: My Own Story.* Dial, 1991. **NF**
Teenager Ryan White not only fights AIDS but also prejudice and his own fears in a personal account about the medical disaster facing all of us.

Whitmore, Arvella. *Trapped between the Lash and the Gun: A Boy's Journey.* Dial, 1999. **F**
After stealing his grandfather's heirloom watch to gain admission to a gang, 12-year-old Jason finds himself transported back to the days of slavery.

Whitney, Kim Ablon. *See You down the Road.* Knopf, 2004. **F**
Bridget, a 16-year-old Traveler and part of a family of roaming con artists, is not sure she wants to stay in the life now that she has been promised in marriage.

Whitney, Phyllis A. *Hunter's Green*. Doubleday, 1968. **F**

Returning to Athmore for a reconciliation with her husband, Eve North finds herself the pawn in a deadly game of chess with the black rook out to destroy her.

Wibbelsman, Charles, and Kathy McCoy. *The Teenage Body Book*. Pocket, 1979. **NF**

Changes in the physical development of both girls and boys, nutrition, personal hygiene, and emotions are covered in this illustrated guide. An updated edition was published in 1999.

Wibberley, Leonard. *The Mouse on Wall Street*. Morrow, 1969. **F**

Gloriana, ruler of Grand Fenwick, conqueror of the United States, sender of the first rocket to the moon, now is possessed by a "Midas touch" which almost wrecks the simple economy of her country.

Wieler, Diana. *Bad Boy*. Delacorte, 1992. **F**

AJ and Tulley have been best friends both on and off the ice for years, but AJ's discovery of Tulley's secret threatens their friendship and AJ's control over his own violence.

Wiesenthal, Simon. *The Murderers among Us: The Simon Wiesenthal Memoirs*. McGraw-Hill, 1967. **NF**

A survivor of the concentration camps searches out and brings to justice Adolf Eichmann, the Gestapo officer, Karl Silberbauer, who arrested Anne Frank, and some 900 other Nazi murderers.

Wilcox, Fred A. *Waiting for an Army to Die: The Tragedy of Agent Orange*. Random House, 1983. **NF**

Based on interviews with Vietnam veterans and on government documents, this comprehensive look at the effects of the defoliant Agent Orange also points to the callous disregard for its victims.

Wilford, John Noble. *The Riddle of the Dinosaur*. Knopf, 1985. **NF**

The science editor of the *New York Times* has produced a humorous and readable history of paleontology, including surprising new discoveries that have revolutionized dinosaur theory.

Wilhelm, Kate. *Where Late the Sweet Birds Sang*. Harper & Row, 1976. **F**

When humankind is faced with annihilation by the sterilizing effects of pollution and plague, cloning becomes the only hope of man's continued existence—or is it?

Wilkinson, Brenda. *Ludell and Willie*. Harper & Row, 1977. **F**

Two high school seniors from a poor, black Georgia community fall in love but are separated because of family tragedy.

Wilkomirski, Binjamin. *Fragments: Memories of a Wartime Childhood*. Schocken, 1996. **NF**

Found wandering near Auschwitz at the end of the war, a small boy has no language or knowledge of who he is. Here, he shares his fragmented memories of surviving as a toddler.

Willard, Nancy. *Things Invisible to See*. Knopf, 1984. **F**

Mystical visions, romance, and the struggle of making choices are intertwined in the story of twins, Ben and Willie, and Clare Bishop after Ben's stray ball paralyzes Clare.

Willeford, Charles. *I Was Looking for a Street*. Countryman, 1988. **NF**

A writer's memoir of his survival from age eight when he was orphaned to his life on the road as a teenager during the Great Depression.

Willey, Margaret. *The Bigger Book of Lydia*. Harper & Row, 1983. **F**

Lydia Bitte is small and unhappy and her rock-musician boyfriend calls her "Littlebit." She acquires a new perspective when she meets Michelle, who has anorexia.

————. *Finding David Dolores*. Harper & Row, 1986. **F**

"Oh God, I whispered. At last I've found someone." Thirteen-year-old Arly experiences the intensity of a first crush when she secretly follows handsome, older David Dolores.

————. *Saving Lenny*. Bantam, 1990. **F**

When Jesse falls in love with handsome, mysterious Lenny, she willingly gives up everything for him—family, friends, and college.

Williams, Carol Lynch. *The True Colors of Caitlynne Jackson*. Delacorte, 1997. **F**

Caitlynne and her sister, forced to fend for themselves when their mother storms out and never returns, take off on their bikes to search for a grandmother they barely know.

Williams, Juan. *Eyes on the Prize: America's Civil Rights Years, 1954–1965*. Viking, 1987. **NF**

A history of the dramatic events of the years between the Supreme Court's ruling against segregated schools in 1954 and the approval of the Voting Rights Act of 1965.

Williams, Lori Aurelia. *When Kambia Elaine Flew in from Neptune.* Simon & Schuster, 2000. **F**

When Shayla befriends the new girl next door who tells wild stories about lizard people and memory beetles, she doesn't realize at first the desperate and dangerous situation Kambia Elaine is in.

Williams, Martin. *Where's the Melody? A Listener's Introduction to Jazz.* Pantheon, 1966. **NF**

Listeners are introduced to jazz using record notes.

Williams, Michael. *Crocodile Burning.* Lodestar, 1992. **F**

Joining the cast of a play about apartheid headed for the New York stage, Seraki leaves his native Soweto, where life under white rule has become unbearable.

Williams, Ted, and John Underwood. *My Turn at Bat: The Story of My Life.* Simon & Schuster, 1969. **NF**

One of baseball's greatest hitters, Ted Williams, explains himself and his controversial career with honesty and frankness.

Williams-Garcia, Rita. *Every Time a Rainbow Dies.* HarperCollins, 2001. **F**

Thulani is drawn out of his grief over the death of his mother when he comes to the aid of a rape victim and is obsessed with forming a relationship with her.

———. *Fast Talk on a Slow Track.* Lodestar, 1991. **F**

Denzel Watson has always been a star; now he faces his first taste of failure the summer before his freshman year at Princeton.

———. *Like Sisters on the Homefront.* Lodestar, 1995. **F**

When Gayle, a streetwise mother at 14, becomes pregnant again, she is sent south to stay with relatives.

———. *No Laughter Here.* HarperCollins, 2004. **F**

When Victoria returns from a family visit to Nigeria, she is uncharacteristically distant from her best friend, Akilah, who learns that her friend was circumcised in a coming-of-age ritual.

Willis, Connie. *To Say Nothing of the Dog, or How We Found the Bishop's Bird Stump at Last.* Bantam, 1997. **F**

When time-traveling historian Ned Henry rescues a cat in Victorian England, the 21st century begins to unravel.

Wilson, Budge. *The Leaving, and Other Stories.* Philomel, 1992. **F**

Nine stories about growing up female reveal the roller coaster of teenage emotions.

Wilson, David Henry. *The Coachman Rat.* Carroll & Graf, 1989. **F**

When the clock tolls midnight, the rat the fairy godmother had turned into a coachman accidentally remains human in all but physical form; will he be as inhumane as the people he encounters?

Wilson, Diane Lee. *I Rode a Horse of Milk White Jade.* Orchard, 1998. **F**

Through sheer determination, crippled Oyuna rides her magical horse in search of the great Kublai Khan.

Wilson, F. Paul. *Dydeetown World.* Baen, 1989. **F**
Private detective Sigmundo Dreyer takes on the underworld and corporate crime when he helps a client in this futuristic hard-boiled detective saga.

Wilson, Robert Charles. *Gypsies.* Doubleday, 1989. **F**

Fifteen-year-old Michael suddenly realizes his mom shares his unusual psychic ability, and now they must flee for their lives.

———. *Mysterium.* Bantam, 1994. **F**

Following an explosion at a secret government installation, the town of Two Rivers wakes up in a parallel dimension, where the church rules and teens are hanged for rebelling.

Windsor, Patricia. *The Summer Before.* Harper & Row, 1973. **F**

Alexandra fights her way back to reality with the help of her parents and a psychiatrist, after the death of her special friend Bradley.

Winick, Judd. *Pedro and Me: Friendship, Loss, and What I Learned.* Holt, 2000. **NF**

Through a graphic format, Winick chronicles his friendship with AIDS victim and educator Pedro Zamora, a friendship that began on MTV's *Real World.*

Winthrop, Elizabeth. *Knock, Knock, Who's There?* Holiday House, 1978. **F**

While Sam and Michael try to cope with their father's death, they discover that their mother has a problem even more devastating to their lives.

Winton, Tim. *Lockie Leonard, Human Torpedo.* Joy Street, 1991. **F**

Lockie gets thrown out of class his first day at his new high school—a good start, he decides. Things look even better when the prettiest girl in school takes an interest in him.

Wirths, Claudine G., and Mary Bowman-Kruhm. *I Hate School: How to Hang In and When to Drop Out.* Crowell, 1986. **NF**
This self-help manual for potential dropouts offers usable, nonpreachy suggestions for improving academic performance and coping with problems.

Wisler, G. Clifton. *Red Cap.* Lodestar, 1991. **F**
Starvation, disease, and despair destroy the lives of Union soldiers at Andersonville. How can Ransom, a 13-year-old prisoner of war, expect to survive?

Wittlinger, Ellen. *Blind Faith.* Simon & Schuster, 2006. **F**
Liz's grieving mother joins a spiritualist church despite objections from her atheist father. With the help of a friend, Liz, who feels trapped in the middle, finds her own path.

———. *Hard Love.* Simon & Schuster, 1999. **F**
Sixteen-year-old John meets fellow zine writer Marisol and falls in love with her, even though he knows she can't love him back.

———. *Lombardo's Law.* Houghton Mifflin, 1993. **F**
When 15-year-old Justine finally finds a boy who loves the same things she does, such as foreign films, she fights her feelings for him because he is only 13.

———. *Razzle.* Simon & Schuster, 2001. **F**
Newly arrived in the small, artsy Cape Cod community, Kenyon befriends Razzle, a girl who works at the town dump and has an artistic spirit just like him.

———. *Sandpiper.* Simon & Schuster, 2005. **F**
Two lonely teens, each with secrets that set them apart, are changed completely when they meet each other.

———. *What's in a Name.* Simon & Schuster, 2000. **F**
While a town debates whether to change its name, the lives of ten of its teenage residents are changing as well.

———. *Zigzag.* Simon & Schuster, 2003. **F**
Robin discovers more than the sights during her cross-country trip with her Aunt Dory and younger cousins.

Wolf, Allan. *New Found Land.* Candlewick, 2004. **F**
Fourteen members of the Corps of Discovery, including the dog, tell the story of the Lewis and Clark Expedition.

Wolf, David. *Foul! The Connie Hawkins Story.* Holt, Rinehart and Winston, 1972. **NF**
Slum beginnings and a college basketball scandal do not keep Connie Hawkins from becoming a superstar with the Phoenix Suns.

Wolf, Sylvia. *Focus: Five Women Photographers.* Whitman, 1994. **NF**
Wolf views the creative process from very different perspectives through crisp, well-selected photographs by Julia Margaret Cameron, Margaret Bourke-White, Flor Garduno, Sandy Skoglund, and Lorna Simpson.

Wolfe, Tom. *The Right Stuff.* Farrar, Straus & Giroux, 1979. **F**
Wolfe provides a fascinating and often irreverent history of manned space flight from the late 1940s exploits of Chuck Yeager to the NASA missions of John Glenn, Alan Shepard, and Gus Grissom—who all had the "right stuff."

Wolff, Tobias. *This Boy's Life: A Memoir.* Atlantic Monthly, 1989. **NF**
A witty, wrenching autobiography of Wolff's coming-of-age with a loving mother and a cruel stepfather.

Wolff, Virginia Euwer. *Make Lemonade.* Holt, 1993. **F**
High-school student LaVaughn, determined to earn money for college, babysits for Jolly, an unwed teenage mother of two, and matures in the process.

———. *The Mozart Season.* Holt, 1991. **F**
Allegra Shapiro plays Mozart on her violin with the same intensity that she plays softball; her decision to enter a music competition turns her 12th summer into the "Mozart season."

———. *Probably Still Nick Swansen.* Holt, 1988. **F**
Slow but proud special education student Nick Swansen must deal with the pain of rejection and the lingering guilt over his sister's death.

———. *True Believer.* Atheneum, 2001. **F**
In this poetic sequel to *Make Lemonade*, LaVaughn finds that her changing goals and relationships bring her both pain and joy.

Wood, Bari. *The Killing Gift.* Putnam, 1975. **F**
Does Jennifer Gilbert really have the psychic power to kill?

Wooding, Chris. *The Haunting of Alaizabel Cray.* Orchard, 2004. **F**
Possession, wych-kin, airships, and Stitch-face all pose tremendous challenges to Thaniel and Cathaline as they fight to rid London of the evil Fraternity.

———. *Poison.* Orchard, 2005. **F**
When her sister is kidnapped by Phaeries, Poison is determined to get her back but doesn't realize that she is part of a much larger and darker story.

———. *Storm Thief.* Orchard, 2006. **F**
After stealing a powerful device, street thieves Rail and Moa flee their city's ruthless leaders with the help of a strange creature.

Woodrell, Daniel. *Winter's Bone.* Little, Brown, 2006. **F**
To save home and family, 17-year-old Ree sets out on a perilous search for her missing father in their isolated and dangerous Ozark mountain community.

Woodson, Jacqueline. *Behind You.* Putnam, 2004. **F**
Family, friends, and Ellie—the love of Jeremiah's life—deal with his tragic death.

———. *From the Notebooks of Melanin Sun.* Blue Sky, 1995. **F**
Melanin Sun finds being a teenager is hard enough without learning that his mother's new boyfriend is a woman.

———. *Hush.* Putnam, 2002. **F**
Toswiah Green struggles toward a new identity as Evie Thomas when her family joins the Witness Protection Program and everything she ever knew is lost to her.

———. *I Hadn't Meant to Tell You This.* Delacorte, 1994. **F**
Marie and Lena become friends despite race and class differences, but can their friendship protect Lena from the terrifying secret she is forced to keep?

———. *If You Come Softly.* Putnam, 1998. **F**
Jeremiah, who is white, and Ellie, who is African American, feel an immediate connection and then must cope with the reactions to their relationship by the people around them.

———. *Locomotion.* Putnam, 2003. **F**
In this verse novel, 11-year-old Lonnie recovers from the trauma that results when his parents are killed in a fire.

———. *Maizon at Blue Hill.* Delacorte, 1992. **F**
After winning a scholarship to a mostly white boarding school, Maizon is forced to confront issues of racism, friendship, and fitting in.

———. *Miracle's Boys.* Putnam, 2000. **F**
Three brothers cope with their mother's death, each one in his own unique way.

Woolley, Persia. *Child of the Northern Spring.* Poseidon, 1987. **F**
The first book in an Arthurian trilogy views life through the eyes of lively 15-year-old Guinevere.

———. *Queen of the Summer Stars.* Poseidon, 1990. **F**
Young Queen Guinevere is torn between loyalty to her king and love for his closest companion, Lancelot, in this sequel to *Child of the Northern Spring.*

Wrede, Patricia C. *Dealing with Dragons.* Harcourt Brace Jovanovich, 1990. **F**
Unconventional Cimorene, fed up with her dull life as a princess, runs away to join the dragons in this fun book that turns fairy tales upside down.

———. *Searching for Dragons.* Harcourt Brace Jovanovich, 1991. **F**
Princess Cimorene and Mendabar, king of the Enchanted Forest, triumph over wizards to rescue Kazul, the king of the dragons.

Wrede, Patricia C., and Caroline Stevermer. *Sorcery and Cecelia, or The Enchanted Chocolate Pot.* Harcourt, 2003. **F**
Cousins Cecelia and Kate, who have grown up a bit wild in the country, correspond in lively letters during the course of Kate's first season in London.

Wyden, Peter. *Day One: Before Hiroshima and After.* Simon & Schuster, 1984. **NF**
The author not only chronicles the making of the atomic bomb and its first use, but also follows the aftermath to the present day.

Wynne-Jones, Tim. *A Thief in the House of Memory.* Farrar, Straus & Giroux, 2005. **F**
When a dead man is found in his family's house, Declan finds himself drawn into a vortex of memories and lies.

Wyss, Thelma Hatch. *Here at the Scenic-Vu Motel.* Harper & Row, 1988. **F**
Living too far away to be bused to the local high school, a coed group of teens room at a motel, with 17-year-old Jake in charge—but by no means ready for such awesome responsibilities.

Yang, Gene. *American Born Chinese.* Roaring Brook, 2006. **F**
Combining three different stories, one drawn from Chinese mythology, this graphic novel explores racism and self-hatred as a young boy struggles to come to terms with his heritage.

Yeager, Chuck, and Leo Janos. *Yeager: An Autobiography.* Bantam, 1985. **NF**
Air Force general Chuck Yeager, World War II ace and first man to break the sound barrier, candidly shares the drama of his life and career.

Yee, Paul. *Breakaway.* Groundwood, 1997. **F**
Eighteen-year-old Kwok Wong desperately wants to play soccer and attend the university—it's his way out of his Chinese family's traditions and their dirt-poor farm.

Yep, Laurence, ed. *American Dragons: Twenty-five Asian American Voices.* HarperCollins, 1993. **NF**
Growing up can be agonizing and traumatic, yet filled with hope and love, as these short stories, poems, and excerpts from plays poignantly demonstrate.

Yolen, Jane. *Briar Rose.* TOR, 1992. **F**
Grandmother Gemma always told the story of Briar Rose, and after she dies, her granddaughter discovers that Gemma was a real-life Sleeping Beauty—a Holocaust survivor.

————. *Dragon's Blood.* Delacorte, 1982. **F**
In an original and engrossing fantasy, Jakkin's freedom is ensured when the dragon he steals and secretly trains wins its first fight.

————. *Gift of Sarah Barker.* Viking, 1981. **F**
Vivacious Sarah and stalwart Abel create havoc in a quiet, modest Shaker community when they fall in love.

————. *Heart's Blood.* Delacorte, 1984. **F**
Jakkin wants only to possess and train his own red dragon—until his love for Akki leads him into the maze of Austarian politics.

————. *Sword of the Rightful King: A Novel of King Arthur.* Harcourt, 2003. **F**
Assassins, treachery, and sorcery abound in this inventive version of King Arthur's early days of rule, including the magician's very risky staging of the test of the sword in the stone.

Yolen, Jane, and Bruce Coville. *Armageddon Summer.* Harcourt Brace, 1998. **F**
In alternating chapters, Marina and Jed tell how they witnessed a cult's preparation for the end of the world.

Yolen, Jane, and Martin H. Greenberg, eds. *Vampires: A Collection of Original Stories.* HarperCollins, 1991. **F**
Meet the vampire of your dreams—in the mall, in a neighbor's garden, or haunting the streets at night.

Yolen, Jane, and Robert J. Harris. *Girl in a Cage.* Philomel, 2002. **F**
Imprisoned in a cage by King Edward Longshanks, Princess Marjorie wages her own small war on him while her father, the newly crowned King of Scotland, defends his country from the ruthless King of England.

————. *Prince across the Water.* Philomel, 2004. **F**
Duncan MacDonald and his cousin Ewan are eager to answer the call to restore Prince Charlie to the Scottish throne, a quest that will lead to the end of the Highland clans at the bloody battle of Culloden.

————. *Queen's Own Fool.* Philomel, 2000. **F**
When 12-year-old Nicola leaves Troupe Brufort to serve as the fool for Mary, Queen of Scots, she experiences political and religious upheaval in France and Scotland.

Young, Al. *Snakes.* Holt, Rinehart and Winston, 1970. **F**
MC, a young ghetto musician, makes the stormy journey through adolescence with the help of his grandmother, a hit record, and his friends.

Young, Jean. *Woodstock Craftsman's Manual.* Praeger, 1972. **NF**
This how-to book covers everything from beads to batik.

————. *Woodstock Craftsman's Manual 2.* Praeger, 1973. **NF**
In this second how-to volume, such crafts as needlepoint, appliqué, quilting, songwriting, and woodblock printing are covered along with how to make stained glass, bronze jewelry, sandals, and videotapes.

Young, Karen Romano. *The Beetle and Me: A Love Story.* Greenwillow, 1999. **F**
A young girl falls in love with the 1957 purple Volkswagen beetle that was her father's first car, and launches a campaign to convince her parents to let her renovate it.

Zahn, Timothy. *Dragon and Thief: A Dragonback Adventure.* TOR, 2003. **F**
Jack Morgan's efforts to be cleared of a false accusation of theft are complicated when he allows Draycos, a symbiotic dragon, to take up residence on his back in the form of a moving tattoo.

Zambreno, Mary Frances. *Plague of Sorcerers.* Harcourt Brace Jovanovich, 1991. **F**
A magic plague is infecting the wizards in the land. Only 16-year-old Jermyn can break the spell, with the help of his most unusual familiar—an overprotective skunk.

Zassenhaus, Hiltgunt. *Walls: Resisting the Third Reich—One Woman's Story.* Beacon, 1974. **NF**

Refusing to be intimidated by the Nazi regime in Germany, Hiltgunt uses her knowledge of the Scandinavian language to help, at some risk to herself, the Scandinavian prisoners in Germany.

Zelazny, Roger. *Doorways in the Sand.* Harper & Row, 1976. **F**

Interstellar espionage is magical and fantastic with two zany alien agents, disguised as a wombat and a kangaroo, and an acrophobic earthman hero.

Zenatti, Valérie. *When I Was a Soldier: A Memoir.* Bloomsbury, 2005. **NF**

This true account features French immigrant and Israeli citizen Valerie Zenatti, who enters into adulthood via compulsory army duty, changing her life forever.

Zerman, Melvyn Bernard. *Taking on the Press: Constitutional Rights in Conflict.* Crowell, 1986. **NF**

The Black Panthers, Vietnam, and nuclear secrets are only some of the legal issues explained in Zerman's lively, entertaining book.

Zindel, Paul. *A Begonia for Miss Applebaum.* Harper & Row, 1989. **F**

Henry and Zelda use a cash card to help their offbeat favorite teacher and her homeless friends.

———. *Confessions of a Teenage Baboon.* Harper & Row, 1977. **F**

Sixteen-year-old Chris Boyd gains self-confidence and control over his life after a tragic encounter with a 30-year-old misfit who befriends lonely teenagers.

———. *The Effect of Gamma Rays on Man-in-the-Moon Marigolds.* Harper & Row, 1971. **F**

An alcoholic mother stifles the lives of her two teenage daughters, one who is bordering on madness and the other who is a sensitive, loving person, in this prize-winning drama.

———. *Pardon Me, You're Stepping on My Eyeball!* Harper & Row, 1976. **F**

Marsh Mellow, an offbeat teenager with an alcoholic mother and a missing father, begins to accept himself when Edna, a new acquaintance, decides to shed her aloofness and help him.

———. *The Pigman and Me.* HarperCollins, 1992. **NF**

Zindel recounts his bizarre adventures growing up on Staten Island, when his neighbor's father becomes his personal "pigman" and teaches him to cope with his rootless family.

———. *The Pigman's Legacy.* Harper & Row, 1980. **F**

John and Lorraine befriend an old man who is hiding from the IRS in the Pigman's house, and through the hilarious and poignant experiences they share with him, they discover the legacy of love which the Pigman left them.

Zolotow, Charlotte, ed. *Early Sorrow: Ten Stories of Youth.* Harper & Row, 1986. **F**

Themes range from the end of a special relationship to the loss of a special possession, from the death of a loved one to a loss of self, in these stories about the first sorrows of youth.

Zusak, Markus. *The Book Thief.* Knopf, 2006. **F**

Death colors (and narrates) Liesel Meminger's attempt to survive Hitler's regime in a small German town. Orphaned and devastated, Liesel finds salvation through stolen books.

———. *Fighting Ruben Wolfe.* Arthur A. Levine, 2001. **F**

Two brothers from the wrong side of the tracks spar in defense of family and on the Australian underground boxing circuit.

———. *I Am the Messenger.* Knopf, 2005. **F**

Aimless and amiable 19-year-old cab driver Ed Kennedy foils a bank robber and then begins to receive mysterious messages assigning him to intervene in the lives of strangers.

The Books
by Year

In 1989, to clarify the currency of a given list, YALSA began to refer to the list by the year of its release rather than the year during which the books were chosen. So the section "1988 Selections" includes books published between September 1987 and December 1988, and the section "1990 Selections" includes books published between September 1988 and December 1989.

1966 SELECTIONS

Abel, Elie. *Missile Crisis.*

Asimov, Isaac. *Fantastic Voyage.*

Bach, Richard. *Biplane.*

Barker, S. Omar. *Little World Apart.*

Boyd, Malcolm. *Are You Running with Me, Jesus? Prayers.*

Brooks, Earle, and Rhoda Brooks. *The Barrios of Manta: A Personal Account of the Peace Corps in Ecuador.*

Capps, Benjamin. *A Woman of the People.*

Clifford, Francis. *The Naked Runner.*

Dufresne, Frank. *My Way Was North.*

Durrell, Gerald. *Two in the Bush.*

Friel, Brian. *Philadelphia, Here I Come!*

Fuller, John G. *Incident at Exeter: The Story of Unidentified Flying Objects over America Today.*

Gallery, Daniel V. *Stand by-y-y to Start Engines.*

Gilman, Dorothy. *The Unexpected Mrs. Pollifax.*

Hallet, Jean-Pierre. *Congo Kitabu.*

Hollinger, Carol. *Mai Pen Rai Means Never Mind.*

Lindall, Edward. *Northward the Coast.*

MacLean, Alistair. *When Eight Bells Toll.*

Manry, Robert. *Tinkerbelle.*

Nader, Ralph. *Unsafe at Any Speed: The Designed-In Dangers of the American Automobile.*

Parks, Gordon. *A Choice of Weapons.*

Plimpton, George. *Paper Lion.*

Russell, Bill, and William McSweeny. *Go Up for Glory.*

Ryan, Cornelius. *The Last Battle.*

Sherman, D. R. *Brothers of the Sea.*

Walker, Margaret. *Jubilee.*

Williams, Martin. *Where's the Melody? A Listener's Introduction to Jazz.*

1967 SELECTIONS

Amosov, Nikolai. *The Open Heart.*

Armstrong, Charlotte. *The Gift Shop.*

Bagley, Desmond. *Landslide.*

Ball, John. *The Cool Cottontail.*

Cole, Ernest, and Thomas Flaherty. *House of Bondage.*

Conot, Robert. *Rivers of Blood, Years of Darkness.*

de Hartog, Jan. *The Captain.*

Hardy, William M. *U.S.S.* Mudskipper: *The Submarine That Wrecked a Train.*

Head, Ann. *Mr. and Mrs. Bo Jo Jones.*

Inouye, Daniel K., and Lawrence Elliott. *Journey to Washington.*

Kuznetsov, Anatoly. *Babi Yar.*

Levitt, Leonard. *African Season.*

Lord, Walter. *Incredible Victory.*

Maas, Peter. *Rescuer.*

Mather, Melissa. *One Summer in Between.*

Olsen, Jack. *Black Is Best: The Riddle of Cassius Clay.*

Peters, Ellis. *Black Is the Colour of My True-Love's Heart.*

Potok, Chaim. *The Chosen.*

Ridgway, John, and Chay Blyth. *A Fighting Chance.*

Rosten, Leo. *A Most Private Intrigue.*

Schaap, Dick. *Turned On.*

Sheehan, Susan. *Ten Vietnamese.*

Simak, Clifford D. *The Werewolf Principle.*

Styron, William. *The Confessions of Nat Turner.*

Szulc, Tad. *The Bombs of Palomares.*

Thompson, Jean. *The House of Tomorrow.*

Walsh, John, and Robert Gannon. *Time Is Short and the Water Rises.*

Wiesenthal, Simon. *The Murderers among Us: The Simon Wiesenthal Memoirs.*

1968 SELECTIONS

Adler, Bill, et al. *Growing Up Black.*

Bagley, Desmond. *The Vivero Letter.*

Bradford, Richard. *Red Sky at Morning.*

Braithwaite, E. R. *Paid Servant.*

Cleaver, Eldridge. *Soul on Ice.*

Collins, Larry, and Dominique Lapierre. *Or I'll Dress You in Mourning.*

Courlander, Harold. *The African.*

Davies, Hunter. *The Beatles: The Authorized Biography.*

Durrell, Gerald. *Rosy Is My Relative.*

Kellogg, Marjorie. *Tell Me That You Love Me, Junie Moon.*

Kramer, Jerry. *Instant Replay: The Green Bay Diary of Jerry Kramer.*

Kuper, Jack. *Child of the Holocaust.*

Leslie, Robert Franklin. *The Bears and I: Raising Three Cubs in the North Woods.*

Lynd, Alice. *We Won't Go: Personal Accounts of War Objectors.*

MacInnes, Helen. *The Salzburg Connection.*

Parks, David. *GI Diary.*

Portis, Charles. *True Grit.*

Sanderson, Ivan T. *Uninvited Visitors: A Biologist Looks at UFO's.*

Schulz, Charles M. *Peanuts Treasury.*

Taylor, Gordon Rattray. *Biological Time Bomb.*

Teague, Bob. *Letters to a Black Boy.*

Watson, James D. *Double Helix: A Personal Account of the Discovery of the Structure of DNA.*

Whitney, Phyllis A. *Hunter's Green.*

1969 SELECTIONS

Ball, John. *Johnny Get Your Gun.*

Bradbury, Ray. *I Sing the Body Electric! Stories.*

Brown, Turner, Jr. *Black Is.*

Cohn, Nik. *Rock from the Beginning.*

Crichton, Michael. *The Andromeda Strain.*

Decker, Sunny. *An Empty Spoon.*

Durrell, Gerald. *Birds, Beasts, and Relatives.*

Ferris, Louanne. *I'm Done Crying.*

Gaines, William M., and Albert F. Feldstein, eds. *The Ridiculously Expensive MAD: A Collection of the Worst from 17 Years of MAD.*

Granatelli, Anthony. *They Call Me Mister 500.*

Hay, Jacob, and John M. Keshishian. *Autopsy for a Cosmonaut.*

King, Coretta Scott. *My Life with Martin Luther King, Jr.*

Kunen, James S. *The Strawberry Statement: Notes of a College Revolutionary.*

Lester, Julius. *Search for the New Land: History as Subjective Experience.*

Lowenfels, Walter, ed. *The Writing on the Wall: 108 American Poems of Protest.*

Michaels, Barbara. *Ammie, Come Home.*

Moody, Anne. *Coming of Age in Mississippi.*

Olsen, Jack. *Night of the Grizzlies.*

Potok, Chaim. *The Promise.*

Stewart, Fred Mustard. *The Mephisto Waltz.*

Wibberley, Leonard. *The Mouse on Wall Street.*

Williams, Ted, and John Underwood. *My Turn at Bat: The Story of My Life.*

1970 SELECTIONS

Angelou, Maya. *I Know Why the Caged Bird Sings.*

Birmingham, John. *Our Time Is Now: Notes from the High School Underground.*

Blum, Ralph. *Simultaneous Man.*

Bouton, Jim. *Ball Four: My Life and Hard Times Throwing the Knuckleball in the Big Leagues.*

Brenner, Joseph H., et al. *Drugs and Youth: Medical, Psychiatric, and Legal Facts.*

Chisholm, Shirley. *Unbought and Unbossed.*

Cousteau, Jacques-Yves, and Philippe Cousteau. *The Shark: Splendid Savage of the Sea.*

Dorman, Michael. *Under 21: A Young People's Guide to Legal Rights.*

Dowdey, Landon, comp. *Journey to Freedom: A Casebook with Music.*

Dribben, Judith Strick. *A Girl Called Judith Strick.*

Eisen, Jonathan, ed. *Altamont: Death of Innocence in the Woodstock Nation.*

Fall, Thomas. *The Ordeal of Running Standing.*

Finney, Jack. *Time and Again.*

Gaylin, Willard. *In the Service of Their Country: War Resisters in Prison.*

Goro, Herb. *The Block.*

Greenberg, Joanne. *In This Sign.*

Gregory, Susan. *Hey, White Girl!*

Hammer, Richard. *One Morning in the War: The Tragedy at Son My.*

Hedgepeth, William, and Dennis Stock. *The Alternative: Communal Life in New America.*

Hillerman, Tony. *The Blessing Way.*

Hough, John T., Jr. *A Peck of Salt: A Year in the Ghetto.*

Howard, Jane. *Please Touch: A Guided Tour of the Human Potential Movement.*

Jordan, June, ed. *Soulscript: Afro-American Poetry.*

Kavaler, Lucy. *Freezing Point: Cold as a Matter of Life and Death.*

Kim, Richard E. *Lost Names: Scenes from a Korean Boyhood.*

Meriwether, Louise. *Daddy Was a Number Runner.*

O'Leary, Brian. *The Making of an Ex-Astronaut.*

Segal, Erich. *Love Story.*

Shaw, Arnold. *The World of Soul: Black America's Contribution to the Pop Music Scene.*

Stewart, Mary. *The Crystal Cave.*

Swarthout, Glendon. *Bless the Beasts and Children.*

Tyler, Anne. *A Slipping-Down Life.*

Wersba, Barbara. *Run Softly, Go Fast.*

Young, Al. *Snakes.*

1971 SELECTIONS

Anonymous. *Go Ask Alice.*

Balducci, Carolyn. *Is There a Life after Graduation, Henry Birnbaum?*

Barjavel, Rene. *The Ice People.*

Brown, Dee. *Bury My Heart at Wounded Knee: An Indian History of the American West.*

Campbell, Hope. *No More Trains to Tottenville.*

Cousteau, Jacques-Yves, and Philippe Diole. *Life and Death in a Coral Sea.*

Gaines, Ernest J. *The Autobiography of Miss Jane Pittman.*

Goodall, Jane. *In the Shadow of Man.*

Goulart, Ron. *What's Become of Screwloose? and Other Inquiries.*

Guffy, Ossie, and Caryl Ledner. *Ossie: The Autobiography of a Black Woman.*

Henderson, Zenna. *Holding Wonder.*

Heyerdahl, Thor. *The Ra Expeditions.*

Hinton, S. E. *That Was Then, This Is Now.*

Houriet, Robert. *Getting Back Together.*

Houston, James. *The White Dawn: An Eskimo Saga.*

Jordan, June. *His Own Where.*

Lavallee, David. *Event 1000.*

Lydon, Michael. *Rock Folk: Portraits from the Rock 'n' Roll Pantheon.*

Michaels, Barbara. *The Dark on the Other Side.*

Moore, Gilbert. *A Special Rage.*

Nolen, William A. *The Making of a Surgeon.*

Parks, Gordon. *Born Black.*

Pierce, Ruth I. *Single and Pregnant.*

Plath, Sylvia. *The Bell Jar.*

Portola Institute. *The Last Whole Earth Catalog: Access to Tools.*

Postman, Neil, and Charles Weingartner. *The Soft Revolution: A Student Handbook for Turning Schools Around.*

Powers, Thomas. *Diana: The Making of a Terrorist.*

Renvoizé, Jean. *A Wild Thing.*

Sorrentino, Joseph N. *Up from Never.*

Stevenson, Florence. *The Curse of the Concullens.*

Townsend, John Rowe. *Good Night, Prof, Dear.*

Whipple, Dorothy V. *Is the Grass Greener? Answers to Questions about Drugs.*

Zindel, Paul. *The Effect of Gamma Rays on Man-in-the-Moon Marigolds.*

1972 SELECTIONS

Allen, Terry, ed. *The Whispering Wind: Poetry by Young American Indians.*

Blum, Ralph. *Old Glory and the Real-Time Freaks: A Children's Story and Patriotic Goodtime Book, with Maps.*

Carlson, Dale. *The Mountain of Truth.*

Conrat, Maisie, and Richard Conrat. *Executive Order 9066: The Internment of 110,000 Japanese Americans.*

Crichton, Michael. *The Terminal Man.*

Del Rey, Lester. *Pstalemate.*

Durham, Marilyn. *The Man Who Loved Cat Dancing.*

Elfman, Blossom. *The Girls of Huntington House.*

Fair, Ronald. *We Can't Breathe.*

Fast, Howard. *The Hessian.*

Friedman, Philip. *Rage.*

Giovanni, Nikki. *Gemini: An Extended Autobiographical Statement on My First Twenty-five Years of Being a Black Poet.*

Graham, Robin Lee, and Derek L. T. Gill. *Dove.*

Hall, Lynn. *Sticks and Stones.*

Herbert, Frank. *Soul Catcher.*

Holland, Isabelle. *The Man without a Face.*

Krents, Harold. *To Race the Wind: An Autobiography.*

Lee, Mildred. *Fog.*

Libby, Bill, and Vida Blue. *Vida: His Own Story.*

Mathis, Sharon Bell. *Teacup Full of Roses.*

O'Brien, Robert C. *A Report from Group 17.*

Potok, Chaim. *My Name Is Asher Lev.*

Scaduto, Anthony. *Bob Dylan.*

Schiff, Ken. *Passing Go.*

Sheehan, Carolyn, and Edmund Sheehan. *Magnifi-Cat.*

Smith, Dennis. *Report from Engine Co. 82.*

Teitz, Joyce. *What's a Nice Girl Like You Doing in a Place Like This?*

Wallace, Duncan R. *The Mountebank.*

White, Robb. *Deathwatch.*

Wolf, David. *Foul! The Connie Hawkins Story.*

Young, Jean. *Woodstock Craftsman's Manual.*

1973 SELECTIONS

Aldridge, James. *A Sporting Proposition.*

Bickham, Jack M. *Katie, Kelly, and Heck.*

Carlson, Dale. *Girls Are Equal Too: The Women's Movement for Teenagers.*

Carrighar, Sally. *Home to the Wilderness.*

Castaneda, Carlos. *Journey to Ixtlan: The Lessons of Don Juan.*

Childress, Alice. *A Hero Ain't Nothin' but a Sandwich.*

Clarke, Arthur C. *Rendezvous with Rama.*

Cooper, Henry S. F., Jr. *Thirteen: The Flight That Failed.*

Freemantle, Brian. *Good-bye to an Old Friend.*

Friedman, Myra. *Buried Alive: The Biography of Janis Joplin.*

Giovanni, Nikki. *My House: Poems.*

Glasser, Ronald J. *Ward 402.*

Gray, Martin, and Max Gallo. *For Those I Loved.*

Greenburger, Ingrid. *A Private Treason: A German Memoir.*

Guy, Rosa. *The Friends.*

Habenstreit, Barbara. *"To My Brother Who Did a Crime . . .": Former Prisoners Tell Their Stories in Their Own Words.*

Harris, Marilyn. *Hatter Fox.*

Hillerman, Tony. *Dance Hall of the Dead.*

Huffaker, Clair. *The Cowboy and the Cossack.*

James, P. D. *An Unsuitable Job for a Woman.*

Lawson, Donna. *Mother Nature's Beauty Cupboard.*

Lieberman, E. James, and Ellen Peck. *Sex and Birth Control: A Guide for the Young.*

Logan, Jane. *The Very Nearest Room.*

Maas, Peter. *Serpico.*

Maynard, Joyce. *Looking Back: A Chronicle of Growing Up Old in the Sixties.*

Michaels, Barbara. *Witch.*

O'Brien, Tim. *If I Die in a Combat Zone, Box Me Up and Ship Me Home.*

Peck, Robert Newton. *A Day No Pigs Would Die.*

Robertson, Dougal. *Survive the Savage Sea.*

Schwarz-Bart, Andre. *A Woman Named Solitude.*

Stewart, Mary. *The Hollow Hills.*

Wagenheim, Kal. *Clemente!*

Windsor, Patricia. *The Summer Before.*

Young, Jean. *Woodstock Craftsman's Manual 2.*

1974 SELECTIONS

Adams, Richard. *Watership Down.*

Angelou, Maya. *Gather Together in My Name.*

Baldwin, James. *If Beale Street Could Talk.*

Benchley, Nathaniel. *Bright Candles: A Novel of the Danish Resistance.*

Blum, Ralph, and Judy Blum. *Beyond Earth: Man's Contact with UFOs.*

Cherry, Mike. *On High Steel: The Education of an Ironworker.*

Cormier, Robert. *The Chocolate War.*

Craven, Margaret. *I Heard the Owl Call My Name.*

Demas, Vida. *First Person, Singular.*

Fields, Jeff. *A Cry of Angels.*

Frazier, Walt, and Ira Berkow. *Rockin' Steady: A Guide to Basketball and Cool.*

Greenfeld, Josh, and Paul Mazursky. *Harry and Tonto.*

Hamilton, Virginia. *M.C. Higgins, the Great.*

Herriot, James. *All Things Bright and Beautiful.*

Herzog, Arthur. *The Swarm.*

Holman, Felice. *Slake's Limbo.*

Jacopetti, Alexandra. *Native Funk and Flash: An Emerging Folk Art.*

Jacot, Michael. *The Last Butterfly.*

Johnston, Jennifer. *How Many Miles to Babylon?*

Le Guin, Ursula K. *The Dispossessed: An Ambiguous Utopia.*

Levit, Rose. *Ellen: A Short Life Long Remembered.*

MacCracken, Mary. *A Circle of Children.*

Mathis, Sharon Bell. *Listen for the Fig Tree.*

Niven, Larry, and Jerry Pournelle. *The Mote in God's Eye.*

Page, Thomas. *The Hephaestus Plague.*

Read, Piers Paul. *Alive: The Story of the Andes Survivors.*

Rose, Louise Blecher. *The Launching of Barbara Fabrikant.*

Samuels, Gertrude. *Run, Shelley, Run!*

Scoppettone, Sandra. *Trying Hard to Hear You.*

Sleator, William. *House of Stairs.*

Slesar, Henry. *The Thing at the Door.*

Tidyman, Ernest. *Dummy.*

Wagoner, David. *The Road to Many a Wonder.*

Wells, Evelyn. *I Am Thinking of Kelda.*

Zassenhaus, Hiltgunt. *Walls: Resisting the Third Reich—One Woman's Story.*

1975 SELECTIONS

Ali, Muhammad, and Richard Durham. *The Greatest: My Own Story.*

Beck, Calvin Thomas. *Heroes of the Horrors.*

Bell, David. *A Time to Be Born.*

Bleier, Rocky, and Terry O'Neil. *Fighting Back.*

Cavagnaro, David, and Maggie Cavagnaro. *Almost Home.*

Coleman, Lonnie. *Orphan Jim.*

Davis, Mildred. *Tell Them What's-Her-Name Called.*

Dixon, Paige. *May I Cross Your Golden River?*

Ellison, Harlan. *Deathbird Stories: A Pantheon of Modern Gods.*

Ferazani, Larry. *Rescue Squad.*

Gilman, Dorothy. *The Clairvoyant Countess.*

Giovanni, Nikki. *The Women and the Men.*

Higgins, Jack. *The Eagle Has Landed.*

Hinton, S. E. *Rumble Fish.*

Holland, Isabelle. *Of Love and Death and Other Journeys.*

Horan, James D. *The New Vigilantes.*

Hotchner, A. E. *Looking for Miracles: A Memoir about Loving.*

Hunter, Kristin. *The Survivors.*

Kerr, M. E. *Is That You, Miss Blue?*

Lockley, Ronald. *Seal-Woman.*

Lund, Doris. *Eric.*

MacLaine, Shirley. *You Can Get There from Here.*

MacLean, Alistair. *Circus.*

Montandon, Pat. *The Intruders.*

O'Brien, Robert C. *Z for Zachariah.*

Peck, Richard. *Representing Super Doll.*

Platt, Kin. *Headman.*

Powers, John R. *Do Black Patent-Leather Shoes Really Reflect Up? A Fictionalized Memoir.*

Roueche, Berton. *Feral.*

Ryden, Hope. *God's Dog.*

Sargent, Pamela, ed. *Women of Wonder: Science Fiction Stories by Women about Women.*

Scortia, Thomas N., and Frank G. Robinson. *The Prometheus Crisis.*

Sherman, D. R. *Lion's Paw.*

Simak, Clifford D. *Enchanted Pilgrimage.*

Smith, W. Eugene, and Aileen M. Smith. *Minamata.*

Sullivan, Tom, and Derek Gill. *If You Could See What I Hear.*

Switzer, Ellen. *How Democracy Failed.*

Trudeau, G. B. *The Doonesbury Chronicles.*

Vonnegut, Mark. *The Eden Express.*

Wersba, Barbara. *The Country of the Heart.*

West, Jessamyn. *Massacre at Fall Creek.*

Wood, Bari. *The Killing Gift.*

1976 SELECTIONS

Angelou, Maya. *Singin' and Swingin' and Gettin' Merry Like Christmas.*

Archer, Jeffrey. *Not a Penny More, Not a Penny Less.*

Boston Women's Health Book Collective. *Our Bodies, Ourselves: A Book by and for Women,* 2nd ed.

Bova, Ben. *The Multiple Man: A Novel of Suspense.*

Bradley, Bill. *Life on the Run.*

Bridgers, Sue Ellen. *Home before Dark.*

Claire, Keith. *The Otherwise Girl.*

Clarke, Arthur C. *Imperial Earth.*

Conford, Ellen. *The Alfred G. Graebner Memorial High School Handbook of Rules and Regulations.*

Derby, Pat, and Peter Beagle. *The Lady and Her Tiger.*

Eagan, Andrea Boroff. *Why Am I So Miserable If These Are the Best Years of My Life? A Survival Guide for the Young Woman.*

Fuller, John G. *The Ghost of Flight 401.*

Gordon, Sol, and Roger Conant. *You! The Psychology of Surviving and Enhancing Your Social Life, Love Life, Sex Life, School Life, Home Life, Work Life, Emotional Life, Creative Life, Spiritual Life, Style of Life, Life.*

Guest, Judith. *Ordinary People.*

Guy, Rosa. *Ruby.*

Haley, Alex. *Roots.*

Konecky, Edith. *Allegra Maud Goldman.*

Konigsburg, E. L. *Father's Arcane Daughter.*

Kovic, Ron. *Born on the Fourth of July.*

Le Guin, Ursula K. *Very Far Away from Anywhere Else.*

Levin, Ira. *The Boys from Brazil.*

Lueders, Edward, and Primus St. John, comps. *Zero Makes Me Hungry: A Collection of Poems for Today.*

MacCracken, Mary. *Lovey: A Very Special Child.*

Margolies, Marjorie, and Ruth Gruber. *They Came to Stay.*

Mazer, Norma Fox. *Dear Bill, Remember Me? and Other Stories.*

Meltzer, Milton. *Never to Forget: The Jews of the Holocaust.*

Mojtabai, A. G. *The 400 Eels of Sigmund Freud.*

Moody, Raymond A., Jr. *Life after Life: The Investigation of a Phenomenon—Survival of Bodily Health.*

Patterson, Sarah. *The Distant Summer.*

Peck, Richard. *Are You in the House Alone?*

Pohl, Frederik. *Man Plus.*

Purdy, Anne, and Robert Specht. *Tisha: The Story of a Young Teacher in the Alaska Wilderness.*

Samson, Joan. *The Auctioneer.*

Schulke, Flip, ed. *Martin Luther King, Jr.: A Documentary, Montgomery to Memphis.*

Walsh, M. M. B. *The Four-Colored Hoop.*

Wersba, Barbara. *Tunes for a Small Harmonica.*

Wilhelm, Kate. *Where Late the Sweet Birds Sang.*

Zelazny, Roger. *Doorways in the Sand.*

Zindel, Paul. *Pardon Me, You're Stepping on My Eyeball!*

1977 SELECTIONS

Anson, Jay. *The Amityville Horror.*

Atwood, Ann. *Haiku-Vision in Poetry and Photography.*

Banks, Lynne Reid. *Dark Quartet: The Story of the Brontës.*

Begley, Kathleen A. *Deadline.*

Brancato, Robin F. *Winning.*

Bredes, Don. *Hard Feelings.*

Brooks, Terry. *The Sword of Shannara.*

Cook, Robin. *Coma.*

Cormier, Robert. *I Am the Cheese.*

Dolan, Edward F., Jr. *How to Leave Home—and Make Everybody Like It.*

Elfman, Blossom. *A House for Jonnie O.*

Garfield, Brian. *Recoil.*

Gedge, Pauline. *Child of the Morning.*

Gerani, Gary, and Paul H. Schulman. *Fantastic Television.*

Hall, Elizabeth. *Possible Impossibilities: A Look at Parapsychology.*

Hayes, Billy, and William Hoffer. *Midnight Express.*

Heyman, Anita. *Exit from Home.*

Highwater, Jamake. *Anpao: An American Indian Odyssey.*

Horwitz, Elinor Lander. *Madness, Magic, and Medicine: The Treatment and Mistreatment of the Mentally Ill.*

Houston, James. *Ghost Fox.*

Huygen, Wil, and Rien Poortvliet. *Gnomes.*

Jenner, Bruce, and Phillip Finch. *Decathlon Challenge: Bruce Jenner's Story.*

Koehn, Ilse. *Mischling, Second Degree: My Childhood in Nazi Germany.*

Kopay, David, and Perry Deane Young. *The David Kopay Story: An Extraordinary Self-Revelation.*

Larrick, Nancy, ed. *Crazy to Be Alive in Such a Strange World: Poems about People.*

Lipsyte, Robert. *One Fat Summer.*

Mazer, Harry, and Norma Fox Mazer. *The Solid Gold Kid.*

McCaffrey, Anne. *Dragonsinger.*

McCartney, Linda. *Linda's Pictures: A Collection of Photographs.*

McConnell, Joan. *Ballet as Body Language.*

Miller, Jim, ed. *The Rolling Stone Illustrated History of Rock and Roll.*

Mohr, Nicholasa. *In Nueva York.*

Peck, Richard. *Ghosts I Have Been.*

Pelé, and Robert L. Fish. *My Life and the Beautiful Game: The Autobiography of Pelé.*

Petty, Richard. *King of the Road.*

Powers, John R. *The Unoriginal Sinner and the Ice-Cream God.*

Rather, Dan, and Mickey Herskowitz. *The Camera Never Blinks: Adventures of a TV Journalist.*

Robinson, Spider. *Callahan's Crosstime Saloon.*

Rothenberg, Mira. *Children with Emerald Eyes: Histories of Extraordinary Boys and Girls.*

Ruby, Lois. *Arriving at a Place You've Never Left.*

Schwarzenegger, Arnold, and Douglas Kent Hall. *Arnold: The Education of a Bodybuilder.*

Sharpe, Roger C. *Pinball!*

Sussman, Alan N. *The Rights of Young People: The Basic ACLU Guide to a Young Person's Rights.*

Taylor, David. *Zoo Vet: Adventures of a Wild Animal Doctor.*

Telander, Rick. *Heaven Is a Playground.*

Trevor, Elleston. *The Theta Syndrome.*

Uhlman, Fred. *Reunion.*

Wilkinson, Brenda. *Ludell and Willie.*

Zindel, Paul. *Confessions of a Teenage Baboon.*

1978 SELECTIONS

Adoff, Arnold, ed. *Celebrations: A New Anthology of Black American Poetry.*

Arrick, Fran. *Steffie Can't Come Out to Play.*

Ash, Brian, ed. *The Visual Encyclopedia of Science Fiction.*

Blankfort, Michael. *Take the A Train.*

Burnford, Sheila. *Bel Ria.*

Campbell, R. Wright. *Where Pigeons Go to Die.*

Curtis, Edward S. *The Girl Who Married a Ghost, and Other Tales from the North American Indian.*

de Larrabeiti, Michael. *The Borribles.*

Duncan, Lois. *Killing Mr. Griffin.*

Durán, Cheli, ed. *The Yellow Canary Whose Eye Is So Black.*

Elder, Lauren, and Shirley Streshinsky. *And I Alone Survived.*

Francke, Linda Bird. *The Ambivalence of Abortion.*

Fuller, John G. *The Poison That Fell from the Sky.*

Glass, Frankcina. *Marvin and Tige.*

Guy, Rosa. *Edith Jackson.*

Hamilton, Eleanor. *Sex with Love: A Guide for Young People.*

Hautzig, Deborah. *Hey, Dollface.*

Hayes, Kent, and Alex Lazzarino. *Broken Promise.*

Holliday, Laurel, ed. *Heart Songs: The Intimate Diaries of Young Girls.*

Ives, John. *Fear in a Handful of Dust.*

Jones, Adrienne. *The Hawks of Chelney.*

Kelly, Gary F. *Learning about Sex: The Contemporary Guide for Young Adults.*

Kerr, M. E. *Gentlehands.*

King, Stephen. *Night Shift.*

Leekley, Sheryle, and John Leekley. *Moments: The Pulitzer Prize Photographs.*

LeFlore, Ron, and Jim Hawkins. *Breakout: From Prison to the Big Leagues.*

Leitner, Isabella. *Fragments of Isabella: A Memoir of Auschwitz.*

Levenkron, Steven. *The Best Little Girl in the World.*

London, Mel. *Getting into Film.*

Mazer, Harry. *The War on Villa Street.*

McFarlane, Milton C. *Cudjoe of Jamaica: Pioneer for Black Freedom in the New World.*

McIntyre, Vonda N. *Dreamsnake.*

McKinley, Robin. *Beauty: A Retelling of the Story of Beauty and the Beast.*

Messing, Shep, and David Hirshey. *The Education of an American Soccer Player.*

Meyer, Carolyn. *C.C. Poindexter.*

Nabokov, Peter, ed. *Native American Testimony: An Anthology of Indian and White Relations; First Encounter to Dispossession.*

Peck, Richard. *Father Figure.*

Saleh, Dennis. *Rock Art: The Golden Age of Record Album Covers.*

Scoppettone, Sandra. *Happy Endings Are All Alike.*

Smith, Martin Cruz. *Nightwing.*

Szabo, Joseph. *Almost Grown.*

Trudeau, G. B. *Doonesbury's Greatest Hits.*

Westall, Robert. *The Wind Eye.*

Wetherby, Terry, ed. *Conversations: Working Women Talk about Doing a "Man's Job."*

1979 SELECTIONS

Bachman, Richard. *The Long Walk.*

Bridgers, Sue Ellen. *All Together Now.*

Comfort, Alex, and Jane Comfort. *Facts of Love: Living, Loving, and Growing Up.*

Cormier, Robert. *After the First Death*.

Craig, John. *Chappie and Me*.

Culin, Charlotte. *Cages of Glass, Flowers of Time*.

Davis, Terry. *Vision Quest*.

Dickinson, Peter. *Tulku*.

Dickinson, Peter, and Wayne Anderson. *The Flight of Dragons*.

Forman, James D. *A Ballad for Hogskin Hill*.

Girion, Barbara. *A Tangle of Roots*.

Guy, Rosa. *The Disappearance*.

Hanckel, Frances, and John Cunningham. *A Way of Love, a Way of Life: A Young Person's Introduction to What It Means to Be Gay*.

Hartman, David, and Bernard Asbell. *White Coat, White Cane*.

Helms, Tom. *Against All Odds*.

Hinton, S. E. *Tex*.

Ipswitch, Elaine. *Scott Was Here*.

Jenkins, Peter. *A Walk across America*.

Kaplan, Helen Singer. *Making Sense of Sex: The New Facts about Sex and Love for Young People*.

Keane, John. *Sherlock Bones, Tracer of Missing Pets*.

Leffland, Ella. *Rumors of Peace*.

LeRoy, Gen. *Cold Feet*.

Macaulay, David. *Motel of the Mysteries*.

Marsh, Dave. *Born to Run: The Bruce Springsteen Story*.

Mazer, Harry. *The Last Mission*.

Mazer, Norma Fox. *Up in Seth's Room: A Love Story*.

Meyer, Carolyn. *The Center: From a Troubled Past to a New Life*.

Myers, Walter Dean. *The Young Landlords*.

Nicol, C. W. *The White Shaman*.

Pascal, Francine. *My First Love and Other Disasters*.

Peyton, K. M. *Prove Yourself a Hero*.

Reed, Kit. *The Ballad of T. Rantula*.

Sandler, Martin W. *The Story of American Photography: An Illustrated History for Young People*.

Say, Allen. *The Ink-Keeper's Apprentice*.

Sebestyen, Ouida. *Words by Heart*.

Seed, Suzanne. *Fine Trades*.

Southerland, Ellease. *Let the Lion Eat Straw*.

Summers, Ian, ed. *Tomorrow and Beyond: Masterpieces of Science Fiction Art*.

Thompson, Estelle. *Hunter in the Dark*.

Torchia, Joseph. *The Kryptonite Kid*.

Van Leeuwen, Jean. *Seems Like This Road Goes on Forever*.

Vonnegut, Kurt. *Jailbird*.

Westall, Robert. *The Devil on the Road*.

Wharton, William. *Birdy*.

Wibbelsman, Charles, and Kathy McCoy. *The Teenage Body Book*.

Winthrop, Elizabeth. *Knock, Knock, Who's There?*

1980 SELECTIONS

Adams, Douglas. *The Hitchhiker's Guide to the Galaxy*.

Auel, Jean M. *The Clan of the Cave Bear*.

Bach, Alice. *Waiting for Johnny Miracle*.

Barlowe, Wayne Douglas, and Ian Summers. *Barlowe's Guide to Extraterrestrials*.

Bode, Janet. *Kids Having Kids: The Unwed Teenage Parent*.

Bogle, Donald. *Brown Sugar: Eighty Years of America's Black Female Superstars*.

Boissard, Janice. *A Matter of Feeling*.

Bradshaw, Gillian. *Hawk of May*.

Brancato, Robin F. *Come Alive at 505*.

Brown, Dee. *Creek Mary's Blood*.

Brown, Michael H. *Laying Waste: The Poisoning of America by Toxic Chemicals*.

Butterworth, W. E. *Leroy and the Old Man*.

Calvert, Patricia. *The Snowbird*.

Cohen, Barbara. *Unicorns in the Rain*.

Curtis, Patricia. *Animal Rights: Stories of People Who Defend the Rights of Animals*.

De Veaux, Alexis. *Don't Explain: A Song of Billie Holiday*.

Due, Linnea A. *High and Outside*.

Garfield, Brian. *The Paladin*.

Hall, Lynn. *Leaving*.

Haugaard, Erik Christian. *Chase Me, Catch Nobody!*

Hayden, Torey L. *One Child*.

Hogan, William. *The Quartzsite Trip*.

King, Stephen. *Firestarter*.

Laure, Jason, and Ettagale Laure. *South Africa: Coming of Age under Apartheid*.

Le Guin, Ursula K. *The Beginning Place*.

Lee, Mildred. *The People Therein*.

MacLeish, Roderick. *The First Book of Eppe: An American Romance*.

Maiorano, Robert. *Worlds Apart: The Autobiography of a Dancer from Brooklyn*.

Matthew, Christopher. *The Long-Haired Boy*.

Miller, Frances A. *The Truth Trap*.

Oneal, Zibby. *The Language of Goldfish*.

Paterson, Katherine. *Jacob Have I Loved*.

Pfeffer, Susan Beth. *About David*.

Prince, Alison. *The Turkey's Nest.*

Prochnik, Leon. *Endings: Death, Glorious and Otherwise, as Faced by Ten Outstanding Figures of Our Time.*

Sagan, Carl. *Cosmos.*

Sallis, Susan. *Only Love.*

Sebestyen, Ouida. *Far from Home.*

Shreve, Susan. *Masquerade.*

Silverberg, Robert. *Lord Valentine's Castle.*

Spielman, Ed. *The Mighty Atom: The Life and Times of Joseph L. Greenstein.*

Terkel, Studs. *American Dreams, Lost and Found.*

Thomas, Kurt, and Kent Hannon. *Kurt Thomas on Gymnastics.*

Webb, Sheyann, and Rachel West Nelson. *Selma, Lord, Selma: Girlhood Memories of the Civil-Rights Days.*

Wells, Rosemary. *When No One Was Looking.*

Wolfe, Tom. *The Right Stuff.*

Zindel, Paul. *The Pigman's Legacy.*

1981 SELECTIONS

Alexander, Lloyd. *Westmark.*

Bauer, Steven. *Satyrday: A Fable.*

Bell, Ruth. *Changing Bodies, Changing Lives: A Book for Teens on Sex and Relationships.*

Blume, Judy. *Tiger Eyes.*

Booher, Dianna Daniels. *Rape: What Would You Do If . . . ?*

Bridgers, Sue Ellen. *Notes for Another Life.*

Bykov, Vasil. *Pack of Wolves.*

Chester, Deborah. *The Sign of the Owl.*

Childress, Alice. *Rainbow Jordan.*

Dolan, Edward F., Jr. *Adolf Hitler, a Portrait in Tyranny.*

Duncan, Lois. *Stranger with My Face.*

Eckert, Allan W. *Song of the Wild.*

Grace, Fran. *Branigan's Dog.*

Guy, David. *Football Dreams.*

Hentoff, Nat. *Does This School Have Capital Punishment?*

Herring, Robert. *Hub.*

Hersh, Gizelle, and Peggy Mann. *"Gizelle, Save the Children!"*

Hoover, H. M. *Another Heaven, Another Earth.*

Hughes, Monica. *The Keeper of the Isis Light.*

Jacobs, Anita. *Where Has Deedie Wooster Been All These Years?*

Jaffe, Rona. *Mazes and Monsters.*

Janeczko, Paul B., ed. *Don't Forget to Fly: A Cycle of Modern Poems.*

Jones, Diana Wynne. *The Homeward Bounders.*

Kerr, M. E. *Little Little.*

Knowles, John. *Peace Breaks Out.*

Koehn, Ilse. *Tilla.*

Krementz, Jill. *How It Feels When a Parent Dies.*

Kullman, Harry. *The Battle Horse.*

Lawson, Don. *The United States in the Vietnam War.*

Levoy, Myron. *A Shadow Like a Leopard.*

Marzollo, Jean. *Halfway down Paddy Lane.*

Mayhar, Ardath. *Soul-Singer of Tyrnos.*

Mazer, Harry. *I Love You, Stupid!*

Murphy, Barbara Beasley, and Judie Wolkoff. *Ace Hits the Big Time.*

Myers, Walter Dean. *Hoops.*

———. *The Legend of Tarik.*

Namioka, Lensey. *Village of the Vampire Cat.*

Peck, Richard. *Close Enough to Touch.*

Petersen, P. J. *Would You Settle for Improbable?*

Reader, Dennis J. *Coming Back Alive.*

Santoli, Al, ed. *Everything We Had: An Oral History of the Vietnam War.*

Senn, Steve. *A Circle in the Sea.*

Sheldon, Mary. *Perhaps I'll Dream of Darkness.*

Skurzynski, Gloria. *Manwolf.*

Snyder, Zilpha Keatley. *A Fabulous Creature.*

Strasser, Todd. *Friends till the End.*

Swanson, Walter S. J. *Deepwood.*

Taylor, Mildred D. *Let the Circle Be Unbroken.*

Wallin, Luke. *The Redneck Poacher's Son.*

Yolen, Jane. *Gift of Sarah Barker.*

1982 SELECTIONS

Alexander, Lloyd. *The Kestrel.*

Banks, Lynne Reid. *The Writing on the Wall.*

Bradley, Marion Zimmer. *Hawkmistress!*

Brancato, Robin F. *Sweet Bells Jangled Out of Tune.*

Butterworth, Emma Macalik. *As the Waltz Was Ending.*

Clapp, Patricia. *Witches' Children: A Story of Salem.*

Cohen, Barbara, and Bahija Lovejoy. *Seven Daughters and Seven Sons.*

Davis, Daniel S. *Behind Barbed Wire: The Imprisonment of Japanese Americans during World War II.*

Dragonwagon, Crescent, and Paul Zindel. *To Take a Dare.*

Duncan, Lois. *Chapters: My Growth as a Writer.*

Epstein, Sam, and Beryl Epstein. *Kids in Court: The ACLU Defends Their Rights.*

Ford, Richard. *Quest for the Faradawn.*

Garden, Nancy. *Annie on My Mind.*

Girion, Barbara. *A Handful of Stars.*

Glenn, Mel. *Class Dismissed! High School Poems.*

Goldston, Robert. *Sinister Touches: The Secret War against Hitler.*

Hamilton, Virginia. *Sweet Whispers, Brother Rush.*

Hollman, Peter. *The Auschwitz Album. A Book Based upon an Album Discovered by a Concentration Camp Survivor, Lili Meier.*

Irwin, Hadley. *What about Grandma?*

Kazimiroff, Theodore L. *The Last Algonquin.*

Lawrence, Louise. *Calling B for Butterfly.*

Lehrman, Robert. *Juggling.*

Lester, Julius. *This Strange New Feeling.*

Llywelyn, Morgan. *The Horse Goddess.*

Lynn, Elizabeth A. *Sardonyx Net.*

Magorian, Michelle. *Good Night, Mr. Tom.*

Magubane, Peter. *Black Child.*

McKinley, Robin. *The Blue Sword.*

Murphy, Jim. *Death Run.*

Naylor, Phyllis Reynolds. *A String of Chances.*

Oneal, Zibby. *A Formal Feeling.*

Park, Ruth. *Playing Beatie Bow.*

Petersen, P. J. *Nobody Else Can Walk It for You.*

Pierce, Meredith Ann. *The Dark-angel.*

Riley, Jocelyn. *Only My Mouth Is Smiling.*

Robeson, Susan. *The Whole World in His Hands: A Pictorial Biography of Paul Robeson.*

Schell, Jonathan. *The Fate of the Earth.*

Searls, Hank. *Sounding.*

Sebestyen, Ouida. *IOU's.*

Simon, Nissa. *Don't Worry, You're Normal: A Teenager's Guide to Self-Health.*

Strasser, Todd. *Rock 'n' Roll Nights.*

Terry, Douglas. *The Last Texas Hero.*

Thomas, Joyce Carol. *Marked by Fire.*

Vinge, Joan D. *Psion.*

Voigt, Cynthia. *Tell Me If the Lovers Are Losers.*

Wersba, Barbara. *The Carnival in My Mind.*

Wharton, William. *A Midnight Clear.*

Yolen, Jane. *Dragon's Blood.*

1983 SELECTIONS

Adler, C. S. *The Shell Lady's Daughter.*

Arrick, Fran. *God's Radar.*

Asimov, Isaac, et al., eds. *Creations: The Quest for Origins in Story and Science.*

Bell, Clare. *Ratha's Creature.*

Boulle, Pierre. *The Whale of the Victoria Cross.*

Briggs, Raymond. *When the Wind Blows.*

Chambers, Aidan. *Dance on My Grave: A Life and Death in Four Parts.*

Cormier, Robert. *The Bumblebee Flies Anyway.*

Crutcher, Chris. *Running Loose.*

Faber, Doris. *Love and Rivalry: Three Exceptional Pairs of Sisters.*

Ferry, Charles. *Raspberry One.*

Fretz, Sada. *Going Vegetarian: A Guide for Teen-agers.*

Gaan, Margaret. *Little Sister.*

Gaines, Ernest J. *A Gathering of Old Men.*

Geras, Adele. *Voyage.*

Golden, Frederic. *The Trembling Earth: Probing and Predicting Quakes.*

Goldman, Peter, et al. *Charlie Company: What Vietnam Did to Us.*

Gordon, Suzanne. *Off Balance: The Real World of Ballet.*

Greenberg, Joanne. *The Far Side of Victory.*

Hamilton, Virginia. *The Magical Adventures of Pretty Pearl.*

Hayden, Torey L. *Murphy's Boy.*

Heidish, Marcy. *The Secret Annie Oakley.*

Holman, Felice. *The Wild Children.*

Hughes, Monica. *Hunter in the Dark.*

Janeczko, Paul B., ed. *Poetspeak: In Their Work, about Their Work.*

Kerr, M. E. *Me, Me, Me, Me, Me: Not a Novel.*

Korschunow, Irina. *A Night in Distant Motion.*

Krementz, Jill. *How It Feels to Be Adopted.*

Lasky, Kathryn. *Beyond the Divide.*

Lee, Tanith. *Red as Blood, or Tales from the Sisters Grimmer.*

Liang, Heng, and Judith Shapiro. *Son of the Revolution.*

Madaras, Lynda, and Area Madaras. *What's Happening to My Body? A Growing Up Guide for Mothers and Daughters.*

Mason, Robert. *Chickenhawk.*

Mazer, Norma Fox. *Someone to Love.*

McGuire, Paula. *It Won't Happen to Me: Teenagers Talk about Pregnancy.*

Newton, Suzanne. *I Will Call It Georgie's Blues.*

Nicholls, Peter, ed. *The Science in Science Fiction.*

Page, Tim. *NAM.*

Paulsen, Gary. *Dancing Carl.*

Pollack, Dale. *Skywalking: The Life and Films of George Lucas.*

Reese, Lyn, et al., eds. *I'm on My Way Running: Women Speak on Coming of Age.*

Richards, Arlene Kramer, and Irene Willis. *What to Do If You or Someone You Know Is under 18 and Pregnant.*

Santiago, Danny. *Famous All Over Town.*

Sargent, Pamela. *Earthseed.*

Severin, Tim. *The Sindbad Voyage.*

Singer, Marilyn. *The Course of True Love Never Did Run Smooth.*

Skurzynski, Gloria. *The Tempering.*

Slepian, Jan. *The Night of the Bozos.*

Smith, Robert Kimmel. *Jane's House.*

Smith, Rukshana. *Sumitra's Story.*

Speare, Elizabeth George. *The Sign of the Beaver.*

Steinem, Gloria. *Outrageous Acts and Everyday Rebellions.*

Sutcliff, Rosemary. *The Road to Camlann.*

Tevis, Walter. *The Queen's Gambit.*

Thomas, Lewis. *The Youngest Science: Notes of a Medicine Watcher.*

Trull, Patti. *On with My Life.*

Ure, Jean. *See You Thursday.*

Van Devanter, Lynda, and Christopher Morgan. *Home before Morning: The Story of an Army Nurse in Vietnam.*

Voigt, Cynthia. *A Solitary Blue.*

Von Canon, Claudia. *The Inheritance.*

Wilcox, Fred A. *Waiting for an Army to Die: The Tragedy of Agent Orange.*

Willey, Margaret. *The Bigger Book of Lydia.*

1984 SELECTIONS

Abercrombie, Barbara. *Run for Your Life.*

Alexander, Lloyd. *The Beggar Queen.*

Anthony, Piers. *On a Pale Horse.*

Ashabranner, Brent. *To Live in Two Worlds: American Indian Youth Today.*

Avi. *The Fighting Ground.*

Bond, Nancy. *A Place to Come Back To.*

Bunting, Eve. *If I Asked You, Would You Stay?*

Burch, Jennings Michael. *They Cage the Animals at Night.*

Carter, Alden R. *Growing Season.*

Conover, Ted. *Rolling Nowhere.*

Crichton, Michael. *Electronic Life: How to Think about Computers.*

Dear, William. *Dungeon Master: The Disappearance of James Dallas Egbert III.*

Durkin, Barbara Wernecke. *Oh, You Dundalk Girls, Can't You Dance the Polka?*

Durrell, Gerald, and Lee Durrell. *The Amateur Naturalist.*

Fox, Paula. *One-Eyed Cat.*

Gale, Jay. *A Young Man's Guide to Sex.*

Gallo, Donald R., ed. *Sixteen: Short Stories by Outstanding Writers for Young Adults.*

Godden, Rumer. *Thursday's Children.*

Greenberg, Jan. *No Dragons to Slay.*

Hall, Lynn. *Uphill All the Way.*

Hamilton, Virginia. *A Little Love.*

Harris, Rosemary. *Zed.*

Highwater, Jamake. *Legend Days.*

Hirshey, Gerri. *Nowhere to Run: The Story of Soul Music.*

Janeczko, Paul B., ed. *Strings: A Gathering of Family Poems.*

Jones, Diana Wynne. *Archer's Goon.*

Kohner, Hanna, and Walter Kohner. *Hanna and Walter: A Love Story.*

Kurtis, Bill. *Bill Kurtis on Assignment.*

Lasky, Kathryn. *Prank.*

MacKinnon, Bernie. *The Meantime.*

Magorian, Michelle. *Back Home.*

Mahy, Margaret. *The Changeover: A Supernatural Romance.*

Manchester, William. *One Brief Shining Moment: Remembering Kennedy.*

Mazer, Norma Fox. *Downtown.*

McCullough, Frances, ed. *Love Is Like the Lion's Tooth: An Anthology of Love Poems.*

Montalbano, William D., and Carl Hiaasen. *A Death in China.*

Paton Walsh, Jill. *A Parcel of Patterns.*

Paulsen, Gary. *Tracker.*

Sachs, Marilyn. *The Fat Girl.*

Schrier, Eric W., and William F. Allman, eds. *Newton at the Bat: The Science in Sports.*

Simon, Neil. *Brighton Beach Memoirs.*

Sleator, William. *Interstellar Pig.*

Southall, Ivan. *The Long Night Watch.*

Sterling, Dorothy, ed. *We Are Your Sisters: Black Women in the Nineteenth Century.*

Sweeney, Joyce. *Center Line.*

Terkel, Studs. *"The Good War": An Oral History of World War Two.*

Terry, Wallace, ed. *Bloods: An Oral History of the Vietnam War by Black Veterans.*

Thompson, Joyce. *Conscience Place.*

Tiburzi, Bonnie. *Takeoff! The Story of America's First Woman Pilot for a Major Airline.*

Wain, John. *The Free Zone Starts Here.*

Walker, Alice. *In Search of Our Mothers' Gardens: Womanist Prose.*

Westall, Robert. *Futuretrack 5.*

Yolen, Jane. *Heart's Blood.*

1985 SELECTIONS

Angell, Judie. *One-Way to Ansonia.*

Ballard, J. G. *Empire of the Sun.*

Bridgers, Sue Ellen. *Sara Will.*

Brin, David. *The Postman.*

Brooks, Bruce. *The Moves Make the Man.*

Burchard, Sue. *The Statue of Liberty: Birth to Rebirth.*

Burns, Olive Ann. *Cold Sassy Tree.*

Card, Orson Scott. *Ender's Game.*

Carter, Alden R. *Wart, Son of Toad.*

Conrad, Pam. *Prairie Songs.*

Couper, Heather, and David Pelham. *The Universe: A Three-Dimensional Study.*

Cross, Gillian. *On the Edge.*

Dahl, Roald. *Boy: Tales of Childhood.*

Dickson, Margaret. *Maddy's Song.*

Edelman, Bernard, ed. *Dear America: Letters Home from Vietnam.*

Edmonds, Walter D. *The South African Quirt.*

Ferris, Timothy, and Carolyn Zecca. *Spaceshots: The Beauty of Nature beyond Earth.*

Foster, Rory C. *Dr. Wildlife: The Crusade of a Northwoods Veterinarian.*

Gallagher, Hugh Gregory. *FDR's Splendid Deception.*

Greenbaum, Dorothy, and Deidre S. Laiken. *Lovestrong: A Woman Doctor's True Story of Marriage and Medicine.*

Halberstam, David. *The Amateurs.*

Hall, Lynn. *Just One Friend.*

Hermes, Patricia. *A Solitary Secret.*

Highwater, Jamake. *The Ceremony of Innocence.*

Howker, Janni. *Badger on the Barge, and Other Stories.*

Irwin, Hadley. *Abby, My Love.*

Janeczko, Paul B., ed. *Pocket Poems: Selected for a Journey.*

Jones, Douglas C. *Gone the Dreams and Dancing.*

Kerr, M. E. *I Stay near You: 1 Story in 3.*

Kincaid, Jamaica. *Annie John.*

Lawrence, Louise. *Children of the Dust.*

Lisle, Janet Taylor. *Sirens and Spies.*

Mason, Bobbie Ann. *In Country.*

Matsubara, Hisako. *Cranes at Dusk.*

McKinley, Robin. *The Hero and the Crown.*

Meltzer, Milton. *Ain't Gonna Study War No More: The Story of America's Peace Seekers.*

Michaels, Barbara. *Be Buried in the Rain.*

Miller, Jonathan, and David Pelham. *The Facts of Life: Three-Dimensional, Movable Illustrations Show the Development of a Baby from Conception to Birth.*

Nomberg-Przytyk, Sara. *Auschwitz: True Tales from a Grotesque Land.*

North, James. *Freedom Rising.*

Oneal, Zibby. *In Summer Light.*

Palmer, David R. *Emergence.*

Parnall, Peter. *The Daywatchers.*

Paulsen, Gary. *Dogsong.*

Peck, Richard. *Remembering the Good Times.*

Phipson, Joan. *Hit and Run.*

Pierce, Meredith Ann. *The Woman Who Loved Reindeer.*

Rodowsky, Colby. *Julie's Daughter.*

Ryerson, Eric. *When Your Parent Drinks Too Much: A Book for Teenagers.*

Sleator, William. *Singularity.*

Smith, Mary-Ann Tirone. *The Book of Phoebe.*

Stone, Bruce. *Half Nelson, Full Nelson.*

Strieber, Whitley. *Wolf of Shadows.*

Talbert, Marc. *Dead Birds Singing.*

Voigt, Cynthia. *The Runner.*

Willard, Nancy. *Things Invisible to See.*

Wyden, Peter. *Day One: Before Hiroshima and After.*

Yeager, Chuck, and Leo Janos. *Yeager: An Autobiography.*

1986 SELECTIONS

Angelou, Maya. *All God's Children Need Traveling Shoes.*

Appel, Allen. *Time after Time.*

Archer, Jules. *The Incredible Sixties: The Stormy Years That Changed America.*

Arnosky, Jim. *Flies in the Water, Fish in the Air: A Personal Introduction to Fly Fishing.*

Atwood, Margaret. *The Handmaid's Tale.*

Avi. *Wolf Rider: A Tale of Terror.*

Bess, Clayton. *Tracks.*

Blume, Judy. *Letters to Judy: What Your Kids Wish They Could Tell You.*

Bodanis, David. *Secret House: 24 Hours in the Strange and Unexpected World in Which We Spend Our Nights and Days.*

Branscum, Robbie. *The Girl.*

Brooks, Bruce. *Midnight Hour Encores.*

Brooks, Terry. *Magic Kingdom for Sale—Sold!*

Callahan, Steven. *Adrift: Seventy-Six Days Lost at Sea.*

Calvert, Patricia. *Yesterday's Daughter.*

Caras, Roger. *Mara Simba: The African Lion.*

Card, Orson Scott. *Speaker for the Dead.*

Cohen, Susan, and Daniel Cohen. *A Six-Pack and a Fake I.D.: Teens Look at the Drinking Question.*

Collier, James Lincoln. *When the Stars Begin to Fall.*

Cooney, Caroline B. *Don't Blame the Music.*

Crutcher, Chris. *Stotan!*

Dahl, Roald. *Going Solo.*

Dana, Barbara. *Necessary Parties.*

Dann, Patty. *Mermaids.*

Derby, Pat. *Visiting Miss Pierce.*

Fante, John. *1933 Was a Bad Year.*

Fine, Judylaine. *Afraid to Ask: A Book for Families to Share about Cancer.*

Finnegan, William. *Crossing the Line: A Year in the Land of Apartheid.*

Gingher, Marianne. *Bobby Rex's Greatest Hit.*

Greenberg, Joanne. *Simple Gifts.*

Greene, Constance C. *The Love Letters of J. Timothy Owen.*

Grunwald, Lisa. *Summer.*

Guy, David. *Second Brother.*

Hall, Lynn. *The Solitary.*

Hambly, Barbara. *Dragonsbane.*

Hill, Susan. *The Woman in Black.*

Hunter, Mollie. *Cat, Herself.*

Jones, Diana Wynne. *Howl's Moving Castle.*

Kerr, M. E. *Night Kites.*

Koertge, Ron. *Where the Kissing Never Stops.*

Korman, Gordon. *Son of Interflux.*

Lamb, Wendy, ed. *Meeting the Winter Bike Rider, and Other Prize Winning Plays.*

Lasky, Kathryn. *Pageant.*

LeVert, John. *The Flight of the Cassowary.*

Levoy, Myron. *Pictures of Adam.*

Lopez, Barry. *Arctic Dreams: Imagination and Desire in a Northern Landscape.*

Mahy, Margaret. *The Catalogue of the Universe.*

Mandela, Winnie. *Part of My Soul Went with Him.*

Mazer, Harry. *When the Phone Rang.*

Moll, Richard. *The Public Ivys: A Guide to America's Best Public Undergraduate Colleges and Universities.*

Naylor, Phyllis Reynolds. *The Keeper.*

Okimoto, Jean Davies. *Jason's Women.*

Parini, Jay. *Patch Boys.*

Patent, Dorothy Hinshaw. *The Quest for Artificial Intelligence.*

Pei, Lowry. *Family Resemblances.*

Ramati, Alexander. *And the Violins Stopped Playing: A Story of the Gypsy Holocaust.*

Rinaldi, Ann. *Time Enough for Drums.*

Rostkowski, Margaret I. *After the Dancing Days.*

Rylant, Cynthia. *A Fine White Dust.*

Sanders, Scott R. *Bad Man Ballad.*

Spiegelman, Art. *Maus: A Survivor's Tale.*

Sullivan, Jack, ed. *The Penguin Encyclopedia of Horror and the Supernatural.*

Thompson, Julian F. *A Band of Angels.*

Townsend, Sue. *The Adrian Mole Diaries.*

Voigt, Cynthia. *Izzy, Willy-Nilly.*

Wilford, John Noble. *The Riddle of the Dinosaur.*

Willey, Margaret. *Finding David Dolores.*

Wirths, Claudine G., and Mary Bowman-Kruhm. *I Hate School: How to Hang In and When to Drop Out.*

Zerman, Melvyn Bernard. *Taking on the Press: Constitutional Rights in Conflict.*

Zolotow, Charlotte, ed. *Early Sorrow: Ten Stories of Youth.*

1987 SELECTIONS

Allen, Maury. *Jackie Robinson: A Life Remembered.*

Anson, Robert Sam. *Best Intentions: The Education and Killing of Edmund Perry.*

Bacon, Katherine Jay. *Shadow and Light.*

Benedict, Helen. *Safe, Strong, and Streetwise.*

Bosse, Malcolm. *Captives of Time.*

Bradshaw, Gillian. *The Beacon at Alexandria.*

Bridgers, Sue Ellen. *Permanent Connections.*

Bull, Emma. *War for the Oaks.*

Card, Orson Scott. *Seventh Son.*

Carter, Alden R. *Sheila's Dying.*

Carter, Peter. *Bury the Dead.*

Cole, Brock. *The Goats.*

Collins, Max Allan. *The Dark City.*

Conrad, Pam. *What I Did for Roman.*

Cross, Gillian. *Chartbreaker.*

Crutcher, Chris. *The Crazy Horse Electric Game.*

Cullen, Brian. *What Niall Saw.*

Davis, Jenny. *Good-bye and Keep Cold.*

Dolmetsch, Paul, and Gail Mauricette, eds. *Teens Talk about Alcohol and Alcoholism.*

Dorris, Michael. *A Yellow Raft in Blue Water.*

Einstein, Charles, ed. *The Fireside Book of Baseball, 4th ed.*

Feinstein, John. *A Season on the Brink: A Year with Bob Knight and the Indiana Hoosiers.*

Ferris, Jean. *Invincible Summer.*

Fink, Ida. *A Scrap of Time, and Other Stories.*

Freedman, Russell. *Indian Chiefs.*

Gallo, Donald R., ed. *Visions: Nineteen Short Stories by Outstanding Writers for Young Adults.*

Gibbons, Kaye. *Ellen Foster.*

Gies, Miep, and Alison Leslie Gold. *Anne Frank Remembered: The Story of the Woman Who Helped to Hide the Frank Family.*

Gordon, Ruth, ed. *Under All Silences: Shades of Love; An Anthology of Poems.*

Gordon, Sheila. *Waiting for the Rain.*

Hamlin, Liz. *I Remember Valentine.*

Haskins, James. *Black Music in America: A History through Its People.*

Hearne, Betsy. *Love Lines: Poetry in Person.*

Hentoff, Nat. *American Heroes: In and Out of School.*

Howker, Janni. *Isaac Campion.*

Jacques, Brian. *Redwall.*

Janeczko, Paul B., ed. *Going Over to Your Place: Poems for Each Other.*

Johnson, LouAnne. *Making Waves: A Woman in This Man's Navy.*

Kerr, M. E. *Fell.*

Klass, Perri. *A Not Entirely Benign Procedure: Four Years as a Medical Student.*

Klass, Sheila Solomon. *Page Four.*

Kogan, Judith. *Nothing but the Best: The Struggle for Perfection at the Juilliard School.*

Koontz, Dean R. *Watchers.*

Korman, Gordon. *A Semester in the Life of a Garbage Bag.*

Kropp, Lloyd. *Greencastle and the Denizens of the Sacred Crypt.*

Kuklin, Susan. *Reaching for Dreams: A Ballet from Rehearsal to Opening Night.*

Lackey, Mercedes. *Arrows of the Queen.*

Leder, Jane Mersky. *Dead Serious: A Book for Teenagers about Teenage Suicide.*

L'Engle, Madeleine. *Many Waters.*

Levitin, Sonia. *Return.*

Llewellyn, Chris. *Fragments from the Fire: The Triangle Shirtwaist Company Fire of March 25, 1911.*

MacLean, John. *Mac.*

Mahy, Margaret. *The Tricksters.*

Marshall, Kathryn. *In the Combat Zone: An Oral History of American Women in Vietnam, 1966–1975.*

Mazer, Harry. *The Girl of His Dreams.*

Mazer, Norma Fox. *After the Rain.*

McKillip, Patricia A. *Fool's Run.*

Meltzer, Milton, ed. *The American Revolutionaries: A History in Their Own Words, 1750–1800.*

Meyer, Carolyn. *Denny's Tapes.*

———. *Voices of South Africa: Growing Up in a Troubled Land.*

Michelson, Maureen R., ed. *Women and Work: Photographs and Personal Writings.*

Naylor, Phyllis Reynolds. *Unexpected Pleasures.*

———. *The Year of the Gopher.*

Palmer, Laura. *Shrapnel in the Heart: Letters and Remembrances from the Vietnam Veterans Memorial.*

Paulsen, Gary. *The Crossing.*

Peck, Richard. *Princess Ashley.*

Pfeffer, Susan Beth. *The Year without Michael.*

Pullman, Philip. *The Ruby in the Smoke.*

Rendell, Ruth. *Heartstones.*

Salassi, Otto R. *Jimmy D., Sidewinder, and Me.*

Salzman, Mark. *Iron and Silk.*

Shilts, Randy. *And the Band Played On: Politics, People, and the AIDS Epidemic.*

Sleator, William. *The Boy Who Reversed Himself.*

Smith, Mary-Ann Tirone. *Lament for a Silver-Eyed Woman.*

Tapert, Annette, ed. *Lines of Battle: Letters from American Servicemen, 1941–1945.*

Terris, Susan. *Nell's Quilt.*

Voigt, Cynthia. *Sons from Afar.*

Watson, Lyall. *The Dreams of Dragons: Riddles of Natural History.*

Wells, Rosemary. *Through the Hidden Door.*

Williams, Juan. *Eyes on the Prize: America's Civil Rights Years, 1954–1965.*

Woolley, Persia. *Child of the Northern Spring.*

1988 SELECTIONS

Ashabranner, Brent. *Always to Remember: The Story of the Vietnam Veterans Memorial.*

Bova, Ben. *Welcome to Moonbase.*

Brown, Rita Mae. *Starting from Scratch: A Different Kind of Writer's Manual.*

Cable, Mary. *The Blizzard of '88.*

Cagin, Seth, and Philip Dray. *We Are Not Afraid: The Story of Goodman, Schwerner, and Chaney and the Civil Rights Campaign for Mississippi.*

Cleary, Beverly. *A Girl from Yamhill: A Memoir.*

Coman, Carolyn, ed. *Body and Soul: Ten American Women.*

Cormier, Robert. *Fade.*

Deaver, Julie Reece. *Say Goodnight, Gracie.*

Edgerton, Clyde. *The Floatplane Notebooks.*

Feldbaum, Carl B., and Ronald J. Bee. *Looking the Tiger in the Eye: Confronting the Nuclear Threat.*

Flanigan, Sara. *Alice.*

Fleischman, Paul. *Joyful Noise: Poems for Two Voices.*

Freedman, Russell. *Lincoln: A Photobiography.*

Gelman, Rita Golden. *Inside Nicaragua: Young People's Dreams and Fears.*

Giddings, Robert. *The War Poets.*

Gordon, Jacquie. *Give Me One Wish.*

Greenberg, Joanne. *Of Such Small Differences.*

Greene, Marilyn, and Gary Provost. *Finder: The True Story of a Private Investigator.*

Hailey, Kendall. *The Day I Became an Autodidact, and the Advice, Adventures, and Acrimonies That Befell Me Thereafter.*

Hambly, Barbara. *Those Who Hunt the Night.*

Hamilton, Virginia. *Anthony Burns: The Defeat and Triumph of a Fugitive Slave.*

———. *In the Beginning: Creation Stories from Around the World.*

Haskins, James, and Kathleen Benson. *The 60's Reader.*

Hillerman, Tony. *A Thief of Time.*

Hinton, S. E. *Taming the Star Runner.*

Hoffman, Alice. *At Risk.*

Hoover, H. M. *The Dawn Palace: The Story of Medea.*

Hotze, Sollace. *A Circle Unbroken.*

Janeczko, Paul B., ed. *The Music of What Happens: Poems That Tell Stories.*

Kennedy, William P. *Toy Soldiers.*

Kingsolver, Barbara. *The Bean Trees.*

Knudson, R. R., and May Swenson, eds. *American Sports Poems.*

Koertge, Ron. *The Arizona Kid.*

Komunyakaa, Yusef. *Dien Cai Dau.*

Kozol, Jonathan. *Rachel and Her Children: Homeless Families in America.*

Langone, John. *AIDS: The Facts.*

Lopes, Sal, ed. *The Wall: Images and Offerings from the Vietnam Veterans Memorial.*

Mackay, Donald A. *The Building of Manhattan.*

Madaras, Lynda. *Lynda Madaras Talks to Teens about AIDS: An Essential Guide for Parents, Teachers, and Young People.*

Mahy, Margaret. *Memory.*

Mazer, Norma Fox. *Silver.*

McKinley, Robin. *The Outlaws of Sherwood.*

Meltzer, Milton. *Rescue: The Story of How Gentiles Saved Jews in the Holocaust.*

Mills, Judie. *John F. Kennedy.*

Morrison, Lillian, ed. *Rhythm Road: Poems to Move To.*

Myers, Walter Dean. *Fallen Angels.*

———. *Scorpions.*

Ngor, Haing, and Roger Warner. *A Cambodian Odyssey.*

Noonan, Michael. *McKenzie's Boots.*

Paulsen, Gary. *The Island.*

Pringle, Terry. *The Preacher's Boy.*

Pullman, Philip. *Shadow in the North.*

Riddles, Libby, and Tim Jones. *Race across Alaska: First Woman to Win the Iditarod Tells Her Story.*

Rinaldi, Ann. *The Last Silk Dress.*

Ritter, Lawrence S. *The Babe: A Life in Pictures.*

Rochman, Hazel, ed. *Somehow Tenderness Survives: Stories of Southern Africa.*

Rogasky, Barbara. *Smoke and Ashes: The Story of the Holocaust.*

Ruskin, Cindy. *The Quilt: Stories from the NAMES Project.*

Rylant, Cynthia. *Kindness.*

Scholl, Hans, and Sophie Scholl. *At the Heart of the White Rose: Letters and Diaries of Hans and Sophie Scholl.*

Severin, Tim. *The Ulysses Voyage: Sea Search for the Odyssey.*

Sleator, William. *Duplicate.*

Tang, Xiyang. *Living Treasures: An Odyssey through China's Extraordinary Nature Reserves.*

Vare, Ethlie Ann, and Greg Ptacek. *Mothers of Invention: From the Bra to the Bomb; Forgotten Women and Their Unforgettable Ideas.*

Willeford, Charles. *I Was Looking for a Street.*

Wolff, Virginia Euwer. *Probably Still Nick Swansen.*

Wyss, Thelma Hatch. *Here at the Scenic-Vu Motel.*

1990 SELECTIONS

Amos, James. *The Memorial: A Novel of the Vietnam War.*

Anderson, Joan, and George Ancona. *The American Family Farm.*

Andronik, Catherine M. *Quest for a King: Searching for the Real King Arthur.*

Armor, John, and Peter Wright. *Manzanar.*

Banfield, Susan. *The Rights of Man, The Reign of Terror: The Story of the French Revolution.*

Block, Francesca Lia. *Weetzie Bat.*

Bode, Janet. *New Kids on the Block: Oral Histories of Immigrant Teens.*

Brooks, Bruce. *No Kidding.*

———. *On the Wing: The Life of Birds; From Feathers to Flight.*

Busselle, Rebecca. *Bathing Ugly.*

Carson, Jo. *Stories I Ain't Told Nobody Yet: Selections from the People Pieces.*

Carter, Alden R. *Up Country.*

Childress, Mark. *V for Victor.*

Cohen, Susan, and Daniel Cohen. *When Someone You Know Is Gay.*

Cole, Brock. *Celine.*

Conrad, Pam. *My Daniel.*

Conway, Jill Ker. *The Road from Coorain.*

Crew, Linda. *Children of the River.*

Crutcher, Chris. *Chinese Handcuffs.*

Davis, Lindsey. *The Silver Pigs.*

Deuker, Carl. *On the Devil's Court.*

Dickinson, Peter. *Eva.*

Duder, Tessa. *In Lane Three, Alex Archer.*

Duncan, Lois. *Don't Look Behind You.*

Grant, Cynthia D. *Phoenix Rising, or How to Survive Your Life.*

Green, Connie Jordan. *The War at Home.*

Hayslip, Le Ly, and Jay Wurts. *When Heaven and Earth Changed Places: A Vietnamese Woman's Journey from War to Peace.*

Helprin, Mark. *Swan Lake.*

Hobbs, Will. *Bearstone.*

Hodges, Margaret. *Making a Difference: The Story of an American Family.*

Homes, A. M. *Jack.*

Horner, John R., and James Gorman. *Digging Dinosaurs.*

Hudson, Jan. *Sweetgrass.*

Janeczko, Paul B. *Brickyard Summer: Poems.*

Klass, David. *Wrestling with Honor.*

Klein, Norma. *No More Saturday Nights.*

Krementz, Jill. *How It Feels to Fight for Your Life.*

Kuklin, Susan. *Fighting Back: What Some People Are Doing about AIDS.*

Laird, Elizabeth. *Loving Ben.*

Lanker, Brian. *I Dream a World: Portraits of Black Women Who Changed America.*

Levitin, Sonia. *Silver Days.*

Macaulay, David. *The Way Things Work.*

Maguire, Gregory. *I Feel Like the Morning Star.*

Marsden, John. *So Much to Tell You.*

McCullough, Frances, ed. *Earth, Air, Fire, and Water: Poems.*

McKibben, Bill. *The End of Nature.*

Meltzer, Milton. *Benjamin Franklin: The New American.*

——, ed. *Voices from the Civil War: A Documentary History of the Great American Conflict.*

Mickle, Shelley Fraser. *The Queen of October.*

Miller, Jim Wayne. *Newfound.*

Moeri, Louise. *The Forty-third War.*

Monk, Lorraine. *Photographs That Changed the World: The Camera as Witness, the Photograph as Evidence.*

Murphy, Pat. *The City, Not Long After.*

Murrow, Liza Ketchum. *Fire in the Heart.*

Namioka, Lensey. *Island of Ogres.*

Naughton, Jim. *My Brother Stealing Second.*

Nelson, Theresa. *And One for All.*

Newth, Mette. *The Abduction.*

Norman, David, and Angela Milner. *Dinosaur.*

Paulsen, Gary. *The Voyage of the Frog.*

——. *The Winter Room.*

Pevsner, Stella. *How Could You Do It, Diane?*

Pinkwater, Jill. *Buffalo Brenda.*

Pringle, Terry. *A Fine Time to Leave Me.*

Rhodes, Richard. *Farm: A Year in the Life of an American Farmer.*

Saul, John. *Creature.*

Shannon, George. *Unlived Affections.*

Sieruta, Peter D. *Heartbeats, and Other Stories.*

Smith, K. *Skeeter.*

Staples, Suzanne Fisher. *Shabanu: Daughter of the Wind.*

Tan, Amy. *The Joy Luck Club.*

Taylor, Theodore. *Sniper.*

Turnley, David C., and Alan Cowell. *Why Are They Weeping? South Africans under Apartheid.*

Van Raven, Pieter. *The Great Man's Secret.*

White, Ellen Emerson. *Long Live the Queen.*

Wilson, David Henry. *The Coachman Rat.*

Wilson, F. Paul. *Dydeetown World.*

Wilson, Robert Charles. *Gypsies.*

Wolff, Tobias. *This Boy's Life: A Memoir.*

Zindel, Paul. *A Begonia for Miss Applebaum.*

1991 SELECTIONS

Abdul-Jabbar, Kareem, and Mignon McCarthy. *Kareem.*

Agard, John, comp. *Life Doesn't Frighten Me at All.*

Anderson, Scott. *Distant Fires.*

Ansa, Tina McElroy. *Baby of the Family.*

Appel, Allen. *Till the End of Time.*

Avi. *The True Confessions of Charlotte Doyle.*

Baldwin, J., ed. *Whole Earth Ecolog: The Best of Environmental Tools and Ideas.*

Bell, Clare. *Ratha and Thistle-Chaser.*

Bennett, James. *I Can Hear the Mourning Dove.*

Blake, Jeanne. *Risky Times: How to Be AIDS-Smart and Stay Healthy.*

Bode, Janet. *The Voices of Rape.*

Brooks, Polly Schoyer. *Beyond the Myth: The Story of Joan of Arc.*

Cannon, A. E. *The Shadow Brothers.*

Carter, Peter. *Borderlands.*

Caseley, Judith. *Kisses.*

Chestnut, J. L., Jr., and Julia Cass. *Black in Selma: The Uncommon Life of J. L. Chestnut, Jr.*

Chetwin, Grace. *Collidescope.*

Clarke, J. *The Heroic Life of Al Capsella.*

Clements, Bruce. *Tom Loves Anna Loves Tom.*

Crispin, A. C. *Starbridge.*

Cushman, Kathleen, and Montana Miller. *Circus Dreams: The Making of a Circus Artist.*

Doherty, Berlie. *White Peak Farm.*

Donofrio, Beverly. *Riding in Cars with Boys: Confessions of a Bad Girl Who Makes Good.*

Embury, Barbara, and Thomas D. Crouch. *The Dream Is Alive.*

Ferris, Jean. *Across the Grain.*

Feuer, Elizabeth. *Paper Doll.*

Freedman, Russell. *Franklin Delano Roosevelt.*

Freedman, Samuel G. *Small Victories: The Real World of a Teacher, Her Students, and Their High School.*

Friedman, Ina R. *The Other Victims: First-Person Stories of Non-Jews Persecuted by the Nazis.*

Gallo, Donald R., ed. *Speaking for Ourselves: Autobiographical Sketches by Notable Authors of Books for Young Adults.*

Gilmore, Kate. *Enter Three Witches.*

Hall, Barbara. *Dixie Storms.*

Hamanaka, Sheila. *The Journey: Japanese Americans, Racism and Renewal.*

Hamilton, Virginia. *Cousins.*

Harrison, Sue. *Mother Earth, Father Sky.*

Haskins, James. *Black Dance in America: A History through Its People.*

Hendry, Frances Mary. *Quest for a Maid.*

Ho, Minfong. *Rice without Rain.*

Hudson, Jan. *Dawn Rider.*

Human Rights in China. *Children of the Dragon: The Story of Tiananmen Square.*

James, J. Alison. *Sing for a Gentle Rain.*

Janeczko, Paul B., ed. *The Place My Words Are Looking For: What Poets Say About and Through Their Work.*

Jordan, Robert. *The Eye of the World.*

Katz, William Loren. *Breaking the Chains: African-American Slave Resistance.*

Kilworth, Garry. *The Foxes of Firstdark.*

Kisor, Henry. *What's That Pig Outdoors? A Memoir of Deafness.*

Klause, Annette Curtis. *The Silver Kiss.*

Koertge, Ron. *The Boy in the Moon.*

Korman, Gordon. *Losing Joe's Place.*

Larson, Gary. *The PreHistory of The Far Side: A 10th Anniversary Exhibit.*

Lauber, Patricia. *Seeing Earth from Space.*

Levin, Betty. *Brother Moose.*

Lord, Bette Bao. *Legacies: A Chinese Mosaic.*

Martin, Valerie. *Mary Reilly.*

McCorkle, Jill. *Ferris Beach.*

Meltzer, Milton. *Columbus and the World around Him.*

Myers, Walter Dean. *The Mouse Rap.*

Naar, Jon. *Design for a Livable Planet: How You Can Help Clean Up the Environment.*

Naidoo, Beverley. *Chain of Fire.*

Naylor, Phyllis Reynolds. *Send No Blessings.*

O'Brien, Tim. *The Things They Carried.*

Parks, Gordon. *Voices in the Mirror: An Autobiography.*

Paulsen, Gary. *Woodsong.*

Pershall, Mary K. *You Take the High Road.*

Pierce, Meredith Ann. *The Pearl of the Soul of the World.*

Popham, Melinda Worth. *Skywater.*

Pullman, Philip. *The Tiger in the Well.*

Ray, Delia. *A Nation Torn: The Story of How the Civil War Began.*

Rylant, Cynthia. *A Couple of Kooks, and Other Stories about Love.*

———. *Soda Jerk.*

Sanders, Dori. *Clover.*

Schami, Rafik. *A Hand Full of Stars.*

Sleator, William. *Strange Attractors.*

Snyder, Zilpha Keatley. *Libby on Wednesday.*

Soto, Gary. *Baseball in April, and Other Stories.*

Spinelli, Jerry. *Maniac Magee.*

Stoll, Cliff. *The Cuckoo's Egg: Tracking a Spy through the Maze of Computer Espionage.*

Strauss, Gwen. *Trail of Stones.*

Taylor, Mildred D. *The Road to Memphis.*

Van Raven, Pieter. *Pickle and Price.*

Voigt, Cynthia. *On Fortune's Wheel.*

Weiss, Ann E. *Who's to Know? Information, the Media, and Public Awareness.*

Willey, Margaret. *Saving Lenny.*

Woolley, Persia. *Queen of the Summer Stars.*

Wrede, Patricia C. *Dealing with Dragons.*

1992 SELECTIONS

Aaron, Henry, and Lonnie Wheeler. *I Had a Hammer: The Hank Aaron Story.*

Adams, Douglas, and Mark Carwardine. *Last Chance to See.*

Anastos, Phillip, and Chris French. *Illegal: Seeking the American Dream.*

Arter, Jim. *Gruel and Unusual Punishment.*

Avi. *Nothing but the Truth.*

Bing, Leon. *Do or Die.*

Bode, Janet. *Beating the Odds: Stories of Unexpected Achievers.*

Brooks, Bruce. *Predator!*

Buss, Fran Leeper, and Daisy Cubias. *Journey of the Sparrows.*

Cannon, A. E. *Amazing Gracie.*

Cary, Lorene. *Black Ice.*

Choi, Sook Nyul. *Year of Impossible Goodbyes.*

Cooper, J. California. *Family.*

Corman, Avery. *Prized Possessions.*

Cormier, Robert. *We All Fall Down.*

Counter, S. Allen. *North Pole Legacy: Black, White, and Eskimo.*

Crichton, Michael. *Jurassic Park.*

Crutcher, Chris. *Athletic Shorts: Six Short Stories.*

Davis, Jenny. *Checking on the Moon.*

Durham, Michael S. *Powerful Days: The Civil Rights Photography of Charles Moore.*

Fleischman, Paul. *The Borning Room.*

Fluek, Toby Knobel. *Memories of My Life in a Polish Village, 1930–1949.*

Fox, Paula. *Monkey Island.*

Freedman, Russell. *The Wright Brothers: How They Invented the Airplane.*

Fussell, Samuel Wilson. *Muscle: Confessions of an Unlikely Bodybuilder.*

Gaiman, Neil, and Terry Pratchett. *Good Omens: The Nice and Accurate Prophecies of Agnes Nutter, Witch.*

Glenn, Mel. *My Friend's Got This Problem, Mr. Candler: High School Poems.*

Hall, Lynn. *Flying Changes.*

Hathorn, Libby. *Thunderwith.*

Hayden, Torey L. *Ghost Girl: The True Story of a Child in Peril and the Teacher Who Saved Her.*

Hayes, Daniel. *The Trouble with Lemons.*

Henry, Sue. *Murder on the Iditarod Trail.*

Higa, Tomiko. *The Girl with the White Flag: An Inspiring Tale of Love and Courage in War Time.*

Hobbs, Will. *Downriver.*

Honeycutt, Natalie. *Ask Me Something Easy.*

Jones, Diana Wynne. *Castle in the Air.*

Kingsolver, Barbara. *Animal Dreams.*

Kotlowitz, Alex. *There Are No Children Here: The Story of Two Boys Growing Up in the Other America.*

Kuklin, Susan. *What Do I Do Now? Talking about Teenage Pregnancy.*

Lauber, Patricia. *Summer of Fire: Yellowstone 1988.*

Lee, Tanith. *Black Unicorn.*

Lipsyte, Robert. *Brave.*

Lyons, Mary E. *Sorrow's Kitchen: The Life and Folklore of Zora Neale Hurston.*

MacLachlan, Patricia. *Journey.*

McCaffrey, Anne. *Pegasus in Flight.*

McCammon, Robert R. *Boy's Life.*

Montgomery, Sy. *Walking with the Great Apes: Jane Goodall, Dian Fossey, Birute Galdikas.*

Morpurgo, Michael. *Waiting for Anya.*

Murphy, Jim. *The Boys' War: Confederate and Union Soldiers Talk about the Civil War.*

Myers, Walter Dean. *Now Is Your Time! The African-American Struggle for Freedom.*

Orlev, Uri. *The Man from the Other Side.*

Paterson, Katherine. *Lyddie.*

Paulsen, Gary. *The Cookcamp.*

———. *The Monument.*

Plummer, Louise. *My Name Is Sus5an Smith. The 5 Is Silent.*

Rappaport, Doreen. *American Women: Their Lives in Their Words.*

Rinaldi, Ann. *Wolf by the Ears.*

Savage, Georgia. *The House Tibet.*

Shusterman, Neal. *What Daddy Did.*

Spiegelman, Art. *Maus II: A Survivor's Tale; And Here My Troubles Began.*

Spinelli, Jerry. *There's a Girl in My Hammerlock.*

Sullivan, Charles, ed. *Children of Promise: African-American Literature and Art for Young People.*

Tepper, Sheri S. *Beauty.*

Thesman, Jean. *The Rain Catchers.*

Westall, Robert. *The Kingdom by the Sea.*

White, Ryan, and Ann Marie Cunningham. *Ryan White: My Own Story.*

Williams-Garcia, Rita. *Fast Talk on a Slow Track.*

Wisler, G. Clifton. *Red Cap.*

Wolff, Virginia Euwer. *The Mozart Season.*

Yolen, Jane, and Martin H. Greenberg, eds. *Vampires: A Collection of Original Stories.*

1993 SELECTIONS

Armstrong, Jennifer. *Steal Away.*

Arrick, Fran. *What You Don't Know Can Kill You.*

Avi. *Blue Heron.*

Beattie, Owen, and John Geiger. *Buried in Ice.*

Berry, James. *Ajeemah and His Son.*

Block, Francesca Lia. *Cherokee Bat and the Goat Guys.*

Bonner, Cindy. *Lily.*

Brooks, Bruce. *What Hearts.*

Brooks, Martha. *Two Moons in August.*

Bunting, Eve. *Jumping the Nail.*

Campbell, Eric. *The Place of Lions.*

Caseley, Judith. *My Father, the Nutcase.*

Cooney, Caroline B. *Flight #116 Is Down.*

Cooper, Louise. *The Sleep of Stone.*

Cormier, Robert. *Tunes for Bears to Dance To.*

Craig, Kit. *Gone.*

Currie, Elliott. *Dope and Trouble: Portraits of Delinquent Youth.*

Davis, Terry. *If Rock and Roll Were a Machine.*

Dickinson, Peter. *AK.*

Doherty, Berlie. *Dear Nobody.*

Duncan, Lois. *Who Killed My Daughter?*

Edelman, Marian Wright. *The Measure of Our Success: A Letter to My Children and Yours.*

Ferry, Charles. *Binge.*

Ford, Michael Thomas. *100 Questions and Answers about AIDS: A Guide for Young People.*

Forman, James D. *Becca's Story.*

Freedman, Russell. *Indian Winter.*

Garland, Sherry. *Song of the Buffalo Boy.*

Gould, Steven. *Jumper.*

Gravelle, Karen, and Leslie Peterson. *Teenage Fathers.*

Gregory, Kristiana. *Earthquake at Dawn.*

Grisham, John. *The Pelican Brief.*

Gurney, James. *Dinotopia: A Land Apart from Time.*

Guy, Rosa. *The Music of Summer.*

Hall, Barbara. *Fool's Hill.*

Haskins, James. *One More River to Cross: The Stories of Twelve Black Americans.*

Hesse, Karen. *Letters from Rifka.*

Hobbs, Will. *The Big Wander.*

Hoffman, Alice. *Turtle Moon.*

Horrigan, Kevin. *The Right Kind of Heroes: Coach Bob Shannon and the East St. Louis Flyers.*

Hotze, Sollace. *Acquainted with the Night.*

Johnson, Earvin "Magic." *What You Can Do to Avoid AIDS.*

Johnson, Scott. *One of the Boys.*

Jones, Diana Wynne. *A Sudden Wild Magic.*

Kaye, Geraldine. *Someone Else's Baby.*

Kimble, Bo. *For You, Hank: The Story of Hank Gathers and Bo Kimble.*

Kincaid, Nanci. *Crossing Blood.*

Kittredge, Mary. *Teens with AIDS Speak Out.*

Koertge, Ron. *The Harmony Arms.*

Koller, Jackie French. *The Primrose Way.*

Lackey, Mercedes. *The Lark and the Wren.*

Laird, Elizabeth. *Kiss the Dust.*

Lyons, Mary E. *Letters from a Slave Girl: The Story of Harriet Jacobs.*

Magorian, Michelle. *Not a Swan.*

Marlette, Doug. *In Your Face: A Cartoonist at Work.*

McKissack, Patricia C., and Fredrick L. McKissack. *Sojourner Truth: Ain't I a Woman?*

Meyer, Carolyn. *Where the Broken Heart Still Beats: The Story of Cynthia Ann Parker.*

Mowry, Jess. *Way Past Cool.*

Murphy, Jim. *The Long Road to Gettysburg.*

Myers, Walter Dean. *The Righteous Revenge of Artemis Bonner.*

———. *Somewhere in the Darkness.*

Nelson, Theresa. *The Beggars' Ride.*

Parks, Rosa, and Jim Haskins. *Rosa Parks: My Story.*

Paulsen, Gary. *The Haymeadow.*

Pfeffer, Susan Beth. *Family of Strangers.*

Powell, Randy. *Is Kissing a Girl Who Smokes Like Licking an Ashtray?*

Pullman, Philip. *The Broken Bridge.*

Reaver, Chap. *A Little Bit Dead.*

Reidelbach, Maria. *Completely Mad: A History of the Comic Book and Magazine.*

Reiss, Kathryn. *Time Windows.*

Rice, Robert. *The Last Pendragon.*

Rinaldi, Ann. *A Break with Charity: A Story about the Salem Witch Trials.*

Robertson, James I., Jr. *"Civil War!": America Becomes One Nation.*

Rylant, Cynthia. *Missing May.*

Salisbury, Graham. *Blue Skin of the Sea.*

Scieszka, Jon, and Lane Smith. *The Stinky Cheese Man, and Other Fairly Stupid Tales.*

Sherman, Josepha. *Child of Faerie, Child of Earth.*

Simon, Neil. *Lost in Yonkers.*

Steffan, Joseph. *Honor Bound: A Gay American Fights for the Right to Serve His Country.*

Stevermer, Caroline. *River Rats.*

Stoehr, Shelley. *Crosses.*

Taylor, Clark. *The House That Crack Built.*

Taylor, Theodore. *The Weirdo.*

Thesman, Jean. *When the Road Ends.*

Uchida, Yoshiko. *The Invisible Thread.*

Ure, Jean. *Plague.*

Westall, Robert. *Stormsearch.*

———. *Yaxley's Cat.*

White, Ruth. *Weeping Willow.*

Wieler, Diana. *Bad Boy.*

Williams, Michael. *Crocodile Burning.*

Wilson, Budge. *The Leaving, and Other Stories.*

Winton, Tim. *Lockie Leonard, Human Torpedo.*

Woodson, Jacqueline. *Maizon at Blue Hill.*

Wrede, Patricia C. *Searching for Dragons.*

Yolen, Jane. *Briar Rose.*

Zambreno, Mary Frances. *Plague of Sorcerers.*

Zindel, Paul. *The Pigman and Me.*

1994 SELECTIONS

Alcock, Vivien. *Singer to the Sea God.*

Anderson, Rachel. *The Bus People.*

Ashe, Arthur, and Arnold Rampersad. *Days of Grace: A Memoir.*

Atkin, S. Beth. *Voices from the Fields: Children of Migrant Farmworkers Tell Their Stories.*

Berg, Elizabeth. *Durable Goods.*

Block, Francesca Lia. *Missing Angel Juan.*

Blume, Judy. *Here's to You, Rachel Robinson.*

Brandenburg, Jim. *To the Top of the World: Adventures with Arctic Wolves.*

Bruchac, Joseph. *Dawn Land.*

Conly, Jane Leslie. *Crazy Lady!*

Cooney, Caroline B. *Whatever Happened to Janie?*

Crutcher, Chris. *Staying Fat for Sarah Byrnes.*

Delany, Sarah, and A. Elizabeth Delany. *Having Our Say: The Delany Sisters' First 100 Years.*

Deuker, Carl. *Heart of a Champion.*

Dickinson, Peter. *A Bone from a Dry Sea.*

Drucker, Olga Levy. *Kindertransport.*

Esquivel, Laura. *Like Water for Chocolate: A Novel in Monthly Installments, with Recipes, Romances, and Home Remedies.*

Feelings, Tom. *Soul Looks Back in Wonder.*

Fleischman, Paul. *Bull Run.*

Freedman, Russell. *Eleanor Roosevelt: A Life of Discovery.*

Gaines, Ernest J. *A Lesson before Dying.*

Garland, Sherry. *Shadow of the Dragon.*

Gee, Maurice. *The Champion.*

Gibbons, Kaye. *Charms for an Easy Life.*

Grant, Cynthia D. *Shadow Man.*

———. *Uncle Vampire.*

Hahn, Mary Downing. *The Wind Blows Backward.*

Haynes, David. *Right by My Side.*

Hobbs, Will. *Beardance.*

Hodge, Merle. *For the Life of Laetitia.*

Isaacson, Philip M. *A Short Walk around the Pyramids and through the World of Art.*

Janeczko, Paul B., ed. *Looking for Your Name: A Collection of Contemporary Poems.*

———. *Stardust Hotel: Poems.*

Johnson, Angela. *Toning the Sweep.*

Jordan, Sherryl. *Winter of Fire.*

Kaysen, Susanna. *Girl, Interrupted.*

LeMieux, A. C. *The TV Guidance Counselor.*

Levine, Ellen. *Freedom's Children: Young Civil Rights Activists Tell Their Own Stories.*

Littlefield, Bill. *Champions: Stories of Ten Remarkable Athletes.*

Lowry, Lois. *The Giver.*

Lynch, Chris. *Shadow Boxer.*

MacLachlan, Patricia. *Baby.*

Macy, Sue. *A Whole New Ball Game: The Story of the All-American Girls Professional Baseball League.*

Mazer, Harry. *Who Is Eddie Leonard?*

Mazer, Norma Fox. *Out of Control.*

McKinley, Robin. *Deerskin.*

Merrick, Monte. *Shelter.*

Meyer, Carolyn. *White Lilacs.*

Mori, Kyoko. *Shizuko's Daughter.*

Myers, Walter Dean. *Malcolm X: By Any Means Necessary.*

Napoli, Donna Jo. *The Magic Circle.*

Paulsen, Gary. *Harris and Me: A Summer Remembered.*

———. *Nightjohn.*

Philbrick, Rodman. *Freak the Mighty.*

Qualey, Marsha. *Revolutions of the Heart.*

Rendell, Ruth. *The Crocodile Bird.*

Reynolds, Marilyn. *Detour for Emmy.*

Rinaldi, Ann. *In My Father's House.*

Roberson, Jennifer. *Lady of the Forest.*

Rochman, Hazel, and Darlene Z. McCampbell, eds. *Who Do You Think You Are? Stories of Friends and Enemies.*

Rol, Ruud van der, and Rian Verhoeven. *Anne Frank, beyond the Diary: A Photographic Remembrance.*

Ruby, Lois. *Miriam's Well.*

Sleator, William. *Oddballs: Stories.*

Smith, Wayne. *Thor.*

Staples, Suzanne Fisher. *Haveli.*

Sutcliff, Rosemary. *Black Ships before Troy: The Story of the Iliad.*

Sweeney, Joyce. *The Tiger Orchard.*

Tamar, Erika. *Fair Game.*

Taylor, Theodore. *Timothy of the Cay.*

Temple, Frances. *Grab Hands and Run.*

Vick, Helen Hughes. *Walker of Time.*

Volavková, Hana, ed. *I Never Saw Another Butterfly: Children's Drawings and Poems from Terezin Concentration Camp, 1942–1944,* 2nd ed.

Walker, Kate. *Peter.*

Watson, Larry. *Montana 1948.*

Weaver, Will. *Striking Out.*

Wittlinger, Ellen. *Lombardo's Law.*

Wolff, Virginia Euwer. *Make Lemonade.*

Yep, Laurence, ed. *American Dragons: Twenty-five Asian American Voices.*

1995 SELECTIONS

Alvarez, Julia. *In the Time of the Butterflies.*

Bachrach, Susan D. *Tell Them We Remember: The Story of the Holocaust.*

Bauer, Marion Dane, ed. *Am I Blue? Coming Out from the Silence.*

Beake, Lesley. *Song of Be.*

Bennett, James. *Dakota Dream.*

Bode, Janet, and Stan Mack. *Heartbreak and Roses: Real-Life Stories of Troubled Love.*

Bonner, Cindy. *Looking after Lily.*

Bosse, Malcolm. *The Examination.*

Brooks, Martha. *Traveling On into the Light, and Other Stories.*

Brown, Mary. *Pigs Don't Fly.*

Bull, Emma. *Finder: A Novel of the Borderlands.*

Butler, Octavia E. *Parable of the Sower.*

Carlson, Lori M., ed. *Cool Salsa: Bilingual Poems on Growing Up Latino in the United States.*

Cooney, Caroline B. *Driver's Ed.*

Coville, Bruce. *Oddly Enough.*

Cushman, Karen. *Catherine, Called Birdy.*

Farmer, Nancy. *The Ear, the Eye, and the Arm.*

Fletcher, Susan. *Flight of the Dragon Kyn.*

Freedman, Russell. *Kids at Work: Lewis Hine and the Crusade against Child Labor.*

French, Albert. *Billy.*

Hambly, Barbara. *Stranger at the Wedding.*

Hayes, Daniel. *No Effect.*

Hesse, Karen. *Phoenix Rising.*

Hite, Sid. *It's Nothing to a Mountain.*

Jones, K. Maurice. *Say It Loud! The Story of Rap Music.*

Jordan, Sherryl. *Wolf-Woman.*

Kerr, M. E. *Deliver Us from Evie.*

Kindl, Patrice. *Owl in Love.*

King, Laurie R. *The Beekeeper's Apprentice, or On the Segregation of the Queen.*

Koebner, Linda. *Zoo Book: The Evolution of Wildlife Conservation Centers.*

Koertge, Ron. *Tiger, Tiger Burning Bright.*

Krisher, Trudy. *Spite Fences.*

Kuklin, Susan. *After a Suicide: Young People Speak Up.*

Lasky, Kathryn. *Beyond the Burning Time.*

Lawlor, Laurie. *Shadow Catcher: The Life and Work of Edward S. Curtis.*

Levitin, Sonia. *Escape from Egypt.*

Lynch, Chris. *Gypsy Davey.*

———. *Iceman.*

Marrin, Albert. *Unconditional Surrender: U. S. Grant and the Civil War.*

Marsden, John. *Letters from the Inside.*

McCall, Nathan. *Makes Me Wanna Holler: A Young Black Man in America.*

Myers, Walter Dean. *The Glory Field.*

Naythons, Matthew. *Sarajevo: A Portrait of the Siege.*

Nelson, Theresa. *Earthshine.*

Nichols, Michael. *The Great Apes: Between Two Worlds.*

O'Donohoe, Nick. *The Magic and the Healing.*

Panzer, Nora, ed. *Celebrate America: In Poetry and Art.*

Paulsen, Gary. *Winterdance: The Fine Madness of Running the Iditarod.*

Porte, Barbara Ann. *Something Terrible Happened.*

Power, Susan. *The Grass Dancer.*

Qualey, Marsha. *Come In from the Cold.*

Rapp, Adam. *Missing the Piano.*

Reuter, Bjarne. *The Boys from St. Petri.*

Reynolds, Marilyn. *Too Soon for Jeff.*

Rivers, Glenn, and Bruce Brooks. *Those Who Love the Game: Glenn "Doc" Rivers on Life in the NBA and Elsewhere.*

Rodowsky, Colby. *Hannah in Between.*

Ross, Stewart. *Shakespeare and Macbeth: The Story behind the Play.*

Roybal, Laura. *Billy.*

Rylant, Cynthia. *Something Permanent.*

Salisbury, Graham. *Under the Blood-Red Sun.*

Schulman, Audrey. *The Cage.*

Shoup, Barbara. *Wish You Were Here.*

Sinclair, April. *Coffee Will Make You Black.*

Springer, Nancy. *Toughing It.*

Stolz, Mary. *Cezanne Pinto: A Memoir.*

Sutton, Roger. *Hearing Us Out: Voices from the Gay and Lesbian Community.*

Sweeney, Joyce. *Shadow.*

Temple, Frances. *The Ramsay Scallop.*

Voigt, Cynthia. *When She Hollers.*

Watkins, Yoko Kawashima. *My Brother, My Sister, and I.*

Wilson, Robert Charles. *Mysterium.*

Wolf, Sylvia. *Focus: Five Women Photographers.*

Woodson, Jacqueline. *I Hadn't Meant to Tell You This.*

1996 SELECTIONS

Adoff, Arnold. *Slow Dance: Heart Break Blues.*

Alder, Elizabeth. *The King's Shadow.*

Ayer, Eleanor H., et al. *Parallel Journeys.*

Banks, Russell. *Rule of the Bone.*

Bauer, Joan. *Thwonk.*

Begay, Shonto. *Navajo: Visions and Voices across the Mesa.*

Bennett, James. *The Squared Circle.*

Blais, Madeleine. *In These Girls, Hope Is a Muscle.*

Block, Francesca Lia. *Baby Be-Bop.*

Boas, Jacob, ed. *We Are Witnesses: Five Diaries of Teenagers Who Died in the Holocaust.*

Bober, Natalie S. *Abigail Adams: Witness to a Revolution.*

Brandenburg, Jim. *An American Safari: Adventures on the North American Prairie.*

Carlson, Lori M., ed. *American Eyes: New Asian-American Short Stories for Young Adults.*

Carter, Alden R. *Between a Rock and a Hard Place.*

Childers, Thomas. *Wings of Morning: The Story of the Last American Bomber Shot Down over Germany in World War II.*

Christiansen, C. B. *I See the Moon.*

Clute, John. *Science Fiction: A Visual Encyclopedia.*

Cofer, Judith Ortiz. *An Island Like You: Stories of the Barrio.*

Colman, Penny. *Rosie the Riveter: Women Working on the Home Front in World War II.*

Cormier, Robert. *In the Middle of the Night.*

Crutcher, Chris. *Ironman.*

Curtis, Christopher Paul. *The Watsons Go to Birmingham—1963.*

Cushman, Karen. *The Midwife's Apprentice.*

D'Aguiar, Fred. *The Longest Memory.*

Denenberg, Barry. *Voices from Vietnam.*

Dijk, Lutz Van. *Damned Strong Love: A True Story of Willi G. and Stefan K.*

Draper, Sharon M. *Tears of a Tiger.*

Feelings, Tom. *The Middle Passage: White Ships/ Black Cargo.*

Feintuch, David. *Midshipman's Hope.*

Ford, Michael Thomas. *The Voices of AIDS: Twelve Unforgettable People Talk about How AIDS Has Changed Their Lives.*

Frank, Anne. *The Diary of a Young Girl: The Definitive Edition.*

Fraustino, Lisa Rowe. *Ash.*

Fremon, Celeste. *Father Greg and the Homeboys: The Extraordinary Journey of Father Greg Boyle and His Work with the Latino Gangs of East L.A.*

Frey, Darcy. *The Last Shot: City Streets, Basketball Dreams.*

Galloway, Priscilla. *Truly Grim Tales.*

Garland, Sherry. *Indio.*

Giblin, James Cross. *When Plague Strikes: The Black Death, Smallpox, AIDS.*

Goldman, E. M. *Getting Lincoln's Goat: An Elliot Armbruster Mystery.*

Gordon, Ruth, ed. *Pierced by a Ray of Sun: Poems about the Times We Feel Alone.*

Grant, Cynthia D. *Mary Wolf.*

Greenberg, Jan, and Sandra Jordan. *The American Eye: Eleven Artists of the Twentieth Century.*

Hamilton, Virginia. *Her Stories: African American Folktales, Fairy Tales, and True Tales.*

Hobbs, Valerie. *How Far Would You Have Gotten If I Hadn't Called You Back?*

Hockenberry, John. *Moving Violations: War Zones, Wheelchairs, and Declarations of Independence.*

Hopkins, Lee Bennett. *Been to Yesterdays: Poems of a Life.*

Hughes, Langston. *The Block: Poems.*

Hurwin, Davida Wills. *A Time for Dancing.*

Laird, Christa. *But Can the Phoenix Sing?*

Lester, Julius. *Othello.*

Lopez, Steve. *Third and Indiana.*

Lynch, Chris. *Slot Machine.*

Marrin, Albert. *Virginia's General: Robert E. Lee and the Civil War.*

Marsden, John. *Tomorrow, When the War Began.*

McCants, William D. *Much Ado about Prom Night.*

McKissack, Patricia C., and Fredrick L. McKissack. *Red-Tail Angels: The Story of the Tuskegee Airmen of World War II.*

Meyer, Carolyn. *Drummers of Jericho.*

Miller, E. Ethelbert, ed. *In Search of Color Everywhere: A Collection of African-American Poetry.*

Moore, Martha. *Under the Mermaid Angel.*

Mori, Kyoko. *One Bird.*

Morpurgo, Michael. *The War of Jenkins' Ear.*

Murphy, Jim. *The Great Fire.*

Nye, Naomi Shihab, ed. *The Tree Is Older Than You Are: A Bilingual Gathering of Poems and Stories from Mexico with Paintings by Mexican Artists.*

Ousseimi, Maria. *Caught in the Crossfire: Growing Up in a War Zone.*

Peck, Richard. *The Last Safe Place on Earth.*

Pierce, Tamora. *The Emperor Mage.*

Powell, Randy. *Dean Duffy.*

Preston, Douglas, and Lincoln Child. *Relic.*

Preston, Richard. *The Hot Zone.*

Psihoyos, Louie, and John Knoebber. *Hunting Dinosaurs.*

Randle, Kristen D. *The Only Alien on the Planet.*

Rochman, Hazel, and Darlene Z. McCampbell, eds. *Bearing Witness: Stories of the Holocaust.*

Ryan, Joan. *Little Girls in Pretty Boxes: The Making and Breaking of Elite Gymnasts and Figure Skaters.*

Scieszka, Jon, and Lane Smith. *Math Curse.*

Taylor, Theodore. *The Bomb.*

Testa, Maria. *Dancing Pink Flamingos, and Other Stories.*

Thornton, Yvonne S., and Jo Coudert. *The Ditchdigger's Daughters: A Black Family's Astonishing Success Story.*

Vande Velde, Vivian. *Companions of the Night.*

Weaver, Will. *Farm Team.*

White, Ellen Emerson. *The Road Home.*

Williams-Garcia, Rita. *Like Sisters on the Homefront.*

Woodson, Jacqueline. *From the Notebooks of Melanin Sun.*

1997 SELECTIONS

Atkin, S. Beth. *Voices from the Streets: Young Former Gang Members Tell Their Stories.*

Avi. *Beyond the Western Sea, Book One: The Escape from Home.*

Barron, T. A. *The Lost Years of Merlin.*

Berry, Liz. *The China Garden.*

Blum, Joshua, et al., eds. *The United States of Poetry.*

Bode, Janet, and Stan Mack. *Hard Time: A Real Life Look at Juvenile Crime and Violence.*

Card, Orson Scott. *Pastwatch: The Redemption of Christopher Columbus.*

Cart, Michael. *My Father's Scar.*

Chambers, Veronica. *Mama's Girl.*

Coles, William E., Jr. *Another Kind of Monday.*

Conly, Jane Leslie. *Trout Summer.*

Cooney, Caroline B. *The Voice on the Radio.*

Dash, Joan. *We Shall Not Be Moved: The Woman's Factory Strike of 1909.*

de Vries, Anke. *Bruises.*

Denenberg, Barry. *An American Hero: The True Story of Charles A. Lindbergh.*

Dessen, Sarah. *That Summer.*

Farmer, Nancy. *A Girl Named Disaster.*

Fleischman, Paul. *Dateline: Troy.*

Fleischman, Sid. *The Abracadabra Kid: A Writer's Life.*

Freedman, Russell. *The Life and Death of Crazy Horse.*

Freeman, Suzanne. *The Cuckoo's Child.*

Gilstrap, John. *Nathan's Run.*

Glenn, Mel. *Who Killed Mr. Chippendale? A Mystery in Poems.*

Gould, Steven. *Wildside.*

Haddix, Margaret Peterson. *Don't You Dare Read This, Mrs. Dunphrey.*

———. *Running Out of Time.*

Hanauer, Cathi. *My Sister's Bones.*

Hautman, Pete. *Mr. Was.*

Hesse, Karen. *The Music of Dolphins.*

Hobbs, Will. *Far North.*

Huth, Angela. *Land Girls.*

Ingold, Jeanette. *The Window.*

Keillor, Garrison, and Jenny Lind Nilsson. *The Sandy Bottom Orchestra.*

Klass, David. *Danger Zone.*

Kozol, Jonathan. *Amazing Grace: The Lives of Children and the Conscience of a Nation.*

Krakauer, Jon. *Into the Wild.*

Lane, Dakota. *Johnny Voodoo.*

Levy, Marilyn. *Run for Your Life.*

Macy, Sue. *Winning Ways: A Photohistory of American Women in Sports.*

Matas, Carol. *After the War.*

McKissack, Patricia C., and Fredrick L. McKissack. *Rebels against Slavery: American Slave Revolts.*

Mead, Alice. *Adem's Cross.*

Meyer, Carolyn. *Gideon's People.*

Myers, Walter Dean. *One More River to Cross: An African American Photograph Album.*

———. *Slam!*

Napoli, Donna Jo. *Song of the Magdalene.*

Nix, Garth. *Sabriel.*

Nye, Naomi Shihab, and Paul B. Janeczko, eds. *I Feel a Little Jumpy around You: A Book of Her Poems and His Poems Collected in Pairs.*

Paschen, Elise, and Neil Neches, eds. *Poetry in Motion: 100 Poems from the Subways and Buses.*

Paterson, Katherine. *Jip: His Story.*

Paulsen, Gary. *Puppies, Dogs, and Blue Northers: Reflections on Being Raised by a Pack of Sled Dogs.*

Pausewang, Gudrun. *The Final Journey.*

Pennebaker, Ruth. *Don't Think Twice.*

Pullman, Philip. *The Golden Compass.*

Rinaldi, Ann. *Hang a Thousand Trees with Ribbons: The Story of Phillis Wheatley.*

Salzman, Mark. *Lost in Place: Growing Up Absurd in Suburbia.*

Savage, Candace. *Cowgirls.*

Schmidt, Gary D. *The Sin Eater.*

Shevelev, Raphael, and Karine Schomer. *Liberating the Ghosts: Photographs and Text from the March of the Living with Excerpts from the Writings of Participants.*

Southgate, Martha. *Another Way to Dance.*

Spinelli, Jerry. *Crash.*

Staples, Suzanne Fisher. *Dangerous Skies.*

Thesman, Jean. *The Ornament Tree.*

Thomas, Rob. *Rats Saw God.*

Turner, Megan Whalen. *The Thief.*

Wallace, Rich. *Wrestling Sturbridge.*

Welter, John. *I Want to Buy a Vowel.*

Westall, Robert. *Gulf.*

White, Ruth. *Belle Prater's Boy.*

Wilkomirski, Binjamin. *Fragments: Memories of a Wartime Childhood.*

1998 SELECTIONS

Alexander, Lloyd. *The Iron Ring.*

Appelt, Kathi. *Just People, and Other Poems for Young Readers; and Paper/Pen/Poem: A Young Writer's Way to Begin.*

Bartoletti, Susan Campbell. *Growing Up in Coal Country.*

Berg, Elizabeth. *Joy School.*

Bernstein, Sara Tuvel. *The Seamstress: A Memoir of Survival.*

Bitton-Jackson, Livia. *I Have Lived a Thousand Years: Growing Up in the Holocaust.*

Bloor, Edward. *Tangerine.*

Brooks, Martha. *Bone Dance.*

Buck, Rinker. *Flight of Passage.*

Carroll, Joyce Armstrong, and Edward E. Wilson, comps. *Poetry after Lunch: Poems to Read Aloud.*

Carter, Alden R. *Bull Catcher.*

Chadwick, Douglas H., and Joel Sartore. *The Company We Keep: America's Endangered Species.*

Chang, Pang-Mei Natasha. *Bound Feet and Western Dress.*

Cook, Karin. *What Girls Learn.*

Cooney, Caroline B. *What Child Is This? A Christmas Story.*

Corbett, Sara. *Venus to the Hoop: A Gold-Medal Year in Women's Basketball.*

Cormier, Robert. *Tenderness.*

Creech, Sharon. *Chasing Redbird.*

de Lint, Charles. *Trader.*

Del Calzo, Nick, et al. *The Triumphant Spirit: Portraits and Stories of Holocaust Survivors, Their Messages of Hope and Compassion.*

Deuker, Carl. *Painting the Black.*

Dorris, Michael. *The Window.*

Draper, Sharon M. *Forged by Fire.*

Dyer, Daniel. *Jack London: A Biography.*

Elders, Joycelyn, and David Chanoff. *Joycelyn Elders, M.D.: From Sharecropper's Daughter to Surgeon General of the United States of America.*

Fleischman, Paul. *Seedfolks.*

Fogle, Bruce. *The Encyclopedia of the Cat.*

Fradin, Dennis Brindell. *The Planet Hunters: The Search for Other Worlds.*

Gallo, Donald R., ed. *No Easy Answers: Short Stories about Teenagers Making Tough Choices.*

Giblin, James Cross. *Charles A. Lindbergh: A Human Hero.*

Glenn, Mel. *Jump Ball: A Basketball Season in Poems.*

———. *The Taking of Room 114: A Hostage Drama in Poems.*

Greenfield, Susan A., ed. *The Human Mind Explained: An Owner's Guide to the Mysteries of the Mind.*

Griffin, Adele. *Sons of Liberty.*

Haddix, Margaret Peterson. *Leaving Fishers.*

Hayes, Daniel. *Flyers.*

Hesse, Karen. *Out of the Dust.*

Hogan, James P. *Bug Park.*

Howe, James. *The Watcher.*

Jiang, Ji-li. *Red Scarf Girl: A Memoir of the Cultural Revolution.*

Kelton, Elmer. *Cloudy in the West.*

Kerner, Elizabeth. *Song in the Silence: The Tale of Lanen Kaelar.*

Kindl, Patrice. *The Woman in the Wall.*

Klause, Annette Curtis. *Blood and Chocolate.*

Krakauer, Jon. *Into Thin Air: A Personal Account of the Mount Everest Disaster.*

Krisher, Trudy. *Kinship.*

Lantz, Frances. *Someone to Love.*

Lee, Marie G. *Necessary Roughness.*

Levenkron, Steven. *The Luckiest Girl in the World.*

Levine, Gail Carson. *Ella Enchanted.*

Maxwell, Robin. *The Secret Diary of Anne Boleyn.*

Mazer, Anne, ed. *Working Days: Stories about Teenagers and Work.*

Mazer, Norma Fox. *When She Was Good.*

McDonald, Joyce. *Swallowing Stones.*

McKinley, Robin. *Rose Daughter.*

McLaren, Clemence. *Inside the Walls of Troy: A Novel of the Women Who Lived the Trojan War.*

Meyer, Carolyn. *Jubilee Journey.*

Myers, Walter Dean. *Harlem: A Poem.*

Napoli, Donna Jo. *Stones in Water.*

Naylor, Phyllis Reynolds. *Outrageously Alice.*

Nix, Garth. *Shade's Children.*

Nolan, Han. *Dancing on the Edge.*

Nye, Naomi Shihab. *Habibi.*

Orr, Wendy. *Peeling the Onion.*

Oughton, Jerrie. *The War in Georgia.*

Paulsen, Gary. *The Schernoff Discoveries.*

Penman, Sharon Kay. *The Queen's Man: A Medieval Mystery.*

Philip, Neil, ed. *In a Sacred Manner I Live: Native American Wisdom.*

Pullman, Philip. *The Subtle Knife.*

Reynolds, Marjorie. *The Starlite Drive-In.*

Rinaldi, Ann. *An Acquaintance with Darkness.*

Rochman, Hazel, and Darlene Z. McCampbell, eds. *Leaving Home: Stories.*

Shoup, Barbara. *Stranded in Harmony.*

Shusterman, Neal. *The Dark Side of Nowhere.*

Skurzynski, Gloria. *Virtual War.*

Soto, Gary. *Buried Onions.*

Steger, Will, and Jon Bowermaster. *Over the Top of the World: Explorer Will Steger's Trek across the Arctic.*

Sullivan, Charles, ed. *Imaginary Animals: Poetry and Art for Young People.*

Tate, Sonsyrea. *Little X: Growing Up in the Nation of Islam.*

Thomas, Rob. *Doing Time: Notes from the Undergrad.*

Tillage, Leon. *Leon's Story.*

Wersba, Barbara. *Whistle Me Home.*

Williams, Carol Lynch. *The True Colors of Caitlynne Jackson.*

Yee, Paul. *Breakaway.*

1999 SELECTIONS

Abelove, Joan. *Go and Come Back.*

Alabiso, Vincent, et al., eds. *Flash! The Associated Press Covers the World.*

Arnoldi, Katherine. *The Amazing True Story of a Teenage Single Mom.*

Bauer, Joan. *Rules of the Road.*

Bennett, Cherie. *Life in the Fat Lane.*

Blackwood, Gary. *The Shakespeare Stealer.*

Bolden, Tonya, ed. *33 Things Every Girl Should Know: Stories, Songs, Poems, and Smart Talk by 33 Extraordinary Women.*

Burgess, Melvin. *Smack.*

Clinton, Catherine, ed. *I, Too, Sing America: Three Centuries of African-American Poetry.*

Colman, Penny. *Corpses, Coffins, and Crypts: A History of Burial.*

Cormier, Robert. *Heroes.*

Dessen, Sarah. *Someone Like You.*

Farrell, Jeanette. *Invisible Enemies: Stories of Infectious Disease.*

Ferris, Jean. *Love among the Walnuts.*

Flake, Sharon G. *The Skin I'm In.*

Fleischman, Paul. *Whirligig.*

Fletcher, Susan. *Shadow Spinner.*

Freedman, Russell. *Martha Graham: A Dancer's Life.*

Griffin, Adele. *The Other Shepards.*

Haddix, Margaret Peterson. *Among the Hidden.*

Hardman, Ric Lynden. *Sunshine Rider: The First Vegetarian Western.*

Helfer, Ralph. *Modoc: The True Story of the Greatest Elephant That Ever Lived.*

Hesser, Terry Spencer. *Kissing Doorknobs.*

Hill, Ernest. *A Life for a Life.*

Hobbs, Will. *The Maze.*

Holt, Kimberly Willis. *My Louisiana Sky.*

Jimenez, Francisco. *The Circuit: Stories from the Life of a Migrant Child.*

Johnson, Angela. *Heaven.*

Koller, Jackie French. *The Falcon.*

Larson, Gary. *There's a Hair in My Dirt! A Worm's Story.*

Lawrence, Iain. *The Wreckers.*

Laxalt, Robert. *Dust Devils.*

Lester, Julius. *From Slave Ship to Freedom Road.*

Lobel, Anita. *No Pretty Pictures: A Child of War.*

Marrin, Albert. *Commander-in-Chief Abraham Lincoln and the Civil War.*

Mastoon, Adam. *The Shared Heart: Portraits and Stories Celebrating Lesbian, Gay, and Bisexual Young People.*

Matcheck, Diane. *The Sacrifice.*

McCaughrean, Geraldine. *The Pirate's Son.*

McKee, Tim, ed. *No More Strangers Now: Young Voices from a New South Africa.*

McKissack, Patricia C., and Fredrick L. McKissack. *Young, Black, and Determined: A Biography of Lorraine Hansberry.*

Mikaelsen, Ben. *Petey.*

Napoli, Donna Jo. *Sirena.*

Newth, Mette. *The Dark Light.*

Nicholson, Joy. *The Tribes of Palos Verdes.*

Nye, Naomi Shihab, ed. *The Space between Our Footsteps: Poems and Paintings from the Middle East.*

Paulsen, Gary. *Soldier's Heart: A Novel of the Civil War.*

Peck, Richard. *A Long Way from Chicago.*

———. *Strays Like Us.*

Philip, Neil, ed. *War and the Pity of War.*

Porter, Tracey. *Treasures in the Dust.*

Potok, Chaim. *Zebra, and Other Stories.*

Quarles, Heather. *A Door Near Here.*

Ritter, John H. *Choosing Up Sides.*

Rottman, S. L. *Hero.*

Rowling, J. K. *Harry Potter and the Sorcerer's Stone.*

Sachar, Louis. *Holes.*

Salisbury, Graham. *Jungle Dogs.*

Silvey, Anita, ed. *Help Wanted: Short Stories about Young People Working.*

Spinelli, Jerry. *Knots in My Yo-Yo String: The Autobiography of a Kid.*

Springer, Nancy. *I Am Mordred: A Tale from Camelot.*

Sweeney, Joyce. *The Spirit Window.*

Thomas, Jane Resh. *Behind the Mask: The Life of Queen Elizabeth I.*

Thomas, Velma Maia. *Lest We Forget: The Passage from Africa to Slavery and Emancipation.*

Turner, Ann. *A Lion's Hunger: Poems of First Love.*

Walter, Virginia. *Making Up Megaboy.*

Weaver, Will. *Hard Ball.*

Werlin, Nancy. *The Killer's Cousin.*

Willis, Connie. *To Say Nothing of the Dog, or How We Found the Bishop's Bird Stump at Last.*

Wilson, Diane Lee. *I Rode a Horse of Milk White Jade.*

Woodson, Jacqueline. *If You Come Softly.*

Yolen, Jane, and Bruce Coville. *Armageddon Summer.*

2000 SELECTIONS

Abelove, Joan. *Saying It Out Loud.*

Alexander, Caroline. *The* Endurance: *Shackleton's Legendary Antarctic Expedition.*

Allison, Anthony. *Hear These Voices: Youth at the Edge of the Millennium.*

Anderson, Laurie Halse. *Speak.*

Armstrong, Jennifer. *Shipwreck at the Bottom of the World: The Extraordinary True Story of Shackleton and the* Endurance.

Atkins, Catherine. *When Jeff Comes Home.*

Barrett, Tracy. *Anna of Byzantium.*

Bat-Ami, Miriam. *Two Suns in the Sky.*

Calabro, Marian. *The Perilous Journey of the Donner Party.*

Calhoun, Dia. *Firegold.*

Carbone, Elisa. *Stealing Freedom.*

Card, Orson Scott. *Ender's Shadow.*

Cart, Michael, comp. *Tomorrowland: Ten Stories about the Future.*

Chbosky, Stephen. *The Perks of Being a Wallflower.*

Cooper, Susan. *King of Shadows.*

Curtis, Christopher Paul. *Bud, Not Buddy.*

Dessen, Sarah. *Keeping the Moon.*

Dominick, Andie. *Needles: A Memoir of Growing Up with Diabetes.*

Ferris, Jean. *Bad.*

Fleischman, Paul. *Mind's Eye.*

Freedman, Russell. *Babe Didrikson Zaharias: The Making of a Champion.*

Friesen, Gayle. *Janey's Girl.*

Gaiman, Neil. *Stardust.*

Garner, Eleanor Ramrath. *Eleanor's Story: An American Girl in Hitler's Germany.*

Gaskins, Pearl Fuyo, ed. *What Are You? Voices of Mixed-Race Young People.*

Gilmore, Kate. *The Exchange Student.*

Gourley, Catherine. *Good Girl Work: Factories, Sweatshops, and How Women Changed Their Role in the American Workforce.*

Haddix, Margaret Peterson. *Just Ella.*

Hewett, Lorri. *Dancer.*

Hickam, Homer H., Jr. *Rocket Boys: A Memoir.*

Hobbs, Will. *Jason's Gold.*

Hoffman, Alice. *Local Girls.*

Holt, Kimberly Willis. *When Zachary Beaver Came to Town.*

Holtwijk, Ineke. *Asphalt Angels.*

Holubitsky, Katherine. *Alone at Ninety Foot.*

Hoobler, Dorothy, and Thomas Hoobler. *The Ghost in the Tokaido Inn.*

Howe, Norma. *The Adventures of Blue Avenger.*

Jennings, Peter, and Todd Brewster. *The Century for Young People.*

Johnson, Scott. *Safe at Second.*

Jordan, Sherryl. *The Raging Quiet.*

Kalergis, Mary Motley. *Seen and Heard: Teenagers Talk about Their Lives.*

King, Stephen. *The Girl Who Loved Tom Gordon.*

Krizmanic, Judy. *The Teen's Vegetarian Cookbook.*

Kuhn, Betsy. *Angels of Mercy: The Army Nurses of World War II.*

Lawrence, Iain. *The Smugglers.*

Levine, Gail Carson. *Dave at Night.*

Lubar, David. *Hidden Talents.*

Mah, Adeline Yen. *Chinese Cinderella: The True Story of an Unwanted Daughter.*

Marchetta, Melina. *Looking for Alibrandi.*

Marrin, Albert. *Terror of the Spanish Main: Sir Henry Morgan and His Buccaneers.*

Mattison, Chris. *Snake.*

Maurer, Richard. *The Wild Colorado: The True Adventures of Fred Dellenbaugh, Age 17, on the Second Powell Expedition into the Grand Canyon.*

McNamee, Graham. *Hate You.*

McNeal, Laura, and Tom McNeal. *Crooked.*

Meyer, Carolyn. *Mary, Bloody Mary.*

Morris, Gerald. *The Squire, His Knight, and His Lady.*

Myers, Walter Dean. *Monster.*

Namioka, Lensey. *Ties That Bind, Ties That Break.*

Nye, Naomi Shihab. *What Have You Lost?*

Okutoro, Lydia Omolola. *Quiet Storm: Voices of Young Black Poets.*

Opdyke, Irene Gut. *In My Hands: Memories of a Holocaust Rescuer.*

Partridge, Elizabeth. *Restless Spirit: The Life and Work of Dorothea Lange.*

Porter, Connie. *Imani All Mine.*

Powell, Randy. *Tribute to Another Dead Rock Star.*

Qualey, Marsha. *Close to a Killer.*

Randle, Kristen D. *Breaking Rank.*

Reich, Susanna. *Clara Schumann: Piano Virtuoso.*

Rottman, S. L. *Head above Water.*

Rowling, J. K. *Harry Potter and the Chamber of Secrets.*

———. *Harry Potter and the Prisoner of Azkaban.*

Rubin, Susan Goldman. *Margaret Bourke-White: Her Pictures Were Her Life.*

Savage, Deborah. *Summer Hawk.*

Schmidt, Thomas, and Jeremy Schmidt. *The Saga of Lewis and Clark: Into the Uncharted West.*

Schwager, Tina, and Michele Schuerger. *Gutsy Girls: Young Women Who Dare.*

Shusterman, Neal. *Downsiders.*

Skurzynski, Gloria. *Spider's Voice.*

Sones, Sonya. *Stop Pretending: What Happened When My Big Sister Went Crazy.*

Stanley, Diane. *A Time Apart.*

Thesman, Jean. *The Other Ones.*

Tomey, Ingrid. *Nobody Else Has to Know.*

Vande Velde, Vivian. *Never Trust a Dead Man.*

Voigt, Cynthia. *Elske.*

Whitmore, Arvella. *Trapped between the Lash and the Gun: A Boy's Journey.*

Wittlinger, Ellen. *Hard Love.*

Young, Karen Romano. *The Beetle and Me: A Love Story.*

2001 SELECTIONS

Almond, David. *Kit's Wilderness.*

Anderson, Laurie Halse. *Fever 1793.*

Appelt, Kathi. *Kissing Tennessee, and Other Stories from the Stardust Dance.*

Armstrong, Lance, and Sally Jenkins. *It's Not about the Bike: My Journey Back to Life.*

Bachrach, Susan D. *The Nazi Olympics: Berlin 1936.*

Bagdasarian, Adam. *Forgotten Fire.*

Bartoletti, Susan Campbell. *Kids on Strike!*

Bauer, Cat. *Harley, Like a Person.*

Bauer, Joan. *Hope Was Here.*

Beckett, Sister Wendy. *My Favorite Things: 75 Works of Art from Around the World.*

Blackwood, Gary. *Shakespeare's Scribe.*

Brooks, Martha. *Being with Henry.*

Cabot, Meg. *The Princess Diaries.*

Calhoun, Dia. *Aria of the Sea.*

Chevalier, Tracy. *Girl with a Pearl Earring.*

Coman, Carolyn. *Many Stones.*

Creech, Sharon. *The Wanderer.*

Crichton, Michael. *Timeline.*

Cross, Gillian. *Tightrope.*

Dessen, Sarah. *Dreamland.*

Deuker, Carl. *Night Hoops.*

Fienberg, Anna. *Borrowed Light.*

Fogelin, Adrian. *Crossing Jordan.*

Fradin, Dennis Brindell, and Judith Bloom Fradin. *Ida B. Wells: Mother of the Civil Rights Movement.*

Franco, Betsy, ed. *You Hear Me? Poems and Writing by Teenage Boys.*

Freedman, Russell. *Give Me Liberty! The Story of the Declaration of Independence.*

Giff, Patricia Reilly. *Nory Ryan's Song.*

Glenn, Mel. *Split Image: A Story in Poems.*

Glover, Savion, and Bruce Weber. *Savion! My Life in Tap.*

Gottlieb, Lori. *Stick Figure: A Diary of My Former Self.*

Gray, Dianne E. *Holding Up the Earth.*

Haruf, Kent. *Plainsong.*

Hyde, Catherine Ryan. *Pay It Forward.*

Isaacs, Anne. *Torn Thread.*

Karr, Kathleen. *The Boxer.*

Katz, Jon. *Geeks: How Two Lost Boys Rode the Internet Out of Idaho.*

Kessler, Cristina. *No Condition Is Permanent.*

Konigsburg, E. L. *Silent to the Bone.*

Koss, Amy Goldman. *The Girls.*

Lalicki, Tom. *Spellbinder: The Life of Harry Houdini.*

Lanier, Shannon, and Jane Feldman, eds. *Jefferson's Children: The Story of One American Family.*

Lawrence, Iain. *Ghost Boy.*

Lebert, Benjamin. *Crazy.*

Levine, Ellen. *Darkness over Denmark: The Danish Resistance and the Rescue of the Jews.*

Logue, Mary. *Dancing with an Alien.*

Lynch, Chris. *Gold Dust.*

Marillier, Juliet. *Daughter of the Forest.*

Marrin, Albert. *Sitting Bull and His World.*

Morris, Gerald. *The Savage Damsel and the Dwarf.*

Murphy, Rita. *Night Flying.*

Myers, Walter Dean. *145th Street: Short Stories.*

Oughton, Jerrie. *Perfect Family.*

Paulsen, Gary. *The Beet Fields: Memories of a Sixteenth Summer.*

Peck, Richard. *A Year down Yonder.*

Peters, Julie Anne. *Define Normal.*

Philbrick, Rodman. *The Last Book in the Universe.*

Platt, Randall Beth. *The Likes of Me.*

Plummer, Louise. *A Dance for Three.*

Plum-Ucci, Carol. *The Body of Christopher Creed.*

Rennison, Louise. *Angus, Thongs, and Full-Frontal Snogging: Confessions of Georgia Nicolson.*

Ryan, Pam Muñoz. *Esperanza Rising.*

Schwartz, Virginia Frances. *Send One Angel Down.*

Spinelli, Jerry. *Stargirl.*

St. George, Judith. *In the Line of Fire: Presidents' Lives at Stake.*

Trueman, Terry. *Stuck in Neutral.*

Turner, Ann. *Learning to Swim: A Memoir.*

Ung, Loung. *First They Killed My Father: A Daughter of Cambodia Remembers.*

Wallace, Rich. *Playing without the Ball.*

Wells, Ken. *Meely LaBauve.*

Whelan, Gloria. *Homeless Bird.*

White, Ruth. *Memories of Summer.*

Williams, Lori Aurelia. *When Kambia Elaine Flew in from Neptune.*

Winick, Judd. *Pedro and Me: Friendship, Loss, and What I Learned.*

Wittlinger, Ellen. *What's in a Name.*

Woodson, Jacqueline. *Miracle's Boys.*

Yolen, Jane, and Robert J. Harris. *Queen's Own Fool.*

2002 SELECTIONS

Bell, Hilari. *A Matter of Profit.*

Brashares, Ann. *The Sisterhood of the Traveling Pants.*

Brenner, Barbara, ed. *Voices: Poetry and Art from Around the World.*

Brooks, Bruce. *All That Remains.*

Card, Orson Scott. *Shadow of the Hegemon.*

Cart, Michael, ed. *Love and Sex: Ten Stories of Truth.*

Clement-Davies, David. *Fire Bringer.*

Colton, Larry. *Counting Coup: A True Story of Basketball and Honor on the Little Big Horn.*

Cooper, Michael L. *Fighting for Honor: Japanese Americans and World War II.*

Cormier, Robert. *The Rag and Bone Shop.*

Crutcher, Chris. *Whale Talk.*

Ferris, Jean. *Eight Seconds.*

———. *Of Sound Mind.*

Fisher, Antwone Quenton, and Mim Eichler Rivas. *Finding Fish*.

Fleischman, Paul. *Seek*.

Flinn, Alex. *Breathing Underwater*.

Fradin, Dennis Brindell. *Bound for the North Star: True Stories of Fugitive Slaves*.

Franco, Betsy, ed. *Things I Have to Tell You: Poems and Writing by Teenage Girls*.

Gallo, Donald R., ed. *On the Fringe*.

Geras, Adele. *Troy*.

Greenberg, Jan, ed. *Heart to Heart: New Poems Inspired by Twentieth Century American Art*.

Greenberg, Jan, and Sandra Jordan. *Vincent Van Gogh: Portrait of an Artist*.

Griffin, Adele. *Amandine*.

Heneghan, James. *The Grave*.

Holm, Jennifer L. *Boston Jane: An Adventure*.

Hoose, Phillip. *We Were There, Too! Young People in U.S. History*.

Howe, James, ed. *The Color of Absence: Twelve Stories about Loss and Hope*.

Jenkins, A. M. *Damage*.

Jimenez, Francisco. *Breaking Through*.

Jordan, Sherryl. *Secret Sacrament*.

Kendall, Martha E. *Failure Is Impossible! The History of American Women's Rights*.

Ketchum, Liza. *Into a New Country: Eight Remarkable Women of the West*.

King, Daniel. *Chess: From First Moves to Checkmate*.

Klass, David. *You Don't Know Me*.

Koertge, Ron. *The Brimstone Journals*.

Lawlor, Laurie. *Helen Keller: Rebellious Spirit*.

Lee, Bruce, ed. John Little. *Bruce Lee: The Celebrated Life of the Golden Dragon*.

Les Becquets, Diane. *The Stones of Mourning Creek*.

Lynch, Chris. *Freewill*.

Marrin, Albert. *George Washington and the Founding of a Nation*.

McCormick, Patricia. *Cut*.

McDonald, Janet. *Spellbound*.

McDonald, Joyce. *Shades of Simon Gray*.

Mikaelsen, Ben. *Touching Spirit Bear*.

Moriarty, Jaclyn. *Feeling Sorry for Celia*.

Mosher, Richard. *Zazoo*.

Murphy, Jim. *Blizzard! The Storm That Changed America*.

Myers, Walter Dean. *Bad Boy: A Memoir*.

———. *The Greatest: Muhammad Ali*.

Na, An. *A Step from Heaven*.

Naidoo, Beverley. *The Other Side of Truth*.

Nam, Vickie, ed. *Yell-oh Girls! Emerging Voices Explore Culture, Identity, and Growing Up Asian American*.

Nelson, Marilyn. *Carver: A Life in Poems*.

Nix, Garth. *Lirael, Daughter of the Clayr*.

Nolan, Han. *Born Blue*.

Orgill, Roxane. *Shout, Sister, Shout! Ten Girl Singers Who Shaped a Century*.

Owen, David. *Hidden Evidence: Forty True Crimes and How Forensic Science Helped Solve Them*.

Park, Linda Sue. *A Single Shard*.

Peck, Richard. *Fair Weather*.

Pierce, Meredith Ann. *Treasure at the Heart of the Tanglewood*.

Pierce, Tamora. *Squire*.

Pratchett, Terry. *The Amazing Maurice and His Educated Rodents*.

Pullman, Philip. *The Amber Spyglass*.

Rees, Celia. *Witch Child*.

Rice, David. *Crazy Loco: Stories*.

Rochelle, Belinda, ed. *Words with Wings: A Treasury of African-American Poetry and Art*.

Ryan, Sara. *Empress of the World*.

Salisbury, Graham. *Lord of the Deep*.

Sanchez, Alex. *Rainbow Boys*.

Shinn, Sharon. *Summers at Castle Auburn*.

Sones, Sonya. *What My Mother Doesn't Know*.

Stratton, Allan. *Leslie's Journal*.

Tashjian, Janet. *The Gospel according to Larry*.

Taylor, Mildred D. *The Land*.

Tingle, Rebecca. *The Edge on the Sword*.

Vance, Susanna. *Sights*.

Vande Velde, Vivian. *Being Dead: Stories*.

Vijayaraghavan, Vineeta. *Motherland*.

Weaver, Beth Nixon. *Rooster*.

Werlin, Nancy. *Black Mirror*.

Williams-Garcia, Rita. *Every Time a Rainbow Dies*.

Wittlinger, Ellen. *Razzle*.

Wolff, Virginia Euwer. *True Believer*.

Zusak, Markus. *Fighting Ruben Wolfe*.

2003 SELECTIONS

Alvarez, Julia. *Before We Were Free*.

Anderson, Laurie Halse. *Catalyst*.

Anderson, M. T. *Feed*.

Armstrong, Jennifer, ed. *Shattered: Stories of Children and War*.

Auch, Mary Jane. *Ashes of Roses*.

Bardi, Abby. *The Book of Fred*.

Barker, Clive. *Abarat*.

Bartoletti, Susan Campbell. *Black Potatoes: The Story of the Great Irish Famine, 1845–1850.*

Bechard, Margaret. *Hanging on to Max.*

Black, Holly. *Tithe: A Modern Faerie Tale.*

Blackwood, Gary. *The Year of the Hangman.*

Breslin, Theresa. *Remembrance.*

Chambers, Aidan. *Postcards from No Man's Land.*

Clements, Andrew. *Things Not Seen.*

Cohn, Rachel. *Gingerbread.*

Crowe, Chris. *Mississippi Trial, 1955.*

Datlow, Ellen, and Terri Windling, eds. *The Green Man: Tales from the Mythic Forest.*

de Lint, Charles. *Seven Wild Sisters.*

Desai Hidier, Tanuja. *Born Confused.*

Dessen, Sarah. *This Lullaby.*

Ellis, Deborah. *Parvana's Journey.*

Etchemendy, Nancy. *Cat in Glass, and Other Tales of the Unnatural.*

Fama, Elizabeth. *Overboard.*

Farmer, Nancy. *The House of the Scorpion.*

Ferris, Jean. *Once upon a Marigold.*

Fleischman, John. *Phineas Gage: A Gruesome but True Story about Brain Science.*

Frank, E. R. *America.*

Frank, Hillary. *Better Than Running at Night.*

Freymann-Weyr, Garret. *My Heartbeat.*

Froese, Deborah. *Out of the Fire.*

Gaiman, Neil. *Coraline.*

Gantos, Jack. *Hole in My Life.*

Giff, Patricia Reilly. *Pictures of Hollis Woods.*

Giles, Gail. *Shattering Glass.*

Grimes, Nikki. *Bronx Masquerade.*

Halam, Ann. *Dr. Franklin's Island.*

Hampton, Wilborn. *Meltdown: A Race against Nuclear Disaster at Three Mile Island; A Reporter's Story.*

Hiaasen, Carl. *Hoot.*

Holeman, Linda. *Search of the Moon King's Daughter.*

Jordan, Sherryl. *The Hunting of the Last Dragon.*

Kidd, Sue Monk. *The Secret Life of Bees.*

Koertge, Ron. *Stoner and Spaz.*

Korman, Gordon. *Son of the Mob.*

Lawrence, Iain. *The Lightkeeper's Daughter.*

Leavitt, Martine. *The Dollmage.*

McCaughrean, Geraldine. *The Kite Rider.*

McPherson, James M. *Fields of Fury: The American Civil War.*

Miller, Mary Beth. *Aimee.*

Moore, Christopher. *Lamb: The Gospel according to Biff, Christ's Childhood Pal.*

Nelson, Peter. *Left for Dead: A Young Man's Search for Justice for the USS* Indianapolis.

Nye, Naomi Shihab. *19 Varieties of Gazelle: Poems of the Middle East.*

Oates, Joyce Carol. *Big Mouth and Ugly Girl.*

Park, Linda Sue. *When My Name Was Keoko.*

Partridge, Elizabeth. *This Land Was Made for You and Me: The Life and Songs of Woody Guthrie.*

Philbrick, Nathaniel. *Revenge of the Whale: The True Story of the Whaleship* Essex.

Placide, Jaira. *Fresh Girl.*

Plum-Ucci, Carol. *What Happened to Lani Garver.*

Powell, Randy. *Three Clams and an Oyster.*

Rall, Ted. *To Afghanistan and Back: A Graphic Travelogue.*

Rottman, S. L. *Stetson.*

Santana, Patricia. *Motorcycle Ride on the Sea of Tranquility.*

Savage, Deborah. *Kotuku.*

Sebold, Alice. *The Lovely Bones.*

Sheppard, Mary C. *Seven for a Secret.*

Smith, Kevin, *Green Arrow: Quiver.*

Smith, Sherri L. *Lucy the Giant.*

Steinberg, Jacques. *The Gatekeepers: Inside the Admissions Process of a Premier College.*

Tolan, Stephanie S. *Surviving the Applewhites.*

Toten, Teresa. *The Game.*

Van Pelt, James. *Strangers and Beggars: Stories.*

Woodson, Jacqueline. *Hush.*

Yolen, Jane, and Robert J. Harris. *Girl in a Cage.*

2004 SELECTIONS

Adichie, Chimamanda Ngozi. *Purple Hibiscus.*

Bell, Hilari. *The Goblin Wood.*

Bird, Eugenie. *Fairie-ality: The Fashion Collection from the House of Ellwand.*

Bray, Libba. *A Great and Terrible Beauty.*

Brennan, Herbie. *Faerie Wars.*

Brooks, Kevin. *Lucas.*

Brooks, Martha. *True Confessions of a Heartless Girl.*

Buckingham, Dorothea N. *Staring Down the Dragon.*

Burt, Guy. *Sophie.*

Calhoun, Dia. *White Midnight.*

Capuzzo, Michael. *Close to Shore: The Terrifying Shark Attacks of 1916.*

Coburn, Jake. *Prep.*

Cofer, Judith Ortiz. *The Meaning of Consuelo.*

Crowe, Chris. *Getting Away with Murder: The True Story of the Emmett Till Case.*

Crutcher, Chris. *King of the Mild Frontier: An Ill-Advised Autobiography.*

Davis, Amanda. *Wonder When You'll Miss Me.*

Donnelly, Jennifer. *A Northern Light.*

Fleming, Candace. *Ben Franklin's Almanac: Being a True Account of the Good Gentleman's Life.*

Fradin, Dennis Brindell, and Judith Bloom Fradin. *Fight On! Mary Church Terrell's Battle for Integration.*

Frank, E. R. *Friction.*

Freedman, Russell. *In Defense of Liberty: The Story of America's Bill of Rights.*

Freese, Barbara. *Coal: A Human History.*

Frost, Helen. *Keesha's House.*

Going, K. L. *Fat Kid Rules the World.*

Goodman, Alison. *Singing the Dogstar Blues.*

Greenberg, Jan, and Sandra Jordan. *Runaway Girl: The Artist Louise Bourgeois.*

Haddon, Mark. *The Curious Incident of the Dog in the Night-Time.*

Hampton, Wilborn. *September 11, 2001: Attack on New York City.*

Hautman, Pete. *Sweetblood.*

Hearn, Lian. *Across the Nightingale Floor.*

Henkes, Kevin. *Olive's Ocean.*

Hoffman, Nina Kiriki. *A Stir of Bones.*

Holt, Kimberly Willis. *Keeper of the Night.*

Horvath, Polly. *The Canning Season.*

Jenkins, A. M. *Out of Order.*

Johnson, Angela. *The First Part Last.*

Johnson, Kathleen Jeffrie. *Target.*

Juby, Susan. *Alice, I Think.*

Koja, Kathe. *Buddha Boy.*

Korman, Gordon. *Jake, Reinvented.*

Krisher, Trudy. *Uncommon Faith.*

Levithan, David. *Boy Meets Boy.*

Little, Jason. *Shutterbug Follies.*

Lowachee, Karin. *Burndive.*

Mack, Tracy. *Birdland.*

Mackler, Carolyn. *The Earth, My Butt, and Other Big, Round Things.*

Martinez, Manuel Luis. *Drift.*

Maynard, Joyce. *The Usual Rules.*

McNamee, Graham. *Acceleration.*

Meyer, L. A. *Bloody Jack: Being an Account of the Curious Adventures of Mary "Jacky" Faber, Ship's Boy.*

Murphy, Jim. *An American Plague: The True and Terrifying Story of the Yellow Fever Epidemic of 1793.*

———. *Inside the Alamo.*

Murray, Jaye. *Bottled Up.*

Myracle, Lauren. *Kissing Kate.*

Naidoo, Beverley. *Out of Bounds: Seven Stories of Conflict and Hope.*

Napoli, Donna Jo. *Breath.*

November, Sharyn, ed. *Firebirds: An Anthology of Original Fantasy and Science Fiction.*

Osa, Nancy. *Cuba 15.*

Parker, Jeff. *The Interman.*

Pattou, Edith. *East.*

Paulsen, Gary. *How Angel Peterson Got His Name, and Other Outrageous Tales about Extreme Sports.*

Peck, Richard. *The River between Us.*

Pierce, Tamora. *Trickster's Choice.*

Pratchett, Terry. *The Wee Free Men.*

Rapp, Adam. *33 Snowfish.*

Rees, Celia. *Pirates! The True and Remarkable Adventures of Minerva Sharpe and Nancy Kington, Female Pirates.*

Reeve, Philip. *Mortal Engines.*

Roach, Mary. *Stiff: The Curious Lives of Human Cadavers.*

Rowling, J. K. *Harry Potter and the Order of the Phoenix.*

Rylant, Cynthia. *God Went to Beauty School.*

Satrapi, Marjane. *Persepolis: The Story of a Childhood.*

Sis, Peter. *The Tree of Life: A Book Depicting the Life of Charles Darwin, Naturalist, Geologist, and Thinker.*

Slade, Arthur. *Dust.*

Spinelli, Jerry. *Milkweed.*

Stroud, Jonathan. *The Amulet of Samarkand.*

Thompson, Craig. *Blankets.*

Trueman, Terry. *Inside Out.*

Vance, Susanna. *Deep.*

Vande Velde, Vivian. *Heir Apparent.*

Wittlinger, Ellen. *Zigzag.*

Woodson, Jacqueline. *Locomotion.*

Wrede, Patricia C., and Caroline Stevermer. *Sorcery and Cecelia, or The Enchanted Chocolate Pot*

Yolen, Jane. *Sword of the Rightful King: A Novel of King Arthur.*

Zahn, Timothy. *Dragon and Thief: A Dragonback Adventure.*

2005 SELECTIONS

Aidinoff, Elsie V. *The Garden.*

Allen, Thomas B. *George Washington, Spymaster: How the Americans Outspied the British and Won the Revolutionary War.*

Almond, David. *The Fire-Eaters.*

Bass, L. G. *Sign of the Qin.*

Bausum, Ann. *With Courage and Cloth: Winning the Fight for a Woman's Right to Vote.*

Bolden, Tonya. *Wake Up Our Souls: A Celebration of Black American Artists.*

Braff, Joshua. *The Unthinkable Thoughts of Jacob Green.*

Burgess, Melvin. *Doing It.*

Choldenko, Gennifer. *Al Capone Does My Shirts.*

Chotjewitz, David. *Daniel Half Human, and the Good Nazi.*

Corrigan, Eireann. *Splintering.*

Curtis, Christopher Paul. *Bucking the Sarge.*

de Lint, Charles. *The Blue Girl.*

Dunkle, Clare B. *The Hollow Kingdom.*

Farmer, Nancy. *The Sea of Trolls.*

Fisher, Catherine. *The Oracle Betrayed.*

Flake, Sharon G. *Who Am I without Him? Short Stories about Girls and the Boys in Their Lives.*

Flinn, Alex. *Nothing to Lose.*

Freedman, Russell. *The Voice That Challenged a Nation: Marian Anderson and the Struggle for Equal Rights.*

Fusco, Kimberly Newton. *Tending to Grace.*

Greenberg, Jan, and Sandra Jordan. *Andy Warhol: Prince of Pop.*

Halpin, Brendan. *Donorboy.*

Hautman, Pete. *Godless.*

Hoose, Phillip. *The Race to Save the Lord God Bird.*

Horowitz, Anthony. *Eagle Strike.*

Janeczko, Paul B. *Worlds Afire.*

Jocelyn, Marthe. *Mable Riley: A Reliable Record of Humdrum, Peril, and Romance.*

Johnson, Angela. *Bird.*

Johnson, Kathleen Jeffrie. *A Fast and Brutal Wing.*

Johnson, Maureen. *The Key to the Golden Firebird.*

Koertge, Ron. *Margaux with an X.*

Koja, Kathe. *The Blue Mirror.*

Konigsburg, E. L. *The Outcasts of 19 Schuyler Place.*

Kubert, Joe. *Yossel, April 19, 1943: A Story of the Warsaw Ghetto Uprising.*

Lawrence, Iain. *B for Buster.*

Lawrence, Michael. *A Crack in the Line.*

Leavitt, Martine. *Heck, Superhero.*

Levithan, David. *The Realm of Possibility.*

Marchetta, Melina. *Saving Francesca.*

McKinley, Robin. *Sunshine.*

McNaughton, Janet. *An Earthly Knight.*

McWhorter, Diane. *A Dream of Freedom: The Civil Rights Movement from 1954 to 1968.*

Meyer, L. A. *Curse of the Blue Tattoo: Being an Account of the Misadventures of Jacky Faber, Midshipman and Fine Lady.*

Morgan, Nicola. *Fleshmarket.*

Moriarty, Jaclyn. *The Year of Secret Assignments.*

Morpurgo, Michael. *Private Peaceful.*

Myers, Walter Dean. *Here in Harlem: Poems in Many Voices.*

Napoli, Donna Jo. *Bound.*

Nelson, Blake. *Rock Star, Superstar.*

Noyes, Deborah, ed. *Gothic! Ten Original Dark Tales.*

Oppel, Kenneth. *Airborn.*

Peck, Richard. *The Teacher's Funeral: A Comedy in Three Parts.*

Peters, Julie Anne. *Luna.*

Pratchett, Terry. *A Hat Full of Sky.*

Rapp, Adam. *Under the Wolf, under the Dog.*

Reeve, Philip. *Predator's Gold.*

Robinson, Sharon. *Promises to Keep: How Jackie Robinson Changed America.*

Rosoff, Meg. *How I Live Now.*

Saenz, Benjamin Alire. *Sammy and Juliana in Hollywood.*

Satrapi, Marjane. *Persepolis 2: The Story of a Return.*

Schmidt, Gary D. *Lizzie Bright and the Buckminster Boy.*

Seagle, Steven T. *It's a Bird.*

Shinn, Sharon. *The Safe-Keeper's Secret.*

Shusterman, Neal. *The Schwa Was Here.*

Silverstein, Ken. *The Radioactive Boy Scout: The True Story of a Boy and His Backyard Nuclear Reactor.*

Sones, Sonya. *One of Those Hideous Books Where the Mother Dies.*

Steer, Dugald A., ed. *Dr. Ernest Drake's Dragonology: The Complete Book of Dragons.*

Strasser, Todd. *Can't Get There from Here.*

Stratton, Allan. *Chanda's Secrets.*

Stroud, Jonathan. *The Golem's Eye.*

Tocher, Timothy. *Chief Sunrise, John McGraw, and Me.*

Townley, Roderick. *Sky.*

Turnbull, Ann. *No Shame, No Fear.*

Unger, Zac. *Working Fire: The Making of an Accidental Fireman.*

Updale, Eleanor. *Montmorency: Thief, Liar, Gentleman?*

Van Der Vat, Dan. *D-Day: The Greatest Invasion; A People's History.*

Weeks, Sarah. *So B. It.*

Werlin, Nancy. *Double Helix.*

Westerfeld, Scott. *So Yesterday.*

Whedon, Joss. *Fray.*

Whitney, Kim Ablon. *See You down the Road.*

Williams-Garcia, Rita. *No Laughter Here.*

Wolf, Allan. *New Found Land.*

Wooding, Chris. *The Haunting of Alaizabel Cray.*

Woodson, Jacqueline. *Behind You.*

Yolen, Jane, and Robert J. Harris. *Prince across the Water.*

2006 SELECTIONS

Adlington, L. J. *The Diary of Pelly D.*

Akbar, Said Hyder, and Susan Burton. *Come Back to Afghanistan: A California Teenager's Story.*

Bartoletti, Susan Campbell. *Hitler Youth: Growing Up in Hitler's Shadow.*

Bechard, Margaret. *Spacer and Rat.*

Black, Holly. *Valiant: A Modern Tale of Faerie.*

Blumenthal, Karen. *Let Me Play: The Story of Title IX; The Law That Changed the Future of Girls in America.*

Bolden, Tonya. *Maritcha: A Nineteenth-Century American Girl.*

Bray, Libba. *Rebel Angels.*

Bruchac, Joseph. *Code Talker: A Novel about the Navajo Marines of World War Two.*

Buckhanon, Kalisha. *Upstate.*

Castellucci, Cecil. *Boy Proof.*

Coburn, Jake. *Love Sick.*

Cummings, Priscilla. *Red Kayak.*

Deem, James M. *Bodies from the Ash: Life and Death in Ancient Pompeii.*

Delaney, Joseph. *Revenge of the Witch.*

Delisle, Guy. *Pyongyang: A Journey in North Korea.*

Dendy, Leslie, and Mel Boring. *Guinea Pig Scientists: Bold Self-Experimenters in Science and Medicine.*

Eisner, Will. *The Plot: The Secret Story of the Protocols of the Elders of Zion.*

Farrell, Jeanette. *Invisible Allies: Microbes That Shape Our Lives.*

Flake, Sharon G. *Bang!*

Fleischman, Paul. *Zap.*

Fleming, Candace. *Our Eleanor: A Scrapbook Look at Eleanor Roosevelt's Remarkable Life.*

Frank, E. R. *Wrecked.*

Frank, Mitch. *Understanding the Holy Land: Answering Questions about the Israeli-Palestinian Conflict.*

Gaiman, Neil. *Anansi Boys.*

Galloway, Gregory. *As Simple as Snow.*

Giblin, James Cross. *Good Brother, Bad Brother: The Story of Edwin Booth and John Wilkes Booth.*

Green, John. *Looking for Alaska.*

Griffin, Adele. *Where I Want to Be.*

Grimes, Nikki. *Dark Sons.*

Gruber, Michael. *The Witch's Boy.*

Halam, Ann. *Siberia.*

Hartnett, Sonya. *Stripes of the Sidestep Wolf.*

Hautman, Pete. *Invisible.*

Hearn, Julie. *The Minister's Daughter.*

Hiaasen, Carl. *Flush.*

Holub, Josef. *An Innocent Soldier.*

Jacobson, Jennifer Richard. *Stained.*

Johnson, Maureen. *13 Little Blue Envelopes.*

Jurmain, Suzanne. *The Forbidden Schoolhouse: The True and Dramatic Story of Prudence Crandall and Her Students.*

Kass, Pnina Moed. *Real Time.*

Kibuishi, Kazu. *Daisy Kutter: The Last Train.*

Krovatin, Christopher. *Heavy Metal and You.*

Lanagan, Margo. *Black Juice.*

Larbalestier, Justine. *Magic or Madness.*

LaRochelle, David. *Absolutely, Positively Not.*

Lavender, Bee. *Lessons in Taxidermy.*

Lester, Julius. *Day of Tears: A Novel in Dialogue.*

Levithan, David. *Are We There Yet?*

Lubar, David. *Sleeping Freshmen Never Lie.*

Lynch, Chris. *Inexcusable.*

Lynch, Jim. *The Highest Tide.*

Martinez, A. Lee. *Gil's All Fright Diner.*

McGhee, Alison. *All Rivers Flow to the Sea.*

Mercado, Nancy E., ed. *Every Man for Himself: Ten Short Stories about Being a Guy.*

Meyer, Stephenie. *Twilight.*

Myers, Walter Dean. *Autobiography of My Dead Brother.*

Nelson, Marilyn. *A Wreath for Emmett Till.*

———. *Fortune's Bones: The Manumission Requiem.*

O'Donnell, Joe. *Japan 1945: A U.S. Marine's Photographs from Ground Zero.*

Oppel, Kenneth. *Skybreaker.*

Partridge, Elizabeth. *John Lennon: All I Want Is the Truth.*

Pearson, Mary E. *A Room on Lorelei Street.*

Peet, Mal. *Keeper.*

Peña, Matt de la. *Ball Don't Lie.*

Perkins, Lynne Rae. *Criss Cross.*

Qualey, Marsha. *Just Like That.*

Riordan, Rick. *The Lightning Thief.*

Rowling, J. K. *Harry Potter and the Half-Blood Prince.*

Salisbury, Graham. *Eyes of the Emperor.*

Spillebeen, Geert. *Kipling's Choice.*

Staples, Suzanne Fisher. *Under the Persimmon Tree.*

Stein, Tammar. *Light Years.*

Taylor, Yuval, ed. *Growing Up in Slavery: Stories of Young Slaves as Told by Themselves.*

Thal, Lilli. *Mimus.*

Tiffany, Grace. *Ariel.*

Tingle, Rebecca. *Far Traveler.*

Tullson, Diane. *Red Sea.*

Vaughan, Brian K. *Runaways.*

Vaught, Susan. *Stormwitch.*

Volponi, Paul. *Black and White.*

Waid, Mark, et al. *Superman: Birthright.*

Weaver, Will. *Full Service.*

Westerfeld, Scott. *Peeps.*

———. *Uglies.*

Whitcomb, Laura. *A Certain Slant of Light.*

Wittlinger, Ellen. *Sandpiper.*

Wooding, Chris. *Poison.*

Wynne-Jones, Tim. *A Thief in the House of Memory.*

Zenatti, Valérie. *When I Was a Soldier: A Memoir.*

Zusak, Markus. *I Am the Messenger.*

2007 SELECTIONS

Almond, David. *Clay.*

Anderson, M. T. *The Astonishing Life of Octavian Nothing, Traitor to the Nation, Volume 1: The Pox Party.*

Bausum, Ann. *Freedom Riders: John Lewis and Jim Zwerg on the Front Lines of the Civil Rights Movement.*

Benanav, Michael. *Men of Salt: Crossing the Sahara on the Caravan of White Gold.*

Bondoux, Anne-Laure. *The Killer's Tears.*

Booth, Coe. *Tyrell.*

Brooks, Kevin. *The Road of the Dead.*

Budhos, Marina. *Ask Me No Questions.*

Cohn, Rachel, and David Levithan. *Nick and Norah's Infinite Playlist.*

Cornish, D. M. *Monster Blood Tattoo: Foundling.*

Dessen, Sarah. *Just Listen.*

Eldred, Tim. *Grease Monkey: A Tale of Growing Up in Orbit.*

Engle, Margarita. *The Poet Slave of Cuba: A Biography of Juan Francisco Manzano.*

Fleischman, Sid. *Escape! The Story of the Great Houdini.*

Fletcher, Susan. *Alphabet of Dreams.*

Fradin, Judith Bloom, and Dennis Brindell Fradin. *5,000 Miles to Freedom: Ellen and William Craft's Flight from Slavery.*

Freedman, Russell. *Freedom Walkers: The Story of the Montgomery Bus Boycott.*

Frost, Helen. *The Braid.*

Gantos, Jack. *The Love Curse of the Rumbaughs.*

Giles, Gail. *What Happened to Cass McBride?*

Glass, Linzi. *The Year the Gypsies Came.*

Going, K. L. *Saint Iggy.*

Gratz, Alan. *Samurai Shortstop.*

Green, John. *An Abundance of Katherines.*

Harper, Hill. *Letters to a Young Brother: MANifest Your Destiny.*

Hartnett, Sonya. *Surrender.*

Hoffman, Alice. *Incantation.*

Hopkinson, Deborah. *Up before Daybreak: Cotton and People in America.*

Hubner, John. *Last Chance in Texas: The Redemption of Criminal Youth.*

Hunt, Scott. *Twice Told: Original Stories Inspired by Original Art.*

Jacobson, Sid, and Ernie Colón. *The 9/11 Report: A Graphic Adaptation.*

Jansen, Hanna. *Over a Thousand Hills I Walk with You.*

Jaramillo, Ann. *La Línea.*

Johnson, Harriet McBryde. *Accidents of Nature.*

Johnson, Maureen. *Devilish.*

Knox, Elizabeth. *Dreamhunter: Book One of the Dreamhunter Duet.*

Koss, Amy Goldman. *Side Effects.*

Krech, Bob. *Rebound.*

Lanagan, Margo. *White Time.*

Lansens, Lori. *The Girls.*

Larson, Kirby. *Hattie Big Sky.*

Lat. *Kampung Boy.*

Lisle, Janet Taylor. *Black Duck.*

Lynch, Scott. *The Lies of Locke Lamora.*

McClafferty, Carla Killough. *Something Out of Nothing: Marie Curie and Radium.*

McCormick, Patricia. *Sold.*

Miller, Kirsten. *Kiki Strike: Inside the Shadow City.*

Mitchell, David. *Black Swan Green.*

Murdock, Catherine Gilbert. *Dairy Queen.*

Murphy, Sean. *Off Road.*

Myers, Walter Dean. *Street Love.*

Na, An. *Wait for Me.*

November, Sharyn, ed. *Firebirds Rising: An Anthology of Original Science Fiction and Fantasy.*

Noyes, Deborah. *One Kingdom: Our Lives with Animals; The Human-Animal Bond in Myth, History, Science, and Story.*

Pfeffer, Susan Beth. *Life as We Knew It.*

Pierce, Tamora. *Terrier.*

Portman, Frank. *King Dork.*

Pratchett, Terry. *Wintersmith.*

Price, Charlie. *Dead Connection.*

Reinhardt, Dana. *A Brief Chapter in My Impossible Life.*

Robertson, James I., Jr. *Robert E. Lee: Virginian Soldier, American Citizen.*

Rosoff, Meg. *Just in Case.*

Sayres, Meghan Nuttall. *Anahita's Woven Riddle.*

Sedgwick, Marcus. *The Foreshadowing.*

Selvadurai, Shyam. *Swimming in the Monsoon Sea.*

Smelcer, John. *The Trap.*

Stahler, David, Jr. *Doppelganger.*

Stassen, Jean-Philippe. *Deogratias, a Tale of Rwanda.*

Sturtevant, Katherine. *A True and Faithful Narrative.*

Tharp, Tim. *Knights of the Hill Country.*

Thimmesh, Catherine. *Team Moon: How 400,000 People Landed Apollo 11 on the Moon.*

Turner, Megan Whalen. *The King of Attolia.*

Vaught, Susan. *Trigger.*

Vizzini, Ned. *It's Kind of a Funny Story.*

Volponi, Paul. *Rooftop.*

Vrettos, Adrienne Maria. *Skin.*

Werlin, Nancy. *The Rules of Survival.*

Wittlinger, Ellen. *Blind Faith.*

Wooding, Chris. *Storm Thief.*

Woodrell, Daniel. *Winter's Bone.*

Yang, Gene. *American Born Chinese.*

Zusak, Markus. *The Book Thief.*

The Best of the Best
from the
2005 Preconference

Publication information is provided for books
that do not appear on any annual BBYA list.

Alexander, Caroline. *The* Endurance:
  Shackleton's Legendary Antarctic Expedition.
Alvarez, Julia. *In the Time of the Butterflies.*
Anderson, Laurie Halse. *Fever 1793.*
———. *Speak.*
Anderson, M. T. *Feed.*
Barron, T. A. *The Lost Years of Merlin.*
Bauer, Joan. *Hope Was Here.*
Bauer, Marion Dane, ed. *Am I Blue? Coming
  Out from the Silence.*
Bitton-Jackson, Livia. *I Have Lived a Thousand
  Years: Growing Up in the Holocaust.*
Block, Francesca Lia. *Baby Be-Bop.*
———. *Girl Goddess #9: Nine Stories.*
  HarperCollins, 1996.
Bloor, Edward. *Tangerine.*
Brashares, Ann. *The Sisterhood of the Traveling
  Pants.*
Calabro, Marian. *The Perilous Journey of the
  Donner Party.*
Card, Orson Scott. *Ender's Shadow.*
Carlson, Lori M., ed. *Cool Salsa: Bilingual Poems
  on Growing Up Latino in the United States.*
Chbosky, Stephen. *The Perks of Being a
  Wallflower.*
Cofer, Judith Ortiz. *An Island Like You: Stories
  of the Barrio.*
Cohn, Rachel. *Gingerbread.*
Colman, Penny. *Corpses, Coffins, and Crypts: A
  History of Burial.*
Cormier, Robert. *Heroes.*
———. *The Rag and Bone Shop.*
———. *Tenderness.*
Crowe, Chris. *Getting Away with Murder: The
  True Story of the Emmett Till Case.*

Crutcher, Chris. *Ironman.*
———. *Whale Talk.*
Curtis, Christopher Paul. *The Watsons Go to
  Birmingham—1963.*
Cushman, Karen. *Catherine, Called Birdy.*
Donnelly, Jennifer. *A Northern Light.*
Farmer, Nancy. *The Ear, the Eye, and the Arm.*
———. *A Girl Named Disaster.*
———. *The House of the Scorpion.*
Feelings, Tom. *The Middle Passage: White Ships/
  Black Cargo.*
Flake, Sharon G. *The Skin I'm In.*
Fleischman, John. *Phineas Gage: A Gruesome
  but True Story about Brain Science.*
Fleischman, Paul. *Whirligig.*
Flinn, Alex. *Breathing Underwater.*
Frank, E. R. *America.*
———. *Life Is Funny.* DK Ink, 2000.
Gantos, Jack. *Hole in My Life.*
Giles, Gail. *Shattering Glass.*
Going, K. L. *Fat Kid Rules the World.*
Haddix, Margaret Peterson. *Among the Hidden.*
Haddon, Mark. *The Curious Incident of the Dog
  in the Night-Time.*
Hautman, Pete. *Mr. Was.*
Hobbs, Will. *Far North.*
Holt, Kimberly Willis. *When Zachary Beaver
  Came to Town.*
Johnson, Angela. *The First Part Last.*
Junger, Sebastian. *The Perfect Storm: A True
  Story of Men against the Sea.* Norton, 1997.
Klass, David. *You Don't Know Me.*
Klause, Annette Curtis. *Blood and Chocolate.*
Kluger, Steve. *Last Days of Summer.* Bard, 1998.

Korman, Gordon. *Son of the Mob.*

Krakauer, Jon. *Into the Wild.*

Lawrence, Iain. *The Lightkeeper's Daughter.*

Levine, Gail Carson. *Ella Enchanted.*

Levithan, David. *Boy Meets Boy.*

Marsden, John. *Letters from the Inside.*

———. *Tomorrow, When the War Began.*

McDonald, Joyce. *Swallowing Stones.*

Mosher, Richard. *Zazoo.*

Murphy, Jim. *An American Plague: The True and Terrifying Story of the Yellow Fever Epidemic of 1793.*

Myers, Walter Dean. *Monster.*

Nelson, Peter. *Left for Dead: A Young Man's Search for Justice for the USS* Indianapolis.

Nix, Garth. *Lirael, Daughter of the Clayr.*

Nye, Naomi Shihab. *Habibi.*

Opdyke, Irene Gut. *In My Hands: Memories of a Holocaust Rescuer.*

Pattou, Edith. *East.*

Paulsen, Gary. *Winterdance: The Fine Madness of Running the Iditarod.*

Philbrick, Rodman. *The Last Book in the Universe.*

Plum-Ucci, Carol. *The Body of Christopher Creed.*

Porter, Connie. *Imani All Mine.*

Pullman, Philip. *The Golden Compass.*

Roach, Mary. *Stiff: The Curious Lives of Human Cadavers.*

Rowling, J. K. *Harry Potter and the Prisoner of Azkaban.*

———. *Harry Potter and the Sorcerer's Stone.*

Ryan, Pam Muñoz. *Esperanza Rising.*

Rylant, Cynthia. *Something Permanent.*

Sachar, Louis. *Holes.*

Shusterman, Neal. *The Dark Side of Nowhere.*

Silverstein, Shel. *Falling Up.* HarperCollins, 1996.

Spinelli, Jerry. *Stargirl.*

Tashjian, Janet. *The Gospel according to Larry.*

Taylor, Mildred D. *The Land.*

Thomas, Rob. *Rats Saw God.*

Thompson, Craig. *Blankets.*

Vande Velde, Vivian. *Companions of the Night.*

Voigt, Cynthia. *When She Hollers.*

Wallace, Rich. *Wrestling Sturbridge.*

Werlin, Nancy. *The Killer's Cousin.*

Whelan, Gloria. *Homeless Bird.*

White, Ellen Emerson. *The Road Home.*

Williams-Garcia, Rita. *Like Sisters on the Homefront.*

Winick, Judd. *Pedro and Me: Friendship, Loss, and What I Learned.*

Wittlinger, Ellen. *Hard Love.*

Wolff, Virginia Euwer. *True Believer.*

Woodson, Jacqueline. *From the Notebooks of Melanin Sun.*

———. *I Hadn't Meant to Tell You This.*

———. *If You Come Softly.*

———. *Miracle's Boys.*

Ten Years
of BBYA Top Tens,
1997–2006

Akbar, Said Hyder, and Susan Burton. *Come Back to Afghanistan: A California Teenager's Story.*

Anderson, Laurie Halse. *Catalyst.*

———. *Speak.*

Anderson, M. T. *Feed.*

Bagdasarian, Adam. *Forgotten Fire.*

Bartoletti, Susan Campbell. *Growing Up in Coal Country.*

———. *Hitler Youth: Growing Up in Hitler's Shadow.*

Bauer, Joan. *Hope Was Here.*

———. *Rules of the Road.*

Bernstein, Sara Tuvel. *The Seamstress: A Memoir of Survival.*

Bloor, Edward. *Tangerine.*

Blum, Joshua, Bob Holman, and Mark Pellington. *The United States of Poetry.*

Braff, Joshua. *The Unthinkable Thoughts of Jacob Green.*

Brashares, Ann. *The Sisterhood of the Traveling Pants.*

Brooks, Martha. *True Confessions of a Heartless Girl.*

Buckhanon, Kalisha. *Upstate.*

Card, Orson Scott. *Ender's Shadow.*

Chevalier, Tracy. *Girl with a Pearl Earring.*

Colman, Penny. *Corpses, Coffins, and Crypts: A History of Burial.*

Cormier, Robert. *The Rag and Bone Shop.*

———. *Tenderness.*

Crutcher, Chris. *Whale Talk.*

Curtis, Christopher Paul. *Bucking the Sarge.*

Donnelly, Jennifer. *A Northern Light.*

Farmer, Nancy. *A Girl Named Disaster.*

———. *The House of the Scorpion.*

Ferris, Jean. *Love among the Walnuts.*

Flinn, Alex. *Breathing Underwater.*

Frank, E. R. *America.*

Gilstrap, John. *Nathan's Run.*

Glenn, Mel. *Who Killed Mr. Chippendale? A Mystery in Poems.*

Green, John. *Looking for Alaska.*

Haddix, Margaret Peterson. *Among the Hidden.*

Haddon, Mark. *The Curious Incident of the Dog in the Night-Time.*

Hesse, Karen. *Out of the Dust.*

Hobbs, Will. *Far North.*

Holt, Kimberly Willis. *My Louisiana Sky.*

———. *When Zachary Beaver Came to Town.*

Hoose, Phillip. *The Race to Save the Lord God Bird.*

Jenkins, A. M. *Damage.*

Johnson, Angela. *The First Part Last.*

Jordan, Sherryl. *The Raging Quiet.*

Katz, Jon. *Geeks: How Two Boys Rode the Internet Out of Idaho.*

Klause, Annette Curtis. *Blood and Chocolate.*

Konigsburg, E. L. *Silent to the Bone.*

Korman, Gordon. *Son of the Mob.*

Krakauer, Jon. *Into Thin Air: A Personal Account of the Mount Everest Disaster.*

Lawrence, Iain. *The Lightkeeper's Daughter.*

Levithan, David. *Boy Meets Boy.*

———. *The Realm of Possibility.*

Lobel, Anita. *No Pretty Pictures: A Child of War.*

Lynch, Chris. *Inexcusable.*

Marchetta, Melina. *Saving Francesca.*
Maynard, Joyce. *The Usual Rules.*
McDonald, Joyce. *Swallowing Stones.*
McNeal, Laura, and Tom McNeal. *Crooked.*
Meyer, Carolyn. *Mary, Bloody Mary.*
Meyer, Stephenie. *Twilight.*
Mikaelsen, Ben. *Petey.*
Moore, Christopher. *Lamb: The Gospel according to Biff, Christ's Childhood Pal.*
Morpurgo, Michael. *Private Peaceful.*
Mosher, Richard. *Zazoo.*
Myers, Walter Dean. *Harlem: A Poem.*
———. *Monster.*
———. *One More River to Cross: An African American Photograph Album.*
Namioka, Lensey. *Ties That Bind, Ties That Break.*
Nelson, Peter. *Left for Dead: A Young Man's Search for Justice for the USS* Indianapolis.
Nix, Garth. *Lirael, Daughter of the Clayr.*
Nye, Naomi Shihab. *19 Varieties of Gazelle: Poems of the Middle East.*
Opdyke, Irene Gut. *In My Hands: Memories of a Holocaust Rescuer.*
Oppel, Kenneth. *Airborn.*
Partridge, Elizabeth. *This Land Was Made for You and Me: The Life and Songs of Woody Guthrie.*
Pattou, Edith. *East.*
Paulsen, Gary. *The Beet Fields: Memories of a Sixteenth Summer.*

Porter, Connie. *Imani All Mine.*
Pullman, Philip. *The Golden Compass.*
Rapp, Adam. *33 Snowfish.*
———. *Under the Wolf, under the Dog.*
Reynolds, Marjorie. *The Starlite Drive-In.*
Rowling, J. K. *Harry Potter and the Sorcerer's Stone.*
Ryan, Pam Muñoz. *Esperanza Rising.*
Sachar, Louis. *Holes.*
Saenz, Benjamin Alire. *Sammy and Juliana in Hollywood.*
Spinelli, Jerry. *Stargirl.*
Stroud, Jonathan. *The Amulet of Samarkand.*
Taylor, Mildred D. *The Land.*
Thomas, Rob. *Rats Saw God.*
Thompson, Craig. *Blankets.*
Vaughan, Brian K. *Runaways.*
Wallace, Rich. *Wrestling Sturbridge.*
Weeks, Sarah. *So B. It.*
Westerfeld, Scott. *Peeps.*
Whelan, Gloria. *Homeless Bird.*
White, Ruth. *Memories of Summer.*
Wilkomirski, Binjamin. *Fragments: Memories of a Wartime Childhood.*
Williams-Garcia, Rita. *Every Time a Rainbow Dies.*
Wolff, Virginia Euwer. *True Believer.*
Wooding, Chris. *Poison.*
Woodson, Jacqueline. *If You Come Softly.*
Zusak, Markus. *I Am the Messenger.*

INDEX

Authors, titles, and subjects are interfiled in one alphabet. Authors print in roman, titles in italics, and subjects in boldface. Annotations are indicated by bold page numbers.

Holly Koelling is the Outreach Services Manager for the King County Library System in Washington State, following many years in both management and teen services positions in Colorado and Washington public libraries. Holly has been involved with the American Library Association's Young Adult Library Services Association for more than ten years, serving on a number of selection committees; has contributed articles to the professional literature; and is the author of *Classic Connections: Turning Teens On to Great Literature*. She reviews teen literature for *Booklist* magazine. Holly earned her master's degree in library science at the University of Texas at Austin in 1993 and is currently a fellow in the Urban Libraries Council's Executive Leadership Institute.